ENCYCLOPEDIA
OF AMERICAN
NATIONAL PARKS

VOLUME ONE

ENCYCLOPEDIA OF AMERICAN NATIONAL PARKS

EDITED BY HAL K. ROTHMAN AND SARA DANT EWERT

VOLUME ONE

SHARPE REFERENCE
an imprint of M.E. Sharpe, Inc.

SHARPE REFERENCE

Sharpe Reference is an imprint of M.E. Sharpe, Inc.

M.E. Sharpe, Inc.
80 Business Park Drive
Armonk, NY 10504

Library of Congress Cataloging-in-Publication Data

Rothman, Hal, 1958-
     Encyclopedia of American national parks/Hal K. Rothman, Sara Dant Ewert.
          p. cm.
     Includes bibliographical references and index.
     ISBN 0-7656-8057-2 (cloth : alk. paper)
     1. National parks and reserves—United States—Encyclopedias. 2. Historic sites—United States—Encyclopedias. 3. United States—History, Local—Encyclopedias. 4. United States—Biography. I. Ewert, Sara Dant. II. Title.

E160.R54 2004
973′.03—dc21

2003053985

Printed and bound in the United States

The paper used in this publication meets the minimum requirements of American National Standard for Information Sciences—Permanence of Paper for Printed Library Materials, ANSI Z 39.48.1984.

MV (c) 10 9 8 7 6 5 4 3 2 1

Publisher: Myron E. Sharpe
Vice President and Editorial Director: Patricia Kolb
Vice President and Production Director: Carmen Chetti
Executive Editor and Manager of Reference: Todd Hallman
Project Editor: Laura Brengelman
Editorial Assistant: Cathleen Prisco
Cover and Text Design: Jesse Sanchez

For Lauralee, Talia, and Brent

For Eric and Claire

CONTENTS

VOLUME 1

Parks by State and Territory xv

Maps
    New England xxiii
    Mid-Atlantic xxiv
    The South xxv
    The Southwest xxvi
    The Midwest xxvii
    The West xxviii
    Alaska and Hawaii xxix
    United States Territories xxx

Preface xxxi

National Park System:
Overview and History 1

BIOGRAPHIES
Albright, Horace M. 15
Cammerer, Arno B. 16
Demaray, Arthur E. 17
Dickenson, Russell E. 17
Drury, Newton B. 18
Everhardt, Gary 19
Hartzog, George B., Jr. 20
Hewett, Edgar L. 21
Kennedy, Roger 22
Mainella, Fran P. 22

Mather, Stephen T. 23
Mott, William Penn, Jr. 25
Pinkley, Frank 26
Stanton, Robert M. 26
Walker, Ronald H. 27
Whalen, William J. 28
Wirth, Conrad L. 29

AMERICAN NATIONAL PARKS
Abraham Lincoln Birthplace National
    Historic Site 33
Acadia National Park 35
Adams National Historical Park 38
Agate Fossil Beds National
    Monument 41
Aleutian World War II National
    Historic Area 42
Alibates Flint Quarries National
    Monument 42
Allegheny Portage Railroad National
    Historic Site 43
American Memorial Park 45
Amistad National Recreation Area 47
Andersonville National Historic Site 48
Andrew Johnson National Historic
    Site 49
Aniakchak National Monument &
    Preserve 52
Antietam National Battlefield 53
Apostle Islands National Lakeshore 56
Appomattox Court House National
    Historical Park 58
Arches National Park 60

Arkansas Post National Memorial 62

Arlington House, the Robert E. Lee
Memorial 63

Assateague Island National Seashore 65

Aztec Ruins National Monument 67

Badlands National Park 71

Bandelier National Monument 73

Bent's Old Fort National Historic Site . . . 75

Big Bend National Park 76

Big Cypress National Preserve 79

Big Hole National Battlefield 80

Bighorn Canyon National Recreation
Area 83

Big South Fork National River and
Recreation Area 85

Big Thicket National Preserve 86

Biscayne National Park 88

Black Canyon of the Gunnison National
Park 89

Blackstone River Valley National
Heritage Corridor 91

Blue Ridge Parkway 93

Booker T. Washington National
Monument 95

Boston African American National
Historic Site 96

Boston Harbor Islands National
Recreation Area 98

Boston National Historical Park 100

Brices Cross Roads National
Battlefield 102

Brown v. Board of Education National
Historic Site 103

Bryce Canyon National Park 104

Buck Island Reef National Monument . . 107

Cabrillo National Monument 109

Canaveral National Seashore 110

Cane River Creole National Historical
Park and Heritage Area 111

Canyon de Chelly National
Monument 113

Canyonlands National Park 114

Cape Cod National Seashore 117

Cape Hatteras National Seashore 119

Cape Lookout National Seashore 121

Capitol Reef National Park 123

Capulin Volcano National Monument . . 125

Carl Sandburg Home National Historic
Site 126

Carlsbad Caverns National Park 127

Casa Grande Ruins National
Monument 129

Castillo de San Marcos National
Monument 130

Castle Clinton National Monument 132

Catoctin Mountain Park 134

Cedar Breaks National Monument 136

Central High School National Historic
Site 137

Chaco Culture National Historical
Park 138

Chamizal National Memorial 139

Channel Islands National Park 141

Charles Pinckney National Historic
Site 142

Chattahoochee River National
Recreation Area 143

Chickamauga and Chattanooga
National Military Park 144

Chickasaw National Recreation Area . . . 146

Chimney Rock National Historic Site . . 147

Chiricahua National Monument 148

Christiansted National Historic Site 150

City of Rocks National Reserve 151

Clara Barton National Historic Site 153

Colonial National Historical Park 154

Colorado National Monument 156

Congaree National Park 157

Constitution Gardens 158

Coronado National Memorial 159

Cowpens National Battlefield 160

Crater Lake National Park 162

Craters of the Moon National
Monument and Preserve 164

Cumberland Gap National Historical
Park 166

Cumberland Island National
Seashore 167

Curecanti National Recreation Area . . . 168

Cuyahoga Valley National Park 170

Dayton Aviation Heritage National
   Historical Park 173
Death Valley National Park 174
Delaware and Lehigh Navigation Canal
   National Heritage Corridor 177
Delaware Water Gap National
   Recreation Area and Delaware
   National Scenic River 178
Denali National Park and Preserve 179
De Soto National Memorial 182
Devils Postpile National Monument 183
Devils Tower National Monument 184
Dinosaur National Monument 186
Dry Tortugas National Park 188
Ebey's Landing National Historical
   Reserve 191
Edgar Allan Poe National Historic
   Site 192
Edison National Historic Site 193
Effigy Mounds National Monument 195
Eisenhower National Historic Site 196
Eleanor Roosevelt National Historic
   Site 198
Ellis Island National Monument 200
El Malpais National Monument 201
El Morro National Monument 202
Eugene O'Neill National Historic Site . . 204
Everglades National Park 205
Federal Hall National Memorial 211
Fire Island National Seashore 212
Florissant Fossil Beds National
   Monument 214
Ford's Theatre National Historic Site . . . 215
Fort Bowie National Historic Site 216
Fort Caroline National Memorial 217
Fort Clatsop National Memorial 219
Fort Davis National Historic Site 220
Fort Donelson National Battlefield 222
Fort Frederica National Monument 223
Fort Laramie National Historic Site 224
Fort Larned National Historic Site 226
Fort Matanzas National Monument 228
Fort McHenry National Monument
   and Historic Shrine 229
Fort Necessity National Battlefield 230

Fort Point National Historic Site 231
Fort Pulaski National Monument 233
Fort Raleigh National Historic Site 235
Fort Scott National Historic Site 236
Fort Smith National Historic Site 237
Fort Stanwix National Monument 240
Fort Sumter National Monument 241
Fort Union National Monument 243
Fort Union Trading Post National
   Historic Site 245
Fort Vancouver National Historic Site . . 246
Fossil Butte National Monument 247
Frederick Douglass National Historic
   Site 247
Frederick Law Olmsted National
   Historic Site 249
Fredericksburg and Spotsylvania
   National Military Park 251
Friendship Hill National Historic Site . . . 253
Gates of the Arctic National Park and
   Preserve 255
Gateway National Recreation Area 256
Gauley River National Recreation
   Area 257
General Grant National Memorial 258
George Rogers Clark National Historical
   Park 260
George Washington Birthplace National
   Monument 262
George Washington Carver National
   Monument 264
Gettysburg National Military Park 265
Gila Cliff Dwellings National
   Monument 268
Glacier Bay National Park and
   Preserve 269
Glacier National Park 271
Glen Canyon National Recreation
   Area 273
Glen Echo Park 275
Gloria Dei (Old Swedes') Church
   National Historic Site 276
Golden Gate National Recreation
   Area 277
Golden Spike National Historic Site . . . 279

Grand Canyon National Park 280
Grand Portage National Monument 284
Grand Teton National Park 286
Grant-Kohrs Ranch National Historic
    Site................................ 289
Great Basin National Park 290
Great Sand Dunes National Monument
    and Preserve 292
Great Smoky Mountains National
    Park 293
Greenbelt Park..................... 297
Green Springs National Historic
    Landmark District 298
Guadalupe Mountains National Park ... 299
Guilford Courthouse National Military
    Park 300
Gulf Islands National Seashore 302
Hagerman Fossil Beds National
    Monument 305
Haleakala National Park 306
Hamilton Grange National Memorial ... 307
Hampton National Historic Site 309
Harpers Ferry National Historical
    Park 310
Harry S Truman National Historic
    Site................................ 312
Hawaii Volcanoes National Park 314
Herbert Hoover National Historic Site .. 317
Historic Camden 318
Home of Franklin D. Roosevelt
    National Historic Site 319
Homestead National Monument of
    America 321
Hopewell Culture National Historical
    Park 322
Hopewell Furnace National Historic
    Site................................ 324
Horseshoe Bend National Military
    Park 325
Hot Springs National Park 326
Hovenweep National Monument 327
Hubbell Trading Post National
    Historic Site 329

Index I-1

VOLUME 2

Parks by State and Territory xi

Maps
    New England xix
    Mid-Atlantic xx
    The South xxi
    The Southwest xxii
    The Midwest xxiii
    The West xxiv
    Alaska and Hawaii xxv
    United States Territories xxvi

Illinois and Michigan Canal National
    Heritage Corridor 331
Independence National Historical
    Park 332
Indiana Dunes National Lakeshore 335
Isle Royale National Park 338
James A. Garfield National Historic
    Site................................ 341
Jean Lafitte National Historical Park
    and Preserve 342
Jefferson National Expansion
    Memorial 343
Jewel Cave National Monument 345
Jimmy Carter National Historic Site ... 346
John D. Rockefeller, Jr. Memorial
    Parkway 347
John Day Fossil Beds National
    Monument 348
John Fitzgerald Kennedy National
    Historic Site 349
John Muir National Historic Site 351
Johnstown Flood National Memorial ... 353
Joshua Tree National Park 354
Kalaupapa National Historical Park 357
Kaloko-Honokohau National
    Historical Park 358
Katmai National Park and Preserve 359
Kenai Fjords National Park 361
Kennesaw Mountain National
    Battlefield Park 362

Keweenaw National Historical Park 364
Kings Mountain National Military
    Park 365
Klondike Gold Rush National
    Historical Park 367
Knife River Indian Villages National
    Historic Site 369
Lake Clark National Park and
    Preserve 371
Lake Mead National Recreation Area . . 372
Lake Meredith National Recreation
    Area 375
Lake Roosevelt National Recreation
    Area 376
Lassen Volcanic National Park 378
Lava Beds National Monument 380
Lincoln Boyhood National Memorial . . 381
Lincoln Home National Historic Site . . . 383
Little Bighorn Battlefield National
    Monument 384
Little River Canyon National Preserve . . 386
Longfellow National Historic Site 387
Lowell National Historical Park 388
Lyndon B. Johnson National Historical
    Park 390
Maggie L. Walker National Historic
    Site 393
Mammoth Cave National Park 395
Manassas National Battlefield Park 397
Manzanar National Historic Site 399
Marsh-Billings-Rockefeller National
    Historical Park 401
Martin Luther King, Jr. National
    Historic Site 403
Martin Van Buren National Historic
    Site 404
Mary McLeod Bethune Council House
    National Historic Site 406
Mesa Verde National Park 408
Minidoka Internment National
    Monument 410
Minute Man National Historical Park . . . 411
Mississippi National River and
    Recreation Area 413
Mojave National Preserve 415

Monocacy National Battlefield 418
Montezuma Castle National
    Monument 419
Moores Creek National Battlefield 420
Morristown National Historical Park . . . 422
Mount Rainier National Park 424
Mount Rushmore National Memorial . . 426
Natchez National Historical Park 429
National Capital Parks 430
National Mall 431
Natural Bridges National Monument . . . 436
Navajo National Monument 437
New Bedford Whaling National
    Historical Park 439
New Orleans Jazz National Historical
    Park 440
Nez Perce National Historical Park 441
Nicodemus National Historic Site 443
Ninety Six National Historic Site 445
North Cascades National Park 446
Ocmulgee National Monument 451
Oklahoma City National Memorial 452
Olympic National Park 454
Oregon Caves National Monument 457
Organ Pipe Cactus National
    Monument 459
Padre Island National Seashore 461
Palo Alto Battlefield National Historic
    Site 462
Pea Ridge National Military Park 464
Pecos National Historical Park 466
Petersburg National Battlefield 467
Petrified Forest National Park 469
Petroglyph National Monument 471
Pictured Rocks National Lakeshore 473
Pinnacles National Monument 474
Pipe Spring National Monument 476
Pipestone National Monument 477
Point Reyes National Seashore 478
Port Chicago Naval Magazine National
    Memorial 480
Poverty Point National Monument/State
    Commemorative Area 481
Prince William Forest Park 482

Pu'uhonua o Honaunau National
    Historical Park 483
Puukohola Heiau National Historical
    Site 484
Rainbow Bridge National Monument . . . 487
Redwood National and State Parks 489
Richmond National Battlefield Park 492
Rock Creek Park 493
Rocky Mountain National Park 494
Roger Williams National Memorial 496
Rosie the Riveter World War II Home
    Front National Historical Park 497
Russell Cave National Monument 499
Sagamore Hill National Historic Site . . . 501
Saguaro National Park 502
Saint Croix Island International
    Historic Site 503
Saint-Gaudens National Historic Site . . . 504
Saint Paul's Church National Historic
    Site 506
Salem Maritime National Historic
    Site 507
Salinas Pueblo Missions National
    Monument 509
Salt River Bay National Historical Park
    and Ecological Preserve 510
San Antonio Missions National
    Historical Park 511
Sand Creek Massacre National Historic
    Site 512
San Francisco Maritime National
    Historical Park 514
San Juan National Historic Site 515
Santa Fe National Historic Trail 516
Santa Monica Mountains National
    Recreation Area 518
Saratoga National Historical Park 518
Saugus Iron Works National Historic
    Site 520
Scotts Bluff National Monument 522
Selma to Montgomery National Historic
    Trail and All-American Road 523
Sequoia and Kings Canyon National
    Parks 527

Shenandoah National Park 529
Shiloh National Military Park 532
Sitka National Historical Park 533
Sleeping Bear Dunes National
    Lakeshore 535
Springfield Armory National Historic
    Site 537
Statue of Liberty National Monument . . 539
Steamtown National Historic Site 540
Stones River National Battlefield 541
Sunset Crater Volcano National
    Monument 542
Tallgrass Prairie National Preserve 545
Thaddeus Kosciuszko National
    Monument 546
Theodore Roosevelt Birthplace National
    Historic Site 548
Theodore Roosevelt Inaugural National
    Historic Site 549
Theodore Roosevelt National Park 550
Thomas Stone National Historic Site . . . 552
Timpanogos Cave National
    Monument 553
Timucuan Ecological and Historic
    Preserve 554
Tonto National Monument 555
Touro Synagogue National Historic
    Site 557
Tumacácori National Historical
    Park 558
Tupelo National Battlefield 560
Tuskegee Airman National Historic
    Site 561
Tuskegee Institute National Historic
    Site 562
Tuzigoot National Monument 564
Ulysses S. Grant National Historic
    Site 565
USS *Arizona* Memorial 566
Valley Forge National Historical
    Park 569
Vanderbilt Mansion National Historic
    Site 570
Vicksburg National Military Park 572

Virgin Islands National Park 574
Voyageurs National Park 576
Walnut Canyon National
    Monument 579
War in the Pacific National Historical
    Park 580
Washita Battlefield National Historic
    Site 581
Weir Farm National Historic Site 584
Western Arctic National Parklands 585
    Bering Land Bridge National
    Preserve 585
    Cape Krusenstern National
    Monument 586
    Kobuk Valley National Park 587
    Noatak National Preserve 588
Whiskeytown National Recreation
    Area 589
White Sands National Monument 591
Whitman Mission National Historic
    Site 592

William Howard Taft National Historic
    Site 594
Wilson's Creek National Battlefield 595
Wind Cave National Park 597
Women's Rights National Historical
    Park 599
Wrangell–St. Elias National Park and
    Preserve 601
Wright Brothers National Memorial . . . 603
Wupatki National Monument 605
Yellowstone National Park 607
Yosemite National Park 609
Yucca House National Monument 612
Yukon-Charley Rivers National
    Preserve 613
Zion National Park 615

Bibliography 619

Index I-1

PARKS BY STATE AND TERRITORY

Alabama

Horseshoe Bend National Military
Park 325
Little River Canyon National
Preserve 386
Russell Cave National Monument 499
Selma to Montgomery National Historic
Trail and All-American Road 523
Tuskegee Airmen National Historic
Site.............................. 561
Tuskegee Institute National Historic
Site.............................. 562

Alaska

Aleutian World War II National
Historic Area 42
Aniakchak National Monument &
Preserve 52
Bering Land Bridge National Preserve .. 585
Cape Krusenstern National
Monument 586
Denali National Park and Preserve 179
Gates of the Arctic National Park and
Preserve 255
Glacier Bay National Park and
Preserve 269
Katmai National Park and Preserve 359

Kenai Fjords National Park 361
Klondike Gold Rush National
Historical Park 367
Kobuk Valley National Park 587
Lake Clark National Park and
Preserve 371
Noatak National Preserve 588
Sitka National Historical Park 533
Western Arctic National Parklands..... 585
Wrangell–St. Elias National Park and
Preserve 601
Yukon-Charley Rivers National
Preserve 613

Arizona

Canyon de Chelly National
Monument 113
Casa Grande Ruins National
Monument 129
Chiricahua National Monument 148
Coronado National Memorial 159
Fort Bowie National Historic Site 216
Glen Canyon National Recreation
Area.............................. 273
Grand Canyon National Park 280
Hubbell Trading Post National Historic
Site.............................. 329
Lake Mead National Recreation Area .. 372
Montezuma Castle National
Monument 419
Navajo National Monument 437
Organ Pipe Cactus National
Monument 459

Petrified Forest National Park 469
Pipe Spring National Monument 476
Saguaro National Park 502
Sunset Crater Volcano National
    Monument 542
Tonto National Monument 555
Tumacácori National Historical Park ... 558
Tuzigoot National Monument 564
Walnut Canyon National Monument... 579
Wupatki National Monument 605

Arkansas
Arkansas Post National Memorial 62
Central High School National Historic
    Site 137
Fort Smith National Historic Site 237
Hot Springs National Park 326
Pea Ridge National Military Park 464

California
Cabrillo National Monument 109
Channel Islands National Park 141
Death Valley National Park 174
Devils Postpile National Monument 183
Eugene O'Neill National Historic Site .. 204
Fort Point National Historic Site 231
Golden Gate National Recreation
    Area 277
John Muir National Historic Site 351
Joshua Tree National Park 354
Kings Canyon National Park 527
Lassen Volcanic National Park 378
Lava Beds National Monument 380
Manzanar National Historic Site 399
Mojave National Preserve 415
Pinnacles National Monument 474
Point Reyes National Seashore 478
Port Chicago Naval Magazine National
    Memorial 480
Redwood National and State Parks 489
Rosie the Riveter World War II Home
    Front National Historical Park 497
San Francisco Maritime National
    Historical Park 514

Santa Monica Mountains National
    Recreation Area 518
Sequoia National Park 527
Whiskeytown National Recreation
    Area 589
Yosemite National Park 609

Colorado
Bent's Old Fort National Historic Site ... 75
Black Canyon of the Gunnison National
    Park 89
Colorado National Monument 156
Curecanti National Recreation Area ... 168
Dinosaur National Monument 186
Florissant Fossil Beds National
    Monument 214
Great Sand Dunes National Monument
    and Preserve 292
Hovenweep National Monument 327
Mesa Verde National Park 408
Rocky Mountain National Park 494
Sand Creek Massacre National
    Historic Site 512
Santa Fe National Historic Trail 516
Yucca House National Monument 612

Connecticut
Weir Farm National Historic Site 584

District of Columbia
Constitution Gardens 158
Ford's Theatre National Historic Site ... 215
Frederick Douglass National Historic
    Site 247
Mary McLeod Bethune Council House
    National Historic Site 406
National Capital Parks 430
National Mall 431
Rock Creek Park 493

Florida
Big Cypress National Preserve 79
Biscayne National Park 88
Canaveral National Seashore 110

Castillo de San Marcos National
    Monument 130
De Soto National Memorial 182
Dry Tortugas National Park 188
Everglades National Park 205
Fort Caroline National Memorial 217
Fort Matanzas National Monument 228
Gulf Islands National Seashore 302
Timucuan Ecological and Historic
    Preserve 554

Georgia
Andersonville National Historic Site 48
Chattahoochee River National
    Recreation Area.................. 143
Chickamauga and Chattanooga
    National Military Park 144
Cumberland Island National Seashore .. 167
Fort Frederica National Monument 223
Fort Pulaski National Monument 233
Jimmy Carter National Historic Site ... 346
Kennesaw Mountain National
    Battlefield Park 362
Martin Luther King, Jr. National
    Historic Site 403
Ocmulgee National Monument........ 451

Guam
War in the Pacific National Historical
    Park............................. 580

Hawaii
Haleakala National Park 306
Hawaii Volcanoes National Park 314
Kalaupapa National Historical Park 357
Kaloko-Honokohau National Historical
    Park............................. 358
Pu'uhonua o Honaunau National
    Historical Park.................... 483
Puukohola Heiau National Historical
    Site.............................. 484
USS *Arizona* Memorial 566

Idaho
City of Rocks National Reserve 151
Craters of the Moon National
    Monument and Preserve 164
Hagerman Fossil Beds National
    Monument 305
Minidoka Internment National
    Monument 410
Nez Perce National Historical Park 441
Yellowstone National Park............ 607

Illinois
Illinois and Michigan Canal National
    Heritage Corridor 331
Lincoln Home National Historic Site ... 383

Indiana
George Rogers Clark National Historical
    Park.............................. 260
Indiana Dunes National Lakeshore 335
Lincoln Boyhood National Memorial ... 381

Iowa
Effigy Mounds National Monument.... 195
Herbert Hoover National Historic Site .. 317

Kansas
Brown v. Board of Education National
    Historic Site 103
Fort Larned National Historic Site 226
Fort Scott National Historic Site 236
Nicodemus National Historic Site...... 443
Santa Fe National Historic Trail 516
Tallgrass Prairie National Preserve 545

Kentucky
Abraham Lincoln Birthplace National
    Historic Site 33
Big South Fork National River and
    Recreation Area................... 85
Cumberland Gap National Historical
    Park.............................. 166
Mammoth Cave National Park 395

Louisiana

Cane River Creole National Historical
    Park and Heritage Area 111
Jean Lafitte National Historical Park and
    Preserve 342
New Orleans Jazz National Historical
    Park 440
Poverty Point National Monument/State
    Commemorative Area 481

Maine

Acadia National Park 35
Saint Croix Island International
    Historic Site 503

Maryland

Antietam National Battlefield 53
Assateague Island National Seashore 65
Catoctin Mountain Park 134
Clara Barton National Historic Site 153
Fort McHenry National Monument
    and Historic Shrine 229
Glen Echo Park 275
Greenbelt Park...................... 297
Hampton National Historic Site 309
Harpers Ferry National Historical
    Park 310
Monocacy National Battlefield 418
Thomas Stone National Historic Site ... 552

Massachusetts

Adams National Historical Park 38
Blackstone River Valley National
    Heritage Corridor 91
Boston African American National
    Historic Site 96
Boston Harbor Islands National
    Recreation Area................... 98
Boston National Historical Park 100
Cape Cod National Seashore 117
Frederick Law Olmsted National
    Historic Site 249
John Fitzgerald Kennedy National
    Historic Site 349
Longfellow National Historic Site 387

Lowell National Historical Park 388
Minute Man National Historical
    Park 411
New Bedford Whaling National
    Historical Park 439
Salem Maritime National Historic
    Site 507
Saugus Iron Works National Historic
    Site 520
Springfield Armory National Historic
    Site 537

Michigan

Isle Royale National Park 338
Keweenaw National Historical Park 364
Pictured Rocks National Lakeshore 473
Sleeping Bear Dunes National
    Lakeshore 535

Minnesota

Grand Portage National Monument 284
Mississippi National River and
    Recreation Area................... 413
Pipestone National Monument 477
Voyageurs National Park 576

Mississippi

Brices Cross Roads National
    Battlefield 102
Gulf Islands National Seashore 302
Natchez National Historical Park 429
Tupelo National Battlefield 560
Vicksburg National Military Park 572

Missouri

George Washington Carver National
    Monument 264
Harry S Truman National Historic
    Site 312
Jefferson National Expansion
    Memorial 343
Santa Fe National Historic Trail 516
Ulysses S. Grant National Historic
    Site 565
Wilson's Creek National Battlefield 595

Montana

Big Hole National Battlefield 80
Bighorn Canyon National Recreation
    Area 83
Glacier National Park 271
Grant-Kohrs Ranch National Historic
    Site 289
Little Bighorn Battlefield National
    Monument 384
Nez Perce National Historical Park 441
Yellowstone National Park 607

Nebraska

Agate Fossil Beds National Monument . . 41
Chimney Rock National Historic Site . . 147
Homestead National Monument of
    America 321
Scotts Bluff National Monument 522

Nevada

Death Valley National Park 174
Great Basin National Park 290
Lake Mead National Recreation Area . . 372

New Hampshire

Saint-Gaudens National Historic Site . . . 504

New Jersey

Delaware National Scenic River 178
Delaware Water Gap National
    Recreation Area 178
Edison National Historic Site 193
Ellis Island National Monument 200
Gateway National Recreation Area 256
Morristown National Historical Park . . . 422

New Mexico

Aztec Ruins National Monument 67
Bandelier National Monument 73
Capulin Volcano National Monument . . 125
Carlsbad Caverns National Park 127
Chaco Culture National Historical
    Park 138
El Malpais National Monument 201
El Morro National Monument 202

Fort Union National Monument 243
Gila Cliff Dwellings National
    Monument 268
Pecos National Historical Park 466
Petroglyph National Monument 471
Salinas Pueblo Missions National
    Monument 509
Santa Fe National Historic Trail 516
White Sands National Monument 591

New York

Castle Clinton National Monument 132
Eleanor Roosevelt National Historic
    Site 198
Ellis Island National Monument 200
Federal Hall National Memorial 211
Fire Island National Seashore 212
Fort Stanwix National Monument 240
Gateway National Recreation Area 256
General Grant National Memorial 258
Hamilton Grange National Memorial . . 307
Home of Franklin D. Roosevelt
    National Historic Site 319
Martin Van Buren National Historic
    Site 404
Sagamore Hill National Historic Site . . . 501
Saint Paul's Church National Historic
    Site 506
Saratoga National Historical Park 518
Statue of Liberty National Monument . . 539
Theodore Roosevelt Birthplace National
    Historic Site 548
Theodore Roosevelt Inaugural National
    Historic Site 549
Vanderbilt Mansion National Historic
    Site 570
Women's Rights National Historical
    Park 599

North Carolina

Blue Ridge Parkway 93
Cape Hatteras National Seashore 119
Cape Lookout National Seashore 121
Carl Sandburg Home National Historic
    Site 126

Fort Raleigh National Historic Site 235
Great Smoky Mountains National
      Park 293
Guilford Courthouse National Military
      Park 300
Moores Creek National Battlefield 420
Wright Brothers National Memorial . . . 603

North Dakota
Fort Union Trading Post National
      Historic Site 245
Knife River Indian Villages National
      Historic Site 369
Theodore Roosevelt National Park 550

Northern Mariana Islands
American Memorial Park 45

Ohio
Cuyahoga Valley National Park 170
Dayton Aviation Heritage National
      Historical Park 173
Hopewell Culture National Historical
      Park 322
James A. Garfield National Historic
      Site 341
William Howard Taft National Historic
      Site 594

Oklahoma
Chickasaw National Recreation Area . . . 146
Fort Smith National Historic Site 237
Oklahoma City National Memorial 452
Santa Fe National Historic Trail 516
Washita Battlefield National Historic
      Site 581

Oregon
Crater Lake National Park 162
Fort Clatsop National Memorial 219
John Day Fossil Beds National
      Monument 348
Nez Perce National Historical Park 441
Oregon Caves National Monument 457

Pennsylvania
Allegheny Portage Railroad National
      Historic Site 43
Delaware and Lehigh Navigation Canal
      National Heritage Corridor 177
Delaware Water Gap National
      Recreation Area and Delaware
      National Scenic River 178
Edgar Allan Poe National Historic
      Site 192
Eisenhower National Historic Site 196
Fort Necessity National Battlefield 230
Friendship Hill National Historic Site . . . 253
Gettysburg National Military Park 265
Gloria Dei (Old Swedes') Church
      National Historic Site 276
Hopewell Furnace National Historic
      Site 324
Independence National Historical
      Park 332
Johnstown Flood National Memorial . . . 353
Steamtown National Historic Site 540
Thaddeus Kosciuszko National
      Monument 546
Valley Forge National Historical Park . . 569

Puerto Rico
San Juan National Historic Site 515

Rhode Island
Blackstone River Valley National
      Heritage Corridor 91
Roger Williams National Memorial 496
Touro Synagogue National Historic
      Site 557

South Carolina
Charles Pinckney National Historic
      Site 142
Congaree National Park 157
Cowpens National Battlefield 160
Fort Sumter National Monument 241
Historic Camden 318

Kings Mountain National Military
    Park 365
Ninety Six National Historic Site 445

South Dakota
Badlands National Park 71
Jewel Cave National Monument 345
Mount Rushmore National Memorial . . 426
Wind Cave National Park 597

Tennessee
Andrew Johnson National Historic Site . . 49
Big South Fork National River and
    Recreation Area 85
Chickamauga and Chattanooga National
    Military Park 144
Cumberland Gap National Historical
    Park 166
Fort Donelson National Battlefield 222
Great Smoky Mountains National
    Park 293
Shiloh National Military Park 532
Stones River National Battlefield 541

Texas
Alibates Flint Quarries National
    Monument 42
Amistad National Recreation Area 47
Big Bend National Park 76
Big Thicket National Preserve 86
Chamizal National Memorial 139
Fort Davis National Historic Site 220
Guadalupe Mountains National Park . . . 299
Lake Meredith National Recreation
    Area 375
Lyndon B. Johnson National Historical
    Park 390
Padre Island National Seashore 461
Palo Alto Battlefield National Historic
    Site 462
San Antonio Missions National
    Historical Park 511

Utah
Arches National Park 60
Bryce Canyon National Park 104
Canyonlands National Park 114
Capitol Reef National Park 123
Cedar Breaks National Monument 136
Dinosaur National Monument 186
Glen Canyon National Recreation
    Area 273
Golden Spike National Historic Site . . . 279
Hovenweep National Monument 327
Natural Bridges National Monument . . . 436
Rainbow Bridge National Monument . . . 487
Timpanogos Cave National
    Monument 553
Zion National Park 615

Vermont
Marsh-Billings-Rockefeller National
    Historical Park 401

Virginia
Appomattox Court House National
    Historical Park 58
Arlington House, the Robert E. Lee
    Memorial 63
Assateague Island National Seashore 65
Blue Ridge Parkway 93
Booker T. Washington National
    Monument 95
Colonial National Historical Park 154
Cumberland Gap National Historical
    Park 166
Fredericksburg and Spotsylvania
    National Military Park 251
George Washington Birthplace National
    Monument 262
Green Springs National Historic Landmark
    District 298
Harpers Ferry National Historical
    Park 310
Maggie L. Walker National Historic
    Site 393
Manassas National Battlefield Park 397

Petersburg National Battlefield 467
Prince William Forest Park 482
Richmond National Battlefield Park 492
Shenandoah National Park 529

Virgin Islands
Buck Island Reef National Monument .. 107
Christiansted National Historic Site 150
Salt River Bay National Historical Park
    and Ecological Preserve 510
Virgin Islands National Park 574

Washington
Ebey's Landing National Historical
    Reserve 191
Fort Vancouver National Historic Site .. 246
Klondike Gold Rush National Historical
    Park 367
Lake Roosevelt National Recreation
    Area............................. 376
Mount Rainier National Park 424
Nez Perce National Historical Park 441
North Cascades National Park 446

Olympic National Park 454
Whitman Mission National Historic
    Site............................. 592

West Virginia
Gauley River National Recreation
    Area............................. 257
Harpers Ferry National Historical
    Park 310

Wisconsin
Apostle Islands National Lakeshore 56

Wyoming
Bighorn Canyon National Recreation
    Area............................. 83
Devils Tower National Monument 184
Fort Laramie National Historic Site 224
Fossil Butte National Monument 247
Grand Teton National Park 286
John D. Rockefeller, Jr. Memorial
    Parkway 347
Yellowstone National Park............ 607

NEW ENGLAND

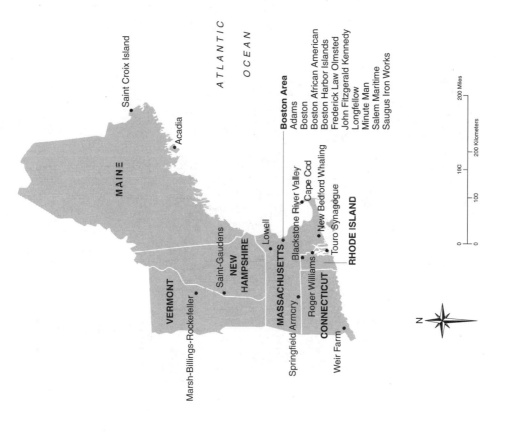

ATLANTIC OCEAN

Saint Croix Island

Acadia

MAINE

VERMONT

Marsh-Billings-Rockefeller

NEW HAMPSHIRE

Saint-Gaudens

Lowell

MASSACHUSETTS

Springfield Armory

Blackstone River Valley

Cape Cod

New Bedford Whaling

Roger Williams

Touro Synagogue

RHODE ISLAND

CONNECTICUT

Weir Farm

Boston Area
Adams
Boston
Boston African American
Boston Harbor Islands
Frederick Law Olmsted
John Fitzgerald Kennedy
Longfellow
Minute Man
Salem Maritime
Saugus Iron Works

N

0   100   200 Kilometers
0   100   200 Miles

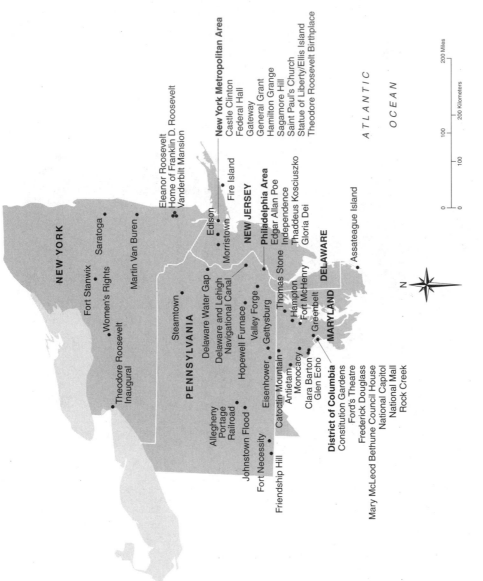

MID-ATLANTIC

NEW YORK

Fort Stanwix
Saratoga
Women's Rights
Martin Van Buren
Theodore Roosevelt Inaugural

Eleanor Roosevelt
Home of Franklin D. Roosevelt
Vanderbilt Mansion

Fire Island

New York Metropolitan Area
Castle Clinton
Federal Hall
Gateway
General Grant
Hamilton Grange
Sagamore Hill
Saint Paul's Church
Statue of Liberty/Ellis Island
Theodore Roosevelt Birthplace

Edison
Morristown
NEW JERSEY
Philadelphia Area
Edgar Allan Poe
Independence
Thaddeus Kosciuszko
Gloria Dei

PENNSYLVANIA
Steamtown
Delaware Water Gap
Delaware and Lehigh Navigational Canal
Hopewell Furnace
Valley Forge
Gettysburg
Thomas Stone

Allegheny Portage Railroad
Johnstown Flood
Fort Necessity
Eisenhower
Catoctin Mountain
Antietam
Monocacy
Clara Barton
Glen Echo
Hampton
Fort McHenry
Greenbelt
DELAWARE
MARYLAND
Assateague Island

Friendship Hill

District of Columbia
Constitution Gardens
Ford's Theatre
Frederick Douglass
Mary McLeod Bethune Council House
National Capitol
National Mall
Rock Creek

N

ATLANTIC

OCEAN

0   100   200 Miles
0   100   200 Kilometers

xxiv

THE SOUTH

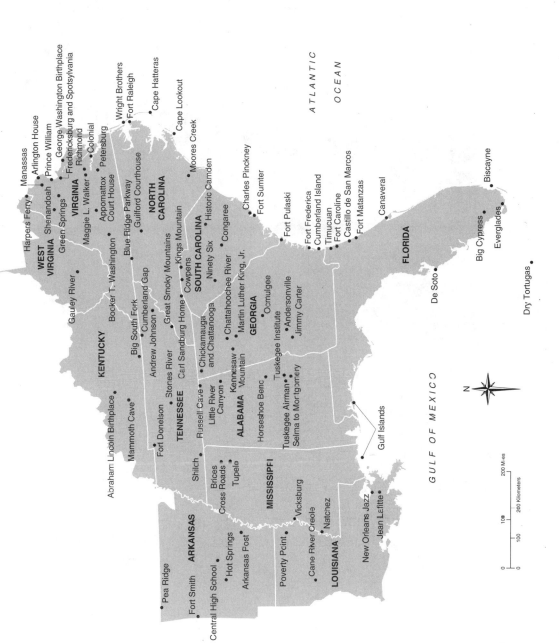

Manassas
Arlington House
Prince William
George Washington Birthplace
Fredericksburg and Spotsylvania
Richmond
Petersburg
Colonial
Wright Brothers
Fort Raleigh
Cape Hatteras

Harpers Ferry
Shenandoah
Green Springs
Maggie L. Walker
Appomattox Court House
Blue Ridge Parkway
Guilford Courthouse
Cape Lookout

WEST VIRGINIA
VIRGINIA
Gauley River

NORTH CAROLINA
Moores Creek

Cumberland Gap
Great Smoky Mountains
Kings Mountain
Cowpens
Historic Camden
Charles Pinckney

Booker T. Washington
Big South Fork
Andrew Johnson
SOUTH CAROLINA
Ninety Six
Congaree
Fort Sumter

KENTUCKY
Abraham Lincoln Birthplace
Mammoth Cave
Stones River
Carl Sandburg Home
Chickamauga and Chattanooga
Chattahoochee River
Martin Luther King, Jr.
Fort Pulaski

TENNESSEE
Fort Donelson
Russell Cave
Little River Canyon
Kennesaw Mountain
Ocmulgee
GEORGIA
Andersonville
Jimmy Carter

Fort Frederica
Cumberland Island
Timucuan
Fort Caroline
Castillo de San Marcos
Fort Matanzas
Canaveral

FLORIDA
Biscayne

Shiloh
Brices Cross Roads
Tupelo
ALABAMA
Horseshoe Bend
Tuskegee Institute
Tuskegee Airmen
Selma to Montgomery

Big Cypress
Everglades
De Soto

ARKANSAS
Pea Ridge
Fort Smith
Central High School
Hot Springs
Arkansas Post

MISSISSIPPI
Vicksburg
Natchez

Poverty Point
Cane River Creole
LOUISIANA
New Orleans Jazz
Jean Lafitte
Gulf Islands

Dry Tortugas

ATLANTIC OCEAN

GULF OF MEXICO

N

200 Miles
200 Kilometers
0   100   200
0   100   200

THE SOUTHWEST

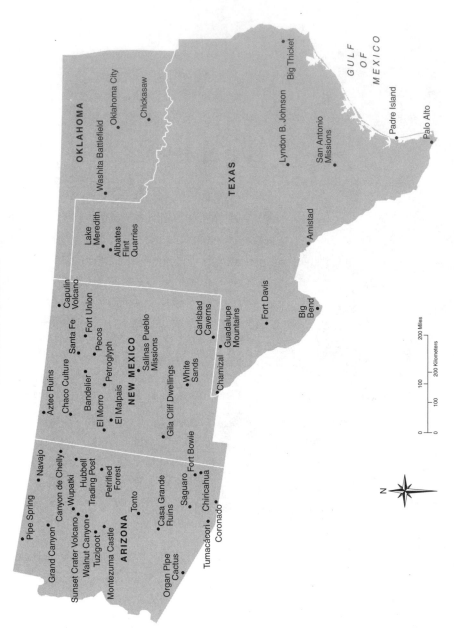

GULF OF MEXICO

OKLAHOMA

Big Thicket

Oklahoma City

Chickasaw

Washita Battlefield

TEXAS

Lyndon B. Johnson

San Antonio Missions

Padre Island

Palo Alto

Lake Meredith

Alibates Flint Quarries

Amistad

Capulin Volcano

Santa Fe

Fort Union

Aztec Ruins

Chaco Culture

Bandelier

El Morro

Petroglyph

Pecos

El Malpais

NEW MEXICO

Salinas Pueblo Missions

Gila Cliff Dwellings

White Sands

Chamizal

Carlsbad Caverns

Guadalupe Mountains

Fort Davis

Big Bend

Pipe Spring

Navajo

Grand Canyon

Canyon de Chelly

Sunset Crater Volcano

Wupatki

Walnut Canyon

Hubbell Trading Post

Tuzigoot

Petrified Forest

Montezuma Castle

Tonto

ARIZONA

Casa Grande Ruins

Saguaro

Fort Bowie

Organ Pipe Cactus

Chiricahua

Tumacácori

Coronado

N

200 Miles

200 Kilometers

100

100

0

0

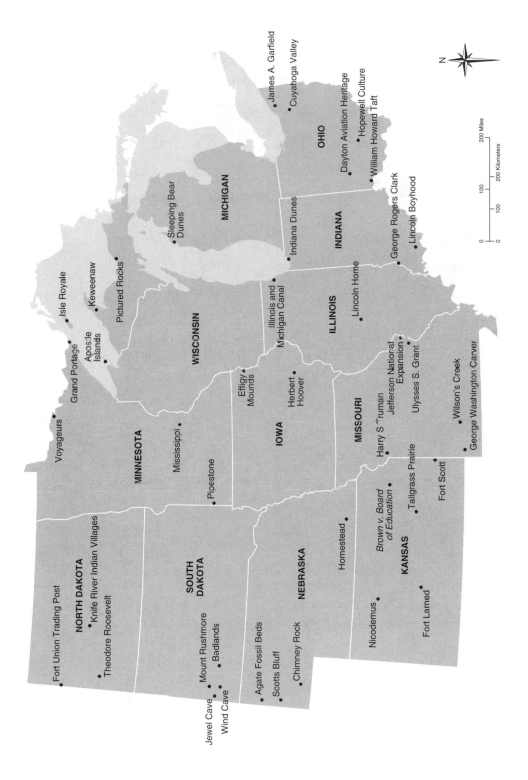

THE MIDWEST

THE WEST

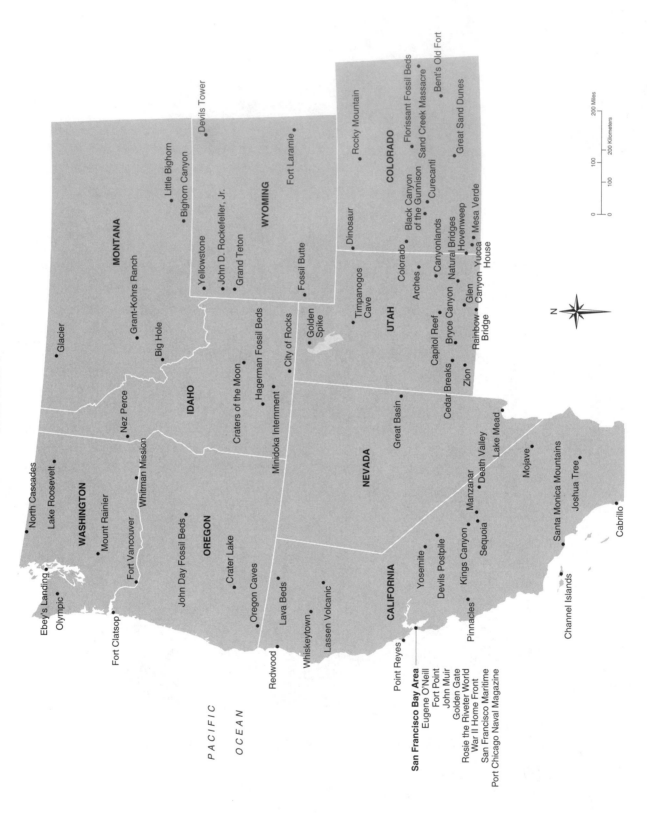

PACIFIC
OCEAN

WASHINGTON
Ebey's Landing
Olympic
North Cascades
Lake Roosevelt
Mount Rainier
Fort Vancouver
Whitman Mission
Fort Clatsop

OREGON
John Day Fossil Beds
Crater Lake
Oregon Caves
Lava Beds
Whiskeytown
Lassen Volcanic

CALIFORNIA
Redwood
Point Reyes
San Francisco Bay Area
Eugene O'Neill
Fort Point
John Muir
Golden Gate
Rosie the Riveter World
War II Home Front
San Francisco Maritime
Port Chicago Naval Magazine
Pinnacles
Yosemite
Devils Postpile
Kings Canyon
Sequoia
Manzanar
Channel Islands
Cabrillo
Santa Monica Mountains
Joshua Tree
Mojave
Death Valley
Lake Mead

MONTANA
Glacier
Grant-Kohrs Ranch
Big Hole
Little Bighorn
Bighorn Canyon

IDAHO
Nez Perce
Craters of the Moon
Hagerman Fossil Beds
Minidoka Internment
City of Rocks

WYOMING
Devils Tower
Yellowstone
John D. Rockefeller, Jr.
Grand Teton
Fort Laramie
Fossil Butte

NEVADA
Great Basin

UTAH
Golden Spike
Timpanogos Cave
Arches
Capitol Reef
Cedar Breaks
Bryce Canyon
Zion
Glen Canyon
Rainbow Bridge

COLORADO
Rocky Mountain
Dinosaur
Colorado
Black Canyon of the Gunnison
Curecanti
Florissant Fossil Beds
Sand Creek Massacre
Bent's Old Fort
Great Sand Dunes
Canyonlands
Natural Bridges
Hovenweep
Mesa Verde
Yucca House

N

200 Miles
200 Kilometers
0   100   200
0   100   200

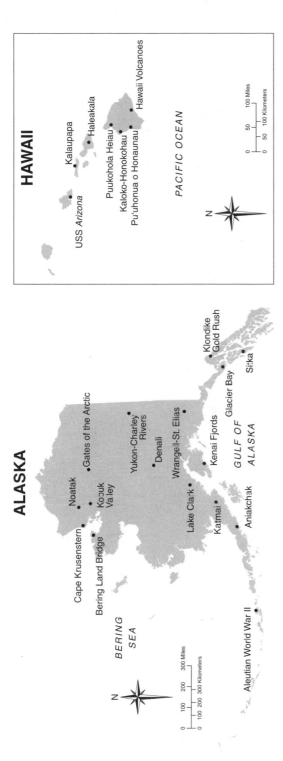

HAWAII

USS *Arizona*

Kalaupapa

Haleakala

Puukohola Heiau
Kaloko-Honokohau
Pu'uhonua o Honaunau

Hawaii Volcanoes

PACIFIC OCEAN

N

0   50   100 Miles
0 50 100 Kilometers

ALASKA

Cape Krusenstern

Bering Land Bridge

Noatak

Kobuk Valley

Gates of the Arctic

Yukon-Charley Rivers

Denali

Wrangell-St. Elias

Lake Clark

Kenai Fjords

Glacier Bay

Klondike Gold Rush

Sitka

GULF OF ALASKA

Katmai

Aniakchak

Aleutian World War II

BERING SEA

N

0   100   200   300 Miles
0 100 200 300 Kilometers

UNITED STATES TERRITORIES

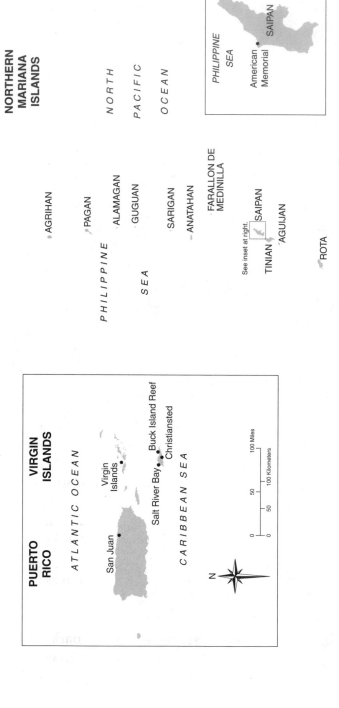

PUERTO RICO

VIRGIN ISLANDS

ATLANTIC OCEAN

Virgin Islands

Buck Island Reef
Salt River Bay
Christiansted

San Juan

CARIBBEAN SEA

N

0   50   100 Miles
0   50   100 Kilometers

NORTHERN MARIANA ISLANDS

FARALLON DE PAJAROS

MAUG ISLANDS

ASUNCION ISLAND

AGRIHAN

PAGAN

ALAMAGAN

GUGUAN

SARIGAN

ANATAHAN

FARALLON DE MEDINILLA

NORTH

PACIFIC

OCEAN

PHILIPPINE

SEA

See inset at right.

SAIPAN

TINIAN

AGUIJAN

ROTA

GUAM

War in the Pacific

N

PHILIPPINE SEA

NORTH PACIFIC OCEAN

American Memorial

SAIPAN

0   50   100 Miles
0   50   100 Kilometers

PREFACE

If there is one genuine contribution that the United States has made to the application of the principles of democracy, the most likely candidate is the national park. Prior to the Age of Enlightenment—the eighteenth-century intellectual and ultimately social revolution that insisted individuals possessed natural rights and added the concept of a relationship between the governors and the governed to human affairs—the idea of a park owned and used by the people was entirely unknown. In most cultures, especially monarchies and other forms of hereditary government, parks were the provinces of the nobility and the wealthy, kept and maintained for their pleasure alone. Common people were forbidden to use designated lands, sometimes on the penalty of death. Many stood outside the boundaries of such areas and looked in with envy, conscious of the wealth of natural resources and aesthetic pleasures within and equally aware of the huge price to be paid for violating the liege's prerogative. Such parks, like the forests set aside for royal hunts, served as manifestations of power, markers of different standing in societies riven by social distinctions. They were also the flash points of class-based tension. The story of Robert of Locksley, a member of the twelfth-century English gentry who, as Robin Hood, took to the woods after defending a man who stole a deer from restricted land to feed his starving family, clearly illustrated the tension inherent in the traditional organization of private parklands.

The history of the United States followed a different vector, for the acquisitive nation of the nineteenth century encompassed more land than its people could then inhabit. The great beauty and uniqueness of much of this land inspired a culture that saw itself as a light to nations, one that believed it was in the process of perfecting human endeavor in a way earlier societies had not. Such lands answered the dilemma of the nineteenth century. They demonstrated distinctiveness in nature that Americans embraced; they served as a counterpoint to European claims that the New World was inferior in every way. Yet nineteenth-century America was a commercial society devoted to economic wealth by the measures of industry. Parkland could not impinge on economic effort, on the process of observing, demarcating, and then harvesting the bounty of the land. The parks' contribution to the purpose of nation-building must be more valuable as symbol than reality; awe-inspiring scenery had to outweigh ranch and agricultural potential at the time when momentum for a park gathered. The first parks, including Yellowstone, Yosemite, Sequoia, General Grant (now part of Kings Canyon), Crater Lake, and their peers, all shared a combination of beauty and inaccessibility for commercial economic purposes that made them valuable manifestations of American cultural needs instead of sources from which to wring wealth.

The crucial feature of these parks in the nation's ideology was the principle of their openness to all Americans. In the eyes of supporters, national parks were testimony to the patrimony and heritage of a country that intended to reinvent the relationships between government and its people. During the late nineteenth century and the first decade of the twentieth, those people who professed goals of community instead of individualism saw in the national parks not only affirmation of their nation, but a clear and distinct way to articulate one of the prime assumptions of the time: that a society's institutions should serve the economic, social, spiritual, and cultural needs of its people. This deeply ingrained principle in the concept of national parks—if not always in the motives behind their creation—became an underlying premise in the evolution of American conservation.

This seemingly contradictory impulse revealed much of the goals and pretensions of the United States as the twentieth century began. Economically and politically powerful families wanted both the feeling of European aristocracy, the sense of having large areas devoted to aesthetic and ultimately recreational purposes, while supporting the democracy that Americans were certain made their nation special. The process of creating a nation that sprawled from the Atlantic to the Pacific challenged many of the ideas of democracy, but in these huge natural parks, Americans could see the fruition of their nineteenth-century idea, a transcontinental nation that practiced democratic ideals. As the twentieth century dawned, no more powerful proof of their commitment to democracy existed than the patrimony of national parks.

Yet an enormous gap existed between the rhetoric of the time and the actuality of the national parks that were created. The language of democracy trumpeted openness, but the parks Americans created catered to only one segment of American society, the people with the time and resources to travel and the education to regard nature as part of their cultural heritage. The Americans who traveled to parks were the winners in the transition to industrial society. The ones who might most benefit from such public patrimony usually lacked the resources, inclination, and even the awareness that such parks existed. As democratic institutions, early national parks functioned more as symbols than as participatory reality.

More than one hundred years later, that equation has been reversed. Today, national parks have evolved into a primary way that Americans declare their Americanness, one of the features of American society that accommodate as wide a cut of the nation's diverse population as any governmental institution. No longer simply national park or national monument, they include an array of categories that house almost 400 places, which have become living proof of the democratization of travel in the United States.

This encyclopedia holds the evidence of the diversity of that vision, of the ways in which national parks not only have changed the character of what is protected within them, but also have come to respond to the transformation of American society. In the heightened variety of what is included in the system, the reasons why such areas are added, and the controversies over the parks, the changing tenor of American society can clearly be seen. In addition, the American national parks are wonderful places to visit.

—*Hal K. Rothman*

ENCYCLOPEDIA
OF AMERICAN
NATIONAL PARKS

VOLUME ONE

NATIONAL PARK SYSTEM: OVERVIEW AND HISTORY

Founded in 1916, the National Park Service (NPS) represented an important advance in the federal system. Until its establishment, each and every federal land management agency had been devised with the express purpose of creating economic opportunity for some segment of the public. The Park Service's mission, the protection of national parks and their management for visitors, was a new innovation, characteristic of the Progressive Era. The moment favored government entities as managers of shared public resources, and the creation of the Park Service met that need as well as the need for some kind of comprehensive administration of the growing number of national parks and monuments.

During the Progressive Era, entities endowed with a mission of managing resources proliferated throughout the federal government. The Reclamation Service—later the Bureau of Reclamation—the U.S. Forest Service, and others came first; the NPS was the last major resource bureaucracy to be established before 1945. The need for the new agency stemmed from a serious management problem: Before 1916, no federal agency, bureau, or department had been assigned specific responsibility for national park areas.

Since the establishment of Yellowstone in 1872, national parks had been stepchildren of the Department of the Interior, with officials devoting only spare moments to management issues. Beginning in 1886, the U.S. Army assumed physical responsibility for Yellowstone, expanding to Yosemite, Sequoia, and other national parks after their establishment in 1890. While cavalry soldiers often enjoyed their posting in the national parks and zealously attended to their duty, they rarely planned the future of the areas under their charge. Jurisdiction fell to the General Land Office, which handled legal issues and inspections. Except for the military presence, seasonal in many national parks, most park areas were protected and preserved simply by warning signs.

Despite the lack of federal administration, national parks garnered much support from the nascent conservation movement. Luminaries such as Theodore Roosevelt, who became the most conservation-minded president in American history until the New Deal, and John Muir, the famed "John of the Mountains" who gave the nation the language to appreciate wilderness, were leading advocates. Organizations such as the Sierra Club, founded in 1892 by Muir and his friends, were devoted to national parks and the solitude and challenge they promised. Such people formed an influential and vocal constituency for national parks.

While this system was never adequate, it passed for administration until the enactment of the Antiquities Act of 1906. This new legislation encouraged the proliferation of national park areas; it allowed the president to use unchecked executive discretionary power to proclaim national monuments from the public domain and led to a rapid increase in the number of designated areas. National parks were soon few in number in comparison to national monuments. Their establishment required congressional approval, a long and often difficult process. Following 1906, the proclamation of new national monuments became a regular feature of the Roosevelt and Taft administrations. By 1911, there were more than thirty national parks and monuments under the administration of the Department of the Interior as well as a number of national monuments administered by the Forest Service in the Department of Agriculture and the War Department.

By then, efforts to establish an agency to administer national parks had a long history. In 1910, Secretary of the Interior Richard Ballinger advocated the idea; in 1912, President William Howard Taft added his voice to a growing clamor. Woodrow Wilson's secretary of the interior, Franklin K. Lane, and public-spirited leaders such as Horace McFarland of the American Civic Association pressed Congress for the creation of a national parks bureau. By 1913, an assistant secretary of the interior responsible for national park matters had become the only person in Washington, D.C., with any direct responsibility for the burgeoning park system.

In 1915, the man who personified the NPS during its first decade got his first taste of government service. During a summer trip in 1914, borax millionaire Stephen T. Mather, a graduate of the University of California, a promotional wizard, and a well-connected individual who knew about power, where to find it, and how to make it work for him, was angered by the poor management of Sequoia and Yosemite national parks. He wrote Lane—like Mather a graduate of the University of California and a member of the Sigma Chi fraternity—to complain, and the secretary replied: "If you don't like the way the parks are being run, come on down to Washington and run them yourself." Mather accepted the challenge, and with his assistant, Horace M. Albright, another Berkeley graduate who had recently graduated from law school and was supposed to shield his boss from red tape, took on the task of inventing an identity and image for the national parks.

The creation of the agency in 1916 was both a first step in this process and a foregone conclusion. In the aftermath of the failure to protect the Hetch Hetchy Valley inside Yosemite National Park from development that culminated in the building of a dam, the idea of preservation received a boost. National parks had been violated, many thought, demonstrating the need for real protection. The piecemeal system of the past had failed. Coupled with existing sentiment that favored a parks bureau, the signing of the National Park Service Act into law on August 25, 1916, gave Mather and Albright the base from which to fashion a national park system worthy of nature's nation, Americans' idea that they were a nation equal to the spectacular continent they felt they had conquered.

The agency experienced a difficult beginning. Initially a small bureau with few resources, the Park Service was forced to grapple with larger land management agencies within the federal government to create a place for itself. The Park Service also received a multifaceted set of obligations. It was to guard the parks, preserving land and resources for the future while simultaneously making them available for use. This seeming contradiction did not much vex the people of the first decades of the twentieth century. Individuals such as Mather and Albright were committed to the ideals of progress as the Progressive Era understood them: Development was good and necessary, and so was the protection of wild nature as a spiritual place and as a vestige of a past quickly fading. They defined this latter space in terms that can be described as sacred, while the temporal world they lived in had become ordinary, trod upon, even profane in a secular sense. Progressives firmly believed that these two kinds of spaces could coexist simultaneously, that the distances between the factories and the mountaintops were so great that they would not ever intersect. At the turn of the century, they were essentially correct, but as the nation grew, population expanded, and technology improved access, this decision to embrace an essentially contradictory mandate lay at the core of many of the policy problems of the agency then and now.

Mather and Albright made a formidable duo. Mather had excellent conservation credentials and came from the right social circle in which to promote national parks. Albright, an assertive young man with an eye on law school, was a fine complement. Endowed with aggressive land-acquisition instincts, Albright grappled with the details in intricate battles in the cloakrooms of Congress while Mather shook hands with dignitaries, smoothed over conflict, and assured the public of the importance of national parks. Together they developed an extraordinary promotional program, building ties with railroads, which brought most of the visitors to national parks, conveying political and civic leaders to national parks on catered recreational and constituency building tours, engineering funding programs for activities in national parks, placing more than 1,000 articles about national parks in American publications between 1917 and 1919 alone, and generally creating an audience where one

had not previously existed. By the end of the 1910s, a mere three years after its founding, the Park Service had forged a clearly defined and established mission and a concrete image with the American public.

The 1920s were pivotal for the new agency. With its emphasis on promotion and leisure, the National Park Service was ideally suited for the cultural revolution that swept the United States after World War I. The world of delayed gratification gave way to one of indulgence, and Americans reveled in the individual freedom spawned by technology and prosperity. More people could afford automobiles, and many had the time with which to travel in them. Mather and Albright recognized the value of highways as a way to allow them to tap into this new constituency. Mather's representatives lobbied governors in nearly every western state, the agency drew up plans for a national park-to-park highway that would link the great western national parks, and a number of highways to national parks were built.

During the 1920s, significant changes also occurred within the agency. National parks developed a primacy in the system that resulted from the difficulty associated with their establishment. National monuments were clearly relegated to lesser status, and areas in the monument category with the attributes of national parks were considered for admission among these "crown jewels" of the system. Beginning with the transfer of the Grand Canyon from monument to park status in 1919, a decade-long procession followed. Zion, Bryce Canyon, and Carlsbad Caverns were among the former monuments that enjoyed a newly enhanced status. Mather and Albright also initiated plans for national parks in the eastern half of the nation, both as a means to build a national constituency and as a way to differentiate the NPS from agencies with similar missions located entirely in the West such as the U.S. Forest Service. As a result, national parks such as Lafayette—now Acadia, in Maine—Shenandoah, Great Smoky Mountains, and Mammoth Cave became part of the primary category of federally reserved parks.

By the beginning of the New Deal in 1933, the NPS had become a formidable agency and the advent of federal programs such as the Civilian Conservation Corps and the Works Progress Administration only added to its position. With a domain that extended from Florida to Alaska, the Park Service administered a wide array of scenic, historic, and prehistoric sites, the most recent of which had come to the agency from the War Department as a result of Franklin D. Roosevelt's reorganization of the government and most of which could benefit from the various development programs the New Deal brought to the American table. As a result, the 1930s were characterized by a level of development never before seen in the national parks. Throughout the system, everything from visitor centers and roads to fire trails and campgrounds were constructed with a singular purpose: to make parks more accessible to the public at large.

The architecture of this early era sought to blend park facilities with the natural features of each region. Colloquially called "parkitecture," this blend of regionalism and available materials created a soft look for national parks, a fundamental quaintness that emphasized the way national parks evoked a preurban past. From Bandelier National Monument to Great Smoky Mountains National Park, the architecture of structures helped to fashion a wistful feeling about a mythic past as it put thousands upon thousands to work. From road builders to stonemasons, from architects to historians, those who implemented the programs of the New Deal not only designed a visual look to the parks, but also created new possibilities for careers within the Park Service.

In this respect, landscape architects became the dominant figures during the Park Service's first twenty-five years. From 1916 until World War II, the agency built and built, and landscape architects drove the process. Their activities made the parks what they were despite the limitations of funding and the constraints of New Deal programs. Landscape architect was the most important profession in the early Park Service. It created the look that drew the public to these new symbols of Americanism.

After World War II, the expansion of the Park Service mirrored the growth in demand for national parks as symbolic proof of reaching the American dream. During the war, few opportunities to spend the money saved from industrial jobs existed, and with rationing of commodities such as gasoline and rubber, most Americans enjoyed only limited opportunities to see the continent. At Navajo National Monument in Arizona, always a remote destination, the custodian, James L. Brewer, reported one visitor in all of July 1942; only half joking, he told an archeologist that he planned to put up a sign on a nearby road offering a free set of dishes to all visitors in an effort to assuage his loneliness. After the war, more widespread distribution of wealth in American society gave greater numbers of people the means to travel, and previously inaccessible places were more easily reached as a result of new and better roads, often built to facilitate wartime activities. The Grand Canyon experienced a harbinger of this change when visitation totals reached new highs each month during fall 1945, as discharged military personnel and departing war-industry workers made their way back to the places they had left when the war began. Sensing that this might be their only chance to see the country, many stopped at the great icons of the American West, national parks such as the Grand Canyon off Route 66, and the Grand Tetons and Yellowstone off the northern Lincoln Highway. The increase in visitors continued throughout 1946, as the stream of workers heading home became a feature of western highways. This movement served as both a precursor and a catalyst of an increase in tourism in the West.

At the same time, a fresh assault on the national parks demonstrated their increased importance in American society. At the turn of the twentieth century, Hetch Hetchy Valley inside Yosemite National Park had been dammed to build a reservoir. After World War II, the proposed Echo Park Dam inside Dinosaur National Monument became a cause célèbre that captured the attention of the nation. Part of the Bureau of Reclamation's nine-dam Colorado River Storage Project (CRSP), the dam was planned to support growth in Utah, Colorado, New Mexico, and Wyoming. After World War II, development was an American watchword, supported by almost everyone. Even the Department of the Interior tacitly agreed that a project of national importance could take priority over previous national park designation in any instance. This philosophy made decisions regarding the sanctity of national parks dependent on the political process in a manner that galled many park advocates.

Spurred by the newly energized conservation movement and its leading light, David Brower of the Sierra Club, the public rose up and defeated the Echo Park Dam. Conservation advocates used every tool at their disposal to stop the dam, even as the Park Service was relegated to the sidelines by the Department of the Interior. Agency Director Newton B. Drury was fired for refusing to support the dam, but many in the Park Service watched as their most sacred principle— the inviolability of national parks—was upheld. The rest of the CRSP, including the controversial Glen Canyon Dam, was eventually built, but Dinosaur National Monument was spared.

The battle to stop the dam in Dinosaur National Monument touched a national nerve, raising questions about the smug faith in progress that Americans had embraced. Parks and wild land within individual states had been saved from a dire threat over the objections of representatives of those states. Local values were superseded by national ones, as people who lived far away from Dinosaur National Monument played an instrumental role in blocking the dam. Many in the conservation movement at the time and many who have written about the controversy since have celebrated the demise of the Echo Park Dam proposal as a signal moment in American history.

After World War II, the traveling public expanded in numbers and breadth, and the expectations of its members reflected a different ethos. The prosperity generated by the war gave more of the American public a chance at the perquisites of the good life, and the constituency for vacation travel grew immensely. Within a few years of the war's end, most Americans enjoyed greater disposable income and more vacation time. A combination of affluence, pent-up demand for leisure after more than a fifteen-year lean period, and new fashions that stressed access to a wider intellectual and conceptual world as part of the pleasures of middle-class life, heightened the importance of the national parks. After the war, automobile ownership became a badge of middle-class status, and the annual two-week auto vacation in the summer became first a requirement of middle-class life and then a caricature of itself. The demand for recreation in national parks soared so rapidly and so greatly that the Park Service could hardly keep pace; not only were available campsites as rare as the American bald eagle, the existing campgrounds were covered with uncollected garbage, timber illegally cut for firewood, and other eyesores. The great symbols in the charge of the

Park Service were simply being overrun; noted author and iconoclast Bernard DeVoto recommended closing the national parks if they could not be better managed.

The transformation of national parks from just symbols to accessible recreational playgrounds inaugurated an unlikely revolution in development. Americans envisioned their parks as both sustenance and pleasure. They admired their culture for preserving such places, and they desperately wanted to get out and visit them. Out of these sentiments grew a program called Mission 66, a ten-year capital development program to refurbish the national parks in time for the fiftieth anniversary of the establishment of the National Park Service, which was to occur in 1966. Park Service officials remember the program as a windfall; the U.S. House of Representatives and the U.S. Senate seemed to be competing with each other to give the agency more money for new buildings such as visitor centers and permanent homes for staff, and for roads, campgrounds, and other developments. Almost every park in the system received some benefit from Mission 66; its most obvious legacy is the dozens of post office–like visitor centers scattered throughout the national park system.

By 1966, when the great capital development program came to an end, the Park Service seemed poised to move beyond the facilities management that long governed its policies to become a comprehensive science-based resources management agency. The structure for that transformation was in place; the 1963 "Leopold Report" offered a vision of the future of the national park system as "vignettes of a primitive America." Written by a team led by A. Starker Leopold, the son of the well-known environmentalist Aldo Leopold, the "Leopold Report" catapulted resource management issues and ecology to a kind of center stage they had never really enjoyed before. An American Academy of Sciences report, called the "Robbins Report," offered many of the same conclusions. Scientists, many trained by the GI Bill at institutions such as the University of California, came to the Park Service in droves, revolutionizing its structure. The mantle passed from landscape architects to scientists, particularly wildlife biologists, who shaped the agenda of the agency.

The moment was brief. Beginning in the late 1960s, the focus of the agency shifted again, toward people management or what might colloquially be called law enforcement. The increase in people in national parks virtually guaranteed greater need for mechanisms to control behavior, and the point was driven home to the Park Service as a result of a riot on July 4, 1970, in Stoneman Meadows in Yosemite. A squad of rangers on horseback rode into a crowd of young people who refused to vacate the meadow, and the fallout illustrated how much the Park Service's paramilitary past was out of touch with the nation's present. Many in the agency were shocked. They had long been the most beloved federal agency, and they could not reconcile this new vision of the Park Service green as part of the oppressive establishment.

The reaction was swift; the Park Service rapidly changed its focus to address these new concerns. Power shifted from managers to law enforcement rangers, and the agency spent much of its time and energy trying to come to grips with new constituencies. With a long history that placed landscape architecture and the development of facilities at the pinnacle of NPS objectives, followed by a short moment of ecology and science, the Park Service now placed people management at center stage, and it has remained there ever since.

The emphasis of the agency also changed rapidly in the 1960s. The prominence of a range of new categories of areas as well as a dramatic broadening of the themes thought worthy of preservation in the national system contributed to a spreading of the mission of the agency and consequently its resources. New historical parks were added to the system in an effort to encompass the emergence of previously ignored aspects of the American past. Places that had significance in African American heritage began to be included in the park system, and the Frederick Douglass National Historic Site in Washington, D.C., established in September 1962, was one example. Women demanded a place for their history among the sites of the system. The Women's Rights National Historical Park in Seneca Falls, New York, added to the system in December 1980, provided further evidence of the trend of inclusiveness.

Recreation also garnered a new position in the agency, helped by the ascendance of Conrad L. Wirth to the directorship in 1953. A development-oriented landscape architect with twenty years in the Park Service, Wirth had a long history of developing amenities in parks and was usually inclined to find opportunities for development in most situations. Under his leadership, the parkways, national lakeshores, and national recreation areas jumped to the fore, and the Park Service took on many of the traits of a recreation management agency.

During the 1960s, the park system grew rapidly. National park areas were part of the optimistic vision of the time, and under Director George B. Hartzog, Jr., who ascended to the head of the agency in 1964, the Park Service moved into the limelight as a federal agency. The genial Hartzog facilitated the addition of almost seventy parks during his eight-year tenure and further broadened the agency's mandate. With a thirty-year history of interest and experience in recreation, and after the filling of Lake Powell behind the Glen Canyon Dam in 1964, the Park Service assumed a primary position in public recreation. It administered not only the symbolic crown jewels of the nation but its outdoor playgrounds as well.

The 1960s inaugurated another important change. The Park Service had always excelled with the public, and as a result, the Park Service could count on a vocal and organized constituency to support its programs, favorable and often extensive press coverage, and, as a result, a willing and usually friendly Congress. Generally, this support system was ready, awaiting the call of the agency, and it usually sprang into action in response to Park Service efforts to mount new programs and increase expenditures. Newspaper editors and influential individuals could be marshaled to contact congressional representatives at a moment's notice. These people were welcome visitors to congressional offices, and federal agencies reciprocated by keeping their constituents informed. This organized campaigning also helped contain independent thinking by supporters. Rarely before the late 1950s did the various private entities that comprised the support system of the Park Service have their own agendas. Even more infrequently did their goals clash with those of the agency.

The Echo Park situation and the subsequent battle for the Wilderness Act began to change the equation. The forced departure of Newton B. Drury over Echo Park in 1951 contributed to a sense that the Park Service could not defend itself. The agency's sometimes laggard, sometimes dilatory approach to the question of wilderness also raised some concerns. Mainstream environmental groups such as the Sierra Club and the Wilderness Society had embraced the idea of a general wilderness bill. Members of these organizations could not help but wonder about the Park Service as it dissembled on the leading environmental issue of the day.

The passage of the Wilderness Act in 1964 posed a challenge to this new picture of the agency. Wilderness became a symbol of all that industrialization had cost the nation, but restrictions in the law made its management difficult. The result was agency ambivalence about wilderness at precisely the moment the public loved it most. Public suspicion of the agency grew as many could not understand why the agency they loved so much could not support what was a strongly preservationist measure.

At the same time, the Park Service faced a crisis in its mission. Since its founding in 1916, the agency had catered to the mainstream of the American public, first with an elite, class-based orientation and later with a democratic approach that facilitated automobiles and the visitors they brought. The Park Service hewed closely to its core mission for most of its first half century; as late as 1964, only six directors had led the agency in its forty-eight-year history and four of them had been with the Park Service since its founding. People came up through the ranks, learned the Park Service way, and implemented it when they reached the top. From Stephen T. Mather through Conrad L. Wirth, this mission meant serving visitors.

In this sense, the NPS understood its core constituency by the 1950s, people with two weeks of vacation each year who chose to see the national parks, often with their children in tow. During the 1960s, the constituencies that government served broadened; urban communities demanded access to national park areas, and after the riots that plagued American cities beginning in 1965, placating urban America became a significant goal of government. Elitism marked federal priorities, people from all walks of life complained, and the bounty of the nation had to be more evenly distributed. In the aftermath of the Wilderness Act of 1964, which many urbanites believed catered precisely to the constituencies that national parks had always served, the need to balance the traditional system with urban parks became paramount.

Worse for the Park Service, its new position located it squarely between constituencies. Park Service officials in the parks and in the regional offices became sensitized to the demands of the environmental constituency and altered the nature of Park Service attractions. In some cases, such as the termination of the firefall at Yosemite National Park and the Rock of Ages ceremony in Carlsbad Caverns—two of many attractions that were unrelated to the features for which the park in question had been established but had been codified by years of practice—agency decisions created controversy and strife. People with long and positive memories of such activities struggled to understand the reasons for their elimination. In other instances, such as the agency's desire to end recreational activities such as skiing within the parks, the changes in policy were insufficient to garner the support of the new environmental movement and simultaneously managed to alienate older supporters, the very constituency for the activities that were terminated. Caught in limbo between its friends and the groups it increasingly sought to cultivate, the Park Service floundered. Urban parks became a prime example of how the Park Service could be caught between two kinds of friends.

The demand for parks in urban areas that were dedicated to recreational use rather than the scenic monumentalism of their predecessors stemmed from far above the Park Service in the hierarchy of the federal government. President Richard M. Nixon and his secretaries of the interior, Walter J. Hickel and C.B. Rogers Morton, coined the idea of "parks for the people, where the people are," a different twist on the older theme of parks for the people. In part a response to the idea that government was out of touch with the people and an equal part salve after the urban riots of the 1960s, urban parks had advantages under this formulation. It provided new experiences to a constituency that had little previous exposure to the national parks themselves.

Despite Hartzog's enthusiasm for the idea, the Park Service responded slowly. Many in the agency were traditionalists, subscribing to a definition of national significance that closely followed the ideas of the first two directors of the agency, Stephen T. Mather and Horace M. Albright. Beautiful mountaintops and historic sites comprised the dominant current of such thinking. Ecology, parks for urban areas or for recreational use, and other similar innovations were far from the mainstream in this view. Hartzog was a tried-and-true Park Service man, sympathetic to such views, but he also was an entrepreneur and leader in the best NPS fashion: He looked for avenues that could expand the agency's reach. In 1972, this movement spawned the first two major urban parks in the nation, Gateway National Recreation Area in greater New York City and Golden Gate National Recreation Area in the San Francisco Bay area.

By the early 1970s, Congress began to regard parks in a new manner. California Representative Phillip Burton, who coined the term "park barreling" to describe his efforts, added places of marginal national significance to omnibus bills to obviate the opposition of colleagues to budget expenditures. When Burton learned that an individual in Congress opposed a spending bill, he routinely sought an area to be added to the park system within the representative's district. Parks meant the expenditure of federal dollars, more job opportunities, and ongoing federal largesse. Even the most conservative members of Congress were loath to vote against bills that provided economic opportunities in their home districts. The result was an even greater expansion in the number of parks created, albeit many with the scorn of park professionals. Some even spoke of the era as "diluting the stock" of the park system.

As these factors came together in the 1970s, the agency began to lose the focus it had generally enjoyed since its founding. Although they differed in philosophy and perspective, Newton B. Drury, who directed the agency from 1940 until 1953, and Conrad L. Wirth were leaders in the mold of Mather and Albright—dynamic individuals who brought to the director's position a vision of what the park system could be. Hartzog was cut from the same cloth. Bold and innovative, such leaders carried the Park Service. But politics torpedoed historical leadership in 1972. President Richard M. Nixon fired Hartzog and appointed Ronald H. Walker, his campaign director and a man with no experience with parks, to the job. Instability followed through three subsequent directors. By 1980, the result was a demoralized agency.

The position of the Park Service improved after 1980 despite the tenure of James Watt as secretary of the interior from 1981 to 1984. An attorney, a staunch advocate of free-market capitalism, and a veteran of more than two decades on the losing side of environmental battles, Watt planned an all-out assault on the reigning value system that supported the reservation of federal land, limits on the use of natural resources for the purposes of development, and the values of the environmental movement. Watt sought to turn the natural resources of the country over to those he called "the people," not the elitists he believed had been managing them for the previous twenty-five years. The National Park Service was squarely in his sights.

Watt emphasized the development of the physical plant in national parks, taking credit for an initiative entitled the Park Restoration and Improvement Program (PRIP) that began before his arrival. "I will err on the side of public use versus preservation," he announced in March 1981 in a statement emblematic of his philosophy. "There are people who want to bring their motorcycles and snowmobiles right into the middle of Yellowstone National Park," he told a group of Park

Service employees, "and our job is to make sure they *can*." Watt's Department of the Interior was different from any since the 1920s, and it was anathema to the people who made their careers in the park system. Many kept their heads down throughout his reign, sighing with relief when his own words forced his resignation.

Yet the Park Service's position did not improve after Watt's departure. It was as if the agency bucked up in the face of visible opposition, buoyed by Director Russell E. Dickenson, a long-time Park Service man who brought the agency together after a series of disastrous appointments. In the late 1980s, the agency again slumped, punished by the great Yellowstone fires of 1988. In the aftermath, NPS Director Roger Kennedy tried to fashion a new direction for the agency, called the Vail Agenda, which brought resource management to the primary position that many in the post-1970 Park Service believed it always had. A planning initiative, the Vail Agenda set goals, but throughout the early 1990s, they remained out of reach. In the most egregious example, a lack of funding set the agency back so far that by 1995, it faced a $5 billion backlog in maintenance alone.

By the mid-1990s, the Park Service was in transition, experiencing changes that promised new options, which also hamstrung the agency. To meet the objectives of Vice President Al Gore's 1995 call to reinvent government, a major component of which was to reduce the size of the federal government, Kennedy made a tactical decision to change the agency's hierarchy. He froze all positions in the parks, forced the central offices to absorb the cuts in staffing and funding, and moved surplus people into the frozen positions at the park level. The strategy was supposed to yield a 30 percent reduction in staffing and $30 million in savings.

Kennedy's decision had a number of consequences that redistributed authority, power, and resources throughout the Park Service. It purposely eviscerated the regional offices, long the mainstay of management, oversight, and specialized expertise, leaving few who could hold park-level management accountable. Each regional director was left with a minimal staff in cultural and natural resources, one representing the rangers, one in administration, and very few others. Interpretation, maintenance, and all other professionals were moved into park support offices and considered noncentral office staff. This created two regional offices where the agency previously had only one, but the two offered less support and assistance than their predecessors, and the oversight long housed in the regional offices evaporated. Clusters of parks, based loosely on geographical similarities, determined regional priorities for research, preventive and rehabilitative maintenance, and most other budget functions previously handled by regional office staff. Parks were supposed to work closely together and share expertise.

By most accounts, the reorganization upended the standard practices of the agency but did not replace them with a viable operating system. When the regional offices were emptied, people moved into leadership positions in parks for which they had no expertise or previous experience. Some parks found themselves with assistant superintendents, the operations chiefs of the park, who had never served in a park and had little conception of how parks worked. Many experienced people took an "early out" retirement option, sometimes with large incentive packages. Often the ones who left had precisely the expertise that the agency needed, leaving not only a gap in institutional memory but also a diminished capacity.

In the new century, the Park Service has yet to regain the power and prestige it enjoyed during most of its first fifty years. As the new millennium begins, the agency faces major challenges, not the least of which is the enormous backlog of maintenance necessary in the park system. A well-developed infrastructure and an agency self-image tied to the culture of consumption helped the Park Service straddle the bifurcated mission given it at its inception. Charged with assuring both the preservation of the parks and their use, the Park Service faced the prospect that any of its decisions could alienate a part of its constituency. This reality has made policy-making a difficult exercise ever since.

–Hal K. Rothman

FURTHER READING

Carr, Ethan. *Wilderness by Design: Landscape Architecture and the National Parks.* Lincoln: University of Nebraska Press, 1997.

Foresta, Ronald. *America's National Parks and Their Keepers.* Washington, DC: Resources for the Future, 1984.

Ise, John. *Our National Park Policy: A Critical History.* Baltimore, MD: Johns Hopkins University Press, 1961.

Rothman, Hal K. *Preserving Different Pasts: The American National Monuments.* Urbana: University of Illinois Press, 1989.

——. *The New Urban Park: Golden Gate National Recreation Area and Civic Environmentalism.* Lawrence: University Press of Kansas, 2003.

Runte, Alfred. *National Parks: The American Experience.* 2d ed. Lincoln: University of Nebraska Press, 1987.

Sellars, Richard. *Natural Resource Management in the National Parks: A History.* New Haven, CT: Yale University Press, 1997.

Shaffer, Marguerite. *See America First: Tourism and National Identity, 1880–1940.* Washington, DC: Smithsonian Institution, 2001.

BIOGRAPHIES

HORACE M. ALBRIGHT

HORACE M. ALBRIGHT, the Park Service's second director, began his career in the agency as Stephen T. Mather's right-hand man, and he was the architect of much of the agency's political success with Congress. Born in Bishop, California, on January 6, 1890, Albright was a recent graduate of the University of California and an assistant to Secretary of the Interior Franklin K. Lane when he was introduced to Mather at the end of 1914. Albright became Mather's closest associate throughout his years as assistant secretary in charge of national parks and later as director

Horace M. Albright. *(National Park Service)*

of the National Park Service (NPS). The two men were an inseparable and insurmountable team. When the Park Service was created in August 1916, Albright went along, rising to director in 1929 when illness finally forced Mather from his life's passion.

Albright was easily the most adept politician and most canny negotiator to ever hold the Park Service's highest office. Under Mather, he served as superintendent of Yellowstone National Park, but his real job was to facilitate relationships with Congress, acquire lands for new park areas and the expansion of existing areas, and solve whatever problems arose. Albright had piranha like land-acquisition instincts. His relentless approach turned the Park Service–Forest Service dispute to the Park Service's favor during the 1920s, largely by his tactic of defining the parameters of individual land acquisition and skewering the foresters with their own logic. Few wanted to face him as they drew their maps; fewer still could even claim to have bested the canny Albright.

Mather was seriously ill three times during his tenure as NPS director, and each time Albright filled in with aplomb. When Mather was finally institutionalized, Albright became director, pursuing an important strategic agenda to broaden the base of the park system. He successfully advocated the acquisition of national parklands east of the Mississippi River, added the impetus for acquiring historic sites, most of which were either managed by the War Department or held in private hands, and prepared the agency to take advantage of Franklin D. Roosevelt's New Deal in 1933. In a famous automobile ride with FDR, Albright outlined how the parks could be part of his back-to-work programs, leading to an enormous Civilian Conservation Corps presence in the national parks. When he left the agency on August 10, 1933, Albright had clearly been the most significant influence on the shape of the national park system.

Only forty-three when he left the agency, Albright continued to a career in the mining industry. He rose in the United States Potash Corporation, and later with the United States Borax and Chemical Corporation. He maintained a strong interest in the national parks, sitting on agency advisory boards, using his congressional connections to further his and the agency's goals, and weighing in on policy in public and private ways. Albright finally died in 1987, having witnessed the expansion of the park system in ways that he foresaw but could not possibly have envisioned.

Albright's legacy had many facets. He taught a strong conservation ethic and relied not only on powerful tactical maneuvering but on the principle of moral suasion. He believed in the values of conservation and in their manifestation in the park system more strongly than any other individual except Mather, and he was uniquely skilled at bringing those values to fruition. In many ways, the national parks and the NPS are what they are because of Horace M. Albright.

FURTHER READING

Albright, Horace M. *Oh, Ranger!* Palo Alto, CA: Stanford University Press, 1928.

Albright, Horace M., as told to Robert Cahn. *The Birth of the National Park Service: The Founding Years, 1913–1933.* Salt Lake City, UT: Howe Brothers, 1985.

Swain, Donald C. *Wilderness Defender: Horace M. Albright and Conservation.* Chicago: University of Chicago Press, 1970.

ARNO B. CAMMERER

The third director of the National Park Service, ARNO B. CAMMERER shepherded the agency through the New Deal. With the enormous base of labor and money the federal programs provided, the agency acquired a physical plant and the ability to serve visitors.

Cammerer was born in Nebraska in 1883, the son of Lutheran minister, and matriculated from Georgetown College of Law in 1911. By that time, he was an experienced federal employee. He had begun a career of public service in the Treasury Department, working for the National Commission on Fine Arts and Public Buildings Commission of Congress before coming to the Park Service in 1919.

Cammerer was the consummate bureaucrat, the agency's inside man under both Mather and Albright. He served as assistant and associate director, spending the summer of 1923 as the agency's acting director during one of Mather's illnesses. Dependable, honest, and careful, Cammerer made the agency work.

He was rewarded with the directorship upon Albright's departure, but the timing turned out to be bad. Cammerer was saddled with an enormous workload, much greater than either of his predecessors experienced, as a result of the New Deal and its many programs. Worse, he instantaneously earned the enmity of the powerful and abrasive secretary of the interior, Harold L. Ickes, who bullied Cammerer with a passion that in retrospect seems shocking. Never good with conflict, Cammerer buckled under the strain, experiencing a powerful heart attack in 1939 that led to his retirement in 1940. He passed away as a result of another heart attack in 1941.

In the end, Cammerer was an outstanding administrator but not a great visionary like his two predecessors. His ascendance to the directorship represented the maturation of the agency; it had gone from movers and shakers, enthusiastic, ground-floor managers who spread the agency as far as it could go, to the hands of a capable manager who sought to consolidate its gains. By 1940, the agency was a different place than it had been even a decade before. Cammerer adroitly managed these changes, leaving a clean slate for his successors.

FURTHER READING
Foresta, Ronald A. *America's National Parks and Their Keepers.* Washington, DC: Resources for the Future, 1984.
Shankland, Robert. *Steve Mather of the National Parks.* New York: Alfred A. Knopf, 1953.

ARTHUR E. DEMARAY

ARTHUR E. DEMARAY, who served as director for nine months in 1951 at the end of a long career with the agency, was the last of the first generation of Park Service officials to hold the agency's highest office. Beginning

Arthur E. Demaray. *(National Park Service)*

with the U.S. Geological Service as a draftsman, Demaray came to Mather's office even before the creation of the Park Service. He served ably for almost forty years, with most of his work in operations, personnel management, budget, fiscal oversight, and similar activities. No particular initiative or programs have been attributed to him. Instead he appears as the consummate organization man, the one who handled the details while others did the planning.

Demaray's short period of directorship was a courtesy, an honor to a man who had been essential to the development of the national parks but had done his work behind the scenes. He was briefly in the limelight, but in his characteristic way, stepped aside late in 1951 to allow the appointment of a new director well before the election of 1952. The directorship of the Park Service had never been a partisan position, and Demaray believed that by stepping away with so much lead time, he could assure the next director the same lack of partisanship that his predecessors enjoyed. Demaray's actions helped stave off the politicization of the directorship for another twenty years.

FURTHER READING
Shankland, Robert. *Steve Mather of the National Parks.* New York: Alfred A. Knopf, 1953.
Wirth, Conrad L. *Parks, Politics, and the People.* Norman: University of Oklahoma Press, 1980.

RUSSELL E. DICKENSON

When he ascended to the directorship of the agency in 1980, RUSSELL E. DICKENSON inherited an agency in turmoil. Dickenson was selected to quell dissension in the agency after nearly a decade in which agency leadership did not meet the challenges it faced. A thirty-five-year veteran of the Park Service when his tenure began, Dickenson was widely respected. Starting as a ranger at the Grand Canyon, he served ably as head of the National Capital Parks, deputy director of the agency under Ron Walker, and regional director in the Pacific Northwest. A true "green-blood," Dickenson marked a change for the agency, a step toward its roots with all the positive sentiment the agency's history conveyed.

In his five years at the top, Dickenson held to an older vision of the national parks, far from the views of his immediate predecessors. In this, he mirrored the sentiments of the Reagan administration, which sought to slow the expansion of government and expressly planned not to increase the number of national park areas. Dickenson's reasons were entirely different from those of an administration hostile to national parks. On the heels of the era of "park barreling," the wholesale creation of national park areas for political reasons, he feared diluting the quality of the park system. Outside of Alaska, only 6 acres were added to the park system under Dickenson.

Dickenson also emphasized rehabilitating the park system, inaugurating the Park Restoration and Improvement Program, which pumped almost $5 billion into the park system during his tenure. Secretary of the Interior James Watt claimed credit for the program, but everyone on Capitol Hill and in the media recognized it as Dickenson's handiwork. This effort to upgrade park facilities was a fitting tribute to Dickenson's tenure.

Dickenson brought steady leadership and continuity in a time when both qualities were lacking. He invigorated the system with a new optimism that stemmed from the high regard in which he was held. His five years served as a high point during a difficult era. He retired in 1985.

FURTHER READING

Everhart, William C. *The National Park Service.* Boulder, CO: Westview, 1983.
Foresta, Ronald. *America's National Parks and Their Keepers.* Washington, DC: Resources for the Future, 1984.

NEWTON B. DRURY

The Park Service's fourth director, NEWTON B. DRURY was the most preservation-oriented of the agency's early leaders. Another of the many Californians who played significant roles in the early history of the agency, Drury began a career in conservation in 1919 when he left his firm, the Drury Brothers Advertising Company, and joined the Save-the-Redwoods League as its executive secretary. Just seven years out of college, Drury had already become a skilled fund-raiser, and the league coveted that skill along with his experience in orchestrating legislation and encouraging public support. Drury already admired Mather's Park Service for its ability to utilize the techniques of modern advertising. He remained close to its sphere throughout the 1920s and 1930s and was offered the directorship in 1933 when Albright departed. Drury demurred, but when Harold L. Ickes came calling again in 1939, Drury accepted.

The agency that Drury inherited in 1940 was entirely different from the one offered him in 1933. The New Deal built an infrastructure for the park system, creating visitor centers, campgrounds, firelines, and headquarters throughout the system. The Park Service had swelled in number, with many people attached to the agency under the aegis of the New Deal. It fell to Drury to fashion a new future.

Although World War II slowed the implementation of Drury's ideas, the years after the war revealed that the Park Service was now led by a man with a strong devotion to the idea of preservation. Always a moderate, Drury strived for reasonable change. He pushed to end the Yosemite firefall, where the concessionaire at the park pushed a pile of flaming brush over the edge of a precipice each night. He lobbied for an end to feeding garbage to bears in Yellowstone National Park, a tactic with no conservation value and

Albright. Drury pointed the Park Service and the park system toward the future, albeit a little before many in the agency were prepared to follow. Yet Drury's leadership and his staunch adherence to principle in the Echo Park controversy set a high standard for leadership in the park system.

FURTHER READING

Fox, Stephen R. *John Muir and His Legacy: The American Conservation Movement.* Boston: Little, Brown, 1981.

Schrepfer, Susan. *The Fight to Save the Redwoods: A History of Environmental Reform, 1917–1978.* Madison: University of Wisconsin Press, 1983.

GARY EVERHARDT

GARY EVERHARDT served one of the shortest tenures of National Park Service directors. He joined the agency as an engineer in 1957, rising to the position of superintendent of Grand Teton National Park in 1972. When Secretary of the Interior C.B. Rogers Morton looked for a successor for Walker within the ranks, he settled on Everhardt.

Everhardt had established a strong track record as an administrator, a skill necessary in the nation's capital. His leadership showed especially in the Park Service's U.S. Bicentennial program, the most sustained of any federal agency and a favorite of the traveling public. In other ways, Everhardt was overwhelmed by the job. He did not understand the politics of the nation's capital and made a number of poorly considered policy judgments that hurt his stature with his superiors. When Jimmy Carter won the 1976 election, Everhardt was as good as gone. The new Democratic administration had its own candidates for the post of directorship, and Everhardt was returned to the superintendency of Blue Ridge Parkway in May 1977.

Everhardt's directorship was too short to leave a significant mark on the agency, but his appointment highlighted the turmoil that

Newton B. Drury. *(National Park Service)*

the sole purpose of assuring that the public saw wildlife. After more than a decade in which he fought valiantly for the parks to be natural, only to find that his superior, Secretary of the Interior Ickes thought him too timid, Drury was finally pushed from office during the Echo Park controversy. Refusing Secretary of the Interior Oscar Chapman's dictate to support the construction of a dam inside Dinosaur National Monument, Drury was unceremoniously dumped from office in 1951. He continued his lifelong interest in conservation until his death in 1978.

Drury was the first to lead the Park Service without rising through its ranks, yet he came to the agency with impeccable conservation credentials. A staunch advocate of nature preservation, he brought a different ethos to the leadership of the Park Service, in some cases even incurring the wrath of Horace characterized the directorship in the 1970s. Everhardt was one of three directors in rapid succession, none of whom were able to last long enough to establish the kinds of programs that line staff and the public could support. The Park Service had begun to drift.

FURTHER READING

Everhart, William C. *The National Park Service.* Boulder, CO: Westview, 1983.

Foresta, Ronald. *America's National Parks and Their Keepers.* Washington, DC: Resources for the Future, 1984.

GEORGE B. HARTZOG, JR.

GEORGE B. HARTZOG, JR., was a throwback, a country boy in an age of Washington bureaucrats. Born in South Carolina in 1920, he

George B. Hartzog, Jr. *(National Park Service)*

became the youngest minister in the Methodist Church when he was ordained at the age of seventeen, read for the bar in the old manner, as an apprentice to an attorney, and was admitted to the practice of law in 1942. In 1946, he joined the Park Service as an attorney, becoming superintendent of the complicated Jefferson National Expansion Memorial in St. Louis in 1959. There he jump-started and oversaw a stalled redevelopment project and the construction of the Gateway Arch. Hartzog brought a fresh spirit to the moribund project, cutting through the bureaucratic rigmarole. Hartzog was so popular in St. Louis that he was enticed away from the agency in 1962 to become executive director of Downtown St. Louis, Inc., the city's private redevelopment entity. He returned to the Park Service as associate director in 1963, replacing Conrad L. Wirth as director in 1964.

A savvy negotiator and a consummate people person, Hartzog inherited the agency at the right moment. Mission 66 had put the Park Service on a solid footing, but the agency had maintained a narrow vision of its place in American society. In 1964, the Park Service still emphasized what it always had: remote national parks with spectacular scenery. Hartzog broadened that approach from the day he took the director's chair. Under his leadership, the agency added seventy new areas, including urban parks. After the urban riots of the 1960s, Hartzog realized that his agency served only a segment of the American public and sought to reach the inner cities. His programs were successful, leading to the creation of the first two great urban national recreation areas, Gateway in New York and Golden Gate in San Francisco. Hartzog also championed the cause of women and minorities, appointing the first African American to head the U.S. Park Police, the first time an African American had been selected to lead a major police force in the United States, and a number of women as park superintendents. He took advantage of the Land and Water Conservation Fund, the Johnson-era program to fund land acquisition for the park system, and played an instrumental role in the resolution of Alaskan native claims to land, the precursor of the Alaskan national park system established during Jimmy Carter's presidency. Hartzog was not a favorite of the Nixon administration, and a few weeks after the Second World Conference on National Parks, which was held at Yellowstone on the hundredth anniversary of its founding in September 1872, Hartzog was unceremoniously dismissed.

A skilled politician, Hartzog extended the reach of the park system to almost every congressional district in the country. In the fashion of Stephen T. Mather, he lobbied incessantly, took congressional representatives on trips, and was the life of the party. A dynamic visionary leader, he shaped the modern Park Service, taking it from its staid origins and giving it the cultural moxie to thrive in the modern U.S. government.

FURTHER READING
Everhart, William C. *The National Park Service.* Boulder, CO: Westview, 1983.
Foresta, Ronald. *America's National Parks and Their Keepers.* Washington, DC: Resources for the Future, 1984.
Hartzog, George B., Jr. *Battling for the National Parks.* Mt. Kisco, NY: Moyer Bell Limited, 1988.

EDGAR L. HEWETT

Known as "El Toro" (the bull), but only behind his back, EDGAR L. HEWETT was a western educator, archeologist, and entrepreneur responsible for the Antiquities Act of 1906 and the revival of Santa Fe, New Mexico. Born in 1865 and raised on a farm in western Illinois, Hewett proceeded to Tarkio College in Missouri. After graduating, he taught there

and at Colorado Normal School in Greeley before becoming president of New Mexico Normal School in Las Vegas, New Mexico, in 1898. Even before Hewett's arrival in New Mexico, the romantic grandeur of the prehistoric Southwest captured his imagination. Archeologist, cultural entrepreneur, and tireless promoter of his causes, Hewett engineered and authored the Antiquities Act of 1906, the single most important piece of preservation legislation passed prior to 1966, while convincing the Archaeological Institute of America to locate a research center, now known as the School of American Research, in Santa Fe. In addition, he became the primary excavator of the Pajarito Plateau region of New Mexico, and developed most of the important cultural institutions in Santa Fe. The Museum of New Mexico, the Museum of Fine Arts, and the revival of both Fiesta and Indian Market were results of his initiative.

As a turn-of-the-twentieth-century institution builder, Hewett ranks in the top echelon. His efforts led to the preservation of much of the archeology in the national park system, and the category of sites that his legislation created became the best tool available to preserve threatened lands through much of the twentieth century. Hewett's actions also saved Santa Fe from the fate of communities bypassed by railroads and created the climate in which artists and writers have felt comfortable ever since. When he died in 1946, he was buried in one of the interior walls of the Museum of Fine Arts in Santa Fe, testimony to both the power he wielded and his commitment to the creation of a cultural heritage.

FURTHER READING
Chauvenet, Beatrice. *Hewett and Friends: A Biography of Santa Fe's Vibrant Era.* Santa Fe: Museum of New Mexico, 1984.
Rothman, Hal K. *On Rims and Ridges: The Los Alamos Area Since 1880.* Lincoln: University of Nebraska Press, 1992.

ROGER KENNEDY

When ROGER KENNEDY succeeded James Ridenour as President Bill Clinton's director of the National Park Service (NPS), he was the first historian to ascend to the agency's top post. Kennedy brought a wealth of public sector experience to the position. For the ten years prior to 1993, he had been director of the Smithsonian's National Museum of American History. The decade before, he served as vice president of the Ford Foundation. Skilled at public life, Kennedy had served on commissions and boards and in many capacities in government. Innovative and creative, he brought new ideas to the agency.

Kennedy's appointment also solidified the political nature of the position. Since Russell Dickenson, no one with a Park Service background had been appointed to lead the agency. This put directors in a difficult position: They had to win the affection of their agency without any experience with its culture. Kennedy was no exception.

As a historian, Kennedy focused on education. Education had always held a truncated position in the agency, a stepchild among its many obligations. Kennedy pushed the Internet as a communications device, laying the basis for the excellent NPS Web site that has become a fixture in national park education.

In an effort to meet the objective of Vice President Al Gore's 1995 call to reinvent government, Kennedy sought to reduce the Park Service workforce by 30 percent and its expenditures by $30 million. The regional offices, long the mainstay of agency operations, bore the brunt of this decision. They lost staff and became shells of their former selves, with many employees leaving through early retirement programs and others transferring to individual national park units. Those who left often had precisely the knowledge and experience that the agency needed. As a result, agency management was left in a shambles. Eviscerated, the regional offices could not serve the functions they always had. The parks attained new levels of responsibility but lacked sufficient staff to carry out the assigned tasks.

It was a demoralizing time for many in the agency. Attrition from early retirement cost the agency much valuable institutional memory, as well as countless skilled professionals. The Park Service became a decentralized agency, and much of the expertise previously shared among the units was lost. Both the parks and their visitors suffered.

In the end, however, Kennedy's reorganization had little long-term effect. After his departure from the Park Service, its impact soon faded. Upon leaving, Kennedy resumed his distinguished career as a lecturer and an educator.

FURTHER READING

Thorsett, Peter E. "Reorganizing the U.S. National Park Service." Unpublished paper, University of Tennessee, Knoxville, 1998.

FRAN P. MAINELLA

FRAN P. MAINELLA ascended to the National Park Service's top post in 2001 as the first woman to head the agency. An appointee of President George W. Bush and a Floridian who served as director of Florida State Parks before assuming the directorship, she had a long and distinguished career as a recreation manager. During her tenure, Florida was awarded the National Sporting Goods Association's Gold Medal for State Parks, a selection denoting the best state park system in the country. Despite her experience and merit, Mainella's appointment was widely seen as political. Her home state had been a battleground in the 2000 election, and the new administration sought to reward the friends that

Fran P. Mainella. *(National Park Service)*

unity to the nation. Mainella recognized that national parks remained powerful symbols of the values of the nation and helped bring the parks to the forefront in a time of crisis. She received the Great Outdoors Award from the American Recreation Coalition for her efforts.

Yet Mainella faced many of the difficulties of leadership in the agency. Despite her focus on the park system's terrifying maintenance backlog, there were few resources available to the agency during the hard economic times of the early twenty-first century. The agency again seemed demoralized and people left in droves for other careers or early retirement. Mainella's position was difficult, but as of 2004, she had not yet negotiated the boundary between politics and leadership.

FURTHER READING
National Park Trust. "NPT Interview with NEW NPS Director Fran Mainella." *Legacy News,* Spring 2002.

helped hand it the presidency. Mainella was among many Floridians in the George W. Bush administration. The conservation community welcomed her in spite of its reservations. She had compiled a strong record of resource stewardship in Florida.

Mainella's greatest accomplishment to date as director was fashioning the National Park Service's response to the atrocities perpetrated on the United States on September 11, 2001. The park system was directly affected: Many of the areas that seemed to be targets, symbols of the nation such as the Washington Monument, were managed by the agency, and security became a major concern. Even more, Americans flocked to their national parks in the aftermath in search of solace and perspective, and Mainella encouraged the agency to meet their needs. She engineered a fee-free weekend in November 2001 in which Americans would visit their parks in an effort to offer hope, healing, and

STEPHEN T. MATHER

The businessman turned civic exemplar who took the reins of the National Park Service at its birth, STEPHEN T. MATHER was an extraordinary individual by any measure. Born on July 4, 1867, Mather was raised in California in an exciting era in the Golden State's young history. He matriculated from the University of California, Berkeley, in 1887, a devoted adherent of the fraternity Sigma Chi and among the many in the era who inhaled the heady fumes of public service that enticed the privileged classes of the United States. Mather first worked as a journalist under the storied Charles A. Dana at the New York *Sun,* leaving the paper to make his fortune in the development of American borax. He took charge of promotion for borax king Francis Marion Smith, creating the Twenty Mule Team brand and making a name for himself in the nascent public relations and advertising community. Mather had a knack for publicity and for keeping a product in the national eye. Following a nervous breakdown that briefly institutionalized him in 1903, Mather left Smith's empire to join an old friend in a new borax-mining endeavor. Eleven years later, he had become sufficiently wealthy to retire and pursue his other passion: public service.

Even before Mather became successful, he had been known to have a strong desire to accomplish civic goals. An inveterate joiner, he belonged to nearly every major civic, social, and charitable organization in every city he lived in. His fraternity remained important to him all his life and expanded to a range of other activities. Mather seemed the classic good citizen; he was involved in so many civic activities that it was hard to find an organization of any significance to which he did not belong. In love with California and perhaps the state's leading cheerleader in the early twentieth century, Mather extended his passion to the outdoors, so remarkable in his native state. This particular fascination drew him to the national parks.

Mather's involvement with the national parks began with an apocryphal story that illustrated much about the cozy nature of the American ruling class at the start of the twentieth century. One of Mather's college classmates, Sidney Mezes, advised President Woodrow Wilson, leading to the appointment of a coterie of Californians—and indeed University of California graduates—to high posts during Wilson's presidency. One of them, Franklin K. Lane, who had been at Berkeley at the same time as Mather, became secretary of the interior. Acquainted with the new secretary, Mather wrote him a scathing letter after a visit to the national parks. Lane purportedly responded: "Dear Steve, if you don't like the way the national parks are being run, come on down to Washington and run them yourself." Mather took up the challenge, coming to the Department of the Interior in 1915 as a special assistant to Lane with national parks as the primary part of his portfolio.

A full eighteen months later, Mather was appointed the first director of the new National Park Service. It had been a dizzying time, full of agitation for the new agency, congressional machinations, and the application of political influence. The result put Mather in a leadership position in which he firmly believed: He had come to see American nature as the extraordinary characteristic of the nation. Leading the Park Service offered him a way to illustrate the importance not only of the physical continent, but of the principles of Bull Moose Republicanism that he had embraced in the 1912 election. Well before 1916, Mather was a dedicated Progressive, among the many who believed in public solutions to issues of the common good in the United States.

Until his death in 1929, Mather led the agency, utilizing his charm and public relations skills to fashion a place for the Park Service—and the national parks they administered—in the federal bureaucracy. Mather built a wide national constituency, courted Congress and influential national leaders, pounded concessions and transportation companies into shape, expanded the park system east of the Mississippi River, and created a formidable agency to protect the parks. Incapacitated by illness and felled at last by a stroke, he was the genesis of the agency and its particular vision of managing the dichotomy between protection and use.

FURTHER READING

Foresta, Ronald A. *America's National Parks and Their Keepers*. Washington, DC: Resources for the Future, 1984.

Shankland, Robert. *Steve Mather of the National Parks*. 3d ed. New York: Alfred A. Knopf, 1970.

WILLIAM PENN MOTT, JR.

With the most distinguished resume in American park management after 1950, WILLIAM PENN MOTT, JR., seemed an ideal choice when he replaced Russell Dickenson in 1985. He began his career in 1933 with the Park Service as a landscape architect, worked as a public planner, and after World War II, became superintendent of the Oakland, California, parks system. In seventeen years, he revolutionized the local park system, creating a national model. When he left to become general manager of the East Bay Regional Park District in 1963, no American city had a better park system than Oakland. He worked similar magic in the East Bay, doubling park acreage and initiating programming during his four-year tenure.

Appointed by Ronald Reagan to head the California Department of Parks and Recreation in 1967, Mott brought the same energy and creativity that he displayed throughout his career. Under his leadership, the agency added more than 150,000 acres of state parkland, increasing park holdings by almost 20 percent. By the time he stepped down in 1974, he was widely acclaimed as the most innovative parks man in California's history.

Mott's relationship with the Park Service was tricky. Initially offered the directorship by Richard Nixon in 1969, he demurred and in fact became an adversary of the Park Service over the possible transfer of lands at Redwood National and State Parks. When another fellow Californian, Ronald Reagan, called in 1985, Mott accepted his offer, well aware that the administration he served was not sympathetic to national parks. Despite opposition, Mott added twelve new areas to the system and defended park values against the onslaught of Reagan-era bean counters. He also was the point man during the terrible fires at Yellowstone in 1988, vociferously explaining the reasoning behind the agency's

William Penn Mott, Jr. *(National Park Service)*

"let burn" strategy as the national media screamed for active suppression of the out-of-control conflagration.

Mott also recognized some of the important threats to national parks. He noted that development around the parks posed a genuine issue, paid attention to revising outdated policies, and provided strong leadership. Following another well-respected leader in Russell Dickenson, Mott helped restore the sense of camaraderie and mission that carried the agency through its first fifty years. After leaving the agency in 1989, he continued to serve as a special assistant and maintained a vigorous schedule. Mott died in 1992.

FURTHER READING
Butler, M.E. *Prophet of the Parks: The Story of William Penn Mott, Jr.* Ashburn, VA: National Recreation and Park Association, 1999.

FRANK PINKLEY

FRANK PINKLEY served as superintendent of the Southwestern National Monuments, a far-flung collection of historical, archeological, and natural park areas in the national park system. Born in 1880 in Missouri, he moved to Arizona in 1900, settling at the Casa Grande Ruins Reservation in 1901. For the next thirty-nine years, "Boss" Pinkley ran an empire by the force of his will, cajoling appropriations from recalcitrant federal officials, creating services for visitors, and maintaining an odd collection of parks and people by applying initiative, charisma, and a set of uncompromising standards. When he began, little systematic administration had been applied to the cultural features of the Southwest. By the time he died of a heart attack at the opening session of his school for national monument personnel in 1940, he had established a network of interrelated parks, procedures and practices for their management, and a tight group of people, loyal to him and his organization, who ran them.

Within the National Park Service, Pinkley was something of a gadfly. In the 1920s, as he put together his system, the emphasis of the agency remained almost exclusively on the large scenic national parks. In an era of limited funding, this meant that Pinkley's national monuments received little support. From his contrary perspective, this seemed to Pinkley a slight; he believed the lack of substantive appropriation revealed a failing on the part of the agency, and comparisons of figures bore out many of his contentions. His stance led to conflict with the national leadership, which sought to create a primary direction for the agency. Pinkley's refusal to follow the stated goals left him with a kind of marginal status within the agency.

Pinkley typified the entrepreneurial generation that created the Park Service during its first fifteen years. He learned the hard way that as the agency became more powerful and more professional, the future lay not in the individualism of the past but in a cooperative relationship between local people and state and federal government.

FURTHER READING

Rothman, Hal K. *Preserving Different Pasts: The American National Monuments.* Urbana: University of Illinois Press, 1989.

ROBERT M. STANTON

ROBERT M. STANTON returned from retirement to ascend to the directorship during President Bill Clinton's second term in August 1997. A career Park Service employee, Stanton became the first African American to head the agency. He worked his way to the top, beginning as a seasonal ranger at Grand

Robert M. Stanton. *(National Park Service)*

Teton National Park in 1962 and serving as a superintendent, deputy regional director, assistant director of the agency, and regional director of the National Capital Region before retiring in January 1997. When the agency needed him once again, he came back to lead it through troubled times.

Stanton was the first career National Park Service person to lead the agency since Russell Dickenson, and his appointment brought hope to many in the organization. Stanton focused on diversity both in staff and in park offerings, adding new dimensions to the agency. He provided a steady hand during the presidential impeachment proceedings, reminding the Park Service that its accomplishments were meritorious and its activities crucial in a time when government was under scrutiny and viewed with suspicion. It was a fitting tribute for a man noted for his calm leadership throughout a lifetime of government service.

Stanton also faced agency issues head on. He apologized to Congress for the Park Service's role in the 2000 Cerro Grande fire that started at Bandelier National Monument in New Mexico and engulfed nearby Los Alamos. Stanton also shepherded the introduction of the Natural Resource Challenge, a program designed to protect park resources and assure their long-term management. It included such innovations as the Vital Signs program, which encouraged close monitoring of air pollution and other environmental indicators in national park areas. Such decisions won him the respect of the rank and file in the Park Service, the first director to enjoy such support in a decade.

Stanton departed the agency in January 2001, returning to the well-deserved retirement he had left four years before.

FURTHER READING

Horton, James O. "An Interview with Robert Stanton." *OAH Newsletter,* May 1999.

RONALD H. WALKER

RONALD H. WALKER was the first political appointee to serve as director of the Park Service. A devoted Richard Nixon supporter, Walker served as an advance man for Nixon's 1972 reelection campaign, endearing himself to the top echelon of the administration. He briefly served in the Department of the Interior under Nixon's first secretary of the interior, Walter Hickel, and with Hartzog's retirement, this limited service was deemed enough to place him in charge of the Park Service. To his credit, Walker recognized his lack of experience and brought Russell E. Dickenson, a long-standing and much-respected park superintendent, into the Washington office as associate director.

Walker pursued a policy of stabilization as director. He recognized that the agency would not receive adequate funding to maintain not only growth but even the new responsibilities associated with the National Environmental Policy Act (NEPA). The result was an effort to consolidate that ran hard against the desires of Congress. Despite Walker's desire to hold the line, fourteen new parks were established during his brief tenure.

Walker spent a great deal of time in the field, engaging in outdoor pastimes such as snowmobiling and floating rivers. He publicly admired the skills of the park rangers who led his tours, and became a genuine national park enthusiast during his tenure. Still, he never won over the rank and file. Even a trip to see the avuncular grand old man of the park system, Horace M. Albright, did not help Walker. "It's impossible not to like the boy," the ever-canny Albright told the press after Walker's departure. "But we simply must return the office to the merit system."

Closely associated with the Nixon administration, Walker was a casualty of the president's resignation. Within a few months of

Nixon's departure, on January 3, 1975, Walker too stepped down. Without the experience to handle the position and with only a short tenure, Walker's administration was at best unremarkable. His appointment represented a new and negative dimension for the agency. It politicized the directorship, costing the agency a good piece of its professional image. Walker continued in a long career in government, serving as special assistant to the president under Ronald Reagan, chairman of the fiftieth presidential inaugural, and associate director of World Championship Tennis. Walker also served on the U.S. Olympic Committee and as chairman of the bicentennial of the U.S. Constitution.

FURTHER READING

Everhart, William C. *The National Park Service.* Boulder, CO: Westview, 1983.

Foresta, Ronald. *America's National Parks and Their Keepers.* Washington, DC: Resources for the Future, 1984.

William J. Whalen. *(National Park Service)*

WILLIAM J. WHALEN

WILLIAM J. WHALEN was the first of a new generation of Park Service directors, those who came to maturity during the tumultuous 1960s. When he attained the directorship in 1977 at the age of thirty-six, his selection confirmed a meteoric rise in the Park Service. Raised in Burgettstown, Pennsylvania, southwest of Pittsburgh, Whalen came to the Park Service in 1965, as part of Sargent Shriver's War on Poverty, when he started a Job Corps Conservation Center at Great Smoky Mountains National Park in Gatlinburg, Tennessee. Whalen remained with the Park Service throughout the rest of the decade, first at Catoctin Mountain Park near Camp David, Maryland, and later in Washington, D.C., developing Job Corps programs. Early in 1969, Director George B. Hartzog, Jr., asked the twenty-nine-year-old Whalen to develop a ranger training program that would provide urban experience for Park Service personnel. Transferred to National Capital Parks later that year, Whalen became chief of the Division of Urban and Environmental Activities. Whalen ran the "Summer in the Parks" program, an endeavor that gave the Park Service urban credibility in the aftermath of the assassination of Reverend Dr. Martin Luther King, Jr., in 1968.

After this stint in the nation's capital, Whalen was regarded as the agency official most in touch with the young in a society bereft of communication across the generations. He became the agency's point man for such issues, moving to Yosemite as assistant superintendent in 1971 in the aftermath of the July 4, 1970, battle in Stoneman's Meadows that offered the image of the Park Service as a military agency. Whalen was selected to work with the youthful constituencies who so vexed the agency. His successes earned him power and significance that exceeded his years and his term of service. Offered the choice of either of the two new urban national recreation areas, Whalen chose the superintendency of Golden Gate National Recreation Area. After five years in the Bay Area, he ascended to the agency's top position for precisely the reasons that spurred his rise: Better than anyone else in the Park Service, he grasped the need for the Park Service to reach out to new constituencies.

Whalen's three-year term as director frustrated him. He sought to expand the agency's reach, appointing an African American, Ira Hutchinson, to an associate director's post. He played an important role in the Alaskan National Interest Lands Act, which led to the establishment of more than 20 million acres of national parklands in Alaska. Yet Whalen pushed the agency in new ways and many of its mainline officials resisted. Nor did he handle the politics of the nation's capital any better than his two immediate predecessors. He antagonized the powerful Representative Morris "Mo" Udall, a long-time friend of the Park Service and a staunch conservationist, prompting Secretary of the Interior Cecil Andrus, already worried about agency morale, to reconsider Whalen's appointment. In May 1980, he was removed from the directorship and returned to the superintendency of Golden Gate National Recreation Area. He remained with the agency until 1983, then continued his career in the business world.

FURTHER READING

Everhart, William C. *The National Park Service.* Boulder, CO: Westview, 1983.

Foresta, Ronald. *America's National Parks and Their Keepers.* Washington, DC: Resources for the Future, 1984.

CONRAD L. WIRTH

CONRAD L. WIRTH was one of the agency's most remarkable directors, with the longest tenure of any leader. Born in 1899, son of Theodore Wirth, who directed the much-admired Minneapolis, Minnesota, park system, Conrad Wirth trained as a landscape architect, the premier profession in the early Park Service. He served as a member of the National Capital Park and Planning Commission from 1928 until 1931, when Horace M. Albright recruited him to the agency as assistant director for land planning. Wirth played an essential role in the Park Service's participation in the Civilian Conservation Corps, coordinating the implementation of the program in the national parks as well as in state parks throughout the country. Wirth's training as a landscape architect made him the agency's premier advocate of features such as parkways, and he was a strong advocate of the recreational use of national parklands as well.

When Wirth ascended to the directorship in 1951, the park system was at its nadir. The capital development of the New Deal era let the agency provide facilities to 1930s levels of visitation, but postwar growth had swamped the system. Wirth conceived of Mission 66, a ten-year capital development program to refurbish the national park system in time for the fiftieth anniversary of the founding of the agency in 1966. He succeeded with Congress, where congressional representatives fell over one another to increase the allocations to the national parks. Beginning in 1956, Wirth's Park Service engaged in a decade-long, $1 billion building program that developed new facilities almost everywhere in the system. Visitor centers, new park headquarters, and staff housing were prominent features of the program.

Wirth also championed the inclusion of

coastline and lakeshore in the park system. The federal government had been lax about preserving such areas. The first such efforts began during the 1930s, and by the late 1950s, only one area, Cape Hatteras in North Carolina, had been established. The growth of American cities between the 1930s and the 1950s put tremendous pressure on shorelines and lakeshores, which seemed likely to become privately owned and off-limits for much of the American public. After the publication of *Our Vanishing Shoreline,* a 1955 Park Service survey, impetus for the establishment of national seashores and lakeshores gained momentum. When Congress established the Outdoor Recreation Resources Review Commission (ORRRC) in 1958, the Park Service embarked upon a comprehensive program to evaluate shoreline resources. Wirth's leadership led to the inclusion of such areas in the park system.

An advocate of Park Service management of public recreation, Wirth ran afoul of the Kennedy administration and Secretary of the Interior Stewart Udall. Udall created the Bureau of Outdoor Recreation (BOR), taking recreation from the Park Service and setting up a conflict between Udall and Wirth that became personal. After a number of incidents, Wirth decided to retire, leaving the agency on January 7, 1964. He continued to be active in conservation until his death in 1993.

Wirth was the agency's most accommodationist director. A brilliant government insider and planner, Wirth embraced the culture of access. His goal was to make the parks more usable and to increase the ways that the public could reach them. His strategy built the strongest congressional support for the park system, but his critics point to a lack of attention to resource protection. In the end, Wirth's accomplishments set the stage for another later onslaught of the park system, the deluge of visitors that followed 1970. Mission 66 anticipated future growth, but so much of it came that the park system again faced inundation.

FURTHER READING

Foresta, Ronald. *America's National Parks and Their Keepers.* Washington, DC: Resources for the Future, 1984.

Sellars, Richard. *Preserving Nature in the National Parks: A History.* New Haven, CT: Yale University Press, 1997.

Wirth, Conrad L., *Parks, Politics, and the People.* Norman: University of Oklahoma Press, 1980.

AMERICAN NATIONAL PARKS

A

ABRAHAM LINCOLN BIRTHPLACE NATIONAL HISTORIC SITE

Location: Hodgenville, Kentucky
Acreage: 344
Established: July 17, 1916

On February 12, 1809, the nation's sixteenth president was born in a one-room log cabin on the 348-acre Sinking Spring Farm in north central Kentucky. More than a century later, on July 17, 1916, Congress set aside the Abraham Lincoln Birthplace National Historic Site to commemorate the birth of the man who steered his country through the turbulent years of the Civil War. Lincoln's parents, Thomas and Nancy Hanks Lincoln, purchased the farm for $200 in 1808, and young Abraham spent the first two years of his life in these richly forested hills. A defective land title, a common problem during an era of rampant fraud and speculation, soon forced the family off the farm, and they moved 10 miles away to Knob Creek. The early nineteenth-century Kentucky cabin that is currently on exhibit at the park was originally touted as the Lincoln birthplace cabin, but many historians doubt its authenticity. Nevertheless, the structure accurately depicts the

Abraham Lincoln Birthplace National Historic Site. *(National Park Service)*

An interior view of the original Lincoln cabin, showing the old fireplace in the west room and Mrs. Lincoln's spinning jenny. *(Library of Congress)*

humble, rural beginnings that shaped Lincoln's childhood.

In about 1900, Robert Collier, Mark Twain, William Jennings Bryan, Samuel Gompers, and others formed the Lincoln Farm Association to preserve Lincoln's birthplace and erect a memorial. The association purchased the farm in 1905 and the cabin in 1906, and raised $350,000 from more than 100,000 people to build a memorial to protect the cabin. In 1909, President Theodore Roosevelt laid the cornerstone for the edifice, and in 1911, President William Howard Taft formally dedicated the neoclassical marble-and-granite memorial building. The combination of interest of prominent people and the reverence in which Lincoln was held contributed to the establishment of Abraham Lincoln National Park in 1916. In 1939, the park was

renamed Abraham Lincoln National Historical Park, acquiring its current nomenclature, Abraham Lincoln Birthplace National Historic Site, in 1959.

The Abraham Lincoln Birthplace is open from 8 A.M. until 4:45 P.M. from September through May, and until 6:45 P.M. during the summer months; there are no entrance fees, but donations are accepted. The park's visitor center displays tools and utensils representative of Lincoln's era as well as the Lincoln family Bible. A short film, "Lincoln: The Kentucky Years," is shown on the hour and half hour. The Park Service holds daily interpretive talks at the memorial building and sponsors a number of events throughout the year, including a Martin Luther King birthday celebration in January, the Abraham Lincoln birthday wreath-laying ceremony in February, Founders Day Weekend in July, U.S. Constitution Week in September, and A Walk Through Lincoln's Life in October. The monument has 2.2 miles of hiking trails and nature walks. One short trail leads to the former site of a giant oak tree that served as a marker for early surveys, as well as the Lincolns' Sinking Spring water source.

The historic site has no food, lodging, or camping facilities. The town of Hodgenville provides all the necessary travel services. Rest rooms and drinking water are available at the park, and there is a picnic area on U.S. Highway 31E, across from the visitor center. A state park with camping facilities is located on U.S. Highway 31E near Bardstown, and a private campground is available in Elizabethtown.

For more information, write Abraham Lincoln Birthplace National Historic Site, 2995 Lincoln Farm Road, Hodgenville, KY 42748, or telephone (502) 358-3137. The park's Web site is www.nps.gov/abli.

FURTHER READING

Donald, David Herbert. *Lincoln.* New York: Simon and Schuster, 1995.

Gienapp, William E. *Abraham Lincoln and Civil War America.* New York: Oxford University Press, 2002.

Oates, Stephen B. *With Malice Toward None: A Life of Abraham Lincoln.* New York: HarperPerennial, 1994.

ACADIA NATIONAL PARK

Location: Bar Harbor, Maine
Acreage: 47,400
Established: July 8, 1916

Where sea and land converge along Maine's rugged glaciated coastline is Acadia National Park, the nation's first national park located east of the Mississippi River. Generously adorned with mountains, lakes, mixed evergreen and hardwood forests, and a complex intertidal zone, the 47,400-acre park provides a sanctuary for 273 species of birds, 40 species of mammals, 24 species of fish, 11 species of amphibians, and 7 species of reptiles. In addition to its vibrant natural diversity, Acadia also boasts a rich cultural history that can be traced back more than five thousand years. The area was first protected in 1916, as the Sieur de Monts National Monument, and three years later, an act of Congress changed the monument's name and status to Lafayette National Park. The explorer Giovanni da Verrazano named the region "Acadia" in the sixteenth century, either because it so impressed him that he labeled it with a favored name for ancient Greece or because the native people pronounced a similar word to describe the place in which they lived. French maps called the northern North American coastline from New Jersey to Nova Scotia "Acadia," and in 1929, the park's name was again changed to Acadia, to indulge several large land donors. Perhaps the most remarkable attraction in the national park is Cadillac Mountain, the highest point on the East Coast, and the first place to see the sunrise in the United States.

The park's extensive archeological record indicates that Native Americans first inhabited the Acadia region at least five thousand years ago. Primarily a hunter-gatherer society, these peoples followed seasonal food supplies, living near the shore in winter and moving inland during the summer. The first Europeans arrived in 1604, when the French explorer Samuel de Champlain came ashore to make boat repairs and became enamored with the jagged landscape. He named the island *l'Isle des Monts-desert*—Isle of Bare Mountains—and thus, nearly twenty years before the arrival of the Pilgrims, this point of land became New France, not New England. In 1613, French Jesuits opened the first French mission in America here, at Fernald Point, but it was soon attacked and destroyed by the English. The park's original name derives from the self-appointed title of the ambitious

Cross-country skiing in Acadia National Park. *(National Park Service)*

Frenchman Antoine Laumet, who called himself "Sieur de la Mothe Cadillac." In 1688, he asked for and received a 100,000-acre land grant along the Maine coastline, which included Mount Desert Island. When his dreams of building a New World feudal empire fizzled, Laumet moved inland, and later founded the city of Detroit.

In the 1760s, following its triumph in the French and Indian War, England claimed the eastern seaboard from France, and over the next two centuries English, and then American, settlers established small farms, small-scale forest industries, and a way of life linked to the sea. By the mid-nineteenth century, the pastoral landscape and the island's magnificent beauty had attracted painters of the Hudson River School. Their canvases popularized the locale, and tourism escalated. During the "Gay Nineties," affluent Americans built elegant "cottages"–summer mansions, really–on

Mount Desert Island; the Morgans, Rockefellers, Fords, Vanderbilts, Carnegies, and Astors all staked out estates. The spectacle of luxury lasted for forty years, until the Great Depression and World War II brought an end to the ostentation. The coup de grâce came in 1947 when a major fire destroyed many of the big mansions. One of these elites, however, George B. Dorr, a rich, progressive conservationist, devoted forty-three years of his "life, energy, and family fortune" to preserving the area. In 1901, he and others formed the "Hancock County Trustees of Public Preservations" to purchase and preserve land on the island for public use and enjoyment. In 1913, when Dorr had acquired more than 6,000 acres on Mount Desert, he offered the lands to the federal government for preservation. When the area finally became a national park in 1919, Dorr became its first superintendent.

During the 1920s, Lafayette National Park, as the area was then known, was the most heavily visited national park in the nation. Located within an easy train trip from Boston and proximate to the rest of the East Coast, where much of the nation's population and most of its wealthy people lived, the park was the easiest to reach. The success of this park led the National Park Service to seek out other national park areas in the East, succeeding with the congressional designation of Shenandoah, Great Smoky Mountains, and Mammoth Cave in the 1920s and 1930s. The result was a national park system, one that truly stretched from east to west and north to south in the United States.

Today, Acadia National Park is divided into three major areas: Mount Desert Island (the main section, which includes the town of Bar Harbor), Schoodic Peninsula (the only mainland section), and Isle au Haut, which can only be reached by boat. Park highlights include a 27-mile scenic drive on the Park Loop Road, 120 miles of hiking trails, and 45 miles of carriage roads for biking and hiking. The park offers several tourist information facilities. The Hulls Cove Visitor Center is open from mid-April through October and features numerous exhibits as well as a fifteen-minute audiovisual program about the park. Visitors can also purchase or rent cassette tape audio tours of Acadia and the surrounding area. Rangers offer numerous programs, including interpretive talks, guided walks, hikes, boat cruises, and evening presentations. Hulls Cove is open daily from 8 A.M. until 4:30 P.M. from mid-April through June, until 6 P.M. during July and August, and for more limited hours during September and October. The Park Headquarters and Winter Visitor Center on Route 233, near Eagle Lake, is open all year from 8 A.M. until 4:30 P.M., though it is closed on weekends from mid-April through October. Three miles south of Bar Harbor is the Sieur de Monts

Nature Center, which is open daily, from 9 A.M. until 3 or 5 P.M. during the summer. Ranger-led walks and talks are scheduled frequently during the season, and exhibits describe the park's natural resources and history. The Islesford Historical Museum on Little Cranberry Island is accessible by mail boat or tour boat and is open daily, from mid-June until mid-September from 10 A.M. until 4:30 P.M. In addition to ranger-guided activities, the museum features exhibits on the maritime history of the Cranberry Isles. On the causeway at the head of Mount Desert Island is the Thompson Island Information Center, which is open from mid-May through mid-October and offers information on the park and area chamber of commerce materials.

Acadia National Park is located on and around Mount Desert Island, Maine, 48 miles southeast of Bangor on state Route 3. Entrance fees are $10 per vehicle and $5 per motorcycle, and are valid for seven days. A $20 annual pass is also available. The majority of the park's 3 million annual visitors come during the summer months to enjoy the mild maritime climate. Although the park is open year-round, winters are cold and snowy and visitors may experience road closures.

There is no lodging in the park proper, but Mount Desert Island and the town of Bar Harbor have hotel and motel facilities for all budgets. Acadia operates 2 campgrounds accessible by car and 1 remote campground linked to the mainland by mail boat. The popular Blackwoods Campground is open all year and is located on Route 3, just 5 miles south of Bar Harbor. Reservations are required from June 15 to September 15 (online or call 800-365-CAMP), and are first-come, first-served during the rest of the year. During the summer, a full range of facilities is available, including comfort stations, cold water, a dump station, picnic tables, fire rings, and spigots; facilities are more limited from December through April, and fees vary accordingly. Seawall Campground is open from late May to October, and is located on Route 102A, just 4 miles south of Southwest Harbor. Sites are available on a first-come, first-served basis, and are in high demand during late July and August. Seawall offers the same amenities as Blackwoods, and all sites are wooded and within a ten-minute walk to the beach. Nearby showers and camping supplies are easily accessible for both campgrounds. The Duck Harbor Campground on Isle au Haut offers 5 lean-to shelters that are available by advance reservation from mid-May through mid-October. Access to the mainland is via the Stonington, Maine, mail boat. Facilities include a fire ring, picnic tables, vault toilet, and hand pump for water, and there is a $25 fee. A free Island Explorer shuttle bus links campgrounds and lodging facilities with park sites; it operates from late June through Labor Day.

For more information, write Acadia National Park, P.O. Box 177, Bar Harbor, ME 04609, or telephone (207) 288-3338. The park's detailed Web site is www.nps.gov/acad.

FURTHER READING

Hill, Ruth Ann. *Discovering Old Bar Harbor and Acadia National Park: An Unconventional History and Guide.* Camden, ME: Down East Books, 1996.

Hobbs-Olson, Laurie. *Discovering Acadia: An Introduction to the Park & Its Environment.* Charlottesville, VA: Elan, 2001.

Perkins, Jack. *Acadia: Visions and Verse.* Camden, ME: Down East Books, 1999.

Roberts, Anne Rockefeller. *Mr. Rockefeller's Roads: The Untold Story of Acadia's Carriage Roads and Their Creator.* Camden, ME: Down East Books, 1990.

ADAMS NATIONAL HISTORICAL PARK

Location: Quincy, Massachusetts
Acreage: 24
Established: December 9, 1946

Established as the Adams Mansion National Historic Site in 1946, renamed the Adams National Historic Site in 1952, and renamed again in 1998, the Adams National Historical Park honors five generations of the Adams family from 1720 to 1927. This first family of American politics showed the way for future generations of leaders, building the first multigenerational political family in American history. Located in Quincy, Massachusetts, 8 miles southeast of Boston, the buildings in the park are the oldest, still-standing presidential birthplaces in America. Although there are 12 structures on site, 4 major units comprise the 24-acre park: the birthplaces of the second and sixth presidents, John Adams and his son John Quincy Adams, the "Old House" that housed them and four subsequent generations, and the United First Parish Church.

No family better tells the complicated political and social history of New England than the tumultuous Adams. John Adams was born on October 30, 1735. An advocate of liberty and democratic government who did not trust common people, he played a crucial role in the formation of the United States. During the Revolutionary War he served as a diplomat in France and Holland, and helped negotiate the 1783 Treaty of Paris, which granted independence to the new United States of America. For the next five years, Adams served as a minister to the Court of St. James, before returning to America to be elected vice president under George Washington. His two terms in the nation's second-highest office were an exercise in frustration: "My country has in its wisdom contrived for me the most insignificant office that ever the invention of man contrived or his imagination conceived." Adams finally ascended to the presidency following the elections of 1796, though he was fated to serve only one term, from 1797 to 1801, and was the last Federalist to hold the office. The first president to live in the new damp and unfinished presidential

The Adams' parlor at the Old House in Adams National Historical Park. *(National Park Service)*

mansion in Washington, D.C., Adams prayed for "Heaven to bestow the best of Blessings on this House and all that shall hereafter inhabit it. May none but honest and wise Men ever rule under this roof." He and his successor, Thomas Jefferson, were lifelong political adversaries who carried on an extensive correspondence until they both died on the fiftieth anniversary of the signing of the Declaration of Independence, on July 4, 1826. The two men disagreed so completely that in his library, Jefferson filed Adams's autobiography under "f" for "fiction."

Abigail Smith Adams, wife of John Adams, was born in 1744 in the Massachusetts colony. Like other women of her time, Abigail lacked a formal education, but her keen intelligence and voracious quest for knowledge attracted the attention of a young Harvard graduate named John Adams, and they

were married in 1764. In ten years she bore three sons and two daughters, including a future president, and maintained a diligent and loving correspondence with her husband. Her vivid letters detail the trials of a woman who stayed at home during the Revolution and struggled to run a farm and raise a family in the midst of wartime shortages and crises. In 1776, she implored her husband to "remember the ladies, and be more generous and favorable to them than your ancestors" when drafting the "new code of laws which I suppose it will be necessary for you to make." Remember, she warned good-naturedly, "all men would be tyrants if they could." Abigail died at the Old House in 1818, leaving behind the legacy of a great woman patriot.

About a mile from the Old House is the John Quincy Adams birthplace, where the sixth U.S. president was born on July 11,

1767. John Quincy Adams is the first president who was the son of a president, and his career often paralleled that of his illustrious father. Young John Quincy watched the Battle of Bunker Hill in the Revolutionary War from the top of Penn's Hill above the family farm. He too was a Harvard-educated lawyer, who at age twenty-six was appointed minister to the Netherlands, then promoted to the Berlin Legation. In 1802, he was elected to the U.S. Senate and six years later, President James Madison appointed him minister to Russia. Under President James Monroe, Adams became one of America's great secretaries of state, arranging for the joint occupation of the Oregon country with England, obtaining the cession of the Floridas from Spain, and formulating the influential Monroe Doctrine. Like his father, John Quincy was fated to serve only one term as president, from 1825 to 1829. He gained office as a minority president, when Henry Clay threw his support to Quincy Adams to prevent Andrew Jackson from securing the presidency. Jackson trounced Quincy Adams four years later. From 1830 until his death, John Quincy, also called "Old Man Eloquent," served with distinction in the House of Representatives and was a leading voice for abolition. In 1848, he collapsed on the floor of the House from a stroke and was carried to the Speaker's Room, where two days later he died.

The Old House, the site's main location, was home to four generations of the Adams family from 1787 to 1927. Originally owned by a wealthy West Indies sugar planter, it housed both presidents, first ladies Abigail and Louisa Catherine Adams, Civil War Minister to Great Britain Charles Francis Adams, and literary historians Henry and James Brooks Adams. Nearly 78,000 artifacts are displayed in the house. Visitors can also tour the Old House grounds, which contain perennial gardens and a carriage house. The site also includes the United First Parish Church, where both presidents and first ladies are entombed in the Adams's family crypt.

The Adams National Historical Park Visitor Center is located off-site, about a mile from the park. The center is open all year from 9 A.M. to 5 P.M. daily, mid-April to mid-November, and from Tuesday through Friday from 10 A.M. to 4 P.M. during the rest of the year. Exhibits include a timeline delineating four generations of the Adams family, models of the Old House and the Church of the Presidents, and video and slide presentations on topics related to the Adams family story and the National Park Service. Rangers conduct regularly scheduled tours of the historic homes and conduct family-oriented special events all year. During the last week of June, the park also hosts an annual lecture series on the legacy of the Adams family. Visitors must register for building tours at the visitor center, and advance reservations are required for groups of eight or more. A free bus trolley is available to transport visitors between the visitor center and the historic homes.

The park is open from April 19 through November 10, from 9 A.M. to 5 P.M. daily. The historic homes are closed in the off-season and park hours are limited. Entrance fees of $2 per person, with children under sixteen admitted free, are valid for seven days, and a $10 annual family pass is available. Visitation is usually highest in May and June; the park displays lovely garden blooms from April through August and beautiful fall foliage from September through November. There are no camping, food, or lodging facilities at the park, but nearby Quincy offers all traveler services. Wompatuck State Park, located 11 miles southeast of the park in Hingham, offers 400 camping sites with toilets, showers, electrical hookups, and other amenities in a quiet, wooded setting.

For more information, write Adams National Historical Park, 135 Adams Street, Quincy, MA 02169-1749, or telephone (617) 770-1175. The park's Web site is www.nps.gov/adam.

FURTHER READING

Cappon, Lester J., ed. *The Adams-Jefferson Letters: The Complete Correspondence Between Thomas Jefferson and Abigail and John Adams.* Chapel Hill: University of North Carolina Press, 1988.

Ellis, Joseph J. *Passionate Sage: The Character and Legacy of John Adams.* New York: Norton, 1993.

——. *Founding Brothers: The Revolutionary Generation.* New York: Alfred A. Knopf, 2000.

McCullough, David. *John Adams.* New York: Simon and Schuster, 2001.

Nagel, Paul C. *The Adams Women: Abigail and Louisa Adams, Their Sisters and Daughters.* New York: Oxford University Press, 1987.

Withey, Lynne. *Dearest Friend: A Life of Abigail Adams.* New York: Simon & Schuster, 2001.

AGATE FOSSIL BEDS NATIONAL MONUMENT

Location: Harrison, Nebraska
Acreage: 3,055
Established: June 5, 1965

Established on June 5, 1965, Agate Fossil Beds National Monument protects three renowned quarries containing well-preserved prehistoric mammal fossils dating back 19.2 million years. Located on the Niobrara River in northwestern Nebraska, about 23 miles south of Harrison, the 3,055-acre prairie-covered monument was first excavated in 1904, when two scientists from Pittsburgh's Carnegie Institute discovered the fossils. One year later, the University of Nebraska sent a professor and four students to open a quarry on what is known as University Hill, and excavations have occurred there periodically ever since. The most common fossils found here are from a small, rhinoceros-type creature that roamed the plains in great numbers during the Miocene epoch.

The visitor center houses 3 rooms of exhibits, a life-size fossil diorama, the Hitchcock Theater, and the Cook Collection Gallery. Open daily from 8 A.M. to 5 P.M. from September through May, and until 6 P.M. during the summer, the center also features an interactive computer tour of the monument's 2 trails with information about the variety of geologic deposits and features in this part of the Niobrara River drainage. Other interactive exhibits allow visitors to test their skills in observing evidence of fossils and rocks. Once part of "Captain" James H. Cook's Agate Springs Ranch, the monument was an important gathering site for Oglala Lakota (Sioux). The Cook Collection of American Indian artifacts contains nearly 200 gifts brought by the Indians during visits to the ranch from the 1880s through the early 1900s.

Visitors can enjoy the numerous hiking trails that exist in the monument. The Fossil Hills Trail surveys Carnegie and University Hills, where most of the mammal fossils were quarried. The Bone Cabin Loop allows visitors to see the historic Bone Cabin or Harold Cook Homestead Cabin where bone hunters stayed while working the Agate bone bed. The Daemonelix (Devil's Corkscrew) Trail leads from a parking lot trailhead near the monument's west entrance through the nearby fossil hills. From Memorial Day through Labor Day rangers conduct talks and guided walks, which begin at the visitor center.

A seven-day pass to the monument is $2 per person, or $5 per vehicle, and a $15 annual pass is also available. The park is open year-round, from 8 A.M. to 5 P.M. daily, with extended hours during the summer. Visitation is highest during the summer months and lowest in January; late May through September is the best time for wildflowers. The climate is sunny and dry in the summer, with occasional afternoon thundershowers, and is windy and cold in winter. Good walking shoes are recommended for use on hiking trails.

There is no food, lodging, or camping in the monument. The nearest motel and RV camping facilities are available in Harrison. Three trailer pads with full hookups are located near the pool in the city park of Harrison. Primitive camping can be found at Gilbert Baker State Recreation Area, located 5 miles north of Harrison down Monroe Canyon.

For more information, write Agate Fossil Beds National Monument, 301 River Road, Harrison, NE 69346-2734, or telephone (308) 668-2211. The park's Web site is www.nps.gov/agfo.

FURTHER READING

Agate Fossil Beds: Agate Fossil Beds National Monument, Nebraska. Washington, DC: Government Printing Office, 1988.

Cockrell, Ron. *Bones of Agate: An Administrative History of Agate Fossil Beds National Monument, Nebraska.* Omaha, NE: National Park Service, 1986.

ALEUTIAN WORLD WAR II NATIONAL HISTORIC AREA

Location: Unalaska/Dutch Harbor, Alaska
Acreage: 81
Established: November 12, 1996

Archeologists believe that the Aleuts are descendants of what some have called the Bering Sea Mongoloids, the people who first migrated from Asia to the Americas across Beringia (a land bridge formed during the last ice age). When water levels rose and inundated the passageway between the two continents, the Aleuts and their Eskimo cousins were isolated in the "New World." Like the Eskimos, the Aleuts were oceangoing hunters who plied the cold waters in kayaks, but unlike the Eskimos, their primary subsistence derived from salmon and birds. Aleut people also shared some traditions with Pacific Northwest coastal groups, such as creating carved wooden hats and beautiful woven basketry.

In the eighteenth century, Russian adventurers began pressing the Aleuts into the fur trade, especially in exchange for trade items. But Euro–Native American contact triggered a devastating population decline, as it did throughout the Americas, and even resulted in the enslavement and forcible relocation of these native inhabitants. During World War II, the Aleutian Islands formed a critical link in the Pacific theater. To protect the Dutch Harbor Naval Operating Base, the U.S. Army constructed Fort Schwatka, at Ulakta Head on Mount Ballyhoo, one of four coastal defense posts built between 1942 and 1943.

In 1996, Congress set aside the Aleutian World War II National Historic Area to educate the public about "the history of the Aleut people, and the role of the Aleut people and the Aleutian Islands in the defense of the United States in World War II." The historic area is located on Amaknak Island in the Aleutian Island chain, about 800 miles west of Anchorage, the nearest large urban center, and can be reached by air through commercial and charter flights from Anchorage. In the summer, access to the Aleutian World War II National Historic Area is via an unimproved gravel switchback road from Unalaska, while winter access is via snowshoes or skis. There are no traveler facilities at the historic area, but all services are available in Anchorage.

For more information, write Aleutian World War II National Historic Area, Ounalashka Corporation, P.O. Box 149, Unalaska, AK 99685, or telephone (907) 581-1276. The park's Web site is www.nps.gov/aleu.

FURTHER READING

Garfield, Brian. *The Thousand-Mile War: World War II in Alaska and the Aleutians.* Fairbanks: University of Alaska Press, 1995.

Jochelson, Waldemar. *History, Ethnology, and Anthropology of the Aleut.* Salt Lake City: University of Utah Press, 2002.

Josephy, Alvin M. *The Indian Heritage of America.* Boston: Houghton Mifflin, 1991.

Morison, Samuel Eliot. *History of United States Naval Operations in World War II.* Urbana: University of Illinois Press, 2001.

ALIBATES FLINT QUARRIES NATIONAL MONUMENT

Location: Fritch, Texas
Acreage: 1,371
Established: August 21, 1965

Distinctive for its varied coloration, Alibates Flint is a hard, sharp-edged rock that occurs in dolomite outcrops in the Canadian River breaks northeast of Amarillo, Texas. Alibates Flint Quarries history dates back nearly twelve thousand years, to the time of the Ice Age Clovis culture, when pre-Columbian native peoples quarried the stones to form sharp projectiles, knives, scrapers, and other tools. Flint tools that originated from this area have been found in many locations throughout the Great Plains and in the desert Southwest. Rich archeological evidence suggests that the entire region of the Texas Panhandle was a prime area for flint tool manufacture, with the Alibates Flint Quarries producing tools from about 10,000 B.C.E. to the late 1800s. Between 1200 and 1450 C.E., some Native Americans settled briefly in the area to farm, mine, and barter flint, but much of the flint "mining" was done by nomadic tribes who fashioned the flint into spear points to hunt the now-extinct mammoth.

This over-1,300-acre monument was originally authorized as part of the Texas Panhandle Pueblo Culture National Monument in 1965, and was redesignated as Alibates Flint Quarries National Monument in November 1978. No fees are charged. Almost completely undeveloped, the monument receives only 3,000 visitors per year. The Bates Canyon Contact Station is open daily from 8:30 A.M. until 5 P.M. between Memorial Day and Labor Day, and has no exhibits or water. Visitors may only experience the monument on a guided tour with a park ranger or volunteer. Tours are available daily at 10 A.M. and 2 P.M. during the summer, and by appointment during the rest of the year, and include information on the site's early inhabitants. The Park Service suggests allowing at least two hours for the guided tour. Occasional flint-knapping demonstrations are held by park officials, although flint- and artifact-collecting is not permitted in the park.

No lodging or camping is available at the monument. The nearest camping is at McBride Canyon Campground in the Lake Meredith National Recreation Area. Meals and lodging are available in Fritch and Borger, about 18 miles east of the monument.

The climate varies from cold and rainy in the winter, with lows dipping to 0 degrees, to hot and dry in the summer, with temperatures approaching 100 degrees. Visitors should be prepared for diverse conditions and carry plenty of water. To reach the monument, follow Highway 136 to the Cas Johnson Road 25 miles north of Amarillo. Continue on the Cas Johnson Road 5 miles to the Bates Canyon Contact Station. A ranger or volunteer will meet visitors there and escort them and their vehicles 3 miles farther to the monument.

For more information, write Alibates Flint Quarries National Monument, Box 1460, Fritch, TX 79036-1460, or telephone (806) 857-3151. The park's Web site is www.nps.gov/alfl.

FURTHER READING

Potter County Historical Survey Committee. *Alibates Flint Quarries: A National Monument.* Canyon, TX: Potter County Historical Survey Committee, 1963.

Yancey, Franklin D. *The Mammals of Lake Meredith National Recreation Area and Adjacent Areas, Hutchinson, Moore, and Potter Counties, Texas.* Lubbock: Museum of Texas Tech University, 1998.

ALLEGHENY PORTAGE RAILROAD NATIONAL HISTORIC SITE

Location: Gallitzen, Pennsylvania
Acreage: 1,249
Established: August 31, 1964

The high lonesome whistle of the Allegheny Railroad told nineteenth-century Americans that change was coming. The Allegheny Portage Railroad officially opened in March 1834, making history as the first railroad constructed over the rugged Allegheny Mountains in western Pennsylvania. In 1826, concerned over the growth of New York and

Baltimore, the Pennsylvania legislature had authorized the construction of a canal to the west, but the Alleghenies posed a formidable problem. The innovative solution was the 36-mile-long Allegheny Portage Railroad, comprised of ten inclined planes, five ascending and five descending, that utilized stationary engines to lift and lower canal boats, loaded on railroad-type flatcars, over the mountains.

Considered a technological wonder in its day, the railroad accelerated the pace of westward movement. It changed not only the way in which travel occurred, but also the pace at which it happened. A train track cut across the countryside, conveying its riders at as much as 20 miles per hour. By comparison,

The south portal at the Allegheny Portage Railroad National Historic Site. Considered a technological wonder in its day, the Allegheny Portage Railroad played a critical role in opening the interior of the United States to trade and settlement. *(Library of Congress)*

a wagon team that covered that distance in a day accomplished a considerable feat. Trains could also carry considerably more goods than wagons, facilitating the beginning of a national economy linked in a daily fashion. It is not a stretch to suggest that the world of today began with railroads such as the Allegheny Portage.

Combined with the Pennsylvania Main Line Canal, the Allegheny Portage Railroad helped slash the travel time from Philadelphia to Pittsburgh from three weeks to four days. The total cost of the public works system was in excess of $16.5 million, with the railroad system itself costing $1.8 million. The system flourished for twenty years, ushering in an era of prosperity for the state. In February 1854, the newly completed all-rail Pennsylvania Railroad linked Philadelphia and Pittsburgh far more efficiently, and three years later, the Allegheny Portage Railroad, already a relic, was closed and dismantled. It had served its purpose but was no longer equal to the task of national expansion. Newer, faster trains conveyed more freight and people on better rails as the nation pushed west of the Mississippi River in earnest. The Allegheny Portage remained as a symbol of innovation, of the first step in a powerful process that transformed the nation. In August 1964, the 1,249-acre historic site was established to commemorate the railroad's important role in opening the country's interior to trade and settlement.

The park is open daily from 9 A.M. to 5 P.M. all year, and until 6 P.M. during the summer. The $2-per-person entrance fee is valid for seven days; a $15 annual Southwest Pennsylvania Park Pass is available for families (and also includes admission to Fort Necessity National Battlefield and the Johnstown Flood National Monument). Park visitation is usually highest in July, August, and October, and it is lowest from December through February. April and May offer the best wildflower displays, and October is ideal for fall colors. Summer weather is generally warm, with cool mornings and evenings. Winters can be very harsh, with cold temperatures, high winds, and snow from November through March. The Allegheny Portage Railroad National Historic Site is located approximately 12 miles west of Altoona and 10 miles east of Ebensburg; visitors should take the Gallitzin exit off U.S. Highway 22 and follow the signs.

The Summit Level Visitor Center is open year-round from 9 A.M. to 5 P.M. daily, and until 6 P.M. during the summer months. The visitor center contains a full-scale model of the Lafayette locomotive and a twenty-minute orientation film, as well as numerous artifacts and exhibits. A small bookstore, rest rooms, phone, and a water fountain are also available. Located nearby is the historic Lemon House, a restored tavern adjacent to the railroad that was a common rest and dining stop for passengers. The Engine House #6 Exhibit Shelter is adjacent to the Lemon House and was built to preserve the remains of the original building at the head of Inclined Plane 6. It features a full-scale model of a stationary steam engine and interactive exhibits on the railroad's technology. The nation's first railroad tunnel, Staple Bend Tunnel, is located outside of the main park in a remote location approximately 4 miles east of Johnstown, Pennsylvania. Although the site is closed to the general public, ranger-guided hikes are available at the visitor center. Park rangers in period dress offer unique programs and events throughout the year, including demonstrations of building skills, "People of the Portage," a living history-like program, and "Lifestyles of the Past," a demonstration of 1840s-era skills such as yarn spinning, medical care, and washing/ironing, and children's programs.

There is no camping or lodging within the park, but there are rest rooms, grills, and picnic tables. Full-facility camping is available at Prince Gallitzin State Park, 20 miles northwest of Altoona. Restaurants, lodging, and all other travel services are located in nearby Cresson.

For more information, write Allegheny Portage Railroad National Historic Site, 110 Federal Park Road, Gallitzin, PA, 16641, or telephone (814) 886-6150. The park's informative Web site is www.nps.gov/alpo.

FURTHER READING

Daniels, Rudolph. *Trains Across the Continent: North American Railroad History.* Bloomington: Indiana University Press, 2000.

Lewie, Chris J. *Two Generations on the Allegheny Portage Railroad: The First Railroad to Cross the Allegheny Mountains.* Shippensburg, PA: Burd Street, 2001.

Rau, William Herman. *Traveling the Pennsylvania Railroad: The Photographs of William H. Rau.* Philadelphia: University of Pennsylvania Press, 2002.

Saylor, Roger B. *The Railroads of Pennsylvania.* University Park: Pennsylvania State University, 1964.

Taber, Thomas Townsend. *Railroads of Pennsylvania: Encyclopedia and Atlas.* T.T. Taber, 1987.

AMERICAN MEMORIAL PARK

Location: Saipan, MP
Acreage: 133
Established: August 18, 1978

The war for the Mariana Islands was the beginning of the end of World War II in the Pacific theater. Although the Japanese attack on Pearl Harbor had thrust the United States into World War II in December of 1941, President Franklin D. Roosevelt made the defeat of Adolf Hitler and Germany the nation's priority and committed the bulk of American troop strength to the European front. By 1944, as combined American, British, and Soviet forces had begun to turn the tide of war in favor of the Allies, the United States focused greater attention on the Pacific. Operating in tandem, American General Douglas MacArthur and Admiral Chester W. Nimitz increased the pressure on Japanese holdings throughout the Pacific. American troops went from island to island, pushing ever closer to the Japanese isles.

After four days of air assault, at 08:40 on June 15, 1944, the United States invaded the island of Saipan, in the Northern Mariana Islands. The island was populated by as many as 20,000 Japanese, Okinawans, and others, making it an important cog in Japan's inner circle of island defenses. The Japanese and other migrants had pushed the native people aside, inspiring animosity and creating support for the Americans when the invasion finally came. The 2nd and 4th U.S. Marine divisions stormed ashore, securing a narrow beachhead. Caught beneath powerful and well-manned enemy guns, the soldiers were bombarded. Shells rained down on the marines, making the beach a living hell. It took three days to close the gap between the two units. Supported by naval and army air corps bombardment, and joined by the U.S. Army's 27th Infantry Division, the marines broke free, starting nearly one month of slow and inexorably painful advance.

By the time the island was secure on July 9, Saipan had become synonymous with death to the American public. In the savage battle, as many as 5,000 Americans died. Yet, by August 10, the United States was in control of Saipan, Tinian, and Guam; the islands provided a perfect location from which to launch long-range B-29 strategic bombers at Tokyo and other major Japanese cities. By the close of this campaign, American naval superiority in the Pacific had become sufficient to sustain an open-ocean invasion of Japan if necessary.

Established in 1978 as a "living memorial" and day-use recreational center for locals and tourists alike, American Memorial Park is a commemorative park that honors the American and Marianas people who died during the Marianas campaign of World War II. More than 5,000 names are inscribed on a memorial, which was dedicated June 15,

1994, during the fiftieth anniversary of the invasion of Saipan. The park's U.S. Memorial Court of Honor and Flag Circle flies the U.S. flag twenty-four hours a day, surrounded by the flags of the U.S. Army, Marine Corps, Navy, and Air Force. Nearby, the Carillon Belltower is dedicated to the American and Northern Marianas people who died during World War II. Bells chime every half hour from 8 A.M. to 8 P.M. in remembrance. The park also contains many remnants from World War II, including Japanese pillboxes, buildings, fuel storage tanks, bunkers, and a bathhouse/garden complex.

The Carolinians were among the native people of the islands, and the initial Carolinian village site is marked by an exhibit at Micro Beach. In addition to its many recreational and cultural sites, American Memorial Park protects a 30-acre wetland and mangrove forest. A remnant ecosystem habitat of the Northern Marianas, the wetlands contain numerous species of plants, trees, flowers, and birds, including the endangered nightingale reed-warbler. The adjacent mudflats are also an important migratory bird site. A picturesque bike and walking path runs from Micro Beach, past the Court of Honor and Flag Circle and the Smiling Cove Marina. All park areas are accessible by paved or well-groomed roads and trails.

Within the 133-acre boundary of the park are beaches, sports fields, picnic sites, boat marinas, playgrounds, and walkways, which support activities such as baseball, bicycling, running, tennis, picnicking, and swimming. Micro Beach, one of Saipan's finest white sand beaches, is a magnet for windsurfers, snorkelers, sunbathers, and picnickers. The park hosts a great number of tourists en route to aquatic activities, is a central gathering place for the community, and plays host to many events throughout the year.

One of the nation's most distant national park units, American Memorial Park is located adjacent to the north end of downtown Garapan on the island of Saipan in the western Pacific, 6,000 miles southwest of Los Angeles. Despite its remote location, the park receives an estimated 1 million visitors each year. Saipan's year-round average temperature is 81.5 degrees. Although the weather is generally warm and sunny throughout the year, a heavy, wet monsoon season runs from July through October. Comfortable summer attire, walking shoes, sunglasses, a hat, and sunscreen are recommended.

There are currently no fees for noncommercial use of the park. The park's hours are from 7:30 A.M. to 4:30 P.M. daily, and there is no visitor center. For more information, visit the ranger's station in the 1,200-seat amphitheater.

To reach the park, proceed north on Airport Road (Tun Herman Pan Highway) until the road ends at Monsignor Guerrero Road (Highway 16). Turn left on Monsignor Guerrero Road, and continue until the road ends at Beach Road. Turn right onto Beach Road, and keep going until the road ends at the park's mall entrance. The park is within easy walking distance from hotels in Garapan's tourist district. From other locations, the park can easily be reached by taxi, rental car, or tourist shuttle bus. There is no camping in the park, but all lodging and meal services are available nearby.

For more information, write American Memorial Park, National Park Service, P.O. Box 5189-CHRB, Saipan, MP 96950, or telephone (670) 234-7207. The park's Web site is www.nps.gov/amme.

FURTHER READING

Ciardi, John. *Saipan: The War Diary of John Ciardi.* Fayetteville: University of Arkansas Press, 1988.

Hoffman, Carl. *Saipan: The Beginning of the End.* Reprint. Nashville, TN: Battery, 1987.

Morison, Samuel Eliot. *New Guinea and the Marianas: March 1944–August 1944.* Vol. 8, *History of United States Naval Operations in World War II.* Urbana: University of Illinois Press, 2001–2002.

Petty, Bruce M. *Saipan: Oral Histories of the Pacific War.* Jefferson, NC: McFarland, 2001.

AMISTAD NATIONAL RECREATION AREA

Location: Del Rio, Texas
Acreage: 58,500
Established: November 28, 1990

A stark land of contrasts, Texas's Amistad—which means "friendship"—National Recreation Area (NRA) is also a land of hidden treasures. This arid desert environment, which at times appears desolate, becomes vibrant with color after a rainstorm. Situated on the U.S.-Mexico border near Del Rio, Texas, the 58,500-acre park is known primarily for excellent year-round, water-based recreation, including scuba diving, water-skiing, boating, fishing, and swimming. The park's 540 miles of lakeshore also provide opportunities for picnickers, campers, birders, wildlife watchers, and hunters. In addition to offering fine recreation, Amistad NRA preserves a rich cultural region. The same water that draws people to boating and fishing activities today sustained more than 300 generations of prehistoric hunters and gatherers. The Native American rock art along the Lower Pecos River region is among the finest in the world, and the park protects some of the oldest and best-preserved archeological deposits in North America.

The roots of the park date to the administration of Lyndon B. Johnson, who strove to bring national-caliber amenities to his home state of Texas. In 1965, the area was first established as Amistad Recreation Area, which was administered in cooperation with the International Boundary and Water Commission. The reservoir, which lies at the confluence of the Rio Grande, Devils, and Pecos rivers, was created in 1969, with the completion of Amistad Dam. The dam was another of Johnson's gifts to his home state, a characteristically Johnson-like use of power and the kind of project he favored early in his political career. A true multipurpose dam, the 256-foot-high structure was developed as a cooperative project between the United States and Mexico for flood control, hydroelectric, water conservation, and recreation purposes. In November 1990, the area was redesignated as a national recreation area. Near the dam's center are a customs station, an international monument, and a water-commission/National Park Service visitor center. The visitor center is open daily, year-round, from 10 A.M. to 6 P.M., and is usually unstaffed. Exhibits at the center tell the story of the dam's construction and detail the natural and cultural resources surrounding Amistad Reservoir.

Amistad's weather is fairly consistent: sunny, humid, hot summers and mild winters. The NRA's most popular activities are boating, fishing, and camping. Major boat ramps are located at Pecos River, Diablo East, and Rough Canyon. Boat rentals, temporary slips, bait, and fuel are available at Diablo East and Rough Canyon. To boat on the lake, you must have a daily or annual permit: $4 a day or $40 annual, and with Golden Age or Golden Access cards fees are halved.

From late spring to early fall, the water in the lake's many coves is warm enough for swimming and water-skiing. Swimming is prohibited in the harbors, and there are no lifeguards on duty. Primary sport fishing is for bass, channel catfish, striped bass, yellow catfish, crappie, and sunfish. A valid Texas fishing license is required, and fishing is prohibited in the harbors. Amistad is also a hunter's paradise, with deer, javelina, and wild turkey available. Those wishing to hunt should check with the Amistad National Park Service office for specific information, regulations, and designated hunting areas.

Four primitive Park Service campsites with vault toilets, covered picnic tables, and grills are scattered throughout the park and are open year-round. Only the Governor's Landing Campground has water, and all are operated on a first-come, first-served basis. Camping fees are $4 a day, and are $2 a day with Golden Age or Golden Access cards. Park rangers frequently offer morning and evening educational programs at the campgrounds. Commercial campgrounds with all facilities are located near Diablo East, Rough Canyon, and Pecos River ranger stations. Park headquarters, located on U.S. Highway 90, has drinking water, and RV water and dumping stations are located on the Diablo East entrance road and at the Del Rio Civic Center. For food and other supplies, Diablo East and Rough Canyon have concessionaire-operated stores. There is no lodging within the park, but motels and restaurants are available in Del Rio and Rough Canyon, and near the lake along U.S. Highway 90.

For more information, write Amistad National Recreation Area, HCR-3, Box 5J, Del Rio, TX 78840, or telephone (830) 775-7491. The park's informative Web site is www.nps.gov/amis.

FURTHER READING

McGregor, Roberta. *Prehistoric Basketry of the Lower Pecos, Texas.* Madison, WI: Prehistory, 1992.
Shafer, Harry J. *Ancient Texans: Rock Art and Lifeways Along the Lower Pecos.* Houston, TX: Gulf, 1992.

ANDERSONVILLE NATIONAL HISTORIC SITE

Location: Andersonville, Georgia
Acreage: 515
Established: October 16, 1970

Georgia's Andersonville National Historic Site is the only American national park area to serve as a memorial to all of America's prisoners of war throughout history. Originally built in early 1864 to house 10,000 Union prisoners of war from Richmond, Virginia, Andersonville held 33,000 captives by summer, and offered no shade or shelter.

During the worst weeks of that sweltering summer, 100 prisoners died each day of disease, exposure, overcrowding, poor sanitation, or malnutrition. In all, during the fourteen months that the prison existed, more than 45,000 Union soldiers were confined here and, of these, nearly 13,000 died. The conditions were so appalling that after the war, the camp's commander, Frederick Wirt, was tried and hung for the conditions he permitted, the only Confederate so penalized.

Officially known as Camp Sumter, Andersonville was one of the largest of many Confederate military prisons established during the Civil War. In 1970, Congress authorized the historic site "to provide an understanding of the overall prisoner of war story of the Civil War, to interpret the role of prisoner of war camps in history, to commemorate the sacrifice of Americans who lost their lives in such camps, and to preserve the monuments located within the site." Today, the 515-acre park encompasses not only the infamous prison site, but also the Andersonville National Cemetery, which shelters more than 16,000 graves.

In 1998, the National Prisoner of War Museum opened at the park, dedicated to all American men and women who have suffered captivity. The museum offers an audiovisual program entitled "Echoes of Captivity" every half hour and features prisoner of war artifacts and exhibits depicting conflicts from the American Revolution to the Gulf War. Sections of the prisoner stockade from Andersonville have been reconstructed, and a central corridor contains more specific interpretation of Civil War prisons and the Andersonville National Cemetery. Often, former American prisoners of war, who volunteer with the park's program, serve as hosts at the museum. Ranger-guided cemetery walks and prison-site talks are also available.

Andersonville National Historic Site is located 10 miles north of Americus, Georgia, on Georgia Route 49. There is no admission fee to the park, but a donation box is available at the National Prisoner of War Museum Visitor Center. The site is open year-round from 8 A.M. until 5 P.M. daily, and a driving-tour cassette tape is available for a $1 rental fee. Visitation is typically highest in April and July and lowest in December and January. Summers are generally hot and humid, while winters are mild and rainy.

There is no food or lodging in the park, but many establishments located close to Andersonville provide these services. There is also no camping, but several campgrounds are located nearby, including one at Georgia Veteran's Memorial State Park, between Americus and Cordele on U.S. Highway 280. This campground offers tables, grills, flush toilets, and showers.

For more information, write Park Headquarters, Andersonville National Historic Site, Route 1, Box 800, Andersonville, GA 31711, or telephone (229) 924-0343. The park's Web site is www.nps.gov/ande.

FURTHER READING

Futch, Ovid. *History of Andersonville Prison.* Gainesville: University of Florida Press, 1968.

Kantor, MacKinlay. *Andersonville.* New York: Plume, 1993.

Marvel, William. *Andersonville: The Last Depot.* Chapel Hill: University of North Carolina Press, 1994.

Ransom, John. *John Ransom's Andersonville Diary/Life Inside the Civil War's Most Infamous Prison.* New York: Berkley Books, 1994.

ANDREW JOHNSON NATIONAL HISTORIC SITE

Location: Greeneville, Tennessee
Acreage: 17
Established: August 29, 1935

Until 1998, only one American president had suffered the humiliation of impeachment. The Andrew Johnson National Historic Site depicts the stormy life of the nation's seventeenth president, who in 1868 fell one vote short of being judged guilty of various (mainly political) charges and removed from office. Authorized in 1935, the site preserves Johnson's early home, his homestead, the tailor shop, and his burial site in a national cemetery.

Andrew Johnson rose to political infamy in a slow and winding fashion. Born in 1808, he had a difficult early life. His father died in 1812, when young Andrew Johnson was just four years old, and at the age of fourteen, he apprenticed as a tailor. In 1826, Johnson and his family moved to Greeneville, Tennessee, where he married Eliza McArdle the following year. Johnson became a successful tailor, winning a seat as an alderman in 1929 and becoming mayor of Greeneville in 1835. After serving as a state representative and senator for eight years, he won election to the

U.S. House of Representatives in 1843 and served five terms. In 1853, he became governor of Tennessee, and then a U.S. senator in 1857. One of the first bills he put forward in the U.S. Senate was the Homestead Act, a piece of legislation entirely repellent to southern slaveholders, who felt it would assure the end to the parity between slave and free states. Johnson cast his lot with the North against the slave-holding South even though he represented the Democratic Party. He was rewarded for his allegiance. An ardent opponent of secession, he became Tennessee's military governor during the Civil War, and in 1864 ran with the Republican Abraham Lincoln as his vice president. When Lincoln was assassinated in April 1865, Johnson began his stormy tenure as president.

Johnson faced a difficult situation when he

Exterior view of Andrew Johnson's tailor shop in Greeneville, Tennessee. *(Library of Congress)*

Corner of Andrew Johnson's bedroom at his residence in Greeneville, Tennessee. *(Library of Congress)*

ascended to the nation's highest office. Unpopular with Republicans, especially the powerful Radical Republicans who controlled Congress, and lacking Lincoln's standing and presence, he found his position under siege from the day he was sworn in. His policies did not help build a close relationship with Congress. Johnson initiated presidential reconstruction while Congress was not in session. He pardoned all who would take an oath of allegiance to the Union but required Confederate leaders and men of wealth to obtain special presidential pardons. By the time Congress convened in December of 1865, most southern states were "reconstructed" and slavery was being abolished, but "Black Codes," an insidious form of legal control di-

rected at limiting the rights of freedmen and women, were beginning to appear. Even though Johnson disbanded military control of the South and helped reestablish governments in the former Confederate states, his tactics alienated a suspicious Congress. Believing that the South was quickly returning to a prewar status quo, Radical Republicans in Congress quickly mounted an attack on the president's program. The legislative body started its own reconstruction program without his support. When he attempted to remove Secretary of War Edwin Stanton, Congress considered this a direct violation of the Tenure of Office Act, which prohibited the removal of cabinet members by the president without Senate approval. Congress had passed the law to protect Stanton's position in Johnson's cabinet. As a result, the House of Representatives approved eleven impeachment charges against Johnson and found him guilty. The Senate failed to convict and remove him from office by one vote. He did not run for the presidency in 1868 and returned to Greeneville after his term expired. Johnson never reconciled himself to the events of his presidency and continued to seek office. After various unsuccessful attempts, he was elected U.S. senator from Tennessee early in 1875, but he died six months later.

The 17-acre historic site is located in northeastern Tennessee in the town of Greeneville, 29 miles southwest of Johnson City via U.S. Highway 11E. The Andrew Johnson Visitor Center is open daily from 9 A.M. until 5 P.M. and features a short film called *Andrew Johnson, Defender of the Constitution*, which details the president's life from boyhood to death. The center also houses numerous exhibits, including Johnson's original tailor shop, his tools, and presidential gifts. An interactive "One Vote Counts" exhibit presents information on Johnson and the impeachment crisis, and even allows visitors to cast their vote to acquit or convict the president. Across the street is Johnson's early home, in which he lived from the 1830s to 1851. In 1851, he moved into the homestead on Main Street, which has been fully restored with many Johnson family artifacts. Ranger-guided tours of the homestead are $2 per person, with those under eighteen and over sixty-one admitted for free. Special events at the historical site include a Memorial Day program in May, a week-long celebration of the Constitution in September, a commemorative birthday program on December 29, and a Christmas tour of the homestead. Johnson is buried in the Andrew Johnson National Cemetery, located at the end of Monument Avenue.

There is no food, lodging, or camping in the park, but nearby Greeneville offers all traveler services, and many national forest campgrounds are located southeast of Greeneville. Park visitation is usually highest in May, and lowest in February.

For more information, write Andrew Johnson National Historic Site, P.O. Box 1088, Greeneville, TN 37744-1088, or telephone (423) 638-3551. The park's Web site is www.nps.gov/anjo.

FURTHER READING
Benedict, Michael Les. *The Impeachment and Trial of Andrew Johnson.* New York: W.W. Norton, 1999.
McKitrick, Eric L. *Andrew Johnson and Reconstruction.* New York: Oxford University Press, 1988.
Trefousse, Hans Louis. *Andrew Johnson: A Biography.* New York: W.W. Norton, 1997.

ANIAKCHAK NATIONAL MONUMENT & PRESERVE
Location: King Salmon, Alaska
Acreage: 601,294
Established: December 1, 1978

One of the finest dry volcanic calderas in the world, Alaska's Aniakchak Caldera covers 10 square miles on the remote Alaska Peninsula. Located in the volcanically active Aleutian Mountains, this crater, discovered in 1922, contains many notable volcanic features including cinder cones, lava flows, and explosion pits. Nearly 6 miles in diameter, the caldera was formed by millennia of frequent volcanic activity; the Aniakchak last erupted in 1931. The same year, it was the subject of a national monument proposal, but no designation was achieved at that time. Only with the Alaska native lands issue in the 1960s did Aniachak attract new attention. In December of 1978, President Jimmy Carter granted federal protection to this over-600,000-acre natural wonder, as Aniakchak National Monument in 1978, which subsequently became a national monument and preserve in 1980.

The caldera also cradles Surprise Lake, source of the Aniakchak National Wild River, which plunges through a 1,500-foot gash in the crater wall called "the Gates." In its first 15 miles, as it cascades southward toward Aniakchak Bay through shrub- and tundra-covered foothills, the rock-strewn river drops 60 feet per mile, creating Class-2 through Class-4 whitewater. The remaining 17 miles of the Aniakchak are gentler, however, and rate only a Class-1. Brown bear, caribou, bald eagles, and sea otters (near the coast) are common sights along the river.

In many ways, Aniakchak provides a kind of wilderness experience that is hard to match in the lower forty-eight states. The few visitors to the park engage in a number of outdoor activities, including fly-fishing, rafting, kayaking, and hiking. Camping is possible and hunting is permitted with the appropriate licenses. Mountain climbing, fishing, and bird-watching are other popular activities for visitors.

As are many of Alaska's national parks and monuments, Aniakchak is undeveloped and difficult to reach, and is often plagued by terrible weather. For those seeking solitude, the park is nearly unparalleled: in 1999, fewer than 500 hardy souls made the journey to this peninsular preserve. There are no federal facilities and no formal trails, although open ash fields do provide hiking and backpacking opportunities. Access to the remote park is by plane or float plane from King Salmon, Alaska, or by power boat from the Pacific coastline. Reeve Aleutian Airways (800-544-2248) flies between Anchorage and Port Heiden, leaving visitors with an extremely arduous 10-mile hike to the monument. Other charter flights are available from King Salmon. Weather conditions can be extreme, and visitors should be prepared for windy conditions, especially through the "Gates" area, and coastal fog and rain. The nearest food and lodging are in King Salmon, and backcountry park permits are available from the Aniakchak office there.

For more information on this rugged, isolated jewel of a national monument, write Aniakchak National Monument & Preserve, P.O. Box 7, King Salmon, AK 99613-0007, or telephone (907) 246-3305. The park's Web site is www.nps.gov/ania.

FURTHER READING

Hubbard, Bernard R. "A World Inside a Mountain: Aniakchak, the New Volcano Wonderland of the Alaska Peninsula, Is Explored." *National Geographic Magazine* 60 (September 1931): 319–46.

Morseth, Michele. *Puyulek Pu'irtuq!: The People of the Volcanoes: Aniakchak National Monument and Preserve Ethnographic Overview and Assessment.* Anchorage, AK: National Park Service, 1998.

Norris, Frank B. *Isolated Paradise: An Administrative History of the Katmai and Aniakchak NPS Units.* Anchorage, AK: National Park Service, 1996. Available at www.nps.gov/katm/adhi/adhi.htm.

Smith, Walter R. *Aniakchak Crater, Alaska Peninsula.* Washington, DC: Government Printing Office, 1925.

ANTIETAM NATIONAL BATTLEFIELD

Location: Sharpsburg, Maryland
Acreage: 3,244
Established: August 30, 1890

Known as the bloodiest single day in American military history, the day the Battle of Antietam raged in western Maryland resulted in 23,000 soldiers killed, wounded, and missing. On September 17, 1862, the Army of the Potomac, 40,000 Confederate troops under the leadership of Robert E. Lee, met 87,000 Union soldiers under George B. McClellan in a decisive battle that ended in a draw but halted Lee's advance.

During the first half of September 1862, Lee attempted to invade the North after his stunning victory in the second Battle of Bull Run. He hoped to draw Union troops out of Virginia and strike a decisive blow against the North. He also sought to bring Maryland over to the Confederate side. The border state had strong Southern leanings. As Lee anticipated, McClellan rallied his troops, but instead of the weeks the Southerners expected, McClellan's men pursued the Army

National Cemetery at Antietam National Battlefield. This site marks the end of General Robert E. Lee's first invasion of the North in September 1862. *(National Park Service)*

of Northern Virginia within days. Lee had split his forces, and when his orders were found by a Union private, McClellan closed quickly to catch the vulnerable Lee without his full complement of soldiers.

On the chilly, damp morning of September 17, Lee's forces collided with the Union's Army, just north of the village of Sharpsburg, in northwestern Maryland. Lee took the high ground to the west of Antietam Creek; McClellan's command charged forward at dawn and a daylong battle ensued.

The conflict raged across 12 square miles. Despite being outnumbered by more than two to one, the Confederates held their ground, amid "a terrific storm of shell, canister, and musketry," as one officer wrote. The losses on both sides were staggering. The Texas brigade endured some of the fiercest

fighting, and by the end of the day, 186 of the unit's original 226 men were dead, wounded, or missing. The carnage along Bloody Lane, as the road subsequently became known, was among the worst in the entire Civil War. In one horrible twenty-four-hour period, more than 23,000 men—12,410 Union and 10,700 Confederate soldiers and officers—were killed, wounded, captured, or missing. Although ultimately a tactical stalemate, the battle resulted in the Union successfully halting Lee's advance.

Antietam was also an emboldening moment for the Union. Not only had it blunted the Confederate advance after a year of defeats in the east, it also hardened the resolve of Lincoln and the antislavery congressmen on whom he increasingly depended. The Civil War had begun as a struggle about whether states could pick up and leave the United States at will. Was the nation a "union," as the North claimed, or a "confederacy," as the South contended? Antietam provided the opportunity to change the terms of the discussion. In no small part as a result of the battle, President Abraham Lincoln issued the Emancipation Proclamation, which freed all slaves in areas still in secession, a few days later. When it took effect four months later, on January 1, 1863, the Civil War had become a battle about much more than union or confederacy. It had become a quest for human manumission, for the extension of the rights guaranteed in the U.S. Constitution and the Bill of Rights to all Americans.

After the Civil War, the 3,244-acre battlefield was the scene of an annual meeting of former soldiers and their families from both sides. They came to commemorate the day of this bloody battle, picnicking and camping sometimes for days. As the war receded further into the past, the scenes of its important moments became protected areas. Established by Congress on August 30, 1890, the Antietam National Battlefield was administered by the Department of War until it was transferred to the National Park Service in 1933. The battlefield contains a national cemetery as well.

The battlefield is located 12 miles south of Hagerstown, Pennsylvania, on state highway 65, and the visitor center is open daily from 8:30 A.M. to 5 P.M., and until 6 P.M. during the summer. In addition to its numerous exhibits, the center also offers an award-winning film called *Antietam Visit*, which re-creates the battle, and various interpretive programs during the summer. Entrance fees are $2 per person or $4 per family, and are good for three days. There is also a $15 annual park pass available. Approximately 270,000 tourists and military buffs visit Antietam each year. Fall and spring weekends are the busiest days, and summer is the busiest season.

Of all America's national battlefields, Antietam offers the most for visitors to see. Perhaps the best way to experience the battlefield is to take the 8.5-mile-long driving tour; walking or biking the route is also possible. Audiotape tours, which enhance the self-guided tour, may be purchased or rented from the bookstore. The route includes eleven stops along the battle's main points of interest, and typically takes from forty-five minutes to one and one-half hours to complete. Highlights include the reconstructed Dunker Church, site of repeated clashes; North Woods, where General Joseph Hooker launched the initial Union attack, but was stopped by General Thomas "Stonewall" Jackson's troops; East Woods, where Union General Joseph Mansfield was fatally wounded; Miller's cornfield, where the battle changed hands several times; West Woods, where Jackson's troops cut down 2,000 federals in twenty minutes; Mumma Farm, burned by Confederates to keep out Union sharpshooters; Bloody Lane, where three hours of fighting resulted in 5,600 casualties; Burnside Bridge, where a few hundred Georgia riflemen held off four Union divisions for four hours; the final attack site; and the Antietam National Cemetery, where 4,776 federal troops are buried.

There is no food or lodging in the park, but all traveler services are located in neighboring Sharpsburg. Water and rest rooms are available in the visitor center. The park's only campground is Rorhbach Campground, a 10-site, walk-in, primitive area available to Boy Scouts and other organized groups. For individuals or small private parties, a walk-in tent campground is available on the C&O (Chesapeake and Ohio) Canal, 5 miles south on Harper's Ferry Road. Greenbrier State Park, 15 miles to the northeast, via Highway 34, has 200 sites with flush toilets, showers, laundry facilities, and a lake for fishing, boating, and swimming.

For more information, write Antietam National Battlefield, P.O. Box 158, Sharpsburg, MD 21782-0158, or telephone (301) 432-5124. The park's Web site is www.nps.gov/anti.

FURTHER READING

Franssanito, William A. *Antietam: The Photographic Legacy of America's Bloodiest Day.* New York: Scribner, 1978.

Luvaas, Jay, and Harold W. Nelson. *U.S. Army War College Guide to the Battle of Antietam: The Maryland Campaign of 1862.* New York: Perennial Library, 1988.

McPherson, James M. *Crossroads of Freedom: Antietam.* New York: Oxford University Press, 2002.

Murfin, James V. *The Gleam of Bayonets: the Battle of Antietam and the Maryland Campaign of 1862.* New York: T. Yoseloff, 1965.

Sears, Stephen W. *Landscape Turned Red.* Norwalk, CT: Easton, 1983.

APOSTLE ISLANDS NATIONAL LAKESHORE

Location: Lake Superior, Wisconsin
Acreage: 69,372
Established: September 26, 1970

Carved by glacial ice, wind, and waves for more than 1 million years, the wild and remote Apostle Islands archipelago juts into Lake Superior, forming the northernmost border of the state of Wisconsin. These sheltered islands on the world's largest freshwater lake feature pristine sand beaches, spectacular sea caves and sandstone cliffs, a variety of wetlands, and remnant old-growth forests. Native Americans, French "voyageurs," loggers, quarry workers, farmers, and commercial fishers have all called this island chain home, as have the islands' resident populations of bald eagles and black bears.

The geologic result of a period when huge sheets of ice covered the region and then receded, the Apostle Island group contains 22 islands, 21 of which are in the National Lakeshore. The name probably derives from the desire of seventeenth-century Jesuit missionaries who wished to honor their apostles by naming a beautiful place after them. French "voyageurs" first established trading posts on the islands, and later settlers built seasonal hunting and fishing camps, summer cabins, farms, and homesteads. During the 1800s, six navigational lighthouses were built to guide approaching ships through the rocky waters, and today, Apostle Islands National Lakeshore boasts the largest collection of lighthouses anywhere in the national park system.

Originally established in September 1970, the over-69,000-acre Apostle Islands National Lakeshore protects 21 Apostle Islands and a 12-mile stretch of Lake Superior shoreline for public educational and recreational purposes. Apostle Islands was the culmination of a fifteen-year trend to preserve lakeshores at a time when waterfront property was rapidly becoming privatized in the United States. Long considered a treasure, the islands were difficult to develop, for the people of the region opposed federal control. Only after long negotiations did the lakeshore finally come to fruition. The park's primary visitor center is located in the old Bayfield County Courthouse. It is open year-round, from 8 A.M. to 5 P.M. (to 6 P.M. Memorial Day to Labor Day) daily, from May through October, and from 8 A.M. to 4:30 P.M., Monday through Friday, from November through April. The center features audiovisual programs and exhibits on the park's history, natural history, and recreational opportunities. The Little Sand Bay Visitor Center is open from 9 A.M. to 5 P.M. daily from Memorial Day until Labor Day, Friday through Sundays in September, and is closed from October to June. The Stockton Island Visitor Center is staffed intermittently from 8 A.M. to 9 P.M. from Memorial Day until Labor Day, and it is closed for the remainder of the year. Park rangers offer tours of the lighthouses located on Raspberry, Sand, Devils, Michigan, and Outer islands, and the historic Manitou Island Fish Camp

Stella Cove at Apostle Islands National Lakeshore, c. 1898. *(Library of Congress)*

allows visitors to experience how commercial fishers lived and worked in the region.

There are more than 50 miles of maintained trails in the national lakeshore, as well as opportunities for sailing, boating, sea kayaking, hiking, fishing, picnicking, swimming, scuba diving (permit required), hunting (state license required), cross-country skiing, snowshoeing, visiting museums and exhibits, and participating in seasonal ranger-guided programs. The Apostle Islands region is one of the best fish-producing habitats in the Great Lakes, and fishing is exceptionally good for lake, brown, and rainbow trout, as well as salmon. A valid Wisconsin fishing license is required.

Although Apostle Islands offers plenty of recreation opportunities on the mainland, most visitors consider the islands to be the most rewarding destinations in the park. The Apostle Islands Cruise Service offers a variety of excursion tours and camper/hiker shuttles to several islands. The Cruise Service also operates a water taxi service between Bayfield and any island, for up to six passengers per trip. Park marinas and local outfitters rent sailboats and sea kayaks, and they can arrange full- or half-day fishing trips. Because of frequently rough conditions on the lake, small open boats are not recommended for inter-island transportation. Summer temperatures range from 75 to 80 degrees during the day, to 55 degrees at night. Frequent summer thunderstorms can create severe, rapidly changing wind and wave conditions. Winter temperatures are extreme, and readings of minus 10 degrees are common. May and June are best for flower displays, July and August for moderate waves, and May and September for bird migrations.

Camping is permitted on 18 of the 21 islands at the national lakeshore. No National Park Service campgrounds are located on the mainland, however, and island campgrounds are not accessible by road. Park Service camping permits are available for $15 per individual campsite and $30 for a group campsite, and are valid for up to fourteen consecutive nights of camping. There is no lodging in the park, but motels are available in Bayfield, Washburn, Cornucopia, and Ashland, and on Madeline Island.

For more information, write Apostle Islands National Lakeshore, Route 1, Box 4, Old Courthouse Building, Bayfield, WI 54814-9599, or telephone (715) 779-3397. The park's helpful Web site is www.nps.gov/apis.

FURTHER READING

Apostle Islands: A Guide to Apostle Islands National Lakeshore, Wisconsin. Washington, DC: National Park Service, 1988.

Cooper, David J., ed. *By Fire, Storm, and Ice: Underwater Archeological Investigations in the Apostle Islands.* Madison: State Historical Society of Wisconsin, 1991.

Merkel, Jim. *Majestic Lights: The Apostle Island Lighthouses.* St. Louis, MO: JCM Press, 2001.

APPOMATTOX COURT HOUSE NATIONAL HISTORICAL PARK

Location: Appomattox, Virginia
Acreage: 1,774
Established: June 18, 1930

On the afternoon of April 9, 1865, Ulysses S. Grant, general in chief of all U.S. forces, sent a simple message to Washington, D.C.: "General [Robert E.] Lee surrendered the army of Northern Virginia this afternoon on terms proposed by myself." Although scattered fighting persisted for a while longer, for all intents and purposes, the great scourge of Civil War passed into history. The 1,774-acre Appomattox Court House National Historical Park commemorates and preserves the closing hours of America's Civil War and the site of Lee's surrender. The war's final days were desperate for the Confederates, as desertion rates soared and hunger menaced the troops. Union forces had marched almost at will through the South in early 1864, destroying not only the Southern army but also the South's will to fight. Now, in April, Grant's heavily entrenched troops had cut off Lee's critical supply lines and successfully blocked the Confederates' escape out of Virginia. On April 6, Union forces slammed into flagging Confederate troops with a massive assault near Appomattox Court House in Virginia. Realizing he could neither fight nor retreat, Lee conceded defeat, and dispatched a lone rider in a gray uniform with a fluttering white flag to surrender his starving, depleted Army of Northern Virginia. On April 9, 1865, four bloody years of Civil War officially ended and a great stillness settled over Appomattox. As the Confederate general handed his sword to the victorious Grant, Lee turned to Ely Parker, the full-blooded Seneca Indian who served as Grant's adjutant, and said, "I'm glad to see one real American here." "We are all Americans," Parker responded. At a cost of more than 620,000 lives, the Union had been saved. The Confederate attempt to create a separate nation had failed, and Grant gently chastened his jubilant Union forces by reminding them that "the war is over—the Rebels are our countrymen again."

The actual site of this momentous meeting was the home of Wilmer McLean, who had been a resident of Manassas Junction before the war, but found his home there in the middle of the Battle of Bull Run. He fled to southwestern Virginia to avoid the conflict, only to

Civilians in front of the hotel at Appomattox Court House, c. 1865. *(Library of Congress)*

find the surrender was taking place in his living room. McLean did not get to keep perhaps the most significant souvenir of the event. Instead, Brevet General George Armstrong Custer rode off from the surrender with the table where the signing occurred on his head; General Phil Sheridan had given it to him as gift for Custer's wife, Libby. In many ways, Wilmer McLean's experience proved an essential fact about the United States during this period: No one could escape the impact of the Civil War. It changed the nation and everyone in it, a feeling driven home at the park.

Originally designated as a national battlefield site in 1930, Appomattox Court House became a national monument in 1935, and achieved national historical park status in 1954. The park is located in southcentral Virginia, 20 miles east of Lynchburg, on state highway 24, 3 miles northeast of Appomattox. Restored to Civil War–era appearance, the site's primary attractions are in the village of Appomattox Court House. The visitor center/museum is located in the reconstructed courthouse building and contains many original artifacts associated with the surrender, as well as interpretive displays, museum exhibits, and audiovisual programs. The center is open year-round from 9 A.M. to 5:30 P.M. Memorial Day through Labor Day, and from 8:30 A.M. to 5 P.M. during the rest of the year. The actual surrender site, the reconstructed McLean House, is open to the public, as are numerous other historic sites such as the Meeks House, the General Store, Woodson Law Office, the County Jail, and the park's oldest structure, the Clover Hill Tavern, built in 1819. A Confederate cemetery lies west of the village, while Lee's headquarters are located northeast of the courthouse. Visitors should also consider following the 100-mile Lee's Retreat Route, featuring 20 wayside stops with radio messages. Park rangers provide living history programs and guided tours during the summer months, and a self-guided, 5-mile walking trail connects all the sites. Entrance fees are $4 per person ($10 maximum per vehicle) during the summer, when a full schedule of daily programs is available, and $2 per person ($5 maximum per vehicle) during the off-season.

There is no food, camping, or lodging in the park. Motels, restaurants, stores, and gas stations are located nearby in the towns of Appomattox and Lynchburg. Camping is available at Holliday Lake State Park, 12 miles northeast of Appomattox, and at numerous private campgrounds. The Holliday Lake campground contains 61 sites (without hookups), flush toilets, showers, a dump station, and a large lake with boat rentals, swimming, and fishing. Visitation is usually highest in the summer months, and lowest in January and February.

For more information, write Appomattox Court House National Historical Park, P.O. Box 218, Appomattox, VA 24522-8987, or telephone (804) 352-8987. The park's Web site is www.nps.gov/apco.

FURTHER READING
Catton, Bruce. *A Stillness at Appomattox.* New York: Anchor Books, 1990.
McPherson, James M. *Battle Cry of Freedom: The Civil War Era.* New York: Oxford University Press, 1988.
Winik, Jay. *April 1865: The Month That Saved America.* New York: HarperCollins, 2001.

ARCHES NATIONAL PARK

Location: Moab, Utah
Acreage: 76,519
Established: April 12, 1929

Located in southeastern Utah, Arches National Park provides one of the most exquisite combinations of desert beauty and remote loneliness in the lower forty-eight states. Established as a national monument in 1929 as director Horace M. Albright envisioned the inclusion of the final pieces of untrammeled spectacular scenery in the national park system, Arches remained largely devoid of development until after World War II. Beautiful and distant, it served as de facto wilderness well into the 1960s. The more than 2,000 sandstone arches within the park's boundaries are the greatest concentration of natural stone openings in the world. A thick bed of salt, deposited deep beneath the surface when a sea flowed through southern Utah more than 300 million years ago, caused the land above it to rise and fall over millions of years. These fissures and cracks, folds and buckles, were smoothed over by millions of years of water that ran across the land, digging deep trenches and shaping the sand into the eerie arch, canyon, and fin formations that today greet the eye.

The stunning and bizarre beauty of the place earned Arches a number of champions, the most noteworthy of whom was the environmentalist writer Edward Abbey. Abbey came to the park as a seasonal national park ranger in the mid-1950s, and it inspired his best—in his case, most passionate and acerbic—writing. "I liked the work and the canyon country and returned the following year for a second season," he wrote in his masterpiece, *Desert Solitaire.* "I would have returned the third year too and each year thereafter, but unfortunately for me, the Arches, a primitive place when I first went there, was developed and improved so well that I had to leave." His gift to the place, the marvelous collection of essays and diatribes contained in *Desert Solitaire,* became one of the bibles of the environmental movement. Abbey himself went on to author numerous books, one of which is *The Monkey Wrench Gang* (1975), which provided one of the rationales and the strategy

Double arch in Windows section of Arches National Park. Windows is one of the park's most visited areas. Graffiti on the rock is the result of vandalism. *(National Archives)*

call to "get out and walk, better yet crawl" to experience the essence of the natural world, could find roads that deposited them at the head of moderately difficult hiking trails, which took them into spectacular and once isolated spaces. Where less than a generation ago only a few hardy souls ventured to Arches, today thousands of visitors come to experience beauty with only a minimum effort on their part. While Arches has achieved a balance between the competing missions of the National Park Service, preservation and use, the nature of that accommodation would gall many of the region's early preservation advocates. The dilemma of the success of Arches National Park is in many ways a microcosm of the entire park system.

While Arches has achieved balance between preservation and use, the nature of that accommodation has led to powerful questions from some park supporters. More than 20 miles of paved roads help the visitor experience the developed national park's many wondrous natural features from behind a windshield; improved dirt roads also branch out from the main roads. Improved hiking trails lead to some of the most noteworthy arches, among them Delicate and Balanced Rock. Landscape Arch, one of the longest arches in the world at over 250 feet, is a favorite with visitors. Located on the Devil's Garden trail (a 5-mile round trip), the path winds through a garden of fin formations, smaller arches, and other unusual natural features. Hikers should be forewarned that summer temperatures can climb well over 100 degrees, with very low humidity. The National Park Service recommends that even on the short trails hikers should carry a minimum of 1 gallon of water per person, and bring sunscreen, cool clothing, and comfortable hiking shoes.

for the radical environmental group Earth First!

The forbidding nature of Arches National Monument made it a focus of the activities of environmentalists. Wild already, it seemed to many worthy of more permanent preservation, and in 1971, Arches National Monument became Arches National Park. Yet such a designation had its drawbacks. Edward Abbey was gone a decade before the area attained national park status, reviling the development that had already occurred. The change in status signaled even greater emphasis on visitor facilities. From its origins as a remote park, Arches became an intermediate step, a place where those who enjoyed natural beauty, but were not up to Abbey's

Located at the park's south entrance off U.S. Highway 191, a visitor center contains a museum and a slide program. Visitors can also get information on guided walks, sight-seeing highlights, maps, and a roadside guide to all the main natural attractions. There are also rest-room facilities and drinking water at the visitor center. There is no food or lodging in the park, but extensive tourist facilities are located in the recreational boomtown of Moab, 5 miles to the south. The park has one improved campground 18 miles north of the park entrance in the Devil's Garden area, with water, tables, grills, and flush toilets, but no RV dump station. No fishing is available in the park.

For more information, write Arches National Park, P.O. Box 907, Moab, UT 84532-0907, or telephone (435) 259-8161. The park's Web site is www.nps.gov/arch.

FURTHER READING

Abbey, Edward. *Desert Solitaire.* New York: Ballantine Books, 1991.

——. *The Monkey Wrench Gang.* New York: Harper-Perennial, 2000.

Baars, Donald L. *Canyonlands Country: Geology of Canyonlands and Arches National Park.* Salt Lake City: University of Utah Press, 1994.

ARKANSAS POST NATIONAL MEMORIAL

Location: Gillett, Arkansas
Acreage: 758
Established: July 6, 1960

The lower Mississippi River Valley was long a meeting place among Europeans and Native Americans, a place where the people of the plains met the people of the hills and where the people who came from across the water encountered both. Arkansas Post National Memorial commemorates more than three centuries of struggle between and among France, Spain, England, and the United States for control over the interior of the North American continent. In 1686, the first permanent French settlement in the lower Mississippi River Valley was estab-lished at the Poste de Arkansea—Arkansas trading post—in the Quapaw Indian village of Osotuoy. Strategically located near the confluence of the Arkansas and Mississippi rivers, this fur-trading outpost soon fell victim to the capriciousness of European fashion; when the fur market collapsed around 1700, so too did the Poste de Arkansea. France was determined to maintain its control over the region, and by 1732, it had built a small fort at the site. In 1763, following its defeat in the French and Indian War, France surrendered the Louisiana Territory—and the Arkansas Post—to Spain. Two decades later, the American Revolution briefly touched the post when the British attacked the now-Spanish garrison, albeit unsuccessfully. In 1800, the French Revolution briefly restored the territory to France, until 1803, when a cash-strapped Napoleon Bonaparte sold the entire Louisiana Territory to the United States for $15 million. By 1819, the post was a thriving river port and the largest city in the region; it was important enough to be selected as the territorial capital of Arkansas, until that honor passed to Little Rock in 1821. During the Civil War, Confederate troops tried to maintain tactical control of the area by constructing an earthen fortification known as Fort Hindman, but in January of 1863, Union troops destroyed the fort and the adjacent river port town, ensuring complete Union control of the Arkansas River.

Originally set aside in 1929 as a state park, Arkansas Post received national recognition in July 1960, when the national memorial park was established. Located in eastern Arkansas 100 miles northwest of Little Rock and 9 miles south of Gillett, the park offers excellent opportunities for fishing, picnicking, and wildlife watching. Arkansas Post National Memorial is open year-round from 8 A.M. to dark daily. Although there is no admission fee, a donation box is available at the visitor center, which is open daily from 8 A.M.

to 5 P.M. The visitor center and museum include exhibits on the history of the park and the fur trade, a fourteen-minute movie about Arkansas Post, and a small bookstore. Visitors can take a self-guided tour of the town site along paved trails, and a nature trail departing from the visitor center skirts the edge of the bayou. Highlights include remnants of the historic town site including a well and cistern, and 50 yards of Civil War earthworks from the Confederate defense lines. Unfortunately, there are few visible remnants of the five different forts and settlements that existed throughout the post's history. The park also features a 2-mile scenic drive, picnic areas, and wayside exhibits. Peak visitation typically occurs between April and June.

Summers in Gillett are generally hot and humid, while winters are mild. Insects are common during much of the year, and appropriate precautions should be observed. Because of the abundance of water in and around the park, a very large population of reptiles and amphibians exists at Arkansas Post. Although most reptiles are nonpoisonous terrestrial and water snakes, there are three species of poisonous snakes that inhabit the area. A small population of American alligators is also found in the park's waters.

Arkansas Post is a day-use-only park, and no camping, lodging, or food is available; all travel services are located in nearby Gillett. The Army Corps of Engineers operates camping and boat ramp facilities at Pendleton Bend, 20 miles southwest of the park off Highway 165, and at Merrisach Lake Park, 25 miles northeast off Highway 144.

For more information, write Arkansas Post National Memorial, 1741 Old Post Road, Gillett, AR 72055, or telephone (870) 548-2207. The park's Web site is www.nps.gov/arpo.

FURTHER READING
Arnold, Morris S. *Colonial Arkansas, 1686–1804: A Social and Cultural History.* Fayetteville: University of Arkansas Press, 1991.

Bearss, Edwin C. *Arkansas Post National Memorial, Arkansas; Structural History Post of Arkansas, 1804–1863, and Civil War Troop Movement Maps, January, 1863.* Washington, DC: Office of History and Historic Architecture, Eastern Service Center, 1971.

Coleman, Roger E. *The Arkansas Post Story: Arkansas Post National Monument.* Santa Fe, NM: Division of History, Southwest Cultural Resources Center, Southwest Region, National Park Service, 1987.

ARLINGTON HOUSE, THE ROBERT E. LEE MEMORIAL

Location: Arlingon, Virginia
Acreage: 28
Established: March 4, 1925

The gallant Robert E. Lee best personified the complicated emotions that accompanied the conflict of the Civil War. A proud American military officer, considered the most capable of his generation, Lee was also a devout supporter of his home state of Virginia. Lee believed in the Union and opposed slavery. As conflict seemed imminent, Lee stood his position as an American, but when his native state seceded, he sadly turned in his federal commission and became a Confederate. The sense that Lee was torn between allegiances, along with his fundamental dignity and decency, made him a heroic figure in American history.

Overlooking the Potomac River and Washington, D.C., the palatial Arlington House is the nation's memorial to this man who retained the respect of Americans both North and South. Constructed between 1802 and 1817 by George Washington Parke Custis, the adopted son of George Washington, Arlington House became the antebellum home of Lee and his family. Named after the Custis family's homestead of Virginia's Eastern Shore, Arlington House was built on a 1,100-acre estate that Custis's father, John Parke Custis, purchased in 1778. In 1804, Custis married Mary Lee Fitzhugh. Their

Arlington House, the Robert E. Lee Memorial. *(Library of Congress)*

only child to survive infancy was Mary Anna Randolph Custis, born in 1808. Young Robert E. Lee, whose mother was a cousin of Mrs. Custis, frequently visited Arlington House. Two years after graduating from West Point, Lieutenant Lee married Mary Custis at Arlington House on June 30, 1831. The Lees lived in the home for the thirty years before the outbreak of the Civil War, when they were forced to abandon the property. During the war, the federal army confiscated the property for use as a headquarters in the defense of Washington, D.C., and it later became part of Arlington National Cemetery.

During the three decades the Arlington House was the Lee and Custis home, the Lees divided their time between various U.S. Army duty stations and Arlington, where six of their seven children were born. When George Washington Parke Custis died in 1857, he left the Arlington estate to Mary Custis for her lifetime and afterward to the Lees' eldest son, George Washington Custis Lee. It was here at Arlington House that Lee felt most comfortable. "My affections and attachments are more strongly placed here than at any other place in the world," he once told a relative.

Although Lee opposed Virginia's secession during the Civil War, he remained loyal to his home state. On April 20, 1861, Lee resigned his commission in the U.S. Army and two days later he left Arlington for Richmond to accept command of Virginia's military forces. He never returned to the home he loved. About a month later, with Union occupation imminent, Mrs. Lee was forced to leave Arlington House, though not before she managed to send some of the family's valuables into safe hands. Later, when Arlington became a headquarters for officers who were monitoring the defenses of nearby Washington, many of the remaining family possessions were moved to the patent office for safekeeping.

Despite the hardships of war, the law required that property owners in areas occupied by Union troops appear in person to pay their land taxes. In 1864, when the Lees were unable to comply, the U.S. War Department confiscated the property and set aside a 200-acre section to serve as a military cemetery—the beginning of Arlington National Cemetery. Over time, it has become the nation's largest military cemetery, protecting the remains of the nation's soldiers, sailors, and marines from the Civil War to the present. Authorized in 1925 as the Custis-Lee Mansion, the property was transferred from the War Department to the Department of the Interior in 1933. It became a permanent memorial in 1955, and was added to the national park system in 1972.

The house is accessible by a shuttle bus or by a ten-minute walk from the Arlington National Cemetery Visitor Center and parking area. Access from Washington is via the Memorial Bridge. Access from Virginia is from the George Washington Memorial Parkway. The memorial is also accessible via the Blue Line of Washington's Metro subway system.

Arlington House is open all year from 9:30 A.M. to 4:30 P.M. The grounds are open 8 A.M. to 7 P.M., from April through September and 8 A.M. to 5 P.M. from October through March. The memorial is closed on Christmas Day and New Year's Day. There are no fees. Visitors tour the house with a self-guided brochure. National Park Activities Service staff in period costumes are stationed in the main areas to talk informally with visitors. Guided tours are available by appointment for groups from October through March. There are no snack bars, restaurants, lodging, or camping facilities in the park or in Arlington National Cemetery.

For more information, write Arlington House, The Robert E. Lee Memorial, George Washington Memorial Parkway, Turkey Run Park, McLean, VA 22101-0001, or telephone (703) 557-0613. The park's Web site is www.nps.gov/arho.

FURTHER READING

Connelly, Thomas Lawrence. *The Marble Man: Robert E. Lee and His Image in American Society.* Baton Rouge: Louisiana State University Press, 1978.
Freeman, Douglas Southall. *R.E. Lee: A Biography.* New York: Scribner's, 1937–1940.
McPherson, James M. *Battle Cry of Freedom.* New York: Oxford University Press, 1988.

ASSATEAGUE ISLAND NATIONAL SEASHORE

Location: Berlin, Maryland, and
  Chincoteague, Virginia
Acreage: 39,727
Established: September 21, 1965

The string bean–like island known as Assateague is a windswept barrier reef formed by sand rising from the ocean floor, then steadily molded by prevailing easterly winds and Atlantic Ocean waves. Thirty-seven miles long, the national seashore covers nearly 40,000 acres of sea and shore in southern Maryland and northern Virginia.

Established in 1965, Assateague was part of the drive to include lakeshores and seashores in the national park system before private owners bought the entire American coast and made it off limits to the general public. Its establishment reflected the growing need for public recreation as well as the many issues involved in acquiring private land for public purposes. In this, Assateague served as a prototype for a broader park system, equally focused on recreational and ecological values.

Assateague is famous for the wild horses that have the run of the island. These feral animals are the descendants of horses that owners brought to barrier islands like Assateague in the late seventeenth century to avoid fencing laws and taxation of livestock. To protect Assateague's natural environment, the ponies are split into two main herds, one on the Virginia side and one on the Maryland side of the island, and the population size of each herd is kept at around 150 animals.

As a result of their poor diet and the harsh environment, the horses are closer to the size of ponies, about 12 to 13 hands high. Coarse, salt-marsh cord grass and American beach grass constitute the bulk of their food supply, and a high concentration of salt in their food supply causes the horses to drink twice as much fresh water as domestic horses. This results in a bloated appearance; many regard the Assateague horses as fat. Some horses removed from Assateague as foals and fed a higher protein diet grow to the size of ordinary horses.

On the Virginia side of the island, the internationally famous "Pony Penning" is the highlight of the year. This event began during the late seventeenth century, when unclaimed horses were captured and claimed and marked by colonists in front of their neighbors during a festival that bound the community together. The modern Pony Penning began in 1924 as an effort to raise money for the Chincoteague Volunteer Fire Company and is still held on the last Wednesday and Thursday of July. The ritual now helps keep the horse population at the size deemed best for the combination of animal needs and island ecology.

Assateague National Seashore offers many opportunities for seashore recreation and nature study. Ocean swimming, camping, bayside canoeing, crabbing, clamming, hunting, surf-fishing and off-road vehicle use are popular activities. The wild horses roam throughout the island and share habitats with a host of other mammals and nearly 300 species of birds. In addition, the seashore has miles of roads and trails. In Maryland, 4 miles of paved roads include an adjacent bike path, with the "Life of Assateague" self-guided trails interpreting 3 different barrier island habitats. In Virginia, 5 miles of paved roads include a bike path. Two short nature trails explore natural habitats and a third leads to the base of the Assateague Lighthouse.

There are only two access points: north near Ocean City, Maryland, and south at Chincoteague, Virginia. Assateague's north entrance is at the end of Route 611, 8 miles south of Ocean City. The south entrance is at the eastern terminus of Route 175, 2 miles from Chincoteague. The Barrier Island Visitor Center at the north end contains publications, exhibits, and information on the island. One paved road extends through the state park and into the national seashore, but sand-capable ATVs are the only vehicles allowed on the island beyond Bayside Drive, and a permit is required. At the park's south end, a 3-mile-long paved road winds into the Wildlife Refuge, where a visitor center provides information. Another sand road leads 5 miles into the seashore beyond Tom's Cove Beach; a permit is required to travel this road.

Visitation is highest from mid-June to Labor Day, and lowest from December to March. Hours are daily, year-round: island open twenty-four hours in Maryland; 5 A.M. to 10 P.M. during daylight savings time in Virginia, with shorter hours during winter. Visitor centers open 9 A.M. to 5 P.M. but closed Thanksgiving and Christmas days. Admission fees are: $5 per weekly vehicle pass, collected separately at each entrance, or $2 per week for cyclists and walk-ins. Golden Age, Golden Access, and Golden Eagle passes are honored. Commercial tour fees are available on request. Fees are $14 per night to camp in the national seashore, $20 per night in Assateague State Park.

There is no lodging in the park. All travel services can be found in Chincoteague or Ocean City. Camping is the only overnight opportunity on the island, and all state and national campgrounds are located in the Maryland portion. National seashore backpacking or canoe-in backcountry camping are also located in Maryland. For more information, call the national seashore at the number listed below or the state park (410-641-2120). Clamming and crabbing are permitted in Chincoteague Bay. Because of the seashore's exposure, it is a good idea to call for possible closures during threats by coastal storms.

For more information, write Assateague Island National Seashore, 7206 National Seashore Lane, Berlin, MD 21811, or telephone (410) 641-1441. The park's Web site is www.nps.gov/asis.

FURTHER READING

Arnosky, Jim. *Wild Ponies.* Washington, DC: National Geographic Society, 2002.

Badger, Curtis J. *The Barrier Islands: A Photographic History of Life on Hog, Cobb, Smith, Cedar, Parramore, Metompkin, & Assateague.* Harrisburg, PA: Stackpole Books, 1989.

Henry, Marguerite. *Misty of Chincoteague.* New York: Simon & Schuster Books for Young Readers, 2000.

Meanley, Brooke. *Bird Life at Chincoteague and the Virginia Barrier Islands.* Centreville, MD: Tidewater, 1981.

AZTEC RUINS
NATIONAL MONUMENT

Location: Aztec, New Mexico
Acreage: 318
Established: January 24, 1923

Long before Columbus reached the New World, Native American peoples in the American Southwest lived in organized permanent communities graced by complicated stone structures. Their masonry buildings dot the southwestern landscape, reminding all who pass by that other people came before and left their mark on the harsh desert and its spare waterways.

Along the Animas River in the town of Aztec, New Mexico, Aztec Ruins National Monument preserves structures and artifacts of Chaco Canyon and Mesa Verde Pueblo peoples between the twelfth and thirteenth centuries. Native Americans associated with Chaco Canyon culture to the south first built and used the structures. They were followed by relatives of the northerly Mesa Verde people, who settled at the site after 1200 C.E.

Aztec's West Ruin is a huge Chaco-style house of nearly 400 rooms and kivas—underground ceremonial chambers. The aboveground West Ruin is only a small portion of a series of unexcavated great houses, plazas, tri-wall and great kivas, and other smaller buildings. Barely visible prehistoric roads connect all the structures within this ancient community, while other more defined road segments suggest connections to numerous other sites in the Animas River valley and other Chaco culture communities in the Four Corners region. Anthropologists theorize that this area might have been an important ceremonial, administrative, and trade center for surrounding Native American populations as late as the 1170s C.E.

By 1200, Chaco culture was in serious decline throughout the region, and many of its locations were abandoned. After the departure of the Chaco culture peoples, Mesa Verde peoples replaced them. They remodeled some of the pueblos, then vacated the buildings sometime in the 1300s. The structures have been uninhabited ever since.

The 318-acre monument was established in 1923, in the middle of the era when archeology was of the most interest to the

Aztec Ruins National Monument preserves the structures and artifacts of ancestral Pueblo people from the 1100s into the 1200s C.E. *(National Park Service)*

American public and when the Park Service routinely added such areas whenever it could. Guarded by a volunteer custodian, a "dollar-a-year-man," Aztec was typical of many smaller southwestern archeological areas during that era. Earl Morris, a noted early southwestern archeologist, did much of the excavating of the region, and in the end left his imprimatur on the site. The park was designated a World Heritage Site in 1987. The highest visitation is June through August; the lowest is December through February. The best time to visit is spring or fall. Winter consists of relatively mild winter days, some occasional snow, and evening temperatures that sometimes drop below zero. Summer day temperatures are in the upper 80s and low 90s, with cool nights, and thundershowers are frequent.

The monument is approximately 2 miles north of U.S. Highway 550 on Ruins Road (County Road 2900) on the north edge of the city of Aztec. Ruins Road is the first street west of the Animas River bridge on U.S. Highway 550 in Aztec. Operating hours are daily, Memorial Day through Labor Day, 8 A.M. to 6 P.M. The rest of the year, the hours are 8 A.M. to 5 P.M.

The visitor center contains an information desk, artifact exhibits, and video programs. The Southwest Parks and Monuments Association sells books, videotapes, calendars, postcards, slides, and other items. A self-guided, quarter-mile-long interpretive trail winds through the West Ruin. Visitors walk through rooms with their original roofs and through the reconstructed Hubbard tri-wall kiva—a partially underground structure once used for community activities.

For more information, write Aztec Ruins National Monument, P.O. Box 640, Aztec, NM 87410-0640, or telephone (505) 334-6174. The park's Web site is www. nps.gov/azru.

FURTHER READING

Koogler, C.V., and Virginia Koogler Whitney. *Aztec: A Story of Old Aztec from the Anasazi to Statehood.* Fort Worth, TX: American Reference, 1972.

Lister, Robert H., and Florence C. Lister. *Aztec Ruins on the Animas. Excavated, Preserved, and Interpreted.* Albuquerque: University of New Mexico Press, 1987.

——. *Aztec Ruins National Monument: Administrative History of an Archeological Preserve.* Santa Fe, NM: National Park Service, Division of History, Southwest Cultural Resources Center, 1990. Available at www.nps.gov/azru/adhi/adhi.htm.

B

BADLANDS NATIONAL PARK
Location: Southwestern South Dakota
Acreage: 242,756
Established: March 4, 1929

The northern plains are eerie and no part of them is more unusual than the area now designated as Badlands National Park. Seventeenth-century French trappers labeled this rugged part of the plains "bad lands to travel across," reflecting its rough, dry, and dramatically intimidating landscape. Covering over 240,000 acres in southwestern South Dakota, the area now known as Badlands National Park is a curious mixture of pinnacles, spires, and buttes, with the largest protected mixed-grass prairie in the United States. Significant in both the past and the present, the park also contains the world's richest Oligocene-epoch fossil beds, dating from 23 million to 38 million years ago, as well as the current reintroduciton site of North America's most endangered land mammal, the black-footed ferret.

Once covered by an ancient inland sea, the land was uplifted and exposed to a warm, humid climate. Saber-toothed cats, small camels, and other prehistoric mammals roamed the land. Fossils of mammalian species such as the horse, sheep, rhinoceros, and pig can be studied in the Badlands formations, created by mudslides from the Black Hills to the west and by widespread volcanic activity. The gray-white layers evident in the soft sedimentary Badlands rock formations were formed by this volcanic activity.

Authorized in 1929, Badlands National Monument required nearly a full decade before it came into existence. The state of South Dakota was to acquire land, and when that land was acquired, the monument could be established. In 1936, Congress gave the president the option of adding up to 250,000 acres to the monument by proclamation, and Franklin D. Roosevelt used this power to add 150,000 acres in 1939. Officially established as Badlands National Monument in 1939, the site was redesignated as a national park in 1978. The park is comprised of 3 separate administrative units: the North, the detached Palmer Creek, and the Stronghold. The Stronghold unit is jointly managed with the Oglala Sioux Nation. It includes Ghost Dance sites of the 1890s, places at which Sioux or Lakota people embraced the faith of the Native American prophet Wovoka. Access to the Stronghold unit is limited because of its status as sacred space to Native Americans.

Hiking and backpacking are common recreational uses of the park. Fossil Exhibit Trail, beginning 5 miles northwest of the Reifel Visitor Center, is the site, during the summer, of fossil history presentations given by park naturalists. Five-mile Castle Trail is the longest hiking trail and the three-quarters-of-a-mile-long Door Trail represents the geological history of the area. Backcountry backpackers are encouraged to speak to rangers at the visitor centers before entering the backcountry. There is one licensed horse packer. Visitors may also explore the unpaved, 10-mile, round-trip drive to Roberts Prairie Dog Town (from Loop Road). A typical visit to the park lasts three to five hours, and it includes the park movie and two walks.

Despite its remote location, the park receives approximately 1.3 million visitors per year. Most visitors arrive between mid-June

Badlands National Park consists of nearly 243,000 acres of sharply eroded buttes, pinnacles, and spires, blended with the largest protected mixed-grass prairie in the United States. Photograph taken c. 1936. *(Library of Congress)*

and September; very few brave the elements from mid-November through March. Summers are hot and dry with occasional violent thunderstorms, while winters are very cold with frequent snow. Extremely high winds and sunshine are common year-round.

Located about 50 miles east of Rapid City, South Dakota, the park is open twenty-four hours a day, seven days per week. An entrance fee of $10 per vehicle, which permits entrance for seven days, is collected all year. Badlands National Park has two visitor centers: Ben Reifel, located 8 miles south of I-90 near the northeast entrance, and White River, at the park's south end off state highway 589. Ben Reifel has exhibits and a slide program

to help orient newcomers to the region's natural history, while White River contains Oglala Sioux Indian cultural exhibits and a video presentation about the tribe's history. The White River Visitor Center is only open from June through August. Full ranger program schedules at the Ben Reifel visitor center are available between June 15 and August 25. The Park Service offers a reduced schedule from August 26 through Labor Day.

The quarter-mile-long Fossil Exhibit Trail is paved and wheelchair accessible. The first 100 yards of Door Trail, located 2 miles northeast of the Ben Reifel Visitor Center, is paved and accessible to athletic wheelchair users. Window Trail, a quarter-mile loop that begins at the Door and Window parking area, is also accessible to athletic wheelchair users. An open-captioned version of the film *Buried Fossils, Living Prairie* is available. An accessibility guide to the park is free upon request.

Cedar Pass Lodge, located near the northeast entrance, offers 23 air-conditioned cabins and full-service dining facilities from April 1 through October 31. The 96-space Cedar Pass campground provides water, tables, flush toilets, and an RV dump station. The cost is $10 per night during summer, with a fourteen-night limit, and $8 per night in winter. Reservations are required for group campsites and school groups. Located near the Pinnacles entrance station, the Sage Creek Wilderness campground has no facilities, but is free and open year-round. Limited traveler supplies are available in Interior, 3 miles from the park near Cedar Pass.

For more information, write Badlands National Park, P.O. Box 6, Interior, SD 57750, or telephone (605) 433-5361. The park's Web site is www.nps.gov/badl.

FURTHER READING

Hall, Philip S. *Reflections of the Badlands.* Vermillion: University of South Dakota Press, 1993.

Hauk, Joy Keve. *Badlands: Its Life and Landscape; The Natural History Story of Badlands National Monument.* Interior, SD: Badlands Natural History Association, 1969.

BANDELIER NATIONAL MONUMENT

Location: Los Alamos, New Mexico
Acreage: 33,677
Founded: February 11, 1916

Late in the afternoon of October 23, 1880, a lean and craggy forty-year-old, Swiss-American, self-trained archeologist named Adolphe F.A. Bandelier stood atop a mesa, a flat ridge in northcentral New Mexico, alongside his guide, Juan José of nearby Cochiti Pueblo. Before the two men unfolded a remarkable sight, a small valley tucked between two enormous cliffs that was dotted with the ruins of a prehistoric civilization. With a shout, Bandelier rushed down the side of the mesa into Frijoles Canyon. His discovery played a large role in creating not only southwestern archeology, but also the peculiar mythic status of the Southwest in American life. Heir to the traditions of taxonomy, the science of classification, he pulled out his walking stick and measured the height, depth, and width of the vast array of cliff dwellings he found.

Located in northcentral New Mexico, about 25 miles as the crow flies northwest of Santa Fe and just to the south of Los Alamos, the 33,677-acre Bandelier National Monument protects spectacular remnants of American prehistory and a more than 23,000-acre wilderness area. The park contains Frijoles Canyon, a 2-mile-long and half-mile-wide area that includes Tyuonyi, an archeoastronomical site with openings that line up with the winter equinox, thousands of cave dwellings—some with plastered or painted walls and ceilings—talus houses, prehistoric fields, and other archeological remains.

In the backcountry, inside the designated wilderness area that can be reached only by foot, a pair of hand-carved stone mountain lions serve ceremonial purposes for Native Americans of the region. Called the "Shrine of the Stone Lions," the place draws visitors as well as Native Americans seeking to commune with their deities. Offerings of various kinds that people leave as tokens of their trip often can be found in the trees that surround the stone lions. Elsewhere in the backcountry, the "Cueva Pintada," the painted cave, a thirteenth-century cave covered with prehistoric paintings, sits above the Rio Grande. The monument also contains an array of trees and plants, a variety of wildlife, including bald eagles, and other natural features as well as a national historic district, a collection of Park Service buildings built during the New Deal in the vernacular "parkitecture" style of the 1930s.

Bandelier National Monument was the scene of intense battles between federal agencies. Created in response to the efforts of turn-of-the-century Santa Fe archeologist and impresario Edgar L. Hewett's national park proposals for the region, the park was established in 1916, two years after Bandelier's death, and was named for him. Initially administered by the National Forest Service (NFS), Bandelier National Monument caught the eye of Horace M. Albright. Throughout the 1920s, efforts to make the area a national park and change its administration to the Park Service took place, although the NFS was able to successfully resist these attempts. In 1932, however, the Park Service took over responsibility for the monument, even though park status was never attained. Today it is a popular destination for people in northern New Mexico—the town of Los Alamos, where the atomic bomb was developed during World War II, is nearby—as well as for travelers from around the globe.

Bandelier National Monument illustrates two of the important issues facing the national park system: the problem of managing differing constituencies of users and the issue of impact in specific areas within the park. It is both a destination for visitors from afar and a day-use park for residents of the region. These two categories of users come with different expectations; the facilities and amenities both demand overlap, creating greater impact than either group would alone and forcing difficult and seemingly arbitrary management decisions. Despite the fact that Bandelier includes more than 33,000 acres of land, more than 95 percent of visitors remain in Frijoles Canyon along the paved trail. This small confined area experiences a remarkable amount of use while much of the rest of the park rarely sees a visitor, yet the mandates of the agency require that its resources are

spread across the entire park. Balancing mandate and use remains a complicated task.

The monument's visitor center houses museum exhibits on the Pueblo cultures that inhabited the canyons, along with an audiovisual presentation. During the summer, rangers conduct guided walks and evening campfire discussions. Paved roads lead into the monument visitor center and the campgrounds; no other roads are usable by visitors. Approximately 70 miles of backcountry trails are available for overnight use. The weather is generally warm and dry, with rain in the early summer months. Snowstorms can occur from October through May. The elevation in Frijoles Canyon is 6,000 feet, which can cause breathing difficulties for people visiting from lower elevations.

Operating hours and seasons are daily in the summer: visitor center, 8 A.M. to 6 P.M.; daily in the winter: visitor center, 8 A.M. to 4:30 P.M.; spring/fall: visitor center, 9 A.M. to 5:30 P.M.; Frijoles Canyon: dawn to dusk. The monument is closed December 25 and January 1. Visitation is highest from May through September, and lowest in December and January. The entrance fee is $10 per car for a seven-day permit. Commercial and recreational group fees vary. Golden Eagle, Golden Age, and Golden Access passports are honored.

There is no lodging in the park. All traveler services can be secured in nearby White Rock and Los Alamos. The 93-space Juniper campground near the visitor center provides tables, fireplaces, water, flush toilets, and an RV dump station; it is closed from December through February. Ponderosa group campground, 6 miles northeast of the main entrance, has 4 spaces, and it is open from April 15 through November 1; reservations are required. Camping fees are $10 per site per night. Many wilderness campsites are located in the park, and you must have a wilderness permit to camp.

For more information, write Bandelier National Monument, HCR 1, P.O. Box 1, Suite 15, Los Alamos, NM 87544, or telephone (505) 672-0343. The park's Web site is www.nps.gov/band.

FURTHER READING

Bandelier National Monument: An Administrative History. Santa Fe, NM: National Park Service, 1988. Available at www.nps.gov/band.

Lange, Charles H., and Carroll L. Riley. *Bandelier: The Life and Adventures of Adolph Bandelier.* Salt Lake City: University of Utah Press, 1996.

Rothman, Hal. *On Rims and Ridges: The Los Alamos Area Since 1880.* Lincoln: University of Nebraska Press, 1997.

BENT'S OLD FORT NATIONAL HISTORIC SITE

Location: La Junta, Colorado
Acreage: 799
Established: June 3, 1960

Southeastern Colorado's Bent's Old Fort National Historic Site is a reconstructed trading post located in what was considered the "Great American Desert" by mid-nineteenth-century travelers and explorers. The site is a version of the original 1830s post, recreated from descriptions in journals, depictions in drawings, and evidence gleaned from archeological excavations. Built in the 1830s, the original post became one of the primary trading sites for Southern Cheyenne and Arapaho Indians and trappers on the Santa Fe Trail's Mountain Branch. For most of its history, Bent's Old Fort was the only major permanent European settlement between Missouri and the New Mexican settlements on the Santa Fe Trail. It provided supplies, wagon repairs, livestock, food, water, rest, and protection for traders and travelers. It was also a border outpost, situated at the very edge of American territory. Just to its south lay the Arkansas River, the border between the United States and Mexico until the Mexican War in 1846.

Owned by the partnership of Charles and William Bent and Ceran St. Vrain, the fort played a prominent role as a supply base for the expeditions of explorer John C. Frémont and for General Stephen W. Kearney's troops during the Mexican War. In 1849–1850, during a cholera epidemic that swept not only the densely populated parts of the country, but also the more sparsely inhabited plains, William Bent set fire to the fort and abandoned it. He moved 38 miles down the Arkansas River to build a second fort, leaving the ruins with the name of the "old fort." More than epidemic disease likely contributed to the move; the murder of William Bent's brother Charles Bent at his home during the Taos uprising against the American presence in 1847, St. Vrain's unsuccessful attempts to sell the fort to the U.S. Army the same year, and the remarkable depletion of timber and grass by Native Americans' herds of ponies and passing cattle contributed to the abandonment. Except for brief use as a stage stop, the old fort remained in ruins until 1975. By then, it had deteriorated considerably. When the National Park Service (NPS) rebuilt the fort on its original foundation, every effort was made to replicate its appearance during the Mexican War.

Bent's Old Fort receives about 40,000 visitors per year. Most people visit with school tours during the spring and return as vacationing families throughout the summer and fall. Summer daytime temperatures range between 80 and 105 degrees, nights from 50 to 75 degrees. Winter daytime temperatures range from 0 to 65 degrees, nights minus 20 to 30 degrees. Precipitation is minimal, although brief afternoon thunderstorms with lightning, hail, and gusty winds occur during the summer. Winter snow accumulations are light, but heavy snows are possible.

The 799-acre Bent's Old Fort National Historic Site became part of the NPS in 1960. It is located along the Arkansas River in southeastern Colorado, 7 miles east of La Junta and 13 miles west of Las Animas on state highway 194. The park is open every day except Thanksgiving, Christmas, and New Year's Day. Summer hours (Memorial Day through Labor Day) are 8 A.M. to 5:30 P.M.; winter hours are 9 A.M. to 4 P.M.

Special events include: Old Time Fourth of July, National Park Service Founders' Day on August 25, and Kid's Quarters in early August. The visitor center has a fully stocked bookstore and a trade room, as well as a twenty-minute history film *Castle on the Plains.* There are guided tours hourly from Memorial Day through Labor Day.

There is no food, lodging, or camping at the fort. All travel services can be found in Las Animas or in La Junta, which has private campgrounds. Thirty-five miles east of the fort along U.S. Highway 50 is John Martin Reservoir, which has an improved, 51-space Army Corps of Engineers campground.

For more information, write Bent's Old Fort National Historic Site, 35110 Highway 194 East, La Junta, CO, 81050-9523, or telephone (719) 383-5010. The park's Web site is www.nps.gov/beol.

FURTHER READING

Comer, Douglas C. *Ritual Ground: Bent's Old Fort, World Formation, and the Annexation of the Southwest.* Berkeley: University of California Press, 1996.

Moore, Jackson W., Jr. *Bent's Old Fort: An Archeological Study.* Denver: State History Society of Colorado, 1973.

BIG BEND NATIONAL PARK

Location: Rio Grande River, Texas
Acreage: 801,163
Established: 1944

Vast and remote, Big Bend National Park in west Texas is a land of borders. Situated on the international border with Mexico along the Rio Grande River, it is a place where countries and cultures meet. Natural environments, from desert mountain ranges to steepwalled canyons to stretches of green along the river, merge in its canyons. It is also a place

where all points on the compass converge to create a wide diversity of plants and animals. The park includes more than 801,000 acres where the Rio Grande makes a sharp turn known as the "Big Bend."

Established in 1944, Big Bend National Park includes a considerable percentage of the U.S.-Mexico border. The Rio Grande forms the international boundary between Mexico and the United States from the Gulf of Mexico to El Paso, where it bends to the north. Big Bend National Park administers approximately one quarter of that 1,000-mile boundary. The 118 serpentine miles of river define the park's southern boundary. Along this stretch, the river's southeasterly flow changes abruptly to the northeast and forms the bend in the Rio Grande that gives the park and the surrounding region its name.

The Rio Grande is an international boundary, complicating the mission of park managers. Big Bend National Park faces unusual constraints as it administers the park. American jurisdiction extends only to the center of the deepest river channel in the Rio Grande. The rest of the river belongs to the Republic of Mexico. South of the river, the Mexican states of Chihuahua and Coahuila include new protected areas for flora and fauna, which are comprised of regions known as the Maderas del Carmen and the Cañon de Santa Elena.

Despite such constraints, the park contains the largest protected area of Chihuahuan Desert topography and ecology in the United States. The park abounds with geologic and paleontological resources. Cretaceous and tiary fossils exist in stunning variety and abundance. Archeologists have discovered nine-thousand-year-old artifacts, and historic buildings and landscapes illustrate the nature of life along the international border at the turn of the twentieth century.

The climate at Big Bend National Park is extreme. Elevation plays a significant role in

The Old Farm House at Big Bend National Park. *(National Park Service)*

the climate as it does in much of the desert Southwest. Dry, hot, late-spring and early-summer days often top 100 degrees at lower elevations. Winters at the same elevations are usually mild, but subfreezing temperatures do occur. The Chisos Mountains, at 7,800 feet in elevation, about 6,000 feet above the river, experience colder winters and cooler summers. The mountains contribute to a wide variation in rainfall and temperature throughout the park. These variations, in turn, contribute to an exceptional diversity of plant and animal species.

The park boundary along the Rio Grande reveals the geological impact of the river. The spectacular canyons of Santa Elena, Mariscal, and Boquillas—cut as the Rio Grande meandered through this portion of the Chihuahuan Desert—have nearly vertical walls where the river has carved a path through three uplifts

comprised primarily of limestone. Throughout the open desert areas, the Rio Grande riparian zone includes various plant and animal species and significant cultural resources. The vegetative belt extends into the desert along creeks and arroyos.

Nearly every period of human habitation is represented in the park. The Paleo-Indian period ten thousand five hundred years ago offers the earliest evidence, but the region was inhabited through the prehistoric period. Throughout the prehistoric period, humans found shelter and maintained open campsites throughout the park. The archeological record reveals an archaic-period desert culture whose inhabitants developed a nomadic hunting and gathering lifestyle that remained virtually unchanged for several thousand years. Recently, Native American groups, such as the Chisos, Mescalero Apache, and

Comanche, all lived in or used the area. More recently, Spanish, Mexican, and American settlers farmed, ranched, and mined in the area.

The recent history of Big Bend is rich and varied. Listed on the National Register of Historic Places, the Castolon District offers a window into Hispanic agricultural life from the early twentieth century. It also acquired a military presence during the Mexican Revolution of 1910–1920. National Guard camps were established at three locations within the park, and later, in 1929, the Army Air Corps established a landing field.

Big Bend's remoteness and ruggedness makes it less heavily used than most national parks. Uncrowded much of the year, park visitation peaks in March and April, and in October and November. In recent years, 300,000 people per year have visited the park, staying an average of three days, far longer than in most parks. Easter and Thanksgiving weekends—and the week between Christmas and New Year's Day—are also very busy. All lodging and campsites are usually full during these periods. Visitation is lowest in the hot late-summer months.

Big Bend National Park headquarters is located in Brewster County, Texas, 70 miles south of Marathon, Texas, and 108 miles from Alpine, Texas, via Highway 118. The park is open twenty-four hours daily, year-round. The Panther Junction Visitor Center is open daily from 8 A.M. to 6 P.M., but may be closed on Christmas Day. Other visitor centers have variable seasons and hours. A weekly pass is $10 per passenger vehicle; $5 per person for cyclists, bus passengers, and walk-ins. Golden Age, Golden Access, and Golden Eagle passes are honored. A Big Bend annual pass is available for $20 and is good for one year from date of purchase.

There are 4 visitor centers: Persimmon Gap, Panther Junction, Chisos Basin, and Rio Grande Village. There is also a visitor contact station at Castolon. The Panther Junction and Chisos Basin visitor centers are open year-round. The Persimmon Gap Visitor Center is open most of the year, staff permitting. The Rio Grande Village Visitor Center is open from November through April. All visitor centers provide information, backcountry permits, and limited exhibits. Nature walks, workshops, and evening slide programs are provided by park naturalists year-round. Several programs per day are offered November to April; fewer programs are offered in summer. Check park bulletin boards and visitor centers for current weekly program schedules.

Several paved roads give the visitor an introduction to the park scenery. The Ross Maxwell Scenic Drive and the road to the Chisos Mountains Basin are not recommended for trailers over 20 feet or RVs over 24 feet. Numerous dirt roads, suitable only for high-clearance vehicles, are located throughout the desert. There are over 200 miles of hiking trails and routes through desert and mountains. Cross-country hiking is permitted.

Lodging—including the 72-room, motel-style Chisos Mountain Lodge—meals, and service stations are available in the park, with limited grocery stores near all campgrounds. Gas is available at Panther Junction (park headquarters) and Rio Grande Village. Showers and laundry facilities are available only at Rio Grande Village. There is a restaurant in the Chisos Basin. There are 3 developed campgrounds at Rio Grande Village, Chisos Basin, and Cottonwood. All have water and rest rooms, but no hookups. Fees are currently $7 per night but are subject to change. All campsites are available on a first-come, first-served basis only. There are also numerous backcountry roadside campsites throughout the park, but no services or facilities at the primitive campsites. A backcountry permit is required to camp, and it can be obtained free of charge at any visitor center.

Open (zone) camping is available in desert areas with a backcountry permit. Designated backcountry campsites in the high Chisos Mountains are available with a backcountry permit on a first-come, first-served basis.

For more information, write Big Bend National Park, P.O. Box 129, Big Bend National Park, TX 79834, or telephone (915) 477-2251. The park's Web site is www.nps.gov/bibe.

FURTHER READING

Maxwell, Ross A. *The Big Bend of the Rio Grande: A Guide to the Rocks, Landscape, Geologic History, and Settlers of the Area of Big Bend National Park.* Austin: University of Texas, 1990.

Steele, D. Gentry. *Land of the Desert Sun: Texas' Big Bend Country.* College Station: Texas A&M University Press, 1998.

Tyler, Ronnie C. *The Big Bend: A History of the Last Texas Frontier.* College Station: Texas A&M University Press, 1996.

Wright, Bill. *Portraits from the Desert: Bill Wright's Big Bend.* Austin: University of Texas Press, 1998.

BIG CYPRESS NATIONAL PRESERVE

Location: Ochopee, Florida
Acreage: 720,567
Established: October 11, 1974

Subtropical swamps, pines, hardwoods, dry and wet prairies, and mangrove forests are many of the diverse natural features comprising southwestern Florida's 720,567-acre Big Cypress National Preserve. The preserve was set aside in 1974 to ensure the preservation and protection of the natural scenic, floral and faunal, and recreational values of the Big Cypress Watershed. Another major consideration in the preserve's creation was the importance of this freshwater watershed to adjacent Everglades National Park.

The name Big Cypress refers to the large cypress trees found in this area. Although few giant cypress trees remain, the preserve contains many vast stands of smaller cypress and dwarf pond cypress trees. Commercial exploitation began in 1928 with the opening of the Tamiami Trail (presently U.S. Highway

41), and a lumber boom ensued in the 1930s and 1940s. The region also attracted outdoor recreationalists and cattle raisers. The area also contained oil; in 1943, Florida's first producing oil well was drilled here. In the 1950s and 1960s, land developers began draining swamps and selling land for commercial purposes. It was also the proposed site of the famous Florida Jetport, scrapped as a result of the environmental revolution of the late 1960s. Such unchecked development threatened the Everglades watershed, and in the climate of "full stomach environmentalism," the era in which the nation seemed to agree that most everybody had most everything they needed and resources could be protected for eternity, led to the creation of the national preserve category and to the establishment of Big Cypress as the nation's first national preserve.

There is no entrance fee to the preserve. A yearly fee of $35 is charged for an off-road-vehicle permit. The preserve is open daily except Christmas Day, from 8:30 A.M. to 4:30 P.M. Visitation is highest from Christmas through Easter, when the weather is cooler and less humid. The climate is subtropical, with mild winters and hot, wet summers. Lightweight clothing is suggested. Hikers must wear long sleeves, pants, and sturdy shoes, and pack bug repellant.

The visitor center, located 55 miles east of Naples on U.S. Highway 41, offers a fifteen-minute movie about the preserve, a wildlife exhibit, and book sales. Two roadside picnic areas are located along the Tamiami Trail. Big Cypress National Preserve is home to many forms of wildlife, including herons, egrets, alligators, wild turkeys, deer, mink, bald eagles, woodpeckers, and the wood stork. The preserve is also home to the endangered Florida panther.

To help visitors view this wildlife, many roads and trails are available. The preserve includes 31 miles of the Florida Trail, which can be very wet in the rainy season. The Tree Snail Hammock Nature Trail is a short, self-guided trail located on Loop Road. Two scenic drives through the preserve provide leisurely wildlife viewing. The Loop Road is a 26-mile, single-lane, unimproved road beginning and ending on Highway 41. Turner River Road and Birdon Road form a U-shaped, 17-mile, graded-dirt drive. In the Bear Island area, swamp buggies, ATVs, and four-wheel-drive vehicles with permits are restricted to designated improved trails. Bicycles are allowed on some of the improved trails in Bear Island and on all roads. The preserve's canals are a fisherman's paradise; bass, bluegill, and catfish are available, and a valid Florida license is required.

There is no food or lodging available. These services can be found in Naples or Everglades City. Camping includes a private (free) campground in the preserve at Ochopee, and more developed campgrounds in Collier-Seminole State Park, Everglades City, Naples, and Alligator Alley. The Park Service provides 6 primitive campgrounds on U.S. Highway 41 and Loop Road, state highway 94.

For more information, write Big Cypress National Preserve, HCR61, P.O. Box 110, Ochopee, FL 34141, or telephone (941) 695-4111. The park's Web site is www.nps.gov/bicy.

FURTHER READING
Bransilver, Connie. *Florida's Unsung Wilderness: The Swamps.* Englewood, CO: Westcliffe, 2000.
Ripple, Jeff. *Big Cypress Swamp and the Ten Thousand Islands: Eastern America's Last Great Wilderness.* Columbia: University of South Carolina Press, 1992.

BIG HOLE NATIONAL BATTLEFIELD
Location: Wisdom, Montana
Acreage: 1,011
Established: June 23, 1910

Located in the Big Hole Valley of southwestern Montana, the Big Hole National Battle-field was established to commemorate the Battle of Big Hole in the Nez Perce War of 1877. On August 9 and 10, 1877, the five-month pursuit of the Nez Perce Indians by the U.S. Army culminated in a bloody battle near Big Hole, Montana. In the spring of that year, the U.S. Army was called out to force the last of the Nez Perce onto a smaller 1,200-square-mile area, about one-tenth the original size of their reservation in Idaho and eastern Oregon. The discovery of gold there in 1863 brought a typical wave of miners, panners, and others, and some of the Nez Perce resisted this encroachment. By 1877, tensions were rife. About 800 nontreaty Nez Perce Indians, under the leadership of Chief Joseph, fled across the Bitterroot Mountains in defiance of government demands that all Nez Perce move onto a minuscule reservation. The army was enforcing a national policy of placing all Native Americans on reservations to make way for the westward expansion of the United States. After a number of killings, the Nez Perce, who rejected the smaller reservation, fled into Montana, certain that the army would not follow them. They were correct that soldiers from Idaho would not come; they did not realize that a group of nearly 200 soldiers and volunteers had come west under Colonel John Gibbon from Fort Shaw, Montana, to intercept the fleeing people.

On the morning of August 9, 1877, these soldiers silently positioned themselves around the Nez Perce camp and waited for the signal to attack. An elderly Nez Perce man stumbled upon them while checking on his horses; the soldiers shot him and the battle commenced. Soldiers and civilian volunteers attacked the village while most of the Nez Perce slept; the warriors quickly mounted a resistance and forced the attackers to retreat to a nearby wooded hill. The soldiers dug trenches for protection, but the determined warriors surrounded the fortified hill and held the soldiers there. Meanwhile, the older men, women,

An incident in the defeat and capture of Chief Joseph by General Nelson A. Miles, during the Nez Perce War, c. 1877. *(Library of Congress)*

and children in the camp buried the dead and fled again. The Battle of the Big Hole lasted less than thirty hours and casualties were high. Between sixty and ninety Nez Perce men, women, and children were killed. Twenty-two soldiers and six civilian volunteers were killed, and thirty-nine more were severely wounded. Although the Nez Perce wanted to avoid bloodshed—the singular purpose of their nearly 1,700-mile flight from their homeland in eastern Oregon—they were prepared to fight for their freedom. In the course of the following day, the Nez Perce escaped the trap and fled to Canada. From the Big Hole, they traveled east through Yellowstone National Park, where they captured a group of tourists, then turned northward toward the Canadian border. There were several skirmishes and encounters with federal troops in the weeks that followed the Battle

of the Big Hole, but it was not until early October that the army finally succeeded in forcing most of the Nez Perce to surrender in the Bear Paw Mountains of northcentral Montana. Troops under General Nelson A. Miles finally caught them about 40 miles from the Canadian border, and, after a five-day standoff, the Nez Perce surrendered. However, some of the Nez Perce escaped into Canada.

Big Hole National Battlefield has one of the most unusual histories of management within the park system. Beginning as a memorial to soldiers administered by the War Department, it became a national monument in 1910, after the passage of the Antiquities Act of 1906. Under the terms of this law, it remained under War Department administration until 1933, when Franklin D. Roosevelt's reorganization of the federal government transferred all the national monuments to National Park Service administration. At the same time, a 115-acre surrounding tract, called the "Gibbons Battlefield Administrative Site" by its managers, the U.S. Forest Service, was also transferred to the park system. Operated first by Yellowstone National Park and later by the Grant-Kohrs Ranch National Historic Site, the monument was designated a national battlefield in 1963. In 1992, Big Hole National Battlefield was added to the Nez Perce National Historical Park, expanding the holdings of the park from 24 to 38 sites and from three states to four.

The inclusion of Big Hole National Battlefield in the Nez Perce National Historical Park also revealed a significant change in the meaning of the site. Initially preserved by the War Department as a memorial to soldiers, the battlefield came to include all participants in the fray in its commemoration. In this transformation, Big Hole National Battlefield represented important shifts not only in the meaning of American history to the American public and in what historic sites meant to the nature of history in the United States, but also to the Park Service's efforts to protect the historic fabric of a more inclusive history of the nation.

Big Hole National Battlefield is located 10 miles west of Wisdom, Montana, on state highway 43, approximately 75 miles southwest of Butte and about 110 miles southeast of Missoula. There is a summertime-only admission fee of $2 per person, or $4 per family. Golden Age, Golden Access, and Golden Eagle passes are honored. Hours are daily in the summer from 8:30 A.M. to 6 P.M., and daily in the winter from 9 A.M. to 5 P.M. The park is closed Thanksgiving, Christmas, and New Year's Day. About 60,000 people visit the park per year, with the highest visitation from June through September, and the lowest from November through January.

The visitor center houses a small museum with Nez Perce cultural exhibits, military clothing and equipment, a twelve-minute introductory video presentation, book sales, area information, and a Junior Ranger activity program for first through eighth grades. Visitors are encouraged to take the self-guided walk through the battlefield from sunrise to sunset daily. The Nez Perce Camp Trail leads to the site where the Nez Perce were camped and attacked by U.S. Army soldiers and civilian volunteers on the night of August 9, 1887. The shorter Siege Trail leads to where the soldiers and volunteers were held under siege by Nez Perce warriors.

Summers are generally cool and breezy, with numerous mosquitoes in June and early July. Summer thunderstorms are not uncommon. Winters are cold and frigid with deep snow. Bug repellent is necessary in early summer and layers of warm clothing are advised year-round.

There is no camping, lodging, or food service at the park. Camping is available at several U.S. Forest Service campgrounds within a 20-mile radius, while 2 motels in Wisdom, 10 miles west, offer rooms. Additional accommodations are available in Jackson, Lost Trail Pass, Dillon, Butte, Hamilton, and Missoula. Wisdom has 2 cafés and a small grocery store.

For more information, write Big Hole National Battlefield, P.O. Box 237, Wisdom, MT 59761, or telephone (406) 689-3155. The park's Web site is www.nps.gov/biho.

FURTHER READING

Beal, Merrill D., and Herman J. Deutsch. *I Will Fight No More Forever: Chief Joseph and the Nez Perce War.* New York: Ballantine Books, 1971.

Catton, Theodore, and Ann Hubber. *Commemoration and Preservation: An Administrative History of Big Hole National Battlefield.* Missoula, MT: Historical Research Associates, 1999.

Hampton, Bruce. *Children of Grace: The Nez Perce War of 1877.* Lincoln, NE: Bison Books, 2002.

Josephy, Alvin M. *The Nez Perce Indians and the Opening of the Northwest.* Boston: Houghton Mifflin, 1997.

BIGHORN CANYON NATIONAL RECREATION AREA

Location: Fort Smith, Montana and
  Wyoming
Acreage: 120,296
Established: October 15, 1966

Containing one of the most beautiful man-made lakes in America, Bighorn Canyon National Recreation Area encompasses more than 120,000 acres in southern Montana and northern Wyoming. Bighorn Lake itself is 70 miles long, of which 55 miles are within the spectacular limestone Bighorn Canyon. This canyon bisects the northern end of the Bighorn mountain range, where the mid-Rockies border the northern Great Plains.

National recreation areas were problematic additions to the national park system for most of the Park Service's first fifty years.

Simply put, the NPS was supposed to preserve and protect beautiful, meaningful, and historical places in the United States. Recreation did not qualify for agency approval until the 1950s, and even then, many felt it was a dubious goal for an agency devoted to the pageant of American experience. By the 1960s, Park Service interest in recreation grew, and even man-made lakes were at least worthy of its consideration. When Congress established Bighorn Canyon National Recreation Area on October 15, 1966, following the completion of the Bureau of Reclamation's Yellowtail Dam, the Park Service added another man-made lake to its growing list of recreation areas. Named after the famous Crow tribal chair Robert Yellowtail, the multipurpose dam harnessed the Bighorn River's fluctuating waters, transforming it into today's

Fishing at Bighorn Canyon National Recreation Area. *(National Park Service)*

magnificent lake. Although fishing and boating are the two primary recreational activities at the park, recreation is only one designated use for Bighorn Lake and Yellowtail Dam. As are most Bureau of Reclamation dams in the West, the lake is also used for flood control, irrigation, power generation, and water supply.

One of the dam's visitor centers, the Lovell Visitor Center, is the first NPS building to utilize solar energy. The panels on the building's south side collect heat and send it to a bed of rocks in the subbasement, which helps heat the building. A reflecting pond has been built to accentuate the sunlight on the panels. During the summer, the water from this pond is pumped over the bed of rocks and helps cool the building. After two decades, the pond has developed its own ecosystem. Many plants and animals have taken up residence here, and it is a rest stop for migratory birds.

There are over 280,000 visitors per year, with most people visiting between Memorial Day and Labor Day. The Park Service warns that the weather can vary greatly year-round throughout the day. Summer daytime temperatures range between 50 and 90 degrees, nights from 40 to 60 degrees. Winter daytime temperatures range between minus 20 and 40 degrees, nights from minus 30 to 20 degrees. Wind is frequent and precipitation is minimal; brief afternoon thunderstorms can occur during the summer, while snow accumulation can vary greatly from year to year. Appropriate seasonal layered clothing is highly recommended.

About 50 miles from Cody, Wyoming, and its Buffalo Bill Historical Center, the Bighorn Canyon National Recreation Area is open year-round. The National Recreation Area's (NRA) entrance fees vary by category: annual, $30, or $15 for Golden Age and Golden Access passport visitors; daily, $5 per car for each twenty-four-hour period or $2.50 per car for Golden Age and Golden Access passport visitors. To access the NRA via Montana, use Montana Highway 313. Bighorn Canyon is 43 miles from Hardin, Montana. From Wyoming the NRA is accessible through the town of Lovell; take Wyoming Highway 14A to Wyoming state road 37. The park is 11 miles from Lovell.

The recreation area has 2 visitor centers and other developed facilities in Ft. Smith, Montana, and near Lovell, Wyoming. Operating hours are: Yellowtail Visitor Center, Memorial Day to Labor Day, daily 9 A.M. to 5 P.M., closed the remainder of the year; Lovell Visitor Center, open year-round, daily 8:15 A.M. to 5 P.M. and closed Thanksgiving, Christmas, and New Year's Day. Both visitor centers offer exhibits of interest, including the dam's construction, information about the native peoples, flora, and fauna in the area.

Developed campgrounds are located in the North District at Afterbay Campground, Black Canyon (primitive and only accessible by boat), Cottonwood Camp, and Bighorn RV Park. South District camping locations include Horseshoe Bend, Barry's Landing, Medicine Creek, Bighorn RV Park, and Lovell Camper Park. There is no lodging in the park; all travel services can be found in Lovell, Wyoming, and Hardin and Fort Smith, Montana.

The Park Service operates 2 marinas: the Ok-A-Beh Marina and the Marina at Horseshoe Bend, both open seven days a week from mid-May to mid-September. To fish the lake and river, you must have a valid state license, depending on the spot selected.

Unfortunately, due to national security issues, at press time, the Yellowtail Dam was no longer accessible to visitors and all tours had been cancelled.

For more information, write Bighorn Canyon National Recreation Area, P.O. Box 7458, Fort Smith, MT 59035, or telephone (406) 666-2412. The park's Web site is www.nps.gov/bica.

FURTHER READING

Hoxie, Frederick. *Parading Through History: The Making of the Crow Nation in America, 1805–1935*. New York: Cambridge University Press, 1997.

Knight, Dennis. *Vegetation Ecology in the Bighorn Canyon National Recreation Area*. Laramie: University of Wyoming, 1987.

BIG SOUTH FORK NATIONAL RIVER AND RECREATION AREA

Location: Kentucky and Tennessee
Acreage: 125,310
Established: March 7, 1974

Straddling Kentucky and Tennessee, the free-flowing Big South Fork of the Cumberland River and its tributaries pass through 90 miles of some of the most rugged terrain of the Cumberland Plateau. As a national recreation area, the park protects both the river and the region's deep, scenic gorges and eroded cliffs and arches. This ensures visitor access to historic features and many kinds of recreation, including camping, whitewater rafting, kayaking, canoeing, hiking, horseback riding, mountain biking, hunting, and fishing.

Authorized in 1974, the more than 125,000-acre Big South Fork National River and Recreation Area is part of a comprehensive effort by the federal government to retain the natural, free-flowing character of American rivers. The Big South Fork and its major tributaries were among the few major American waterways that had not been dammed, and with development pressure on all kinds of waterways, legislation that protected such rivers became a priority of the 1970s. The U.S. Army Corps of Engineers, with extensive experience managing river basins, acquired the land and planned the development of facilities to allow the river and its adjacent plateau to be utilized for recreation. Now completed, these facilities are operated and maintained by the National Park Service.

Big South Fork National River and Recreation Area typifies one dimension of the later additions to the park system. Its lands had been heavily used, and once their commercial economic potential had been exhausted and the land denuded of its timber and the ground stripped of its mineral resources, the remaining economic option became tourism. Because the Big South Fork had not suffered the fate of most American rivers, it held a tremendous attraction for the nation as the United States re-embraced its older self-image as "nature's nation" during the 1960s and 1970s.

The river ran free, but the land was trammeled by human development. With the establishment of the park area, former homestead and mine sites, as well as logging camps and roads, were gradually replaced by lush vegetation. This second-generation natural environment held a human past as well. Adjacent to the Big South Fork is Historic Rugby, a restored 1880s settlement built for the sons of British gentry. Another attraction is the Blue Heron Mining Community in Kentucky, an outdoor museum that interprets the Stearns Coal and Lumber Company, as well as company town coal mining and life. Other sites include the Daniel Boone National Forest, Pickett State Park, and the Sergeant York gristmill. Recreational activities include river floating, hiking, mountain biking, and horseback riding, as well as viewing the beautiful vistas, sandstone arches, and abundant wildlife.

The Big South Fork National River and Recreation Area is located in a humid part of the country, typified by mild winters and moist warm to hot summers. Storm systems typically bring heavy rains from December through March and may cause local flooding. Summer thunderstorms are common. Winter snowfall occurs intermittently in the area and averages 17 inches per year. Visitation at the recreation area is highest during the summer months of June, July, and August, and during October.

Located in northeastern Tennessee and southeastern Kentucky, the park is open year-around. Park visitor centers are located in Tennessee 15 miles west of Oneida off Tennessee Highway 297, and in Kentucky in Stearns on Kentucky Highway 92.

The park headquarters is located 9 miles west of Oneida on Tennessee 297. The Bandy Creek Visitor Center is open daily, except Christmas. Visitor center hours are 8 A.M. to 4:30 P.M. from November through May, and from 8 A.M. to 6 P.M. from June through October. The Kentucky Visitor Center is open daily from May through October from 9 A.M. to 5:30 P.M. From November through April, the hours may vary.

No entrance fees are charged to use the National Recreation Area (NRA). Visitor fees are charged for the Bandy Creek and Blue Heron Campgrounds. Rates effective January 1, 1999, are: Bandy Creek $15 per night (no electricity) and $18 per night (with electricity); Blue Heron $12 per night (with or without electricity); Bandy Creek Pool $2 per day (noncampers). NRA campground reservations are recommended and available through the National Park Reservations Service at (800) 365-CAMP (2267). Other smaller private or government campgrounds are available in the area. Charit Creek Lodge is a rustic lodge reached by foot or horseback; call (423) 429-5704 for more information. Groceries, food, and lodging are available in the surrounding towns.

For more information, write Big South Fork National River and Recreation Area Headquarters, 4564 Leatherwood Road, Oneida, TN 37841, or telephone (931) 879-3625. The park's Web site is www.nps.gov/biso.

FURTHER READING

Faragher, John Mack. *Daniel Boone: The Life and Legend of an American Pioneer.* New York: Holt, 1992.

Manning, Russ. *The Historic Cumberland Plateau: An Explorer's Guide.* Knoxville: University of Tennessee Press, 1999.

BIG THICKET NATIONAL PRESERVE
Location: Beaumont, Texas
Acreage: 97,168
Established: October 11, 1974

In a biological convergence of unusual diversity in a relatively small area, Texas's Big Thicket National Preserve contains a mixture of flora and fauna common to eastern hardwood forests, southern swamp wetlands, western prairies, and arid southwestern ecosystems. Among the numerous plant species are 85 varieties of trees, 60 species of shrubs, and almost 1,000 assorted flowering plants, including 20 different types of orchids and 4 carnivorous plants. Many varieties of wildlife thrive in the preserve, some of which are nocturnal. Nearly 175 different species of birds have been spotted and recorded during the migratory season. Big Thicket is also home to several endangered species, including the paddlefish, the American alligator, and the red-cockaded woodpecker. As a result, the region has been the subject of scientific study since the 1930s and is sometimes called the "biological crossroads of North America" or more simply the "American Ark."

Biological diversity was low on the list of congressional priorities until the environmental crisis of the 1960s. As a result, all kinds of lands that lacked the earlier attributes of national parks, the scenic monumentalism of the great natural parks, or even the representative areas of the second generation, were included in the park system. In an age of plenty, arguing for the preservation of biodiversity became easier, and a range of areas under a variety of labels were added to the system. Big Thicket National Preserve, established in 1974, was among such additions. At 97,168 acres, it comprises 9 separate land units and 4 water corridors north and northeast of Beaumont, Texas. In 1981, the preserve was officially designated as an International Biosphere Reserve as part of the United Nations'

Education, Scientific, and Cultural Organization's Man and the Biosphere program.

The establishment of the preserve required adept political management through a decade-long battle. Located near the Golden Triangle of Beaumont, Port Arthur, and Orange, Texas, the area that became Big Thicket was integral to oil and natural gas development in the region. Added to the opposition were timber companies such as Eastex. Advocates such as Lance Rosier, known as "Mr. Big Thicket," sought a national park for the area, but industry recognized that such legislation would eliminate their activities. As owners of considerable amounts of land that was desired for the park, Eastex and others held an important trump card. A classic struggle emerged between landowners with an economic investment and those who sought preservation goals.

The effort to attain protection for Big Thicket began at the grass roots level in the early 1960s, but took shape at the national level when Texas Senator Ralph Yarborough introduced a bill that would proclaim his beloved Big Thicket as a national park. After his defeat in the 1970 Democratic primary in Texas, his Senate colleagues passed the bill as a tribute to the much-beloved senator. The House of Representatives, with the powerful Wayne Aspinall in the lead, refused to meet to hear the bill, and it died at the end of the session. Lloyd Bentsen, who succeeded Yarborough, also supported a park, as did Congressman George H.W. Bush.

After a series of back-and-forth proposals, an agreement was finally reached that brought Eastex into the coalition in favor of the park. The trade-off was a change in status from "national park" to "national preserve," which allowed continued oil and gas activity within the new area. While some advocates might have charged that the new park was compromised from its inception, Big Thicket National Preserve resulted from the complicated forces that surrounded national park-land acquisitions in the post–World War II era.

There is no entrance fee and all programs are free in the preserve. Visitation is highest in April and October, and lowest in January. An information station, open from 9 A.M. to 5 P.M. daily, contains brochures and hand-outs, an interpretive publication sales area, some video programs, and assorted exhibits. It is located on Farm to Market Road 420, 22 miles east of U.S. Highway 69, 7 miles north of Kountze. There are no regularly scheduled tours. All guided walks, special tours, off-site talks, and environmental education programs are by reservation only.

The best way to see the preserve's holdings are from the park's 9 trails, which range from one-quarter to 18 miles long. Trail guide booklets are available at the Kirby and Sundew Nature Trails, and trail maps are available at other trailheads. Pets and vehicles are not permitted on trails, while all-terrain bicycles and horses are permitted only on the Big Sandy Trail.

Visitors are advised that the preserve's climate can be brutal, especially in the summer. Rain, heat, and humidity are typical. An average rainfall of 55 inches is well distributed throughout the year. Summers are hot and humid with daytime temperatures ranging between 85 and 95 degrees. Moderate temperatures in the mid-50s are normal for winter. Spring and fall are the most pleasant seasons for outdoor activity. Wear comfortable sportswear and walking shoes, and carry rain gear. Trail flooding is frequent during and after thunderstorms.

The preserve has no overnight accommodations or developed campgrounds. Back-country camping is allowed by permit only in designated units. Permits are available at the information station. Campgrounds with flush toilets are available at Martin Dies State Park, 13 miles west of Jasper on U.S. Highway 190, and at Village Creek State Park. Contact the preserve for a listing of other private campgrounds.

Restaurants, grocery, and convenience stores, as well as limited lodging may be found in nearby communities. Beaumont contains a wide variety of traveler services.

For more information, write Big Thicket National Preserve, 3785 Milam, Beaumont, TX 77701, or telephone the information station at (409) 246-2337, or the administrative offices at (409) 839-2689. The park's Web site is www.nps.gov/bith.

FURTHER READING

Gunter, Pete A.Y. *The Big Thicket: A Challenge for Conservation.* New York: Viking, 1972.
——. *The Big Thicket: An Ecological Reevaluation.* Denton: University of North Texas Press, 1993.
Sitton, Thad. *Backwoodsmen: Stockmen and Hunters Along a Big Thicket River Valley.* Norman: University of Oklahoma Press, 1995.

BISCAYNE NATIONAL PARK

Location: Miami, Key Biscayne, and
  Homestead, Florida
Acreage: 172,924
Established: October 18, 1968

Regarded by locals in southern Florida as a fantastic recreation area, Biscayne National Park is one of the few units in America's national park system where water and water wildlife are the main attractions. The almost-173,000-acre park is 95 percent water. It protects and preserves a nationally significant marine ecosystem with mangrove shorelines, a shallow bay, undeveloped islands, and living coral reefs. The world's third longest coral reef begins in the park.

The shoreline of Biscayne Bay is lined with a deep green forest of mangroves. These trees, with their complex system of prop roots, help stabilize the shoreline and provide shelter for animals, birds, and marine life. Mangrove leaves become a vital part of the food chain when they fall into the waters. Lush sea grass beds found throughout the bay are another

major component of the food chain. The Florida spiny lobster depends on this rich food chain; the bay has been designated a sanctuary for year-round lobster protection. Shrimp, fish, sea turtles, and manatees also utilize these productive underwater pastures.

On the eastern edge of Biscayne Bay are the northernmost Florida Keys. The interiors of these mangrove-edged emerald islands contain tropical hardwood forests. The park's establishment in 1968 protected these islands from planned commercial and residential development, allowing them to retain their natural beauty.

On the Atlantic side of the islands lie the most beautiful of the underwater communities: the coral reefs. This fragile ecosystem supports a kaleidoscope of life: numerous varieties of fish, plants, and other animals abound in the astounding color.

Natural features are not the only resources protected within Biscayne National Park. The cultural resources here represent more than two thousand years of human history, with some perhaps as much as ten thousand years old. Rich with archeological remains, Biscayne prserves not only a crossroads of international maritime trade and exploration since the arrival of the first Europeans, but also the history of the earliest inhabitants of this area.

The park encompasses more than 100 known archeological sites (the majority are submerged), 10 historic structures, 3 National Historic Register listings, and 16,000 museum objects, covering the maritime history of southern Florida and ranging from eighteenth-century shipwrecks to the results of twentieth-century development. In addition, the park's 40 keys, or islands, located north of Key Largo, offer a look at the way the Florida Keys were before development.

The park was founded amid turmoil in the post–World War II era. Florida was invaded by visitors and new residents after the war, and developers sought to capitalize on this by creating new communities and even dredging shallow bays to build new cities. At the same time, postwar conservation gathered momentum, and a group of Floridians sought to protect the Key Biscayne area with federal protection. A struggle that lasted more than a decade ensued, with advocates of a town bulldozing a broad road labeled "Spite Highway" down the center of Elliott Key. Conservation advocates pushed forward, and Biscayne National Monument came into existence just before the 1968 election. It was reclassified as a national park in 1980.

Opportunities abound in Biscayne National Park for recreation, including boating, sailing, fishing, snorkeling, diving, and camping. Park visitation is highest from January to April, and from July to September. The climate is subtropical. Summers are hot and humid, with brief afternoon thundershowers; winters are mild and dry.

The main access to the park is at Convoy Point, at the end of Miami's Southwest 328th Street (North Canal Drive). The park's first permanent visitor center opened in July 1997. The Dante Fascell Visitor Center offers a video orientation to the park, museum exhibits, book sales, and information and assistance. The visitor center is open daily from 8 A.M. to 5 P.M., except on Christmas. Glass-bottom boat tours start here at 10:30 A.M. daily.

While there is no entrance fee, the park does charge an overnight docking fee of $15 per night at Boca Chita Key Harbor and Elliott Key Harbor ($7.50 per night for holders of Golden Age or Golden Access passports).

The park can only be seen by boat; visitors who have their own boats have almost unlimited access to the park's resources. Access for visitors who do not have their own boats is provided by boat tours and the snorkel and dive trips offered by the park concessionaire at Convoy Point (call Biscayne National Underwater Park at 305-230-1100 for schedules, rates, and reservations). In fact, Convoy Point is the only place in the park accessible by car. In addition to the park's new visitor center, picnic tables and grills, and the concession operation are located here.

Not surprisingly, there is no lodging in the park, but Homestead, Miami, and the Florida Keys offer all traveler services. Elliot Key campground has 35 sites and a group site, with grilles, rest rooms, showers, and other improvements. Boca Chita campground is less developed, with no fresh water. Both are only accessible via boat. Camping fees are $10 per night (maximum 6 people and 2 tents per site) for individual camp sites, $25 per night (maximum 25 people and 6 tents) for the Elliott Key group campsite. The $15 per night overnight docking fee at the Boca Chita Key and Elliott Key harbors includes the use of an individual campsite. There is a 50 percent discount for holders of Golden Age or Golden Access Passport holders.

For more information, write Biscayne National Park, 9700 Southwest 328th Street, Homestead, FL 33033-5634, or telephone (305) 230-7275. The park's Web site is www.nps.gov/bisc.

FURTHER READING

Barnes, Jay. *Florida's Hurricane History.* Chapel Hill: University of North Carolina Press, 1998.
Blank, Joan Gill. *Key Biscayne: A History of Miami's Tropical Island and the Cape Florida Lighthouse.* Sarasota, FL: Pineapple, 1998.
Landrum, Wayne L. *Biscayne: The Story Behind the Scenery.* Las Vegas, NV: KC Publications, 2001.
Sites, George Lytrelle. *Boater's Guide to Biscayne Bay: Miami to Jewfish Creek.* Coral Gables, FL: University of Miami Press, 1971.

BLACK CANYON OF THE GUNNISON NATIONAL PARK

Location: Montrose, Colorado
Acreage: 30,244
Established: March 2, 1933

Black Canyon of the Gunnison presents an American paradox. As spectacular as Arizona's Grand Canyon, it received little of the attention lavished on the Great Chasm of the Colorado. Its location contributed to this neglect, as did the steep depth of the canyon: Whereas in Arizona, the view to the bottom can be seen from the rim, Black Canyon of the Gunnison leaves the river at its bottom in shadows most of the day.

No other North American canyon combines the narrow opening, sheer walls, and startling depths offered by the Black Canyon of the Gunnison. This spectacular western Colorado landscape was slowly formed over 2 million years by the corrosive effects of the Gunnison River and its tributaries scouring down through hard, Proterozoic crystalline rock. At times during the summer, there are points along the Gunnison River, at the canyon's narrowest confines, that receive less than two hours of sunshine a day—and none during the winter.

A national monument since 1933, Black Canyon of the Gunnison achieved national park status during 1999. With a total area measuring less than 30,000 acres, it is one of the smallest units to receive national park designation.

The Gunnison River's flow has created a canyon ranging in depth from 1,730 to 2,689 feet—with widths as narrow as 1,100 feet (at Chasm View). The river's erosive actions are much faster than those of its tributaries, and this has resulted in the creation of smaller canyons overhanging the main gorge. The river cuts through softer volcanic rock and then into the harder crystalline rock of the present canyon. Numerous spires in the park's eastern end illustrate this progressive erosive action.

The original national monument was among the many established during the lame-duck era after Herbert Hoover's defeat in the 1932 election. It protects a 12-mile stretch of the unspoiled Gunnison River canyon, and today's national park shares its eastern boundary with the Curecanti National Recreation Area.

The river is named for Lieutenant John Gunnison of the U.S. Corps of Topographical Engineers, who first ventured west as part of the Stansbury expedition to Mormon Utah in 1849. Gunnison fancied himself a mediator, someone who could talk across cultural lines and be understood. This served him well for a number of years, but in a subsequent western exploration in 1853, one of the many designed to discern a route for a transcontinental railroad, Gunnison and his party were attacked by a group of Paiutes seeking revenge for the murder of their leader, and he and six of his party of eleven were killed. In his explorations, Gunnison had avoided the Black Canyon that is now a natural park, believing it impenetrable. Its beauty and mystery were not his concern. Like many early explorers, Gunnison's objectives were economic and political.

Characterized by high deserts, deep canyons, and pygmy forests, Black Canyon of the Gunnison National Park is typical of high elevation desert environments. Home to branches of the Ute people before the arrival of explorers, the region offers many recreational opportunities. Rainbow and brown trout inhabit the Gunnison River, but access for fishing is very difficult, and you must have a valid Colorado license. Free backcountry permits are required for access to all inner-canyon routes to the river, as well as for such activities as kayaking, bouldering, and rock climbing.

Weather can vary greatly between the canyon rim and floor. Summer daytime temperatures range between 60 and 100 degrees, nights from 30 to 50 degrees. Winter daytime temperatures range between 20 and 40 degrees, and from minus 10 to 20 degrees at night. While precipitation is minimal, brief afternoon thunderstorms can occur during the summer. Layered clothing appropriate for the season is recommended. An average of 230,000 visitors come to Black Canyon per year, with the majority of people visiting the more-accessible South Rim between Memorial Day and Labor Day.

The South Rim is 15 miles east of Montrose, via U.S. Highway 50 and Colorado Highway 347. The North Rim is 11 miles south of Crawford, via Colorado Highway 92 and North Rim Road, which is closed in winter. Open year-round, many of the canyon's spectacular overlooks are easily accessed by car and very short walks. The South Rim is open every day, with limited access in the winter. The North Rim is open every day, but the ranger station is closed in winter. The South Rim Visitor Center contains detailed information on hiking trails and automobile access to the canyon's numerous vista points.

Entrance and camping fees vary with location. South Rim: $7 per vehicle per week entrance fee, with a $15 annual entrance pass for Black Canyon available, and an $8-per-night camping fee. North Rim: no entrance fee, with an $8-per-night camping fee. Golden Eagle, Golden Age, and Golden Access passports are honored. No lodging is available in the park, but the nearby towns of Gunnison and Montrose offer all traveler services. The Rim House on the South Rim offers lunch, refreshments, souvenirs, and limited grocery and camping supplies during the summer. There are 2 campgrounds in the park: North Rim has tables, grills, water, and pit toilets; South Rim campground is similar. Both are open from May through October. Camping is on a first-come, first-served basis. There are also commercial campgrounds located near Montrose.

For more information, write Black Canyon of the Gunnison National Park, 102 Elk Creek, Gunnison, CO 81230, or telephone (970) 641-2337. For general information, you also can call the South Rim Visitor Center at (970) 249-1914, extension 23. The park's Web site is www.nps.gov/blca.

FURTHER READING

Dolson, John. *The Black Canyon of the Gunnison: A Story in Stone: The Natural and Human History of Black Canyon of the Gunnison National Monument.* Boulder, CO: Pruett, 1982.

Houk, Rose. *Black Canyon of the Gunnison.* Tucson, AZ: Southwest Parks and Monuments Association, 1991.

Mumey, Nolie. *John Williams Gunnison (1812–1853), The Last of the Western Explorers: A History of the Survey Through Colorado and Utah, with a Biography and Details of His Massacre.* Denver, CO: Artcraft, 1955.

BLACKSTONE RIVER VALLEY NATIONAL HERITAGE CORRIDOR

Location: Blackstone Valley, Massachusetts and Rhode Island
Acreage: 400,000 (approximate)
Established: November 10, 1986

As the birthplace of America's Industrial Revolution, New England's Blackstone River Valley preserves the earliest phases of a major social, economic, and cultural transformation in American life. Contained in approximately 400,000 designated acres along 46 miles of the Blackstone River between Worcester, Massachusetts, and Providence, Rhode Island, the valley's villages, farms, cities, and river ways offer a cultural landscape dotted with artifacts from the era. In 1790, American craftsmen used a British model to build the first machines that successfully used waterpower to spin cotton. America's first factory, Slater Mill, was built on the banks of the Blackstone River in Pawtucket, Rhode Island. It was here that industrial America was born, and the revolutionary method of using waterpower to augment labor quickly spread throughout the valley and all of New England.

More than two hundred years later, the story of the American Industrial Revolution's origins is visible in the Blackstone River Valley. Today, rural and urban landscapes chronicle this revolution in American history. Native Americans, European colonizers, farmers, craftsmen, industrialists, and continuing waves of immigrants all left the imprint of their work and culture on the land.

The Blackstone River Valley National Heritage Corridor reveals changing ideas about how to create and manage national park areas. Unlike traditional national park areas, Blackstone is not owned or managed by the federal government. Its nearly 400,000 acres were set aside on November 10, 1986, to preserve and interpret the significant historical value of the Blackstone Valley. Cities, towns, and villages and more than 1 million people thrive within the boundaries of the corridor, yet the region manages to evoke the past. The Park Service, two state governments, local municipalities, businesses, nonprofit historical and environmental organizations, educational institutions, private citizens, and a unifying commission jointly seek to protect and maintain the valley's identity. This concept, initially called "greenline parks," became an important Park Service strategy during the 1980s and 1990s. It evolved into the idea of preservation of cultural landscapes and helped the agency expand its presence from largely uninhabited to inhabited parts of the nation.

There are no admission fees to the corridor or to most of its regular programs. Some of the private, nonprofit, historical, and environmental sites of interest do charge admission or accept donations for special events and programs. Visitation is highest during spring and fall, and lowest during January and February. Route 146 is the main highway running north and south between Providence and Worcester, with major intersections at I-95 and I-295 in Rhode Island. Exit 11 on I-90 (Massachusetts Turnpike) will give access to Route 122 and the visitor information centers in Worcester and Uxbridge. The valley is bordered on the east by I-495 and on

the west by I-395. Follow signs to visitor information centers. Visitors traveling north–south on I-95 may take exit 27 or 28 in Rhode Island for the Pawtucket Visitor Center and Slater Mill Historic Site. The corridor office operates year-round, Monday to Friday, from 8 A.M. to 5 P.M. The visitor contact centers are usually open daily between 9 A.M. and 4 P.M.

There are 4 regional welcome centers with rest rooms and visitor information. In Worcester, the Broad Meadow Brook Wildlife Sanctuary, at 414 Massasoit Road, is operated by the Massachusetts Audubon Society. In Uxbridge, the River Bend Farm Visitor Center is located at 287 Oak Street within the Blackstone River and Canal Heritage State Park. It is operated by the Massachusetts Department of Environmental Management. In Woonsocket, the Museum of Work and Culture, at 42 South Main Street, traces the origins of the Blackstone valley's labor movement. The museum is open seven days a week and offers full visitor services. In Pawtucket, the visitor center is located at 171 Main Street and is operated by the Blackstone Valley Tourism Council.

In addition to the numerous facilities offering lodging in Worcester and Providence, the valley offers a plethora of privately owned motels, country inns, bed and breakfasts, campgrounds, and recreational trailer parks. A full range of restaurants, groceries, general merchandise, and specialty stores are found throughout the Heritage Corridor.

For more information, write Blackstone River Valley National Heritage Corridor, One Depot Square, Woonsocket, RI 02895-9501, or telephone (401) 762-0250. There is a general information line at (401) 762-0440. The park's Web site is www.nps.gov/blac.

FURTHER READING

Leavitt, Sarah. *Slater Mill.* Dover, NH: Arcadia, 1997.
Leveillee, Alan. *An Old Place, Safe and Quiet: A Blackstone River Valley Cremation Burial Site.* Westport, CT: Bergin & Garvey, 2002.

Mattson, Thomas. *Small Town: Reflections of People, History, Religion and Nature in Central New England.* Grafton, MA: Northfield, 1992.

Monjo, F.N. *Slater's Mill.* New York: Simon and Schuster, 1972.

BLUE RIDGE PARKWAY

Location: Blue Ridge Mountains, North
  Carolina and Virginia
Acreage: 92,667
Established: June 30, 1936

The Blue Ridge Parkway extends 469 miles along the crest of the Blue Ridge Mountains, through the southern Appalachians of Virginia and North Carolina, linking Shenandoah and Great Smoky Mountain national parks. Designed as a national "scenic drive," the parkway provides both stunning landscapes and close-up looks at the natural and cultural history of these mountains. It is one of the many areas in the national park system that illustrate the beauty of the American land.

Along the trail, the cultural history of the Appalachian Mountains surrounds the parkway. A careful observer can see the past along the road—from prehistoric and historic Native American settlements to the relics and remains of Appalachian mountain culture. The Cherokee of North Carolina, and the Monacan, Saponi, and Tutelo of western Virginia made the Blue Ridge their home, altering the landscape to fit their needs. The fields often visible at the base of mountains testify to Native American practices of burning and girdling trees and underbrush to clear land for crops and grazing for their stock. The names of mountains and rivers along the Blue Ridge also reflect the Native American influence in the area.

Early Appalachian pioneer artifacts attest to the arrival of eighteenth-century Americans. These mountain people left behind their structures, and a notable aggregation of nineteenth-century farm buildings can be seen along the parkway. One such collection, the Johnson Farm at the Peaks of Otter (milepost 85.9), shows where generations of this family lived and worked with other members of the now-vanished community. Log cabins throughout the Blue Ridge illustrate the isolated existence of mountain families and attest to the efforts of the original park planners to save these historic structures.

The Blue Ridge Parkway idea reflected the changing emphasis of the Park Service during the 1930s. Even with the immense support the New Deal provided the agency, its reach in the eastern half of the nation was limited. As it acquired the three major eastern national parks, agency leaders realized that to serve this vast majority of the American population, the Park Service needed a greater presence. The Blue Ridge Parkway provided one avenue, for the parkway allowed use of New Deal resources even as it promoted the ideals of preservation and scenic beauty.

Overlooks and trails offer breaks during a drive, and there are ranger programs at most developed areas during the summer and autumn months. The parkway provides wonderful opportunities for hiking, photography, bird-watching, bicycling, historical and cultural demonstrations, and ranger-guided walks at developed areas. The traditional mountain music programs at Roanoke Mountain, Rocky Knob, and the Folk Art Center represent an interesting facet of local culture.

The parkway passes through western Virginia and North Carolina, and is accessible from several major highways and cities. Asheville, North Carolina, and Roanoke, Virginia, are the largest metropolitan areas along the parkway. It is open year-round, although severe weather may close many sections during the winter months. The parkway's speed limit is 45 miles per hour (35 in developed areas). It takes twelve or more hours of driving to safely traverse the parkway between its north-

A charming farm stand on the Blue Ridge Parkway in North Carolina. *(National Park Service)*

ernmost point and its southern end at the Great Smokey Mountains. The road's winding nature may make it difficult for large recreational vehicles, but all personal vehicles, motorcycles, tour buses, and bicycles are allowed. There is no fee for traveling the parkway, or for visitor centers and picnic areas.

Approximately 17 million people per year travel the Blue Ridge Parkway, making it the most visited area in the National Park System. The greatest visitation is during summer holidays and during the fall color season in mid-October. The parkway ranges from 650 feet above sea level to over 6,000 feet, so expect rapidly changing weather conditions. Visitor centers are open from May through October, and campgrounds are open from April through October. All lodges and facilities are closed during the winter, with the exception of the Peaks of Otter Lodge and its restau-

rant, and the Linville Falls and Otter Creek campgrounds.

Eleven visitor facilities are spaced out along the entire length of the parkway in North Carolina and Virginia, 5 in Virginia, and 6 in North Carolina. Each is designed to provide information on the activities and facilities in the area, as well as information about the parkway. Facilities include 3 concessionaire-operated lodges and a cabin complex along with 7 restaurants and three service stations. Nine developed campgrounds have tent pads, trailer sites, picnic tables, fire pits, dump stations, and comfort stations with cold running water sinks, but no hookups or shower facilities. Camping is allowed only in designated areas. There are picnic tables in all developed areas, as well as tables at some overlooks along the motor road. Private campgrounds, restaurants, and hotels may be found in many towns adjoining the parkway.

Camping fees are $12 per night for families or groups with 2 adults, plus $2 for each additional adult over age eighteen. No reservations are taken on the parkway, except at lodgings operated by concessionaires. Permits are required for hang gliding, commercial activities, weddings, and other park uses. These can be obtained through parkway headquarters in Asheville, North Carolina.

For more information, write Blue Ridge Parkway, 400 BB&T Building, Asheville, NC 28801, or telephone (828) 298-0398. The park's Web site is www.nps.gov/blri.

FURTHER READING

Alderman, J. Anthony. *Wildflowers of the Blue Ridge Parkway.* Chapel Hill: University of North Carolina Press, 1997.

Humphries, George. *Along the Blue Ridge Parkway.* Englewood, NJ: Westcliffe, 1997.

Jolley, Harley E. *Blue Ridge Parkway: The First 50 Years.* Boone, NC: Appalachian Consortium, 1985.

BOOKER T. WASHINGTON NATIONAL MONUMENT

Location: Hardy, Virginia
Acreage: 239
Founded: April 5, 1956

On April 5, 1856, Booker T. Washington was born into slavery on a 207-acre tobacco farm, the son of an enslaved woman and a white neighbor. Gaining his freedom at the age of nine, he left for West Virginia with his mother, brother, and sister.

Washington's legacy was a passionate activism on behalf of African American education. His earliest memories of school centered on his own exclusion from the system. As a young boy, he had carried the books for his master's daughter, but knew that it was illegal to teach a slave to read. He recalled later that at a young age he "had the feeling that to get into a schoolhouse and study would be about the same as getting into paradise." At age sixteen, he entered the Hampton Institute, a school for former slaves, paying his way as a laborer at the school. Washington believed that full political citizenship for African Americans could only be attained through education and self-help.

In 1881, Washington was asked to head Tuskegee Institute in Tuskegee, Alabama, with thirty students and a $2,000 budget. He directed the institute through an era of rapid growth that eventually resulted in a campus of 1,500 students and an endowment of $2 million. Tuskegee became the foremost African American institution for vocational training before Washington's death on November 14, 1915.

Booker T. Washington became an important figure in the debate about the role of African Americans in the late nineteenth and early twentieth centuries. During this era, the South reverted to a pre-Civil War–like social setting. The advances that resulted from the war and reconstruction were rescinded, and segregation laws, called "Jim Crow" laws, were enacted in every southern state and many north of the Mason-Dixon line as well. At the Cotton States and International Exposition in Atlanta in 1895, Washington gave a famous speech forever after known as the Atlanta Compromise. "In all things that are purely social, we can be as separate as the fingers," he intoned to the all-white audience, "yet one as the hand in all things essential to mutual progress." Washington believed that for African Americans to find a place in American society, they would have to demonstrate their economic usefulness to white America. His perspective stemmed from his time, when African American options were diminishing and threats to the safety of the community were vast. He has often been attacked for his perspective in the century since he spoke, for he was willing to accept a less-than-equal position for African Americans. In the context of his time, facing circumstances that included violence, such as lynching against African American communities, he crafted a strategy that helped preserve African American communities even as it revealed the limited options of the time.

Established in 1956, the 239-acre Booker T. Washington National Monument preserves the tobacco plantation of his birth and early childhood. There is a living history farm, trails, and a picnic area on the grounds. The Plantation Trail is a quarter-mile walking trail through the historic area of the park. Jack-O-Lantern Branch Trail is a 1.5-mile walk through woods and fields. There are regularly scheduled guided tours. Exhibits and an audiovisual program in the visitor center tell Washington's story. A visit to the historic area offers a look back at life more than a century ago and an additional hour walking Jack-O-Lantern Branch Trail reveals regional nature as well.

Visitation to the national monument is highest in July and August and lowest in November, December, and January. The climate is fairly consistent: hot and humid during July and August, with frequent afternoon thunderstorms, while the coldest months are December, January, and February. The spring and fall seasons are long, with moderate temperatures. Trails are unpaved and may be muddy at times. The area is prone to lightning strikes and may be closed periodically to visitors during summer thunderstorms, which occur most frequently in the late afternoon. During the winter months of December, January, and February, the historic area may be closed due to icy conditions.

The park is located 20 miles southeast of Roanoke, Virginia, via Highways 220 and 122. There is no admission fee. The visitor center contains exhibits, an audiovisual program, and a bookstore. The hours of operation are daily, 9 A.M. to 5 P.M. year-round, closed Thanksgiving, Christmas, and New Year's days.

Reservations for school and other groups should be made as far in advance as possible, especially for the most popular school tour seasons, mid-April to mid-June and September through October. For additional information concerning reservations, or special use or filming permits, call (540) 721-2094. There are no lodging or traveler services in the park. A variety of hotels and motels are available within a 30-mile radius, and there are local restaurants and grocery stores located within a 5-mile radius. There is no camping in the park, although there are some private campgrounds nearby. The Roanoke Mountain Campground, located on the Blue Ridge Parkway, is operated by the National Park Service and provides tables, grills, water, and flush toilets, but no hookups.

For more information, write Booker T. Washington National Monument, 12130 Booker T. Washington Highway, Hardy, VA 24101, or telephone (540) 721-2094. The park's Web site is www.nps.gov/bowa.

FURTHER READING

Harlan, Louis R. *Booker T. Washington: The Wizard of Tuskegee, 1901–1915*. New York: Oxford University Press, 1983.

Norrell, Robert J. *Reaping the Whirlwind: The Civil Rights Movement in Tuskegee*. New York: Knopf, 1985.

Washington, Booker T. *Education of the Negro*. Albany, NY: J.B. Lyon, 1904.

——. *Up from Slavery*. Edited by William L. Andrews. New York: W.W. Norton, 1995.

BOSTON AFRICAN AMERICAN NATIONAL HISTORIC SITE

Location: Boston, Massachusetts
Acreage: .59
Established: October 10, 1980

Although it was located in the North, the area of the nation that most Americans believe was free of slavery, Boston was a slave-holding city before the nineteenth century. The ear-

The Robert Gould Shaw Memorial, part of the Black Heritage Trail in Boston, Massachusetts. *(Library of Congress)*

liest African Americans arrived in Boston in 1678 as slaves, and slavery existed in the city throughout the colonial period. At the same time, a significant number of free blacks flourished in a community in Beacon Hill. The social and economic systems of colonial Massachusetts did not offer opportunities for a slave labor system. The fields were not expansive enough, the need for labor too small to permit the mass slavery of the plantation South. As a result, slaves were manumitted (freed) far more often in this region of the colonies than any other. Without economic motivation and absent the class and status system of the South, slavery made little sense in

Massachusetts. Free blacks eventually outnumbered the enslaved population, and at the end of the eighteenth century, the federal census listed the state of Massachusetts as having no slaves.

Established in 1980 as part of Representative Phil Burton's omnibus bill and located in the heart of Beacon Hill, the Boston African American National Historic Site preserves and commemorates the city's free African American community's pursuit of civil rights, including recognition in the political process, and an end to school segregation. The site, which contains 15 pre–Civil War structures, includes the African Meeting

House, the oldest standing African American church in the United States. The 1.6-mile Black Heritage Trail connects the 15 sites and provides the best way to see the park. In the summer, there are living history presentations and films on African American history.

Other attractions include a school built in 1834 by a white abolitionist businessman for the education of black children, one of the city's first integrated schools, and Augustus Saint-Gaudens' memorial to Civil War General Robert Gould Shaw and his Massachusetts 54th Regiment, whose story was detailed in the movie *Glory*. There are also many private residences not open to the public.

There are no entrance fees, but visitor donations support the Museum of Afro-American History. The site is open five days a week year-round: winter, spring, and fall from 10 A.M. to 4 P.M., and summer from 9 A.M. to 5 P.M. The site can be reached from the Massachusetts Turnpike (Route 90). Take the Copley Square exit to Stuart Street, then turn left on Route 28 (Charles Street) to Boston Common. From Route 93, take Storrow Drive to the Copley Square exit; turn left on Beacon Street, right on Arlington Street, left on Boylston Street, and left on Charles Street (Route 28). Driving and parking are difficult on Beacon Hill. There are several parking garages in the vicinity within walking distance of the site. The site is also accessible by public transportation. Park-and-ride facilities at MBTA subway (T) stations are alternative options to driving into the congested downtown area. MBTA subway stops closest to the site are the Park Street stop of the red and green lines, or the Bowdoin Square stop of the blue line.

Visitation is highest in July and August, and lowest in January and February. Temperatures range from warm, humid summer days to cold, harsh winter days. Wear appropriate clothing for the season and comfortable walking shoes.

There are no National Park Service RV or camping sites. Many hotels and motels are located throughout the city. Private and state camping and RV facilities are open seasonally in outlying areas. A list of overnight accommodations in Boston is available at the site office. Food and supplies are available on Charles Street, Cambridge Street, and throughout the Beacon Hill area.

For more information, write Boston African American National Historic Site, 14 Beacon Street, Suite 506, Boston, MA 02108, or telephone (617) 742-5415. The park's Web site is www.nps.gov/boaf.

FURTHER READING

Burchard, Peter. *One Gallant Rush: Robert Gould Shaw and His Brave Black Regiment.* New York: St. Martin's, 1965.

Schneider, Mark L. *Boston Confronts Jim Crow, 1890–1920.* Boston: Northeastern University Press, 1997.

Siebert, Wilbur Henry. *The Underground Railroad from Slavery to Freedom.* 1898. Reprint, New York: Arno, 1968.

Sterling, Dorothy. *Freedom Train: The Story of Harriet Tubman.* Garden City, NY: Doubleday, 1954.

Trudeau, Noah A. *Like Men of War: Black Troops in the Civil War, 1862–1865.* Boston: Little Brown, 1998.

BOSTON HARBOR ISLANDS NATIONAL RECREATION AREA

Location: Boston, Massachusetts
Acreage: 1,482
Established: November 12, 1996

Boston Harbor Islands National Recreation Area is made up of 30 islands, ranging in size from less than an acre to more than 200 acres. The islands are situated within the large C shape of the Greater Boston shoreline. Most are within 2 to 4 miles of mainland points and all of the islands are within a 10-mile radius of Boston proper. In this transition between the open sea and the populated shores of Boston, Massachusetts, the park celebrates both a rich cultural past and a diverse natural present. The islands figure prominently in the colonial history of the region. In 1675, during King Philip's War between Indians and colonists in New England, fearful English settlers forcibly relocated many Native Americans to the Boston Harbor Islands. Conditions were horrific, and as many as half of the incarcerated native people died of starvation, disease, and exposure. Today, the islands still protect the burial sites of those who lost their lives.

Boston Harbor itself is an estuary system where the salt water of Massachusetts Bay mixes with fresh water from the Charles, Mystic, and the Neponset rivers, and it provides valuable wildlife habitat and a vital nursery for marine organisms, as well as water filtration and flood control benefits for humans. Comprehensive planning for this relatively new park, established on November 12, 1996, is still under way. This unique national recreation area is managed by a thirteen-member Partnership and Advisory Council, including officials from the National Park Service, as well as assorted public and private organizations. Such private-public partnerships increasingly appear to be a hallmark of future national park area management. There is frequent ferry and water taxi service to these islands, and private boaters can anchor around any of the 30 islands. Each island has different physical characteristics, and public access varies from island to island.

The undeveloped islands can be enjoyed like any other natural area: hiking, beach-combing, enjoying the spectacular views, picnicking, watching birds and other wildlife, and studying horticulture. The multicolored outcropping of Cambridge Argillite, the type of slate that makes up the harbor's bedrock, is located on Grape Island. And Little Brewster Island's Boston Light, the oldest continuous aid to maritime navigation operating in America, is an interesting attraction.

During the summer season, 6 islands are open daily to the general public, while during the spring and fall the islands are open only during the weekends. In addition to self-guided, walking tours, there are ranger-led walks on George's Island in summer; park rangers also give regular tours corresponding to the ferry schedule on other islands.

Passenger-only ferries operate from Long Wharf, Boston, to George's Island, a forty-five-minute ride. From there, visitors can take various water taxis to 4 or 5 other islands. On George's Island, you can talk with the park rangers to plan your trip to other islands. The round-trip ferry costs $8 for adults, $6 for children under twelve, and $7 for seniors. The water taxis and the islands are free. On rare occasions, ferry service may be interrupted because of poor weather. Generally, all activities continue in either rain or shine, but be prepared for a sudden rainsquall, wind, or cool temperatures. The islands offer limited shelter and protection from the elements.

Weather in New England is variable, from clear, crisp days to stormy, chilly days. Summers are often hot and humid (high 80s) with occasional showers. Spring and fall temperatures can also range broadly, but 60s is typical. Water breezes make for cooler ferry rides, requiring jackets or windbreakers. Walking shoes, hats, and sunscreen are essential. None of the islands has drinking water, and only George's Island has a concessions stand. Visitors are advised to bring provisions and plenty of water. All islands have toilet facilities and boat piers.

Free overnight camping is available on Bumpkin, Grape, Lovell, and Peddocks islands; call (617) 223-8666 for a full schedule and to obtain a permit.

For more information, write Boston Harbor Islands National Recreation Area, National Park Service Office of the Project Manager, 408 Atlantic Avenue, Boston, MA 02210-3350, or telephone (617) 223-8666. The park's Web site is www.nps.gov/boha.

FURTHER READING

Finnerty, Cheryl Anne. *Lighthouses of Boston Harbor Past & Present.* Seminole, FL: Harbor Productions, 2001.

Lepore, Jill. *The Name of War: King Philip's War and the Origins of American Identity.* New York: Alfred A. Knopf, 1998.

Levering, Dale. *An Illustrated Flora of the Boston Harbor Islands.* Boston: Northeastern University Press, 1978.

Mallory, Kenneth. *Boston Harbor Islands: National Park Area.* Camden, ME: Down East Books, 2003.

Perkins, William D. *Chestnuts, Galls, and Dandelion Wine: Useful Wild Plants of the Boston Harbor Islands.* Halifax, MA: Plant, 1982.

Snow, Edward Rowe. *The Islands of Boston Harbor, 1630–1971.* New York: Dodd, Mead, 1971.

BOSTON NATIONAL HISTORICAL PARK

Location: Boston, Massachusetts
Acreage: 43
Established: October 1, 1974

Reflecting the city's lengthy and illustrious history, Boston National Historical Park is a unique collection of Boston's oldest and most significant historic structures. Established in 1974, it is a group of federal, private, and municipal sites with related historical themes. The intellectual energy that sustained the American Revolution was manifest in these places. John Hancock and Samuel Adams denounced British policies at town meetings in Faneuil Hall and the Old State House. In 1775, lanterns were hung in the Old North Church's steeple to warn the Charlestown militia of British troop movements near Concord; Paul Revere saw those lights and shouted a warning on his famous midnight ride. During the Revolutionary War, after landing at the present-day Charlestown Navy Yard, British redcoats clashed with American soldiers in the Battle of Bunker Hill.

Sixteen separate historic sites, including the downtown and Charlestown sites of Boston National Historical Park, are connected by the 3-mile Freedom Trail that runs through downtown Boston and Charlestown. A red painted or brick line on the pavement marks the trail. Seven of the 8 privately, municipally, and federally owned and managed historic sites that comprise Boston National Historical Park are connected by the Freedom Trail, including the Old State House, Old South Meeting House, Faneuil Hall, Paul Revere House, Old North Church, the Bunker Hill Monument, and Charlestown Navy Yard. The eighth site, Dorchester Heights Monument, is located in the residential neighborhood of South Boston.

Boston National Historical Park sites present information in various ways, including tours, lectures, costumed programs, exhibits, and publications. National Park Service rangers are at the Charlestown Navy Yard, Bunker Hill Monument, Faneuil Hall, and the downtown visitor center, and conduct ninety-minute walking tours of the downtown portion of Boston's Freedom Trail daily, from mid-April through November, and present historical talks at Faneuil Hall and the Bunker Hill Monument year-round. At the Charlestown Navy Yard, rangers conduct tours of the Navy Yard, Commandant's House, and the World War II destroyer USS *Cassin Young.* The U.S. Navy conducts tours of USS *Constitution* (Old Ironsides)—America's oldest commissioned warship—from 9:30 A.M. to 3:50 P.M. daily.

Fees are collected at the privately owned and operated sites by self-supporting associations working cooperatively with the park, including the Old South Meeting House, Old State House, Paul Revere House, and USS *Constitution* Museum. There is no fee at the federally owned sites, including the Bunker Hill Monument, USS *Constitution,* and Dorchester Heights Monument. Ranger-led programs on the Freedom Trail and at Faneuil Hall are also free.

Paul Revere's house at Boston National Historical Park. *(National Park Service)*

All Boston National Historical Park sites are accessible by public transportation. Park-and-ride facilities at MBTA subway (T) stations are an alternative to driving congested downtown streets. The downtown visitor center is at the State Street stop of the blue and orange subway lines. Water transportation runs frequently between downtown Boston (Long Wharf) and the Charlestown Navy Yard. If driving from Route 1 south and Route 93 north and south, follow the signs to the Charlestown Navy Yard (berth of USS *Constitution*). Further directions to downtown Boston are available there. There are many parking garages in the downtown area.

Visitor centers and sites are open year-round. The downtown visitor center at 15 State Street and the Charlestown Navy Yard Visitor Information Center are open 9 A.M. to 5 P.M. daily and until 6 P.M. from mid-June through Labor Day. Most historic sites are open 9:30 A.M. to 5 P.M. peak season and 10 A.M. to 4 P.M. off-season. The USS *Constitution* is open Thursday through Sunday 10 A.M. to 4 P.M.

There are no National Park Service RV or camping sites, but a wide range of hotels and motels are located throughout the city and in outlying areas. Private and state-run camping and RV facilities are open seasonally in outlying areas.

For more information, write Boston National Historical Park, Charlestown Navy Yard, Boston, MA 02129-4543, or telephone (617) 242-5644. The park's Web site is www.nps.gov/bost.

FURTHER READING
Alden, John R. *A History of the American Revolution.* New York: DaCapo, 1989.

Bahne, Charles. *The Complete Guide to Boston's Freedom Trail.* Cambridge, MA: Newtowne, 1993.

Ellis, Joseph J. *Founding Brothers: The Revolutionary Generation.* New York: Alfred A. Knopf, 2000.

Fischer, David Hackett. *Paul Revere's Ride.* New York: Oxford University Press, 1994.

Shaara, Jeff. *Rise to Rebellion.* New York: Ballantine Books, 2001.

BRICES CROSS ROADS NATIONAL BATTLEFIELD

Location: Tupelo, Mississippi
Acreage: 1
Established: February 21, 1929

The depleted, demoralized Confederate Army found themselves on the defensive in the Civil War's last two years, and desperately needed victories to boost low morale. The battle of Brices Cross Roads near Tupelo, Mississippi, was significant because it provided a lift for dwindling Confederate hopes. On June 10, 1864, 3,500 Confederate soldiers led by General Nathan Bedford Forrest routed 8,500 Union troops under General Samuel Sturgis. Military historians and tacticians consider Forrest's battle plan and leadership that day as one of the textbook-perfect examples of generalship in military history.

Although the tide had turned in the Union's favor after Gettysburg in 1863, General Ulysses S. Grant still wanted to strike at the heart of the Confederacy and destroy its ability to wage war. As General William Sherman's forces fought throughout northern Georgia, Confederate leaders decided to attack what they considered their enemy's most vulnerable element: a single-track railroad supply line between Nashville and Chattanooga, Tennessee. The Confederacy believed that if they captured this railroad, they could cut off the Union's supply line to the east, which included Georgia.

On June 1, Forrest set out from Tupelo to destroy the line. Sherman soon discovered Forrest's objective, and sent Sturgis and his soldiers to ward off the attack. Learning of this, Forrest concentrated 3,500 troops along the rail line between Guntown, Baldwyn, and Booneville, and waited patiently for Sturgis. On June 10, the two forces met on Baldwyn Road, about a mile east of Brices Cross Roads. The daylong battle became a stunning Confederate victory, a reversal of the decline in rebel fortunes. Forrest's surprise attack initially wore down the Union cavalry, routed the opposition across the bridge over Tishomingo Creek, and captured many Union artillery pieces and 1,500 troops as northern soldiers fled for their lives. In the end, the Union lost 2,240 men killed, wounded, or captured, while the Confederates suffered 492 casualties—96 killed and 396 wounded.

Military historians assert that the key to victory was Forrest's ability to attack on his own, familiar terrain, several daring flank movements, and the extremely hot, humid weather that wore down Union troops. In the end, the victory was hollow, for it did nothing to stop the flow of Union troops and supplies into northern Georgia from Tennessee. The battle occurred too far west to provide any tactical advantage in the East, and, in any event, by 1864, the Confederacy lacked the materiel, manpower, and ultimately the resilience to fight much longer.

Established as a national battlefield on February 21, 1929, Brices Cross Roads was transferred from the War Department to the National Park Service on August 10, 1933, along with many other areas. The tiny 1-acre site is located 6 miles west of Baldwyn, Mississippi, on Mississippi 370. Open year-round, the site has no entrance fee, nor are there facilities or park personnel. Folders are available both at the site and at the Natchez Trace Parkway Visitor Center in Tupelo. Site monuments and markers describe the battle. A short drive northwest on the Ripley-Guntown Road leads to Tishomingo Creek, the site of the bridge where the Union retreat turned into a Confederate rout. Confederate soldiers killed in the battle are buried in the adjacent Bethany Church cemetery.

No camping is permitted in the park. J.P. Coleman State Park, east of Corinth, and Tombigbee and Trace State Parks, near Tupelo, offer developed camping facilities.

For more information, write Brices Cross Roads National Battlefield, c/o Superintendent, Natchez Trace Parkway, 2680 Natchez Trace Parkway, Tupelo, MS 38804, or telephone (622) 680-4025. The park's Web site is www.nps.gov/brcr.

FURTHER READING
Hurst, Jack. *Nathan Bedford Forrest: A Biography.* New York: Alfred A. Knopf, 1993.

Sherman, William T. *Memoirs of W.T. Sherman.* New York: Library of America, 1990.

Wills, Brian Steel. *A Battle from the Start: The Life of Nathan Bedford Forrest.* New York: HarperCollins, 1992.

BROWN v. BOARD OF EDUCATION NATIONAL HISTORIC SITE
Location: Topeka, Kansas
Acreage: 2
Established: October 26, 1992

> We conclude that, in the field of public education, the doctrine of "separate but equal" has no place. Separate educational facilities are inherently unequal.

On May 17, 1954, with these simple eloquent words, Chief Justice Earl Warren, delivering the unanimous decision of the United States Supreme Court, struck down nearly a century of legalized segregation and set in motion the dismantling of Jim Crow. On October 26, 1992, Congress authorized the *Brown v. Board of Education* National Historic Site to commemorate this landmark ruling. The site itself is located at Monroe Elementary School in Topeka, Kansas, the newest of four schools that were segregated and served Topeka's African American community, and the one that the lead plaintiff's daughter, Cheryl Brown,

attended when *Brown v. Board of Education of Topeka* was first filed in 1951.

When Oliver and Linda Brown found that their nine-year-old daughter would have to walk from their home across the street from a grade school all the way across town, through downtown, and across railroad tracks and the Kaw River to attend the segregated school, they sued for relief. The U.S. District Court in Kansas first heard the case in 1951 and ruled against the plaintiffs. This decision was not surprising at the time. Segregation was the national norm in both the North and South, and Kansas's school segregation law had been in place since 1906. District Court Judge Walter Huxman later explained that his court's ruling was intended to force the Supreme Court to rule on the separate but equal doctrine enshrined in the 1896 *Plessy v. Ferguson* decision. *Plessy* allowed the creation of two societies, theoretically separate but equal. In reality, facilities were never equal and generations of African American—and Hispanic and Native American children— were deprived of the educational opportunities routinely afforded white children. The *Plessy* decision came in a case about public transportation, but before 1910, it became the legislation most frequently cited to create segregation, or "Jim Crow," laws not only in the South, but in the rest of the country as well.

When the U.S. District Court ruled against the Browns, NAACP (National Association for the Advancement of Colored People) attorneys immediately filed appeals, and other district courts around the country heard five similar cases. The courts had to decide whether or not school segregation was unconstitutional, a violation of the fourteenth amendment's equal protection clause. In 1952, the Supreme Court decided to consolidate all the cases and hear them together. On May 17, 1954, the Supreme Court voted unanimously to overturn the "separate but equal" doctrine detailed in *Plessy v. Ferguson.* In writing the opinion, Chief Justice Earl Warren commented that separate educational facilities were inherently unequal and violated the fourteenth amendment. "To separate them from others of similar age and qualifications solely because of their race," Warren stated, "generates a feeling of inferiority as to their status in the community that may affect their hearts and minds in a way unlikely ever to be undone."

The *Brown v. Board of Education* decision began the rights revolution in the United States. The Supreme Court dragged the rest of the country into the twentieth century, putting law ahead of custom. It was a bold decision, one that led to social strife, new legislation, amendments to the Constitution of the United States, and ultimately to the end of legal segregation in the United States.

The park is located on the corner of 15th and Monroe streets in southeast Topeka, Kansas, approximately 55 miles west of Kansas City. The grand opening of the site occurred on May 17, 2004, the fiftieth anniversary of the landmark decision. It is now open from 8 A.M. to 5 P.M., Monday through Friday year-round, and is closed on all federal holidays. Topeka contains all traveler services, and private campgrounds are located in the outlying areas.

The Monroe School serves as an interpretive and resource center for information about *Brown v. Board of Education* and its crucial role in the American civil rights movement. Audiovisual programs, exhibits, and literature are available, and a research library is open to the public. There is no admission fee, although donations are accepted. A variety of tours and off-site interpretive programs are available through the National Park Service and a cooperative agreement with the Brown Foundation for Educational Equity, Excellence, and Research.

For more information, write Brown v. Board of Education National Historic Site, 155 SE Monroe Street, Topeka KS 66612-1143, or telephone (785) 354-4273. The park's Web site is www.nps.gov/brvb.

FURTHER READING

Howard, John. *The Shifting Wind: The Supreme Court and Civil Rights from Reconstruction to Brown.* Albany: State University of New York Press, 1999.
Kluger, Richard. *Simple Justice.* New York: Alfred A. Knopf, 1975.
Martin, Waldo. *The Brown Decision: A Brief History with Documents.* Boston: Bedford Books, 1998.
Tushnet, Mark. *Making Civil Rights Law: Thurgood Marshall and the Supreme Court, 1936–1961.* New York: Oxford University Press, 1994.

BRYCE CANYON NATIONAL PARK

Location: Bryce Canyon, Utah
Acreage: 35,835
Founded: June 8, 1923

Truly one "hell of a place to lose a cow," as one pioneer labeled it, Bryce Canyon National Park is one of America's most colorful and spectacular vistas. Located in southcentral Utah, approximately 85 miles northeast of Zion National Park, Bryce Canyon is one of many horseshoe-shaped amphitheaters carved from the eastern edge of the Paunsaugunt Plateau in southern Utah. Only 35,835 acres, it is one of America's most popular national parks and is a regular stop for tourists visiting other nearby National Park Service (NPS) areas such as Zion, the Grand Canyon, Capitol Reef, and Cedar Breaks National Monument. Extensive wind and water erosion over hundreds of millennia shaped colorful Claron limestones, sandstones, and mudstones into thousands of spires, fins, pinnacles, and mazes. Collectively called "hoodoos," these unique formations are whimsically arranged and tinted with numerous vivid hues that span the spectrum from fairly mild to truly wild.

Located on a high rim, Bryce Canyon National Park contains numerous amphitheaters cut into cliffs. The park's cliffs are the end result of accumulated sand, silt, and lime washed into inland lakes, then compacted into rock layers. As the land uplifted over the millennia, persistent wind and water erosion cut the unusual, colorful rock shapes. The park itself was named after Ebenezer Bryce, a Mormon settler who homesteaded at the canyon's mouth in 1875. Regional folklore maintains that Bryce was the first to utter the now-famous "lose a cow" phrase. Other settlers coined colorful descriptions for the numerous natural features, including Fairyland Point, Queen's Garden, Peekaboo Loop, Silent City, and Chinese Wall.

Anglo-Americans first saw the mysterious spires of Bryce Canyon in the nineteenth century, when representatives of the Church of Jesus Christ of Latter-Day Saints established a frontier in southern Utah. By the turn of the twentieth century, the valleys around the park were inhabited by Mormon settlers, and as a result of the "See America First" movement, which was founded in Salt Lake City in 1906 to promote tourism within the United States, the area came to the attention of Stephen T. Mather, the first director of the NPS. Mather first visited the area in 1919, following a narrow and difficult Paiute Indian trail to the Bryce Canyon overlook, where he let out an enthusiastic whoop. Mather had a vision of a string of national parks with smaller national monuments interspersed as a way to promote auto travel to the park system. Well connected in Utah, he developed a strong local cadre to support park establishment for Bryce. As a result, Bryce Canyon was established as a national monument in 1923. With

Bryce Canyon National Park is famous for its remarkable geology. This area also boasts some of the world's best air quality and features panoramic views of three states. *(National Park Service)*

the assistance from the Union Pacific Railroad, which operated a lodge within the park and brought visitors by train by the thousands, Bryce Canyon attained national park status five years later in 1928.

Bryce Canyon receives close to 1.75 million visitors annually. Visitation peaks from June through September and ebbs in December, January, and February. The park's roads can be extremely congested during the summer, and a shuttle system has been added to reduce auto traffic and pollution from May through September.

Visitors can enjoy Bryce Canyon during any season. Located 8,000 to 9,000 feet above sea level, the canyon enjoys pleasant summer days and cool nights. July is the warmest month, with an average daytime high temperature of 83 degrees and a nighttime low of 47 degrees. Much of the canyon's precipitation comes as afternoon thundershowers during mid- to late summer. Spring and fall weather is highly variable. Cold winter days are offset by high altitude sun and dry climate, while winter nights are subfreezing. During some winters, Alaskan cold fronts descend on the Colorado Plateau region bringing temperatures as low as minus 30 degrees. Although March is the snowiest month, the area can have snowstorms from October through April. Snowfall averages 95 inches annually, providing excellent opportunities for cross-country skiing and snowshoeing.

The park is open twenty-four hours per day year-round. There may be temporary road closures during and shortly after winter snowstorms until conditions are safe for visitor traffic. Road maintenance may require brief closures of individual areas at other times. Passenger cars are charged $10 per seven-day visit, or $20 per year, valid only at Bryce Canyon National Park. Noncommercial tours (scouts, church groups, school groups on recreational outings), as well as foot and bicycle travelers are charged $5 per person age seventeen and older. Golden Eagle ($50 annual fee) and Golden Age ($10 one-time fee) passports allow half-price admission. Campsites are $10 per site per night. (Golden Age and Golden Access passport holders receive a 50 percent discount.) Backcountry permits are required and are $5 each.

The park visitor center is open year-round except Thanksgiving, Christmas, and New Year's. A ten-minute slide program, exhibits, rest rooms, information, and backcountry permits are available. In addition, maps and other publications are available for purchase through Bryce Canyon Natural History Association. The park has over 50 miles of hiking trails with a wide range of difficulties, distances, and elevation changes; check with the visitor center for maps and details. Assess your ability and know your limits, and use caution if you are unaccustomed to high altitudes.

Lodging is available at Bryce Canyon Lodge, near the rim of Bryce amphitheater. In addition to the main lodge, it offers motel and cabin-style accommodations. The main lodge has a dining room and gift shop. A store near Sunrise Point offers all traveler services, but no lodging. Because the park is so popular, there are other accommodations located away from the park in nearby small towns and in Panguitch, 26 miles northwest.

Camping in Bryce Canyon is available at 2 areas: North Campground, immediately east of the visitor center, and Sunset Campground, 2 miles south. Both provide tables, grills, and flush toilets. North Campground has an RV dump station, and because it is much closer to the park's developed facilities, it fills much more quickly than Sunset. For information on Bryce Canyon Lodge, write Amfac Parks and Resorts, Inc., 14001 East Iliff Avenue, Suite 600, Aurora, CO 80014, or call (303) 297-2757.

For more information, write Bryce Canyon National Park, P.O. Box 170001, Bryce Canyon, UT 84717-0001, or telephone (435) 834-5322. The park's Web site is www.nps.gov/brca.

FURTHER READING
Bezy, John V. *Bryce Canyon: The Story Behind the Scenery.* Las Vegas, NV: KC Publications, 1980.
Lindquist, Robert C. *The Geology of Bryce Canyon National Park.* Bryce Canyon, UT: Bryce Canyon Natural History Association, 1977.
Shankland, Robert. *Steve Mather of the National Parks.* 3d ed. New York: Alfred A. Knopf, 1970.

BUCK ISLAND REEF NATIONAL MONUMENT
Location: Christiansted, St. Croix, Virgin Islands
Acreage: 19,015
Established: December 28, 1961

One of four national park sites in the U.S. Virgin Islands, Buck Island Reef National Monument contains some of the Caribbean Sea's finest marine gardens, as well as numerous colorful coral grottoes, sea fans, gorgonians, and tropical fishes. Located off the island of St. Croix, and open year-round, Buck Island has both marked underwater interpretive trails for novice and expert snorkelers, and an overland nature trail that allows visitors to enjoy the park's uncrowded beaches. In addition to its recreational functions, Buck Island also serves as an important rookery for frigate birds and endangered brown pelicans, and a protected nesting area for hawksbill and leatherback sea turtles, and the threatened green turtle.

Beginning in the 1750s, Buck Island was used for pasturage and timber. Within two centuries, this unchecked activity had resulted in severe overgrazing by huge goat herds, and the widespread depletion of lignum vitae trees, locally called Pokholdt trees, on the island. By 1940, most commercial activity ended, and in the 1950s, the voracious goats were removed. Over time, the environmental scars began to heal; vegetation has largely recolonized the desertified lands left behind by overgrazing, though the island still struggles to protect native flora and fauna from the nonnative plants and animals, called "exotics," that accompanied commercial activity.

Authorized under the Antiquities Act in 1961, Buck Island Reef National Monument followed a relatively arduous process of establishment. After 1945, Congress insisted that the executive branch cease to establish new national monuments without its permission. Although the law permitted such a designation, Congress insisted that it would not provide funding. As a result, Buck Island and other similar additions to the system were reviewed and informally approved by Congress prior to executive proclamation. President Jimmy Carter brought this prohibition to an end with his bold use of the Antiquities Act in Alaska in 1978, and in 2001, an executive order signed by President Bill Clinton enlarged Buck Island Reef National Monument by 18,185 marine acres.

Visitors can take in the crystal clear water, extraordinary array of underwater life, and tropical vegetation through a variety of activities that include swimming, snorkeling, boating, hiking, bird watching, and picnicking. Snorkelers are advised to exercise caution in the water because cuts from coral can inflict painful wounds. The spiny sea urchins are also a common hazard, as are the poisonous jellyfish and the Portuguese man-of-war. It is recommended that visitors practice snorkeling in shallower waters before attempting the more dangerous reefs, and respect all underwater wildlife by maintaining a safe distance.

While the park itself charges no entrance fees, boat concessionaires do, and the monument is accessible only by concessionaire craft or private boat. Concession boats are available at Christiansted Wharf to make the 5-mile journey to the park on St. Croix. Private boats should be maneuvered slowly

Sailing in Buck Island Reef National Monument. *(National Park Service)*

through the monument's waters. Because it is warm year-round—summers are hot and humid—lightweight clothing is suggested. Long-sleeve shirts, pants, sturdy shoes, and bug repellant are recommended for hiking, and visitors must take necessary precautions to avoid sunburn.

Camping is permitted on boats, but not on the island, and overnight accommodations are available in Christiansted and St. Croix. There is no food or lodging on the island, but the Park Service provides picnic tables, charcoal grills, a changing house, a sheltered picnic pavilion, rest rooms, and a nature trail. First aid is available on Buck Island.

For more information, write Buck Island Reef National Monument, Danish Custom House, Kings Wharf, 2100 Church Street, #100, Christiansted, VI 00820-4611, or telephone (340) 773-1460. The park's Web site is www.nps.gov/buis.

FURTHER READING

Kasler, Ben. *Priceless Heritage: History and Lore of Estate St. George, Home of the St. George Village Botanical Garden of St. Croix.* St. Croix, U.S. Virgin Islands: privately published, 1980.

Sandburg, H., and G. Crile. *Above and Below: A Journey Through Our National Underwater Parks.* New York: McGraw-Hill, 1969.

C

CABRILLO NATIONAL MONUMENT

Location: San Diego, California
Acreage: 160
Established: October 14, 1913

Sailing from Navidad, Mexico, Spanish explorer Juan Rodriguez Cabrillo inched his way into a narrow channel along the extreme southern California coast in late September 1542. On September 28, Cabrillo set foot on land off San Diego Bay. It was the first time Europeans landed on what eventually became the West Coast of the United States. Six days later, Cabrillo departed from San Diego and sailed north to explore California's uncharted coastline. His explorations contributed to the Spanish colonization of the American coast.

In 1913, Cabrillo's journey was memorialized with the establishment of the 160-acre Cabrillo National Monument, located on the southern tip of San Diego's Point Loma peninsula. As was typical of early national monuments, Cabrillo National Monument's establishment resulted from the efforts of local people. The Order of Panama, a San Diego–area civic organization devoted to publicizing the efforts of Juan Rodriquez Cabrillo, spearheaded the drive, which created the monument in advance of the Panama-California Exposition in San Diego in 1915. At its establishment, the monument was a mere acre, encompassing the lighthouse, and was entirely surrounded by military land.

The monument offers various interpretive programs and houses a small museum about Cabrillo. It also offers a superb view of San Diego harbor, the Pacific Ocean, and the winter gray whale migration. The monument preserves the Old Point Loma Lighthouse, the remains of Fort Rosecrans's World War II coastal defense system, a coastal sage scrub ecosystem, and the Cabrillo Tidepools.

Programs vary throughout the year. Rangers conduct talks on natural history themes, including tide pools, whales, and coastal sage scrub during the fall, winter, and spring. Cultural history presentations on topics such as Spanish exploration, lighthouses, and military

Old Point Loma Lighthouse at Cabrillo National Monument. *(National Park Service)*

history are given year-round. Bayside Trail is a self-guided, mile-long hiking trail through a coastal sage scrub forest. It follows a downhill slope toward San Diego Bay, then returns along the same route. Interpretive panels along the trail provide information about Point Loma's ecology. Open daily, the Old Point Loma Lighthouse is a restored structure with 1880s furnishings. The Whale Overlook's protected shelter houses exhibits, a tactile model of an adult gray whale and calf, and recorded messages.

Visitation is fairly even throughout the year, with annual numbers approaching 1.2 million people. Winter and spring are the best seasons to visit. The annual migration of gray whales occurs December through February. The peak tide-pool season is November through February, and the blooming of coastal sage scrub occurs February through April. The clearest visibility for the spectacular views of San Diego Bay, downtown San Diego, Mexico, and the ocean occur in winter and spring.

The monument is located on the southern tip of Point Loma, approximately 10 miles from downtown San Diego. It can be reached by following state highway 209 south from I-5 or I-8 to the tip of Point Loma. The monument is open year-round, daily from 9 A.M. to 5:15 P.M., and until 6:15 P.M. from July 4 through Labor Day. Entrance fees are $5 per vehicle, or $2 per person for those who walk in or ride bicycles and motorcycles.

The monument has no food or lodging. Metropolitan San Diego provides traveler services for all budgets. Mission Bay, north of the monument, has private campgrounds. Surf fishing is available on the monument's west side off Gatchell Road. A valid California license is required.

For more information, write Cabrillo National Monument, 1800 Cabrillo Memorial Drive, San Diego, CA 92106-3601, or telephone (619) 557-5450. The park's Web site is www.nps.gov/cabr.

FURTHER READING

Kelsey, Harry. *Juan Rodriguez Cabrillo.* San Marino, CA: Huntington Library, 1986.

Lavender, David Sievert. *Desoto, Coronado, Cabrillo: Explorers of the Northern Mystery.* Washington, DC: Government Printing Office, 1992.

Nauman, James D. *An Account of the Voyage of Juan Rodriguez Cabrillo.* San Diego, CA: Cabrillo National Monument Foundation, 1999.

Reupsch, Carl F., ed. *The Cabrillo Era and His Voyage of Discovery.* San Diego, CA: Cabrillo Historical Association, 1982.

CANAVERAL NATIONAL SEASHORE

Location: Titusville and New Smyrna
  Beach, Florida
Acreage: 57,662
Established: January 3, 1975

Located just north of NASA's (National Aeronautics and Space Administration) Kennedy Space Center and south of Daytona Beach, Florida's 57,662-acre Canaveral National Seashore is part of a barrier island made up of 24 miles of undeveloped beaches and wetland environments. Designated as a national seashore, the park protects the natural environment of the area from development and provides sanctuary for more than 1,000 species of plants and 300 species of birds, including 14 threatened or endangered species. Manatees inhabit Mosquito Lagoon; whales and dolphins are frequently spotted offshore; and armadillos, bobcats, raccoons, rattlesnakes, turtles, and crabs inhabit the inland and beach areas. Canaveral National Seashore offers a microcosm of the natural habitat of the Florida coast.

Originally part of the Kennedy Space Center, the stretch of land known as Merritt Island entered the park system during President Gerald Ford's administration. On January 3, 1975, Congress established the national seashore to protect one of the last remaining wilderness areas on Florida's Atlantic Coast. Another section on the south side of the island, the Merritt Island National Wildlife Refuge, is administered by the U.S. Fish and Wildlife Service. This form of management, by more than one federal land management agency, is common in Alaska but less in the lower forty-eight states. Federal agencies have always relied on their neighbors; in the case of Canaveral National Seashore, that interdependence is both more crucial and more apparent.

Beaches abound in the park. Apollo Beach, located in the North District, can be reached by car, while Klondike Beach requires foot, bicycle, or horseback access; it is less crowded and offers more solitude. The South District's Playalinda Beach is also accessible by car. Swimmers must watch for potential riptides, and be careful to avoid jellyfish, including the poisonous Portuguese man-of-war. Most hiking trails within the park are gentle and less than a mile in length. Bug repellent is recommended. Boat launch sites provide access to Mosquito and Indian River Lagoons.

The seashore is open throughout the year, and entrance fees are $5 per day, per vehicle, or $3 per person; an annual pass is also available for $28. Visitation is typically highest from January through August, and lowest from September through December. There are two districts to the park: the North District is accessible via state highway A1A in New Smyrna Beach, exit 84A off I-95; the South District is reached via state highway 406 in Titusville, exit 80 off I-95. Operating hours are daily in the summer from 6 A.M. to 8 P.M.; daily in the winter from 6 A.M. to 6 P.M. The park's South District closes three days before a shuttle launch, then reopens the day after. The park closes when parking lots fill up, mostly during busy summer weekends.

The North District Information Center in New Smyrna Beach offers exhibits and maps of trails. Year-round, ranger-led programs in the North District include walks, talks, canoe programs, and seasonal "Sea Turtle Watch" programs. A visitor center at Merritt Island National Wildlife Refuge, in the South District, offers exhibits and limited tours. Other than the wildlife refuge programs, the park's South District has no programs.

There is no food or lodging in the park, but all traveler services can be found in nearby Titusville and New Smyrna Beach. Klondike Beach has limited backcountry camping from November 1 through April 30, while wilderness camping is available in Mosquito Lagoon year-round. Both require free permits, which are available at the New Smyrna Beach information center. Many private campgrounds are located nearby.

For more information, write Canaveral National Seashore, 308 Julia Street, Titusville, FL 33943, or telephone (407) 267-1110. The park's Web site is www.nps.gov/cana.

FURTHER READING

Childers, Frank M. *History of the Cape Canaveral Lighthouse.* Cocoa, FL: Brevard Museum of History and Natural Science, 1997.

Merritt Island National Wildlife Refuge. *Protecting Endangered Species.* New York: Time Life, 1996.

CANE RIVER CREOLE NATIONAL HISTORICAL PARK AND HERITAGE AREA

Location: Natchez, Louisiana
Acreage: 116,000 (approximate)
Established: November 2, 1994

Still under construction and development, the Cane River Creole National Historical Park and Heritage Area in eastcentral Louisiana will preserve significant landscapes, sites, and structures associated with the development of southern Louisiana's multiracial and multiethnic culture called Creole. On November 2, 1994, Congress approved legislation creating the Cane River Creole National Historical Park and the Cane River National Heritage Area. The park's mission is to provide a comprehensive understanding of the region's broad historic and cultural heritage. The park's preserved buildings, records of the region's elite families, and an extensive collection of tools, equipment, and furniture serve to reconstruct and interpret the history of this fascinating region.

Cane River Creole National Historical Park is located within the heritage area, which extends for a mile on both sides of the Cane River from the southern boundary of Natchitoches to Monette's Ferry. Cumulatively, the park represents the cultural history of French and English colonization, French Creole architecture, slavery and sharecropping systems in the United States, cotton agriculture, and social relations between African American and Anglo-American residents over two centuries. It reveals a culture now largely lost, a multiracial ethnic group with clearly defined customs of its own and ways of being that pulled together influences from Europe, Africa, the Caribbean, and beyond. The Cane River National Heritage Area includes the Kate Chopin House, home of the author of *The Awakening,* one of the early twentieth century's important woman writers, and the state commemorative areas of Los Adaes, Fort Jesup, and Fort St. Jean Baptiste. The heritage area includes approximately 40,000 acres of privately and publicly owned lands. Forty-two acres of Oakland Plantation and 18 acres of Magnolia Plantation outbuildings are also preserved in the park.

The Oakland Plantation provides a good example of eighteenth- and early nineteenth-century plantation life. The founder of Bermuda (later Oakland) Plantation was Pierre Emmanuel Prudhomme, a second-generation native of French descent. Prudhomme was in the forefront of southern agriculture, experimenting with multiple crops, equipment, and techniques while most of the antebellum South was engaged in a one-crop economy.

When Union General Nathaniel Banks' Red River Campaign swept through the Cane River area in early 1864, Bermuda was spared the worst of its ravages; the main plantation house and some outbuildings survived. In 1873, the Prudhomme brothers partitioned the plantation, renaming the right-bank portion Oakland. Both the Prudhomme family and their laborers' descendants occupied and farmed the plantation until recently, continuing an agricultural relationship with the land that has spanned three centuries.

Magnolia Plantation was founded in 1835 by Julia Buard and her husband Ambroise Lecomte. By 1860 they were the largest slaveholders in Natchitoches Parish. Most of Magnolia Plantation's structures are from the early- to mid-antebellum era, 1790 to 1830. The park preserves the agricultural complex, which tells the story of the work that created and sustained the plantation. The main house, a reconstruction of the original, which was burned by retreating Union troops during the Civil War, lies outside the park's boundary. The park's buildings include Magnolia's blacksmith shop, plantation store, a former slave hospital—that at various times also housed the owners while the main house was being rebuilt—brick cabins, and a gin barn. Magnolia's 8 brick cabins are a rare surviving example of a masonry slave village.

At press time, the park was still undergoing extensive renovation, but it was open to the public on a restricted basis. Tours of Oakland are given at 1 P.M. daily, and self-guided grounds maps are also available. The park's administrative offices are located at Oakland Plantation in Natchez. Office hours are Monday through Friday, 8 A.M. to 4:30 P.M.

For more information, including tour reservations, write Cane River Creole National Historical Park and Heritage Area, 4386 Highway 494, Natchez, LA 71456, or telephone (318) 352-0383. The park's Web site is www.nps.gov/cari.

FURTHER READING

Chopin, Kate. *The Awakening and Other Stories.* New York: Modern Library, 2000.

Gould, Philip. *Natchitoches and Louisiana's Timeless Cane River.* Baton Rouge: Louisiana State University Press, 2002.

Kein, Sybil, ed. *Creole: The History and Legacy of Louisiana's Free People of Color.* Baton Rouge: Louisiana State University Press, 2000.

Mills, Gary B. *The Forgotten People: Cane River's Creoles of Color.* Baton Rouge: Louisiana State University Press, 1977.

CANYON DE CHELLY NATIONAL MONUMENT

Location: Chinle, Arizona
Acreage: 83,840
Established: February 14, 1931

Pronounced "d'shay," Canyon de Chelly National Monument in northeastern Arizona preserves the remnants of prehistoric Anasazi and Pueblo Indian cultures. Ruins of Native American villages built between 350 and 1300 C.E. are located at the base of sheer, red sandstone cliffs and in canyon wall caves. Located 85 miles northwest of Gallup, New Mexico, the 83,840-acre monument offers visitors the chance to learn about Southwestern Indian history ranging from the earliest Basket Maker cultures to the Navajo Indians who currently live and farm in the area.

The canyon's earliest known native cultures lived in pit houses (semisubterranean structures built within pits), grew maize and squash, and wove baskets for transporting and storing water and food. Many centuries later, from about 1100–1300 C.E., Anasazi Indians made pottery and constructed rectangular masonry cliff houses high in the canyon walls. After an extended drought in the thirteenth century forced all native people in the Four Corners area to disperse, although ancestors of the Hopi sporadically occupied the canyon. Around 1700, the Navajo moved into the canyon. For a hundred and fifty years, the Navajos battled the Hopis, the Spanish, and finally the U.S. Army for control of the region. After a Civil War–era attempt by the government to relocate Navajos to eastern New Mexico failed, many tribal members returned to the canyon to live.

In 1931, President Herbert Hoover authorized the area as a national monument. The lands within the established boundaries belonged to the Navajo people, who approved the monument and retained control of most activities within the park. In the 1930s, the Park Service saw the monument as a piece of a larger objective, a great national park in the desert and in the canyonlands. When the Navajo rejected that idea, they called for exclusive control of Canyon de Chelly. The Park Service did not acquiesce, retaining control of a monument on land the agency did not own. The result has been complicated joint management that has left control of most day-to-day activities in Navajo hands and put the Park Service in the position of overseeing activities it does not control. Although since the 1980s, Navajo National Park Service employees have played a more prominent role at the park, local Navajo people remain frustrated by the presence of the Park Service.

Because the Navajo tribe still lives and works in the canyon proper, access is limited. There is no entrance fee. Hiking within the canyon requires a Park Service permit and an authorized Navajo guide, except along the 2.5-mile White House Ruins Trail. One guide may take up to 15 people for $10 per hour. To drive on the canyon bottom, a four-wheel-drive vehicle, a Park Service permit, and an authorized Navajo guide are required. The fee is $10 an hour for 1 vehicle, $5 an hour for each additional vehicle with a 5-vehicle limit per guide. Autos should use paved roads only; the inner canyons are impassable in winter and at certain other times of the year. Quicksand, deep dry sand, cliffs, loose rocks, and flash floods make inner canyon travel hazardous for people unfamiliar with the area.

The visitor center, which is located 3 miles from Route 191 in Chinle, is open daily from 8 A.M. to 5 P.M., October to April, and from 8 A.M. to 6 P.M., May to September. It is suggested that visitors stop here to orient themselves, view the many Native American exhibits and displays, and obtain the necessary permits for inner-canyon travel or camping. The visitor center also contains a guidebook for those who wish to drive the 22-mile south rim drive, which does not require a guide or permit. Six scenic overlooks dot the rim drive, and a trail leads down to White House Ruin. This grueling, 2.5-mile hike is the only opportunity to see the ruin without having to sign up for a tour, and offers many vantage points to see both Anasazi and Pueblo Indian pictographs.

Cottonwood Campground, with 104 sites, is located near the entrance. Set in a grove of Cottonwood trees, it contains grills, tables, and, in the summer, water and flush toilets. It is available on a first-come, first-served basis year-round, with a maximum stay of five days. Reservations for group sites for 15 or more people can be made by contacting the monument. Backcountry camping is allowed only with an authorized guide. Lodging is available at Thunderbird Lodge near the monument entrance. Other overnight accommodations are available in Chinle and Window Rock, Arizona, and Gallup, New Mexico. The Thunderbird Lodge serves meals, but the monument has no food or supplies. Chinle offers all traveler services.

For more information, write Canyon de Chelly National Monument, P.O. Box 588, Chinle, AZ 86503, or telephone (520) 674-5500. The park's Web site is www.nps.gov/cach.

FURTHER READING

Grant, Campbell. *Canyon de Chelly: Its People and Rock Art.* Albuquerque: University of New Mexico Press, 1978.

Noble, David Grant, ed. *Houses Beneath the Rock: The Anasazi of Canyon de Chelly and Navajo National Monument.* Santa Fe, NM: Ancient City, 1992.

Simonelli, Jeanne M. *Crossing Between Worlds: The Navajos of Canyon de Chelly.* Santa Fe, NM: School of American Research, 1997.

CANYONLANDS NATIONAL PARK

Location: Moab, Utah
Acreage: 337,598
Established: September 12, 1964

During his 1869 exploration of the Colorado River, John Wesley Powell described the strangely carved landscape of southeastern Utah as "a wilderness of rocks." In 1964, this wild and unruly land became Canyonlands National Park, a geologic wonderland of colorful and fantastic pinnacles, clefts, mazes, arches, balanced rocks, and mesas. One of America's most expansive and rugged national parks, Canyonlands encompasses 527 square miles of striking landscapes and vistas, shaped over the past 300 million years by oceans, winds, floods, and the erosive action of the Colorado and Green rivers. The park's distinctive sandstone formations are underlaid by massive salt deposits, leftover from an ancient inland sea, which, under the tremendous pressure from the rock above, liquefy and push upward, forming domes that collapse and leave crater-like depressions, such as Upheaval Dome.

Human inhabitation of the area has been sporadic even in recent times. Evidence of humans dates back about ten thousand years, but only five thousand years ago did Paleo-Indian hunter-gatherers begin to settle in the area of the park. They left traces of their existence, most prominently in rock art, known as the "Barrier Canyon style," that illustrated their lifeways. By about 250 C.E., the an-

Canyonlands National Park. *(National Park Service)*

cestors of the Pueblo people of the Southwest brought their agricultural techniques to this dry region, lasting almost one thousand years. They were succeeded by the Navajos, Utes, and Paiutes, the native people Anglo-Americans met when they reached the Canyonlands. The Dominguez-Escalante expedition in 1776 traversed the region, bringing the first known Europeans to the area, and the region remained remote. A trapper named Denis Julien carved his name repeatedly in the area between 1836 and 1838, but only when the U.S. Army Corps of Topographical Engineers, an arm of the U.S. Army Corps of Engineers created to explore the West, reached the region in 1859 did the first real map of the region become reality. Soon after, Powell came down the Colorado River, bringing its wonders to the attention of the American public.

The Colorado and Green rivers carve the park into 3 land districts—Island in the Sky, the Needles, and the Maze—in addition to the Horseshoe Canyon detached unit. All 4 share an arid, high-desert environment, but also offer unique opportunities for exploration and the study of natural and cultural history. Most of the park's 446,000 annual visitors travel to the high-altitude Island in the Sky district, which is accessible via state highway 313, a few miles north of Moab. The 6,300-foot Grand View Point provides a sweeping panorama of the park that is certainly worthy of its name. From here, visitors gaze down 1,500 feet to the White Rim formation, a vast plateau deeply incised by the canyons of Monument Basin, and at the shimmering snow-capped La Sal Mountains in the distance. The White Rim Road, one of the park's most popular jeep and mountain bike roads, meanders for more than 100 miles through prime desert bighorn sheep country, and includes the harrowing Shafer Trail, a zigzag, thrilling switchback ribbon of a dirt road that provides the only other access to Island in the Sky via "The Neck."

The Needles district is a vast rock "forest" landscape of twisted spires and convoluted canyons, and is accessible only by a 35-mile paved road that begins 56 miles south of Moab off U.S. Highway 191. The road ends at Squaw Flat, and all passenger cars must stop at Elephant Hill—a brutal 40 percent grade traversed only by high-clearance four-wheel-drive vehicles. Many hiking trails take off from Squaw Flat and lead into the Needles backcountry. Area attractions include the Native American ruins and the pictographs of Salt Creek Canyon and Horse Canyon.

West of the Green and Colorado rivers lies the remote Maze district. This is the perfect area for those who might find the other 2 districts too crowded, for this is the least-accessible portion of the park. To get to the Maze, take U.S. Highway 191 north to I-70, head west to exit 147, then head south about 50 miles on Utah 24—about 120 miles from Moab, one-way. Passenger cars can get as far as Hans Flat Ranger Station. Four-wheel-drive vehicles can continue for an additional 34 miles to the Maze Overlook, another classic jeep route in the park. Most of the Maze district is only accessible by foot. This district contains a "maze" of sheer-walled canyons that lead nowhere, as well as a confusing array of rock spires. Because it is so rugged and remote, the Park Service recommends that visitors contact headquarters before visiting this area.

Northwest of the Maze lies Horseshoe Canyon, a detached unit of Canyonlands National Park added in 1971. Its intriguing rock art is considered by many to be the most significant in North America. The archeology of the canyon dates back thousands of years, to as early as 9000–7000 B.C.E. The majority of Native American rock art found in Horseshoe Canyon is painted in a style known as "Barrier Canyon," which dates from 2000 B.C.E. to 500 C.E., and is characterized by tapered, life-size figures, lacking arms and legs and frequently containing intricate designs. The Great Gallery is the best known and most spectacular of the Horseshoe Canyon panels, and includes both pictographs (painted figures) and petroglyphs (figures etched in the rock with a sharp stone). In the 1800s, hundreds of years after the prehistoric artists left the area, outlaws like Butch Cassidy made use of Horseshoe Canyon, taking refuge in its confusing network of canyons. Later, in the early 1900s, ranchers built several stock trails into Horseshoe so cows and sheep could reach water and feed in the canyon bottom. Horseshoe Canyon also boasts beautiful spring wildflower displays, sheer sandstone walls, and mature cottonwood trees that shade the canyon floor.

Canyonlands National Park came into being as part of the Johnson administration's commitment to the growing sentiment for environmentalism. Secretary of the Interior Stewart Udall, author of the book *The Quiet Crisis*, an early but influential environmental tract, was a native Arizonan who worked to conserve lands in the desert Southwest. Canyonlands can be attributed to his influence and to the acerbic environmental writer Edward Abbey, whose writing also played an important role in alerting the American public to the beauty of the desert.

Visitation to the park is typically highest during the pleasant spring and fall seasons, and lowest during the cold winters and hot summers. Entrance fees, good for seven days, are $10 for private vehicles and $5 for individuals. There is also a $25 annual pass available which covers entrance fees for Arches, Canyonlands, Hovenweep, and Natural Bridges. Permits are required for four-wheel-drive day use ($5), four-wheel-drive and mountain bike camping ($25), backpacking ($10), overnight flat-water trips on the Colorado and Green rivers ($25 for fourteen days), and overnight white-water trips in Cataract Canyon ($25 for fourteen days).

The park has 3 visitor or information centers, 1 for each district. The visitor centers are open year-round from 8 A.M. to 4:30 P.M. daily, and all can issue backcountry permits. The Island in the Sky and the Needles visitor centers have a park orientation video, exhibits describing the natural and cultural history of the area, a small bookstore, and limited drinking water. Hans Flat Ranger Station serves the Maze district of the park and features exhibits and a book sales outlet.

Canyonlands National Park has numerous camping opportunities. Individual sites for ten or fewer people are available on a first-come, first-served basis. The Squaw Flat Campground is located in Needles district and has 26 sites with water, bathrooms, fire grates, and picnic tables for $10 per night. In the Island in the Sky District, there is the Willow Flat Campground, which has 12 sites with picnic tables, fire grates, and vault toilets—but no water—for $5 per night. Primitive campsites with no water are located along many of the four-wheel-drive roads throughout the park. Canyonlands has no lodging or food services. The towns of Moab, Monticello, Green River, and Hanksville (near the Maze) offer a full range of traveler facilities. The Needles Outpost, near the Needles entrance, offers limited supplies, as well as scenic flights over the park from March through October.

For more information, write Canyonlands National Park, 2282 SW Resource Blvd., Moab, UT 84532, or telephone (435) 259-7164. The park's informative Web site is www.nps.gov/cany.

FURTHER READING

Baars, Donald L. *Canyonlands Country: Geology of Canyonlands and Arches National Parks.* Salt Lake City: University of Utah Press, 1993.
Barnes, F.A. *Canyonlands National Park: Early History and First Descriptions: An Illustrated Guide to the Study and Appreciation of the Early History of Canyonlands National Park.* Moab, UT: Canyon Country, 1988.
deBuys, William, ed. *Seeing Things Whole: The Essential John Wesley Powell.* Washington, DC: Island, 2001.
Worster, Donald. *A River Running West: The Life of John Wesley Powell.* New York: Oxford University Press, 2001.

CAPE COD NATIONAL SEASHORE

Location: Wellfleet, Massachusetts
Acreage: 43,605
Established: August 7, 1961

> Being thus arrived in a good harbor, and brought safe to land, they fell upon their knees and blessed the God of Heaven who had brought them over the vast and furious ocean . . .

With these words, William Bradford and the Pilgrims claimed Cape Cod as their new home in 1620. The first English settlers in New England were religious dissenters-separatists—convinced that the Church of England had become so corrupt that they must establish their own, independent church. Their six-week journey across the Atlantic should have carried them to the familiar shores of Virginia, but navigational errors instead brought the *Mayflower* to the rocky November coast of Massachusetts. Here, their land patent was invalid; they had no authority to establish a government.

To preserve their social experiment from anarchy, the men on the expedition agreed to sign "a covenant and combine our selves together into a civil body politick"—the Mayflower Compact. Hailed as the first document of European self-government in North America, the Mayflower Compact nevertheless was ineffective at warding off disease and hunger. During the first months in Plymouth, death claimed approximately half of the 102 Pilgrims, weakened by scurvy and malnutrition, who had initially set out from England. Only friendly relations with the neighboring native people proved the salvation of the rest. Massasoit, sachem leader of the Wampanoags, offered the colonists food and advice in exchange for alliance with the newcomers against the warring Narragansetts. Massasoit's adviser Squanto, the last surviving member of the Pautuxet tribe, spoke English and taught the Pilgrims to grow maize. By autumn, the Pilgrims had a bumper crop of corn, a flourishing fur trade, and a supply of lumber for shipment.

Though the Pilgrims arrived safely on the shores of Cape Cod, many seafarers were not so fortunate. Treacherous sand bars lie hidden just off the coast, and the 50 miles of sea stretching from Chatham to Provincetown have been called an "ocean graveyard." In its three hundred years of maritime history, the cape has witnessed more than 3,000 shipwrecks. In the early 1800s, winter took a deadly toll—an average of two shipwrecks each month. Finally, in 1872, Congress created the U.S. Life Saving Service, a series of staffed lifesaving stations along the eastern seaboard.

By the beginning of the twentieth century, advances in radio, telegraphy, and weather forecasting dramatically reduced the number of shipwrecks on Cape Cod. The 1914 opening of the Cape Cod Canal further reduced navigational dangers and, the following year, the U.S. Life Saving Service was incorporated into the newly formed U.S. Coast Guard.

In August 1961, this infamous fist of land that Thoreau once described as "boxing with northeast storms," was preserved as Cape Cod National Seashore. It stemmed from the rush to protect the coastline that followed the publication of *Our Vanishing Shoreline*, a 1955 Park Service survey sponsored by the Mellon family, and was easily the most popular of the national seashores. Comprising some 43,605 acres of shoreline and upland landscapes,

Cape Cod remains one of the most popular national park units. Numerous historic structures lie within the seashore's boundary, including lighthouses, lifeguard stations, and several Cape Cod–style houses. In 1996, Highland Light and Nauset Light, two historic lighthouses within the park, were relocated away from the eroding cliffs of the Outer Cape.

Many visitors enjoy the park's 6 developed beaches—which include rest rooms, changing facilities, cold showers, and lifeguard protection—10 self-guided nature trails, and 3 paved bicycled trails. Others gravitate toward the 40-mile-long stretch of pristine sandy beach, woodlands, and dozens of deep freshwater ponds and marshes.

The seashore's weather changes significantly with the seasons. Cool and damp in the spring, with temperatures in the mid-40s, gives way to warmer summer days with highs generally ranging between 70 and 80 degrees (but higher temperatures possible), and cool nights. Though winter on Cape Cod is a bit milder than inland, dampness and wind chill can create bitterly cold days.

The park maintains 2 visitor centers: the Salt Pond Visitor Center in Eastham just off Route 6, and the Province Lands Visitor Center off Race Point road in the Provincelands. Both offer numerous interpretive ranger programs from mid-May to Columbus Day, including campfire programs, guided beach hikes, and historic home tours.

Although there is no entrance fee, during the summer season (July through Labor Day), the seashore charges a $7-per-vehicle daily fee at the park's lifeguard-protected swimming beaches (walkers and bicyclists are charged $1 per day). A $20 seasonal pass is also available. Day use fees are waived for holders of valid Golden Eagle, Golden Age, and Golden Access passports, as well as those with a current National Parks Pass.

There are privately operated campgrounds within the boundaries of Cape Cod National Seashore and at nearby Nickerson State Park, located in Brewster. Lodging, food, and other traveler services are available in all towns adjoining the seashore.

For more information, write Cape Cod National Seashore, 99 Marconi Site Road, Wellfleet, MA 02667, or telephone (508) 349-3785. You also can call the Salt Pond Visitor Center at (508) 255-3421. The park also maintains a Web site at www.nps.gov/caco.

FURTHER READING

Finch, Robert. *Common Ground: A Naturalist's Cape Cod.* Boston: D.R. Godine, 1981.

Schneider, Paul. *The Enduring Shore: A History of Cape Cod, Martha's Vineyard, and Nantucket.* New York: Henry Holt, 2000.

CAPE HATTERAS NATIONAL SEASHORE

Location: Manteo, North Carolina
Acreage: 30,321
Authorized: August 17, 1937

The perilous currents, shoals, and storms that characterize North Carolina's Outer Banks have earned the name Graveyard of the Atlantic; it is a grim, but fitting, epithet for the final resting place of more than 600 ships. At Coquina Beach, the remains of a quad-mast schooner stranded in 1921 are accessible to visitors. During World War II, German submarines sank so many Allied tankers and cargo ships off the coast that these treacherous waters earned a second sobering name—Torpedo Junction. Today, Cape Hatteras National Seashore stretches over 70 miles of barrier islands and provides a wealth of history relating to shipwrecks, lighthouses, and the U.S. Lifesaving Service. The nation's tallest lighthouse is also here—the 208-foot, black and white, barber-striped Cape Hatteras Lighthouse, built in 1870. The park's beaches, marshlands, dunes, and woodlands sustain diverse wildlife and are a valuable wintering area for migrating waterfowl.

Cape Hatteras's rich human history includes the mysterious fate of the first English settlement in North America—Roanoke. The Roanoke settlement was to be Walter Raleigh's financial coup. An exploratory expedition in 1584 indicated that local Algonquian peoples, who enjoyed prosperity from hunting, fishing, and agriculture, were interested in an alliance with the English. The following year, then, Raleigh sent an all-male envoy to found Roanoke colony. But Raleigh, like most of his European successors, never intended to establish an equitable partnership with the native people. He anticipated that his colonial investment would return profits via a lucrative fur trade, flourishing agriculture, or, best of all, mines of silver and gold. The Native Americans would provide the labor. Raleigh's soldiers and adventurers made poor colonists and neighbors; their inability to feed and house themselves meant they simply drained the resources of the Algonquians. Before the natives could retaliate, Raleigh's men instigated hostilities, killing several Roanoke leaders, and then returning to England. In 1587, Raleigh arranged for a new, family-oriented colony to settle on Roanoke, but they could not overcome the legacy of violence and hatred left by their predecessors. Three years later, when English ships sailed through Hatteras Inlet to Roanoke Island, they found the settlement destroyed and the colonists gone. The English settlers of Roanoke became known as the Lost Colony, their disappearance and ultimate fate one of the enduring mysteries of colonial history.

Although authorized in 1937 as the nation's first national seashore, Cape Hatteras was not officially established until June 1953. Ignored from the 1930s by the state of North Carolina, a partner in the project, because of the potential for oil drilling, the project came to life in 1952 after a $618,000 donation from

Once dubbed the "Graveyard of the Atlantic" because of its treacherous currents, shoals, and storms, Cape Hatteras National Seashore has a wealth of history relating to shipwrecks, lighthouses, and the U.S. Lifesaving Service. The Cape Hatteras Lighthouse is the tallest in the nation. *(National Park Service)*

the Avalon Foundation and the Old Dominion Foundation. North Carolina matched the donation, and the Park Service was able to acquire much of the land. The state also contributed a gift of 6,490 acres, which, when combined with the 5,880 acres of the Pea Island National Wildlife Refuge that were attached to the project, made the seashore large enough to conform to the congressional minimum of 10,000 acres in the 1937 legislation. By 1956, the Park Service owned or controlled 25,000 acres of the 28,500 it anticipated for the lakeshore, and formal establishment took place. Two years later, the two foundations again gave money to finish land acquisition.

At its establishment, Cape Hatteras National Seashore was an anomaly. It preceded

general federal interest in lakeshores and seashores and, as a result, served as a model for the expansion of federal holdings along coastlines in the 1950s and 1960s. As the first national seashore, it holds an important role in the park system today.

The park is open year-round, with no entrance fee. Its fishing and surfing are considered the best on the East Coast. The park operates 3 concession fishing piers, located in the villages of Rodanthe, Avon, and Frisco. The Oregon Inlet Fishing Marina, another park concession, provides charter boat fishing, gear, and supplies, also for a fee. There are numerous short trails in the park, as well as long stretches of pristine beach, although off-road vehicle access is permitted in several areas. Three visitor centers contain information and exhibits on the seashore. The Hatteras Island Visitor Center, located at the Cape Hatteras Lighthouse in Buxton is open from 9 A.M. to 5 P.M. daily, and the Bodie Island and Ocracoke Island visitor centers are open seasonally. Throughout the summer, park rangers present interpretive activities, including a wide range of history, natural resource, and recreational programs.

There are 3 major accesses to the seashore. From the north, North Carolina Highway 158 accesses the Outer Banks at Kitty Hawk, and then intersects North Carolina Highway 12 (the only road that runs through the park) at the park's northern entrance below Nags Head. U.S. Highway 64 comes in from the west at Roanoke Island, and also intersects North Carolina Highway 12 at the park's northern entrance. State-operated toll ferries access the park's southern entrance at Ocracoke Island from Cedar Island or Swan Quarter; call (800) BY-FERRY for information.

The park currently operates 4 improved campgrounds open from Memorial Day to Labor Day. Lodging and other traveler services are available in all nearby villages and towns.

For more information, write Cape Hatteras National Seashore, Route 1, Box 675, Manteo, NC 27954, or telephone (252) 473-2111. The informative Cape Hatteras Web site is www.nps.gov/caha. Birders may also wish to consult the checklist posted at www.npwrc.usgs.gov/resource/othrdata/chekbird/r4/pealand.htm.

FURTHER READING

Carr, Dawson. *The Cape Hatteras Lighthouse: Sentinel of the Shoals.* Chapel Hill: University of North Carolina Press, 2000.

Kupperman, Karen Ordahl. *Roanoke: The Abandoned Colony.* Totowa, NJ: Rowman & Allanheld, 1984.

Miller, Lee. *Roanoke: Solving the Mystery of the Lost Colony.* New York: Arcade, 2001.

Torres, Louis. *Historic Resource Study of Cape Hatteras National Seashore.* Denver, CO: National Park Service, 1985.

Wallace, David H. *Little Kinnakeet Life-Saving Station (1874–1915)/Coast Guard Station (1915–1954), Cape Hatteras National Seashore, North Carolina.* Harpers Ferry, WV: National Park Service, 1991.

CAPE LOOKOUT NATIONAL SEASHORE

Location: Harkers Island, North Carolina
Acreage: 28,243
Established: March 10, 1966

Cape Lookout National Seashore is a 56-mile-long stretch of North Carolina's Outer Banks, one of the few remaining natural coastal barrier island systems in the world. Constantly buffeted by winds, rains, waves, and currents, this seemingly barren and isolated chain of 3 islands is mostly sandy beaches and dunes covered by thin grasses, though thicker grasslands and salt marshes endure on the western reaches. Yet the park is an ecological wonder. These narrow strips of land harbor numerous endangered species, and the park's native grasslands comprise the only remaining natural grasslands in the eastern United States. To preserve the islands' sensitive natural environment and ecosystems, the park enforces seasonal closures for nesting birds and sea turtles. The seashore marks the northernmost range of the loggerhead turtle, a marine turtle on the federal list of endangered species. The endangered piping plover also calls Cape Lookout home, as do bald eagles, peregrine falcons, and roseate terns. These endangered species share the islands with more than 100 wild horses.

Authorized in March 1966, the seashore reflected a change in federal emphasis about coastal preservation. Until the postwar eras, the government had been lax about preserving seashores and lakeshores; the first such efforts began during the 1930s, more than a half century after the establishment of Yellowstone National Park, and by the late 1950s, only one area, Cape Hatteras in North Carolina, had been established. The growth of American cities between the 1930s and the 1950s put tremendous pressure on shorelines and lakeshores, which seemed likely to become privately owned and off-limits to most of the American public. After the publication of *Our Vanishing Shoreline*, a 1955 Park Service survey sponsored by the Mellon family, impetus for the establishment of national seashores and lakeshores gained momentum. When Congress established the Outdoor Recreation Resources Review Commission (ORRRC) in 1958, the Park Service embarked upon a comprehensive program to evaluate shoreline resources and produced three additional surveys, *A Report on the Seashore Recreation Survey of the Atlantic and Gulf Coasts, Our Fourth Shore: Great Lakes Shoreline Recreation Area Survey*, and *Pacific Coast Recreation Area Survey*. The interest spurred others to action, and in 1959, U.S. Senator Richard Neuberger of Oregon, a longtime conservation advocate, proposed the authorization of ten national shoreline recreation areas, a new and confusing designation to add to the plethora of names that already existed for national park areas. Cape Lookout was established in part as a response to these conditions.

The seashore remains largely undeveloped and most visitors enjoy the park on foot. Hikers will appreciate the essentially trailless nature of Cape Lookout, which allows unlimited exploration across the dunes and along the open beach face. It is an excellent place to explore for shells. Although there are no roads on the seashore, personal four-wheel-drive and all-terrain vehicles are allowed; bicycles and motorcycles are not permitted. The park's only trail provides a self-guided tour of Portsmouth Village, a ghost town built in 1753, but long since abandoned. The Cape Lookout Lighthouse also merits a visit. Built in 1869, the lighthouse is still in operation, and thus is closed to the public, but the adjacent Lighthouse Keeper's Quarters is open seasonally as a visitor center. The park op-

erates 2 additional visitor centers on Harkers Island and in Portsmouth Village. Privately operated beach shuttle services are available to facilitate visitor access to more remote areas of the park. There is no entrance fee.

Cape Lookout National Seashore is accessible only by personal boat or private ferry (some carry vehicles) leaving from Harkers Island, Davis, Atlantic, Beaufort, Morehead City, and Ocracoke. Private ferry service to the park is offered from mid-March to the first weekend in December; the park is accessible by personal boat year-round. Visitation is lowest in January and February and highest in the fall, particularly in October and November, though summers are busy as well. Winter temperatures can dip below freezing, but fall and spring are generally mild. Summers are warm and humid, and biting insects necessitate the use of bug repellent. Rainy periods occur throughout the year, and hurricane season is June through November.

The park offers very little shade or shelter and no sources for supplies, and there is no developed lodging or food service. Camping opportunities are free, yet primitive—no water, toilet, or other amenities. All water must be carried in, trash must be carried out, and campers are advised to take portable radios to keep current on rapidly changing weather conditions. Primitive cabin rentals are available from mid-March to the first weekend in December on 2 of the islands. These cabins have hot and cold water, gas stoves, no refrigerators, and no linens. Nearby towns and villages on the mainland offer all travel services.

For more information, write Cape Lookout National Seashore, 131 Charles Street, Harkers Island, NC 28531, or telephone (252) 728-2250. The park maintains an informative Web site at www.nps.gov/calo.

FURTHER READING

Olson, Sarah. *Portsmouth Village, Cape Lookout National Seashore, North Carolina.* Denver, CO: National Park Service, 1982.

Rankin, Hugh F. *The Pirates of Colonial North Carolina.* Raleigh, NC: State Department of Archives and History, 1965.

CAPITOL REEF NATIONAL PARK

Location: Torrey, Utah
Acreage: 241,904
Established: August 2, 1937

Capitol Reef National Park, located in southern Utah, is named for the unusual geological formations that dominate the area. "Capitol" refers to the rounded white Navajo sandstone found in the park's northern reaches that resemble the Capitol's dome in Washington, D.C., while "Reef" was coined by Mormon explorers and prospectors as an obstacle to travel. These early visitors were no doubt referring to the park's main natural feature, the Waterpocket Fold, a 100-mile-long wrinkle in the earth's crust known to geologists as a monocline. Over millions of years, wind and water erosion shaped this land, once covered by a shallow sea. As the sea retreated, the landscape shifted from flood plain to desert. Assorted sediments deposited by wind and water over the millennia gradually hardened into the colorful, varied shapes seen today. Immense geological forces tilted and buckled the rock formations into the "upwarp" of Waterpocket Fold, while erosion sculpted the fold's steeply pitched rock layers and canyons. Extending from Thousand Lakes Mountain to Lake Powell, the fold allows visitors to view the vertical stratigraphy of 200 million years of geologic history.

The 241,904-acre Capitol Reef National Park protects this grand and colorful geologic feature, as well as the cultural history that abounds in the area. The Fruita district, in the narrow park's northern regions near headquarters, was the most populated. Compared with the desert-like starkness of the surrounding area, the Fruita district is lush and green. Fruita was the first area to be settled, initially by the native people during the ninth century. These people—called the Fremont Culture by archeologists—were contemporaries of the pueblo-building Anasazi of the Four Corners area but were less advanced. In the thirteenth century, all native cultures in this area underwent sudden change; Fremont settlements and fields were abandoned and these hunter-farmers simply disappeared. By the eighteenth century, Ute and Southern Paiute peoples subsisted as hunter-gatherers in the region.

During the 1880s Mormon settlers moved into the area and developed an irrigation system that drew water from the Fremont River and Sulphur Creek, and turned the area into a valley of green among the scrub and sage desert. Difficult to reach, the Fruita district remained isolated until the mid-twentieth century. The first mechanized tractor was not brought into the area until after World War II. The restored old Fruita schoolhouse, built in the early 1900s, is an artifact from this era of settlement, as are the over 2,000 fruit trees that grow in the region.

Capitol Reef's early champion was Ephraim Porter Pectol, born in 1875, who served as Mormon bishop in nearby Torrey from 1911 until 1928. Pectol was sensitive to the rugged beauty of the Capitol Reef area and was an avid Fremont culture relic hunter. In 1921, eager for the "outside world" to appreciate the beauty of the reef, Pectol organized a "Boosters Club," furnishing stories and photos to periodicals and newspapers. By 1924, his efforts led to the organization of a Wayne County–wide "Wayne Wonderland Club." In 1933, Pectol was elected to the legislature and almost immediately contacted President Franklin D. Roosevelt and asked for the creation of "Wayne Wonderland National Monument" out of the federal lands comprising the bulk of the Capitol Reef area. While federal agencies conducted a feasibility study and boundary assessment, Pectol not only guided government investigators on numerous trips, but escorted an increasing number of visitors. Finally, on August 2, 1937, President Roosevelt signed a proclamation creating Capitol Reef National Monument. During the 1960s, the Park Service used money from the Land and Water Conservation Fund to purchase private land parcels at Fruita and Pleasant Creek, and almost all private property passed into public ownership on a "willing buyer–willing seller" basis. In 1971, President Nixon signed legislation creating Capitol Reef National Park.

Today, Capitol Reef is a haven for backcountry hiking. Many trails are available for people of all abilities and time constraints. The park also has a number of scenic roadways, many of them unpaved, that can be taken to all corners of the park. One notable road is the graded-dirt Notom-Bullfrog Road, which runs parallel to the spectacular Waterpocket Fold from Utah Highway 24 all the way to Lake Powell's Bullfrog Marina. Travelers should contact the visitor center about road conditions and trail information. Capitol Reef is subject to flash floods from late June through early October.

The Fruita orchards–all owned by the National Park Service–are maintained at a level of about 2,500 trees, with 1,800 in production. Management of the orchards, especially during picking season, presents some difficult problems to resolve. Because the trees were originally planted in smallish family orchards–each with a wide variety of fruit–fruit ripens in many "mini-orchards" at varying times. However, as the trees age, horticultural workers have slowly replaced the patchwork quilt–like layout of the orchards with a more orderly arrangement consisting of large tracts of monocultures–all peaches in one large orchard, all apricots in another large orchard, and so on. In this way, the gross aspect of the "historic landscape" is maintained but the fruit harvest is much easier to manage. Sea-sonally, visitors can pick free fruit from the orchards, which include cherries, apricots, apples, pears, and peaches.

Capitol Reef National Park is located in southcentral Utah, 30 miles west of Hanksville. The park is open year-round. The visitor center is open daily (except Christmas) from 8 A.M. to 4:30 P.M., with extended hours during the summer season. The fee for entering the scenic drive is $4; there is no charge for this drive for holders of Golden Eagle, Golden Age, or Golden Access passes. Approximately 706,000 visitors see the park each year, mostly between April and October. Visitation is the highest from April through June and in September and October, and lowest in January. The climate is hot in the summer, and mild the rest of the year, with cool winters and little snow.

The park's sole developed campground is the 70-site Fruita Campground, which adjoins the Fremont River. Fees are $10 per night, and sites are available on a first-come, first-served basis. Because it is such a beautiful campground, it fills quickly. The group campground is $3 per person per night with a minimum charge of $50; reservations are required. Cedar Mesa and Cathedral Valley have free primitive campgrounds, and there are national forest campgrounds on the Boulder Plateau, immediately west of the park. There is no lodging or food service in the park. The nearby towns of Hanksville, Loa, and Torrey offer all traveler services, including gas, food, and small motels.

For more information, write Capitol Reef National Park, HC 70 Box 15, Torrey, UT 84775, or telephone (435) 425-3791. The park's thorough Web site is www. nps.gov/care.

FURTHER READING

Davidson, George E. *Red Rock Eden: The Story of Fruita.* Torrey, UT: Capitol Reef National History Association, 1986.

Gilbert, Cathy. *Cultural Landscape Report: Fruita Rural Historic District, Capitol Reef National Park.* Denver,

CO: National Park Service, Intermountain Region, 1997.

CAPULIN VOLCANO NATIONAL MONUMENT
Location: Capulin, New Mexico
Acreage: 793
Established: August 9, 1916

A dark, stark, symmetrical cone on an otherwise-flat landscape, the extinct Capulin Volcano rises more than 1,200 feet above the surrounding High Plains of northeastern New Mexico. Capulin—Spanish for chokecherry—Volcano's last eruption occurred approximately sixty thousand years ago in a sensational explosion that sent "rooster tails" of glowing hot cinders flying through the air. Lava that flowed from fissure vents located at the volcano's flanks covered almost 16 square miles. Long a visual landmark for Native Americans, travelers, and explorers, the cone's pinyon-juniper forested slopes today provide an important habitat for mule deer, wild turkey, black bear, and other wildlife.

The park was established in 1916, and its proclamation stems from a time when federal employees prowled the public domain in search of scientific, natural, and other oddities to include in the nascent park system. That the volcano was on public land only made the task easier, as the Antiquities Act of 1906 allowed the monument's establishment with the mere signing of an order. Yet establishment did not guarantee development, and even now Capulin Volcano National Monument remains far from the main patterns of national park visitation.

The 793-acre park preserves this striking example of a young cinder cone—a dramatic testament to the volcanic processes that shaped northeastern New Mexico. The spiraling, 2-mile paved road to the rim makes it one of the most accessible volcanoes in the world. The panoramic view from Capulin Volcano encompasses four states, numerous volcanoes, and beautiful countryside. In late June and July, a profusion of wildflowers adorns the mountain, and hikers may encounter swarms of ladybugs along the crater rim. Trails leading around the rim and to the bottom of the crater allow a rare opportunity to easily explore a volcano. Unfortunately, as in many other of the nation's parks and monuments, tourist impact has been heavy. Illegal rock collecting has reached alarming levels, and crowded summer conditions often lead to delays along the Volcano Road. Each year more than 65,000 people visit the park, with peak visitation season occurring in July. Consider sightseeing on weekdays or in early morning or late afternoon in the summer to avoid congestion.

The Capulin Volcano Visitor Center contains exhibits about geology, natural history, and human history as well as a ten-minute video detailing Capulin's last eruption and the surrounding Raton-Clayton Volcanic Field. There is also a short nature trail adjacent to the visitor center. Elevations in the park range from approximately 7,000 feet to 8,182 feet on the crater rim. Summers are mild, with highs in the mid-80s. Thunderstorms are common in July and August. Winters are cold, and blizzards may result in temporary park closures.

The monument is located 33 miles east of Raton, New Mexico, via U.S. Highway 64/87 and 58 miles west of Clayton, New Mexico, via the same highway. The park entrance is off New Mexico Highway 325, 3 miles north of Capulin. I-25 connects Raton with Denver, Colorado, from the north and Albuquerque from the south. The entrance fee is $4 per private vehicle, and $2 per person on motorcycle. The monument is open daily. Winter hours (Labor Day to Memorial Day) are from 8 A.M. to 4 P.M., while summer hours (Memorial Day to Labor Day) are 7:30 A.M. to

6:30 P.M. The Volcano Road is closed after park hours except on Friday and Saturday nights during June, July, and August, when it remains open until sunset. Trailers, towed vehicles, bicycles, and pedestrians are prohibited on Volcano Road because it is narrow with no shoulders. Snow, ice accumulation, and severe thunderstorms can close the Volcano Road.

The park has no lodging or camping facilities and there are no food or travel services. Camping facilities are available nearby in the town of Capulin, 3 miles south of the park, and also at Sugarite Canyon State Park and Clayton Lake State Park. Des Moines, Clayton, and Raton, all provide lodging accommodations. The closest tourist services are in Capulin, 3 miles south of the park, and Des Moines, 13 miles east.

For more information, write Capulin Volcano National Monument, P.O. Box 40, Capulin, NM 88414, or telephone (505) 278-2201. The park's Web site is www.nps.gov/cavo.

FURTHER READING
Decker, Robert W. *Volcanoes in America's National Parks.* New York: W.W. Norton, 2001.
Parent, Laurence. *Capulin Volcano National Monument.* Tucson, AZ: Southwest Parks and Monuments Association, 1991.

CARL SANDBURG HOME NATIONAL HISTORIC SITE

Location: Flat Rock, North Carolina
Acreage: 264
Established: October 17, 1968

Carl Sandburg was the son of Swedish immigrants, born in the Land of Lincoln in 1878. His family was desperately poor, and Sandburg's education often suffered because of it. After serving in the Spanish-American War, at the turn of the century, Sandburg enrolled in Lombard College, in Illinois, although he never graduated. Soon, he was working as a reporter at the Chicago *Daily News*, and it was there that he began to write free-verse poetry. In 1916, he published *Chicago Poems*, which, among other themes, celebrated the city:

> Come and show me another city with
>   lifted head
> singing so proud to be
> alive and coarse and strong and
>   cunning.

A fine and gifted writer, Sandburg received the 1940 Pulitzer Prize in history for his passionate biography entitled *Abraham Lincoln: The War Years*, and the 1951 Pulitzer Prize in Literature for his *Complete Poems.* He is revered today as one of the giants of twentieth-century American culture.

In 1968, Congress set aside Connemara, the farm home of America's renowned poet-author for the last twenty-two years of his life, to pay tribute to this literary icon. The historic site is open from 9 A.M. until 5 P.M. daily. Thirty-minute home tours are offered from 9:30 A.M. until 4:30 P.M., and the fees are $3 for adults, with children sixteen and younger admitted free. Park rangers offer walks, talks, and programs throughout the summer celebrating Sandburg's life and works, information about Mrs. Sandburg's dairy goat operation, while dramatic productions of Sandburg's zany "Rootabaga Stories" and other serious works are also available.

There is no food or lodging available at the historic site, but all traveler services can be found in nearby Flat Rock and Hendersonville.

For more information, write Carl Sandburg Home National Historic Site, 81 Carl Sandburg Lane, Flat Rock, NC 28731-8635, or telephone (828) 693-4178. The park's Web site is www.nps.gov/carl.

FURTHER READING
Niven, Penelope. *Carl Sandburg: A Biography.* New York: Scribner's Sons, 1991.
Sandburg, Carl. *The Complete Poems of Carl Sandburg.* New York: Harcourt Brace Jovanovich, 1970.
——. *Abraham Lincoln: The Prairie Years and the War*

Years. San Diego, CA: Harcourt, Brace, Jovanovich, 1982.

Sandburg, Helga. *A Great and Glorious Romance: The Story of Carl Sandburg and Lilian Steichen.* New York: Harcourt Brace Jovanovich, 1978.

CARLSBAD CAVERNS NATIONAL PARK

Location: Carlsbad, New Mexico
Acreage: 46,766
Established: October 25, 1923

Early in the twentieth century, a small boom in guano (bat droppings) mining took place in southeastern New Mexico. Before synthesized fertilizer, guano was highly prized in agriculture, and mining it became a primary industry in the late nineteenth century–the subject of American diplomatic efforts and even imperialism. After the turn of the twentieth century, domestic sources of this natural fertilizer were also valued, and the porous caves beneath the Permian Uplift, an upthrusted reef from the Permian period of the Paleozoic Era, between 280 and 225 million years ago, housed millions of bats and yielded much of the prized material. Among the miners was a Texas cowboy named James Larkin "Jim" White, who had come to that part of New Mexico still known as "Little Texas" before he turned ten years old. In June 1901, White "worked his way through the rocks and brush until I found myself gazing into the biggest and blackest hole I had ever seen out of which the bats literally seemed to boil." White estimated the depth of the cave at 200 feet, watched the remaining bats depart, and returned to his camp.

Jim White likely was not the first to discover the so-called Bat Cave, but he was the first to regard it as more than a curiosity. When he first happened upon the area in 1898, it had been explored by people seeking economic opportunity. But apparently those who saw the bats earlier could not find the caves from which they sprang or simply did not appreciate the value of guano. Perhaps the muckiness of the material, and the idea of making a living from animal excrement, dissuaded others. White clearly believed he found something new and hid his find from others. Certainly, he took greater interest in the caves than any predecessor.

A few days later, White returned, again furtively, but far better equipped. He arrived at midafternoon with a kerosene lamp, several coils of rope, some wire, and a hand axe, and he proceeded to cut wood for a ladder. His companion this time was a young Mexican boy called "Muchacho" (kid or boy), the only one he knew with any interest in the cave. White lowered the completed ladder into the cave, climbed down, and found himself in complete darkness and silence. Lighting his lantern, he maneuvered down to the floor of an awesome space. "I could see ahead of me a darkness so black it seemed a solid," he later wrote. "The light of my lantern was a sickly glow." White forged onward into the network of caves, elated, terrified, awestruck, and oppressed by the silence and the darkness. To calm himself, he spoke aloud; the echoes nearly drove him mad. "Perhaps you can appreciate my sense of satisfaction when I wormed my way back and could see a shaft of sunlight filtering down through the entrance," White later recounted. Later, he felt relieved to be aboveground, somehow bested by the cave.

White anticipated the modern spelunker, attracted to the cave for compelling personal reasons. He returned with whoever would accompany him, making as thorough an exploration as the limits of lighting and his resources would permit. White approached the cave systematically, telling about what he encountered. Many felt that he invented the existence of the cave or at least profoundly exaggerated its size and depth. White actively

King's chamber, Carlsbad Caverns National Park, 1926. *(Library of Congress)*

wanted to persuade everyone of the importance of the cave.

White became the person most closely associated with the bat caves, the tour guide, operator, and manager of the nascent tourist industry that began at the turn of the twentieth century. Title to the land remained in public hands, and White never tried to claim it. He soon offered visitors minuscule comforts, but his operation was not sophisticated. Visitors descended in an old guano bucket. On angular ascents and descents, White pounded discarded automobile axles—usually from Fords, he boasted—into the cracks in the rocks and strung them with galvanized wire to create handholds. Everything about a trip to the caverns was idiosyncratic, typical of the

way life was often held together with baling wire on the peripheries of the nation.

From White's endeavor came first a national monument, then in 1930 a national park, which soon became one of the wonders of the American continent, a place that everyone had to see. Carlsbad Caverns became central to the self-image of the nation at mid-century, a place that people visited to demonstrate their membership in the growing American middle class with its opportunities for travel and leisure. This feeling inaugurated a long-standing tradition of the acquisition of status by bumper sticker, and the subsequent two generations of the American middle class felt incomplete if they lacked a "We Visited Carlsbad Caverns" bumper sticker on their vehicle. In this respect, Carlsbad Caverns became more than a national park; it became an important symbol of American aspirations.

Since 1980, changing travel patterns have curtailed the growth in visitation at the park, as fewer people will venture the more than two-and-one-half-hour drive from I-40 to see the caverns. As Americans and American culture changed, as it became obsessed with MTV and popular attractions, the appeal of Carlsbad Caverns diminished to generations raised on video images that move at the rate of twelve images each second. The park retains a wide constituency, including specialty groups such as cavers and others, but it no longer represents a widely held aspiration of middle-class American society. It is still unique, still beautiful and impressive, but its message has been muted by the cultural obsession with experience.

Facilities at the park are limited to a few aboveground picnic tables at the visitor center and an underground rest area in the cave. All visitor services are available nearby in Carlsbad, New Mexico.

For more information, write Carlsbad Caverns National Park, 3225 National Parks Highway, Carlsbad, NM 88220, or telephone (505) 785-2232. The park's Web site is www.nps.gov/cave.

FURTHER READING
Geluso, Kenneth N., Ronal C. Kerbo, and J. Scott Altenbach. *Bats of Carlsbad Caverns National Park.* Carlsbad, NM: Carlsbad Caverns Natural History Association, 1996.
Hill, Carol A. *Geology of Carlsbad Cavern and Other Caves in the Guadalupe Mountains, New Mexico and Texas.* Socorro: New Mexico Bureau of Mines & Mineral Resources, 1987.
Nymeyer, Robert, and William R. Halliday. *Carlsbad Cavern: The Early Years.* Carlsbad, NM: Carlsbad Caverns, Guadalupe Mountains Association, 1991.
Rothman, Hal K. "Promise Beheld and the Limits of Place: A Historic Resource Study of Carlsbad Caverns and Guadalupe Mountains National Parks and the Surrounding Areas." Washington, DC: National Park Service, 1998.
Stewart, John. *Secret of the Bats: The Exploration of Carlsbad Caverns.* Philadelphia, PA: Westminster, 1972.

CASA GRANDE RUINS NATIONAL MONUMENT
Location: Coolidge, Arizona
Acreage: 473
Established: March 2, 1892

For more than a millennia, prehistoric Hohokam farmers inhabited much of present-day southcentral Arizona. But by the time that the first Europeans arrived, all that remained of this ancient culture were buildings in ruins, dried-up irrigation canals, and intriguing artifacts.

Most prominent among these ancient ruins is the huge Casa Grande, or "Big House," one of the largest and most mysterious prehistoric structures ever built in North America. Casa Grande Ruins, established in 1892 as the nation's first archeological preserve, protects the Casa Grande and other archeological sites within its boundaries.

Casa Grande is located in the Gila River Valley, extensively farmed by these prehistoric Hohokam Indians. To help grow their crops of cotton, corn, beans, and squash, the Hohokam constructed over 1,000 miles of irrigation canals measuring about 8 to 10 feet in width and 7 to 10 feet in depth. About six hundred and fifty years ago, these Gila Valley farmers built the four-story Casa Grande; used only for a relatively short period, it was abandoned by the mid-1400s. When the Jesuit priest Father Eusebio Kino discovered the house in 1694, he gave it the Spanish name that it carries to this day.

Casa Grande has the distinction of being the first prehistoric ruin ever preserved by the U.S. government. After an outcry from explorers and archeologists, in 1892, Congress proclaimed the Casa Grande Ruins Reservation, the first and only example of its kind. After the passage of the Antiquities Act in

1906, the national monument category seemed a better location for the ruins. In 1918, it became Casa Grande Ruins National Monument.

During the 1920s and 1930s, Casa Grande was home to Frank "Boss" Pinkley, who headed the southwestern national monuments groups for the Park Service. Iconoclastic and committed, Pinkley became one of the great protectors of southwestern prehistory. An organizational genius, he forged the people who worked in national monuments—called "custodians" in that era—into a vital, professional force that savored the opportunity to teach the public and protect prehistoric resources. When Pinkley died in 1940, his work had laid the basis for the long-term preservation of prehistory in the federal system.

The monument is open year-round from 8 A.M. to 5 P.M., and is closed December 25. It is located in Coolidge, Arizona, about an hour's drive from either Phoenix or Tucson. From I-10 take the Coolidge exit and follow the signs to the park entrance off Arizona Highway 87/287. Entrance fees are $2 per person, with a maximum of $4 per car; children sixteen and under are admitted free. Casa Grande receives about 165,000 visitors per year. The highest visitation occurs in the cooler months from Thanksgiving through Easter; the lowest is in the sometimes brutally hot summer season from May through September.

The visitor center contains an information counter, a museum exhibit area with Hohokam artifacts, a book store, rest rooms, and drinking fountains. The monument is fully accessible with level paved and packed-dirt surfaces. From the visitor center, there is a 300-yard, self-guided walking trail around the ruins with wayside signs. Regularly scheduled guided tours are held from January through April, while advance-request guided tours are provided for school and tour groups during the rest of the year, depending on staff availability.

There are no lodging, food, or camping facilities at the monument; however, all travel services are available in nearby Coolidge and the surrounding area.

For more information, write the Casa Grande Ruins National Monument, 1100 Ruins Drive, Coolidge, AZ 85228, or telephone (520) 723-3172. The park's Web site is www.nps.gov/cagr.

FURTHER READING
Clemensen, A. Berle. *Casa Grande Ruins National Monument, Arizona: A Centennial History of the First Prehistoric Reserve, 1892–1992.* Coolidge, AZ: National Park Service, 1992.

Houk, Rose. *Casa Grande Ruins National Monument.* Tucson, AZ: Southwest Parks and Monuments Association, 1996.

CASTILLO DE SAN MARCOS NATIONAL MONUMENT
Location: St. Augustine, Florida
Acreage: 20
Established: October 15, 1924

For years, Florida's Castillo de San Marcos demarcated the northernmost outpost of Spain's vast New World empire. Built between 1672 and 1695, this garrison defended the colonial town of St. Augustine, the oldest continuously occupied European settlement in the continental United States. Though not the first fort built by the Spanish, the Castillo was the most formidable; its nine predecessors were all made of wood. A pirate attack on St. Augustine in 1668 convinced the Queen Regent Mariana that only a masonry fort could adequately defend the city and the port. The 1670 founding of British Charles Town (Charleston), less than a two-day sail from St. Augustine, further hastened construction. Originally surrounded by a moat, the massive square-shaped fort contained guardrooms, storage rooms, a chapel, a central courtyard—the *plaza de armas*—and diamond-shaped bastions at each corner. Engineers utilized a local limestone called "coquina"—little shells—for the fort's walls, and in 1702, when the British laid siege to the city, the coquina walls proved impenetrable. The Castillo's strategic location also protected Spain's primary trade route to Europe and the Bahama Channel, today known as the Gulf Stream. In 1821, Spain ceded the fort to the United States, which changed the name to Fort Marion. During its long history, the Castillo has served a number of nations, but it has never been taken by force.

The Spanish founded St. Augustine in 1565, and the heart of the city retains the distinctive design of a sixteenth-century Spanish colonial walled town. St. Augustine's historic district presents an impressive array of period architecture dating from 1703 to 1821. The city is also the site of the oldest African American settlement in the United States. During the sixteenth, seventeenth, and eighteenth centuries, free blacks and slaves found Florida, and St. Augustine in particular, a haven, since the Spanish Crown granted refuge to blacks if they embraced Catholicism. In the late nineteenth century, railroad tycoon and former Standard Oil partner Henry Flagler built the 540-room Ponce de Leon Hotel in St. Augustine. The lavish accommodations soon attracted such notables as the Vanderbilts, Rockefellers, and Morgans, and put Florida on the map as a winter tourist destination.

Initially designated as Fort Marion National Monument in 1924, the 20-acre park, consisting primarily of the Castillo itself and

Castillo de San Marcos National Monument. Throughout its history, the Castillo has never been taken by military force. *(National Park Service)*

its surrounding grounds, was among the first historic places in the national park system. Its proclamation in 1924 gave the Park Service a piece of national history, albeit not exactly what the public regarded as mainstream history. Yet the creation of Fort Marion National Monument provided one of the main starts in the long road to the preservation of American history in the park system. The park was changed to its present name in 1942.

Although the park has no visitor center, it maintains museum exhibits on the premises, and visitors can take a self-guided tour. The Castillo also offers living history events and regularly scheduled ranger programs and junior ranger programs year-round. The Castillo de San Marcos is open to the public from 8:45 A.M. to 4:45 P.M. every day except Christmas Day. Admission fees are $4 for adults, while children sixteen and under are admitted free when accompanied by an adult; senior citizens who hold a National Park Service Golden Age Pass are admitted free. Visitation is highest from July through early September and in December and January, and lowest from the middle of September through early December. Summers can be very hot with high humidity, with afternoon thundershowers highly possible. Winters can be very cool, with possible sudden cold snaps.

Visitors traveling east to west on I-10 should take I-295 or I-95 south and take the St. Augustine Historic Downtown exit. Those traveling north to south on I-95, U.S. Highway 1, or A1A, should make their way into downtown St. Augustine, where the Castillo de San Marcos is located at the bay front, just north of the Bridge of Lions. There is no lodging, food, or camping in the monument, but St. Augustine has all travel services. Developed campsites are available at Anastasia State Park, a short drive south of town on Route A1A. Fishing is allowed from the monument's seawall with a valid saltwater license.

For more information, write Castillo de San Marcos National Monument, One South Castillo Drive, St. Augustine, FL 32084, or telephone (904) 829-6506. The park's Web site is www.nps.gov/casa.

FURTHER READING
Brown, Jennifer D. *Castillo de San Marcos National Monument Historic Resource Study.* Atlanta, GA: National Park Service, 1997. Available at www.nps.gov/casa/hrs/hrs.htm.

Krako, Jere L. *Administrative History of Castillo de San Marcos National Monument and Fort Matanzas National Monument.* Washington, DC: National Park Service, 1986.

Skinner, Woodward B. *The Apache Rock Crumbles: The Captivity of Geronimo's People.* Pensacola, FL: Skinner, 1987.

CASTLE CLINTON NATIONAL MONUMENT
Location: New York, New York
Acreage: 1
Established: August 12, 1946

As a response to increasingly hostile relations between the new nation and European powers prior to the War of 1812, the United States built more than a dozen forts to defend valuable New York Harbor. The Southwest Battery, built between 1808 and 1811, occupied the southern tip of Manhattan Island. Although fully armed and staffed, the fort never fired upon the enemy. After the war, in 1817, the fort was renamed Castle Clinton in honor of New York City Mayor DeWitt Clinton, James Madison's Federalist presidential rival in 1812. Tall, handsome, and somewhat arrogant, Clinton swept into the mayor's office on a tide of popularity generated by his promotion of a statewide canal. The result was the Erie Canal, the most ambitious and successful canal project of the era. Linking New York to the Great Lakes, the 364-mile-long Erie Canal—also derisively called Clinton's ditch—was completed in October 1825. By 1830, the canal carried 50,000 passengers, most of whom journeyed west to the rich farmland of Indiana, Illinois, and territories farther west.

In 1821, the army vacated the fort and deeded it to the city. Three years later, in 1824, a new restaurant and entertainment center opened at the site, now called Castle Garden. Following the addition of a roof in the 1840s, Castle Garden served as an opera house and theater until 1854. In August 1855, the state of New York obtained the Castle Garden lease and operated the facility as an immigrant landing depot. Over the next three and a half decades, more than 8 million people, mostly from Northern and Western Europe, entered the United States through Castle Garden. These early immigrants came from nations such as England, Ireland, Germany, and the Scandinavian countries and constituted the first large wave of immigrants that settled and populated the United States. Throughout the 1800s and intensifying in the latter half of the nineteenth century, ensuing political instability, restrictive religious laws, and deteriorating economic conditions in Europe began to fuel the largest mass human migration in the history of the world. It soon became apparent that Castle Garden was ill-equipped and unprepared to handle the growing numbers of immigrants arriving yearly. In 1890, the federal government intervened and constructed a new immigration station on Ellis Island. Castle Clinton was renovated once again and reopened as the New York City Aquarium on December 10, 1896. It was one of the city's most popular attractions until it closed in 1941. Finally, in August 1946, President Harry S Truman authorized the single-acre Castle Clinton as a national monument. A small museum detailing the history of the structure is located on the site. Ranger-led programs and tours are offered throughout the day and costumed interpreters describe the harbor defenses of New York City during the War of 1812.

Castle Clinton is located in Battery Park at the southern tip of Manhattan; admission, tours, and programs are free. It is open from 8:30 A.M. to 5 P.M. daily except Christmas. Nearly 3 million people visit the monument every year; visitation peaks in July and August, and is lowest in the winter. Driving to the monument is not recommended. Parking in downtown Manhattan is extremely limited and very expensive. The use of taxi or mass transit is suggested: Seventh Avenue #1 and #9 subway trains stop at South Ferry station in Battery Park. Lexington Avenue #4 and #5 subway trains stop at Bowling Green station adjacent to Battery Park; N and R subway trains stop at Whitehall Street station adjacent to Battery Park. Frequent service is provided on all lines twenty-four hours a day, seven days a week. Bus service to South Ferry is via the M-6 route, operating on Broadway seven days a week; the M-1 route, operating on Fifth Avenue, Park Avenue, and Broadway Monday through Friday; and the M-15 route, operating on Second Avenue twenty-four hours a day, seven days a week.

There is no food, camping, or lodging in the park. Abundant lodging and traveler facilities are available throughout New York City and its suburbs. Light refreshments are available from Battery Park vendors. Food and dining facilities are available in the immediate neighborhood.

For more information, write Castle Clinton National Monument, 26 Wall Street, New York, NY 10005, or telephone (212) 344-7220. The park's Web site is www. nps.gov/cacl.

FURTHER READING
Burrows, Evan G., and Mike Wallace. *Gotham: A History of New York to 1898.* New York: Oxford University Press, 1998.

Cornog, Evan. *The Birth of Empire: DeWitt Clinton and the American Experience, 1769–1828*. New York: Oxford University Press, 1998.

Shaw, Ronald E. *Erie Water West: A History of the Erie Canal, 1792–1854*. Lexington: University Press of Kentucky, 1990.

CATOCTIN MOUNTAIN PARK

Location: Thurmont, Maryland
Acreage: 5,810
Established: November 14, 1936

In 1936, the federal government purchased a badly depleted 10,000-acre tract of land in northern Maryland's Monocacy River Valley. Decades of misuse had rendered this once-vibrant forest nearly barren. Though farming had certainly taken a toll on the land, the production of iron ore wreaked a far greater havoc on the natural environment. The region's forests would fire the nation's nascent industrial revolution by providing charcoal to the Catoctin Iron Furnace. While this flourishing enterprise of the late nineteenth century employed hundreds of woodcutters, it also denuded the natural landscape. It took a cord of wood to manufacture six bushels of charcoal, at a cost of approximately eighty bushels of charcoal for every ton of iron manufactured. When the Catoctin Furnace closed in 1903, it left devastation in its wake.

In the 1930s, Conrad L. Wirth, assistant director of the National Park Service, proposed a program to buy land near metro-

Visitors come to Catoctin Mountain Park for camping, fishing, 25 miles of hiking trails, and scenic mountain vistas. *(National Park Service)*

politan areas no longer suitable for agriculture, in order to "provide quality outdoor recreation facilities at the lowest cost for the benefit of people of lower and middle incomes." In 1936, with the goal of creating a productive recreation area, the government brought in workers from the Works Progress Administration (WPA) and the Civilian Conservation Corps (CCC) to rehabilitate the land. Known as the Catoctin Recreational Demonstration Area—jointly managed by the National Park Service and the Maryland Park Service—the project was originally designed to provide recreational camps for federal employees. Eventually, one of the camps became the presidential retreat, Camp David. The CCC's vigorous revegitation program utilized new ideas in agriculture, such as contour planting, to revitalize the worn-out soil, control forest encroachment, restore native species of flora and fauna, and reclaim old logging roads. The CCC also instigated numerous stream-improvement projects along Big Hunting Creek and Owens Creek. Pools were deepened to provide cool water and cover for the fish, which in turn revived moribund sport angling. Over time, these CCC measures helped nature reclaim 800 acres of the area, before the program wound down in 1940 and 1941. In 1954, 5,770 acres were set aside as Catoctin Mountain Park. The preserve protects an area of deciduous hardwood forest approximately 65 miles northwest of Washington, D.C., along an eastern ridge of the Appalachian Mountains.

The park has over 25 miles of hiking trails, with scenic overlooks situated an easy half-mile walk from parking areas. In the summer, visitors can also rock climb (permit required), fish, picnic, and view wildflowers and wildlife. In the winter, Park Central Road, the main road through the park, is closed, as is part of the Manahan Road; however, these closures provide excellent cross-country skiing opportunities.

There is no entrance fee to Catoctin Mountain Park. The park is open year-round during daylight hours, although Camp David is closed to the public. Peak park visitation is in October, when fall colors are at their best, while winter months are considered the low season. Summers are warm and humid, and winters are generally cold and very snowy. The visitor center, which has an exhibit area and a book sales outlet, is open Monday through Thursday, 10 A.M to 4:30 P.M.; Friday, 10 A.M. to 5 P.M.; Saturday and Sunday, 8:30 A.M. to 5 P.M.; it is closed on winter federal holidays and occasional winter days.

Within the park, campers can choose between the Owens Creek Campground, which offers 51 sites on a first-come, first-served basis for $12 per night per site, and the Poplar Grove Youth Group Campground, which is $15 per night per site, for up to 25 people. Catoctin visitors may also rent individual cabins at Camp Misty Mount, starting at $40 per night. There is a seasonal concession facility in Cunningham Falls State Park, as well as additional camping opportunities. Food and limited supplies are available locally in the town of Thurmont.

For more information, write Catoctin Mountain Park, 6602 Foxville Road, Thurmont, MD 21788-1598, or telephone (301) 663-9330 or (301) 663-9388. The park's Web site is www.nps.gov/cato.

FURTHER READING

Nelson, W. Dale. *The President Is at Camp David.* Syracuse, NY: Syracuse University Press, 1995.
Strain, Paula M. *The Blue Hills of Maryland: History Along the Appalachian Trail on South Mountain and the Catoctins.* Vienna, VA: Potomac Appalachian Trail Club, 1993.

CEDAR BREAKS NATIONAL MONUMENT

Location: Cedar City, Utah
Acreage: 6,155
Established: August 22, 1933

Over the last 55 million years, a huge, multicolored natural amphitheater was carved out of the Pink Cliffs east of Cedar City, Utah. The canyon's western exposure accelerated the process of erosion that cut into the limestone cliffs. Softer sections of limestone were eroded by many millennia of rain, wind, snow, and ice, creating the "breaks," a deep canyon of rock walls, fins, spires, and columns that spans 3 miles and is over 2,000 feet deep. The brilliant colors evident in the breaks are the result of the oxidation of impurities (mostly iron and magnesium) contained within the white limestone. Volcanic eruptions contributed to the formation; many lava beds can be seen next to the highways that lead to the monument. The rim of the canyon towers 10,000 feet above sea level—the remnant of a plateau uplifted by an ancient sea—and is forested with islands of Engelmann spruce and subalpine fir and aspen, separated by broad meadows of wildflowers that bloom in the summer with unusual brilliance.

This popular, 6,155-acre national monument was established in 1933 after a long and complex dispute between the National Park Service (NPS) and the Forest Service. During this era, the two agencies often engaged in battles of mission and constituency, and Cedar Breaks became a garden-variety struggle in which the growing Park Service dominance of the struggle became clear. NPS Director Stephen T. Mather spent much time building a constituency for national parks in southern Utah, and his successor, Horace M. Albright, exploited the agency's advantage. Albright outmaneuvered the foresters, and Cedar Breaks was established in August 1933.

The Point Supreme Overlook, adjacent to the visitor center, provides a spectacular view across the Escalante desert. Visibility here is outstanding and often exceeds 100 miles. Three additional developed overlooks are located along the 5-mile scenic drive. There are two designated hiking trails: the Spectra Point/Ramparts trail (2 to 4 miles round-trip), and Alpine Pond self-guided nature trail (a 2-mile loop). Rangers present hourly geology talks at Point Supreme Overlook in the summer, from 10 A.M. to 5 P.M. daily.

Guided nature walks are given on weekends at 10 A.M. during the summer, weather and trail conditions permitting. The walks begin at the Spectra Point trailhead in the visitor center parking lot. The 2-mile round-trip hike travels along the rim of the geologic amphitheater to a stand of bristlecone pines, one of the world's longest-living tree species. This is a good way to see the monument's diverse birds and wildlife: blue grouse, swifts, swallows, the occasional golden eagle, marmots, mule deer, pikas, and red squirrels. This is a moderately strenuous high-altitude hike, and it is not recommended for those with cardiac or pulmonary problems.

Park visitation is highest in July and August, and lowest in January and February. All visitor facilities and the scenic rim drive are located over 10,000 feet above sea level. In the summer, daytime highs are cool, with temperatures in the upper 50s to upper 60s. Overnight lows during the summer are in the upper 30s to lower 50s. Subfreezing temperatures, snow, and high winds can occur at any time of the year—even in July. Afternoon thunderstorms are common in July and August. Winter visitors who enter the park via skis or snowmobiles must be prepared for extreme winter conditions.

The visitor center contains numerous exhibits and a bookstore and is open from late May through mid-October; all visitor facilities are closed during the winter season (mid-

October through late May). Located 23 miles east of Cedar City, Utah, the monument is open year-round as weather permits. Entrance fees are $4 for a single, private, seven-day vehicle permit, and $2 per person, for seven days, for pedestrians and bicyclists.

The park's only camping opportunities are at the 30-site Point Supreme Campground, which is usually open from mid-June through mid-September, and contains grills, tables, water, and flush toilets. Evening campfire programs are also offered at the campground amphitheater through Labor Day. A number of forest service campgrounds are scattered throughout the surrounding Dixie National Forest. There are no food, lodging, or travel services at the monument, though nearby communities such as Panguitch, Cedar City, and Parowan (19 miles north) have all services.

For more information, write Cedar Breaks National Monument, 2390 West Highway 56, Suite #11, Cedar City, UT 84720-4151, or telephone (435) 586-9451. The park's Web site is www.nps.gov/ccbr.

FURTHER READING

Hayle, Buchanan. *Wildflowers of Southwestern Utah: A Field Guide to Bryce Canyon, Cedar Breaks and Surrounding Plant Communities.* Helena, MT: Distributed by Falcon, 1992.

Leach, Nicky. *Cedar Breaks National Monument.* Springdale, UT: Zion Natural History, 1994.

Rothman, Hal K. "Shaping the Nature of a Controversy: The Park Service, the Forest Service and the Cedar Breaks National Monument." *Utah Historical Quarterly,* Summer 1987.

CENTRAL HIGH SCHOOL NATIONAL HISTORIC SITE

Location: Little Rock, Arkansas
Acreage: 27
Established: November 6, 1998

Despite the fame of Martin Luther King, Jr., and others, the real strength of the civil rights movement in America was that ordinary people did extraordinary things. Perhaps no-

where was that strength more evident than in Little Rock, Arkansas, where nine black schoolchildren bravely asserted their right to an equal education. In 1954, the U.S. Supreme Court had unanimously ruled, in *Brown v. Board of Education of Topeka,* that "separate educational facilities are inherently unequal." At the time of this landmark decision, schools in twenty-one states and the District of Columbia were segregated by race. The court urged desegregation "with all deliberate speed," but progress was slow, and the South proved particularly reluctant. The crucial confrontation came here, in Little Rock, which scheduled the desegregation of the all-white Central High School with the token admission of nine black students. Crowds chanting "two, four, six, eight, we ain't gonna integrate," and other much worse taunts, greeted the "Little Rock Nine," and Arkansas Governor Orval Faubus called out the National Guard to prevent the black students from entering the school. Faced with this direct challenge to federal authority, President Dwight D. Eisenhower reluctantly placed the National Guard under federal command and called out 1,000 federal paratroopers to escort the nine children to class. The students finished the school year under armed guard. In the aftermath, Little Rock authorities closed Central High School for two years, to protest desegregation, and when it did reopen, only three African Americans were in classes.

In 1998, Congress set aside Central High School as a memorial to the bravery and courage of those who fought to end segregation in America. The park's visitor center is open from 10 A.M. until 4 P.M. Monday through Saturday, and from 1 P.M. until 4 P.M. on Sunday, and includes an interpretive exhibit about the 1957 crisis. Admission is free. There are no food or lodging facilities at the historic site, but all traveler services are available in Little Rock.

For more information, write Central High School National Historic Site, 2125 Daisy L. Gatson Bates Drive, Little Rock, AR 72202, or telephone (501) 374-1957. The park's Web site is www.nps.gov/chsc.

FURTHER READING

Bates, Daisy. *The Long Shadow of Little Rock: A Memoir.* Fayetteville: University of Arkansas Press, 1987.

Beals, Melba. *Warriors Don't Cry: A Searing Memoir of the Battle to Integrate Little Rock's Central High.* New York: Pocket Books, 1995.

Jacoway, Elizabeth, and C. Fred Williams, eds. *Understanding the Little Rock Crisis: An Exercise in Remembrance and Reconciliation.* Fayetteville: University of Arkansas Press, 1999.

CHACO CULTURE NATIONAL HISTORICAL PARK

Location: Nageezi, New Mexico
Acreage: 33,960
Established: March 11, 1907

Chaco Culture National Historical Park in northern New Mexico preserves the remains of a complex pre-Columbian Pueblo Indian civilization. One of North America's largest archeological sites, the canyon, with hundreds of smaller sites, contains thirteen major archeological digs. Chaco is remarkable for its multistory dwellings, known as "great houses," which required sophisticated planning, organization, and management for construction. Working without metal tools or formal mathematics, the Chaco Canyon Anasazi nevertheless constructed vast communal buildings that still compel admiration. These dwellings provide evidence that their builders had an extensive knowledge of astronomy, because they are oriented to solar, lunar, and cardinal directions.

From 850 to 1150 C.E., the canyon was not just the center of Chaco culture, but the economic and ceremonial center for all Pueblo tribes in the San Juan River basin. Chaco's impressive structures were connected to other great houses in the region by a network of roadways—not foot trails, but roadbeds that demonstrated evidence of advanced engineering knowledge. By 1000 C.E., archeologists estimate that there were between 2,000 and 5,000 people living in some 400 settlements in and around Chaco. In addition to their architectural skills, the Pueblo peoples of the region were admired for their distinctive black-on-white pottery and exquisite turquoise jewelry, both of which were traded as far south as Mexico. By 1200, however, after prevailing for nearly three centuries, Chaco Canyon declined in importance, and construction ceased. Prolonged drought and an overtaxed environment may have led to food shortages that even the sophisticated irrigation works of the Anasazi could not overcome. The culture's influence carried on for about another hundred years at Aztec ruins and other centers that reached north, west, and south. Over the subsequent centuries, the Chacoans dispersed to new areas, reorganized their social structures, and interacted with other Native American, Mexican, and European cultures. Chacoan culture was unique. Its sophisticated architecture, social organization, community complexity, and regional interaction have never been duplicated on the same scale by other Native American cultures.

First established in 1907 as a national monument, the almost-34,000-acre preserve was the scene of some of the primary struggles in American archeology. The cowboy and amateur archeologist from Mancos, Colorado, Richard Wetherill, homesteaded Chaco Canyon in 1896, excavating the most impressive of the ruins, Pueblo Bonito. As a result, the full force of the nascent discipline of archeology was pressed against him, and with much outside pressure, his homestead application was denied. In the end, Wetherill was murdered by a Navajo in 1909, two years after the establishment of the monument. The park was renamed the Chaco Culture National Historical Park in 1980.

The preserve provides excellent hiking opportunities, and all sites and trails are open from sunrise to sunset. Una Vida, the most-excavated great house, is a short walk from the visitor center. A paved, 8-mile-loop road extends from the visitor center and passes near six of the great houses—Pueblo Bonito, Chetro Ketl, Hungo Pavi, Pueblo del Arroyo, Kin Kletso, and Casa Rinconada—where short, hour-long, self-guided trails begin. Hikers can also walk the backcountry to see other remote sites or to view the great houses from different angles; a permit is required. During the summer, rangers provide interpretive walks.

Chaco Canyon weather is inconsistent and unpredictable. Temperatures can fluctuate over 60 degrees during a twenty-four-hour period. As with much of New Mexico, precipitation may be localized, and one end of the canyon will experience a downpour while the sun blazes 5 miles to the east. Lightning and flash floods are real concerns. If hiking in the canyon, be prepared for heat, rain, wind, and unexpected changes in temperature and always carry extra water (available in the visitor center parking lot). Permits are required for backcountry hiking, and they are available at the visitor center or from a ranger. No overnight backpacking is allowed.

Located in remote northwestern New Mexico between Gallup and Farmington, Chaco Culture National Historical Park is open year-round. Entrance fees are $8 per vehicle or $4 per person. Both the northern and southern routes into the park include 16 and 41 miles of dirt roads, respectively. The preferred and recommended route is from the north via Highway 44/550. Although these roads are generally well maintained, they can become impassable during inclement weather. Inquire locally, or call the park for current road conditions. The park's visitor center is open from 8 A.M. to 6 P.M., Memorial Day through Labor Day, and the rest of the year from 8 A.M. to 5 P.M. The center houses films, exhibits, and books explaining Chaco and Pueblo Indian cultures.

Although there are no lodging or travel facilities—including gas—at the park, camping is available for $10 per night at the 67-site Gallo Campground near the visitor center. This popular destination, often filled by noon, is open year-round on a first-come, first-served basis. There is no backcountry camping. Motorists are advised to bring plenty of gas and basic car repair materials and tools. The nearest lodging is a bed and breakfast at Nageezi Trading Post. The distant towns of Bloomfield, Farmington, and Gallup all have travel services.

For more information, write Chaco Culture National Historical Park, P.O. Box 220, Nageezi, NM 87037, or telephone (505) 786-7014. The park's Web site offers detailed information about the cultural and historical heritage of the region at www.nps.gov/chcu.

FURTHER READING

Mathien, Frances Joan, ed. *Environment and Subsistence of Chaco Canyon, New Mexico.* Albuquerque, NM: National Park Service, 1985.

Sebastian, Lynne. *The Chaco Anasazi: Sociopolitical Evolution in the Prehistoric Southwest.* New York: Cambridge University Press, 1992.

Strutin, Michal. *Chaco: A Cultural Legacy.* Tucson, AZ: Southwest Parks and Monuments Association, 1994.

Vivian, R. Gwinn. *Chaco Canyon.* New York: Oxford University Press, 2002.

CHAMIZAL NATIONAL MEMORIAL
Location: El Paso, Texas
Acreage: 55
Authorized: June 30, 1966

Chamizal National Memorial commemorates the peaceful resolution of a century-long international boundary dispute between the United States and Mexico. The 1848 Treaty of Guadalupe Hidalgo defined the border between these two nations as the Rio Grande

River, and stipulated that the international boundary would fluctuate along with the river so long as the shift was gradual; in the event that the river changed course suddenly, the boundary was to remain in the old channel. Before the construction of modern dams and irrigation projects, these shifts occurred frequently, touching off numerous quarrels between the United States and Mexico. One of the most famous was the Chamizal controversy.

The ambiguity of the 1848 treaty created a tense situation in El Paso when, in the late nineteenth century, the Rio Grande severed a 600-acre tract of Mexican land known as the Chamizal (named after a native plant species). Claiming that the change had been sudden rather than gradual, Mexico maintained ownership of this parcel. The United States disputed this claim, and in 1911 an international arbitration decision called for dividing the tract equally between the two countries. When the United States refused to comply with the judgment, Mexican nationalists seized upon the Chamizal controversy as an example of "Yankee imperialism" trying to thwart Mexican sovereignty, and tension between the two nations continued.

Finally, in 1962, President John F. Kennedy and Mexican President Lopez Mateos agreed to divide the land evenly between the two nations and to build a concrete channel through the Chamizal to stabilize the river's course, and thus the international boundary, forever. In 1974, the 55-acre Chamizal National Memorial was established to celebrate this triumph of diplomacy and to encourage goodwill between these two nations with one border. Utilizing the visual and performing arts as a medium of interchange, the park provides a venue for cross-cultural understanding and enrichment that transcends barriers of race, ethnicity, heritage, and language. Across the river, Mexico maintains the 760-acre Chamizal Federal Park, featuring a highly acclaimed archeological museum, as well as other facilities.

Encircling the memorial is the 2-mile-long Cordova Island Trail, which offers views of the Franklin and Juarez mountains, the El Paso skyline, and the international bridge. The park is open daily from 8 A.M. to 5 P.M. and there is no admission fee, though donations are accepted. The visitor center has interpretive exhibits, an acclaimed twelve-minute video on the memorial, art exhibits, and a 500-seat performing arts theater in which cultural performances are presented at various times throughout the year. During the summer, the City of El Paso's Arts Resources Department sponsors the annual Music Under the Stars on Sunday evenings, and the park's outdoor stage features a variety of free events. The Mexican Consulate's Centro Cultural Mexicano sponsors El Grito, a Mexican Independence Day celebration, on the evening of September 15. Each fall, the National Park Service sponsors the annual Border Folk Festival.

The weather at Chamizal is generally sunny with low humidity. Winters are quite mild, while summers are very hot and dry. Comfortable, layered sportswear is recommended along with comfortable shoes.

To reach the memorial, visitors traveling east or west on I-10 should exit at U.S. Highway 54 and follow designated signs; visitors traveling south on U.S. Highway 54 should take the exit marked Juárez, Mexico. *Do not* proceed onto the international bridge, but turn right onto Paisano Street, and continue to follow signs toward the memorial. Although there is no camping, food, or lodging in the park, nearby El Paso has all traveler services, and numerous private campgrounds are located in the vicinity.

For more information, write Chamizal National Memorial, 800 South San Marcial, El Paso, TX 79905, or telephone (915) 532-7273. The park's Web site is www.nps.gov/cham.

FURTHER READING

Griswold del Castillo, Richard. *The Treaty of Guadalupe Hidalgo: A Legacy of Conflict.* Norman: University of Oklahoma Press, 1992.

Lamborn, Alan C., and Stephen P. Mumme. *Statecraft, Domestic Politics, and Foreign Policy Making: The El Chamizal Dispute.* Boulder, CO: Westview, 1988.

Mueller, Jerry E. *Restless River: International Law and the Behavior of the Rio Grande.* El Paso: Texas Western University Press, 1975.

CHANNEL ISLANDS NATIONAL PARK

Location: Ventura, California
Acreage: 249,561
Established: April 26, 1938

One of America's most remarkable ocean parks, Channel Islands National Park comprises five of the eight Channel Islands—San Miguel, Santa Rosa, Santa Cruz, Anacapa, and Santa Barbara—off the coast of southern California, near Los Angeles. The Channel Islands are the mountaintop remnants of a huge coastal landmass that cracked and fell below sea level millions of years ago. Although they lie only a few miles off shore from present-day California's burgeoning population, these isolated islands harbor more than 2,000 species of plants and animals, from microscopic plankton to the endangered blue whale; some 145 species can be found nowhere else in the world.

The islands also have a lengthy human history. For thousands of years—until the early nineteenth century—the Chumash and other southern California coastal tribes occupied the islands, commuting via large plank canoes. Some of the park's islands have native burial and village sites that provide an extensive archeological record dating back ten thousand years.

In 1938, Anacapa and Santa Barbara islands were established as a national monument to provide a wildlife refuge for nesting seabirds and endangered marine species. In 1980, when three additional islands were preserved, Channel Islands also received national park status. Today, the Channel Islands National Marine Sanctuary extends for 6 nautical miles around each island, placing fully half of the park's just under 250,000 acres under water. Each island exhibits notable features. Anacapa Island is a chain of closely linked islets with rocky shorelines and sheer cliffs. It has hiking trails, a visitor center, lighthouse exhibits, a primitive campground, and a picnic area, and offers opportunities for scuba diving, snorkeling, bird-watching, fishing, and observing marine mammals. Santa Barbara Island, 42 miles off the coast, consists of rolling grass hills surrounded by sheer cliffs. Most of the largest island, Santa Cruz, is maintained by the Nature Conservancy, which strictly limits visitors. The National Park Service owns the eastern arm of the island, however, where visitors may observe wildlife, hike, and camp. Santa Rosa and San Miguel contain natural and physical features similar to the other islands. San Miguel also contains the greatest number of Native American burial and village sites, and is the most remote and least visited island.

The greatest challenge to the future of Channel Islands comes from the enormous population base of southern California. The more than 20 million people in the greater Los Angeles area are the natural constituency for park visitation, yet the islands are so fragile that ongoing increases in demand for the use threatened the fragile ecology of the islands. In this sense, Channel Islands National Park shares a dramatic problem with other park areas near urban centers: the very constituencies devoted to their protection are simultaneously a threat to their survival.

Channel Islands National Park is open year-round; there is no entrance fee. Each year between 50,000 and 100,000 people visit the islands. Although most visitation occurs in the summer, migrating gray whales and spectacular wildflower displays attract visitors in the winter and spring. Autumn is an excellent time to travel to the park because the days are usually sunny, with minimal winds, and divers will enjoy the clear ocean water. Each island has a primitive campground and there is a reservation fee of $2.50 per campsite per night. The islands have no stores, restaurants, or overnight lodging accommodations. Visitors must bring their own food, water, and camping equipment. California coastal cities have all traveler services. Park headquarters and the Robert J. Lagomarsino Visitor Center are located in Ventura. The visitor center hours are Labor Day through Memorial Day, 8:30 A.M. to 4:30 P.M. weekdays, 8 A.M. to 5 P.M. weekends; Memorial Day through Labor Day, 8 A.M. to 5 P.M. weekdays, 8 A.M. to 5:30 P.M. weekends.

The Park Service has designated concessionaires that offer boat and air travel to the islands from the California mainland. For boat travel departures from Ventura and Channel Islands harbors, visitors should contact Island Packers at (805) 642-1393. Those boat travelers wishing to depart from Santa Barbara Harbor should contact Truth Aquatics at (805) 962-1127. Channel Islands Aviation, located at the Camarillo airport, offers air travel to Santa Rosa Island at (805) 987-1301. Visitors wishing to travel to the park's islands via private boat should contact park headquarters for information, permits, and docking restrictions.

For more information, write Channel Islands National Park, 1901 Spinnaker Drive, Ventura, CA 93001, or telephone (805) 658-5730. The park's informative Web site is www.nps.gov/chis.

FURTHER READING

Holdman, Annette. *Window to the Channel: A Guide to the Resources of the Channel Islands National Marine Sanctuary.* Santa Barbara, CA: Channel Islands National Marine Sanctuary, Santa Barbara Museum of Natural History, 1990.

Howorth, Peter. *Channel Islands.* Las Vegas, NV: KC Publications, 1982.

Lamb, Susan. *Channel Islands National Park.* Tucson, AZ: Southwest Parks and Monuments, 2000.

CHARLES PINCKNEY NATIONAL HISTORIC SITE

Location: Mount Pleasant, South Carolina
Acreage: 28
Established: September 8, 1988

This National Historic Site was authorized in 1988 to commemorate Charles Pinckney's (1757–1824) role in the drafting of the U.S. Constitution as well as his significant contributions to American politics. A native South Carolinian, Pinckney fought in the American Revolution and was captured defending Charleston. He later served in the Confederated Congress, the South Carolina state assembly, both houses of Congress, and as a four-term governor of South Carolina. From 1801 to 1805, he was President Thomas Jefferson's minister to Spain and facilitated that country's acquiescence to the 1803 Louisiana Purchase between France and the United States. Pinckney is perhaps best known, however, for his participation in the 1787 Constitutional Convention. Anxious to be the youngest delegate, Pinckney lied about his age, claiming to be a youthful twenty-four years of age though he was in fact thirty. Nevertheless, his contributions were substantial and much of the final draft of the Constitution attests to his influence.

While this political renaissance man aided the young republic in its transition from colony to nation-state, Pinckney resided at his family's 700-acre estate, Snee Farm, near Charleston. In 1754, Pinckney's father had acquired the land, which was originally part of a 1698 royal grant, and for nearly two and a half centuries this working plantation grew rice, indigo, cotton, and assorted vegetables. Today, the 28-acre historic site preserves and interprets Pinckney's ancestral home and estate. The park also examines the influences of African Americans in the development and success of Snee Farm, in particular, and South Carolina's agriculture, in general.

Charles Pinckney National Historic Site is an example of the shift in the kind of areas introduced into the park system in the recent past. Simultaneously, it was part of an effort to backfill the park system with a broader national past and a way to assure congressional support from the South Carolina delegation. This melding of purposes has become common; some point to such efforts as a clear way to "thin the blood" of the park system, to dilute its original purposes. Whether such proclamations add to the national heritage or not, it is clear that they will continue to add new areas to the park system on an annual basis.

Located on Long Point Road in Mount Pleasant, South Carolina, 6 miles north of Charleston, the historic site is open year-round from 9 A.M. to 5 P.M. daily. There is no entrance fee. The park's open spaces contain exhibits describing the existing house, archeological excavations, southern agricultural history, and the ways in which neighboring water and wetlands contributed to the plantation's ecosystem. Visitation is typically highest in the summer months and lowest in December in January. Flower enthusiasts may wish to visit in spring, particularly in late March and early April, when the park's azaleas and camellias put on a showy display for visitors.

The self-guided visitor center is located in a small house built around 1828, shortly after Pinckney's death. This well-preserved structure is a rare example of the once-common low-country cottage. Exhibits at the center focus on Pinckney, his family, his political offices, his influence on the Constitution, the impact of slavery in South Carolina's low-country, and some of the archeological discoveries made on-site. The visitor center also offers 2 videos: one on Pinckney and Snee Farm, and the other on the 1787 writing of the Constitution, which features scenes from other national park sites associated with constitutional history.

Although there is no food, lodging, or camping in the park, both Mount Pleasant and Charleston offer all travel services, including hotels and motels, bed and breakfasts, and inns. Camping is available in the Francis Marion National Forest and in several private campgrounds located nearby.

For more information, write Charles Pinckney National Historic Site, 1214 Middle Street, Sullivan's Island, SC 29462–9748, or telephone (843) 881–5516. The park's Web site is www.nps.gov/chpi.

FURTHER READING

Blythe, Robert W., Emily Kleine, and Steven H. Moffson. *Charles Pinckney: Historic Resource Study.* Atlanta, GA: Southeast Regional Office, National Park Service, 2000. Available at www.nps.gov/chpi/hrs/hrs.htm.

Edgar, Walter B. *Historic Snee Farm: A Documentary Record.* Columbia: University of South Carolina Department of History, 1991.

Kaplanoff, Mark D. "Charles Pinckney and the American Republican Tradition." In *Intellectual Life in Antebellum Charleston.* Edited by Michael O'Brien and David Moltke-Hansen. Knoxville: University of Tennessee Press, 1986.

CHATTAHOOCHEE RIVER NATIONAL RECREATION AREA

Location: Atlanta, Georgia
Acreage: 9,167
Established: August 15, 1978

Running slow, clear, and cold, the Chattahoochee River winds for 436 miles through the mountains of northern Georgia all the way to the Gulf of Mexico. Established in 1978 as part of Representative Phil Burton's omnibus parks bill, the Chattahoochee River National Recreation Area (NRA) protects a spectacular 48-mile stretch of the river north and east of Atlanta, Georgia. In addition to providing excellent recreational opportunities, this 9,167-acre, 16-unit park preserves a diverse riparian ecosystem as well as various nineteenth-century historic sites and Native American archeological sites.

Numerous hiking trails wind through 9 of the park's 16 units, including the Vickery Creek unit, which has trails that lead to antebellum-era textile mills and a dam. On the west side of the Sope Creek unit, hikers can follow a loop trail leading to old homestead sites and the ruins of a nineteenth-century paper mill. The NRA even offers a 3-mile fitness trail with exercise stations.

The Chattahoochee River itself provides a scenic route for boaters to "shoot the hooch." Most of the "rapids" in the park are rated no more than Class-2 in terms of difficulty. The biggest obstacles are occasional downed trees and partially submerged boulders that require minimal scouting and maneuvering. Rafts and boats are available from Park Service concessionaires and private companies. Stocked with 23 species of game fish, including trout and bass, the river also boasts excellent year-round fishing opportunities; a valid Georgia fishing license and trout stamp are required.

The Chattahoochee River NRA maintains 2 visitor contact stations—at Paces Mill and Island Ford—which provide orientation, interpretive information, and publications. Shuttle buses operate between Johnson Ferry, Powers Island, and Paces Mill. Each year, nearly 3 million people visit the park to enjoy fishing, canoeing and boating, hiking, horseback riding, and bird-watching. Not surprisingly, visitation is highest in the summer. The climate here is quite temperate, with short, cool winters and hot, humid summers, and a long, mild spring and fall.

This day-use-only park is open year-round from dawn until dark. Although there are no entrance fees, the Chattahoochee River NRA has instituted a $2 daily parking fee for all units of the park; a $20 annual parking permit is available. The NRA offers numerous picnic sites but no camping or lodging. Stores at Johnson Ferry, Powers Island, and Paces Mill offer food and supplies, and the metropolitan Atlanta area has all traveler services. The U.S. Army Corps of Engineers operates a campground at nearby Lake Sidney Lanier, and Stone Mountain Park and other neighboring state parks also have camping facilities.

For more information, write Chattahoochee River National Recreation Area, 1978 Island Ford Parkway, Atlanta, GA 30350, or telephone (770) 399-8070. The park's limited Web site is www.nps.gov/chat.

FURTHER READING

Cook, Joe. *River Song: A Journey Down the Chattahoochee and Apalachiocola Rivers.* Tuscaloosa: University of Alabama Press, 2000.
Willoughby, Lynn. *Fair to Middlin': The Antebellum Cotton Trade on the Apalachicola/Chattahoochee River Valley.* Tuscaloosa: University of Alabama Press, 1993.
——. *Flowing Through Time: A History of the Lower Chattahoochee River.* Tuscaloosa: University of Alabama Press, 1999.

CHICKAMAUGA AND CHATTANOOGA NATIONAL MILITARY PARK

Location: Georgia and Tennessee
Acreage: 9,059
Established: August 19, 1890

Established in 1890 as America's first National Military Park, Chickamauga and Chattanooga National Military Park honors the Civil War soldiers who fought at the September 1863 Battle of Chickamauga and the November 1863 Battle of Chattanooga. An attempt to halt the Union Army's advance toward Georgia, Chickamauga was the last major Confederate victory in the western theater. Yet it was a hollow victory, as the federal army gained control of Chattanooga only two months later.

Following the January 1863 battle at

Stones River, Tennessee, Union forces under General William Rosecrans prepared to attack the Confederate rail center at Chattanooga, Tennessee. Rosecrans's troops effectively surrounded Chattanooga, and the Confederates withdrew to Georgia's Fort Oglethorpe. Rosecrans was unaware that the Confederates had increased their troop strength to 66,000 at Chickamauga. Under the leadership of General Braxton Bragg, the Confederates defeated General George H. Thomas's Union soldiers. The Battle of Chickamauga is widely regarded as one of the Civil War's most bloody battles. Nearly 34,000 soldiers on both sides died in hand-to-hand combat.

Smarting from this defeat, Thomas's remaining forces retreated north to Chattanooga. Soon after, 70,000 Union soldiers under the command of General Ulysses S. Grant successfully drove Bragg's Confederates off Missionary Ridge and Lookout Mountain, and eventually Grant took control of Chattanooga. Over 12,000 soldiers on both sides lost their lives in this battle, and Chattanooga became the staging point for General William Tecumseh Sherman's famed march to Atlanta.

From 1850 to 1933, the War Department administered the park. Like many Civil War battlefields, it became the scene of postwar commemorations; each year on the anniversary of the battle, thousands of veterans and their families, and the families of those who died in the battle, would arrive to remember their losses. This form of public celebration became common in the late nineteenth century and in many ways is a precursor to the creation of public monuments such as the Vietnam Wall and the Oklahoma City Memorial today. In 1933, as part of Franklin D. Roosevelt's reorganization of the federal government, the park was transferred to the Park Service. Its transfer, along with many other Civil War and Revolutionary War battlefields, gave the Park Service the toehold it sought in presenting American history to the public.

The park consists of over 9,000 acres spread over the Georgia/Tennessee border. Visitor centers are located at Chickamauga battlefield and at Point Park on Lookout Mountain. The Cravens House, a strategic location in the Battle of Lookout Mountain, is open on a limited, seasonal basis. Visitation is highest in July, and lowest in January and February. A $2 fee is charged for ages eighteen to sixty-one for tours of the Cravens House. There is no charge for ages seventeen and under. Golden Eagle, Golden Age, and Golden Access passes are accepted. The climate varies little; summers are generally hot and humid, while winters are mild but damp.

At the Chickamauga Battlefield Visitor Center on U.S. Highway 27, there is a 26-minute multimedia presentation, for which a fee is charged. Many trails and drives around both battlefields point to sites of interest. A walking tour on Lookout Mountain helps visitors interpret this important battle, while near Point Park, the Ochs Museum and Overlook provide pictures and battle exhibits.

The Ochs Museum has a signaling exhibit and houses James Walker's painting *The Battle of Lookout Mountain.* The museum also houses a soldier's exhibit as well as an exhibit of the park's dedication. In the summer, rangers provide assorted historical walks and interpretive programs.

Camping is not permitted in the park, but Georgia's Cloudland Canyon State Park, located about 20 miles south of Chattanooga via I-59, has developed camping facilities. Chattanooga and Fort Oglethorpe have all travel services.

For more information, write Chickamauga and Chattanooga National Military Park, P.O. Box 2128, 3370 LaFayette Road, Fort Oglethorpe, GA 30742, or telephone (706) 866-9241. The park's Web site is www. nps.gov/chch.

FURTHER READING

Cozzens, Peter. *This Terrible Sound: The Battle of Chickamauga.* Urbana: University of Illinois Press, 1992.

——. *The Shipwreck of Their Hopes: The Battles for Chattanooga.* Urbana: University of Illinois Press, 1994.

——. *The Civil War in the West: From Stones River to Chattanooga.* Urbana: University of Illinois Press, 1996.

Foote, Shelby. *Chickamauga: And Other Civil War Stories.* New York: Delta, 1993.

Woodworth, Steven E. *Chickamauga: A Battlefield Guide with a Section on Chattanooga.* Lincoln: University of Nebraska Press, 1999.

CHICKASAW NATIONAL RECREATION AREA

Location: Sulphur, Oklahoma
Acreage: 9,889
Established: July 1, 1902

The Chickasaw National Recreation Area lies on the eastern edge of the Great Plains, in southcentral Oklahoma, and occupies the transition zone where eastern deciduous forests give way to the wide western prairie. Various Native American tribes have inhabited this land for nearly seven thousand years, attracted by the healing properties of the region's natural mineral springs. They called it the "peaceful valley of rippling waters." In 1855, the area became part of the Chickasaw Nation, the tribe for whom the park is now named. By the 1880s, white settlers began encroaching on the area, a practice that accelerated with intensity throughout "The Nations," Indian Territory, as Oklahoma was known prior to statehood in 1906. Fearful that uncontrolled use would destroy the springs, the Chickasaws sold 640 acres of their land to the federal government to prevent further degradation, and in 1902, this became the Sulphur Springs Reservation. In 1904, two tracts were added, and, in 1906, the reservation became Platt National Park, named for Connecticut Senator Orville Platt, who had recently died and had been prominent in Native American affairs. As national parks became more powerful symbols, and especially after the Park Service was founded in 1916, there was much criticism of the 900-acre national park and its name. The Park Service frowned on parks named for political figures. In 1910 an effort was made to turn the park over to the state of Oklahoma, but state officials, recognizing the access to federal dollars that any national park granted their state, unanimously insisted that the area remain federal. The area remained a national park, farther and farther from the mainstream of national parks, until 1976, when it was combined with the Arbuckle National Recreation Area and redesignated as the Chickasaw National Recreation Area (NRA). The infrastructure of the NRA was largely developed during the New Deal, when men in the Civilian Conservation Corps (CCC) designed and constructed the trail system that winds through this gently rolling hill country. Today, the 9,889-acre park protects the unique flora and fauna of this edge environment, as well as the rippling waters.

Chickasaw NRA offers something for everyone. The Travertine Information and Nature Center is open all year and offers live-animal exhibits, films of the area's native history, a small bookstore, and an environmental study area. Ranger-led activities include nature walks, campfire programs, and other educational programs. The park also offers 3 different levels of water-based recreation. In the protected zone near the nature center, visitors may enjoy the quiet beauty of the park's natural springs and streams, and at Veteran's Lake, use restrictions have created a park-like atmosphere that nurtures quieter activities. Those visitors wishing to engage in the full range of water recreational activities, including swimming, boating, and fishing, have full access to the 2,235-acre Lake of the Arbuckles. Boat launches are located at Guy

Sandy, The Point, and Buckhorn campgrounds. And finally, the park hosts a variety of annual events including Sulphur Days, Art in the Park, the Hills of Oklahoma Bicycle Tour, Bald Eagle Watch, and the living history program titled the "1906 Historic Candlelight Tour."

With 3.4 million visitors a year, Chickasaw NRA is one of the most heavily visited parks of its size in the national park system. Peak tourist season is from Memorial Day to Labor Day, with activities focusing on water recreation and camping. Summers are hot and humid, and daytime temperatures near 100 degrees are common from July to September. The humidity here frequently exceeds 50 percent, and thunderstorms are common April through July. Winters are generally mild, with temperatures rarely dropping below 32 degrees for more than two or three consecutive days.

The park is open year-round, and it is located on state highway 177, just south of Sulphur, Oklahoma. It is approximately 90 miles south of Oklahoma City, and 120 miles north of Dallas, Texas. There is no fee to enter the park, but fees are charged for camping, boat launching, and reserving picnic pavilions. There are 6 developed campgrounds in the 2 park districts. Rock Creek, Cold Springs, and Central campgrounds are located in the historic Platt District. Buckhorn, The Point, and Guy Sandy campgrounds are situated in the Lake District around Lake of the Arbuckles. All sites have tables, grills, rest rooms, and water. The Buckhorn campground has utility hookups available. Camping is on a first-come, first-served basis except for group camp sites located in Rock Creek (1 site), Central (10 sites), and Cold Springs (2 sites), which may be reserved. Although food and lodging are not available in the park, the nearby towns of Sulphur and Davis have all traveler services.

For more information, write Chickasaw National Recreation Area, P.O. Box 201, Sulphur, OK 73086, or telephone (580) 622-3165 for park information, or (580) 622-3161 for park headquarters. The park's thorough Web site is www.nps.gov/chic.

FURTHER READING

Cushman, H.B. *History of the Choctaw, Chickasaw, and Natchez Indians.* Norman: University of Oklahoma Press, 1999.
Gibson, Arrell Morgan. *The Chickasaws.* Norman: University of Oklahoma Press, 1971.

CHIMNEY ROCK NATIONAL HISTORIC SITE

Location: Bayard, Nebraska
Acreage: 83
Established: August 2, 1956

During the first half of the nineteenth century, powerful forces propelled nearly half a million Americans westward along the Oregon Trail in search of the future. The 2,000-mile journey was slow, dangerous, tedious, and exhausting and usually took seven months. Weary emigrants, traveling west across the wide, flat plains, measured their progress against a series of landmarks beginning with the reassuring spire of Chimney Rock. For centuries an important guidepost for northern Plains Indians, trappers, and traders, this 325-foot sentinel towers dramatically over the Platt River in western Nebraska's hill country, and pioneers regarded it as the symbol of the approaching Rocky Mountains. Most emigrants traveled with their families but usually also joined a larger group, forming a "train." They labored across the most difficult parts of the plains, using natural markers to chart their progress and determine their location. As they passed Chimney Rock, many paused to inscribe their names in stone. Comprised of layered sedimentary rocks that have been sculpted by the erosive forces of wind and water, Chimney Rock became the most noted formation on the Oregon Trail, and in 1956, this enduring symbol of westward migration was set aside as a national historic site.

Located about 25 miles southeast of Scotts Bluff, Nebraska, Chimney Rock National Historic Site is open year-round. This 83-acre site receives around 35,000 visitors every year, primarily in the summer months. There is a $2 admission fee, although Nebraska State Historical Society members and their immediate families are admitted free of charge. The Historical Society operates the Ethel and Christopher J. Abbot Visitor Center, one of the premier interpretive centers on the Oregon Trail, which is open daily from 9 A.M. to 6 P.M. from April 1 through September 30, and from 9 A.M. to 5 P.M. during the rest of the year. The center features museum exhibits on the westward migration experience, a hands-on opportunity to "pack your wagon," and a sixteen-minute introductory film, *Chimney Rock and the American West,* which is shown at regular intervals.

Although there are no lodging, camping, or food facilities on-site, traveler services are available along U.S. Highway 26 and Nebraska Highway 92, and in Scotts Bluff. Developed camping is available 10 miles southeast at Bridgeport State Recreation Area.

For more information, write Chimney Rock National Historic Site, P.O. Box F, Bayard, NE 69334-0680, or telephone (308) 586-2581. The park's Web site is www.nps.gov/chro.

FURTHER READING

Davis, Anita Price. *Chimney Rock and Rutherford County.* Charleston, SC: Arcadia, 2002.

Faragher, John Mack. *Women and Men on the Overland Trail.* New Haven, CT: Yale University Press, 1979.

Unrau, John D., Jr. *The Plains Across: The Overland Emigrants and the Trans-Mississippi West, 1840–1860.* Urbana: University of Illinois Press, 1979.

CHIRICAHUA NATIONAL MONUMENT
Location: Willcox, Arizona
Acreage: 11,985
Established: April 18, 1924

Twenty-seven million years ago, the earth around Chiricahua National Monument in southeastern Arizona rumbled and roared to life. As highly pressurized rhyolitic magma began to push its way through the earth's lower crust and toward the surface, the crust began to bulge like an automobile tire about to burst. Finally, unable to withstand the pressure any longer, the crust of the Turkey Creek Caldera fractured and an immense volcanic explosion, similar to the 1980 eruption of Mount Saint Helens in Washington State but containing an estimated 1,000 times more material, spewed great quantities of ash and pumice and hot, choking gas. Scientists believe the deadly gas cloud and hurled debris likely destroyed every living thing within a 20-mile radius. The pyroclastic flow then fused into a 2,000-foot-thick layer of granite called a welded tuff, topped with a loose ash layer, while the spent magma chamber collapsed into a huge caldera nearly 12 miles wide. The final piece of Chiricahua's volcanic puzzle was a later flow of dacite magma that capped the earlier ash deposits and protected them much like a hat. Powerful forces then heaved and tilted this formation into the Chiricahua Mountain Range, while wind and water eventually eroded exposed rock into the carved spires, massive columns, balanced rocks, hoodoos, and canyons for which Chiricahua is justifiably famous.

Established in 1924, the 11,985-acre Chiricahua National Monument represents one of the most diverse natural and biological regions in the entire northern hemisphere. Here, where the Chihuahuan and Sonoran deserts meet the southern Rocky Mountains and northern Sierra Madre Range, visitors

Chiricahua National Monument, a mecca for hikers and bird watchers. *(National Park Service)*

can view animals and birds not seen outside the desert southwest. Javelina, coatimundi, hog-nosed and hooded skunks, white-tailed and mule deer, bears, and mountain lions all call the monument home. Birders will enjoy looking for black-chinned and rufous hummingbirds, western and mountain bluebirds, Mexican chickadees, Scott's orioles, hepatic tanagers, numerous quail species, painted redstarts, yellow-rumped and red-faced warblers, various woodpeckers, and black-headed grosbeaks.

Although the monument is 90 percent wilderness, Chiricahua features 17 miles of maintained trails that vary in degree of difficulty. The Echo Canyon Trail and the Heart of Rocks Trail offer spectacular views of balanced rocks, spires, and pinnacles. Auto tourists will appreciate the road ascending

through Bonito Canyon that continues to the Sugarloaf parking area, where hikers can pick up the summit trail to Sugarloaf Mountain. Perhaps the most exciting view in the park is from Massai Point, at the road's end, where visitors are rewarded with a sweeping view of the broad Sulfur Springs Valley, the hazy Dragoon Mountains, and the monument's dramatic sculpted columns rising from forested slopes. Of historic interest is the Faraway Ranch, a picturesque pioneer homestead and later a working cattle and guest ranch. Daily tours of the historically furnished house offer glimpses into the lives of this Swedish immigrant family that was one of the first to settle in the area.

Located 120 miles east of Tucson, Chiricahua National Monument is open year-round. Entrance fees are $6 per vehicle, and

$3 per motorcycle, bicycle, or hiker. Each year approximately 100,000 visitors take in Chiricahua's vistas and rock formations, with peak visitation occurring between March and May. The Chiricahua Visitor Center features audiovisual programs, exhibits, a computer information station, and book sales, and is open daily from 8 A.M. to 5 P.M. Park rangers present interpretive programs from March through November, and evening programs are offered at the campground amphitheater. Check at the visitor center for specific times and places.

Temperatures at the park are generally mild with summer daytime highs in the upper 90s and nighttime lows in the 50s. Winter daytime highs range in the 50s to 60s, and nighttime lows are typically in the upper teens or low 20s but can dip into the subzero range. Moisture is evenly distributed, half during the winter as snow, half in the summer as rain. Daily monsoon thunderstorms can occur from July through September, and can cause flash floods.

The monument has one developed campground, the 25-site Bonita Canyon Campground. It features rest rooms with flush toilets, running water, picnic tables, and trash pickup for $8 per night. There are no hook-ups or showers. Camping is limited to fourteen days and is available on a first-come, first-served basis only. There are also many national forest campgrounds nearby in the Coronado National Forest. Backcountry camping is not permitted in the monument. There are no food services, gasoline, or lodging in the monument, but all travel services and supplies are available in Willcox.

For more information, write Chiricahua National Monument, Dos Cabezas Route, Box 6500, Willcox, AZ 85643, or telephone (520) 824-3560. The park's Web site is www.nps.gov/chir.

FURTHER READING

Hayes, Alden C. *A Portal to Paradise: 11,537 Years, More or Less, on the Northeast Slope of the Chiricahua Mountains: Being a Fairly Accurate and Occasionally Anecdotal History of That Part of Cochise County, Arizona, and the Country Immediately Adjacent, Replete with Tales of Glory and Greed, Heroism and Depravity, and Plain Hard Work.* Tucson: University of Arizona Press, 1999.

Kiver, Eugene P., and David V. Harris. *Geology of U.S. Parklands.* New York: John Wiley and Sons, 1999.

Lamberton, Ken. *Chiricahua Mountains: Bridging the Borders of Wildness.* Tucson: University of Arizona Press, 2003.

Sweeney, Edwin R. *Cochise: Chiricahua Apache Chief.* Norman: University of Oklahoma Press, 1991.

CHRISTIANSTED NATIONAL HISTORIC SITE

Location: Christiansted, St. Croix, Virgin Islands
Acreage: 27
Established: March 4, 1952

The colonial development of the Virgin Islands is commemorated by the eighteenth- and nineteenth-century structures at Christiansted National Historic Site, located on St. Croix Island, in the capital of the former Danish West Indies. Although first claimed and named by the French in 1650, the island of St. Croix did not flourish until the eighteenth century, under the influence of Danish sugar merchants. In 1733, the Danish West India and Guinea Company purchased St. Croix Island for sugar production development, and within two decades, sugar-cane cultivation flourished. As wealth flowed into the island, planters and merchants celebrated their prosperity with opulent homes and buildings, some of which survive to the present day. But the sugar boom did not last long. By 1820, international competition from the cultivation of sugar beets triggered a steep drop in sugar prices and signaled prosperity's end on St. Croix. In 1848, planters and merchants also lost the labor force that had made their plantations so profitable: slavery was outlawed. Following the Civil War, the United States began a long campaign to acquire St. Croix, St. Thomas, and St. John islands from Denmark. When their strategic importance as a Caribbean naval base became evident during World War I, Denmark relented, and in 1917, the United States purchased the islands for $15 million. One of four national park sites in the islands, Christiansted was originally designated the Virgin Islands National Historic Site in March 1952, and was renamed Christiansted National Historic Site in January 1961.

This 27-acre park is located in the port town of Christiansted on the West Indian island of St. Croix, U.S. Virgin Islands. The park's headquarters and information center is in Fort Christiansvaern, an outstanding example of Danish colonial fortification architecture built in 1749. The site is open from 8 A.M. to 5 P.M. daily and offers various publications, interpretive materials, and gifts. The entrance fee for the Fort and Steeple Building Museum is $2 for ages sixteen and older. The museum, which contains exhibits and information on the island's colonial history, is open from 8 A.M. to 5 P.M., Monday through Friday, and from 9 A.M. to 5 P.M. on Saturdays and Sundays. Visitors are encouraged to take a self-guided walking tour that begins at the fort and includes the site's five other buildings: the Danish Customs House, where the government collected taxes; the Scalehouse, where trade goods were inspected and weighed; the Government House, which included the governor's residence; the Danish West India and Guinea Company Warehouse; and the Steeple Building, the island's first Danish Lutheran Church later converted to a hospital, bakery, and school. Although there is no food or lodging at the park, Christiansted has all traveler services.

For more information, write Christiansted National Historic Site, P.O. Box 160, Christiansted, VI, 00821, or telephone (340) 773-1460. The park's Web site is www.nps.gov/chri.

FURTHER READING

Greene, Jerome A. *Fort Christiansvaern: Christiansted National Historic Site, Christiansted Virgin Islands.* Harpers Ferry, WV: Harpers Ferry Center, National Park Service, 1988.

Svensson, Ole, ed. *Three Towns: Conservation and Renewal of Charlotte Amalia, Christiansted, and Frederiksted of the U.S. Virgin Islands.* Copenhagen: Danish West Indian Society, 1980.

CITY OF ROCKS NATIONAL RESERVE

Location: Almo, Idaho
Acreage: 14,107
Established: November 18, 1988

"We encamped at the city of the rocks, a noted place from granite rocks rising abruptly out of the ground," wrote James Wilkins in 1849. A pioneer on the California Trail, Wilkins was among the first travelers to fix the name "City of Rocks" to this unique reserve located in southern Idaho on the northern edge of the Great Basin. The surreal rock formations evident throughout the reserve are the geologic product of millions of years of erosion. These weather-sculpted formations

President Harry S Truman delivering a speech at Christiansted, St. Croix, Virgin Islands, February 23, 1948. *(U.S. Navy, Courtesy Harry S Truman Library)*

range in age from the relatively "recent"—25 million years old—to over 2 billion years old.

Originally the home of the Shoshone and Bannock Indians, the City of Rocks area was an important landmark for emigrants on the California Trail and the Salt Lake Alternate Trail. It is estimated that in 1852 alone, 50,000 gold rushers came through this region seeking their fortunes in California. Some pioneers even wrote their names in axle grease on the reserve's rock faces—a feature still visible today. Renowned as one of the world's premier technical rock-climbing sites, the area's historical and geologic features, unique scenery, and opportunities for recreation led to its designation as a national reserve in 1988.

This over-14,000-acre park, a part of Idaho's Minidoka Bird Refuge, is home to eagles, falcons, vultures, hawks, hummingbirds, jays, and the state bird—the mountain bluebird; birding is best in May and June. The reserve's wide range of elevation supports more than 450 plant species, including a 55-foot-tall pinyon pine, Idaho's tallest. In late May, City of Rocks plays host to a fine wildflower display. Wildlife enthusiasts will appreciate the striking array of fauna in the park, including mountain lions, coyotes, badgers, bobcats, porcupines, elk, mule deer, and bats.

The City of Rocks National Reserve contains nearly 20 miles of hiking, biking, and horse trails, and is connected to nearby Mount Harrison via a 21-mile U.S. Forest Service trail (the Skyline Trail) suitable for backpacking, biking, or horseback riding. Open year-round, the park accommodates winter visitors with cross-country skiing, snowshoeing, and snowmobiling. The visitor center, located in Almo, Idaho, provides climbing guides, books, and information on road conditions, camping, and rock climbing. It is open daily in the summer and on weekdays

in the winter, from 8 A.M. to 4:30 P.M. On Friday and Saturday evenings between Memorial Day and Labor Day, park officials offer interpretive talks, guided hikes, and cultural demonstrations.

There are no entrance fees for City of Rocks, and each year more than 72,000 people visit the reserve (visitation peaks in August and September). Access to this isolated reserve is via 9 miles of dirt road from the Almo entrance, and about 17 miles of dirt road from the Oakley entrance. This is a high desert environment, and temperatures can be extreme. Since elevations in the park range from 5,000 to 8,000 feet above sea level, summers can be very hot while winter temperatures can drop well below freezing.

There are approximately 75 primitive campsites scattered throughout City of Rocks. Most are accessible from the road, contain picnic tables and fire rings, and cost $7 per night. Three group sites are also available. There is a sole potable water source in the park, but no hookups, showers, or dump stations. Vault toilets are located throughout the reserve. Backcountry permits are free and available at the visitor center. Visitors should be aware that the nearest motels are about 30 to 40 miles north of the reserve, along the I-84 corridor, although Almo has a bed-and-breakfast. City of Rocks National Reserve has no food or lodging facilities available, but Burley, Idaho, offers all travel services.

For more information, write City of Rocks National Reserve, P.O. Box 169, Almo, ID 83312, or telephone (208) 824-5519. The park's thorough Web site is www.nps.gov/ciro.

FURTHER READING

Elwell, Jean Nicholson. *Idaho's Silent City of Rocks: A Land of "Make-Believe."* Ogden, UT: Ramona's, 1994.

National Park Service. *Historic Resources Study: City of Rocks National Reserve, Southcentral Idaho.* Washington, DC: National Park Service, 1996.

CLARA BARTON NATIONAL HISTORIC SITE

Location: Glen Echo, Maryland
Acreage: 9
Established: October 26, 1974

Men have worshiped war till it has cost a million times more than the whole earth is worth.... war is Hell. ... Only the desire to soften some of its hardships ... ever induced me ... to face its pestilent and unholy breath.

So wrote Clara Barton (1821–1912), humanitarian and founder of the American Red Cross. The Clara Barton National Historic Site, which commemorates her life, was the first-ever dedicated to the accomplishments of a woman. The site's primary facility is Barton's home, located in Glen Echo, Maryland, which also served as the nation's Red Cross headquarters and a warehouse for disaster relief supplies. Originally set aside as a national historic landmark in 1965, the present 9-acre site was redesignated a national historic site in 1974, and is administered by the George Washington Memorial Parkway.

Born in 1821, Barton began her career, like many other women of her time, as a schoolteacher. By the 1850s, women had begun to move into other professions, and Barton seized the opportunity to work as a clerk in the U.S. Patent Office. For a short time, her salary was equal to that of her male counterparts—$1,400 per year—but in 1855, Barton was demoted, on account of her gender, to the position of copyist.

Six years later, however, when the United States became embroiled in the Civil War, Clara Barton found her true vocation. In July 1861, after the First Battle of Manassas (Bull Run), as Barton attended to wounded Union soldiers, she perceived the critical need for more efficient and sanitary field hospitals. By the following year, at the battle of Cedar Mountain, she began directing hospital logistics, organizing nursing staffs, and securing medical supplies. Present at some of the most gruesome battles of the war—Second Manassas, Antietam, Fredericksburg, the Wilderness, and Cold Harbor—Barton saved countless lives through her administrative efforts. At war's end, she helped identify and mark nearly 13,000 graves at Georgia's infamous Andersonville Prison, and raised the flag over the dedication of the Andersonville National Cemetery.

After the war, Barton joined the lecture circuit and became a strong advocate for the women's suffrage movement. "I believe I must have been born believing in the full right of women to all privileges and positions which nature and justice accord her common with other human begins," she said. "Perfectly equal rights—human rights. There was never any question in my mind in regard to this."

In 1881, Barton succeeded in forming the American Association of the Red Cross and served as its first president until 1904. The American Red Cross directed relief efforts for victims of natural disasters and war, including Mississippi River floods, New York's typhoid, and Florida's yellow fever epidemics, the Johnstown flood, the Galveston hurricane, and the Balkan War. Barton herself was on the scene when the USS *Maine* exploded in Havana Harbor in 1898, triggering the Spanish-American War. She died in April 1912, at the age of ninety.

Accessible from the Capital Beltway (I-495), the Clara Barton site is located off MacArthur Boulevard in Glen Echo, Maryland, several miles northwest of Washington, D.C. Admission and parking are free. The 38-room house contains interpretive exhibits and audiovisual programs, and thirty-minute guided tours are available daily from 10 A.M. to 4:30 P.M. These rooms provide visitors with a sense of the life and work of this dedicated woman, whose personal space was linked irrevocably with her public relief work. There is a small picnic area on the grounds, but no lodging, food, or camping facilities. All traveler services are available nearby in Montgomery County, Maryland, Washington, D.C., and northern Virginia. The National Park Service operates campgrounds at Greenbelt Park, Maryland, and Prince William Forest Park, Virginia.

For more information, write Clara Barton National Historic Site, 5801 Oxford Road, Glen Echo, MD 20812, or telephone (301) 492-6245. The park's thorough Web site is www.nps.gov/clba.

FURTHER READING

Oates, Stephen B. *A Woman of Valor: Clara Barton and the Civil War.* New York: Free Press, 1994.
Pryor, Elizabeth Brown. *Clara Barton: Professional Angel.* Philadelphia: University of Pennsylvania Press, 1987.

COLONIAL NATIONAL HISTORICAL PARK

Location: Jamestown and Yorktown, Virginia
Acreage: 8,677
Established: July 3, 1930

Colonial National Historical Park commemorates two of the most historically significant sites in North America—the beginning and end of British colonialism: the first permanent settlement at Jamestown in 1607, and the final major battle of the Revolutionary War at Yorktown in 1781. One of the very first objectives that Horace M. Albright laid out for the National Park Service as it sought to capture American history as one of its offerings, the area was first set aside in 1930, and redesignated a national historical park in 1936 at the height of the New Deal. In addition to its historical and cultural significance, the park also protects the unique environment of the Tidewater area along the James and York rivers, which includes extensive wetlands, forests, fields, shorelines, and streams, as well as threatened and endangered plants and animal species.

In 1607, a group of merchants established the first permanent colony in North America at Jamestown, Virginia. Granted a colonial charter by King James I of England, they operated as a joint-stock company, an early form of a modern corporation. In the early years, profits proved elusive, and the original investors and settlers received a rude shock. Instead of duplicating the remarkable success of the Spanish and Portuguese in Mexico, Peru, and Brazil, the Jamestown colonists died miserably from dysentery, malaria, and malnutrition. Between 1607 and 1609, more than 900 settlers, mostly men, journeyed to Jamestown; only 60 survived. Hampered by the swampy environment and their desire to avoid hard labor, the first colonists struggled for survival. The salvation of Jamestown was tobacco, which flourished in the region, and became the economic foundation for the colony's growth. Unfortunately, the settlers' insatiable need for land to increase tobacco cultivation ultimately led to bloody conflict with the region's native peoples, the Algonquians. Within two short generations, the English had decimated more than half of the native population of the Chesapeake; by 1670 only a dozen tribes and about 2,000 native people remained from the 20,000 natives who had inhabited the area when Jamestown was founded.

Just a hundred and seventy-four years after the founding of Jamestown, the self-declared American nation secured its independence at the decisive 1781 Battle of Yorktown. The hardest and most important fighting of the American Revolution took place in the South. Often outnumbered and usually outfought in traditional battle, the patriots soon adopted a guerrilla-style warfare that proved vexing to the loyalists. During the summer of 1781, British General Charles Cornwallis turned his troops toward the coastal Yorktown garrison to regroup and re-supply. Sensing an opportunity, George Washington coordinated his troop movements with allied French naval operations and moved in for the victory. In September, more than 16,000 American and French troops converged on the 8,000-man British garrison at Yorktown. Desperate for relief, Cornwallis wrote to the British commander in New York, "If you cannot relieve me very soon, you must expect to hear the worst." For the British, the result was "the worst": on October 19, 1781, Cornwallis surrendered. Britain's prime minister, Lord North, exclaimed, "Oh God, it is all over." And indeed it was. In 1783, Britain signed the Treaty of Paris granting independence to the United States and establishing its western boundary at the Mississippi River.

Colonial National Historical Park maintains 2 visitor centers, which are open year-round from 9 A.M. to 5 P.M. daily. The Jamestown Visitor Center houses archeological artifacts from this early settlement, paintings depicting events experienced by the colonists, model replicas of the fort and the 3 ships that brought the settlers to America, and a theater program that explores Jamestown and early colonial history. Walking tours begin at the visitor center and include stops at the Old Church Tower—the only seventeenth-century building still standing above ground level; the seventeenth century home of Sir William Berkeley, Virginia's colonial governor; and the Cape Henry Memorial, which marks the approximate site of the first landing of the Jamestown colonists in April 1607. A special point of interest is the reconstructed Jamestown Glasshouse, where glassblowers demonstrate this ancient craft. Seasonal programs include the Pinch Pot Program, Living History Character tours, and guided ranger tours. The Yorktown Visitor Center offers

exhibits on the original eighteenth- and nineteenth-century earthworks and the colonial architecture of the period, as well as tours of the town of York and the battlefield. Visitors will also want to tour Moore House, where the defeated British and the victorious Americans negotiated the terms of surrender; it is open for tours daily in the summer, and on weekends in the spring and fall. Events at the park include the Lamb's Artillery Firing Program, the 1862 Siege Anniversary, Memorial Day Weekend/Civil War Weekend, Independence Day Celebration, and the Yorktown Victory Celebration. Entrance fees are $5 for Jamestown, $4 for Yorktown, and $7 for a joint Jamestown/Yorktown pass. All park grounds are closed daily at sunset.

Although there are no camping, dining, or lodging facilities in the park, a full range of traveler services is located nearby in Williamsburg, Newport News, Hampton, and Yorktown, and the area has many private campgrounds. A beach picnic area is open seasonally at Yorktown, and some picnic tables are available in the parking lots. Colonial National Historical Park is located a short distance from I-64, about 40 miles southeast of Richmond, near Williamsburg, and the scenic 23-mile Colonial Parkway connects the Jamestown and Yorktown sites.

For more information, write Colonial National Historical Park, P.O. Box 210, Yorktown, VA 23690-0210, or telephone (757) 898-3400. The park's informative Web site is www.nps.gov/colo.

FURTHER READING

Flexner, James Thomas. *George Washington and the New Nation, 1783–1793.* Boston: Little, Brown, 1970.

Griffith, Samuel B. *The War for American Independence: From 1760 to the Surrender at Yorktown in 1781.* Urbana: University of Illinois Press, 2002.

Miller, John C. *The Origins of the American Revolution.* Boston: Little, Brown, 1943.

Rountree, Helen C. *Before and After Jamestown: Virginia's Powhatans and Their Predecessors.* Gainesville: University Press of Florida, 2002.

Royster, Charles. *A Revolutionary People at War: The*

Continental Army and American Character, 1775–1783. Charlottesville: University of Virginia Press, 1979.

COLORADO NATIONAL MONUMENT

Location: Fruita, Colorado
Acreage: 20,534
Established: May 24, 1911

A stunning landscape of towering red sandstone monoliths, spires, sheer-walled canyons, and beautiful vistas, Colorado National Monument has been compared by some to Arizona's famous Monument Valley. The geologic array of sandstone, shale, and dark igneous and metamorphic rocks tells the story of millions of years of earth building and subsequent erosion. Although the area receives a sparse average annual rainfall of only 11 inches, heavy thunderstorms, winter snow and ice, and high winds have had pronounced erosive effect, particularly on the soft sandstone formations. Set aside as a national monument in 1911, this over-20,000-acre park is home to bighorn sheep, golden eagles, mule deer, mountain bluebirds, and mountain lions.

The park's most popular attraction is the 23-mile, winding, narrow, paved Rim Rock Drive. Connecting the park's east and west entrances, the road is renowned as one of the most scenic drives in any national park property in America. As it winds along canyon cliffs, over juniper-forested mesas, and through narrow tunnels carved in sandstone formations, Rim Rock Drive offers many scenic overlooks that provide outstanding views of the monument and the surrounding valley, as well as of Grand Mesa to the east—the world's highest, largest flattop mountain. Several of the park's 13 backcountry hiking trails lead off the Rim Rock Road drive, including the impressive Monument Canyon Trail. In addition to scenery, the Black Ridge and Liberty Cap trails offer views of extensive An-asazi and Ute Indian petroglyphs. There is also a shorter, self-guided Alcove Trail near the visitor center. Hikers should be accustomed to high altitudes before attempting any of the longer, more strenuous trails.

Colorado National Monument (NM) was among the first generation of areas added to the monument category. Its 1911 establishment precedes the founding of the National Park Service by a full half-decade and when the agency began to implement programs in national monuments, Colorado NM was often left out. It lacked the archeological features such as pueblos that characterized the early vision of monuments. As a result, it remained a remote and lightly visited area for most of the twentieth century.

Colorado NM is open all day, year-round. Entrance fees are $4 per vehicle and $2 per person—a $10 annual pass is also available. Located due south of the west entrance, the visitor center is open from 9 A.M. to 5 P.M. daily and offers an audiovisual program, interpretive exhibits, and a small bookstore. Evening campfire programs are held in the campground during the summer months, on Saturdays and Sundays only. Visitors should be prepared for unpredictable weather, particularly in the summer when heavy cloudbursts are frequent. Although the monument's elevation ranges from 4,700 feet to 7,028 feet, temperatures are generally mild, with few extremes, except at the higher elevations where winters can be cold and windy.

In addition to several picnic facilities, the monument operates the 80-site Saddlehorn Campground, which is open year-round. It has rest rooms with flush toilets and sinks, drinking water, charcoal grills, and picnic tables. No wood fires are allowed in the monument and there is no water available in winter. Camping fees are $10 per site year-round; there are also several private campgrounds located nearby. The monument has no lodging or food services, but all travel services can be obtained in Fruita (3 miles north of the west entrance) and Grand Junction (4 miles east of the east entrance).

For more information, write Colorado National Monument, Fruita, CO 81521-9530, or telephone (970) 858-3617. The park's Web site is www.nps.gov/colm.

FURTHER READING
Kania, Alan. *John Otto: Trials and Trails.* Niwot: University Press of Colorado, 1996.

Lohman, Stanley William. *The Geologic Story of Colorado National Monument.* Gunnison: Colorado and Black Canyon Natural History Association, 1965.

Schock-Roberts, Lisa. *A Classic Western Quarrel: A History of the Road Controversy at Colorado National Monument.* Denver, CO: National Park Service, 1997.

CONGAREE NATIONAL PARK

Location: Hopkins, South Carolina
Acreage: 21,744
Established: October 18, 1976

Here in the heart of South Carolina lies a wilderness of big trees and dark, quiet creeks. The area preserved by South Carolina's Congaree National Park was originally the domain of prehistoric hunters and gatherers who hunted and fished the rich waters. Later claimed by the Congaree Indian tribe, the area was first noted by whites in the journals of Spanish explorer Hernando de Soto. By 1700, European settlement had introduced a devastating smallpox epidemic to the region that decimated the Congarees, leaving the land essentially vacant. The new Euro-American residents quickly set about altering the natural environment to make the land suitable for planting and grazing. Although its minor elevation changes and frequent flooding checked agricultural activity, the rich, dense forest thrived, and soon attracted the attention of logging interests. Poor accessibility confined logging operations to tracts near waterways so logs could be floated downriver. Yet in these swamp-like conditions, many of

the cut trees remained too green to float, and operations were soon suspended as unprofitable, leaving the swamp's loblolly pines, bald cypress, sweet gums, ash, hickories, elms, and other tree species basically untouched.

By the 1970s, high timber prices prompted private landowners to consider resuming logging operations, which, in turn, provoked a strong response from the growing environmental movement. Local individuals allied with the Sierra Club in a grassroots campaign to protect this unique, old-growth, floodplain forest ecosystem, and in 1976, Congress authorized the almost-22,000-acre Congaree Swamp National Monument. Further preservation of the area's natural diversity came in June 1983, when the monument was declared an International Biosphere Reserve, again in October 1988, when Congress set aside large portions of the park as wilderness, and finally in November 2003, when the monument became the nation's fifty-seventh national park. Despite the park's previous name, Congaree is not truly a swamp, but a continually renewed nutrient-rich floodplain that boasts some of the largest trees east of the Mississippi and one of the tallest temperate deciduous forest canopies in the world.

None of these designations was strong enough to protect Congaree from Hurricane Hugo in September 1989. The park lost several National Champion Trees to the storm, but overall the forest proved remarkably resilient. The hurricane's winds had snapped treetops, allowing sunlight to penetrate the canopy and promote new growth. Fallen trees provided shelter for many new species of organisms, and standing dead trees became new homes for a variety of plant and animal species, including fungi, insects, reptiles, birds, and bats.

Today, this significant tract of old-growth, bottomland hardwood forest has more than 20 miles of hiking trails–including a 2.3-mile boardwalk that is wheelchair accessible, and

18 miles of marked canoe trails. Both hikers and boaters should wear long-sleeve shirts, long pants, and boots, and bring along industrial-strength bug repellent, a compass, first-aid kit, and drinking water.

Located about 20 miles southeast of Columbia, South Carolina, Congaree is open daily from dawn until dusk, and there is no admission fee. The ranger station is also open daily from 8:30 A.M. to 5 P.M., and features exhibits, an information desk, and a bookstore. Seasonal programs include guided nature walks, school tours, "owl-prowls," guided canoe trips, and a Nature Fest in April. Visitation to the park is highest in spring and fall, and lowest during the hot and humid summer and cool winter months.

There is no lodging or food service in the park; both can be obtained in Columbia. Free backcountry primitive camping is available in the park with a permit obtained from the ranger station, and a few surrounding state parks offer fully developed campgrounds that charge fees. Larger groups may stay at the Bluff Campground, which has Porta-Johns, fire rings, and picnic tables.

For more information, write Congaree National Park, 200 Caroline Sims Road, Hopkins, SC 29061, or telephone (803) 776-4396. The park's Web site is www.nps.gov/cosw.

FURTHER READING
Adams, Edward C.L. *Tales of the Congaree.* Chapel Hill: University of North Carolina Press, 1987.
Michie, James L. *An Archeological Survey of Congaree Swamp: Cultural Resources Inventory and Assessment of a Bottomland Environment in Central South Carolina.* Columbia: Institute of Archeology and Anthropology, University of South Carolina, 1980.
Porcher, Richard D. *A Guide to the Wildflowers of South Carolina.* Columbia: University of South Carolina Press, 2001.

CONSTITUTION GARDENS
Location: Washington, D.C.
Acreage: 52
Established: August 1, 1974

Constitution Gardens is an oasis in the hectic urban Washington, D.C., landscape. The 52-acre park was originally beneath the Potomac River until a turn-of-the-century U.S. Army Corps of Engineers' dredging project created this eventual monument to the founding of the republic. Beginning in World War I, the navy maintained temporary office buildings on this site. Nicknamed "tempos," these structures remained until the 1970s, when President Richard M. Nixon began lobbying for their removal. The buildings were demolished in 1971, and the renowned architectural firm of Skidmore, Owings, and Merrill designed and built the park, which includes a 6.5-acre artificial lake surrounding a 1-acre island.

In May 1976, the Gardens was established as a living legacy for the American Revolution Bicentennial tribute. Six years later, in July of 1982, President Ronald Reagan dedicated the signers of the Declaration of Independence Memorial on the lake's small island. This memorial features fifty-six low granite stones, arranged in a half-circle in thirteen groups representing the thirteen original states. Each stone is inscribed with a signer's signature, his profession, and his hometown. Further recognition for the area came in September 1986, when, in honor of the Constitution's bicentennial, President Reagan issued a proclamation making Constitution Gardens a living legacy tribute to the Constitution. Each year, to celebrate this purpose, the National Park Service hosts a naturalization ceremony for new citizens at the site. Park rangers also offer interpretive programs, talks, and walking tours of the mall.

Located between the Lincoln Memorial, the Washington Monument, Constitution Avenue, and the Reflecting Pool, the park is open year-round, from 8 A.M. to 11:45 P.M. daily. There are no fees to this or any other national mall memorials or sites. The climate in Washington, D.C., is seasonal; summers can be very hot and humid with an average temperature of 82 degrees. Winters are variable and can be very mild to very cold, with an average temperature of 35 degrees.

Parking in Washington, D.C., is extremely scarce but is available on city streets during nonrush-hour times (9 A.M. until 4 P.M.) during the week. There are parking lots at the Washington Monument and Jefferson Memorial that provide two-hour parking. Parking is also available for longer periods along Ohio Drive near the Lincoln and Jefferson memorials. There are several Metro train routes from the suburban areas surrounding the city. The Smithsonian Metro station provides the most direct access to the National Mall.

The Tourmobile provides one method of visiting Constitution Gardens while avoiding parking problems. Tourmobile sightseeing offers daily, narrated shuttle tours to 18 major sites on the National Mall and Arlington National Cemetery. One ticket allows unlimited free reboarding throughout the day. Boarding locations can be found throughout the National Mall, at the major monuments and memorials, and at the Arlington National Cemetery Visitor Center. Advance arrangements are available through TicketMaster at (800) 551-SEAT (outside D.C., Maryland, and Virginia); the local number is (202) 432-SEAT.

Lodging and meals are available in Washington, D.C., and the surrounding metro area. It is advisable to make lodging reservations in advance for the peak late spring, summer, and fall tourist seasons. Private campgrounds are located farther out in the countryside.

For more information, write Constitution Gardens, c/o National Capital Parks-Central, The National Mall, 900 Ohio Drive, SW, Washington, DC 20242, or telephone (202) 426-6841. The park's Web site is www.nps.gov/coga.

FURTHER READING

Bowen, Catherine Drinker. *Miracle at Philadelphia: The Story of the Constitutional Convention May to September, 1787.* New York: Book-of-the-Month Club, 1986.

Wood, Gordon S. *The Creation of the American Republic, 1776–1787.* Chapel Hill: University of North Carolina Press, 1998.

CORONADO NATIONAL MEMORIAL

Location: Hereford, Arizona
Acreage: 4,750
Established: August 18, 1941

Coronado National Memorial lies at the southern end of the Huachuca Mountains, on the U.S.-Mexican border, within sight of the San Pedro River Valley. Near there, in February 1540, Francisco Vasquez de Coronado brought his men north from Mexico and became the first European to enter what later became the United States. Coronado searched for the fabled Seven Cities of Cibola and focused on securing the vast riches he believed could be found there. By spring 1541, his force had made its way north and east before crossing into New Mexico through present-day Albuquerque, northern Texas, and into Kansas. Disappointed at being unable to find and secure riches for the Spanish crown, a wounded Coronado returned to Mexico in spring 1542 under a cloud that stemmed from his handling of a war with the Tiguex people.

While Coronado did not succeed in finding wealth for the crown, his expedition changed the nature of Spanish exploration. Coronado's men remained under government control throughout their two-year journey. They followed the rules set out for them, which included restrictions on using native people as carriers of their equipment, and the missionaries among them attempted to convert these people to Christianity. Coronado's men gave the Spanish in Mexico the first clear account of the lands to their north, and they were followed by countless explorers. Native American cultures paid a price during this initial contact. Thinking he needed a supply base for many smaller, ancillary expeditions, Coronado attacked and occupied a hostile Zuni Pueblo for four months.

Although some tribes welcomed the Spanish—mostly as possible allies against other tribes—many did not like the explorers trespassing on their lands. When Coronado discovered a Plains Indian had duped him about the lost golden city of Quivira—in the hopes that the expedition would get lost and perish on the vast Great Plains—Coronado had the Indian put to death.

Dejected over failure, the demoralized Coronado returned to Mexico, faced trial for his failed mission, and barely avoided being convicted and put to death himself. Even though he did not locate the fabled gold-covered cities, Coronado's expedition opened the way for Spanish colonial development.

First set aside in 1941 on the four hundredth anniversary of Coronado's arrival in the Southwest and renamed in 1952, the 4,750-acre Coronado National Memorial, located on the Arizona-Mexico border, 26 miles west of Bisbee, commemorates both the first major exploration of the American Southwest by Europeans and the region's Hispanic heritage.

There is no fee to enter the memorial; donations are accepted at the visitor center. Hours of operation are daily from 8 A.M. to 5 P.M., and it is closed on Thanksgiving and Christmas Day. The memorial has a small museum with authentic and replica sixteenth-century arms and armor, a nine-minute video on Coronado's expedition, period costumes for visitors to try on, and wildlife and bird exhibits. Rangers offer history and nature programs and tours of Coronado Cave for groups when scheduled in advance, and for the general public on weekends during the busy seasons. Most museum exhibits, some videos, and all wayside signs are in English and Spanish.

Many roads and trails of varying condi-

tion allow for auto or hiking tours of the monument. East Montezuma Canyon Road is paved from Arizona Highway 92 to 1 mile west of the visitor center; then it is a narrow, unpaved mountain road to the scenic overlook at Montezuma Pass. The dirt road continues west into the Coronado National Forest. There are hiking trails from the visitor center west to Montezuma Pass, from Montezuma Pass south to Coronado Peak, from Montezuma Pass north to Miller Peak connecting with trails in the Miller Peak Wilderness; and from the visitor center to Coronado Cave (a permit is required).

There is no lodging, food service, or camping in the park. Lodging and restaurants are available in Sierra Vista and Bisbee. There is abundant camping available in adjacent Coronado National Forest lands.

For more information, write Coronado National Memorial, 4101 East Montezuma Canyon Road, Hereford, AZ 85615, or telephone (520) 366-5515. The park's Web site is www.nps.gov/coro.

FURTHER READING
Flint, Richard, and Shirley Cushing Flint, eds. *The Coronado Expedition to Tierra Nueva: The 1540–1542 Route Across the Southwest.* Niwot: University Press of Colorado, 1997.

Preston, Douglas J. *Cities of Gold: A Journey Across the American Southwest.* Albuquerque: University of New Mexico Press, 1999.

COWPENS NATIONAL BATTLEFIELD
Location: Chesnee, South Carolina
Acreage: 842
Established: March 4, 1929

By the time the sun crept over the horizon in Cherokee County, South Carolina, on January 17, 1781, a battle between Continentals and militia under General Daniel Morgan and the notorious British Dragoon leader Banastre Tarleton was well under way. The British had tracked Morgan across South Carolina; Tarleton had been sent to pursue, harass, and if possible destroy Morgan's forces. Continental scouts observed the British about 6 miles from the Americans' camp in a place called Thicketty Creek, and Morgan was forced to make a difficult tactical decision: ford the Broad River and risk an attack against him when his army was in transition or dig in and find a place to fight. Morgan found the Cowpens, a cattle-penning area slightly above the fields through which the British would approach, and set his troops in three lines there.

In the predawn darkness, the British crossed the Green River Road short of the Cowpens and were surprised by rifle fire from Morgan's crack sharpshooters. Caught off guard, the British advance briefly stalled as fifteen cavalrymen fell in the first volley. The more than 1,100 well-organized regulars regrouped in classic British style and advanced to the second line of Morgan's defense, the militia. The British advance slowed for a moment in the face of withering fire and continued forward until it reached Morgan's third line, the Continentals, who seemed to fall away as the regulars advanced. Pushed back by confusion and then halted by Morgan's loud commands, the Continentals wheeled and sent a devastating barrage into the onrushing British. Patriot militiamen flanked the British on one side; Continental cavalry closed a pincer move from the other, and the vaunted British soldiers turned and ran. In the brief battle, Morgan's men played a decisive role in determining the fate of the South in the Revolutionary War.

Cowpens National Battlefield, an 842-acre tract about 10 miles east of Gaffney and 17 miles northeast of Spartanburg, South Carolina, was established as a national battlefield

Colonel William Augustine Washington at the Battle of Cowpens, January 1781. *(National Archives)*

under the jurisdiction of the War Department on March 4, 1929. With most other War Department holdings, it was transferred to the National Park Service by the reorganization of the federal government under Franklin D. Roosevelt's New Deal. It was one of the many sites commemorating American history transferred to the park system during the New Deal.

At the battlefield, a 1.5-mile loop trail takes visitors around and through this important piece of Revolutionary War history. A 4-mile automobile road circles the park, and its wayside exhibits discuss the battle. Interpretive exhibits in the visitor center, including a video program called *Daybreak at Cowpens* and a fiber-optic map program of the battle, further tell the story of the dramatic battle that helped break British power in the South.

For more information, write Cowpens National Battlefield, P.O. Box 308, Chesnee, SC 29323, or telephone (864) 461-2828. The park's Web site is www.nps.gov/cowp.

FURTHER READING

Babits, Lawrence E. *A Devil of a Whipping: The Battle of Cowpens.* Chapel Hill: University of North Carolina Press, 2001.
Davis, Burke. *The Cowpens-Guilford Courthouse Campaign.* Philadelphia: University of Pennsylvania Press, 2002.

CRATER LAKE NATIONAL PARK

Location: Crater Lake, Oregon
Acreage: 183,224
Established: May 22, 1902

With depths approaching 2,000 feet, Crater Lake in southcentral Oregon is the deepest lake in the United States, the seventh-deepest freshwater lake in the world, and holds the world record for natural water clarity. This 6-mile-wide caldera was created by the eruption and collapse of Mount Mazama almost seven thousand years ago—estimated to be

forty-two times more powerful than the May 1980 Mount Saint Helens explosion. Subsequent lava flows sealed cracks in the bottom, allowing the caldera to fill over the millennia with approximately 4.6 trillion gallons of water from rainfall, snow melt, and warm springs. Although Mazama is now dormant, additional volcanic activity created a cinder cone inside the caldera; Wizard Island rises over 700 feet above the lake's surface. Wildflowers and conifers eventually recolonized the lava-covered landscape surrounding Crater Lake, which is now home to black bears, bobcats, deer, marmots, eagles, and hawks. For centuries, the eruption was retold in Native American creation legends, and the local Klamaths revered both the lake and the surrounding area. Prospectors first happened upon Crater Lake by accident in 1853. "This is the bluest lake we've ever seen," they exclaimed, but the search for gold overshadowed their discovery, and Deep Blue Lake, as they named it, was soon forgotten. Crater Lake's champion was William Gladstone Steel, who devoted his life and fortune to the preservation of this scenic wonder as a national park. His efforts included extensive lake surveys that provided scientific support for his seventeen-year campaign. His persistence paid off. After fighting against ranching, timber, and development interests, and personally appealing to President Theodore Roosevelt, Steel convinced the Congress and the nation that the lake's uniqueness and grandiose scenery rated federal protection.

In 1902, Crater Lake became America's sixth national park. Judge William Gladstone Steel, a Kansan, had become obsessed with the park as a young man and vowed to make the spectacular lake one of the national parks. He and some friends sent a petition in favor of the park to President Grover Cleveland, and bills were offered in Congress as early as 1886. In the 1890s, the state of Oregon became interested, proposing to hire a guardian

Crater Lake National Park in 1942. During the summer months, park visitors may follow the Rim Drive around the lake, enjoy boat tours, or hike the park's various trails. *(Library of Congress)*

for the lake, and its U.S. representatives spearheaded the passage of park legislation. Steel's personal interest and ongoing interest from the Oregon congressional delegation led to the eventual establishment.

At 183,224 acres, Crater Lake is one of the smaller national parks in the western United States. During the summer, visitors may navigate the 33-mile Rim Drive around the lake, enjoy boat tours on the lake surface, stay in the historic Crater Lake Lodge, camp at Mazama Village, or hike one of the park's many trails. Numerous interpretative programs enhance visitors' knowledge and appreciation of this national park, 90 percent of which is managed as wilderness.

Winter brings some of the heaviest snowfall in America—averaging 533 inches per year. Although most park facilities close during this snowy season, visitors may view the lake during fair weather, enjoy cross-country skiing, and participate in weekend ranger-led snowshoe hikes. The months of July through mid-September are mild with little precipitation. Due to the park's elevation (6,500 feet at park headquarters and 7,100 feet at Rim Village), weather conditions can change quickly. From October through June, blizzards, high winds, extreme cold, and low visibility are frequent. About 500,000 people visit the park each year, with the peak season being late summer.

Open year-round, Crater Lake National Park is located in southern Oregon on the crest of the Cascade Range, 57 miles north of Klamath Falls. The entrance fee for cars and motor homes is $10, $5 for bicycles/foot traffic, and is valid for seven days. Boat Tours cost $15 for adults and $8.50 for children. The Steel Information Center, located at park headquarters on the south side of the park, is open year-round. Park rangers can assist with information, trip planning, weather forecasts, and backcountry camping permits. An eighteen-minute video is shown every half-hour in the summer, and upon request in the winter. Books, maps, posters, and educational materials are also available. The Rim Village Visitor Center is located on the south rim of the caldera, approximately 200 yards west of Crater Lake Lodge. Park information, back-country camping permits, and educational materials are available here. It is open June through September. Interpretive exhibits concerning the park's history are located inside Crater Lake Lodge. Activities include nature walks, campfire programs, children's programs, historical tours, narrated boat tours, and winter snowshoe tours.

From mid-May through mid-October, lodging is available at the newly renovated, 71-room Crater Lake Lodge, and at the Mazama Motor Inn in Mazama Village. Advance reservations are strongly recommended and can be obtained on-line. During this season, many restaurant and food facilities are also open. Some restaurants serve light meals in the winter. Groceries and gas can be obtained at Mazama Campground during the summer.

Mazama is the park's most developed campground, and is considered one of the nicest in the National Park System because of its spacious layout and services. It has 200 sites, running water, flush toilets, picnic tables, and fire rings, and is open from June 9 until October 1. The smaller, more primitive Lost Creek Campground is located in the park's east end near the Pinnacles. It has only 16 tent sites and is open from July 1 until October 1. Both campsites are first-come, first-served. Crater Lake originally had no fish but was stocked by Steel many years ago. Some kokanee salmon and rainbow trout still survive, but the lake is so deep and the fish are so few that fishing efforts are not very productive. No license is required for those who relish a challenge.

For more information, write Crater Lake National Park, P.O. Box 7, Crater Lake, OR 97604, or telephone (541) 594-2211, for general information and current weather conditions. For lodging reservations, telephone (541) 830-8700. The park's informative Web site is www.nps.gov/crla.

FURTHER READING

Blakeslee, Charles A., et al. *Wild and Beautiful Crater Lake.* Helena, MT: Farcountry Press, 2001.

Crater Lake National Park at 100: Special Issue of the Oregon Historical Quarterly, Spring 2002.

Harmon, Rick. *Crater Lake National Park: A History.* Corvallis: Oregon State University Press, 2002.

CRATERS OF THE MOON NATIONAL MONUMENT AND PRESERVE

Location: Arco, Idaho
Acreage: 714,727
Established: May 2, 1924

A visit to southcentral Idaho's Craters of the Moon National Monument and Preserve is like setting foot on a desolate lunar landscape. In fact, the geologic features of the monument are so moon-like that American astronauts trained here for the Apollo moon landings during the late 1960s and early 1970s. Craters of the Moon boasts more than twenty cinder cones, including excellent examples of spatter cones, over sixty different lava flows ranging in age from two thousand to fifteen thousand years old, and outstanding examples of pahoehoe and aa lava flows. In addition to its geologic wonder, the park also has a historic aspect: the northern end contains a portion of

Goodale's Cutoff, which is part of the Oregon Trail. Craters of the Moon's seemingly desolate landscape is deceiving, for the park is home to more than 350 species of plants, 43 mammals, more than 160 different species of birds, and 2,000 insect species. All have adapted in order to survive this harsh, high-desert environment.

Established by presidential proclamation in 1924, the monument contains remarkable fissure eruptions and associated volcanic cones, lava tubes, craters, rifts, lava flows, and natural bridges. It is the largest basaltic, dominantly Holocene (last ten thousand years) lava field in the conterminous United States, and Big Cinder Butte is one of the largest basaltic cinder cones in the world. Further protection for the park came in October of 1970, when President Richard M. Nixon signed into law the Craters of the Moon Wilderness Area, preserving approximately 43,000 acres of one of the most astonishing landscapes in America. An additional expansion took place in 2000, and the designation as a National Preserve became official in August 2002.

Extensive lava flows at the Craters of the Moon National Monument and Preserve. *(Library of Congress)*

A flashlight is required to explore the lava tubes (caves), and a hat is highly recommended. Some of the lava caves can be difficult to enter and maneuver; only experts at spelunking should attempt these caves. One cave, Boy Scout, has an ice floor that can be slippery. There is a 7-mile-long loop drive through the monument, and numerous hiking trails ranging from a quarter mile to 8 miles round-trip.

Located about 18 miles southwest of Arco, Idaho, the monument is open all day, year-round. Entrance fees are $4 per vehicle; $2 per individual; and $10 per site per night to camp. The recently remodeled Robert Limber Visitor Center has a museum, art exhibits on natural and cultural history, and a book sales outlet. The visitor center is open daily in the summer from 8 A.M. to 6 P.M., and during the rest of the year from 8 A.M. to 4:30 P.M. Visitation is highest in July and August, and lowest in December and January. Craters of the Moons's weather can vary from warm and dry in the summer, to below freezing in the winter. Precipitation averages 17 inches per year.

There are no food or travel services in the park itself, but nearby Arco has all travel facilities. The monument does offer a unique 52-site campground set among the cinders and lava flows. It has rest rooms, picnic tables, charcoal grills, and scattered water taps. There are no hookups, and no wood fires are allowed.

For more information, write Craters of the Moon National Monument and Preserve, P.O. Box 29, Arco, ID 83213, or telephone (208) 527-3257. The park's informative Web site is www.nps.gov/crmo.

FURTHER READING

Dykes, Fred W. *Jeffrey's Cutoff: Idaho's Forgotten Oregon Trail Route.* Pocatello, ID: Pocatello Copy Cat, 1989.

Louter, David. *Administrative History: Craters of the Moon National Monument, Idaho.* Seattle, WA: Cultural Resources Division, Pacific Northwest Re-

gion, 1992. Available at www.nps.gov/crmo/adhi.
htm.

Schwantes, Carlos. *In Mountain Shadows: A History of Idaho.* Lincoln: University of Nebraska Press, 1990.

CUMBERLAND GAP NATIONAL HISTORICAL PARK

Location: Kentucky, Tennessee,
 and Virginia
Acreage: 20,508
Established: June 11, 1940

The Cumberland Gap is a narrow break in the Appalachian Mountain chain first used by migratory animals like bison and deer, and later by Native Americans. In the late eighteenth and early nineteenth centuries, the Gap became a doorway for Euro-American pioneers; between 1775 and 1810, hundreds of thousands of men, women, and children crossed through the Gap into the mostly unknown wilderness of the American West. The most famous name associated with the Cumberland Gap is Daniel Boone, who blazed the first marked trail–the Wilderness Trail–through the region in 1775. Within a single generation, the relentless tide of human migration had filled Kentucky territory with homesteads, and in 1792, the Bluegrass State became the nation's fifteenth. Statehood triggered an even greater flood of people; by 1830, more than 300,000 emigrants had passed through the Gap on their way to the West. With the advent of canals and railroads in the 1830s, however, the Gap's importance as an east-west route began to subside. During the Civil War, the Cumberland Gap assumed a new strategic importance, as both sides sought to secure this valuable travel corridor. Control of the Gap changed hands several times, yet despite numerous back-and-forth maneuvers and small skirmishes, no significant Civil War battle was ever fought there.

In 1940, Congress authorized Cumberland Gap National Historical Park, set aside to protect a scenic stretch of Cumberland Mountain and to commemorate the opening of the West through this historically significant passage through the central Appalachian Mountains. It was a piece with the era, which saw the creation of the Jefferson National Expansion Memorial in St. Louis as well. During the depression decade, the Park Service became a primary purveyor of American history; much of it showed national expansion in a dramatic light, suggesting that the ideals, lessons, and practices of the past could be applied to the very tough economic times of the 1930s. As did most national park areas in the East, Cumberland Gap required the purchase of much private land, and, only in 1955, did the park acquire enough land (20,000 acres) to allow establishment. Later boundary extension increased the park to its current size.

More than 55 miles of hiking trails meander through this dense eastern deciduous forest park. Trail distances range from a quarter-mile loop trail to the 21-mile-long Ridge Trail. Towering 3,500 feet above the valley, White Rocks was a welcome sight to travelers on the Wilderness Trail. Upon seeing this massive limestone outcropping, the settlers knew they were but a day's journey from the Cumberland Gap. Today, visitors can hike or ride horseback 3 miles to the top of White Rocks. Leaving the visitor center, park visitors can also drive a winding 4-mile-long road up the mountain to the Pinnacle Overlook (elevation 2,440 feet) for a spectacular view into the three states of Kentucky, Virginia, and Tennessee; this road also passes by a small earthen Civil War–era fort.

Located where southeast Kentucky, southwest Virginia, and northeast Tennessee meet, Cumberland Gap National Historical Park is open year-round. There is no entrance fee. The visitor center is open Memorial Day through Labor Day from 8 A.M. to 6 P.M. daily, and from 8 A.M. to 5 P.M. during the rest of the year. Exhibits, artifacts, and a film tell the story of the Gap as a transportation corridor. The park offers numerous ranger-led activities, including tours of the restored Hensley settlement and campfire programs. Visitation peaks in July and in October when the mountains come alive with brilliant fall foliage, and is lowest during the months of January and February.

There is no food or lodging in the park, but both are available in Cumberland Gap and Tazewell, Tennessee, and Middlesboro, Kentucky. The 160-site Wilderness Road campground is open year-round and has all amenities including hot showers. Rates are $10 per night for sites without electricity, $15 per night for sites with electricity, and $20 per night for group sites. Five primitive back-country campgrounds are also available with a free permit.

For more information, write Cumberland Gap National Historical Park, P.O. Box 1848, Middlesboro, KY 40965, or telephone (606) 248-2817. The park's innovative Web site is www.nps.gov/cuga.

FURTHER READING

Aron, Stephen. *How the West Was Lost: The Transformation of Kentucky from Daniel Boone to Henry Clay.* Baltimore, MD: Johns Hopkins University Press, 1996.

Faragher, John Mack. *Daniel Boone: The Life and Legend of an American Pioneer.* New York: Holt, 1992.

Rohrbough, Malcolm J. *The Trans-Appalachian Frontier: People, Societies, and Institutions, 1775–1850.* Belmont, CA: Wadsworth, 1990.

CUMBERLAND ISLAND NATIONAL SEASHORE

Location: St. Marys, Georgia
Acreage: 36,415
Established: October 23, 1972

In 1972, Cumberland Island National Seashore was set aside to protect one of the largest undeveloped barrier islands in the world. The 36,415-acre seashore contains federally designated wilderness and preserves one of the largest maritime forests remaining in the United States. Stretching for 17.5 miles along Georgia's coast, Cumberland Island consists of salt marshes, mud flats, tidal creeks, and dune fields, and is renowned for its sea turtles and abundant shore birds. To protect the island's natural environment and minimize human impact, visitation is limited to no more than 300 people per day. Opportunities for relaxation and solitude on this undisturbed island paradise abound, although more adventurous visitors may wish to visit and tour historic structures such as the Ice House at Dungeness Dock, and the Plum Orchard mansion. In all, the island has witnessed more than four thousand years of human history, and its former residents include Native Americans, Spanish missionaries, English colonials, Revolutionary War heroes, enslaved African Americans, plantation owners, and wealthy Gilded Age industrialists.

Yet the park might never have been established if most of the island's current residents had not banded together with national environmental organizations and the Department of the Interior. Much of the land came from the Carnegie family; Thomas Carnegie, the brother of steel magnate Andrew Carnegie, bought 4,000 acres of the island in the 1880s. Many other smaller landowners agreed to the personal sacrifice of selling their property for the national interest. In the 1990s, the Park Service spent $2 million to acquire 148 million acres and, as 2000 began, more than 1,000 additional acres were slated for eventual purchase.

Visitors will find plenty of roads and trails to hike and explore. One short trail leads to the nineteenth-century Carnegie mansion. Swimming is allowed on the beaches, and saltwater surf fishing is permitted without a license. Bicycles are permitted from the island's south end to the wilderness boundary north of Stafford. Visitors may encounter vehicles on the island, because the island's residents and their guests are permitted to drive their vehicles on historic roadways.

Located near St. Marys, Georgia, 32 miles north of Jacksonville, Florida, Cumberland Island is open year-round. The day-use fee is $4 per person, per visit, and an annual pass is available for $20. The park features one campground called Sea Camp, where campers may choose among one developed and four primitive backcountry sites. Sea Camp features rest rooms, cold showers, drinking water, grills, fire rings, and picnic tables. There are no facilities at the backcountry sites, and campfires are not permitted. Backcountry sites range from 3.5 to 10.8 miles from the ferry dock. Reservations are required and fees are $4 per person, per day for Sea Camp, and $2 per person, per day in the backcountry. The seashore gets about 50,000 visitors per year, with most arriving during March, April, and May, and the fewest in January. The best time to visit is from October through February when visitation has slacked off and the temperature and humidity are more pleasant.

The Mainland Visitor Center is open daily from 8:15 A.M. to 4:30 P.M. year-round, and smaller visitor centers are located at Sea Camp Dock and Dungeness Dock on the island. Cumberland Island is accessible via a concession-operated passenger ferry. From March 1 through September 30, the ferry departs St. Marys at 9 A.M. and 11:45 A.M., and departs from Cumberland Island at 10:15 A.M. and 4:45 P.M. Wednesday through Saturday there is a 2:45 P.M. departure from the island. Between October 1 and the end of February, the ferry does not run on Tuesdays and Wednesdays, and there is no 2:45 departure from the island. The ferry does not transport pets, bicycles, or cars. Ferry tickets are round-trip and include sales tax: Adults are $10.17, senior citizens (sixty-five and older) are $8.03, and children (twelve and under) are $6.05. Small private boats may dock at Sea Camp and larger vessels may anchor off

Sea Camp and dock a dinghy. Other than the concession ferry/charter service, all commercial transportation is prohibited.

For more information, write Cumberland Island National Seashore, P.O. Box 806, St. Marys, GA 31558, or telephone (912) 882-4335 for the reservation line (10 A.M. to 4 P.M., Monday–Friday), or (912) 882-4336 for the information line (8 A.M. to 4:30 P.M., daily). The park's Web site is www.nps.gov/cuis.

FURTHER READING

Bullard, Mary. *Cumberland Island: A History.* Athens: University of Georgia Press, 2002.
Dilsaver, Lary M. *Cumberland Island National Seashore: A History of Conservation Conflict.* Charlottesville: University of Virginia Press, 2004.
Seabrook, Charles. *Cumberland Island: Strong Women, Wild Horses.* Winston-Salem, NC: John F. Blair, 2002.

CURECANTI NATIONAL RECREATION AREA

Location: Gunnison, Colorado
Acreage: 41,972
Established: February 11, 1965

Established in 1965, the almost-42,000-acre Curecanti National Recreation Area encompasses three reservoirs along a 40-mile stretch of the Gunnison River. The park derives its name from Curicata, a leader of the Ute Indians who lived in the region when American settlers arrived in the 1800s. Located in the middle of western Colorado's high mesa country, the area offers visitors a wide array of activities, including fishing, boating, sailing, swimming, waterskiing, windsurfing, camping, cross-country skiing, and hiking. Panoramic mesas, fjord-like lakes, and deep, steep, and narrow canyons abound. Recently discovered dinosaur fossils, a 5,000-acre archeological district, and a narrow-gauge train further enhance the offerings of Curecanti.

The park's three reservoirs—Blue Mesa, Morrow Point, and Crystal—are named for corresponding dams on the Gunnison River, and collectively they are known as the Wayne Aspinall Storage Unit. A prominent western

A successful catch at Curecanti National Recreation Area. *(National Park Service)*

Colorado congressman and longtime chairman of the U.S. House Appropriations Committee known as the "King of the Water Buffalos," the nickname for the collection of western representatives and senators who made their careers by bringing home development projects to their states, Aspinall was instrumental in the creation of the massive Colorado River Storage Project, which includes the Gunnison dams, to meet the growing demand for water and power in the American Southwest. Blue Mesa Lake forms the state's largest body of water and is the largest kokanee salmon fishery in the country. Morrow Point Lake marks the beginning of the famous Black Canyon of the Gunnison, and Crystal Lake is the site of the Gunnison

Diversion Tunnel, a National Historic Civil Engineering Landmark.

Curecanti is situated along the Gunnison River, 25 miles west of Gunnison, Colorado, on U.S. Highway 50, near the Blue Mesa Dam, approximately 200 miles southwest of Denver. The park is open every day of the year, and there are no entrance fees. All private boats must be registered; Blue Mesa Lake boat fees (for all motorized, state-registered vessels) are $4 for two days, $10 for fourteen days, or $30 for an annual pass. All boat ramps are on Blue Mesa Lake, and visitors must have a valid Colorado state fishing license to fish in the park's lakes.

The main visitor center at Curecanti National Recreation Area is Elk Creek, which is open year-round. The facility features interpretive exhibits, video presentations, and a fish observation pond. During the summer, rangers host morning and afternoon interpretive programs, theme hikes, kids' programs on the weekends, fishing tournaments, and evening programs at the Elk Creek Amphitheater. During the winter there are several treks and snowshoe hikes available. The park's 2 other visitor centers, Cimarron and Lake Fork, are open daily from late May through September. Cimarron has an information station, a Morrow Point Dam overlook, and a narrow-gauge railroad exhibit featuring a nineteenth-century trestle, steam locomotive, and several Denver and Rio Grande Railroad cars. The Lake Fork Visitor Center has a photo display on the history and resources of Curecanti as well as a book, poster, and postcard sales outlet. Most of the park's 1.1 million annual visitors come between Memorial Day and Labor Day to enjoy the mild summer weather. Winters here are typically very cold and windy.

Curecanti has numerous first-come, first-served campgrounds, with no hookups. The fee is $10 per night. All campgrounds are usually full during Memorial Day, Fourth of July, and Labor Day holidays, and weekends are often crowded. From east to west, the following campgrounds are available: Stevens Creek, located 12 miles west of Gunnison, has 54 sites, vault toilets, water, boat ramp, and fishing access. Elk Creek, 16 miles west of Gunnison, has 179 sites located on the shore of Blue Mesa Reservoir with a marina, restaurant, flush toilets, water, dump station, showers, and vault toilets in the winter. East Elk Creek, just over 16 miles west of Gunnison, has group sites (reservations required) with vault toilets, water, picnic tables and shelter, and fire grates. The fee here is $2 per person per night with a $30 minimum. Dry Gulch, located 17 miles west of Gunnison, has 10 sites nestled among cottonwood trees with vault toilets, water, and picnic tables. Red Creek, located 19 miles west of Gunnison, has 2 individual sites with vault toilets, water, and picnic tables, and one group site. Lake Fork, located 27 miles west of Gunnison, has 87 mostly paved sites with flush toilets, water, showers, dump station, and a marina. Gateview, located at the extreme southern end of the Lake Fork arm of Blue Mesa Reservoir, has 7 no-fee sites set deep in a canyon with remote access, vault toilets, picnic tables, and water. Ponderosa, located at the end of the Soap Creek Arm of Blue Mesa Reservoir, has 29 sites with vault toilets, water, picnic tables, a boat ramp, and horse corrals. Cimarron, located 20 miles east of Montrose, Colorado, has 22 sites with flush toilets, water, and a dump station. East Portal, located at the bottom of the Black Canyon of the Gunnison below Crystal Dam, has 15 sites with vault toilets, water, picnic tables, and good fishing access. Only Cimarron and Elk Creek campgrounds are open year-round.

There is no overnight lodging in the park. The towns of Gunnison and Montrose have all traveler services. The Elk Creek Marina has a full-service restaurant, Pappy's, open in the summer only, and the marinas at Elk Creek and Lake Fork offer boat repairs, rentals, gas, guided fishing tours, tackle, and groceries.

For more information, write Curecanti National Recreation Area, 102 Elk Creek, Gunnison, CO 81230, or telephone (970) 641-2337. The park's informative Web site is www.nps.gov/cure.

FURTHER READING

Houk, Ro. *Curecanti National Recreation Area.* Tucson, AZ: Southwest Parks and Monuments, 1991.

Schulte, Steven C. *Wayne Aspinall and the Shaping of the American West.* Niwot: University Press of Colorado, 2002.

Sturgeon, Stephen C. *The Politics of Western Water: The Congressional Career of Wayne Aspinall.* Tucson: University of Arizona Press, 2002.

CUYAHOGA VALLEY NATIONAL PARK

Location: Cleveland, Ohio
Acreage: 32,861
Established: December 27, 1974

Authorized in 1974 as the Cuyahoga Valley National Recreation Area and upgraded to national park status by the Clinton administration as a final conservation gift to the nation, this surprising park protects almost 33,000 acres along Ohio's Cuyahoga River between Cleveland and Akron. The headwaters of this sinuous river, called the "ka-ih-ohg-ha" or "crooked" river by Native Americans, lie 30 miles east of its mouth in Cleveland, flowing in a great "U" along the base of the escarpment that supports the city of Akron. Deep forests, rolling hills, and open farmlands frame the Cuyahoga River Valley. In the early 1960s, when suburban development threatened to encroach on this pastoral region, concerned citizens joined forces with state and local governments to save the green space and historic features. Their goals coincided with those of the Park Service, which was in the middle of a program called "parks for the people, where the people are." This program established urban national recreation areas as a way to bring national park experience to city dwellers, especially those without the resources to travel to faraway crown jewels in the system. In Ohio, this resulted in a national recreation area managed by the Park Service in cooperation with others who own property within its boundaries, including Cleveland Metroparks and Summit County Metro Parks.

The change to national park status reflected an important transition in national parks in American society. For more than a century after the establishment of Yellowstone, national parks were considered remote places untrammeled by human use. The creation of national recreation areas in the 1930s acknowledged both the need for recreation for the urban population and the distinct character of national parks. The transformation of Cuyahoga from national recreation area to national park served as an indicator that old distinctions between categories were changing and that national parks in the United States had taken on an entirely new meaning.

Historically, the Cuyahoga Valley was part of an important transportation corridor. In 1832, construction of the Ohio and Erie Canal was completed, providing a crucial link between Cleveland on Lake Erie and Portsmouth on the Ohio River. The Ohio and Erie Canal Towpath Trail follows the historic route of the canal and is open to hikers, bikers, and, in the winter, cross-country skiers. Small portions of the canal still contain some water, and a few of the locks, spillways, an aqueduct, and other canal features still remain. Before the Civil War began in 1861, canal-building ended, replaced by steam engines and the railroad. Visitors to the park today can ride on the Cuyahoga Valley Scenic Railroad, a diesel-locomotive-powered passenger train that follows the historic route of the Valley Railroad, which began opera-

tion in the 1870s. Although the train is owned and operated by a private, nonprofit organization, Park Service interpreters are usually on board to present information on the natural and cultural history of the valley.

Cuyahoga Valley National Park maintains 3 visitor centers, which are open year-round. The Canal Visitor Center is located in Valley View, and serves as both an information center and a museum. Permanent exhibits illustrate twelve thousand years of human history in the valley, including the history of the Ohio and Erie Canal. Park Service staff and volunteers in period costumes conduct canal lock demonstrations seasonally on weekends. A twenty-minute slide show about the park and three thirty-minute videos about the Ohio and Erie Canal are also available. The Happy Days Visitor Center is located in Boston Heights, and offers concerts, lectures, plays, and ranger-led special events. The Hunt Farm Visitor Information Center is located in Cuyahoga Falls, and features exhibits on the area's agricultural history. Its location adjacent to the Ohio and Erie Canal Towpath Trail makes Hunt Farm an ideal starting point for a hike or a bicycle ride. There are no admission fees to the park or its regular programs. Trail users are encouraged to support the Towpath Trail's maintenance through the Towpath Tag donation program. Park visitation is highest on weekends from May through August, and in October when the fall foliage peaks.

In addition to its visitor centers, the park also operates 2 museums. The Boston Store, in Boston, Ohio, was built in 1836 as a warehouse, store, and gathering place, and now houses a boat-building exhibit which is open year-round. The Frazee House was constructed in 1825 and 1826, and offers a fine example of an early federal-style Western Reserve home with exhibits on architectural styles, construction techniques, and the Frazee family. The Frazee House is open from April through October on the weekends from 10 A.M. to 5 P.M.

Lodging is available in the park. Overlooking the 67-foot Brandywine Falls is the Inn at Brandywine Falls, a 6-room bed-and-breakfast built in 1848 and listed on the National Register of Historic Places. The historic Stanford House Hostel is a Greek Revival farmhouse built in 1843 by George Stanford. Both are open year-round and reservations are available on-line. Food, lodging, and other travel services are also available in nearby towns. There is no camping in the park.

For more information, write Cuyahoga Valley National Park, 15610 Vaughn Road, Brecksville, OH 44141, or telephone (216) 524-1497. The park's extensive Web site is www.nps.gov/cuva.

FURTHER READING

Cockrell, Ron. *A Green Shrouded Miracle: An Administrative History of Cuyahoga National Recreation Area.* Omaha, NE: National Park Service, 1992.

Ellis, William Donahue. *The Cuyahoga.* Chicago: Landfall, 1998.

Gieck, Jack. *A Photo Album of Ohio's Canal Era, 1825–1913.* Kent, OH: Kent State University Press, 1992.

Hannibal, Joseph T. *Geology Along the Towpath: Stones of the Ohio & Erie and Miami & Erie Canals.* Columbus: State of Ohio, 1998.

The Nature of the Towpath. Cuyahoga, OH: Cuyahoga Valley Trails Council, 1999.

DAYTON AVIATION HERITAGE NATIONAL HISTORICAL PARK

Location: Dayton, Ohio
Acreage: 86
Established: October 16, 1992

Dayton Aviation Heritage National Historical Park (NHP) commemorates the legacy of three exceptional men–aviators Wilbur and Orville Wright, and poet Paul Laurence Dunbar–and their work in the Miami Valley of Ohio. The 86-acre park is a cooperative effort between the National Park Service and three partners, and it contains 4 separate sites in Dayton, Ohio: The Wright Cycle Company building and the Wright brothers' print-shop building; Huffman Prairie Flying Field at Wright-Patterson Air Force Base; Wright Hall, which contains the restored 1905 Wright Flyer III; and the Paul Laurence Dunbar State Memorial.

Through the development and invention of controlled, powered flight, Wilbur (1867–1912) and Orville (1871–1948) Wright made significant contributions to world history. Their small Dayton, Ohio, bicycle shop became the center of the drive to put humanity into the air. These two brothers taught themselves the art and science of aviation, researched, designed, constructed, and perfected the world's first power-driven, human-piloted, heavier-than-air flying machine. On December 17, 1903, the Wright brothers made history. At Kitty Hawk, North Carolina, Orville and Wilbur Wright took their machine into the air for the first-ever free and sustained flight–120 feet in 12 seconds. They also built and flew the world's first practical, fully controllable airplane, the 1905 Wright Flyer III.

In addition to designing and flying the first airplanes, the Wright brothers taught others how to fly. At their flying school on Huffman Prairie, just northeast of Dayton, they trained more than 100 military and civilian aviators, many of whom became leading aviation figures in the following decades.

Paul Laurence Dunbar (1872–1906)–a business associate and friend of Orville's–was a gifted and prolific African American poet who gave voice to a people forced to endure the bitterness of segregation and Jim Crow laws. "We wear the mask that grins and lies, It hides our cheeks and shades our eyes, This debt we pay to human guile;" he wrote. "With torn and bleeding hearts we smile, And mouth with myriad subtleties." Dunbar achieved national and international acclaim in a literary world that was almost exclusively white, and his work contributed to a growing social consciousness and cultural identity for African Americans. In 1899, just a few years before his death, Dunbar wrote, "It is not a carol of joy or glee, But a prayer that he sends from his heart's deep core. . . . I know why the caged bird sings!"

Visitation to the Dayton Aviation Heritage NHP is highest between June and August, when the weather is most pleasant. Summer's average lows are 65 to 80 degrees, and highs range from 70 to 90 degrees. Hot, humid weather is possible, as well as thunderstorms. Winter temperatures range from lows of 5 to 20 degrees, to highs between 10 and 35 degrees. Heavier clothing and layers are strongly advised, and snow and snowstorms are possible.

In July 2003, the Dayton Aviation Heritage NHP opened the wheelchair-accessible Wright Dunbar Interpretive Center—also known as the Aviation Trail Visitor Center and Museum—with 2 floors of exhibits, an eighteen-minute movie, and a bookstore. Exhibits and visitor services are also available at the Paul Laurence Dunbar State Memorial (admission $5 for adults, $2 for children ages six to twelve, under five free) and at the Carillon Historical Park ($5 for adults, $4 for seniors, free for children under three), which is open April 1 through October 31 and has a café. Self-guided facilities only are available at the free Huffman Prairie Flying Field. At press time, the renovated Wright Cycle Company building was just about to reopen.

Although most facilities are open year-round, their days and hours of operation are subject to change, and visitors should contact the park for specific details. There is no lodging or camping at the park, but Dayton has all traveler services.

For more information, write Dayton Aviation Heritage National Historical Park, Box 9280, Wright Brothers Station, Dayton, OH 45409, or telephone (937) 225-7705. You also can call the Paul Laurence Dunbar State Memorial at (937) 224-7061. The park's Web site is www.nps.gov/daav.

FURTHER READING

Crouch, Tom D. *The Bishop's Boys: A Life of Wilbur and Orville Wright.* New York: W.W. Norton, 2003.

Culick, Fred E., and Spencer Dunmore. *On Great White Wings: The Wright Brothers and the Race for Flight.* New York: Hyperion, 2001.

Wright, Orville. *How We Invented the Airplane: An Illustrated History.* Mineola, NY: Dover, 1989.

DEATH VALLEY NATIONAL PARK

Location: California and Nevada
Acreage: 3,372,402
Established: February 11, 1933

Death Valley National Park is a place of extremes. Bounded on the west by the 11,049-foot Telescope Peak and on the east by the 5,475-foot Dante's View, Badwater, in the heart of the park, is the lowest point in the western hemisphere—282 feet *below* sea level. Death Valley is also the hottest and driest spot in North America. Summer temperatures routinely reach 120–130 degrees—the record is 134 degrees—and in 1972, the Park Service recorded the hottest ground temperature ever in America—201 degrees! The harsh desert climate results from an orographic barrier, a rain-shadow created by the Sierra Nevada Mountains to the west, limiting annual rainfall to about 2 inches. Despite this hyperaridity, Death Valley harbors a complex ecology. The extreme conditions have attracted hardy, adaptable, and unique species of flora and fauna; more than 900 kinds of plants and 98 species of animals live within the park's boundaries. Surrounded by rugged mountain ranges, Death Valley provides unparalleled views of spectacular desert dunes, interesting and rare wildlife, complex geology, and undisturbed wilderness. In the spring, the park even puts on a spectacular wildflower display.

At more than 3.3 million acres, Death Valley National Park is the largest national park south of Alaska. Originally set aside as a national monument in 1933, Death Valley was redesignated as a national park as part of the 1994 California Desert Protection Act. This act added 1.3 million acres of waterfalls, a Joshua Tree forest, canyons, springs, mountains, and other lands crucial to the desert ecosystem. Congress designated the vast majority of the park—3.2 million acres—as the Death Valley Wilderness Area, making it by far the largest wilderness in the lower forty-eight United States.

In addition to its geologic and ecological wonders, the park contains numerous sites of historical and cultural interest. The park headquarters is located at Furnace Creek, an oasis within this desert environment, with a long human history. The Timbisha Shoshone

An elaborate wishing well at Death Valley Ranch.
(Library of Congress)

were the first to settle this region more than a thousand years ago; white emigrants accidentally stumbled upon the lush Furnace Creek valley during the 1849 California gold rush. Gold and silver were on their minds, but these minerals were scarce. Borax, a white water-soluble powder used as cleansing agent, was not, and three decades later in the 1880s, it became the "white gold" of the desert—carried out of the valley by the famed twenty-mule teams. Mining became the dominant economic activity in the desert, with a series of rushes that continued into the 1930s.

Death Valley was also the scene of two major legislative changes. When it came into the park system, mining was allowed to continue within the original monument boundaries. This was unusual, and, over time, it diminished the park's value in the park sys-

tem. A boom in open-pit mining in the 1970s led to the 1976 Mining in the Parks Act, which ended new mining claims in the entire park system, curtailed options on existing claims that had not been worked, and established new ground rules for mining on existing claims within the park system. This landmark decision accompanied a major water case, *F.L. Caeppart et al. v. U.S.* Caeppart believed that an exchange of lands with the federal government granted him water rights that superceded implied rights in an earlier designation of Ash Meadows, a noncontiguous area of Death Valley National Monument. The U.S. Supreme Court ruled that an implied water right existed, preventing Caeppart's cattle ranch from draining the underground aquifer that fed Devil's Hole. It was a major triumph for conservation in the West and in the nation.

Located on the California-Nevada border, 135 miles west of Las Vegas, Death Valley is a remote, often harsh desert environment. Despite modern conveniences like the air-conditioned automobile and year-round resort accommodations, most of the park's 1.5 million annual visitors come in the cooler spring and fall months. A seven-day park pass costs $10 per vehicle or $5 per person, and an annual park pass is available for $20.

Various roads and trails provide access to excellent views and points of interest. California Highway 190, the Badwater Road, the Scotty's Castle Road, and paved roads to Dante's View and Wildrose provide access to major viewpoints and points of interest. Access to more remote wilderness areas, camping, and historical sites, including many old borax mines and ghost towns like Skidoo and Rhyolite, is provided by over 350 miles of unpaved and four-wheel-drive roads.

Death Valley National Park maintains 2 visitor centers, a ranger station, and 2 museums. The Furnace Creek Visitor Center and

Museum, located in the center of the park, is open daily from 8 A.M. to 6 P.M., and features an introductory slide program as well as displays on the geology, climate, wildlife, and natural and human history of the park. During the winter season, park rangers present a wide variety of walks, talks, and evening slide presentations. The Beatty Information Center is located in the town of Beatty, Nevada, and has exhibits about Death Valley natural history, cultural history, and scenic highlights. The Stovepipe Wells Ranger Station is located in the center of Death Valley, and it provides general information and backcountry camping and hiking permits. Scotty's Castle and the Gas House Museum are located at the north end of the park. The castle is a Mediterranean-style architectural gem dating from the early 1920s that was once the retreat of a wealthy Chicago couple. Daily guided living history tours are available for $8 per person. The Gas House Museum contains a new exhibit of artifacts from the Castle Collection, and details the history of Scotty's Castle; both are open from 7 A.M. to 6 P.M. daily.

Death Valley offers a wide variety of lodging and camping possibilities. In the popular Furnace Creek area, the Furnace Creek Inn (760-786-2361) offers first-class resort accommodations, while the Furnace Creek Ranch (760-786-2345) provides motel accommodations. Both Stovepipe Wells Village (760-786-2387) and the Panamint Springs Resort (702-482-7680) offer resort accommodations; there is limited RV camping with full hookups in the Stovepipe Wells area, and Panamint also has camping opportunities. Traveler services are available throughout the park's more developed areas, as well as at Scotty's Castle.

Three campgrounds in the park are open year-round. The popular Furnace Creek Campground is available on a first-come, first-served basis from April through mid-October, and by reservation during the rest of the year. Located 196 feet below sea level, the campground has 136 sites with water, tables, fireplaces, flush toilets, and a dump station, and costs $16 per night during the winter and $10 per night during the summer. Mesquite Spring is 3 miles from Scotty's Castle and has 30 sites with water, tables, fireplaces, flush toilets, and a dump station. The fee is $10 per night. Wildrose Campground is located at 4,100 feet in the Panamint Mountains. This 30-site campground has tables, fireplaces, and pit toilets, but no drinking water, and camping is free. Mahogany Flat Campground and Thorndike Campground are both open from March through November and have 10 sites with tables, fireplaces, and pit toilets. Access to both campgrounds may require a four-wheel-drive vehicle, and conditions are primitive; there is no fee for either campground. Texas Spring, Stovepipe Wells, and Sunset campgrounds are open from October through April; Texas Spring has 92 sites; Stovepipe Wells has 200 sites; and Sunset has 1,000 sites. All 3 campgrounds provide water, flush toilets, and a dump station. Texas Spring campground is $12 per night and the fee for Stovepipe Wells and Sunset is $10 per night.

For more information, write Death Valley National Park, P.O. Box 579, Death Valley, CA 92328, or telephone (760) 786-2331. The park's extensive Web site is www.nps.gov/deva.

FURTHER READING

Clark, Bill. *Death Valley: The Story Behind the Scenery.* Las Vegas, NV: KC Publications, 2002.

Lingenfelter, Richard. *Death Valley and the Amargosa: Land of Illusion.* Berkeley: University of California Press, 1986.

Miller, Martin G., and Lauren Wright. *Geology of Death Valley National Park: Landforms, Crustal Extension, Geologic History.* Dubuque, IA: Kendall/Hunt, 2001.

Siebert, Diane. *Rhyolite: The True Story of a Ghost Town.* New York: Clarion Books, 2003.

DELAWARE AND LEHIGH NAVIGATION CANAL NATIONAL HERITAGE CORRIDOR

Location: Bethlehem, Pennsylvania
Acreage: not applicable
Established: November 18, 1988

Established in November 1988, the Delaware and Lehigh Navigation Canal National Heritage Corridor stretches for 150 miles along the historic routes of the Delaware Canal and the Lehigh Navigation System, from Wilkes-Barre to Bristol, Pennsylvania. These two nineteenth-century canals and their associated railroads linked the rich coal fields of eastern Pennsylvania to the nation's growing industrial cities. Canal and waterway usage peaked between 1830 and 1860, but portions of the Delaware Canal and the Lehigh Navigation System operated until 1942. Today, the Delaware Canal is the most intact towpath canal in America.

The region surrounding the Lehigh and Delaware rivers has a long history. From the early Lenape Indians to William Penn's Quakers, human settlement patterns reveal the important role of these waterways in human endeavor. For centuries, the natural resources in this riparian environment provided ample sustenance to early Native Americans. Later European settlers found their dreams of economic and industrial development hindered by poor roads and inadequate overland transportation. They turned to the rivers for reliable transportation. Settlements and towns, including Allentown and Bethlehem, originally a Moravian community, sprung up along the rivers' corridor. By the early nineteenth century, anthracite coal dominated the economy in this region, and canals, waterways, and towpaths were constructed between 1817 and 1845 to ship it to waiting markets.

Today, the Heritage Corridor consists of many parks, trails, historic villages and structures, museums, and the canals/waterways themselves. Highlights include a restored Quaker village at Historic Fallsington, mule-drawn canal rides at New Hope and Hugh Moore Park, and a steam train ride up the Lehigh River gorge. The Two Rivers Landing Visitor Center is open Tuesday through Sunday from 9 A.M. until 5 P.M. An added attraction is the Crayola Factory and the National Canal Museum, which are both located in the same building. Throughout the Corridor, visitors can enjoy museum programs explaining the industries, people, and wildlife of the region; community walking tours; and numerous ethnic and musical celebrations throughout the year. Operating hours and entrance fees vary from site to site, and much of the park is still under development. Hikers will enjoy the restored towpath between Catasauqua and Bristol, Pennsylvania, which traces the meandering Lehigh and Delaware rivers through pastoral landscapes and bustling communities. The towpath is part of a larger, 160-mile-long trail project that, when complete, will link the Corridor to the Appalachian Trail and more than 20 other regional trails. The Corridor is also an angler's dream, with trout, shad, smallmouth bass, walleye, and muskellunge teeming in both major rivers and in smaller streams. A valid Pennsylvania license is required.

Although there are no Park Service facilities along the canal, a wide range of lodging and camping options are available within the Corridor—from Gilded Age bed-and-breakfast inns to primitive camping opportunities. All towns along the Corridor offer traveler services, and the area's ethnic diversity is evident in the broad selection of restaurants.

For more information, write Delaware and Lehigh Navigation Canal National Heritage Corridor, 10 East Church Street, P-208, Bethlehem, PA 18018, or telephone (610) 861-9345. The park's Web site is www.nps.gov/dele.

FURTHER READING

McClellan, Robert J. *The Delaware Canal: A Picture Story*. New Brunswick, NJ: Rutgers University Press, 1967.

Shaw, Ronald E. *Canals for a Nation: The Canal Era in the United States, 1790–1860*. Lexington: University Press of Kentucky, 1993.

Yoder, Clayton P. *Delaware Canal Journal: A Definitive History of the Canal and the River Valley Through Which It Flows*. Bethlehem, PA: Canal, 1972.

DELAWARE WATER GAP NATIONAL RECREATION AREA AND DELAWARE NATIONAL SCENIC RIVER

Location: New Jersey and Pennsylvania
Acreage: 68,714
Established: September 1, 1965

A former vacation haven for wealthy turn-of-the-twentieth-century Americans, the Delaware Water Gap National Recreation Area—which includes the Delaware National Scenic River—is sandwiched between New Jersey's Kittatinny Ridge and Pennsylvania's Pocono Plateau. The park preserves 40 miles of the middle Delaware River and acreage along the river's New Jersey and Pennsylvania shores. The park's name derives from the mile-wide scenic gap—actually a tight S-curve notch—in the Appalachian Mountains carved by the Delaware River. Authorized in September 1965, the recreation area was initially envisioned as part of the Tocks Island Dam project on the Delaware River. Heated controversy soon erupted over these plans to dam one of the last free-flowing rivers on the East Coast, since the area harbored both threatened and endangered plants and animals as well as significant prehistoric and historic sites. Finally, in 1978, Congress designated the section of the Delaware River within Delaware Water Gap National Recreation Area as part of the National Wild and Scenic Rivers System. In 1992, the Tocks Island Dam project was officially deauthorized.

Today, the Delaware Water Gap National Recreation Area is a popular vacation site. The 5 million annual visitors include spring anglers, summer canoeists and swimmers, autumn hunters, winter cross-country skiers, and year-round hikers. Because the park is in a resort area, the highest visitation occurs in July and August, and is lowest in December and January. Most roadways and access points to the Delaware National Scenic River are open twenty-four hours a day, year-round, unless closed due to heavy snowfall or other hazardous conditions. Boat access and most visitor facilities are open dawn to dusk, year-round. One notable attraction is New Jersey's Historic Millbrook Village. Here, visitors can tour a re-created late-1800s town, including period homes, blacksmith shops, a church, a general store, and a woodworker's cabin. Village grounds are open daily from 9 A.M. to 5 P.M. year-round, but the buildings are closed from November through March. There is no admission fee to the park or scenic river, but during the summer, recreation and boat fees are collected at Smithfield Beach, Milford Beach, Bushkill access, and Dingmans Ferry.

The recreation area maintains 3 visitor centers and a park headquarters. Kittatinny Point, just off I-80 in New Jersey, is open daily from 9 A.M. to 4:30 P.M. from mid-October to mid-April, and until 5 P.M. during the rest of the year. Exhibits include a collection of fossils and highlights of the Appalachian Trail, as well as rotating seasonal displays. Daily ranger programs give visitors a general introduction to the recreation area, and cover topics such as geology, local history, and plant and wildlife identification. Information, audiovisual programs, displays, a sales outlet for park-related items, and boating permit sales are also available. The Bushkill Visitor Center, on U.S. Highway 209 along Bushkill Creek, is open daily from 9 A.M. to 5 P.M. May through mid-October, and on weekends only from mid-October until mid-November. The center is closed from mid-November to mid-April. This center contains information, an audiovisual program, displays, and a sales outlet for park-related items. Special programs include a nature hike to learn about the geology of Dingmans Falls area and presentations on local fauna including bats, bears, and beavers. Park Headquarters, located on River Road 1 mile off Pennsylvania Highway 209 in Bushkill, Pennsylvania, is open Monday through Friday from 8 A.M. to 4:30 P.M. After undergoing extensive reconstruction, the Dingmans Falls area reopened in the spring of 2004; hours for the visitor center are 9 A.M. to 5 P.M. from Memorial Day to Labor Day.

There are no commercial food or lodging facilities in the park proper, but all can be found in the towns adjoining the recreation area. Picnic areas are found throughout the park, and boat launch ramps are located at the Gap, Dingmans Ferry, Pocono, Smithfield Beach, and Milford Beach. The private Dingmans Campground, just south of Dingmans Ferry, is open from April to mid-October and has more than 100 sites with all amenities. Other private and public campgrounds dot the nearby valley, and state forests on both sides of the river have camping facilities. Fishing is abundant, with catfish, carp, shad, smallmouth bass, and walleye popular catches. Ice fishing is popular in the wintertime.

For more information, write Delaware Water Gap National Recreation Area, Bushkill, PA 18324-9999, or telephone (570) 588-2451. The park's informative Web site is www.nps.gov/dewa.

FURTHER READING
Albert, Richard C. *Damming the Delaware: The Rise and Fall of Tocks Island Dam.* State College: Pennsylvania State University Press, 1987.

Kraft, Herbert C. *The Dutch, the Indians and the Quest for Copper: Pahaquarry and the Old Mine Road.* Union, NJ: Lenape Books, 1996.

Sinden, Frank W., Robert H. Socolow, and Harold A. Feiveson, eds. *Boundaries of Analysis: An Inquiry into the Tocks Island Dam Controversy.* Boston: Ballinger, 1976.

DENALI NATIONAL PARK AND PRESERVE
Location: Alaska
Acreage: 6,075,030
Established: February 26, 1917

North America's highest mountain, 20,320-foot-high Mount McKinley, looms like a snow-draped sentinel over central Alaska's Denali National Park and Preserve. Denali (the Athabascan word means "the high one") is a wild, subarctic tundra landscape of vast snowfields, deep-blue glacial lakes, and ice-capped Alaska Range peaks. Denali's almost-6.1 million acres also protect a diverse ecosystem populated by wolves, grizzly bears, caribou, moose, and Dall sheep. Established in 1917 as Mount McKinley National Park, the preserve's original purpose was to protect dwindling herds of moose, sheep, and caribou from exploitation by hunters from Fairbanks and Alaska Railroad construction camps. In 1980, the original park was designated a wilderness area and incorporated into the much larger Denali National Park and Preserve, which expanded the park's boundaries from 1.9 million acres to its present size. In the park, nature takes priority over visitors, an effective management strategy only because visitors must trek so far to reach the park that all but the most hardy never get past the visitor center. In effect, the park is protected by its distance from the traveling public, a condition unlikely to last much longer.

Today, Denali is one of the premier wilderness parks in the world, where visitors often see elusive wildlife and truly spectacular scenery. The park is aggressively managed to prevent tourist overcrowding and damage to the flora and fauna, and rangers frequently close sectors of the park to visitation during breeding season or after a wolf- or bear-kill. Denali is the best example of the difficulties of balancing tourism and ecosystem protection. During the past thirty years, visitation to

Pearson Cabin, near Toklat River, at Denali National Park and Preserve. *(Library of Congress)*

the park has increased by 1,000 percent, stressing the systems set up to manage visitors and threatening all manner of park resources.

Denali is a mountain-climber's paradise, offering one of the world's most challenging and grueling climbs. Mountaineers from all over the world attempt to scale Mount McKinley every year, including those preparing themselves for even higher ascents like K2 and Mount Everest. In 1913, the first climbers reached McKinley's summit, but it was not until 1967 that the first team of adventurers conquered the peak during winter. Today, springtime visitors to the village of Talkeetna will see climbing parties preparing to ascend "the mountain," as it is known to locals, on a daily basis.

The park maintains 2 visitor centers and a ranger station at Talkeetna. The Denali Na-

tional Park Visitor Center, located at mile 1 of the Denali Park Road, is open from late April through September, from 7 A.M. to 8 P.M. during the peak summer season. The center offers an audiovisual program about the park, ranger programs, and backcountry safety information. The annual Winterfest program is also held here in early spring, usually during March. Eielson Visitor Center, located at mile 66 of the Denali Park Road, is accessible only by shuttle or tour bus and is open from June through mid-September, 9 A.M. to 7 P.M. Exhibits on the park's geology, park ranger "porch talks," and daily guided hikes are all offered at Eielson. The Talkeetna Ranger Station, located in Talkeetna, 100 miles north of Anchorage, is open all year from 8 A.M. to 4:30 P.M. The station features interpretive programs on the history of climbing at Denali, a photo exhibit of the Alaska range, and climbing information.

Denali National Park and Preserve accommodates a wide variety of visitor uses, including wildlife viewing, mountaineering, sport fishing, hiking, and backpacking. The park is located along the George Parks Highway, approximately 240 miles north of Anchorage and 125 miles south of Fairbanks. Denali is accessible by car or via the Alaska Railroad from either Anchorage or Fairbanks. In summer, a variety of private bus and van services and the railroad operate daily from both cities. Within the park itself, the Denali Park Road is accessible by private vehicle for the first 14.8 miles, to the Savage River Bridge. Destinations beyond the bridge, including Eielson Visitor Center, require visitors to use shuttle and tour bus services. Bicycles are permitted along the Denali Park Road. The park receives more than a million visitors each year, the vast majority of whom come during the summer months when the park enjoys up to sixteen hours of sunlight every day. Not surprisingly, visitation is lowest during the brutally frigid, twilight-dark winter months. Summers are generally cool and damp with average high temperatures in the mid-60s. Winters are extremely cold with temperatures falling to minus 40 degrees and below, and specialized cold-weather gear is crucial for mountaineering and winter visits.

Entrance fees are $10 per family and $5 per person, and are valid for seven consecutive days. An annual pass is also available for $15. Fees are charged for shuttle and tour bus services, and vary according to age, usage, and destination. Backcountry camping permits are required; they are free and can be obtained only at the visitor center, no more than one day in advance. A camper bus pass ($15) must be purchased in order to reach most backcountry camping units. Denali's mountaineering headquarters is located in Talkeetna, 100 miles north of Anchorage.

Climbers must obtain a permit to climb Denali or any other park peaks. Mountaineering permit registration packets must be submitted at least sixty days in advance of the scheduled climb with a $150 fee.

There are no hotels within the park. Many other accommodations are available within a short distance of the park, but most are open only in the summer. Year-round lodging is available in Healy, 12 miles north of the park entrance, and Cantwell, 29 miles south. The Park Service operates 7 campgrounds in the park. Three campgrounds, Riley Creek, Savage River, and Teklanika River, are open to private vehicles. Morino, near the railroad depot, is for those traveling without vehicles. The other 3 campgrounds, Sanctuary River, Igloo Creek, and Wonder Lake, are shuttle bus–accessible only. Fees are charged for all campgrounds and advanced reservations are available for most. Riley Creek is the only campground open year-round.

A restaurant and snack shop are located within the Denali Park Hotel; a small convenience store, the McKinley Mercantile, is located near the entrance to the hotel. Several other restaurants and convenience stores are located within a few miles of the park entrance. Most food services are available only in summer. Restaurants, convenience stores, and gas stations are open year-round in Healy and Cantwell.

For more park, reservation, or permit information, write Denali National Park and Preserve, P.O. Box 9, Denali Park, AK 99755, or telephone (907) 683-2294. The park's informative Web site is www.nps.gov/dena.

FURTHER READING

Bauer, Erwin A., and Peggy Bauer. *Denali: The Wild Beauty of Denali National Park.* Seattle, WA: Sasquatch Books, 2000.

Catton, Theodore. *Inhabited Wilderness: Indians, Eskimos, and National Parks in Alaska.* Albuquerque: University of New Mexico Press, 1997.

Murie, Adolph. *The Wolves of Mount McKinley.* Seattle: University of Washington Press, 1985.

———. *The Grizzlies of Mount McKinley.* Seattle: University of Washington Press, 2000.

DE SOTO NATIONAL MEMORIAL

Location: Bradenton, Florida
Acreage: 27
Established: March 11, 1948

In May 1539, the Spanish conquistador Hernando de Soto made landfall in North America. Armed with nearly 700 men and orders to "conquer, pacify, and populate" the area that the Spanish crown called "La Florida," de Soto set out to find the rumored golden cities of Cibola. His grueling four-year, 4,000-mile expedition was the first large-scale European exploration into the interior of southeastern North America. De Soto found no gilded cities. The expedition journeyed through the forested wilderness of present-day Florida, Georgia, the Carolinas, southeastern Tennessee, Alabama, Mississippi, Arkansas, and east Texas. In the process, his entourage commandeered supplies and slaves from the Mississippi people along their route, leaving a swath of resentment in their wake. In Alabama, thousands of warriors in the Alibamu chiefdom swarmed the expedition, and a few months later, the ancestors of the modern-day Chickasaws destroyed half of de Soto's army. Despite growing opposition among his own men, de Soto refused to abandon the expedition, and pushed his dwindling troops deep into Arkansas. Finally, in 1542, the defeated conquistador relented and ordered retreat. In May, de Soto succumbed to a fever, perhaps malaria, and died on the banks of the great Mississippi River. Eventually, the ragtag remnants of the expedition, which numbered fewer than 300, made their way down the Mississippi River to the Gulf and sailed home to Mexico. Although the native peoples of the South had successfully re-

pelled the Spanish invasion—indeed the Spanish government considered the expedition a complete failure—they paid a high price for the encounter. De Soto and his men introduced assorted deadly Old World epidemic diseases like smallpox, typhoid, and measles, which ravaged Native American communities and depopulated the countryside. These germs proved far more powerful than the guns of the conquistadors. A century later, when Europeans returned to colonize the area, they found the American bison had extended its range into what is now northern Alabama, populating the niche vacated by the decline in human population. Simple tribal confederacies stood where the once mighty Mississippi culture had flourished.

Established in 1949, this 27-acre park commemorates the intrepid de Soto expedition and attempts to illuminate the sixteenth-century Spanish cultural values that produced the inevitable conflict with Native Americans. There is no admission fee. The De Soto National Memorial Visitor Center is open all year from 9 A.M. until 5 P.M. daily. The center contains exhibits on the de Soto expedition, including many sixteenth-century artifacts such as armor and weapons, as well as Native American pottery and projectile points. A twenty-minute film entitled *Hernando de Soto in America* is shown throughout the day, and depicts his journey through what is now the southeastern United States, describing the expedition's influence on Native Americans and Florida. Peak visitation occurs from mid-December through mid-April, and the park is least crowded in August and September. During the busy season, park rangers in period costumes offer special programs on blacksmithing, cooking, armor repair, and military weapons at Camp Ucita, a reproduction of the sixteenth-century Native American village that de Soto's expedition used as a base camp. Of special interest is the firing of a military crossbow, and of an Arquebus—a primitive black-powder weapon that predated the flintlock.

The memorial is located at the mouth of the Manatee River, 5 miles north of Bradenton on Tampa Bay. There is no food, lodging, or camping at the park, but nearby Bradenton has all travel services, including private campgrounds. Myakka River State Park, just south of Bradenton on U.S. Highway 41 and Florida Highway 72, also has a developed campground.

For more information, write De Soto National Memorial, P.O. Box 15390, Bradenton, FL 34280, or telephone (941) 792-0458. The park's Web site is www.nps.gov/deso.

FURTHER READING

Clayton, Lawrence A., Vernon James Knight, Jr., and Edward C. Moore, eds. *The De Soto Chronicles: The Expedition of Hernando de Soto to North America in 1539–1543.* Tuscaloosa: University of Alabama Press, 1993.

Duncan, David Ewing. *Hernando de Soto: A Savage Quest in the Americas.* Norman: University of Oklahoma Press, 1997.

Hudson, Charles. *Knights of Spain, Warriors of the Sun: Hernando de Soto and the South's Ancient Chiefdoms.* Athens: University of Georgia Press, 1997.

DEVILS POSTPILE NATIONAL MONUMENT

Location: Mammoth Lakes, California
Acreage: 798
Established: July 6, 1911

Devils Postpile National Monument is a geologic wonder set along the picturesque Middle Fork of the San Joaquin River high on the western slope of the Sierra Nevada mountain range in eastern California. Buffeted by nature's most powerful forces, the monument boasts some of the finest examples of columnar basalt in the world. Nearly 1 million years ago, a basalt lava eruption filled the entire Middle Fork of the San Joaquin River Valley. As the lava cooled, it cracked in successive layers, forming 40- to 60-foot columns, or

"posts." Subsequent glaciation overrode the fractured mass of lava and scoured away all but the most resistant sections—a sheer wall of hexagonal gray columns, 2 to 3 feet in diameter, that resemble the pipes of a gigantic organ. When viewed from above, the Postpile formation gives the illusion of a highly polished tile floor, the handiwork of glaciers.

Evidence that this area is still volcanically active exists along the gravel bar of the Middle Fork San Joaquin River just north of the Postpile, in an area known as Soda Springs. Hot gasses rise from fissures in the earth and combine with groundwater to produce highly carbonated mineralized springs. Hot springs enthusiasts enjoy the pools in nearby Reds Meadow, which derives its name from the high concentrations of iron that have stained the river gravel a reddish brown.

Established in 1911, the 798-acre monument is a hiker's paradise—a rough and rugged landscape with quiet pine forests. A notable 2-mile trek to the southern end of the monument leads to stunning Rainbow Falls, where the Middle Fork of the San Joaquin River plunges more than 100 feet over a sheer cliff into a beautiful, deep-green pool. A short, steep trail leads to the bottom of the falls, where a lush garden of trees and flowers thrives. Devils Postpile is also a key stop along the 211-mile John Muir Trail that connects Yosemite and Kings Canyon national parks. Perhaps best known for his efforts to save the Hetch Hetchy Valley in Yosemite, Muir also advocated a strenuous life, centered on backcountry camping and tramping. "Thousands of tired, nerve-shaken, over-civilized people," Muir insisted, "are beginning to find out that going to the mountains is going home; that wilderness is a necessity; and that mountain peaks and reservations are useful not only as fountains of timber and irrigating rivers, but as fountains of life." His turn-of-the-century advocacy anticipated a post–World War II surge in outdoor recreation and tourism that led, ironically, to intensified use of the nation's public lands.

Devils Postpile played an integral role in the battle over Hetch Hetchy. Excised from Yosemite National Park along with the rest of the Minaret section in 1902, it was considered a reservoir for the city of San Francisco in the aftermath of the earthquake of 1906. A private entity, the San Joaquin Water Company, wanted to demolish the formation to create a dam that it could use to store water to sell to San Francisco. The recently founded Sierra Club objected, stymieing the attempt and orchestrating the establishment of the national monument. With this possible source of water eliminated, the pressure increased for municipal control of a reservoir in Hetch Hetchy.

Located 40 miles north of Bishop, California, at the end of a 16-mile paved road off U.S. Highway 395 at Mammoth Lakes, Devils Postpile lies in the heart of a region generously endowed with scenic splendor. The monument's proximity to Yosemite, Sequoia, and Kings Canyon national parks and Mono Lake provides a rich perspective on the varied natural landscape of the American West—from lofty alpine peaks to searing desert playas—with minimal driving. The monument is only open during summer months. Entrance is free, but all visitors must pay to ride shuttle buses over the last 7 miles of the narrow mountain road that connects Minaret Summit with the monument. A ranger station, located near the parking area and shuttle stop, contains information on the monument and its many hiking trails. Accessible only by the shuttle service, a 21-site campground near the ranger station is open from July 1 to mid-October. The monument has no other lodging or restaurant facilities, although traveler services are available in nearby Reds Meadow Resort and in Mammoth Lakes.

For more information, write Sequoia and Kings Canyon National Parks, 47050 Generals Highway, Three Rivers, CA, 93271, or telephone (559) 565-3341.

During the summer season, write Devils Postpile National Monument, P.O. Box 501, Mammoth Lakes, CA 93546, or telephone (619) 934-2289. The park's Web site is www.nps.gov/depo.

FURTHER READING

Chronic, Halka. *Pages of Stone: Geology of Western National Parks and Monuments: Sierra Nevada, Cascades, and Pacific Coast.* Seattle, WA: Mountaineers Books, 1989.

Cohen, Michael. *The Pathless Way: John Muir and American Wilderness.* Madison: University of Wisconsin Press, 1984.

Muir, John. *My First Summer in the Sierra.* New York: Penguin Books, 1997.

DEVILS TOWER NATIONAL MONUMENT

Location: Devils Tower, Wyoming
Acreage: 1,347
Established: September 24, 1906

For first-time visitors, Devils Tower offers an awe-inspiring encounter of the monumental kind. In September 1906, President Theodore Roosevelt set aside Devils Tower as the nation's first national monument. This striking column of rock towers 1,200 feet above the Belle Fourche River Valley in northeastern Wyoming and is considered a sacred site by several Northern Plains Indian tribes, who call the place "Bears Lodge." According to Kiowa legend, seven little girls were being chased by bears that had just about caught them, when the girls jumped onto a low rock, about 3 feet high. They prayed to the rock to take pity on them and save them from the bears. The rock heard their pleas and began to grow upward, pushing the girls higher and higher to safety. The bears, in their anger, clawed and scratched the rock, but they could not reach the girls, who were pushed up into the sky, where they now live—as the seven little stars in a group, the Pleiades. In the winter, in the middle of the night, this constellation hovers right above Devils Tower.

Geologists believe that Devils Tower was

Devils Tower National Monument. On September 24, 1906, President Theodore Roosevelt proclaimed this as the nation's first national monument. Known by several Northern Plains tribes as Bears Lodge, it also is a sacred site of worship for many Native Americans. *(Library of Congress)*

formed millions of years ago when molten lava intruded into softer sedimentary rock. As the lava cooled and contracted, it cracked into vertical pentagonal columns that average 10 feet in diameter. Over time, the erosional forces of water and wind wore away the surrounding stone, leaving behind Devils Tower. During America's westward movement, the tower became an important directional landmark for explorers, trappers, and emigrants. The moniker "Devils Tower" is generally credited to Colonel Richard Dodge, who made a reconnaissance of the Black Hills in 1875. He described the monolith as "one of the most remarkable peaks in this or any country" and translated another Native American name for the shaft–"the bad god's tower"–into Devils Tower. In more contem-

porary times, Devils Tower achieved fame and notoriety as the preferred landing site for extraterrestrials in Steven Spielberg's 1979 sci-fi film classic *Close Encounters of the Third Kind.* Although stark and imposing, the tower is not the park's only feature. The 1,347-acre monument is surrounded by rolling prairie grasslands and the ponderosa and deciduous forests of the Black Hills. Devils Tower is also home to a healthy prairie-dog town as well as deer and other wildlife.

Devils Tower National Monument is located in the northeast corner of Wyoming, approximately 70 miles northeast of Gillette off I-90. Entrance fees are $8 per vehicle and $3 per person/motorcycle/bicycle, and are valid for seven days. A $20 annual pass is also available. The visitor center houses numerous interpretive exhibits on the geology and geography of the park as well as the Devils Tower Natural History Association Bookstore, which offers educational items for children and adults. The center is open daily from 9 A.M. until 4 P.M., and from 8 A.M. until 4 P.M. from mid-April through August. Park rangers offer guided walking tours, cultural events, and evening campfire programs. The park itself is open twenty-four hours a day, seven days a week, and outdoor wayside exhibits can be found throughout the monument. Each year, nearly 400,000 people visit the monument, primarily between Memorial and Labor days. The park is also very crowded during the annual Sturgis Motorcycle Rally, held during the second week of August.

The monument features 7 miles of hiking trails, including the popular Tower Trail, a paved, 1.3-mile loop around the tower's base that affords excellent views of this grandiose monolith. Devils Tower is considered one of the premier "crack climbing" areas in North America, and experienced climbers can scale the tower after registering with park headquarters. Climbers and nonclimbers alike will appreciate the spectacle.

There are no lodging or restaurant facilities in the park. Gillette, Wyoming, and Spearfish, South Dakota, offer all traveler services, and 3 general stores, a few restaurants, and a post office are located just outside the monument. The park's sole developed campground is the 50-site Belle Fourche Campground, located on the banks of the river in a cottonwood grove. Spaces are available on a first-come, first-served basis and cost $12 per night; there are also 3 group sites. The Belle Fourche Campground is open from April through October, weather permitting, and has drinking water and handicap-accessible rest room facilities, but no hookups, showers, or dump stations. There is a private, fully developed campground located just outside the park's main entrance.

For more information, write Devils Tower National Monument, P.O. Box 10, Devils Tower, WY 82714, or telephone (307) 467-5283. The park's Web site is www.nps.gov/deto.

FURTHER READING

Gunderson, Mary Alice. *Devils Tower: Stories in Stone.* Glendo, WY: High Plains, 1988.
Mattison, Ray H. *History of Devils Tower.* Gillette, WY: Devils Tower Natural History Association, 2001.
Norton, Stephen L. *Devils Tower: The Story Behind the Scenery.* Las Vegas, NV: KC Publications, 1992.

DINOSAUR NATIONAL MONUMENT

Location: Dinosaur, Colorado, and
  Vernal, Utah
Acreage: 210,278
Established: October 4, 1915

On the remote northern border between Utah and Colorado lies the internationally significant Earl Douglass Quarry, home to extensive deposits of ancient mammalian and dinosaur fossils. A true Jurassic Park, Dinosaur National Monument offers visitors a rare opportunity to examine prehistoric giants like apatosaurus, allosaurus, diplodocus, and stegosaurus. The monument is considerably more than a dinosaur graveyard. Native American rock art along the corridors of the Yampa and Green rivers and their side canyons testifies to the allure this region had for prehistoric and Ute cultures. In 1869, the beauty of the Yampa River–Green River confluence captivated famed explorer John Wesley Powell, who named the area "Echo Canyon." In 1915, President Woodrow Wilson proclaimed an 80-acre site as Dinosaur National Monument after the entreaties of paleontologist Earl Douglass and his sponsor, the Carnegie Museum of Pittsburgh, Pennsylvania. During the New Deal, the monument was enlarged by more than 200,000 acres. This was typical of the Great Depression, when the only jobs available were on federal work programs such as the Civilian Conservation Corps.

In the 1950s, Echo Canyon and the Yampa, the last free-flowing river in the Colorado River basin, were threatened by a proposed dam. The Colorado River Storage Project, the largest chain of dams proposed until that time, included a dam at the confluence of the Yampa and Green rivers inside the monument. No development plan had threatened a national park area since the Hetch Hetchy dam in the early 1900s, and an energized conservation community responded in anger. A concerted effort by an ever-growing number of conservation organizations built a sophisticated antidam campaign that eventually compelled both Congress and federal agencies to abandon the Echo Canyon Dam project. Writer and historian Bernard DeVoto called for saving Echo Park as one of the few remaining places where "the balance of nature, the web of life, the interrelationships of species, [and] massive problems of ecology" could be recognized and studied. By 1954, mail to Congress ran 80 to 1 against the Echo Park Dam, and the Bureau of Reclamation relented. In 1956, Congress authorized the Colorado River Storage Project, but without the controversial Echo Park Dam. Today, the monument's high-plateau scrub desert, canyon, and river landscapes provide critical habitat for endangered species like the peregrine falcon, bald eagle, Colorado pike minnow, and razorback sucker.

The Headquarters Visitor Center is located 2 miles east of Dinosaur, Colorado, on Highway 40. The center contains exhibits and a ten-minute orientation program, and is open daily from 8 A.M. to 6 P.M. during the summer, and weekdays from 8 A.M. to 4:30 P.M. during the winter. The Dinosaur Quarry Visitor Center is located 7 miles north of Jensen, Utah, on Utah Highway 149, and its pre-mier exhibit is the quarry where dinosaur bones and fossils can be seen. The center also has exhibits on the Jurassic dinosaurs that lived here, their environment, and the science of paleontology. Ranger talks and guided walks are offered during the summer months.

The park has many scenic drives and self-guided trails that lead to scenic areas, including Echo Park, Harpers Corner, Jones Hole, the Gates of Lodore, Canyon Overlook, Rainbow Park, and the rugged Yampa Bench Road. Since park roads vary in condition from paved to unimproved dirt, it is advisable to check with park headquarters in Dinosaur for detailed information on conditions and vehicle restrictions. Most dirt roads, especially the long, isolated Yampa Bench Road, are impassable when wet. Although some outer portions of the monument can be reached by automobile, much of the park is accessible only by boat or raft. Because the monument is so popular with river runners, fees and noncommercial river permits (lottery-drawn) are required for private whitewater river trips on the Green and Yampa rivers. Commercial trips down both river canyons are also available, and are typically one to six days in length.

Dinosaur is high in altitude and semiarid in character. In the summer it is hot, with temperatures reaching into the 90s, but evenings are cool, and there are occasional afternoon thunderstorms. Elevations within the park vary between 4,500 and 9,000 feet, and a hot summer day at the Dinosaur Quarry Visitor Center can be cool at the much-higher Harpers Corner. September and October boast the best weather; winters are cold and windy, with occasional light snowfall.

There are no lodging or restaurant facilities in the park, but the nearby towns of Vernal and Jensen, Utah, and Rangely, Craig, and Dinosaur, Colorado, offer all traveler services. The park's only improved campgrounds are the Green River and Split Mountain campgrounds, and during the summer, Split Mountain is for group camping only. Both campgrounds are located east of the Quarry Visitor Center and have modern rest rooms, tables and fireplaces, firewood for sale, and evening ranger programs. Primitive campgrounds are located at Deerlodge Park (where Yampa River trips begin), Echo Park, Gates of Lodore (where Green River trips begin), and Rainbow Park. These campgrounds only have picnic tables and pit toilets, and only Echo Park, $6 per night, and Gates of Lodore, $5 per night, have drinking water. Deerlodge and Rainbow Park campgrounds are free.

For more information, write Dinosaur National Monument, 4545 East Highway 40, Dinosaur, CO 81610-9724, or telephone (970) 374-3000. For specific information on private river-running fees, equipment, and experience requirements, and how to apply for the permit lottery, call (970) 374-2468. The park's interesting Web site is www.nps.gov/dino.

FURTHER READING

Hagood, Allen. *Dinosaur: The Story Behind the Scenery.* Las Vegas, NV: KC Publications, 1990.

Harvey, Mark W.T. *A Symbol of Wilderness: Echo Park and the American Conservation Movement.* Seattle: University of Washington Press, 2000.

Reisner, Marc. *Cadillac Desert: The American West and Its Disappearing Water.* New York: Perguin, 1993.

Stegner, Wallace, ed. *This Is Dinosaur: Echo Park Country and Its Magic Rivers.* New York: Roberts Rinehart, 1985.

DRY TORTUGAS NATIONAL PARK

Location: Key West, Florida
Acreage: 64,701
Established: January 4, 1935

Seventy miles west of Key West, Florida, in the warm waters of the Gulf of Mexico, lies the chain of seven coral-reef and sand islands called the Dry Tortugas. The Spanish explorer Ponce de Leon first discovered the archipelago in 1513, and named it *las tortugas* after the abundant sea turtles that provisioned his ships with fresh meat. But the islands offered no fresh water, leading to the moniker "dry tortugas." For the next three hundred years, pirates relied on the turtles for meat and eggs, and also raided the nests of the islands' sooty and noddy terns. By the early 1800s, the islands' strategic location in the Florida straits attracted the attention of the U.S. military, and in 1846, construction began on a massive coastal fort, Fort Jefferson; it was never completed. Despite its 50-foot-high, 8-foot-thick walls and room for 450 cannon and a garrison of 1,500 soldiers, Fort Jefferson was rendered obsolete by the invention of the rifled cannon.

Fort Jefferson was used as a prison after the Civil War. The most famous man housed there was Dr. Samuel Mudd, an ancestor of newsman Roger Mudd, who was accused of treating John Wilkes Booth after the assassination of Abraham Lincoln. Mudd set the injured Booth's ankle, for which he was sentenced to Fort Jefferson. He spent four years there and the rest of his life trying to clear his name.

Although it failed as a military outpost, Fort Jefferson, and the Dry Tortugas, were invaluable as a wildlife sanctuary, and in 1935, President Franklin D. Roosevelt set aside the islands as Fort Jefferson National Monument. In October 1992, the almost-65,000-acre site was redesignated Dry Tortugas National Park; it is renowned for its abundant bird and marine life, as well as its legends of pirates and sunken gold. The park is also home to some of the healthiest remaining coral reefs off the North American coastline.

Dry Tortugas is open year-round, with no entrance fee. Access is only by public boat or seaplane from Key West, and personal watercraft like jet skis are not permitted. The park is remote and wild, so visitors must bring everything they will need, including food and water. Private boaters must be fully self-sufficient with water, fuel, and supplies. Nautical charts for the route can be purchased at boating supply outlets in Key West. The park has no boat moorings or slips, and overnight anchorage is limited to the designated area within 1 nautical mile of the Fort Jefferson harbor light. Fort Jefferson on Garden Key is open only during daylight hours. Loggerhead Key is day-use only, and Bush Key is closed to visitors from April to September to protect nesting sooty and noddy terns—over 100,000 of them. Hospital and Long keys are closed all year.

The Dry Tortugas Visitor Center features exhibits on the history of Fort Jefferson and a video describing the park's history and natural resources. The Fort Jefferson Museum has a self-guided tour with interpretive signs, and park rangers often give guided tours of the fort. The Florida National Parks and Monuments Association bookstore at the visitor center contains books, videos, and related products describing the park's flora, fauna, and history.

There are no food or lodging facilities at the park, but camping is permitted at the Garden Key campground. The 13 sites are available on a first-come, first-served basis for $3 per person per night. The campground provides picnic tables, grills, and saltwater flush toilets. All supplies, including fresh water, must be brought in, and all trash must be carried out. Other overnight accommodations, restaurants, and traveler services are available in Key West.

For more information, write Dry Tortugas National Park, P.O. Box 6208, Key West, FL 33041, or telephone (305) 242-7700. Specific information about the public boat and seaplane services may be obtained by contacting the park, or the Key West Chamber of Commerce, Old Mallory Square, Key West, FL 33040 (305) 294-2587. The park's Web site is www.nps.gov/drto.

FURTHER READING

Bethel, Rodman. *A Slumbering Giant of the Past: Fort Jefferson, USA in the Dry Tortugas.* Key West: Florida Flair Books, 1979.

Fuson, Robert Henderson. *Juan Ponce de Leon and the Spanish Discovery of Puerto Rico and Florida.* Granville, OH: McDonald & Woodward, 2000.

Mudd, Nettie, ed. *The Life of Dr. Samuel A. Mudd, Containing His Letters from Fort Jefferson, Dry Tortugas Island, Where He Was Imprisoned Four Years for Alleged Complicity in the Assassination of Abraham Lincoln.* R.D. Mudd, privately published, 1962.

Souza, Donna J. *The Persistence of Sail in the Age of Steam: Underwater Archaeological Evidence from the Dry Tortugas.* Boston: Plenum, 1998.

E

EBEY'S LANDING NATIONAL HISTORICAL RESERVE

Location: Coupeville, Washington
Acreage: 19,324
Established: November 10, 1978

> Come look from this eminence of bluff, now in the soft hour before daybreak, the island's farm fields are leather and corduroy, rich even panels between black-furred stands of forest.
>
> —*Ivan Doig*

Ebey's Landing National Historical Reserve is an island of calm in the midst of the rapidly growing Puget Sound metropolitan area, and preserves the rich historical record and landscape of the Pacific Northwest. Unlike many national park units, this 19,324-acre reserve encompasses a mixture of federal, state, county, and private lands, and includes two state parks and the historic Victorian waterfront town of Coupeville, one of the oldest towns in Washington State. Within the boundaries of the park lie five distinct ecological areas that form the mosaic landscape so distinct to the reserve. These diverse ecosystems include a coastal zone of sparsely vegetated beach and bluff; a prairie of rich fertile soil in both farmland and wetland; wooded areas of second- and third-growth Douglas fir and Western red cedar with an understory of rhododendron; upland hills of pastures and cultivated fields; and Penn Cove's lowland lagoons that shelter waterfowl and migratory birds.

Whidbey Island, where Ebey's Landing is located, was named by Captain George Vancouver when he explored the region in 1792. Vancouver wrote of the island's verdant, lush, fertile lands as ideal for long-term farming and settlement. Later, the English Hudson's Bay Company established a post near present-day Olympia, but the Treaty of 1846 gave all of Oregon Territory to the United States, which opened the floodgates to settlement in the Pacific Northwest. The first American settler on Whidbey Island was Colonel Isaac Ebey—hence the landing's name—and the nearby town of Coupeville was founded by New England sea captains.

Today 48 historic structures are still standing in Coupeville—many are old sea captains' homes—while 50 other buildings of various kinds are sprinkled about the reserve. The open fields between Ebey's Landing and Coupeville have been farmed continuously since the 1850s. Many who still farm the area on homesteads established at that time are direct descendants of the original settlers, and many of their homes are either original or were rebuilt on mid-nineteenth-century foundations.

Established as a national historical reserve in November 1978, Ebey's Landing National Historical Reserve represented the manifestation of an advance in the conceptualization of national park areas. Among of the first of the generation of parks then referred to as "greenline" and now called cultural landscapes, Ebey's Landing National Historical Reserve established a zone on Central Whidbey Island in which to preserve rural life and its patterns in the historic landscape. The reserve protected a historic rural past, nearly unbroken since the nineteenth century, offering a mantle of protection that extended over not only federal property but state and privately owned land as well. The legislative definition of the goals of the reserve gave the Park Service a complicated mandate: how to preserve the past for the present while simultaneously giving the present physical access and simultaneously allowing the many people and activities that fell within its boundaries to continue unimpeded by the agency and visitors to the park. The dimensions of this new kind of management required greater fidelity to the past in a local setting, more sensitivity to local needs than parks without local populations inside their boundaries, and a clear understanding of the history of the relationships between people and their landscapes as well as among different groups of people. The rich historical texture of Whidbey Island became essential in communicating the values of the park to the traveling public.

Ebey's Landing is open year-round, with no admission fee. Although summer is the peak tourist season, the reserve is also popular for short winter weekend trips, due to its relatively mild winters and close proximity to Seattle, Tacoma, and Vancouver, British Columbia. The park is located on central Whidbey Island, Washington, two hours north of Seattle, and is accessible via Washington Highway 20 or by ferry from Port Townsend or Mukilteo.

The reserve is best seen by private car or bicycle, and free, island-wide bus transportation (with bike racks) is available and accessible at both ferries and in Coupeville. Fort Ebey and Fort Casey state parks are both part of the reserve—Fort Casey was built during World War I as a coastal defense garrison, and Fort Ebey was established during World War II for the same purpose—and offer stunning marine views. Visitors should also consider a short hike along the spectacular bluff trail, a visit to the Admiralty Head Lighthouse, and bird-watching at Crockett Lake. The Island County Historical Museum on Coupeville's waterfront is a good place to se-

cure informative brochures and plan visits. Food and lodging are available in Coupeville and further north at Oak Harbor. Both Fort Casey and Fort Ebey state parks have developed campgrounds. Surf fishing and a boat ramp are available at Fort Casey State Park, and Coupeville also has a boat ramp.

For more information, write Ebey's Landing National Historical Reserve, P.O. Box 774, Coupeville, WA 98239-0774, or telephone (360) 678-6084. The park's Web site is www.nps.gov/ebla.

FURTHER READING
Fisher, Robin. *Vancouver's Voyage: Charting the Northwest Coast, 1791–1795.* Seattle: University of Washington Press, 1992.
——, ed. *From Maps to Metaphors: The Pacific World of George Vancouver.* Vancouver: University of British Columbia Press, 1993.
Kellogg, George Albert. *A History of Whidbey Island.* Coupeville, WA: The Island County Historical Society, 1968.
White, Richard. *Land Use, Environment, and Social Change: The Shaping of Island County, Washington.* Seattle: University of Washington Press, 1980.

EDGAR ALLAN POE NATIONAL HISTORIC SITE
Location: Philadelphia, Pennsylvania
Acreage: .52
Established: November 10, 1978

The Edgar Allan Poe National Historic Site celebrates the life of one of America's most famous and influential literary stylists. Although perhaps best known for his dark short stories, Poe (1809–1849) was also a poet, editor, playwright, and critic. Almost from the beginning, Poe's life was beset with difficulty. When he was only two, his mother died and his father disappeared. Raised as a foster child by Frances Allan and her husband, John, Poe attended boarding school in England before returning to the states to study language at the University of Virginia. At age eighteen, Poe published his first set of poems, but his gambling debts provoked his stepfather to withdraw support from the struggling young student, and by the age of twenty-two, Poe's life became one of struggle and poverty.

"From childhood's hour, I have not been as others were," he wrote. "I have not seen as others saw." In 1835, at age twenty-six, he became the editor of the *Southern Literary Messenger* in Richmond, Virginia, and a year later he married Virginia Clemm. In 1837, the couple moved from Richmond to New York City, then to Philadelphia, where they resided for six years. From 1843 to 1844 they made their home in the modest, red-brick, three-story building preserved today. It was here that the prolific Poe wrote some of his most famous stories, such as "The Fall of the House of Usher," "The Tell-Tale Heart," and "The Murders in the Rue Morgue." In 1844, the restless Poe moved back to New York City, where his wife died of tuberculosis in 1847. Following her death, Poe's mental and physical health declined, and he died in Baltimore in 1849.

Of Poe's numerous Philadelphia homes, only one survives. Located at 532 North Seventh Street, the 1-acre site, consisting of Poe's home and 2 connecting buildings, was originally set aside as a national historic landmark in 1962, and became a national historic site in 1978. The park is open year-round from 9 A.M. until 5 P.M. daily, from June through October, and from Wednesday through Sunday for the remainder of the year. Admission is free. Although there is no formal visitor center, audiovisual programs, interpretive exhibits, and ranger-guided house tours are available throughout the year. A "Reading Room" allows visitors to enjoy Poe's literature, including dramatic readings of his works on audio tape, and a library is available for research purposes. Visitation is usually highest in October and lowest in January and February.

The historic site is located about a mile north of Independence Hall, and parking adjacent to and even near the park can be scarce. Visitors are encouraged to use either a taxi or mass transit to get to the site. There are no lodging, restaurant, or camping facilities on-site, but a wide variety of travel services are available in Philadelphia, and local restaurants and grocery stores are within walking distance of the home. Picnic tables are conveniently located on park grounds. The nearest camping facilities are about 20 miles outside the city center in the western suburbs.

For more information, write Edgar Allan Poe National Historic Site, 532 North Seventh Street, Philadelphia, PA 19123, or telephone (215) 597-8780. The park's Web site is www.nps.gov/edal.

FURTHER READING
Poe, Edgar Allan. *Complete Stories and Poems of Edgar Allan Poe.* Garden City, NY: Doubleday, 1966.
Silverman, Kenneth. *Edgar A. Poe: Mournful and Never-ending Remembrance.* New York: HarperCollins, 1991.

EDISON NATIONAL HISTORIC SITE
Location: West Orange, New Jersey
Acreage: 21
Established: December 6, 1955

Thomas Alva Edison (1847–1931) has often been heralded as one of the most important people of the past millennium. Indeed, for more than forty years, the West Orange, New Jersey, laboratory created and operated by this prolific inventor had an enormous impact on the lives of millions of people around the world. Today, the 21-acre Edison National Historic Site preserves Edison's research and development laboratory and his home, Glenmont, and interprets this enduring symbol of American technical ingenuity and productive power.

Born in Milan, Ohio, Thomas Edison was the seventh and last child of Nancy and Samuel Edison. Although he received only a few months of formal school education, Edison was a studious child and learned the 3 Rs

The library at the Edison National Historic Site.
(Library of Congress)

from his mother. By the age of sixteen, Edison struck out on his own, working full-time as a telegrapher. His first successful invention was an improved stock ticker called the "Universal Stock Printer," for which he earned an astonishing $40,000–enough to establish his first laboratory in Newark, New Jersey. In 1876, Edison sold his Newark enterprises and moved to the small community of Menlo Park, near New York City. It was here that Edison, "The Wizard of Menlo Park," developed his most famous invention–a practical incandescent electric light. In 1886, two years after the death of his first wife, Mary Stilwell, Edison remarried and moved to the Glenmont estate in West Orange, New Jersey. In 1887, he opened "the best equipped and largest laboratory extant and the facilities superior to any other for rapid and cheap development of an invention." Edison's pro-

lific "Invention Factory" was awarded 1,093 patents and generated many of the wonders of modern society: the motion picture camera, vastly improved phonographs and sound recordings, silent and sound movies, and the nickel-iron alkaline electric storage battery. The laboratory, which remained in operation after Edison's 1931 death, was the forerunner of the modern technical research and development complex.

The site's visitor center is located in the Edison Laboratory and is open from noon to 5 P.M. Wednesday through Friday, 9 A.M. to 5 P.M. Saturday and Sunday, and is closed on Monday and Tuesday. Sophisticated multimedia and audiovisual presentations, as well as interactive exhibits, tell the story of Edison and his inventions. In addition to special events throughout the year, park rangers offer tours of the laboratory and the 16-acre Glenmont estate. The Laboratory Complex contains 14 structures, 6 of which Edison built in 1887, to serve as his original laboratory. Another unit is the "Black Maria," a replica of the world's first structure exclusively designed as a motion picture studio. Edison's 29-room residence, Glenmont, was built in 1880. This brick-and-timber mansion contains the original furnishings and family items used by Thomas and Mina Edison, their family, and their servants. The estate grounds include gardens, the family greenhouse and barn, and the poured cement garage containing the family's automobiles. The Edisons' graves are located on the estate's grounds.

The museum collection and archives, by far the largest single body of Edison-related material located anywhere, are the products of Thomas Edison's prolific sixty-year career as an inventor, manufacturer, businessman, and private citizen. The collection's size is daunting. The Park Service estimates the artifact collection alone numbers 400,000 items, while the archives contain approximately 5 million documents, including lab notebooks, sketches, working drawings made by Edison and his colleagues, specialized testing equipment and materials, master and unreleased sound recordings, and the prototypes and working models for important inventions, including the first phonograph, improved telegraph equipment, and early motion picture apparatus. Many of these documents are also available on-line, at the park's home page.

The entrance fee for Edison National Historic Site is $2 per person and is valid for seven days. There is no food, camping, or lodging in the park but all are available nearby. Visitation is usually highest in July and August, and lowest in October and January. The site is located in West Orange, New Jersey, about 15 miles west of New York City. Public transportation (800-772-2222) to the park is available.

Note that at press time, the Edison National Historic Site was closed for renovations and scheduled to reopen sometime in 2005.

For more information, write Edison National Historic Site, Main Street and Lakeside Avenue, West Orange, NJ 07052, or telephone (973) 736-0550. The park's Web site is www.nps.gov/edis.

FURTHER READING
Israel, Paul. *Edison: A Life of Invention.* New York: John Wiley and Sons, 1998.
Melosi, Martin V. *Thomas A. Edison and the Modernization of America.* New York: Longman, 1990.

EFFIGY MOUNDS NATIONAL MONUMENT
Location: Harpers Ferry, Iowa
Acreage: 2,526
Established: October 25, 1949

In 1949, President Harry S Truman established Effigy Mounds National Monument in northeastern Iowa to preserve and protect the remarkable remains of the prehistoric Mound Builder's culture. Archeologists estimate that farming cultures in eastern North America emerged about three thousand years ago, along the fertile banks of the Mississippi River.

These peoples, also known as the Woodland culture, combined hunting and gathering with agricultural cultivation to create a sophisticated way of life that could sustain larger populations. While these mound-building peoples inhabited most of the eastern United States and southeastern Canada, the effigy Mound Builders occupied a far more restricted region that included southern Wisconsin, northern Illinois, and neighboring Iowa and Minnesota.

The 2,500-plus-acre national monument contains nearly 200 mounds, 31 of which are effigies—representations of living creatures such as bears, birds, bison, deer, and reptiles measuring up to 70 feet wide, 137 feet long, and 2 to 4 feet high. Built between 500 B.C.E. and 1300 C.E., the mounds were most likely used for burials. Scientific excavation of the mounds has unearthed human remains, large chipped blades, dart points, spherical copper beads, tools, and pottery. The oldest excavated mound in the park, one belonging to a culture known as the Red Ocher, is estimated to be about twenty-five hundred years old.

The study of Mound Builders became an American obsession as the nation expanded westward, and, before 1800, articles about mounds in Ohio and in the east and hypotheses about their builders were common. In 1838, Richard C. Taylor produced the first accurate descriptions of effigy mounds in central Wisconsin, and in the late 1850s and early 1860s, federal officials assessed mounds from Ohio to Missouri. Only in 1881, when Alfred J. Hill and Theodore Lewis joined together to explore the mounds of Upper Mississippi Valley did the Effigy Mounds National Monument area attract similar attention. Local interest in the mounds took shape, with Elison Orr of Waukon, Iowa, playing a catalytic role in initiating study of the mounds in the region. The New Deal added resources for survey endeavors and Orr himself played a role in developing an inventory of the Iowa mounds. By 1945, the mounds were widely regarded as an important feature of Iowa's prehistory. Their establishment as a national monument in 1949 resulted from the increase in estimation of their importance, a long campaign by Iowa's congressional delegation, and willingness of the Iowa Conservation Commission, which owned much of the land in the area, to cede the acreage to the federal government for a national park.

Effigy Mounds is open daily, year-round, from 8 A.M. to 4:30 P.M., with extended hours during the summer. Entrance fees are $4 per car or $2 per person and are valid for seven days. A $10 annual pass is also available. The park's visitor center contains a museum, archeological exhibits, and information on the region's natural history. Park rangers give guided walks, hikes, and prehistoric tool demonstrations from Memorial Day through Labor Day. The park also hosts several special events in the autumn, including Archeological Week in September, which highlights the monument's various archeological programs, and Hawk Watch, held the last weekend in September, which features the migration of birds of prey and raptors along the Mississippi River. Each year, more than 80,000 people visit Effigy Mounds, and visitation is typically highest in August and also October, when colorful fall foliage graces the park.

Hiking opportunities through the tall-grass prairies and forests are plentiful, and no vehicles are allowed in the park beyond the visitor center. Eleven miles of trails lead the hiker around many of the more unusual mounds and unique effigies. The popular Fire Trail point is a moderately strenuous 2-mile, self-guided interpretive trail to scenic overlooks and the park's major points of interest, like Little Bear Mound and Great Bear Mound. The park's South Unit contains the spectacular Marching Bears Mound Group, the park's best integrated collection of effigy mounds: 10 bears and 3 birds.

Effigy Mounds is located in northeastern Iowa, along the Mississippi River, 3 miles north of Marquette. There are no food, lodging, or camping facilities in the park. The nearest camping is at Pikes Peak State Park and Yellow River State Forest (both 8 miles away) in Iowa and Wyalusing State Park (15 miles away) in Wisconsin. Motel and restaurant accommodations can be found nearby in Marquette and McGregor, Iowa, and Prairie du Chien, Wisconsin.

For more information, write Effigy Mounds National Monument, 151 Highway 76, Harpers Ferry, IA 52146, or telephone (319) 873–3491. The park's Web site is www.nps.gov/efmo.

FURTHER READING

Benn, David W., ed. *Woodland Cultures on the Western Prairies: The Rainbow Site Investigations.* Iowa City: Office of the State Archaeologist, University of Iowa, 1990.

O'Bright, Jill York. *The Perpetual March: An Administrative History of Effigy Mounds National Monument.* Omaha, NE: National Park Service, 1989.

EISENHOWER NATIONAL HISTORIC SITE

Location: Gettysburg, Pennsylvania
Acreage: 690
Established: November 27, 1967

On June 6, 1944–D-Day in World War II– the voice of Supreme Allied Commander Dwight David Eisenhower announced news of the Normandy invasion to the people of Western Europe: "I call upon all who love freedom to stand with us now. Together we shall achieve victory." On that day, hope returned to a Europe ravaged by war and stunned by the rise of Adolf Hitler. Less than a year later, on May 7, Eisenhower accepted the German surrender that ended the European war.

Dwight D. "Ike" Eisenhower's (1890–1969) rise to greatness had been steady and measured. He was born in Denison, Texas, and grew up in America's heartland, Abilene,

Kansas. In 1915 he graduated from West Point and began a twenty-seven-year career of army service, including a tour of duty as an aide to General Douglas MacArthur in the Philippines. When the Japanese attacked Pearl Harbor on December 7, 1941, however, Eisenhower quickly rose to international prominence. After a brief stint in the War Department, he commanded American forces in Europe, then successfully directed the North Africa campaign, before becoming the Supreme Allied Commander. After the war, Eisenhower resigned from active duty to become president of Columbia University, but returned to service in 1950 to become the supreme commander of the newly created NATO (North Atlantic Treaty Organization) forces. Although he had no political experience, Eisenhower had tremendous national appeal, and in 1952 and again in 1956, American voters sent this moderate Republican to the White House. The eight years he was in office were marked largely by peace and prosperity, as the nation moved beyond the Korean War, developed the interstate highway system, and enjoyed the most prosperous decade it had ever known. Although Eisenhower had been a product of the military, he used the occasion of his 1961 farewell address to warn the country of the dangers posed by unchecked expansion: "In the councils of government, we must guard against the acquisition of unwarranted influence, whether sought or unsought, by the military-industrial complex. The potential for the disastrous rise of misplaced power exists and will persist."

The Eisenhower National Historic Site preserves Dwight and Mamie Eisenhower's only home, a 230-acre estate in southcentral Pennsylvania, as well as an additional 460 acres of adjoining farmland donated to the park over time. During his presidency, Eisenhower used the property both as a weekend retreat and an informal setting for meetings with international dignitaries such as Charles de Gaulle, Nikita Khrushchev, and Winston Churchill. Although the Eisenhowers continued to live at the residence until their deaths—Ike in 1969 and Mamie in 1979—in 1967, the couple deeded the estate to the United States for administration by the National Park Service.

The Eisenhower Reception Center, once the Secret Service Office, is open daily from 9 A.M. until 5 P.M. The center contains interpretive exhibits on Eisenhower's life, and offers an illustrated brochure that narrates a self-guided tour of the grounds, including the Eisenhowers' prized Black Angus cattle operation. Park rangers offer regularly scheduled talks and living history programs, as well as a guided tour of the Eisenhower home, which features almost all of the original furnishings.

The Eisenhower National Historic Site adjoins Gettysburg National Military Park in Gettysburg, Pennsylvania, about 80 miles north of Washington, D.C. Except for four weeks during the winter, it is open year-round; hours are daily, from April 1 through October 31 from 9 A.M. to 4 P.M. The rest of the year the site is open from Wednesday through Sunday. Entrance fees vary according to age: Adults (seventeen years or older) are $5.25, children ages thirteen to sixteen are $3.25, and children ages six to twelve are $2.25 each. Due to a lack of on-site parking and space limitations in the Eisenhower home, visits can only be made by a shuttle bus (fee charged) leaving from the Gettysburg National Military Park Visitor Center. The center opens at 8 A.M., and the first scheduled shuttle leaves one hour later. Visitation is highest from mid-June to mid-August and October, and is lowest during the winter.

There is no food or lodging on-site, but nearby Gettysburg has all traveler services. Developed camping is available at the adjacent Gettysburg National Military Park.

For more information, write Eisenhower National Historic Site, 97 Taneytown Road, Gettysburg, PA 17325, or telephone (717) 338–9114. The park's Web site is www.nps.gov/eise.

FURTHER READING

Ambrose, Stephen E. *Eisenhower: Soldier and President.* New York: Simon and Schuster, 1990.

D'Este, Carlo. *Eisenhower: A Soldier's Life.* New York: Henry Holt, 2002.

Eisenhower, Dwight D. *Crusade in Europe.* Baltimore, MD: Johns Hopkins University Press, 1997.

ELEANOR ROOSEVELT NATIONAL HISTORIC SITE

Location: Hyde Park, New York
Acreage: 181
Established: May 27, 1977

Eleanor Roosevelt National Historic Site in Hyde Park, New York, is the only Park Service unit dedicated to a first lady, and one of only five national park sites that celebrate women in American history. Set aside in May 1977 by President Jimmy Carter, the 181-acre site preserves Roosevelt's modest home and grounds along the Hudson River called Val-Kill, "in order to commemorate for the education, inspiration, and benefit of present and future generations the life and work of an outstanding woman in American history."

Anna Eleanor Roosevelt was born in October 1884 into the elite and wealthy New York Roosevelt clan. "I was a shy, solemn child," she remembered, and by the age of ten, she was also an orphan. Raised by her mother's family, Eleanor left for boarding school in England when she was fifteen, and there she commenced what she called "my real education," which included a growing concern for the oppressed—the hallmark of her long career. In 1902, she returned to New York and soon married her distant cousin, a dashing young man named Franklin Delano Roosevelt. A typical woman of the time, she quickly began a family that soon swelled to five children. In 1921, however, the idyllic world of the Roosevelts came crashing down

Eleanor Roosevelt and her dog Fala at Val-Kill in Hyde Park, New York, 1948. *(National Archives)*

when Franklin contracted a near-fatal case of polio. Though he survived, his physical activity was extremely limited, and he came to rely on his formerly shy wife to help him reestablish his political career. Eleanor took to the task with a relish and revolutionized the role of the political wife. By the time Franklin was elected president in 1932, Eleanor was already traveling the country promoting various liberal political agendas. Although she never held elective office, her political influence was significant. "Sometimes I acted as a spur," she confessed, "even though the spurring was not always wanted." After Franklin's death in 1945, Eleanor retired to Val-Kill for a year, until President Harry S Truman named her as a delegate to the UN General Assembly. She served for six years before resigning to become a "good will ambassador" to the world. Her vigorous public schedule continued through the 1950s and early 1960s, when President John F. Kennedy asked her to chair his Presidential Commission on the Status of Women. The commission's 1963 report was the most comprehensive study of women's lives ever produced by the federal government, and it was a fitting end to a brilliant career. Anna Eleanor Roosevelt died on November 7, 1962, shortly before the report was published.

Val-Kill and the surrounding grounds were a popular Roosevelt family retreat from the early 1920s to 1945. The Val-Kill estate grew out of a suggestion Franklin made in 1924 that a cottage should be built on Val-Kill stream, a favorite family fishing spot. In 1925, a fieldstone cottage was constructed, but it originally served as a furniture storage facility for Val-Kill Industries, which encouraged local craftsmen in the production of furniture and pewter items—indeed, many of the home's furnishings were fabricated here. When the business ceased operations in 1936, the original cottage was converted to a residence, and Eleanor entertained guests and foreign dignitaries in this lovely natural setting until her death.

Established in 1977, Eleanor Roosevelt National Historic Site resulted from the major transformation of the idea of history in the United States. After 1960, the older definitions of historical significance did not hold; history ceased to be simply the achievements of great men. In the search for a more inclusive history, the Park Service added numerous sites about the history of women, African American history, and other less-told narratives about the past. Eleanor Roosevelt was the preeminent woman of her generation and a national figure who often served as the nation's conscience. Her life and experience helped shed light on a broader national past.

The historic site is located in southeastern New York, about 6 miles north of Poughkeepsie on U.S. 9-G. The grounds are free and open year-round, and they feature elegant gardens, a formal Rose Garden and Cutting Garden, a pond, and several trails. The Stone Cottage, also on the grounds, is operated as a conference center by Eleanor Roosevelt's Val-Kill Inc., a nonprofit organization. Val-Kill Cottage is open daily from 9 A.M. until 5 P.M. from May through October, and on weekends from November through April. Access to the cottage is by guided tour only, which costs $5 for adults; children under seventeen are admitted free. The tour includes an introductory film, and park rangers conduct talks and programs on a variety of topics dealing with Mrs. Roosevelt's political activities, personal challenges, home life, and international diplomatic efforts. Visitation is usually highest in August and October, and lowest in January and February. Visitors can also purchase a combination pass to the Franklin Roosevelt National Historic Site, FDR Library and Museum, Eleanor Roosevelt National Historic Site, and Vanderbilt Mansion National Historic Site at a reduced cost of $18.

There is no food, camping, or lodging on-site, but the town of Hyde Park has all traveler services. The closest camping facilities are located near Vanderbilt Mansion National Historic Site, 6 miles north of Poughkeepsie, and at nearby Mills-Norrie State Park.

For more information, write Eleanor Roosevelt National Historic Site, 519 Albany Post Road, Hyde Park, NY 12538, or telephone (914) 229–9115. The park's informative Web site is www.nps.gov/elro.

FURTHER READING

Black, Allida M. *Casting Her Own Shadow: Eleanor Roosevelt and the Shaping of Postwar Liberalism.* New York: Columbia University Press, 1996.

Hoff-Wilson, Joan, and Marjorie Lightman, eds. *Without Precedent: The Life and Career of Eleanor Roosevelt.* Bloomington: Indiana University Press, 1984.

Purcell, Sarah J. *The Life and Work of Eleanor Roosevelt.* Indianapolis: Alpha, 2002.

ELLIS ISLAND NATIONAL MONUMENT

Location: New Jersey and New York
Acreage: 28
Established: May 11, 1965

On a small island in New York Harbor stands the unassuming building that, for many immigrants, symbolized the gateway to hope and freedom. Between 1892 and 1954, more than 12 million newcomers from around the world passed through the portal of Ellis Island and into the United States. The men, women, and children that came through Ellis Island were not the elites nor the well-to-do; those passengers underwent only a cursory inspection on-board the steamships since they were unlikely to become an economic "burden" in America. Ellis Island processed the "others"–"steerage" or third-class passengers who had traveled for weeks in crowded and often unsanitary conditions in the hulls of the great steamships. Even with proper documen-

tation and excellent health, the Ellis Island inspection process could stretch three to five hours. Doctors examined every immigrant for physical ailments, while immigration officials asked each person twenty-nine different questions about their plans and their past. Although the island soon gained the moniker "Island of Tears," only 2 percent of arriving immigrants were barred from entry; immigrants were usually blocked if they had a contagious disease or falsified papers. The Ellis Island National Monument was set aside in May 1965 and incorporated into the Statue of Liberty National Monument. During the late 1980s, Ellis Island underwent a massive restoration effort, and the island's main building is now a museum dedicated to the history of immigration and this island's important role during the great mass migration of the late nineteenth and early twentieth centuries.

The Ellis Island Immigration Museum–the former processing building–offers a vari-

Immigrants arriving at Ellis Island, c. 1907. *(Library of Congress)*

ety of self-guided permanent exhibits and programs about the island's history and the immigration process. "Through America's Gate" provides a step-by-step synopsis of the actual immigrant inspection process. "Peak Immigration Years" (1880–1924) covers the journey of immigrants to America and their settlement. "Treasures from Home" contains displays of personal objects and stories of immigrants. "The Peopling of America" offers a look at immigration trends using statistics, timelines, and graphs. Historic photographs of immigrants, official and personal papers, and artifacts help to re-create the entire immigration experience. The short thirty-minute documentary film *Island of Hope, Island of Tears* is shown in 2 theaters on a continuous basis. The museum also includes a research library that contains materials related to the Statue of Liberty, Ellis Island, and immigration history. The Oral History Collection includes 2,000 taped and transcribed interviews of actual Ellis Island immigrants and staff. Both the library and Oral History Collection are open to the public during the museum's regular operating hours.

Ellis Island is open year-round from 9 A.M. to 5:30 P.M. daily, with extended hours during the summer. Admission is free. Each year more than 5 million people visit Liberty and Ellis islands, with July and August being the busiest months. During the summer, temperatures average 80 to 95 degrees, while spring and fall are milder, with temperatures ranging from the mid-50s to the mid-70s. Winter temperatures can be extreme and visitors should check the local weather forecast prior to their visit. The islands are accessible only by the Statue of Liberty–Ellis Island ferries. One round-trip ferry ticket includes visits to both islands; tickets cost $7 for adults, $3 for children, and $6 for seniors. Ferries depart from Battery Park in New York and Liberty State Park in New Jersey. Private vessels are not permitted to dock at the islands.

Neither Ellis Island nor Liberty Island has restaurants or lodging, but the New York metropolitan area has all traveler services. Private campgrounds can be found away from the city in New York and New Jersey.

For more information, write Statue of Liberty National Monument and Ellis Island, Liberty Island, New York, NY 10004, or telephone (212) 363-3200. Call the ferry operator directly at (212) 269–5755 for additional information and schedules. The park's Web site is www. nps.gov/elis.

FURTHER READING
Bell, James B. *In Search of Liberty: The Story of the Statue of Liberty and Ellis Island.* Garden City, NY: Doubleday, 1984.
Overland, Orm. *Immigrant Minds, American Identities: Making the United States Home, 1870–1930.* Urbana: University of Illinois Press, 2000.
Yans-McLaughlin, Virginia, and Margorie Lightman. *Ellis Island and the Peopling of America.* New York: New Press, 1997.

EL MALPAIS NATIONAL MONUMENT
Location: Grants, New Mexico
Acreage: 114,277
Established: December 31, 1987

El Malpais National Monument and National Conservation Area protects a unique volcanic wilderness ecosystem that includes ancient and recent lava flows, cinder cones, complex ice caves, and a 17-mile-long lava tube system. Established in 1987, El Malpais, which means "the badlands," also safeguards important cultural resources. The site preserves ancestral Pueblo Indian ruins and grounds that continue to serve contemporary Native American groups such as the Acoma, Laguna, Zuni, and Ramah Navajo. These peoples still gather medicines and herbs and perform traditional ceremonies on their historic lands, providing a powerful reminder of the ten thousand years of human history at El Malpais.

The 114,277-acre national monument is jointly managed by the National Park Service and the Bureau of Land Management and offers a broad array of recreational opportunities. Hiking trails throughout the park allow visitors to explore volcanic features such as lava flows, cinder cones, pressure ridges, and lava tubes and caves. The Zuni-Acoma Trail, for example, follows an ancient trade route between the two pueblos; it is a strenuous, 72-mile one-way hike across four of the region's major lava flows. The Big Tubes area is home to one of the largest ice cave/lava tube systems in North America. Other natural attractions are accessible by car. The Sandstone Bluffs Overlook is reached via an easy dirt road drive to a sandstone ridge, and the overlook affords excellent views of the El Malpais lava flows and the surrounding countryside. The nearby El Calderon is a forested area that includes Junction Cave, Double Sinks, El Calderon cinder cone, lava flows, and sandstone formations.

There are 2 visitor centers associated with El Malpais. The Northwest New Mexico Visitor Center is located in Grants just south of I-40 at exit 85, and is open daily from 8 A.M. until 5 P.M. (which switches to 9 A.M. until 6 P.M. for daylight savings). The center features exhibits on the natural and cultural history of the area, local artwork, and a variety of interpretive programs, cave explorations, special events, and demonstrations throughout the year. The El Malpais Information Center is located 23 miles south of Grants on state highway 53, and is open all year from 8:30 A.M. until 4:30 P.M. The information center offers a variety of ranger-guided programs and interpretive hikes as well as exhibits on volcanology and natural history. Of particular note is the park's Bat Flight program, conducted from June through August, where rangers lead guided hikes to observe bats in their natural environment.

There are no entrance fees for El Malpais and visitation usually peaks in July and August. The monument ranges in elevation from 6,500 to 8,300 feet above sea level, which can lead to unpredictable weather throughout the year. Monsoon thunderstorms are a common occurrence during July and August afternoons, and lightning can pose a hazard to hikers. Regardless of the outside temperature, spelunkers planning to explore ice and lava tube caves should be prepared for cool, damp conditions and are advised to bring warm clothing, protective headgear, three light sources, and leather gloves.

Although the monument has no lodging or restaurant facilities, nearby Grants has all traveler services. El Malpais does not have a developed campground, but overnight primitive camping is allowed in the Narrows Camping Area with a free backcountry permit available from the monument's information center. There are developed RV campgrounds in Grants and near El Morro National Monument, and the U.S. Forest Service operates campgrounds in the adjacent Cibola National Forest.

For more information, write El Malpais National Monument, P.O. Box 846, Grants, NM 87020-0846, or telephone (505) 783-4774 or (505) 287-7911. The park's informative Web site is www.nps.gov/elma.

FURTHER READING

Beck, Warren A. *New Mexico: A History of Four Centuries.* Norman: University of Oklahoma Press, 1987.

Mangum, Neil C. *In the Land of Frozen Fires: A History of Occupation in El Malpais Country.* Santa Fe, NM: National Park Service, 1990. Available at www.nps.gov/elma/hist/hist.htm.

Minge, Ward A. *Acoma: Pueblo in the Sky.* Albuquerque: University of New Mexico Press, 1976.

EL MORRO NATIONAL MONUMENT

Location: Ramah, New Mexico
Acreage: 1,279
Established: December 8, 1906

Established in 1906, El Morro National Monument's showcase attraction is the "guest register" etched into this sandstone mesa, which bears witness to seven centuries of human history in the region. Known as Inscription Rock, this bluff served as a critical rest area for weary travelers who slaked their thirst at the dependable natural pool at the cliff base and carved their names in the soft rock. Prehistoric Anasazi petroglyphs date from 1000 to 1400 C.E., while the earliest European inscription is that of Spanish explorer Don Juan de Oñate in 1605. The 200-foot-high monolith was also home to two significant pueblos: North Ruin and A'ts'ina, which once housed at least 1,000 people. Both were built during the thirteenth century and abandoned by the late fourteenth century, although the latter continues to occupy an important place in Zuni tradition and folklore.

Among the first national monuments es-

tablished after the passage of the Antiquities Act in June 1906, El Morro reflected the interest in American archeology of that era. As the United States found itself as a nation, it searched for a continental past; El Morro's collection of names scratched in rock helped affirm that human experience and offered a look into a murky if romantic past.

Located 60 miles southeast of Gallup, New Mexico, on New Mexico Highway 53, El Morro is open year-round. Entrance fees are $2 per individual and $4 per vehicle, and are valid for seven days. The monument's visitor center is open daily from 9 A.M. until 5 P.M. and offers a fifteen-minute video introduction to the park, interpretive exhibits on the human history of the region and the hun-

Inscription Rock at El Morro National Monument. *(Library of Congress)*

dreds of inscriptions, as well as arts and crafts demonstrations by local artisans. During the summer, park rangers offer interpretive talks at the visitor center, and 2 of the park's self-guided trails begin here. The Inscription Rock Trail is a half-mile loop that passes by the inscriptions and carvings at the cliff's base. The Mesa Top Trail is a 2-mile loop that winds over the top of the mesa past ancient pueblo ruins; it also provides one of the area's best panoramic views. Mesa Top Trail is usually closed in the winter due to heavy snowfall. Most of El Morro's 96,000 annual visitors come during May and June, while December and January are the least crowded. Visitors should be aware that New Mexico weather can be unpredictable. Summers days are often hot, with frequent monsoonal afternoon thundershowers and unusually heavy lightning, while winters can be cold, with frequent wind and snow.

The 1,279-acre monument has no food or lodging facilities, but all traveler services can be obtained in nearby communities, as well as Gallup and Grants. There is a small, family-run café just outside the park, and food service is available in Ramah, 13 miles west of the monument. El Morro has one small, 9-site campground located about a mile from the visitor center. It is open from late April through mid-October and offers picnic tables, grills, water, and pit toilets. Sites are available on a first-come, first-served basis, and a fee is charged during the summer months. There is also a private RV park just outside the monument's entrance.

For more information, write El Morro National Monument, Route 2, Box 43, Ramah, NM 87321, or telephone (505) 783-4226. The park's Web site is www.nps.gov/elmo.

FURTHER READING

Greene, Jerome A. *The Historic Pool, El Morro National Monument, New Mexico.* Denver, CO: Denver Service Center, National Park Service, 1978.

Murphy, Dan. *El Morro National Monument.* Tucson, AZ: Southwest Park and Monuments Association, 1989.

Noble, David Grant. *Zuni and El Morro Past and Present.* Santa Fe, NM: Ancient City Press, 1993.

Slater, John M. *El Morro, Inscription Rock, New Mexico: The Rock Itself, the Inscriptions Thereon, and the Travelers Who Made Them.* Los Angeles: Plantin, 1961.

EUGENE O'NEILL NATIONAL HISTORIC SITE

Location: Danville, California
Acreage: 13
Established: October 12, 1976

Eugene O'Neill (1888–1953) was born in a Broadway hotel and raised amid the bright lights of the American theater. His father was a famous actor, and O'Neill's early childhood was spent touring the country in traveling theatrical companies. Expelled from Princeton University after his freshman year for a drunken prank and "general hell-raising," O'Neill wandered the world until an attack of tuberculosis focused his energies on writing drama. During the 1920s and early 1930s, O'Neill ascended to the height of popularity with a series of theatrical triumphs that included *The Emperor Jones, Desire Under the Elms,* and his 1931 masterpiece *Mourning Becomes Electra.* At the pinnacle of his career, O'Neill withdrew into retirement and seclusion, and his works soon vanished from the popular stage. Yet his most enduring plays, all based on family tragedies—*The Iceman Cometh, Long Day's Journey into Night,* and his last, *A Moon for the Misbegotten*—were produced during these later years, 1937 to 1944, when he lived at Tao House near Danville, California. Today, the Eugene O'Neill National Historic Site commemorates the significant contributions of this architect of the modern American theater, the winner of four Pulitzer Prizes, and the only Nobel Prize–winning playwright from the United States.

The Eugene O'Neill National Historic Site (NHS) was established in 1976, as part of the expansion of the national park system to encompass a comprehensive national history. Although many of the parks added in this era reflected the themes of diversity, arts and culture played an important role. Even more, Representative Phil Burton, the congressional mastermind who engineered the establishment of many of these parks, represented the Bay Area and looked to add to Park Service holdings in his home area. The O'Neill NHS was an intersection of these trends.

Nestled in the Corduroy Hills above the San Ramon Valley 30 miles east of San Francisco, Tao House, built in 1937, was named by O'Neill and his wife, Carlotta, after the Chinese philosophy of Tao. The unusual house and surrounding gardens employ Chinese landscape design elements within a distinctly California-Monterey-style of architecture. Since 1980, the National Park Service has been restoring Tao House and the surrounding grounds.

Although there is no admission fee, guided tours are available by advance reservation only, which the Park Service recommends making two weeks prior to visiting. Directions to the site's free shuttle service are provided when reservations are confirmed. The historic site is open Wednesday through Sunday, year-round, and visitation is usually highest in April and June, and lowest in January.

The park's visitor center has a revolving series of displays on O'Neill's life, and visitors can take a self-guided tour of the grounds and orchards. Performances of O'Neill's works are offered as special programs during the summer months, and a bookstore provides a wide variety of material related to O'Neill's life and work.

There are no lodging, restaurant, or camping facilities on-site. Nearby local and Bay Area communities have all travel services, and a few private campgrounds are located in the surrounding area.

For more information and reservations, write Eugene O'Neill National Historic Site, P.O. Box 280, Danville, CA 94526, or telephone (925) 838-0249. The park's Web site is www.nps.gov/euon.

FURTHER READING

Alexander, Doris. *Eugene O'Neill's Creative Struggle: The Decisive Decade, 1924–1933.* University Park: Pennsylvania State University Press, 1992.

Bogard, Travis. *Eugene O'Neill at Tao House.* Tucson, AZ: Southwest Parks and Monuments, 1989.

——. *From the Silence of Tao House: Essays About Eugene and Carlotta O'Neill and the Tao House Plays.* Danville, CA: Eugene O'Neill Foundation, 1993.

O'Neill, Eugene. *Eugene O'Neill.* Broomall, PA: Chelsea House, 2000.

EVERGLADES NATIONAL PARK

Location: Miami, Florida
Acreage: 1,508,538
Established: May 30, 1934

Unlike early national parks that were set aside to protect the scenery, southern Florida's over-1.5-million-acre Everglades National Park was the first established to preserve a rapidly disappearing ecosystem. The largest remaining subtropical wilderness in the continental United States, Everglades is a unique wetlands environment—a shallow "river of grass" 120 miles long, 50 miles wide, and less than a foot deep, covering much of the southern half of the Florida Peninsula from Lake Okeechobee south to the Gulf of Mexico. By the early twentieth century, this ecosystem was in peril; water that once flowed freely through this flat landscape was being siphoned off to slake the thirst of Florida's growing human population. The Everglades' flora and fauna paid the price as the loss of habitat and the invasion of nonnative species disrupted thousands of years of evolution and decimated species. In 1934, Congress passed a park bill to protect Everglades—which opponents dubbed the "alligator and snake swamp bill"—and in 1947, President Harry S Truman formally dedicated about a quarter of this fragile and complex ecosystem as a national park.

Everglades National Park resulted from a three-decade-long struggle to protect natural Florida against the encroachment of a rapidly expanding population. In this, it was typical of the national parks founded as World War II ended. Everglades resulted from the concerns of conservationists worried about the rapidly dropping numbers of birds and alligators. Thousands of birds—egrets, spoonbills, flamingos, white herons, pelicans—were killed for their colorful plumage, and alligators were hunted almost to extinction for their hides. Park advocates had begun to take an interest as early as 1915, and the National Park Service coveted the lands as early as the 1920s.

Like most eastern parks, Everglades required purchase of private land and cooperation of the state. In 1929, an organization to spearhead a campaign of giving formed, and in 1934, Congress authorized the acquisition of private or public land by gift for the national park. Little occurred for the better part of a decade until a federal wildlife refuge was established in 1944; this served as an important catalyst. Two years later, in 1946, the Florida legislature allotted $2 million to buy land for the park, and, the next year, the park was formally established.

In many ways, the battle for the Everglades repeated earlier conflicts between local hunters who made their living close to nature and national conservationists, often hunters themselves, who regarded the hunt as sport. In the 1940s, such conservationists were close

Chokoloskee rookery in Everglades National Park. *(National Archives)*

Forest fires are fairly common in the Everglades in dry seasons or years. The year 1973, when this photograph was taken, however, was not dry. There were reports that the condition was caused by drainage of the land for commercial development. *(National Archives)*

to power in American society, albeit not yet infused with the spirit of wilderness that later came to dominate the movement. Yet Everglades was established as a wild park, and that moniker held as an important component of the public's perception of the park throughout the remainder of the twentieth century and beyond.

A mere 35 miles due west from Miami, Everglades hosts more than 700 temperate and tropical plant species in fresh and saltwater swamps, saw-grass prairies, and mangrove and cypress forests, which, in turn, shelter abundant wildlife. Everglades is renowned for its rich bird life–over 300 species–including large wading birds such as the roseate spoonbill, wood stork, great blue heron, and egrets. The park is also the last refuge for fourteen officially listed threatened and endangered species, including the Florida panther, the West Indian manatee, and the American crocodile, and it is the only place in the world where alligators and crocodiles coexist. In addition to its biological abundance, the park is also home to many ancient Calusa Culture Mounds that demonstrate the importance of the region to Native Americans. Some of the region's canoe trails date back to the Seminole Wars (1818–1855), when the federal government attempted to forcibly relocate Everglades natives. The Miccosukee and Seminole tribes still live in the Everglades on small reservations north of the park, adjoining Big Cypress National Preserve.

The main entrance access to Everglades National Park is via Florida Highway 9336 southeast of Homestead. Seven-day admission fees are $10 per vehicle or $5 per person, and a $20 annual pass is available. Visitation is highest from December through April, when the weather is mild and pleasant, and lowest from May through November. Summers are very hot and humid, and afternoon thunderstorms are common. The Atlantic hurricane season runs from June through November and tropical storms may affect the park. Mosquitoes are very abundant in Everglades, and visitors should be prepared with insect repellent and long-sleeve clothing.

The park maintains 5 visitor centers scattered throughout the reserve. The Ernest F. Coe Visitor Center is located at the main park entrance west of Homestead and Florida City, and open year-round from 8 A.M. until 5 P.M. Although there are no trailheads here, the center does have educational displays, orientation films, and a bookstore (which sells insect repellent). The Flamingo Visitor Center is located 38 miles southwest from the main entrance at the southern end of the park, and is open from 7:30 A.M. until 5 P.M. from December through April and intermittently during the summer. It contains natural history exhibits and information in the Florida Bay Museum. The Gulf Coast Visitor Center is located in Everglades City in the northwest corner of the park, and is open year-round from 7:30 A.M. to 5 P.M. from mid-October through April, and from 8:30 A.M. to 4:30 P.M. for the rest of the year. In addition to exhibits on the park's natural history, the center offers a one-hour-and-forty-five-minute narrated boat tour of the Everglades' saltwater ecosystem. The Shark Valley Visitor Center is located on the northern border of the park on U.S. Highway 41 (Tamiami Trail), and is open year-round from 8:30 A.M. until 4 P.M. from May through October, and until 5:15 P.M. during the rest of the year. The center has exhibits and information, and numerous trailheads, including a 15-mile elevated boardwalk that extend into the marsh and provides an up-close-and-personal opportunity to view alligators and other marsh fauna. The center also offers a two-hour narrated Everglades overview tram ride. The Royal Palm Visitor Center is located 4 miles west of the main entrance and is open year-round from 8 A.M. until 4:15 P.M. Exhibits include an artist's stylized images of Everglades wildlife and interpretive recordings on the park's unique ecosystems. Two ranger-led programs, the Anhinga Amble and Glades Glimpses, provide a fine introduction to the unique environment of the Everglades.

Although all traveler services are available in neighboring communities, Everglades offers limited facilities within the park's boundaries. Flamingo Lodge (800-600-3813), the only lodging within the park, features 103 rooms and 24 cottages with kitchen facilities, and is open year-round. During the winter, a restaurant and café are also available. Campgrounds are located at three places in the park: Chekika, Flamingo, and Long Pine Key. All have tent and RV sites, rest rooms, dump stations, and water. Chekika and Flamingo have showers, and all 3 campgrounds are open year-round. Reservations for Long Pine Key and Flamingo campgrounds are available online or through the National Park Reservation Service at (800) 365-2267. Chekika is first-come, first-served, and in 1999, this campground sustained heavy hurricane damage that forced its closure "until further notice." (It was still closed at press time.) Backcountry camping (fee charged) is also available in the park, and reservations for designated campsites may be made in person up to twenty-four hours before entering the backcountry. There are 3 sites accessible by foot and 43 additional sites available in Florida Bay, along the Gulf Coast and inland, all accessible by canoe or boat. All camping supplies must be carried in—and out—of the backcountry, including drinking water and waste.

Boating is popular in the Everglades, as many parts of the park are only accessible from the water. The park charges a boat launch fee of $5 (for a seven-day pass) or $60 (for an annual pass). The seven-day-pass fee for a nonmotorized boat is $3.

Fishing in the inland and coastal waters of the Everglades is also excellent and can be enjoyed year-round. Freshwater and saltwater fishing require separate valid Florida fishing licenses.

For more information, write Everglades National Park, 4000l State Road 9336, Homestead, FL 33034-6733, or telephone (305) 242-7700. The park's informative Web site is www.nps.gov/ever.

FURTHER READING

Cerulean, Susan, ed. *The Book of the Everglades.* Minneapolis, MN: Milkweed Editions, 2002.

Douglas, Marjory Stoneman. *The Everglades: River of Grass.* Sarasota, FL: Pineapple, 1997.

Griffin, John W. *Archaeology of the Everglades.* Gainesville: University Press of Florida, 2002.

Lodge, Thomas E. *The Everglades Handbook: Understanding the Ecosystem.* Boca Raton, FL: St. Lucie, 1998.

McCally, David. *The Everglades: An Environmental History.* Gainesville: University Press of Florida, 1999.

Simmons, Glen. *Gladesmen: Gator Hunters, Moonshiners, and Skiffers.* Gainesville: University Press of Florida, 1998.

F

FEDERAL HALL NATIONAL MEMORIAL

Location: New York, New York
Acreage: .45
Established: May 26, 1939

Federal Hall National Memorial commemorates the rich history made at 26 Wall Street in lower Manhattan, New York City. In the eighteenth century, this was the location of New York City's City Hall, the seat of New York's colonial government, and the meeting place of the Stamp Act Congress, which assembled in October 1765 to protest against "taxation without representation." After the American Revolution, the Continental Congress, the nation's first government, met here, and in 1787, they passed the Northwest Ordinance, which established procedures for creating new states. When the United States

Federal Hall National Memorial, c. 1915. *(Library of Congress)*

ratified the new Constitution in 1788, the nation's capital remained in New York, and Federal Hall became the temporary seat of the new American federal government. The next year, George Washington took the oath of office as the first president of the United States on the hall's second-floor balcony.

When the nation's capital moved to Philadelphia in 1790, the building reverted back to its original function as city hall. Despite its lustrous history, the building fell into disrepair and was demolished in 1812. The current Greek Revival structure on the site was built as the Federal Customs House between 1834 and 1842. In 1862, Customs moved up the street, and the building became the home of the U.S. Subtreasury. Millions of dollars of gold and silver were stored in its basement vaults until the Federal Reserve Bank replaced the subtreasury system. The location was originally set aside in May 1939 as a national historic site and was redesignated a national memorial in August 1955.

Located in downtown Manhattan, Federal Hall National Memorial is open year-round, with no admission or tour fees. Hours are 9 A.M. to 5 P.M., Monday through Friday. The park has interpretive films and exhibits about George Washington, along with late-eighteenth-century artifacts, information on the old Federal Hall, and a large bronze statue of Washington sculpted by John Quincy Adams Ward in 1883. Ranger-led programs and tours are offered throughout the day, along with an orientation video program. The rotunda features classical music concerts on Wednesdays, as well as Friday afternoon movie programs. Visitation is usually highest in July and August, and it is lowest in January.

Parking in downtown Manhattan is very limited and expensive, and driving is not recommended. The use of cabs or mass transit is preferable: Seventh Avenue #2 and #3 subway trains stop at Wall and William streets, 1

block east of Federal Hall; Lexington Avenue #4 and #5 subway trains stop at Wall Street and Broadway, 1 block west of Federal Hall; J, M, and Z subway trains stop at Wall and Broad streets, Monday through Friday. There are no food, lodging, or camping facilities at the memorial, but New York City and the surrounding suburbs have all traveler services.

For more information, write Federal Hall National Memorial, 26 Wall Street, New York, NY 10005, or telephone (212) 825-6888. The park's Web site can be found at www.nps.gov/feha.

FURTHER READING

Alexander, James. *A Brief Narrative of the Case and Trial of John Peter Zenger, Printer of the New York Weekly Journal.* Edited by Stanley Nider Katz. Cambridge, MA: Belknap Press of Harvard University Press, 1972.

Onuf, Peter S. *Statehood and Union: A History of the Northwest Ordinance.* Bloomington: Indiana University Press, 1987.

Weslager, C.A. *The Stamp Act Congress: With an Exact Copy of the Complete Journal.* Newark: University of Delaware Press, 1976.

Williams, Frederick D., ed. *The Northwest Ordinance: Essays on Its Formulation, Provisions, and Legacy.* East Lansing: Michigan State University Press, 1989.

FIRE ISLAND NATIONAL SEASHORE

Location: Patchogue, New York
Acreage: 19,579
Established: September 11, 1964

Disputes linger over how Fire Island National Seashore, located parallel to the south shore of New York's Long Island, received its name. Local legends tell of pirates, who burned fires to lure their cargo ship prey into the shore. Others claim the barrier-beach island was named for the abundant native plant poison ivy, which produces an itch described by sufferers as "fiery." The park was established in 1964 as part of the federal government's effort to bring more national parks closer to eastern urban areas, the idea of "parks for the people, where the people are." It embodied many of the ideals of Lyndon B.

Johnson's Great Society, for it provided the nation's largest urban population with a federally managed recreational seashore. Today, the almost-20,000-acre seashore preserves natural and cultural features ranging from ocean-washed beaches, dunes, and salt marshes to the Fire Island Light Station and the colonial estate of William Floyd. This very narrow, 32-mile-long seashore, only an hour east of New York City, also includes the Otis Pike Wilderness Area—the only federally designated wilderness in New York state—and the Sunken Forest, a three hundred-year-old holly forest.

Fire Island National Seashore maintains 3 visitor centers. The Wilderness Visitor Center is located on the eastern portion of Fire Island near the Smith Point County Park, and it is open all year. In addition to seasonal interpretive programs, the center has exhibits on natural history topics and a boardwalk nature trail. The Sailors Haven and Watch Hill visitor centers are located in the middle of Fire Island and are open only during the summer. The centers offer interpretive programs and exhibits, nature trails, bathhouses, a marina, and a seasonally lifeguarded ocean beach.

The Fire Island Light Station museum is located on the western end of Fire Island and is open year-round, with seasonal hours. Park rangers offer history talks, nature walks, and special evening programs, and tower tours are available by reservation. The museum and exhibit room feature displays on shipwrecks and rescues off Long Island, video programs, historical photos, and information

Fire Island National Seashore has many educational opportunities for visitors, who can enjoy the area's salt-water marshes, a "sunken" forest of three hundred-year-old holly trees, hiking trails, and a wilderness area.

(National Park Service)

about the restoration of the Fire Island Light Station.

Visitors will also appreciate the two hundred and seventy-five-year-old William Floyd estate, a separate unit of the seashore located on Washington Avenue in Mastic Beach. Floyd was one of the original signers of the Declaration of Independence, and his estate includes 12 outbuildings, a cemetery, and surrounding grounds and trails. Exhibits throughout the mansion include historical photographs of the Floyd family and estate; ranger-guided and self-guided tours of the mansion and seasonal interpretive programs are available.

Located a scant 50 miles from New York City, most sections of Fire Island National Seashore are open year-round, weather permitting, with no admission fees. The Sailors Haven and Watch Hill units are dependent on water travel and are open from mid-May through mid-October. Fire Island is reached by automobile via bridges from Bayshore and Shirley on opposite ends of the park. Visitors must park at Robert Moses State Park or Smith Point County Park lots and walk in to the seashore, for no automobiles are allowed. Visitors may also take ferries (for a fee) from Bayshore, Sayville, and Patchogue from May to November. The seashore receives about 500,000 visitors annually, mostly New York City urbanites escaping summertime heat. All seashore visitors are advised to check themselves thoroughly for ticks, especially after wet weather. The island has three varieties of ticks: dog, lone star, and northern deer—the primary carrier of Lyme disease.

Other than the seasonal food and snack concessions at Sailors Haven and Watch Hill, there are no restaurant or lodging facilities on-site. Nearby Fire Island and Long Island towns offer complete traveler services. There is a developed, fee-charged campground at Watch Hill, and reservations are required from May to October. During the off-season,

no water or toilets are available, and no fee is charged. Access is by scheduled ferry or private boat only. A permit is required for free backcountry camping.

For more information and reservations, write Fire Island National Seashore, 120 Laurel Street, Patchogue, NY 11772, or telephone headquarters (631) 289-4810, Fire Island Light Station (631) 661-4876, or the William Floyd Estate (631) 399-2030. The park's Web site is www.nps.gov/fiis.

FURTHER READING
Johnson, Madeleine C. *Fire Island, 1650s–1980s.* Mountainside, NJ: Shoreland, 1983.
Shaw, Edward R. *Legends of Fire Island Beach and the South Side.* Port Washington, NY: I.J. Friedman, 1969.

FLORISSANT FOSSIL BEDS NATIONAL MONUMENT
Location: Florissant, Colorado
Acreage: 5,998
Established: August 20, 1969

Florissant Fossil Beds National Monument preserves and protects an internationally renowned collection of fossils—particularly of insects and plants—found in prehistoric Lake Florissant in central Colorado. As geologist Arthur C. Peale wrote, "when the mountains are overthrown and the seas uplifted, the universe at Florissant flings itself against a gnat and preserves it." Millions of years ago, this ancient lake bed became the final resting place for the components of an ecosystem buffeted by volcanic eruptions. During this volcanic process, a remarkable variety of plants, animals, and insects were caught in the plume of ash and rock and swept away into the lake's bottom, while massive mudflows buried and petrified the redwood trees surrounding the lake. Over millions of years, Lake Florissant filled with volcanic materials that preserved the fossils, until erosion broke through the volcanic cover and exposed the lakebed—and the extensive fossil collection within. More than 1,000 species of insects,

140 plants, and numerous fish, bird, and small mammal species have been excavated from the Florissant shale beds. Today, these fragments of life, 33 to 35 million years old, provide a striking contrast between this primeval warm and humid lake environment and the present-day montane ecosystem.

The monument provides numerous recreational opportunities, from cross-country skiing and snow-shoeing in the winter, to hiking and birding in the summer. There are nearly 14 miles of trails through ponderosa pine forests and high mountain meadows. The self-guided Petrified Forest and Walk Through Time trails are the most popular and feature close-up views of massive sequoia stumps. June and July are the best months for wildflowers, while September and October feature beautiful fall colors and elk activity.

Established in 1969, the almost-6,000-acre monument is open year-round, daily from 8 A.M. to dusk. Admission fees are $2 per person, or $4 per family, and are valid for seven days. A $10 annual pass is also available. The park's visitor center serves as a museum and information center. Fossil exhibits are on display and include dragonflies, beetles, ants, butterflies, spiders, fish, birds, and mammals; some plant fossil leaves include earlier forms of beech, maple, willow, and hickory trees. Another point of interest is the 1878 Hornbek Homestead, which is listed on the National Register of Historic Buildings and serves as an example of early settlement in the Florissant Valley. In addition to interpretive talks and walks, park rangers conduct a series of miniseminars on various weekends throughout the summer. Visitation is usually highest in July and August, and lowest in January and February. Because of the high altitude, summers here are generally short with warm days and cool nights, and freezing temperatures can sometimes occur during summer months. Subzero lows and heavy snow are common in the winter.

There are no food, lodging, or camping facilities at the monument, but all nearby towns have travel services, including tourism-geared Colorado Springs. Although camping is not permitted at the monument, there are many private campgrounds in the nearby area and along U.S. Highway 24 to Colorado Springs. The U.S. Forest Service also has many campgrounds in the adjoining Pike National Forest.

For more information, write Florissant Fossil Beds National Monument, P.O. Box 185, Florissant, CO 80816-0185, or telephone (719) 748-3253. The park's Web site is www.nps.gov/flfo.

FURTHER READING

Emmel, Thomas C. *Florissant Butterflies: A Guide to the Fossil and Present-day Species of Central Colorado.* Stanford, CA: Stanford University Press, 1992.

Meyer, Herbert W. *The Fossils of Florissant.* Washington, DC: Smithsonian Institution, 2003.

FORD'S THEATRE NATIONAL HISTORIC SITE

Location: Washington, D.C.
Acreage: .29
Established: February 12, 1932

Ford's Theatre has the macabre distinction of being the site of the nation's preeminent presidential assassination. On the night of April 14, 1865, just as the Civil War ended, a disgruntled Southern actor, John Wilkes Booth, approached President Abraham Lincoln's box as the president and first lady enjoyed a play at Washington, D.C.'s Ford's Theatre, placed a derringer behind his ear, fired at point-blank range, hopped over the rail, landed shouting "death to tyrants," fractured his ankle, and disappeared into the night. The mortally wounded president was carried across the street to a small bedroom in the back of the Petersen Boarding House, where he never regained consciousness. In the early morning hours of April 15, just six days after Robert E. Lee had surrendered his Confederate forces, the nation's sixteenth president died, with his wife and son at his side. Having fled the theater, Booth remained at large for nearly two weeks. But on April 26, Booth and an accomplice were cornered by Union troops in a tobacco shed in Port Royal, Virginia; Booth refused to surrender and was shot while the shed burned down around him. The federal government purchased Ford's Theatre in 1866 and the Petersen House in 1896. Both structures were transferred to the Park Service in 1932, and then combined to create the Ford's Theatre National Historic Site in June 1970.

The Ford's Theatre site is open year-round from 9 A.M. to 5 P.M. daily, and admission is free. The theater contains the Lincoln Museum, which houses many interpretive exhibits and artifacts associated with the assassination. The Petersen House has been preserved and historically furnished to depict the scene from that tragic evening. An excellent fifteen-minute interpretive talk on the assassination occurs at quarter past the hour, beginning at 9:15 A.M. and concluding with the 4:15 P.M. presentation. Since it is still a live venue, the theater is subject to closure for matinees and rehearsals. Matinees generally run on Thursday and Sunday afternoons, and information on theater closures is available by calling the site. The museum and William Petersen Boarding House always remain open.

Since there is only minimal parking on or near the site—and traffic is so heavy in the area—taxi or public transportation is recommended. Although the site has no lodging, restaurant, or camping facilities, Washington, D.C., has all traveler services. Annual visitation exceeds 1 million people; it is usually highest in March, April, and May, and lowest in January and September. It is highly recommended that visitors make advance reservations for lodging during the peak tourist season.

For more information, write Ford's Theatre National Historic Site, 511 10th Street NW, Washington, DC 20004 or telephone (202) 426-6924. The park's informative Web site is www.nps.gov/foth.

FURTHER READING

Steers, Edward, Jr. *Blood on the Moon: The Assassination of Abraham Lincoln.* Lexington: University Press of Kentucky, 2001.
Swanson, James L., and Daniel R. Weinberg. *Lincoln's Assassins: Their Trial and Execution.* Santa Fe, NM: Arena Editions, 2001.

FORT BOWIE NATIONAL HISTORIC SITE

Location: Willcox, Arizona
Acreage: 999
Established: August 30, 1964

For several centuries, southeastern Arizona was home to nomadic Chiricahua Apache Indians. But in 1853, the Gadsden Purchase transferred 30 million acres of southern Arizona and New Mexico—and their homeland—from Mexico to the United States. The United States quickly established a military

President Lincoln's box at Ford's Theater, c. 1865.
(Library of Congress)

presence and stage routes–the Butterfield Overland Mail opened in 1858–in the region, but there was no violence between Apaches and whites until 1861, when the Chiricahua Apaches were wrongly accused of abducting a toddler during a stage raid. The army dispatched Lieutenant George Bascomb to the area to quell the unrest, but it soon escalated into bloody violence when Bascomb captured the Apache leader Cochise and held him hostage. Known as the Bascomb Affair, it initiated an extended period of violence between whites and Chiricahuas.

In 1862, during the Civil War, a contingent of Union soldiers from California headed to the Rio Grande River to stop the advance of Confederate forces into New Mexico and Arizona. As the Union soldiers reached Apache Pass, a large force of armed Chiricahua Apaches led by Mangas Coloradas and Cochise fought the California contingent. It was futile, for superior federal firepower soon overwhelmed the Native Americans, and they retreated. As a result of this skirmish, however, the army ordered the construction of a fortification at the pass to protect this strategic route and important water supplies. Known as Fort Bowie, the garrison was the focal point of the nation's far southwestern military operations and Apache/white conflicts–known as the Indian Wars–which eventually culminated in the 1886 surrender of Geronimo and the removal of the Chiricahuas to reservations in Florida and Alabama. In 1894, the army abandoned the fort.

Located between the Chiricahua and Dos Cabezas mountains 25 miles south of Willcox, Arizona, the 999-acre Fort Bowie National Historic Site preserves and interprets the remains of Fort Bowie, the adobe walls of various post buildings, the ruins of a Butterfield stage station, and other related structures and sites of interest. There is no admission fee to the site, which is open daily from dawn to dusk. The Fort Bowie Visitor Center is open daily from 8 A.M. until 5 P.M. and contains historic exhibits on the Butterfield mail route, military life at the fort, and Apache Indians. The 3-mile, round-trip, strenuous hike into the fort is the site's main activity. The trail winds past the remains of the Butterfield stage station, the post cemetery, an Apache wickiup, the Chiricahua Apache Indian Agency, Apache Springs, and the visitor center. The park service recommends a minimum of two hours for the round trip, and hikers should carry their own water. Picnic facilities are located at the trailhead and visitor center. Relatively few people visit Fort Bowie, and because summers are so hot, and winters so cold and windy, the peak tourist season is in the mild spring months from March to May.

The site has no camping, lodging, or restaurant facilities, but nearby Bowie and Willcox have all traveler services. Chiricahua National Monument, 25 miles south of Fort Bowie, has a small campground, and Bowie and Willcox each have a private campground.

For more information, write Fort Bowie National Historic Site, P.O. Box 158, Bowie, AZ 85643, or telephone (520) 847-2500. The park's informative Web site is www.nps.gov/fobo.

FURTHER READING

Opler, Morris Edward. *An Apache Life-Way: The Economic, Social, and Religious Institutions of the Chiricahua Indians.* Lincoln: University of Nebraska Press, 1996.

Sweeney, Edwin R. *Cochise: Chiricahua Apache Chief.* Norman: University of Oklahoma Press, 1991.

——. *Mangas Coloradas: Chief of the Chiricahua Apaches.* Norman: University of Oklahoma Press, 1998.

Utley, Robert Marshall. *A Clash of Cultures: Fort Bowie and the Chiricahua Apaches.* Washington, DC: Office of Publications, National Park Service, 1977.

FORT CAROLINE NATIONAL MEMORIAL

Location: Jacksonville, Florida
Acreage: 138
Established: September 21, 1950

Although the French presence in sixteenth-century Florida was fleeting, Fort Caroline National Memorial, a site situated within the Timucuan Ecological and Historic Preserve near Jacksonville, memorializes their efforts to establish a permanent colony amidst this Spanish stronghold. In May 1562, French explorer Jean Ribault sailed several miles up the St. Johns River and claimed the surrounding area for France. Two years later, some 200 French Huguenots, seeking refuge from continental religious wars, established a colony at the site, comprised of a village and a small earthen and timber fortification, which they named La Caroline—literally, the colony of Charles, King of France. Relations between the Huguenots and the native Timucuas were friendly and hospitable, although short-lived. The French colony soon provoked conflict with another European power, for the Spanish had also claimed sovereignty over Florida. And Fort Caroline was manned not only by Frenchmen, but by French Protestants—sworn enemies of the Catholic monarchs of Spain. In September 1565, in partial response to French piracy of Spanish ships in the Caribbean, Spanish forces marched 40 miles overland from their newly established settlement at St. Augustine to crush the Huguenots. The well-armed Spanish quickly overran the beleaguered French colony, killing many of the French defenders. The Spanish commander wrote home to his king, "I put Jean Ribault and all the rest of them to the knife, judging it to be necessary to the service of the Lord Our God and of Your Majesty." In all, more than 500 Frenchmen were killed in the conflict, and the conquerors renamed Fort Caroline "San Mateo." The determined French, however, exacted their revenge. Two years later, a combined French and Timucuan Indian force led a successful surprise attack on San Mateo and burned it to the ground. Unable to establish a secure foothold in the re-

gion, however, the French soon left Florida for points north.

Although nothing remains of the original Fort de la Caroline today, Congress established Fort Caroline National Memorial in September of 1950 to honor the first Europeans who came to North America seeking freedom. A near full-scale interpretive rendering of the fort, together with exhibits in the nearby visitor center, provide information on the French colony's history, French interaction with the Timucuan Indians, and the colonists' brief struggle for survival.

The free, 138-acre memorial is located about 14 miles northeast of downtown Jacksonville, Florida, and is open daily during daylight hours. The visitor center also serves as the principal interpretive center of the more than 46,000-acre Timucuan Ecological and Historic Preserve, and it is open daily from 9 A.M. until 5 P.M. The center contains exhibits on the rich human history of the region and the unique ecology of the St. Johns River estuary—called "Where the Waters Meet"—as well as detailed information about the maritime environment of northeastern Florida, and the other visitor sites within the preserve, including the Theodore Roosevelt Area, Cedar Point, and Kingsley Plantation. Visitation is usually highest in cool February and March, and lowest in hot and humid June and July.

A quarter-mile walk from the visitor center along the Old French Trail brings visitors to an exhibit of Fort de la Caroline. While the fort exhibit is not the original historic structure, the exhibit offers some insight into the efforts the French undertook to protect their colonists from a harsh new environment and their powerful Spanish enemy. In addition to the fort trail, there is a 1-mile, self-guided loop trail (Hammock Trail) with interpretive placards that focus on the site's natural and cultural history. Other points of interest include the freshwater wetland surrounding the Spanish Pond area, the scenic view from Ribault Monument, and the 600-acre Theodore Roosevelt Area nature preserve.

Fort Caroline has no lodging, restaurant, or camping facilities, but Jacksonville and all nearby towns have all traveler services. Camping is available within the Timucuan Preserve at Little Talbot Island State Park, and at Huguenot Memorial Park, operated by the city of Jacksonville.

For more information, write Fort Caroline National Memorial, 12713 Fort Caroline Road, Jacksonville, FL 32225-1240, or telephone (904) 641-7155. The park's informative Web site is www.nps.gov/foca.

FURTHER READING
Bennett, Charles E. *Laudonniere and Fort Caroline: History and Documents.* Tuscaloosa: University of Alabama Press, 2001.

FORT CLATSOP NATIONAL MEMORIAL
Location: Astoria, Oregon
Acreage: 125
Established: May 29, 1958

The Lewis and Clark "voyage of discovery" from 1804 to 1806 is the most famous government-sponsored expedition of exploration into the American West. As the first white men to cross into western North America within the present boundaries of the United States, Captains Meriwether Lewis and William Clark finally ended the long, and ultimately unsuccessful, search for a transcontinental water route—the fabled Northwest Passage—launched soon after Columbus's arrival in the New World. President Thomas Jefferson had commissioned the Lewis and Clark Expedition to survey the newly acquired Louisiana Purchase and make contact with the Native Americans. They departed from St. Louis in 1804, journeying across wild and unknown terrain until they arrived at the Pacific Ocean, near present-day Astoria. In December of 1805, the thirty-three-member expedition constructed a small, fortified log-cabin compound 2 miles up the Netul (now Lewis and Clark) River near the Oregon coast and settled in for a long, soggy winter.

In this compound, named Fort Clatsop for the friendly native people the expedition encountered, Lewis and Clark spent three and a half dreary months consolidating maps and journals, hunting, trading, making buckskin clothing, and preparing foodstuffs for the long springtime journey back to St. Louis. The Clatsops proved enormously valuable allies, providing food, herbal medicines, and hides, and Lewis spent much of his time detailing the cultural nuances and traditions of the local tribes, as well as the native flora and fauna. The expedition's winter camp was wet, cold, and rough as constant, penetrating rain and wind plagued the camp, rotted buckskin, and made life miserable. Lewis noted in his detailed log that from December 1805 until their departure, it rained all but twelve days, and the sun came out on only six. Finally, on March 23, 1806, the restocked expedition abandoned Fort Clatsop and headed east toward St. Louis, where six months to the day later, overdue and feared lost, they arrived in triumph and received a hero's welcome.

Established in 1958, Fort Clatsop National Memorial commemorates the 1805–1806 winter encampment of the Lewis and Clark Expedition. Although the 1955 community-built replica of the explorers' compact, 50-foot by 50-foot Fort Clatsop is the focal point of visitor interest and activity at this 125-acre park, the memorial also protects a rich mixture of forest and estuarine wetland resources. The fort replica, historic canoe landing site, and salt works are all nestled in the convergence zone between the Oregon Coast Range and the Lower Columbia River estuary, and visitors are encouraged to embrace a landscape-scale perspective to fully appreciate the significance of the encampment and the Lewis and Clark Expedition.

Located 5 miles south of Astoria off U.S. Highway 101, the memorial is open daily year-round during daylight hours, and admission fees, good for seven days, are $2 per person, or $4 per vehicle. An annual pass for the fort is also available for $10; both the five-day Oregon Coast pass ($10) and the Oregon Coast annual pass ($35) are valid for the park. The visitor center is open daily from 8 A.M. until 5 P.M. from Labor Day through mid-June, and until 6 P.M. during the summer. It contains an exhibit hall, laser disk demonstrations, a movie, and a slide presentation. In addition, each day during the summer, costumed rangers at the fort offer free living-history programs about the Lewis and Clark Expedition, bringing to life some activities such as flintlock muzzle loading and firing demonstrations, candle making, and hide tanning and sewing. The park also celebrates "Explorers' Christmas" from December 25 through January 1. Walking trails, bordered by native plants, connect the visitor center, the fort replica, the historic canoe landing on the Lewis and Clark River, and the picnic area. Park trails total about a mile. Visitation is typically highest in July and August, and lowest from December through February, though visitors wishing to experience the more "authentic" expedition weather come during the winter months.

No food, lodging, or camping facilities are available in the park, but nearby communities such as Astoria, Cannon Beach, Gearhart, Seaside, and Warrenton have travel services. Fort Stevens State Park, 8 miles northwest of Fort Clatsop, offers a very large, developed campground with all facilities, including hookups, and there are 2 private campgrounds located near the memorial.

For more information, write Fort Clatsop National Memorial, 92343 Fort Clatsop Road, Astoria, OR 97103, or telephone (503) 861-2471. The park's informative Web site is www.nps.gov/focl.

FURTHER READING
Ambrose, Stephen E. *Undaunted Courage: Meriwether Lewis, Thomas Jefferson, and the Opening of the American West.* New York: Simon and Schuster, 1996.
Cannon, Kelly June. *Administrative History: Fort Clatsop National Memorial.* Seattle, WA: National Park Service, Pacific Northwest Region, 1995.
Moulton, Gary E., ed. *The Definitive Journals of Lewis and Clark: Down the Columbia to Fort Clatsop.* Lincoln: University of Nebraska Press, 2002.
Ronda, James P. *Lewis and Clark Among the Indians.* Lincoln: University of Nebraska Press, 2002.

FORT DAVIS NATIONAL HISTORIC SITE
Location: Fort Davis, Texas
Acreage: 474
Established: September 8, 1961

A key southwestern military post from 1854 to 1891, Fort Davis in western Texas helped open the area to white settlement and protected travelers and merchants along the San Antonio–El Paso Road. Named after President Franklin Pierce's Secretary of War (and future Confederate president) Jefferson Davis, Fort Davis is regarded as one of the best preserved historic sites in the Southwest. The fort's first structures consisted of mostly pine-slab jacales covered with canvas and thatched grass. A few years later, six stone barracks were constructed to house enlisted men, quarters vastly superior to the wood, thatch, and canvas structures.

When Texas seceded from the Union in 1861, Union troops abandoned Fort Davis and other west Texas military installations. The Confederacy occupied the fort for a year, and then abandoned it after the Union repeatedly pushed back Confederate attempts to expand into New Mexico. After being wrecked by Apaches, the fort lay deserted until after the Civil War. In 1867, the Union sent a black cavalry regiment under the lead-

Inside a barracks building at Fort Davis, one of the best-preserved frontier forts, May 1972. *(National Archives)*

ership of Colonel Wesley Merritt to construct a second fort not far from the original site. Much more sophisticated and tougher than the rustic original, the new Fort Davis, completed in 1880, consisted of more than 50 stone and adobe structures that housed both infantry and cavalry units.

During the 1870s and 1880s, as white settlers poured into the West, Apache raids against soldiers, travelers, and settlers escalated. In 1880, the Apache leader Vittorio and his men, who had been hiding out in Mexico, crossed the Rio Grande to launch a series of raids on local settlements. To answer this threat, Fort Davis dispatched Troop H—the famed African American "buffalo soldier" cavalry contingent—to pursue Vittorio. Although they were unsuccessful in capturing

him, the soldiers did drive him back into Mexico, where he and his warriors were killed by Mexican troops. By the mid-1880s, Native American hostilities had subsided in West Texas, and in 1885, the army transferred Troop H to Fort Bowie in Arizona territory to help capture Geronimo and his band of Chiricahua Apaches. As with many forts in the American West, maintaining Fort Davis became too expensive in the post–Indian Wars period, and in 1891, the army abandoned the fort.

In 1961, Congress authorized Fort Davis National Historic Site to protect perhaps the best-preserved historic U.S. military installation in the Southwest. The Fort Davis Visitor Center/Museum is located in the restored enlisted men's barracks, and special activities and programs are offered regularly. Of the 50 buildings that made up the second fort, the exteriors of 15 officer's quarters, 2 enlisted barracks, kitchens, servants' quarters, a commissary, and a hospital have been restored. Recently, a number of the first fort's foundations have been uncovered. Five of the fort's buildings have had their interiors recently refurbished and restored in 1880s style, and are open on a self-guided basis. Park Service interpreters dressed in period costumes are stationed at some of these buildings during the summer months, and bugle calls and a sound representation of an 1875 dress retreat parade can be heard over the parade ground at scheduled times. The Friends of Fort Davis festival is held on the Saturday of Columbus Day weekend, and the park offers a special evening tour of the fort on a Saturday in November, called "From Retreat to Tattoo."

Located on the northern edge of the town of Fort Davis on Texas Highway 17, the 474-acre site is open daily, year-round, during daylight hours. Entrance fees are $2 per person and are valid for seven days. Visitation is usually highest in March, April, and July, and lowest in December and January. There is no food, camping, or lodging on-site, but Fort Davis has all traveler services and developed camping is available at Davis Mountains State Park, 4 miles south of town.

For more information, write Fort Davis National Historic Site, P.O. Box 1456, Fort Davis, TX 79734, or telephone (915) 426-3224. The park's Web site is www.nps.gov/foda.

FURTHER READING

Greene, Jerome A. *Historic Resource Study: Fort Davis National Historic Site.* Denver, CO: National Park Service, 1986.

Thybony, Scott. *Fort Davis National Historic Site.* Tucson, AZ: Southwest Parks and Monuments Association, 1990.

——. *Fort Davis: The Men of Troop H.* Tucson, AZ: Southwest Parks and Monuments Association, 1990.

Utley, Robert Marshall. *Fort Davis National Historic Site, Texas.* Washington, DC: National Park Service, 1965.

Welsh, Michael. *A Special Place, a Sacred Trust: Preserving the Fort Davis Story.* Santa Fe, NM: Intermountain Cultural Resources Center, National Park Service, 1996. Available at www.nps.gov/foda/adhi/adhi.htm.

Wooster, Robert. *Fort Davis: Outpost on the Texas Frontier.* Austin: Texas State Historical Association, 1994.

FORT DONELSON NATIONAL BATTLEFIELD

Location: Dover, Tennessee
Acreage: 552
Established: March 26, 1928

Prior to the February 16, 1862, Battle of Fort Donelson, Tennessee, Ulysses S. Grant was just another obscure Union general, frustrated by the military success of the Confederate States of America during the first year of the Civil War. But Grant's skillful capture of Fort Donelson and 13,000 Confederate soldiers delivered a devastating blow to the Confederacy and set the stage for the Union's invasion of the deep South. More significantly, certainly to Grant, the Union's first major victory of the Civil War catapulted the general

from an unknown into national prominence, earning him the undying favoritism of President Abraham Lincoln and eventual command of the Union Army.

Early in the war, the Confederate Army had achieved decisive victories at Manassas in July 1861, and at Wilson's Creek in August 1861, but no other major campaigns occurred until the battle at Fort Donelson. During this lull, the Union eyed two potential Confederate targets that could help turn the war in their favor: the Tennessee River's Fort Henry and the Cumberland River's Fort Donelson. In addition to being vital strategic military posts along the Confederacy's line of defense from the Mississippi River to the Appalachians, both forts were on tributaries of the Ohio River—a key Confederate route of access. On February 6, 1862, a fleet of four ironclad Union gunboats easily pounded Fort Henry into submission, but most of the Confederate garrison escaped east to Fort Donelson. On February 14, the Union ironclads moved into position on the Cumberland River against Fort Donelson, but it was better protected and more heavily armed, and Confederate cannons forced the ironclads' retreat.

General Grant sensed an opportunity. Noticing vulnerabilities in the 15-acre fort's landward fortifications, he encircled Donelson and persistently breached various spots in the breastwork. An intense battle ensued, but Grant held his position on the fort's right side and redoubled his efforts on the left, thereby blocking the main Confederate escape route. For the Confederacy, offense quickly turned to defense, but the soldiers' resistance was futile. Grant's strategy had enabled his men to encircle the fort, and although Donelson's top two commanders eventually abandoned the fort and escaped down the Cumberland River, Grant captured the garrison and nearly 13,000 soldiers. When the remaining Confederate commander asked for surrender conditions, Grant replied that surrender was unconditional, thus earning him the nickname "Unconditional Surrender" Grant. Following the loss of Donelson, Confederate forces retreated from Kentucky and a major portion of western Tennessee. More than 4,300 soldiers died in the battle.

Fort Donelson was first set aside as a national military park in March 1928, was transferred to the Park Service in Franklin D. Roosevelt's reorganization of the federal government in 1933, and was redesignated as a national battlefield in August 1985. Today, the 552-acre National Battlefield includes a visitor center, the Dover Hotel (Surrender House), Fort Donelson itself with its earthen rifle pits and river cannon batteries, and Fort Donelson National Cemetery (established in 1867), the final resting place for Union soldiers killed in the battle and American veterans from seven wars.

The Fort Donelson Visitor Center is open daily from 8 A.M. until 4:30 P.M. and contains information and exhibits on the battle and an audiovisual program depicting the battle. During the summer, park staff conduct a variety of interpretive programs and living-history demonstrations. The Dover Hotel, the partially restored historic building where Confederate General Simon Buckner unconditionally surrendered to Grant, is open for afternoon tours from June to September. Five miles of trails are available for walking and hiking at Fort Donelson National Battlefield, and there are several short foot trails along the auto tour route. A cassette tour tape is also available from the visitor center.

Located in western Tennessee on the west side of Dover, the park is open year-round with free admission. Visitors can enjoy spring flowers from April through June and smaller crowds in March and September. Although the park has no food, lodging, or camping facilities, the town of Dover has all travel services. The TVA (Tennessee Valley Authority) Land Between the Lakes Park offers full, developed camping facilities, and some nearby state parks also have campgrounds.

For more information, write Fort Donelson National Battlefield, P.O. Box 434, Dover, Tennessee 37058-0434, or telephone (931) 232-5706. The park's Web site is www.nps.gov/fodo.

FURTHER READING

Catton, Bruce. *Grant Takes Command.* Boston: Little, Brown, 1969.
Chester, Edward W. *Fort Donelson National Battlefield: A Botanical and Historical Perspective.* Clarksville, TN: Center for Field Biology, Austin Peay State University, 1997.
Cooling, B. Franklin. *Fort Donelson's Legacy: War and Society in Kentucky and Tennessee, 1862–1863.* Knoxville: University of Tennessee Press, 1997.

FORT FREDERICA NATIONAL MONUMENT

Location: Saint Simons Island, Georgia
Acreage: 241
Established: May 26, 1936

Originally established in 1736, southeastern Georgia's Fort Frederica was the southernmost outpost of Britain's North American colonies. While the fort's military purpose was the protection of Georgia and South Carolina from the Spanish in Florida, Frederica is also known for its exceptional beauty: stately oaks, grape vines, and Spanish moss grace this historic site and lend it an air of antiquity that is unequaled on the coast.

General James Edward Oglethorpe, founder of the Georgia colony, established Fort Frederica to defend his humanitarian experiment against Spanish attack. Oglethorpe had hoped to create in Georgia a haven for poor British farmers squeezed out of a country with too many people and too little land. But the colony lay in the midst of "debatable" land—territory claimed by both Great Britain and Spain. To buffer his settlement from Spanish Florida, Oglethorpe selected a site 60 miles south of Savannah for the military headquarters of his new colony: Fort Frederica, named for the Prince of Wales, Frederick Louis. In addition to building a fortification, Oglethorpe's colonists also laid out a town that included permanent homes and shops. Each family received a 360-square-foot lot for a house, plus 50 additional acres for farming. In time, the village housed about 500 people.

In 1740, during King George's War, Oglethorpe led a major British offensive against key Spanish military targets in Florida, capturing two small forts near Jacksonville. But his efforts only antagonized the Spanish, who responded in 1742 by sending an armada north from Florida to wipe out all British settlements and fortifications in Georgia. Frederica was never captured, and by 1743, the fort sheltered nearly 1,000 people. When Great Britain and Spain signed a peace treaty in 1748, however, the garrison was withdrawn and disbanded. A decade later, fire destroyed what remained of the largely abandoned town.

Fort Frederica National Monument was authorized in May 1936 to commemorate this early British colony, and the park's visitor center contains museum exhibits depicting colonial life in Frederica, a twenty-five-minute film (*This Is Frederica*), interactive touch-screen information computers, and a National Park Service Cooperating Association Museum Store. The monument is primarily an archeological site, and park rangers offer guided tours of the town site, which contains the exposed foundations of many houses. Although no whole structures remain, visitors can see the ruins of the fort's magazine and barracks.

During the first weekend in March, the park also hosts the annual Frederica Festival, a family-oriented day of fun, food, and activities that captures many aspects of colonial life in Frederica. A self-guided walking trail leads past wayside exhibits and signs explaining daily life in "Frederica Town." A self-guided audio tour is also available for rent in the visitor center for a nominal fee.

Located 12 miles from Brunswick, Georgia, Fort Frederica is open daily during daylight hours, and fees for a seven-day pass are $4 per vehicle, or $2 per person for cyclists and hikers. Visitation is typically highest in June, July, and August, and lowest in September and February.

While there are no food, lodging, or camping facilities in the park, all traveler services are available on Saint Simons Island, in Brunswick, and in Jekyll. Jekyll Island State Park, 13 miles southeast of Brunswick on Georgia Highway 50, and Blythe Island Regional Park have developed campgrounds, and private campgrounds are available on the mainland.

For more information, write Fort Frederica National Monument, Route 9, Box 286-C, Saint Simons Island, GA 31522-9710, or telephone (912) 638-3639. The park's Web site is www.nps.gov/fofr.

FURTHER READING

Spalding, Phinizy. *Oglethorpe in America.* Athens: University of Georgia Press, 1984.

Spalding, Phinizy, and Harvey H. Jackson, eds. *Oglethorpe in Perspective: Georgia's Founder after Two Hundred Years.* Tuscaloosa: University of Alabama Press, 1989.

FORT LARAMIE NATIONAL HISTORIC SITE

Location: Fort Laramie, Wyoming
Acreage: 833
Established: July 16, 1938

Eastern Wyoming's Fort Laramie, near the confluence of the Laramie and Platte rivers, played an important role in the westward expansion of the young American nation. Founded in 1834 as the fur-trading post Fort William, it was a regional trade center for beaver pelts, buffalo robes, and other hides as well as a place for mountain men, frontier entrepreneurs, and Plains Indians to rendezvous and barter. In 1841, the center was rebuilt as a more substantial, fortified adobe complex and renamed Fort John on the Laramie. The new post quickly became a welcome rest and replenishment stop for emigrants migrating westward along the Oregon and Mormon trails.

As the unrelenting tide of western emigration increased, so did the anxiety levels of Northern Plains Indian tribes. As this cultural conflict escalated, so did the hostilities. In 1849, in response to this unrest, the U.S. Army purchased the post, renamed it Fort Laramie, and expanded it into a major military fort. The garrison served as the locus of American military presence on the high plains for the next forty years, drawing native people to it in a sometimes dangerous embrace. The most significant battle that took place in the area started as a result of the kill-

ing of an ox and ended with thirty U.S. soldiers dead in a nearby native encampment in 1854. Fort Laramie was an important command post, a staging area for infantry and cavalry, and a strategic communication and transportation depot. The Pony Express, the transcontinental telegraph, and the Deadwood Stage route all passed through Fort Laramie.

Fort Laramie also played an important role in a series of Native American peace negotiations and treaties. Of these, perhaps the most significant was the 1868 Fort Laramie Treaty with the Lakotas (Sioux). Wagon train traffic and military forts had invaded the Lakotas' principal buffalo range and violated sacred tribal grounds, and the Fort Laramie Treaty attempted to mitigate these trespasses by assigning inviolate reservations to the La-

Hospital ruins at Fort Laramie National Historic Site. *(Library of Congress)*

kotas and other Plains Indians. The peace was only temporary. Six years later, white prospectors discovered gold in South Dakota's Black Hills, the heart of the Lakota territory and a profoundly sacred site. Determined to fight for their lands, Lakota and allied Cheyenne warriors won a decisive victory at Greasy Grass (Little Bighorn) in June of 1876, but ultimately lost their war for independence. Fort Laramie soldiers fought in battles and skirmishes that eventually forced all Lakotas and other Northern Plains tribes onto reservations. In 1890, with the threat of hostilities ended, the military decommissioned the post and sold the fort's land and buildings.

Nearly a half century later, in 1938, Fort Laramie was established as a national monument, and in 1960, the park was redesignated as a National Historic Site. Today, the 833-acre park commemorates the forty-one-year history of Fort Laramie's military service. Eleven of the fort's original buildings, along with the parade grounds, have been restored and elaborately refurnished, and they are open to visitors. The foundations or lime grout shells of other buildings are also preserved.

Fort Laramie is located 3 miles southwest of the town of Fort Laramie, Wyoming, off U.S. Highway 26, about 95 miles north of Cheyenne. Admission fees are $2 per person, with children under sixteen admitted free. The fort grounds are open year-round during daylight hours, and the park's museum/visitor center is open daily, year-round, at 8 A.M., with extended hours during the summer season. The center has a short orientation film that provides information on the fort's role in American westward expansion and the Indian Wars, as well as interpretive exhibits, information, and a bookstore. In addition to its self-guided tours, the park also has an excellent living-history program. Regularly scheduled fort tours and interpretive programs are offered during the peak summer season, and

each day, park rangers present talks focused on an aspect of the fort's history. Visitation at Fort Laramie is usually highest in the mild and warm summer months and lowest in the frigid, windy winter months.

There is no food, lodging, or camping at the park, but all travel services and facilities—including campgrounds—can be found in the nearby towns of Fort Laramie, Guernsey, Lingle, Torrington, and Wheatland. Private tent campgrounds are also available at Fort Laramie, Lingle, Torrington, and Guernsey.

For more information, write Fort Laramie National Historic Site, HC 72, Box 389, Fort Laramie, WY 82212, or telephone (307) 837-2221. The park's Web site is www.nps.gov/fola.

FURTHER READING

Hafen, Le Roy Reuben. *Fort Laramie and the Pageant of the West, 1834–1890.* Lincoln: University of Nebraska Press, 1984.

Hedren, Paul L. *Fort Laramie in 1876: Chronicle of a Frontier Post at War.* Lincoln: University of Nebraska Press, 1988.

——. *Fort Laramie and the Great Sioux War.* Norman: University of Oklahoma Press, 1998.

Lavender, David Sievert. *Fort Laramie and the Changing Frontier: Fort Laramie National Historic Site, Wyoming.* Washington, DC: National Park Service, 1983.

Mattes, Merrill J. *Fort Laramie Park History, 1834–1977.* Washington, DC: National Park Service, 1980. Also available at www.nps.gov/fola/history/index.htm.

Nadeau, Remi A. *Fort Laramie and the Sioux.* Lincoln: University of Nebraska Press, 1982.

FORT LARNED NATIONAL HISTORIC SITE

Location: Larned, Kansas
Acreage: 718
Established: August 31, 1964

Named for Army Paymaster General Benjamin Larned, Fort Larned was established in 1859 to serve as a base of military operations against hostile Central Plains Indians, and to protect U.S. mail and traveler traffic on the Santa Fe Trail. Between 1861 and 1868, the fort also served as an agency for the U.S. Indian Bureau's administration of Central Plains tribes.

The Santa Fe Trail spanned 900 miles of the Great Plains and connected Independence, Missouri, with Santa Fe, New Mexico. A vital trade route, the trail also provided easy access for white emigrants eager to settle in the new American West. By the 1860s, as the Civil War drew to a close, the flood of white migration led to conflict with the Great Plains Indians whose lands were being engulfed. In 1864, the Arapaho, Cheyenne, Comanche, and Kiowa peoples retaliated by attacking wagon trains and stagecoaches on the trail. Strong military responses only provoked further raids, creating an escalation of violence, and the U.S. War Department soon prohibited all travel on the trail between Fort Larned and Fort Union in New Mexico without an armed escort. In 1867, the army rebuilt the fort, and Larned became the region's most important military post. Finally, in November 1868, a brash young lieutenant colonel named George A. Custer defeated Black Kettle and the Cheyenne at the Battle of Washita, ending the Indian Wars in the region around the fort. Larned's role shifted to protecting construction workers on the Santa Fe Railroad. In 1872, the railroad was completed, rendering the Santa Fe Trail obsolete, and in 1878, the army abandoned Fort Larned.

Established in 1964, the 718-acre fort reflected the post–World War II obsession with American expansion. In 1966, William H. Goetzmann published the Pulitzer Prize–winning *Exploration and Empire: The Explorer and the Scientists in the Winning of the American West*, the culmination of a generation of scholarship about expansion. In an era when printed matter still dominated, this widely influential book played a significant role in the creation of parks such as Fort Larned.

Fort Larned National Historic Site is located in southwestern Kansas, 6 miles west of the town of Larned. With 9 restored buildings, Fort Larned survives as one of the best examples of an Indian Wars–era fort, and most buildings are furnished to their original appearance. Entrance fees are $4 per family or $2 per person, with children sixteen and younger admitted free. The Fort Larned Visitor Center is open daily from 8 A.M. until 6 P.M. from Memorial Day through Labor Day, and from 8:30 A.M. until 5 P.M. during the rest of the year. The center has an introductory slide presentation, a museum, a library, a bookstore, and a self-guided nature trail. When available, personnel in period costume staff the barracks, blacksmith shop, hospital, blockhouse, commissary, and officers quarters. During the summer, there are weekend living-history demonstrations that offer a look at life in the 1860s. The Santa Fe Trail Ruts Area, a detached unit of the park, is 44 acres of virgin prairie that features a prairie-dog town and the visible ruts from wagons that traveled the Santa Fe Trail.

Food, lodging, and all traveler services are available in the town of Larned, Dodge City, Hays, and Great Bend. There is no camping on-site, but campgrounds are located in Larned, Jetmore City Lake, and La Crosse.

For more information, write Fort Larned National Historic Site, Route 3, Larned, KS 67550, or telephone (316) 285-6911. The park's Web site is www.nps.gov/fols.

FURTHER READING

Fort Larned National Historic Site, Kansas: Cultural Landscape Report. Omaha, NE: Midwest Support Office, National Park Service, 1999.

Goetzmann, William H. *Exploration and Empire: The Explorer and the Scientist in the Winning of the American West.* New York: Norton, 1978.

Oliva, Leo E. *Fort Larned on the Santa Fe Trail.* Topeka: Kansas State Historical Society, 1982.

——. *Fort Larned: Guardian of the Santa Fe Trail.* Topeka: Kansas State Historical Society, 1997.

Utley, Robert Marshall. *Fort Larned National Historic Site.* Tucson, AZ: Southwest Parks and Monuments Association, 1993.

FORT MATANZAS NATIONAL MONUMENT

Location: St. Augustine, Florida
Acreage: 300
Established: October 15, 1924

Fort Matanzas National Monument commemorates the site of a grizzly massacre and a later Spanish garrison, and today serves as a historic remnant of the early Spanish empire in the New World. Almost two hundred years before the construction of the fort, nearly 250 French Huguenots were slaughtered as heretics near the inlet that became known as Matanzas–the Spanish word for "massacre." The French had a tenuous hold in New World Florida in the sixteenth century, and in 1565, they set out from Fort Caroline to bolster their claims by attacking the Spanish at St. Augustine. The French force was captured and ordered to surrender and to renounce Protestantism in favor of Catholicism. Although the defeated men duly surrendered, they refused to disavow their faith, and their Spanish captors cut them down with swords.

The Matanzas massacre ended French aspirations in Florida, but the French were not the only threat to Spanish sovereignty. In 1733, Britain established a colonial foothold in southern Georgia near Savannah. They quickly made their presence felt in small skirmishes and blockades, provoking the Spanish military to erect a small, but sturdy, stone fort at Matanzas Inlet, which was completed in 1742. From this masonry watchtower fort, the Spanish could observe all maritime traffic approaching St. Augustine from the south. And her cannons blocked potential enemies from attacking via the city's backdoor–the Matanzas River. Although the fort thwarted British military advances, it could not defend against diplomacy, and in 1763, the Peace of Paris gave the British what they had failed to take by military force: all of Florida. During the Revolutionary War, the Spanish regained Florida and held the region until the United States purchased it in 1821. By this time, Fort Matanzas had long been abandoned and had fallen into ruin.

Established in 1924, the 300-acre Fort Matanzas National Monument preserves this unique style of Spanish colonial military architecture as well as the intact barrier island ecosystem surrounding Rattlesnake and Anastasia islands. During the summer months, the park's beaches harbor nesting sea turtles, including the endangered green and leatherback, and the threatened loggerhead. Sharp-eyed visitors may also see ghost crabs, least terns, the endangered Anastasia Island beach mouse, herons, egrets, ospreys, dolphins, and even the rare, endangered manatee.

The Fort Matanzas Visitor Center is open daily from 9 A.M. until 4:30 P.M. and contains interpretive exhibits including a model of the fort, a timeline, and a map illustrating the relationship of Matanzas to St. Augustine, as well as a video and a bookstore. Special living-history programs and guided nature walks are presented on weekends throughout the year. Weather permitting, park rangers offer guided, forty-five-minute boat tours to Fort Matanzas itself, which is located across the Matanzas River on Rattlesnake Island. The park also features a half-mile, self-guided boardwalk trail that winds through a coastal maritime forest, and another boardwalk through the dunes to a beach overlook. There is no charge for admission to the monument or for the boat tour to the fort, and peak visitor seasons are usually March through Labor Day, and after hurricane season, from November to early January.

Fort Matanzas has no food, lodging, or camping facilities in the park, but all traveler services are located nearby. Camping is available at Anastasia State Park, just south of St. Augustine.

For more information, write Fort Matanzas National Monument, 8635 Highway A1A South, St. Augustine, FL 32086, or telephone (904) 471-0116. The park's Web site is www.nps.gov/foma.

FURTHER READING

McGrath, John T. *The French in Early Florida.* Gainesville: University Press of Florida, 2000.

Milanich, Jerald T. *The Timucua.* Cambridge, MA: Blackwell, 1996.

Waterbury, Jean Parker, ed. *Defenses and Defenders at St. Augustine.* St. Augustine, FL: St. Augustine Historical Society, 1999.

FORT McHENRY NATIONAL MONUMENT AND HISTORIC SHRINE

Location: Baltimore, Maryland
Acreage: 43
Established: March 3, 1925

August 1814 was a difficult time for the United States. The war with Great Britain, which had begun in 1812, had not gone well, and there had been no bleaker moment than the arrival of a twenty-warship British fleet under the command of Admiral Alexander Cochrane in the Chesapeake Bay. Cochrane's ships delivered veteran soldiers, under Major General Robert Ross, who assaulted the new American capital, Washington, D.C., burning the White House, the Capitol, and other national buildings. With the arrogance of winners, they returned to their ships and headed north toward Baltimore with every expectation of another devastating victory.

The British assault on Baltimore was two-pronged. Ross's men were put ashore to march to the less-well-protected landward side of the city, while Cochrane's fleet began an all-out assault on Fort McHenry from the sea. Neither attack succeeded; Ross's men were driven back by militia and trapped near a place called Rodgers' Bastion. Cochrane's attack did little to dislodge Major George Armistead and his garrison.

On the rainy night of September 14, the British tried again from the sea. Cochrane's cannons delivered barrage after barrage against the fort, the orange and yellow glow of exploding rockets, the traceries of shell fuses, and the cannon fire reflected against the rain clouds that hugged the ground. The bombardment created an eerie glow, a combination of the terrifying colors of the explosions and the reflected glow of the night. Hour after hour, the bombardment continued, letting up only when dawn broke.

Aboard one of the British ships, two Americans, Colonel John Skinner and Francis Scott Key, a thirty-one-year-old attorney, were held hostage. They had been sent under a flag of truce to negotiate the release of an American physician held hostage by the British. The British released the doctor, but held Skinner and Key in his place. The two men had an excellent view of an event they preferred not to see happen at all: the bombardment of the fort that defended their city, graced by the flag of their country.

When morning broke, the men anxiously peered for signs that the American flag still flew over Fort McHenry. As the haze of the battle cleared, the two men saw the 42-foot by 30-foot, star-spangled banner waving in the breeze. The fort had not fallen. Excitedly, Key jotted down a few lines of poetry to commemorate the American success in a war that had seemed to be failure after failure. Within a few days, Key began to expand upon his poem, and a Baltimore newspaper published it under the title "The Defense of Fort McHenry." Retitled "The Star-Spangled Banner," the poem was widely reprinted from Georgia to Maine, and the words set to the music of a popular song of the time, "Anacreon in Heaven." Despite the odd melody, the words and music resonated, and in the twentieth century, "The Star-Spangled Banner" became the national anthem of the United States.

Despite renovation for use in the Civil War, Fort McHenry remains one of the most complete structures that commemorate the War of 1812. It is also the only unit in the park system designated as a national monument and historic shrine. The fort's visitor center has interpretive exhibits and a video about the battle of Fort McHenry, and there is a self-guiding tour of the fort that displays the ravelin, a V-shaped defensive structure at the Sally Port, the entrance; bombproof shelters where the soldiers stayed during the bombardment; the parade ground; and the location of the original flagpole, from which flew the flag that Key saw and memorialized.

The park is open daily from 8 A.M. until 5 P.M., with later hours during the summer. The climate is mostly sunny, with humid, rainy periods throughout the year. Cold winters are common and the area tends to be windy throughout the year. Summers are generally hot and humid. Entrance fees are $5 for adults and are valid for seven days. Located within 10 miles of BWI Airport, the park is easily accessible from the Baltimore-Washington area. It is 3 miles southeast of the Baltimore Inner Harbor and just off I-95. From northbound or southbound I-95, take exit 55 to Key Highway. From Key Highway turn left on Lawrence Street and left on Fort Avenue. Proceed 1 mile to the park. From the Baltimore Inner Harbor, take Light Street south to Fort Avenue. Turn left on Fort Avenue and proceed to the park.

For more information, write Fort McHenry National Monument, End of East Fort Avenue, Baltimore, MD 21230-5393, or telephone (410) 962-4290. The park's Web site is www.nps.gov/fomc.

FURTHER READING

Molotsky, Irvin. *The Flag, the Poet and the Song: The Story of the Star-Spangled Banner.* New York: Dutton, 2001.

Sheads, Scott, and Merle T. Cole. *Fort McHenry and Baltimore's Harbor Defenses.* Charleston, SC: Arcadia, 2001.

Svejda, George J. *History of the Star-Spangled Banner from 1814 to the Present.* Washington, DC: Division of History, Office of Archeology and Historic Preservation, 1969.

FORT NECESSITY NATIONAL BATTLEFIELD

Location: Farmington, Pennsylvania
Acreage: 903
Established: March 4, 1931

In July 1754, colonial troops commanded by a young colonel named George Washington were defeated by combined French and native forces near a small, southwestern Pennsylvania stockade known as Fort Necessity, or the "Great Meadow." This defeat was the opening salvo in a seven-year struggle between Britain and France for control of North America—the French and Indian War, also known as the Seven Years' War.

This strategic area in the upper Ohio River Valley had long been disputed by the two nations. French troops and fur trappers were moving south from Canada into the region, while the English colony of Virginia claimed the same area. It was here that their geopolitical aspirations collided.

In early 1754, hoping to convince the French to leave, Virginia's governor sent a small militia under then Major George Washington to the region. When negotiations failed, the governor ordered troops to establish a British fort at the junction of the Allegheny and Monongahela rivers (the location of present-day Pittsburgh). The French, however, had other plans. French forces quickly drove off the British detachment and proceeded to construct their own small fortification at the site, named Fort Duquesne.

In April 1754, determined to assert British sovereignty in the region, Washington led another expedition westward, establishing a camp at the Great Meadows in late May. Several days later, Washington and his men surprised a nearby French encampment under the leadership of Joseph Coulon de Villiers, Sieur de Jumonville, killing ten Frenchmen, including Jumonville, and capturing twenty-one prisoners. Fearing "we might be attacked by considerable forces," Washington returned to Great Meadows, where his men erected a small, circular fortification, which they named Fort Necessity.

Shortly thereafter, on the morning of July 3, the French and their Native American allies from Fort Duquesne launched a retaliatory strike upon Colonel Washington's troops at Fort Necessity. During the fierce eight-hour battle, Washington's forces proved no match for the combined 700 French soldiers and Native American warriors. That evening, Washington surrendered his command for the first and only time in his illustrious military career. After the French commander permitted his retreat, Washington and his troops returned to Virginia, and the French torched the fort.

Established in 1931, the 903-acre Fort Necessity National Battlefield is located in southwestern Pennsylvania 11 miles southeast of Uniontown on U.S. Highway 40. It contains 3 separate sites. The main unit contains the visitor center, the reconstructed Fort Necessity, and the historic Mount Washington Tavern. The Braddock Grave unit is about 1.5 miles west of the main unit, and the Jumonville Glen Unit is approximately 7 miles northwest of the main unit; it is the site of Washington's first encounter with the French. Admission fees are $2 per adult, with children sixteen and under admitted free, and are valid for seven days. The annual Southwest Pennsylvania Park Pass, which includes Fort Necessity, is also available for $15.

The Fort Necessity Visitor Center near the restored stockade is open daily from 9 A.M. until 5 P.M. and contains information, exhibits, and a slide program that help interpret the battle. Visitors will also enjoy touring the Mount Washington Tavern, originally built as a stagecoach stop for travelers on the Na-

tional Road (1828–1855), and refurbished to reflect early-nineteenth-century tavern life. From mid-June through Labor Day, a variety of talks, tours, and living-history demonstrations are available at the fort, the visitor center, and Mount Washington Tavern. During the winter, cross-country skiing is available on the trails.

There are no food, lodging, or camping facilities on site, but nearby Uniontown offers all traveler services. Ohiopyle State Park, located just northeast of the battlefield, has a developed campground, and camping is also available in Chalk Hill and Farmington.

For more information, write Fort Necessity National Battlefield, 1 Washington Parkway, Farmington, PA 15437, or telephone (724) 329-5512. The park's informative Web site is www.nps.gov/fone.

FURTHER READING

Alberts, Robert C. *A Charming Field for an Encounter: The Story of George Washington's Fort Necessity.* Washington, DC: National Park Service, 1975.

Fort Necessity Memorial Association. *A Young Colonel from Virginia and the Blow He Struck for American Independence in the Year 1754, Together with Its Significance as a Feature of the Approaching Bicentennial of His Birth.* Uniontown, PA: Fort Necessity Memorial Association, 1931.

Higginbotham, Don. *George Washington and the American Military Tradition.* Athens: University of Georgia Press, 1985.

FORT POINT NATIONAL HISTORIC SITE

Location: San Francisco, California
Acreage: 29
Established: October 16, 1970

Built on the location of a tiny Spanish adobe gun battery called Castillo de San Joaquin, Fort Point was the first major American installation in the Bay Area. Conceived as a first-line defense against a harbor attack, Fort Point was constructed by the U.S. Army Corps of Engineers between 1853 and 1861 to prevent a hostile fleet from invading the

San Francisco Bay. During the Civil War, the imposing, three-story, brick-and-granite fortification was continuously occupied by Company I of the 3rd U.S. Artillery Regiment, although the company never fired a single shot.

Designed to mount 126 cannons and house 600 soldiers, the massive fort boasted walls averaging 5 to 12 feet in thickness, but the advent of the more powerful rifled cannon rendered Fort Point obsolete. In 1886, the army withdrew its last troops—in 1900, the last of the cannons was removed—and the fort reverted to a storage facility and training ground. By the 1920s, it was part of the Presidio, the primary military installation in the Bay Area. In 1926, the fort was abandoned,

and between 1933 and 1937, during construction of the Golden Gate Bridge, discussions about its demolition became serious. Only intervention by Joseph Strauss, the powerful and authoritarian chief engineer of the Golden Gate Bridge project, prevented its destruction.

During World War II, the army stationed about 100 soldiers at the fort to operate searchlights and rapid-fire cannons to protect a submarine net strung across the bay's entrance. After the end of the war, the fort was again abandoned and stood vacant in the shadow of the Golden Gate Bridge. Today, this unique coastal fortification offers stunning views of the bay, San Francisco, and the massive bridge that towers above it.

Fort Point National Historic Site at the Golden Gate National Recreation Area. Although occupied throughout the Civil War, Fort Point and similar brick forts became obsolete with the advent of faster, more powerful rifled cannon. *(National Park Service)*

Located under the south anchorage of the Golden Gate Bridge in the Presidio of San Francisco, Fort Point had attracted the interest of preservationists since the 1920s. In 1959, a group of military retirees and civilian engineers, impressed with the structure, formed an organization called the Fort Point Museum Association. They raised funds for preservation and lobbied for the establishment of a national historic site at the fort. A decade-long grassroots movement took shape. With the support of the Sixth Army, the association cleaned up the fort, built safety barricades, sponsored special events, hosted school groups and civic organizations, and entertained growing numbers of weekend visitors. In 1968, local congressional representatives introduced bills to establish Fort Point National Historic Site. The proposals encountered little resistance; the area was small and already in federal hands, and the structure was intriguing. The House of Representatives and the U.S. Senate passed the bills, and on October 16, 1970, the park came into existence.

Part of Golden Gate National Recreation Area, Fort Point National Historic Site offers free entrance and parking. The visitor center contains several museum displays of early-nineteenth-century armament and soldier life, as well as 3 photography exhibits on the African American Soldier Experience, Women in U.S. Military History, and the Construction of the Golden Gate Bridge. The visitor center's theater offers a seventeen-minute video on the fort's history, "Guardian of the Golden Gate," and a thirty-minute video on the bridge's construction. Park rangers offer daily, guided tours and cannon-loading demonstrations, where visitors can get a hands-on opportunity to learn about the firing of Civil War–era artillery. The Fort Point Bookstore, operated by the Golden Gate National Parks Association, is located inside the fort and has a large number of titles, with primary emphases on the Civil War, westward expansion, African American history, lighthouses, seacoast defense, women's history, and San Francisco history and guides. The 29-acre site also has numerous hiking and biking trails that connect the fort with the Coastal Trail, the Golden Gate Promenade, and the bridge itself. Views are outstanding.

There are no camping, lodging, or restaurant facilities in the park, but a wide variety of traveler services are available in San Francisco and the Bay Area. Private campgrounds are available in Marin County, just north of San Francisco.

For more information, write Fort Point National Historic Site, P.O. Box 29333, Presidio of San Francisco, CA 94129-0333, or telephone (415) 556-1693. The park's informative Web site is www.nps.gov/fopo.

FURTHER READING

Grassick, Mary K. *Fort Point: Fort Point National Historic Site, Presidio of San Francisco, California.* Harpers Ferry, WV: Division of Historic Furnishings, Harpers Ferry Center, National Park Service, 1994.

Martini, John A. *Fort Point: Sentry at the Golden Gate.* San Francisco: Golden Gate National Park Association, 1991.

FORT PULASKI NATIONAL MONUMENT

Location: Savannah, Georgia
Acreage: 5,623
Established: October 15, 1924

In 1829, construction began on an imposing military fortification at the mouth of the Savannah River, on Georgia's northern coast. Intended as one in a series of twenty-nine coastal defense fortifications stretching from Maine to Louisiana, Fort Pulaski—named after Polish count and Revolutionary War hero Casimir Pulaski—took eighteen years to build and purportedly contained 25 million bricks in 7.5-foot thick walls. The massive garrison was the first military assignment for a young second lieutenant fresh out of West Point named Robert E. Lee, and when Georgia seceded from the Union on January 19, 1861, Pulaski became a Confederate fort.

The strategy of coastal defense was a feature common to the age of sail, and the presence of the British, Spanish, and French in the Caribbean and Mexico enhanced America's need. As Americans attempted to repel British attacks during the War of 1812 and then experienced the subsequent allure of Manifest Destiny, the need for a series of coastal forts became clear. Called the "Third System," this network established a presence along American coasts that could protect, first, the continent and then, later, the hemisphere. During the Civil War, part of the Union's overall strategy was to recapture all of the coastal fortifications that had fallen into Confederate hands. Because it guarded the city of Savannah, Fort Pulaski was considered a prime strategic target. Due to its sturdy construction, and its location just out of the harmful range of traditional, inaccurate, smoothbore cannons and mortars, Pulaski was also considered one of the most formidable. But the fort's aura of invincibility was shattered on April 10 and 11, 1862, when a Union artillery barrage commanded by Engineer Captain Quincy Adams Gillmore directed new, rifled cannon artillery fire at the fort from nearly a mile away on Tybee Island. For thirty long hours, more than 5,000 bullet-shaped shells pounded the fort's massive walls and gun placements. Pulaski proved no match. Realizing that the new technology could completely demolish the fort, Confederate Colonel Charles Olmstead surrendered. But the scope of this Union victory had even wider ramifications. In a two-day stretch, all of America's seemingly impenetrable coastal fortifications had been rendered obsolete by the powerful and accurate rifled cannon technology. Defensive military strategy worldwide would never be the same. Interestingly, despite the intensity of the battle, there were only two casualties—one Confederate and one Union soldier.

Established in 1924, the 5,623-acre Fort Pulaski National Monument preserves the fort and some of the most pristine marshland on the Georgia coast. Entrance fees are $2 per person or $4 per family, and an annual Fort Pulaski National Monument pass is available for $10. The park's visitor center is open from 9 A.M. until 5 P.M. daily, and it contains museum exhibits on the history and significance of the site, a seventeen-minute film called "The Battle for Fort Pulaski," and a small bookstore. Ranger-led talks and demonstrations are presented at the fort daily during the summer, and on weekends the rest of the year. In addition, encampments of troops, special living-history programs, and military demonstrations are presented on major holiday weekends. A quarter-mile, self-guided nature trail meanders through the monument and grasslands, terminating at the John Wesley Memorial, while a longer, 2-mile earthen dike circuit affords excellent views of the fort. Visitors may also wish to take a private boat to the Cockspur Island Lighthouse, built in 1857.

There is no food, lodging, or camping at the monument, but both Savannah and Tybee Island offer all traveler services. Hotels and campgrounds are available on Tybee Island, 4 miles to the east, and Skidway Island State Park, located a short distance southeast of Savannah, has a small developed campground.

For more information, write Fort Pulaski National Monument, P.O. Box 30757, U.S. Highway 80 East, Savannah, GA 31410-0757, or telephone (912) 786-5787. The park's Web site is www.nps.gov/fopu.

FURTHER READING

Kajencki, Francis C. *Casimir Pulaski, Cavalry Commander of the American Revolution.* El Paso, TX: Southwest Polonia, 2001.

Schiller, Herbert M. *Sumter Is Avenged! The Siege and Reduction of Fort Pulaski.* Shippensburg, PA: White

Mane, 1995.

——. *Fort Pulaski and the Defense of Savannah*. Conshohocken, PA: Eastern National Park and Monument Association, 1997.

FORT RALEIGH NATIONAL HISTORIC SITE

Location: Manteo, North Carolina
Acreage: 513
Established: April 5, 1941

Fort Raleigh National Historic Site commemorates the first English attempts at colonization in the New World. Between 1558 and 1603, England's Queen Elizabeth I charted an ambitious course of unprecedented global expansion for her island nation. As a Protestant, she frequently had to contend with Philip II, the Catholic king of Spain, and this rivalry spurred British interest in the New World, where Spain had made a fortune. One of Elizabeth's favorite courtiers was a thirty-one-year-old soldier-poet named Sir Walter Raleigh, and in 1584, he obtained a charter from the crown for a reconnaissance voyage to the New World, a place where England could amass great wealth and imperial prosperity. Raleigh's expedition landed in present-day North Carolina, and he named the region Virginia, in honor of Elizabeth, the Virgin Queen. His glowing descriptions of the rich land and its "very handsome and goodly people" were encouraging, and in 1585, Raleigh sent out another expedition to establish a formal colonial foothold. The colonists settled on Roanoke Island and constructed a small fortification, mostly as a defense against French and Spanish incursions.

Ostensibly settled to bring the Protestant faith to the godless "savages," the Virginia colony was primarily a militaristic operation, dependent on the home country and exploitative of the Native Americans. Although trading relations had been established between the two groups, the colonists were simply incapable of supporting themselves, and as fall turned to winter, they began to rob the food stores and fish traps of the Algonquians. Disenchantment swelled into resentment after measles and smallpox brought by the settlers began to kill the native people. By the next spring, when Sir Francis Drake stopped at the colony on his way back from the West Indies, he found starving, destitute, and homesick colonists fending off constant attacks from hostile natives. Drake loaded up all the relieved colonists and took them back to the homeland. The first attempt at English colonization had failed.

This failure did not deter the persistent Raleigh, and in 1587, he sent a new group of men, women, and children to establish an agrarian colony on the southern end of Chesapeake Bay, under the governorship of John White. Through an unfortunate twist of fate and timing, the new colonists were forced to settle on Roanoke Island, placing the "Cittie of Ralegh" squarely in the middle of a hostile situation. Despite the colonists' good intentions, they could not overcome the legacy of violence and hatred left by the former settlement. Desperately needing provisions and reinforcements, the settlers urged White to return to England, where his ship was immediately pressed into service to fend off the Spanish Armada. Finally, in 1590, White returned to Roanoke only to find the settlement destroyed and the colonists gone. Only a few mysterious clues remained—such as the word "Croatan" (the Native American name for the Outer Banks island off Cape Hatteras) carved in wood. For more than a decade, Raleigh attempted to locate these colonists, but failed, and the fate of the "lost colony" remains a mystery to this day.

Established in 1941, Fort Raleigh National Historic Site preserves the small earthen fort (rebuilt in 1950) constructed by White and the "lost" colonists. In 1990, Congress enlarged the site to incorporate American Indian cultures, Roanoke Island's role in the Civil War, the Freedman's colony, and the activities of radio pioneer Reginald Fessenden. There is no admission fee for the 513-acre park, which is located on eastern North Carolina's Roanoke Island 3 miles north of Manteo, but admission is charged for "The Lost Colony" musical drama and the Elizabethan Gardens attraction. The Lindsay Warren Visitor Center is open from 9 A.M. until 5 P.M. daily, with extended hours during the summer, and houses a museum with exhibits on the history of the English expeditions and colonies on Roanoke Island, a seventeen-minute introductory video, exhibits on the Civil War and Freedman's colony, and a gift shop operated by the Roanoke Island Historical Association. Every August 18, the park and "The Lost Colony" cast commemorate the birthday of Virginia Dare, the first child born to English parents in the New World, born on Roanoke Island in 1587.

There is no food, lodging, or camping at the historic site, but all traveler services are available in nearby communities, and Cape Hatteras National Seashore has Park Service campgrounds.

For more information, write Fort Raleigh National Historic Site, National Park Service, 1401 National Park Drive, Manteo, NC 27954, or telephone (252) 473-5772. The park's informative Web site is www.nps.gov/fora.

FURTHER READING
Fort Raleigh Historic Resource Study. Atlanta, GA: Southeast Regional Office, National Park Service, 1999. Available at www.nps.gov/fora/hrs/hrs.htm.
Kupperman, Karen Ordahl. *Roanoke: The Abandoned Colony.* Totowa: Rowman and Allanheld, 1984.
Lacey, Robert. *Sir Walter Raleigh.* London: Phoenix, 2000.
Miller, Lee. *Roanoke: Solving the Mystery of the Lost Colony.* New York: Arcade, 2001.
Seitz, Frederick. *The Cosmic Inventor: Reginald Aubrey Fessenden (1866–1932).* Philadelphia, PA: American Philosophical Society, 1999.

FORT SCOTT NATIONAL HISTORIC SITE
Location: Fort Scott, Kansas
Acreage: 17
Established: October 19, 1978

Perhaps no state in the union has lost its nineteenth-century centrality more than Kansas. The crossroads of the nation throughout the century of expansion, the scene of frontier contact between Native Americans and incoming settlers, the battleground between free- and slave-state forces, and finally the locus of the populist rebellion, nineteenth-century Kansas spoke to the concerns of the nation in dulcet tones. "Bleeding Kansas" and the Civil War cut the nation to the quick, redefining its very essence; the expulsion of Native Americans from Kansas so typified a process central to the age of Manifest Destiny in the legal structure and the celerity with which it occurred; populism reflected the urban-rural tension fostered by industrialization at the moment when thousands first acquired the land they thought would make them independent, only to find that it often bound them in another form of servitude. What happened in the Kansas Territory and then in the Sunflower State not only reflected the most vexing and contentious concerns of the nation in the nineteenth century, it shaped the nature and perception of those situations and the actions that surrounded them.

Between 1838 and 1873, no place stood on the front lines of those conflicts more than the military post at Fort Scott, Kansas. It was the only fort whose sole function was to support the concept of the Permanent Indian Frontier, a mid-nineteenth-century idea that proposed to separate the native peoples in the useless plains beyond the settled fields of western Missouri. Established in 1842 to help secure this barrier, Fort Scott helped support exploration of the West, acted as a supply point for military operations in the Mexican-

American War and the Civil War, and served as the headquarters for military operations to protect railroad crews from 1869 to 1873.

The town that grew up around Fort Scott, incorporated in 1855, was a center for pro-slavery forces during the years of "Bleeding Kansas," and army patrols were frequently called into the area to help quell civil violence. The army buildings sold at auction after troops were withdrawn in 1854 were crucial to the town's development, with buildings serving as hotels, post offices, stores, saloons, and schools.

In its relatively brief life as a military post, Fort Scott reprised a role long played by frontier military posts. The garrison at Fort Scott guarded the line between (in the parlance of the nineteenth century) civilization and savagery, between the institutions of a democracy and the turmoil of the world beyond. On one side of this line, the laws of the American republic were in force. Beyond it, only the military stood between an individual and the chaos of a lawless world without rules or reason.

This boundary role—first between the settlers and Native Americans, then between proslavery and free-soil settlers, and, later, between the rugged past and the prosperous future—gave Fort Scott genuine significance between 1838 and 1873. Fort Scott was the fulcrum on which the Kansas frontier turned, the place where the institutions of American society found their best representation. The fort even became the catalyst for the formation of a town, the kind of permanent settlement that proved the strategy of siting a military post.

Fort Scott possessed a centrality in the settlement process of nineteenth-century Kansas, and with that crucial role, a place of significance that has been long overlooked in American history. As did so many other places—the boomtowns and military installations that defined their moment—Fort Scott slipped into oblivion, until it was preserved in the national park system in 1978. Its central-

ity to the nineteenth century offers a lens on the past, a new way of seeing the world from which the modern American nation sprang.

Fort Scott National Historic Site is open year round, from 8 A.M. until 5 P.M. April to October and from 9 A.M. to 5 P.M. from November to March. Entrance fees are $2 per person or $4 per family.

Spring and autumn here are pleasant with mild temperatures. Summers are generally hot and humid, while winters are mild with periods of cold weather and varying snowfall. Thunderstorms are common throughout the spring and summer. Heavy coats should be worn in winter; if traveling in other seasons, bring rain gear.

Fort Scott National Historic Site is located in downtown Fort Scott, Kansas (U.S. Highways 69 and 54 intersect here), about 90 miles south of Kansas City and 60 miles northwest of Joplin, Missouri. It is 4 miles from the Kansas–Missouri border. Approaches from all directions are clearly signed.

For more information, write Fort Scott National Historic Site, P.O. Box 918, Fort Scott, KS 66701-0918, or telephone (620) 223-0310. The park's Web site is www. nps.gov/fosc.

FURTHER READING

Goodrich, Thomas. *War to the Knife: Bleeding Kansas, 1854–1861.* Mechanicsburg, PA: Stackpole Books, 1998.

Oliva, Leo E. *Fort Scott: Courage and Conflict on the Border.* Topeka: Kansas State Historical Society, 1996.

Shoemaker, Earl Arthur. *The Permanent Indian Frontier: The Reason for the Construction and Abandonment of Fort Scott, Kansas, During the Dragoon Era: A Special History Study.* Washington, DC: National Park Service, 1986.

FORT SMITH NATIONAL HISTORIC SITE

Location: Fort Smith, Arkansas and Oklahoma

Acreage: 75

Established: September 13, 1961

Fort Smith National Historic Site. *(National Park Service)*

Fort Smith was the quintessential early-nineteenth-century fort, a reflection of the national aspirations of the American republic, and one of the first U.S. military posts in the Louisiana Territory. In 1817, the army ordered the construction of the first Fort Smith, a small, log-and-stone stockade measuring 132 feet on each side. The fort served as the base of operations for enforcing federal policy regarding Native Americans and for maintaining the peace among native Osage Indians, displaced Cherokees moving west to Indian Territory, and white settlers moving into western Arkansas. Hoping to segregate whites and native people, the government had created an imaginary line between the two groups called the "Permanent Indian Frontier," which purported to demarcate inviolate Native American lands. But this un-

realistic boundary would quickly disappear as the relentless tide of whites poured into the West.

The initial Fort Smith succeeded in keeping the peace, leading to its demise and abandonment in 1824. By this time, however, the federal government was firmly committed to a policy of relocating Native Americans, and it continued to uproot more Cherokee, Choctaw, Chickasaw, Creek, and Seminole Indians—the Five "Civilized Tribes"—from their southeastern homelands to Indian Territory in Oklahoma. The most infamous of these relocations was the forcible removal of the Georgia Cherokee; perhaps as many as 4,000 of the 16,000 Cherokees died along the Trail of Tears. Anglo-American settlers, now well ensconced in the rich lands of western Arkansas, became increasingly nervous, and in

1838, a second Fort Smith—a larger, more fortified facility—was constructed near the original fort's ruins to allay the settlers' fears.

Again the purpose of the fort and the mission it served diverged. Despite settlers' fears, displaced native people posed little threat to western Arkansas. As a result, the army converted the second fort into a supply depot. Occupied by Arkansas volunteers during the Mexican-American War, and fought over by the Confederacy and the Union during the Civil War, the fort was a military prize for almost three decades. But like other forts on the edge of the prairie, its moment passed. The military abandoned Fort Smith in 1871, when it was deemed too far east to serve as a supply center for the ever-expanding western frontier. Soon thereafter, the soldier's barracks were converted into a courthouse and jail for the federal court for the Western District of Arkansas. At the time, this district covered not only the thirteen western Arkansas counties, but most of the "lawless" Indian Territory (now Oklahoma), a post–Civil War refuge for outlaws and criminals. Between 1875 and 1896, federal judge Isaac C. Parker presided over 9,000 convictions or pleas of guilt, and hung 76 prisoners. Eventually, more federal courts were established as more settlers arrived in the region. As Parker's jurisdiction diminished in size, so did his responsibilities, and he presided over his last federal case in 1896.

Located on Rogers Avenue in downtown Fort Smith, the 75-acre historic site, established in 1961, comprises what remains of the 2 frontier forts and the federal court for the Western District of Arkansas. Admission fees are $3 per person or $6 per family and are valid for seven days. The park's visitor center is located in the Barracks/Courthouse/Jail building and is open daily from 9 A.M. until 5 P.M. The center has numerous exhibits that focus on Fort Smith's military history between 1817 and 1871, federal policy, removal of Native Americans and the Trail of Tears, U.S. deputy marshals and outlaws, and the impact of the federal court on Indian Territory. The newly renovated facility also contains an extensive artifact and photography collection. Visitors will appreciate the careful 1880s restoration of "Hanging Judge" Isaac C. Parker's courtroom, the original "Hell on the Border" jail used between 1871 and 1889, and the Gallows, the original site used for federal executions between 1873 and 1896. The main exhibit is a partial, full-sized replica of the 1890s jail interior, reconstructed from original historic blueprints. The center also offers several audiovisual programs, including an introductory video, a fifteen-minute film about Parker's deputy marshals, and 3 video stations displaying Native American perspectives on the Trail of Tears. Park rangers offer guided tours of the courtroom, jail, and gallows during the summer months, and special programs, exhibits, and military encampments occur throughout the year. There are several maintained trails that lead visitors through this urban park, including the half-mile Arkansas River Trail, which follows the river's shoreline and leads to the site of the first Fort Smith and the Trail of Tears Overlook.

There are no food, lodging, or camping facilities at the historic site, but the city of Fort Smith has all traveler services, and there are 2 developed Army Corps of Engineers campgrounds located nearby.

For more information, write Fort Smith National Historic Site, P.O. Box 1406, Fort Smith, AR 72902, or telephone (501) 783-3961. The park's helpful Web site is www.nps.gov/fosm.

FURTHER READING

Bearss, Edwin C. *Fort Smith, Little Gibraltar on the Arkansas.* Norman: University of Oklahoma Press, 1979.

Butler, William James. *Fort Smith, Past and Present: A Historical Summary.* Fort Smith: First National Bank of Fort Smith, Arkansas, 1972.

Mapes, Ruth B. *Old Fort Smith: Cultural Center on the*

Southwestern Frontier. Little Rock, AR: Pioneer, 1965.

FORT STANWIX NATIONAL MONUMENT

Location: Rome, New York
Acreage: 16
Established: August 21, 1935

Strategically located at the centuries-old Oneida Carrying Place along the Iroquois Confederacy portage between the Atlantic Ocean and the Great Lakes, Fort Stanwix seemed destined for a pivotal role in the imperial struggle for the New World. In an effort to secure their New World claims, the British began construction on the fort in 1758, but the 1759 conquest of Canada, culminating in the great battle for Quebec on the Plains of Abraham, effectively destroyed the French empire in America and temporarily reduced the strategic significance of Fort Stanwix. The garrison nevertheless served an important role in defining Native American–white relations in the region. In 1768, the Iroquois reluctantly signed the Treaty of Fort Stanwix, which relinquished their claims to the Ohio Valley, in the hope that it would deflect English settlement away from their own homeland. The effort would prove futile. In 1784, in the second Treaty of Fort Stanwix, congressional commissioners forced the Iroquois to cede more of their territory in eastern Ohio, in an attempt to meet western settlers' nearly insatiable demand for land.

Fort Stanwix reasserted its military significance during the American Revolution. In 1776, rebellious Americans seized the fort as part of a defensive strategy to protect the nascent nation from a British invasion out of Canada. British officials had endeavored to divide and conquer in the northern colonies, and in early August 1877, British Colonel Barry St. Leger moved eastward from Lake Ontario to the Mohawk River to join British Generals John Burgoyne and Sir William Howe. Their plan was to seize the strategic Lake Champlain–Hudson River corridor between Canada and New York City, which would effectively cut off New York from the New England colonies. On his way to the Hudson, however, St. Leger stopped to try and regain Fort Stanwix, now occupied by 800 Americans. The resolute rebels, under the leadership of Colonel Peter Gansevoort, refused to surrender. During the next three weeks, as 1,700 British soldiers, Loyalists, and native allies besieged the fort, the Americans held firm. A little subterfuge aided the patriots' cause. Gansevoort knew that more than two thirds of St. Leger's force were "irregulars"—colonists who supported the crown and natives who favored the British. Irregular troops generally lacked the discipline and devotion of regular soldiers, and were more prone to discard their loyalty at the first sign of a genuine threat. While the fort was surrounded, Gansevoort "leaked" information that General Benedict Arnold, a vaunted American leader (before his treason was exposed), and a much larger force of Americans were rushing to the defense of Fort Stanwix. Upon hearing this, many of the irregulars abandoned the British, and in one afternoon St. Leger lost more than two thirds of his fighting force. Fearing Arnold's arrival, commanding fewer men than the Americans already had at Fort Stanwix, and suddenly unable to make a military difference at Lake Champlain or along the Hudson River, St. Leger faced a dilemma. He could wait and presumably face a more powerful foe, or he could retreat. He chose the latter. On August 22, St. Leger reluctantly withdrew his troops to Canada. Two days later, Arnold and his troops arrived at the fort and secured it for the new nation. The British rarely challenged the area again, and the fort stood until it was abandoned in 1781.

Established in 1935, the 16-acre Fort Stanwix National Monument preserves and interprets the site of this important battle. Located in the city of Rome, New York, Fort Stanwix is open daily from April 1 through December 31, and admission to the monument is free. The visitor center, open from 9 A.M. until 5 P.M., is located inside the Gregg barracks, and it contains an orientation diorama, a theater, and a bookstore. Visitors are invited to get a "feel" for archeology at the Discovery Table Exhibit, and a five-minute slide show depicts the archeological excavation and reconstruction of the fort. Hundreds of artifacts on display also help interpret more than two hundred years of regional history. Park rangers conduct interpretive programs daily, averaging about forty-five minutes in length, and special living-history programs, including military drill demonstrations, are offered throughout the summer. Visitors can even "enlist" and experience life in a wilderness fort for themselves. In addition to the fully reconstructed fort, the monument has 3 short, self-guided trails that encircle the fort. One of the trails follows a portion of the Oneida Carrying Place, while the other 2 interpret the events of the August 1777 siege. Since mud is a frequent problem, closed-toe shoes or boots are highly recommended. Each year the monument receives nearly 55,000 visitors, mostly during the late summer when most of the special events and programs are offered.

There are no food, lodging, or camping facilities at the monument, but all traveler services are available locally. Delta Lake State Park, 6 miles northeast of Rome, has developed camping accommodations, and there is a private campground 7 miles west of Rome.

For more information, write Fort Stanwix National Monument, 112 East Park Street, Rome, NY 13440, or telephone (315) 336-2090. The park's Web site is www. nps.gov/fost.

FURTHER READING

Lowenthal, Larry, ed. *Days of Siege: A Journal of the Siege of Fort Stanwix in 1777.* New York: Eastern Acorn, 1983.

Luzader, John F. *The Construction and Military History of Fort Stanwix.* Washington, DC: U.S. Office of Archeology and Historic Preservation, Division of History, 1969.

FORT SUMTER NATIONAL MONUMENT

Location: Charleston Harbor, South Carolina
Acreage: 200
Established: April 28, 1948

On April 12, 1861, secessionist forces under Brigadier General Pierre G.T. Beauregard loaded their cannons and fired on the Union's Fort Sumter in Charleston Harbor, South Carolina. Their artillery fanned the flames of passion that had smoldered almost from the birth of the American republic in 1776. The United States had been founded on the principles of "life, liberty, and the pursuit of happiness," but the forefathers had neglected to resolve the nagging issue of slavery when they drafted the Constitution in 1787, and the problem had festered for nearly a century. In late 1860, following the hotly contested presidential election that gave the White House to Republican Abraham Lincoln, the delicate fabric of union began to unravel. In December, South Carolina seceded from the Union. One month later, the other six Deep South states followed South Carolina's lead. In February, delegates from the seven seceding states met in Montgomery, Alabama, and reconstituted themselves as the Confederate States of America. The country hovered at the brink of war and all eyes turned to Washington, D.C., for the inauguration of the man who had once pledged to place slavery on a course of "ultimate extinction."

On March 4, 1861, Lincoln spoke to a

The interior of Fort Sumter, 1863. *(Library of Congress)*

deeply divided nation. Hoping to appeal to moderates on both sides of the controversy, the president reminded the country that "we are not enemies, but friends. We must not be enemies. Though passion may have strained, it must not break our bonds of affection." But Lincoln's eloquence could not overcome a long legacy of anger and mistrust, and the president's first crisis occurred the following month at Fort Sumter. The fort was an imposing federal military installation poised on a granite island at the entrance to Charleston Harbor in the middle of rebellious South Carolina. Beyond its strategic importance, Sumter held enormous symbolic value. For as long as federal troops held the post, they could immobilize secessionist sentiment. By early April, the fort was dangerously low on supplies, and Lincoln had to decide whether to withdraw, acknowledging the southern insurrection, or reinforce, at the risk of provoking war. His cautious solution was to resupply the garrison with food, but not weapons. This left Confederate President Jefferson Davis with little choice but to demand the surrender of the fort, and when commander Major Robert Anderson refused, Davis ordered Beauregard to attack. Just before dawn on April 12, 1861, the Confederate bombardment began. Some of the shelling came from nearby Fort Moultrie, which the Union had abandoned shortly after South Carolina's secession. After thirty-four hours of fierce fighting, Major Anderson surrendered the battered fort to Beauregard and was allowed to evacuate his troops. Despite the heavy damage—Beauregard lobbed over 3,000 shots at the fort—no Union soldiers were killed.

Although it remained unfinished in 1861, Fort Sumter's roots were nearly a half century old. It had originally been conceived as part of America's post–War of 1812 coastal defense system, a response to the shocking British attacks on the American mainland. The aging Revolutionary War–era Fort Moultrie served Charleston until construction of the pentagon-shaped 135-cannon Fort Sumter began in 1829. Fort Sumter was also central to later phases of the Civil War. Between 1863 and early 1865, this Confederate stronghold withstood an unrelenting twenty-two-month siege by Union forces. During this time, most of the fort was reduced to brick rubble. In February 1865, as Union General William T. Sherman's army approached the area, Confederates abandoned the fort and, along with it, any reasonable expectation that they could retain Charleston. On April 14, 1865, exactly four years to the day after Major Anderson had surrendered Fort Sumter, he returned to raise the same Union flag he had lowered in 1861.

Established in 1948, the 200-acre Fort Sumter National Monument preserves and interprets both Fort Sumter and Fort Moultrie. Located in Charleston Harbor, Fort Sumter is accessible only by boat. Tour boats leave from the Charleston City Marina and from Patriots Point in Mount Pleasant, and private boats can dock at the monument. The concession fee for the boat ride is $11 for adults, $10 for seniors, and $6 for children ages six to eleven. Fort Moultrie is accessible via South Carolina Highway 703 through Mount Pleasant at Sullivan's Island. The monument is open daily, year-round, and visitation is usually highest in April and July and lowest in December and January. Although Fort Sumter does not have a formal visitor center, an extensive museum is located on-site, and contains many artifacts, interpretive exhibits, and a bookstore. Interpretive wayside exhibits are located throughout the fort for self-guided tours. A history tape is played during the tour boat ride to Fort Sumter, and ranger-led orientations are given on every tour boat.

There are no food, lodging, or camping facilities at the monument, but Charleston and Mount Pleasant have traveler services, and the nearby Frances Marion National Forest has U.S. Forest Service campgrounds.

For more information, write Fort Sumter National Monument, 1214 Middle Street, Sullivan's Island, SC 29482, or telephone (843) 883-3123. For boat tour information, call Fort Sumter Tours at (843) 722-2628. The park's Web site is www.nps.gov/fosu.

FURTHER READING

Current, Richard Nelson. *Lincoln and the First Shot.* Philadelphia, PA: Lippincott, 1963.

Stampp, Kenneth M. *And the War Came: The North and the Secession Crisis, 1860–1861.* Westport, CT: Greenwood, 1980.

Swanberg, W.A. *First Blood: The Story of Fort Sumter.* New York: Scribner, 1957.

FORT UNION NATIONAL MONUMENT

Location: Watrous, New Mexico
Acreage: 721
Established: April 5, 1956

In 1848, as the spoils for its victory in the Mexican-American War, the United States annexed much of northern Mexico and thereby assumed the entire burden of protecting the busy and lucrative Santa Fe Trail. Since the 1820s, the Santa Fe Trail had been a major route of commerce, but it had also been the repeated target of the Plains Indians. These frequent raids on white travelers and settlers eventually brought 1,300 soldiers to New Mexico, and in 1851, Lieutenant Colonel Edwin V. Sumner, the commander of the Department of New Mexico, decided to establish Fort Union—the first of three different forts constructed at the site—at the junction of the two branches of the Santa Fe Trail, to provide more effective protection for the region. A decade later, when the Civil War broke out, the Confederacy attempted to seize the post as part of an ambitious plan to carry the war into the far West. The Confederate defeat in the battle of Glorieta Pass at the hands of Fort Union soldiers dashed that dream, however. For the remainder of the nineteenth century, the garrison's primary role was to aid white American settlers in their quest to claim and tame the West. Notably, at one time, the fort was the largest military post west of the

Mississippi River, functioning as a military garrison, territorial arsenal, and military supply depot for the entire Southwest. After the arrival of the Santa Fe Railroad in Las Vegas, New Mexico, in 1879, the fort's utility diminished. In 1891, a year after the census led Americans to believe the frontier had closed, Fort Union was abandoned. During the next sixty-five years, the site suffered at the hands of a private owner, the Union Land and Grazing Company. Because the company's primary focus was on ranching, the fort itself quickly deteriorated.

Established in April 1956, the 721-acre Fort Union National Monument, located in the Mora Valley in northeastern New Mexico, preserves the ruins of this military garrison as well as the largest visible network of Santa Fe Trail ruts in the nation. The park's visitor center is open year-round and features exhibits on the construction of the 3 forts, the frontier army at Fort Union, the New Mexico volunteers, the Civil War in New Mexico, and the Santa Fe Trail. Admission is $3 per person. During the summer months, living-history talks and demonstrations are offered on weekends, and a 1.6-mile, self-guided interpretive trail enables visitors to tour the ruins all year. The Park Service also offers several special programs, including the First Fort Anniversary in June; Cultural Encounters on the Santa Fe Trail, which is a living-history camp with talks and demonstrations, in July; and An Evening at Fort Union, a guided evening walk through the fort's ghostly ruins, in August.

Fort Union, the historical guardian of the Santa Fe Trail, offers visitors a chance to reconnect with the past through living-history demonstrations and other special events, such as Cultural Encounters Weekend each July. *(National Park Service)*

There are no food, lodging, or camping facilities at the monument, but all traveler services are available in Las Vegas, New Mexico.

For more information, write Fort Union National Monument, P.O. Box 127, Watrous, NM 87753, or telephone (505) 425-8025. The park's Web site is www.nps.gov/foun.

FURTHER READING

Emmett, Chris. *Fort Union and the Winning of the Southwest.* Norman: University of Oklahoma Press, 1965.

Oliva, Leo E. *Fort Union and the Frontier Army in the Southwest.* Santa Fe, NM: Division of History, National Park Service, 1993.

Utley, Robert Marshall. *Fort Union National Monument.* Washington, DC: National Park Service, 1984.

——. *Fort Union and the Santa Fe Trail.* El Paso: Texas Western, 1989.

Zhu, Liping. *Fort Union National Monument: An Administrative History.* Santa Fe, NM: Southwest Cultural Resources Center, National Park Service, 1992. Available at www.nps.gov/foun/adhi/adhi.htm.

FORT UNION TRADING POST NATIONAL HISTORIC SITE

Location: Williston, North Dakota
Acreage: 444
Established: June 20, 1966

In its heyday, John Jacob Astor's Fort Union Trading Post, located near the junction of the Missouri and Yellowstone rivers in what is now North Dakota, was a bustling hive of activity. Built in 1828 to house the American Fur Company's headquarters, the post employed as many as 100 people to trade bison hides and other furs with the Assiniboine Indians to the north, the Crow Indians on the upper Yellowstone, and the Blackfeet who lived farther up the Missouri River. It served as the most important nineteenth-century fur-trading center on the Missouri River until disease ravaged the tribes. In 1837 and again in 1857, smallpox swept through the Assiniboines and Crows, decimating their popula-

tions, which, in turn, doomed the trading post. In the 1860s, the U.S. Army dismantled the fort to provide materials for the construction of nearby Fort Buford.

Since its acquisition of the 444-acre Fort Union Trading Post property in 1966, the National Park Service has excavated the stone foundations and most of the building sites of the original fort, and reconstructed the fort to appear as it did in 1851. Reconstruction remains a controversial technique, yet a number of Fur Trade–era posts besides Fort Union have been rebuilt. Scholars and the general public debate whether significance is lost or altered by reconstruction and whether a more authentic past is retained if only the foundations of such sites remain. It is an ongoing debate.

The park's visitor center, located in Bourgeois House, is open from 8 A.M. until 8 P.M. from June through August, and from 9 A.M. until 5:30 P.M. for the remainder of the year. Admission is free. The center features interpretive exhibits on life at the Fort Union Trading Post and a video program, and park rangers offer guided tours of the reconstructed fort grounds during the summer.

There are no food, lodging, or camping facilities at the historic site, but all traveler services are available in Williston, North Dakota, and Sidney, Montana. Camping is also available nearby at Fort Buford State Park.

For more information, write Fort Union Trading Post National Historic Site, 15550 Highway 1804, Williston, ND 58801, or telephone (701) 572-9083. The park's Web site is www.nps.gov/fous.

FURTHER READING

Barbour, Barton H. *Fort Union and the Upper Missouri Fur Trade.* Norman: University of Oklahoma Press, 2001.

De Vore, Steven Leroy. *Beads of the Bison Robe Trade: The Fort Union Trading Post Collection.* Williston, ND: Friends of Fort Union Trading Post, 1992.

Peterson, Lynelle A. *The 1987 Investigations at Fort Union Trading Post: Archeology and Architecture.* Lincoln, NE: National Park Service, Midwest Archeological Center, 1990.

FORT VANCOUVER NATIONAL HISTORIC SITE

Location: Vancouver, Washington
Acreage: 209
Established: June 19, 1948

Fort Vancouver, located in southwestern Washington and named in honor of British explorer George Vancouver, served for more than two decades as the administrative headquarters and main supply depot for the Hudson's Bay Company's (HBC) fur-trading operations. In addition to its strategic and agricultural advantages, the location of the fort also gave the British a stronghold in their dispute with the Americans over the jointly occupied Oregon country. At the helm of the HBC's sprawling Columbia district (a 700,000-square-mile area that stretched from Russian Alaska to Mexican California, and from the Rocky Mountains to the Pacific Ocean) was Dr. John McLoughlin, a tall, intense, feisty Scottish-Irishman with a flowing mane of white hair who the native people called the "White Headed Eagle." Under his leadership, the HBC grew into a mighty fur empire. Fort Vancouver itself was modeled after a small, self-sustaining European village, and in time it became the center of political, cultural, and commercial activities in the Pacific Northwest. Known as Jolie Prairie or Belle Vue Point because of its natural beauty, Fort Vancouver attracted a diverse population of Native Americans and Europeans.

Finally, in 1846, the United States and Great Britain peacefully resolved their territorial differences and divided the Oregon country at the 49th Parallel, although the HBC did not formally abandon the fort until 1860. The 209-acre Fort Vancouver National Historic Site was set aside in 1948, and in 1996, the larger 366-acre Vancouver National Historic Reserve was established to protect adjacent, historically significant areas, including Fort Vancouver National Historic Site, as well as Vancouver Barracks, Officers' Row, Pearson Field, the Water Resources Education Center, and portions of the Columbia River waterfront. Admission is $2 per person or $4 per family. The Fort Vancouver Visitor Center is open year-round from 9 A.M. until 4 P.M. (and until 5 P.M. from November through February) and offers a fifteen-minute video and numerous exhibits depicting Fort Vancouver and its role in the exploration, settlement, and development of the Pacific Northwest. The General O.O. Howard House, which serves as the visitor center for the reserve, is also open year-round, and it features a fifteen-minute introductory video, daily interpretive walks and talks on a variety of topics, historic exhibits, and living-history demonstrations in the kitchen, blacksmith shop, carpenter shop, bakehouse, and period garden. On summer weekends, cultural programs and evening programs are also available.

There are no food, lodging, or camping facilities at the site, but all traveler services are available in Portland and Vancouver.

For more information, write Fort Vancouver National Historic Site, 612 East Reserve Street, Vancouver, WA 98661-3897, or telephone (360) 696-7655, extension 17, or (800) 832-3599. The park's Web site is www.nps.gov/fova.

FURTHER READING
Fort Vancouver: Fort Vancouver National Historic Site, Washington. Washington, DC: National Park Service, 1981.

Merritt, Jane T. *The Administrative History of Fort Vancouver National Historic Site.* Seattle, WA: National Park Service, Pacific Northwest Region, 1993.

Schwantes, Carlos. *The Pacific Northwest: An Interpretive History.* Lincoln: University of Nebraska Press, 1996.

Taylor, Terri A., and Patricia C. Erigero. *Cultural Landscape Report: Fort Vancouver National Historic*

Site, Vancouver, Washington. Seattle, WA: National Park Service, Pacific Northwest Region, 1992.

FOSSIL BUTTE NATIONAL MONUMENT

Location: Kemmerer, Wyoming
Acreage: 8,198
Established: October 23, 1972

In southwestern Wyoming, amid the flat, rolling topography so typical of the Great Plains, lies a remarkable geologic treasure, the best site in the Americas for paleontological research. Some 50 million years ago, this sea of grass was instead a land of lakes, covering the region of present-day Wyoming, Utah, and Colorado. These ancient waters—Lake Gosiute, Lake Uinta, and Fossil Lake (which is the smallest)—supported what was a dynamic forest ecosystem, and, in their sediments, they preserved the most noteworthy historical record of freshwater fossil fish ever found in the United States. The shaley limestone, known as the Green River Formation, records an exceptional 2-million-year span of plant, insect, fish, reptile, and mammal life, and the fossilized details are simply exceptional. Many of the more than twenty species of fish, for example, retain not only their entire skeletons but their teeth, delicate scales, and skin as well. While the monument's fossils have unlocked many secrets of the ancient world for scientists, there is strong evidence of massive fish die-offs here, and the answer to this mystery has remained elusive.

Fossil Butte National Monument was established on October 23, 1972, in order to preserve these internationally significant fossil-bearing rock formations. The 8,198-acre park is located just 15 miles west of the town of Kemmerer in southwestern Wyoming. Admission is free. The park's visitor center is open from 8 A.M. until 4:30 P.M. from September through May and until 7 P.M. June through August. It features a display of museum-quality fossils, video programs, a bookstore, and an information desk. During the summer months, park rangers offer fossil preparation demonstrations, interpretive programs, and guided nature hikes. Visitors can also enjoy two self-guided trails available in the monument: The Historic Quarry Trail provides the opportunity for a closer look at a high desert environment and the site of a historic fossil quarry, while the Fossil Lake Trail winds through an aspen grove and affords visitors a look at the wildflowers and wildlife of the region. Herds of elk, pronghorn antelope, mule deer, and even a few moose frequent the park, while smaller mammals such as jackrabbits, badgers, porcupines, coyotes, and prairie dogs are resident year-round. Hiking is allowed throughout the monument, except for those areas that are clearly marked as closed. Elevations within the park range from 6,600 feet to over 8,000 feet above sea level. Summers bring hot, sunny days and pleasantly cool nights, while winters are cold with moderate snowfall.

There are no food, lodging, or camping facilities at the monument, but all traveler services are available in Kemmerer.

For more information, write Fossil Butte National Monument, P.O. Box 592, Kemmerer, WY 83101-0592, or telephone (307) 877-4455. The park's Web site is www.nps.gov/fobu.

FURTHER READING

Kiver, Eugene P., and David V. Harris. *Geology of U.S. Parklands.* New York: John Wiley and Sons, 1999.

McGrew, Paul Orman, and Michael Casilliano. *The Geological History of Fossil Butte National Monument and Fossil Basin.* Washington, DC: National Park Service, 1975.

FREDERICK DOUGLASS NATIONAL HISTORIC SITE

Location: Washington, D.C.
Acreage: 9
Established: September 5, 1962

Frederick Douglass, one of the most prominent abolitionists of his time, c. 1879. *(National Archives)*

No individual more clearly demonstrated the ills of slavery to nineteenth-century America than did Frederick Douglass. Born the son of a plantation owner and a slave girl in 1818, Douglass escaped from slavery as a young man and became one of the most prominent abolitionists—antislavery advocates—and certainly the most prominent African American opponent of slavery in mid-nineteenth-century America. The publication of his autobiography, *Narrative of the Life of Frederick Douglass, An American Slave*, in 1846 forced him to flee to England and Scotland to avoid slave catchers. While he was in England, British abolitionists purchased his freedom, an event that made Douglass an even more persistent opponent of slavery. Douglass returned to the United States and published an antislavery weekly newspaper, *The North Star*, in Rochester, New York. The symbolism of the title was significant; the North Star was

the guide for many slaves who escaped and followed the Underground Railway to freedom.

Despite his vehement position, Douglass advocated a political end to slavery. In a dramatic meeting just before the conflagration that was to start a slave insurrection, Douglass declined to support the efforts of John Brown to raid the federal arsenal at Harpers Ferry, testimony to Douglass's faith in other ways to end the peculiar institution. Some have called him the father of civil rights, and his involvement in causes beyond the antislavery movement, such as women's rights and general human rights, attests to the breadth of his vision of equality. "I am not only an American slave, but a man," Douglass wrote fellow abolitionist William Lloyd Garrison in 1846. "As such [I] am bound to use my powers for the welfare of the whole human brotherhood." His vision of an inclusive nation free of discrimination foreshadowed efforts to achieve human rights and civil rights in the twentieth century.

Douglass enjoyed a distinguished career as a journalist, speaker, author, publisher, and social reformer. He published a second autobiography, *My Bondage and My Freedom*; gave many famous speeches, including the famous "What to the Slave Is the Fourth of July"; and served as an adviser to presidents, including Abraham Lincoln, Ulysses S. Grant, Rutherford B. Hayes, James A. Garfield, and Benjamin Harrison. Lincoln often called Douglass the most meritorious man of the nineteenth century; Harrison appointed him U.S. ambassador to the Caribbean nation of Haiti. He was nominated for the vice presidency of the United States in 1872 on the Equal Rights Party ticket, topped by feminist Victoria Woodhull. Throughout his life, he maintained a vigorous speaking schedule, carrying his ideas throughout the nation. In 1894, the year before he died, Douglass gave a torrid antilynching speech called "Lessons of the Hour." Observers said that the aging Douglass mustered all the passion and fury of his youth in one of his last public speeches.

In 1872, Douglass moved from Rochester, New York, to the nation's capital, settling in his home at Cedar Hill in 1878. The home created there played a central role in the struggle for civil rights in the late nineteenth century. It is filled with his personal effects, gifts from well-known figures such as Harriet Beecher Stowe, the author of *Uncle Tom's Cabin*, Abraham Lincoln, and others. His most treasured books are located there, as are mementos of a career in public life. The 9-acre site contains Douglass's home and a visitor center, and a range of interpretive materials that allow visitors to delve more deeply into Douglass's life can be found there.

The park is open from 9 A.M. to 5 P.M. daily during the spring and summer and from 9 A.M. to 4 P.M. during the fall and winter. The historic site can be reached from the Eleventh Street Bridge (toward Anacostia) by going to Martin Luther King Avenue; continue straight for 3 blocks and turn left on W Street; follow W Street for 4 blocks to the visitor center parking lot on the right. The Anacostia Metro Station on the Green Line is the closest stop. Connect to a B-2 (Mount Rainer) bus. A bus stop is directly in front of the home. Continue down W Street to Fifteenth Street. The visitor center is about 2 blocks from the stop on your right. Home tours cost $3 for the day, and space is limited to 47 visitors per tour. It is recommended that all visitors make a reservation. Groups of 10 persons or more must make reservations in advance. Home tours for seniors (sixty-two and over) are $1.50 for the day. Children five years and younger are admitted without charge.

For more information, write Frederick Douglass National Historic Site, 1411 W Street SE, Washington, DC 20020, or telephone (202) 426-5961. The park's Web site is www.nps.gov/frdo.

FURTHER READING

Douglass, Frederick. *Frederick Douglass: Autobiographic Narrative of the Life of Frederick Douglass, an American Slave/My Bondage and My Freedom/Life and Times of Frederick Douglass.* Edited by Henry Louis Gates. New York: Library of America, 1994.

Lampe, Gregory P. *Frederick Douglass: Freedom's Voice, 1818–1845.* East Lansing: Michigan State University Press, 1998.

FREDERICK LAW OLMSTED NATIONAL HISTORIC SITE

Location: Brookline, Massachusetts
Acreage: 7
Established: October 12, 1979

> It is one great purpose of the Park to supply to the hundreds of thousands of tired workers, who have no opportunity to spend their summers in the country, a specimen of God's handiwork that shall be to them, inexpensively, what a month or two in the White Mountains or the Adirondacks is, at great cost, to those in easier circumstances.

So wrote Frederick Law Olmsted (1822–1903) of perhaps his most famous accomplishment: New York City's Central Park, the first of thousands of urban parks and landscapes attributed to Olmsted, his sons, and successors. The founder of the profession of landscape architecture in the United States and the nation's premier urban park designer, Olmsted created a remarkable legacy of 5,000 public and private landscapes that endure to the present day and comprise a vital part of our national heritage.

A native New Englander, Olmsted developed a love for countryside landscapes early in life. In 1850, after a few years as an engineer's apprentice, he traveled to Europe to study the designs and landscapes of various estate grounds and urban parks. Just prior to the Civil War, in 1858, Olmsted teamed with renowned architect Calvert Vaux to design and oversee the construction of New York City's Central Park, which they envisioned as "a single work of art." After its completion in 1865, Olmsted turned his talents to other urban areas, creating Boston's Fenway Park system, New York's Prospect Park, and the community of Riverdale near Chicago, among others. During the mid-1860s, this dedicated conservationist also headed a commission to investigate the possibility—and potential problems—of turning California's Yosemite River Valley into a park for public recreational purposes. His imprint remains in the Yosemite Valley today.

In 1883, Olmsted moved into a Brookline, Massachusetts, farm to establish the nation's first professional landscape architecture firm. Olmsted's firm was part of an important revolution in American professions, the distinction increasingly being made between aficionados—amateurs who practiced—and the empirical and often science-based credentialed professionals who followed them. Olmsted foreshadowed the nation's first trained forester, Gifford Pinchot, as well those in biology, archeology, and countless other professions. The practice remained in the family, with Olmsted's office complex serving as the base of operations for his sons John Charles (1852–1920) and Frederick Jr. (1870–1957), both of whom were trained in landscape design and worked at the firm. During his lifetime, Olmsted's fame seemed to know no bounds. His commissions included exclusive private estates such as George Vanderbilt's Biltmore, national monuments such as the Jefferson Memorial, whole city park systems for Seattle and Louisville, Stanford University, and the site for the 1893 Chicago Exposition.

Established in 1979, the 7-acre Frederick Law Olmsted National Historic Site preserves and interprets the home and office of America's foremost landscape architect, while the grounds form a living exhibit of Olmsted's design ideals. Guided tours are available Friday through Sunday, and admission is free. Located on the first floor of the historic Olmsted home is the visitor information area, which is open all year from 10 A.M. until 4:30 P.M. and contains information, a bookstore, and interpretive exhibits featuring a variety of Olmsted landscapes throughout the United States. A seventeen-minute orientation video, "From Pencil to Park: Preserving Olmsted Landscapes," is shown prior to guided tours. Park rangers also lead guided walks, and the park sponsors a lecture series from January through March. Parking at the site is limited, and the best times to visit are in the spring and fall.

The Olmsted Archives is one of the largest and most widely researched museum collections in the National Park Service. When the Park Service assumed responsibility for the site in 1979, most of the archival records were rapidly deteriorating and inaccessible to the public. Park Service staff quickly set to work inventorying and preserving the documents, making accessible nearly 1 million records dating from the 1860s, including an estimated 150,000 landscape architectural plans and drawings and thousands of photographic prints and negatives, planting lists, lithographs, letters, financial records, and reports. Every year park and urban planners from across the country and around the world use these documents to restore, rehabilitate, and rebuild public landscapes. In all, the Olmsted Archives house records for 5,000 projects including many of America's most treasured landscapes—the U.S. Capitol and White House grounds, Great Smoky Mountains and Acadia National Parks, New York City's Central Park—as well as planned residential communities, school and college campuses, arboretums and reservations, institutional grounds, and private estates.

Although there are no traveler services in the park, a wide variety of restaurants and many opportunities for overnight lodging and camping are located within close proximity to the park and the greater Boston metropolitan area.

For more information, write Frederick Law Olmsted National Historic Site, 99 Warren Street, Brookline, MA 02146-5998 or telephone (617) 566-1689. The park's Web site is www.nps.gov/frla.

FURTHER READING

Carden, Marie L. *Fairsted: Home and Office of Frederick Law Olmsted: Frederick Law Olmsted National Historic Site.* Brookline, MA: Northeast Cultural Resources Center, Northeast Region National Park Service, 1998.

Fein, Albert. *Frederick Law Olmsted and the American Environmental Tradition.* New York: Braziller, 1972.

Fisher, Irving D. *Frederick Law Olmsted and the City Planning Movement in the United States.* Ann Arbor, MI: UMI Research, 1986.

FREDERICKSBURG AND SPOTSYLVANIA NATIONAL MILITARY PARK

Location: Fredericksburg, Virginia
Acreage: 8,352
Established: February 14, 1927

The Civil War was the bloodiest war in American history, and the fierce fighting that occurred in the vicinity of Fredericksburg, Virginia, made this ground the bloodiest on the North American continent. Approximately 110,000 casualties occurred during four major battles fought here: Fredericksburg (December 11–13, 1862); Chancellorsville (April 27–May 6, 1863); the Wilderness (May 5–6, 1863); and Spotsylvania Court House (May 8–21, 1864). In 1927, Congress established the Fredericksburg and Spotsylvania National Military Park to commemorate these significant battles and to honor the men who gave their lives. Today, the widely scattered park also includes the historic structures of Chatham, Ellwood, Salem Church, and the "Stonewall" Jackson Shrine. It is the world's largest military park.

On November 7, 1862, Union General Ambrose E. Burnside inherited the Army of the Potomac from indecisive George McClellan. Burnside, whose facial hair inspired the term "sideburns," determined to move decisively against Confederate General Robert E. Lee and swiftly marched his troops to Fredericksburg. Though he should have had the upper hand, Burnside's leadership left much to be desired and his forces failed to halt the rebels. Lee suffered 5,300 casualties but inflicted more than twice that many losses on his opponent. It was a hollow victory for Lee. The North, though discouraged by the defeat, quickly made up the battle's losses in manpower and material, but by 1862, Lee found it increasingly difficult to replace lost soldiers from the depleted Confederacy and he needed supplies. Fredericksburg established a pattern repeated at Chancellorsville. Confederate success at Chancellorsville was often referred to as "Lee's greatest victory," but the tangible results were not impressive. Although Lee's Army of Northern Virginia had sustained fewer total casualties than the federals—13,000 and 17,000, respectively, the percentages were significant: 13 percent of Union troops and 22 percent of Lee's troops were lost. Even more important, Lee lost Thomas J. "Stonewall" Jackson, his greatest cavalry general and most respected peer, creating a vacancy that could never be filled.

Lee's triumph at Chancellorsville also provided Lee with false security. The victory imbued him with a sense of invincibility, and he confidently marched north to Gettysburg. The new Union general, Ulysses S. Grant, decided to squeeze the Confederacy into submission by wearing down Lee's forces. Because the North possessed such vast resources, including men, Grant knew he could win a war of attrition, and he fought relentlessly at the Wilderness, described by one observer as the war's most bloody, chaotic

Burial place, Fredericksburg, Virginia, c. 1860–1865. *(National Archives)*

battle. Those who fought at Spotsylvania might argue this claim. As Grant pressed east, his troops again met Lee's forces at Spotsylvania Court House. For twenty hours, both sides fought in an unrelenting hand-to-hand slaughter in fog and thick mud, a confusing bedlam that even saw the use of bloody fisticuffs when weapons were lost in the confusion. Losses during the two weeks at Spotsylvania were staggering; the Union suffered 18,000 casualties, while the Confederacy endured 10,000 casualties, but Lee suffered disproportionately. His officer corps had been devastated, and replacing them this late in the war was impossible. Although Grant did not win the decisive victory he sought here, his

merciless hammering of the Confederacy continued at Cold Harbor and Petersburg and eventually forced Lee to surrender at Appomattox.

The 8,352-acre National Military Park was established in 1927 and assigned to the War Department for administration. Until 1933, the War Department managed most battlefields, maintaining a patriotic feeling about them. Each year on the anniversary of the battle, the families and descendants of Confederate and Union soldiers met on the Civil War battlefields and picnicked and camped out in commemoration of the battle. Such public sentiment led to preservation efforts. In 1933, Roosevelt's reorganization of the government transferred all federal battlefields to the Park Service.

The park is open year-round from dawn to dusk, and entrance fees are $3 per person. The military park maintains 2 visitor centers—at Chancellorsville and Fredericksburg battlefields—which are open all year from 9 A.M. until 5 P.M. Both facilities offer guided walking tours led by historians on weekends during the spring and fall, and daily during the peak summer tourist season. Each center contains exhibits about the battles fought there as well as a twelve-minute slide presentation. The Wilderness Battlefield Exhibit Shelter and the Spotsylvania Battlefield Exhibit Shelter are staffed by historians daily during the summer and on weekends in the spring and fall, and both feature exhibits on the battles. The historic Chatham Manor is open from 9 A.M. until 5 P.M. and has exhibits on the house's place in Civil War history and the fifteen families who owned the home. The "Stonewall" Jackson Shrine, where Lee's beloved general died, contains interpretive exhibits and is staffed by a historian. Salem Church and Ellwood also contain exhibits and are open seasonally. There are many outdoor exhibits, as the park is designed as an "outdoor classroom" for those interested in studying the battles, and park roads link tour stops on all four of the battlefields. Numerous walking trails provide access to additional areas. These walks include: Sunken Road, National Cemetery, Marye's Heights, Chancellorsville History Trail, Hazel Grove, Salem Church, Gordon Flank Attack, Widow Tapp Field, Spotsylvania History Trail, and the Bloody Angle. Folders for these trails are available in the visitor centers.

There are no food, lodging, or camping facilities located in the park, but Fredericksburg has all traveler services, and there are numerous developed campgrounds in the area.

For more information, write Fredericksburg and Spotsylvania National Military Park, 120 Chatham Lane, Fredericksburg, VA 22405, or telephone (540) 373-6122. The park's informative Web site is www.nps.gov/frsp.

FURTHER READING

Krick, Robert K. *Stonewall Jackson at Cedar Mountain.* Chapel Hill: University of North Carolina Press, 1990.

Matter, William D. *If It Takes All Summer: The Battle of Spotsylvania.* Chapel Hill: University of North Carolina Press, 1988.

O'Reilly, Francis Augustin. *The Fredericksburg Campaign: Winter War on the Rappahannock.* Baton Rouge: Louisiana State University Press, 2003.

Robertson, James I., Jr. *Stonewall Jackson: The Man, the Soldier, the Legend.* New York: Macmillan, 1997.

Sears, Stephen W. *Chancellorsville.* Boston: Houghton Mifflin, 1996.

FRIENDSHIP HILL NATIONAL HISTORIC SITE

Location: Point Marion, Pennsylvania
Acreage: 675
Established: November 10, 1978

Friendship Hill National Historic Site preserves the country estate of Swiss emigrant Albert Gallatin (1761–1849) and commemorates his thirteen years of service as secretary of the treasury during the presidential administrations of Thomas Jefferson and James Madison. Gallatin was a remarkable man, along with Alexander Hamilton, an early financial wizard who transformed the new republic through the application of capital. Gallatin's tenure in office was quite notable by any measure; between 1801 and 1813, he reduced the national debt, purchased the Louisiana Territory from France, funded the Lewis and Clark Expedition, and was instrumental in negotiating an end to the War of 1812.

A businessman by trade, Gallatin first arrived in southwestern Pennsylvania in the mid-1780s. Because the area was at the edge of the westward-expanding frontier, Gallatin believed the region around the Monongahela River might prove vital for increased business opportunities. In 1789, Gallatin began construction on an estate that he called Friendship Hill, at a point about 3 miles north of Point Marion, Pennsylvania, and for more than forty years he called Friendship Hill home. In addition to his career as a public servant, Gallatin was also a scholar, and his later years were largely devoted to the study of Native American languages. His meticulous attention to facts and procedures brought him international recognition, and in 1842 he became a founder of the American Ethnological Society.

Authorized in 1978, the 675-acre Friendship Hill National Historic Site was part of the revolution in national park–area establishment, engineered by Representative Phil Burton of California. Burton expanded the range of the park system by judiciously using his power in the House of Representatives to add park bills to omnibus bills. Parks such as Friendship Hill allowed political ends as well as broadening the themes preserved in the national park system.

Friendship Hill is open daily, year-round, and there is no admission fee. The Gallatin House Visitor Center contains interpretive exhibits and special programs on Gallatin's multifaceted life. Rangers lead tours of the house during the summer, and it is open the rest of the year for self-guided audio tours. The park features special programs, concerts, and lectures on summer weekends, and a "FestiFall" on the last Sunday in September. The site also has nearly 10 miles of hiking trails that lead around the expansive estate. A short loop trail passes by the graves of Gallatin and his first wife, Sophia, while another trail follows the Monongahela River through verdant meadows, woods, and streams.

While there are no food, lodging, or camping facilities at the site, Point Marion has restaurants and cafés, while Uniontown and Morgantown, West Virginia, have food and lodging. Coopers Rock State Forest, located about 10 miles east of Morgantown, offers a developed campground.

For more information, write Friendship Hill National Historic Site, 1 Washington Parkway, Farmington, PA 15437, or telephone (724) 725-9190. The park's Web site is www.nps.gov/frhi.

FURTHER READING

Kuppenheimer, L.B. *Albert Gallatin's Vision of Democratic Stability: An Interpretive Profile.* Westport, CT: Praeger, 1996.

Walters, R. *Albert Gallatin: Jefferson Financier and Diplomat.* New York: Macmillan, 1957.

G

GATES OF THE ARCTIC NATIONAL PARK AND PRESERVE

Location: Bettles, Alaska
Acreage: 8,472,506
Established: December 1, 1978

Located in the isolated central Brooks Range in northern Alaska, Gates of the Arctic National Park and Preserve is a vast 8.4-plus-million-acre area of untrammeled natural beauty and exceptional scientific value. America's second largest national park, Gates of the Arctic survived into the twentieth century without significant defilement because of its remote location and its rugged and inhospitable nature. The park is a maze of wild glaciated valleys and rugged mountains covered with boreal forest and arctic tundra, all inhabited by populations of caribou, Dall sheep, wolves, and grizzly and black bears.

Established as a national monument as part of the Alaskan Native Claims Settlement Act of 1978, Gates of the Arctic became a national park during the lame duck portion of President Jimmy Carter's term in 1980. After Carter's trouncing in the 1980 election, the departing proconservation Congress moved to complete a number of initiatives. Conservation goals loomed large among these objectives. Reagan ran on an antigovernment platform and pledged his allegiance to the Sagebrush Rebellion, a late-1970s movement that sought to end federal land ownership in a number of western states. Gates of the Arctic and many other Alaskan parklands were put on sound footing by the departing Congress's courageous action.

Located about 200 miles northwest of Fairbanks in the Brooks Range, Gates of the Arctic is the park system's northernmost park. The Brooks Range plays an important part in the history of American conservation, for Wilderness Society founder Robert Marshall, a prolific author and thinker about nature and wilderness, spent much of his short life in its development. The park incorporates several other elements, including the national park, national preserve, a wilderness, six Wild Rivers, and two national natural landmarks, under the park's heading. True to its wild nature, the park has few visitor improvements, including roads, trails, or visitor services. Information is available at the Bettles Ranger Station/Visitor Center in Bettles Field and seasonally at the Coldfoot Interagency Visitor Center in Coldfoot. One Alaska Indian community is located within the park's boundaries; its residents and those of eight other adjacent communities use the park's lands and waters for subsistence hunting, fishing, trapping, and gathering.

The central Brooks Range has long, severe winters and relatively short, rainy, cool summers. The entire region receives continuous sunlight during the summer for at least thirty days. The south side of the Brooks Range is generally a subarctic climate zone, with low precipitation. June through September is the wettest time of year, and freezing temperatures may occur at any time, but particularly from mid-August on. July may be the only month that snow does not fall. Winters are extreme, long, and cold. Snow is guaranteed to fall eight or nine months of the year, averaging 60 to 80 inches. Average minimum and maximum January temperatures are minus 10 and minus 30 degrees. Each year, approximately 4,000 recreationists visit the park, primarily in the perpetual-daylight summer months.

Because there are no roads to or in the park, access is often a challenge. The Dalton Highway comes within about 5 miles of the park's eastern boundary, but necessitates a rugged hike into the park (from the Dalton Highway between milepost 190 to milepost 276 and across one or two rivers then over mountain passes), so most visitors arrive by air. Scheduled air taxis from Fairbanks serve Anaktuvuk Pass, Bettles, and Coldfoot, and charter flights may also be arranged.

There are no food, lodging, or camping facilities in Gates of the Arctic. Limited commercial facilities exist in Anaktuvuk Pass, Bettles, Coldfoot, and Wiseman, and there is a Bureau of Land Management campground at Dalton Highway milepost 180, 5 miles north of Coldfoot, which is open from June through mid-September. Supplies are not available within the park; visitors must be completely self-sufficient. All visitors must adhere to Alaska state hunting and fishing guidelines and regulations. Sport hunting is allowed in the Gates of the Arctic Preserve areas. As in other national parks, artifact collection is prohibited, including (but not limited to) antlers, wildflowers, bark, and so on. Since Alaska is a relatively young state, items from as recently as the 1960s (tin cans, tools, newspapers, magazines, etc.) may be considered historical artifacts and should not be collected.

For more information, write Gates of the Arctic National Park and Preserve, P.O. Box 74680, Fairbanks, AK 99707, or telephone (907) 456-0281. The park's Web site is www.nps.gov/gaar.

FURTHER READING

Catton, Theodore. *Inhabited Wilderness: Indians, Eskimos, and National Parks in Alaska.* Albuquerque: University of New Mexico Press, 1997.

Cohen, Michael P. *The History of the Sierra Club, 1892–1970.* San Francisco, CA: Sierra Club Books, 1988.

Glover, James M. *A Wilderness Original: The Life of Bob Marshall.* Seattle, WA: Mountaineers Books, 1986.

Sutter, Paul. *Driven Wild: How the Fight Against Automobiles Launched the Modern Wilderness Movement.* Seattle: University of Washington Press, 2002.

GATEWAY NATIONAL RECREATION AREA

Location: New Jersey and New York
Acreage: 26,607
Established: October 27, 1972

Established in 1972 as one of America's first urban national recreation areas, Gateway National Recreation Area comprises 26,000 acres at the entrance to New York City's harbor. Divided into 4 units across 2 states, the park extends from Sandy Hook, New Jersey, through Staten Island, New York and into the Jamaica Bay and Rockaway Peninsula areas of Brooklyn and Queens boroughs. The thin arms of land that are the Breezy Point and Sandy Hook Units stretch out to make a literal "gateway" to New York harbor. The other 2 units, Staten Island and Jamaica Bay, lie near or within the arms themselves.

Gateway National Recreation Area was part of the revolution in national park proclamation that began with the Johnson administration's idea of "parks for the people where the people are." After the race riots in 1965 and 1966, the administration looked to extend the reach of the park system to American cities, creating places where people could play and learn. The Nixon administration embraced this concept as well, developing the first two urban national recreation areas, Gateway and its counterpart in San Francisco, Golden Gate National Recreation Area. Such parks represented a broader and less elite vision of what national parks could be.

Gateway is the country's fifth most visited national park site, with nearly 7 million visitors each year. During the spring and fall, more than 365 species of birds migrate through the recreation area, while September and October feature monarch butterflies in profusion. The recreation area protects and preserves a variety of natural and historical features, including saltwater marshes, beaches, wildlife habitats, historic forts and airfields, the nation's oldest operating lighthouse, New York City's first municipal airport, and the oldest military site in America.

New York's Breezy Point Unit contains 2 National Register of Historic Places sites: the bathhouse at Jacob Riis Park and a former harbor defense site, historic Fort Tilden. It also has numerous beaches, as well as other recreational facilities for swimming, surf fishing, baseball, rugby, and other sports. During the Memorial Day weekend, this unit hosts an Irish festival and from June through August visitors can enjoy the Fort Tilden Concert Series. Call (718) 318-4300 for detailed information on special unit programs and activities.

The Jamaica Bay Unit contains a wildlife refuge which provides a critical habitat for more than 300 species of birds. It also contains New York City's first airport, the historic Floyd Bennett Field, which serves as the refuge's headquarters. The visitor center features exhibits on the natural history of the area and a description of how this bird sanctuary was created in the 1950s. In addition to its scenic wonders, Jamaica Bay also boasts fine beach recreational facilities. Call (718) 338-3799 for updated program and activity information, including tours of the airfield.

The Sandy Hook Unit, located in Monmouth County, New Jersey, includes a holly forest, the colonial-era Fort Hancock, and another National Register structure—the oldest continuously operated lighthouse in America. Ranger-led tours of the forest and the fort are offered daily. The Beach Concert Series runs from June through August, and in September, the Sandy Hook Unit hosts the Shore Heritage festival. Call the unit at (732) 872-5970 for updated schedules and other activities.

The Staten Island Unit has yet another historic airfield, Miller Field, which served seaplanes of the U.S. Air Service after World War I. It also includes historic Fort Wadsworth, a 200-year-old fort designed to protect New York's harbor from attack. Ranger-led tours of the fort and airfield are offered daily. The Staten Island Unit is the location for the New York City Five-Borough Bike Tour in May and the New York City Marathon in November. For more information, call (718) 354-4500 for updated information and hours of operation.

Gateway National Recreation Area is a day-use area only, and it is open year-round, including major holidays, from dawn to dusk. It is best to call a specific unit to get updated information on hours of operation for tour-specific locations like the forts and lighthouse. Although there is no admission fee to each unit, some visitor sites charge admission for tours and special events. In addition, beach parking fees are charged at Sandy Hook and Jacob Riis Park during the summer; annual passes are available for Sandy Hook. Camping is limited to organized groups by reservation only at 4 primitive sites in the Sandy Hook Unit. The New York City metropolitan area has all other travel services.

For more information, write Gateway National Recreation Area Headquarters, Floyd Bennett Field Building 69, Brooklyn, NY 11234-7097, or telephone (718) 338-33688. The park's Web site is www.nps.gov/gate.

FURTHER READING

Bearss, Edwin C. *Historic Resource Study, Fort Hancock 1895–1948, Gateway National Recreation Area, New York.* Denver, CO: Denver Service Center, Historic Preservation Division, National Park Service, 1981.

GAULEY RIVER NATIONAL RECREATION AREA

Location: Glen Jean, West Virginia
Acreage: 11,507
Established: October 26, 1988

West Virginia's Gauley River National Recreation Area protects 25 miles of the free-flowing Gauley River and 6 miles of the Meadow River, which tumble and roar through dramatic gorges and bucolic valleys. The park is also home to some of the most challenging whitewaters in the eastern United States; several Class-5+ rapids make the Gauley one of the most difficult whitewater boating stretches in the East. Dropping around 28 feet per mile through a scenic, 300-foot-deep gorge, the Gauley River challenges even the most experienced rafters. It is prized by the whitewater rafting community as one of the gems of the United States.

Established in 1988, the more-than-11,000-acre Gauley River National Recreation Area also protects numerous sites of cultural significance, including Carnifex Ferry Battlefield State Park, where a September 10, 1861, Union victory assured West Virginia's petition for statehood. The National Recreation Area is located between Summersville and Fayetteville in central West Virginia; it is open year-round, with no admission fees. The park maintains 2 visitor centers. The U.S. Army Corps of Engineers visitor information station is located at Summersville Dam, and tours are offered daily. The nearest Park Service visitor center is at Canyon Rim, approximately 20 miles south on U.S. Highway 19. It contains information and exhibits on the area's natural and cultural history. Ranger-led hikes are available year-round, and in September, visitors can witness Civil War battle reenactments at Carnifex Ferry Battlefield State Park. Visitation is usually highest in September and October, during the peak whitewater season, and lowest in winter. Vehicle access is from West Virginia Highway 129 at Summersville Dam, and from Swiss Road off West Virginia Highway 39. Much of the land within the authorized boundaries of the national recreation area remains private property, a result of the recent establish-

ment of the area and the lack of a federal allocation to acquire additional acreage. As a result, Gauley River National Recreation Area feels very wild, apart from the development above and below the park. A new hydropower facility, under construction beginning in 1999, will provide greater access but may change the wild feel of the area.

There are no food, lodging, or camping facilities available in the recreation area, but nearby communities offer all traveler services. The Park Service operates a primitive campground at the Tailwaters Area suitable for RVs as well as tents, and camping is also available at nearby Babcock State Park and at Summersville Lake. Lodging is available at Hawk's Nest and Babcock state parks and in neighboring towns.

For more information, write Gauley River National Recreation Area, c/o New River Gorge National River, P.O. Box 246, Glen Jean, WV 25846-0246, or telephone (304) 465-0508. The park's interesting Web site is www.nps.gov/gari.

FURTHER READING

Connely, John Ed Grove, John Porterfield, and Charlie Walbridge. *Appalachian Whitewater: The Northern States.* 4th ed. Birmingham, AL: Menasha Ridge, 2001.

Mozier, Jeanne. *Way Out in West Virginia: A Must-Have Guide to the Oddities and Wonders of the Mountain State.* Charleston, WV: Quarrier, 1999.

Rice, Otis K., and Stephen W. Brown. *West Virginia: A History.* Lexington: University Press of Kentucky, 1993.

GENERAL GRANT NATIONAL MEMORIAL

Location: New York, New York
Acreage: .76
Established: April 27, 1897

Popularly known as Grant's Tomb, General Grant National Memorial in New York City is the final resting place of Ulysses S. Grant and his wife, Julia Dent Grant. Born on April 27, 1822, Grant graduated from West Point in 1843 and served as a quartermaster during the Mexican-American War. Although he resigned from the army in 1854, Grant returned to military service with the outbreak of Civil War, and he quickly rose to the rank of brigadier general through his leadership abilities and tactical skills.

Decisive victories at Fort Henry, Fort Donelson, and Vicksburg earned Grant his second general's star in 1863. After the successful siege of Chattanooga the following year, Lincoln promoted Grant to lieutenant general and placed him in full command of all Union armies. The Army of the Potomac under his command finally forced Robert E. Lee's Army of Northern Virginia to withdraw from Richmond the following spring, and on April 9, 1865, Grant accepted Lee's surrender at Appomattox Court House. In 1866, Congress made Grant the first full General of the Armies in American history.

Because the war hero's popularity was at an all-time high, Grant accepted the Republican Party's nomination for president in 1868. From 1869 to 1877, he served two terms as president. While his administration was marked by scandal, Grant did sign the 1872 act creating Yellowstone National Park. After the presidency, he entered private business on Wall Street. A heavy cigar smoker his entire life, Grant died of advanced throat cancer on July 23, 1885. He was laid to rest in New York City on August 8, with 60,000 marchers in his funeral procession and a million spectators. In 1897, a public ceremony dedicated the 150-foot-high imposing granite

General Grant National Memorial, photographed in the early twentieth century. *(Library of Congress)*

tomb, and in 1959, the National Park Service assumed responsibility for the site, which overlooks the Hudson River in Manhattan's Riverside Park.

Designed by architect John Duncan and completed in 1897, the granite and marble tomb is the largest mausoleum in North America. Located at 122nd Street and Riverside Drive, the General Grant National Memorial is open daily, year-round. Admission, programs, and tours are free. An extensive on-site museum interprets the life and accomplishments of the general and president. Rangers lead programs and tours throughout the day, and costumed interpreters provide living-history descriptions of Grant's role during the Civil War. Visitation is usually highest in July and August, and lowest in February and March.

There are no food, lodging, or camping facilities at the memorial, but New York City has all traveler services. Restaurants are in adjoining neighborhoods and private campgrounds can be found in suburban New York and New Jersey.

For more information, write General Grant National Memorial, 26 Wall Street, New York, NY 10005, or telephone (212) 666-1640. The park's Web site is www.nps.gov/gegr.

FURTHER READING

Catton, Bruce. *Grant Moves South.* Boston: Little, Brown, 1960.
——. *Grant Takes Command.* Boston: Little, Brown, 1969.
Fuller, J.F.C. *The Generalship of Ulysses S. Grant.* New York: Da Capo, 1991.
Grant, Ulysses S. *The Civil War Memoirs of Ulysses S. Grant.* New York: Forge, 2002.

GEORGE ROGERS CLARK NATIONAL HISTORICAL PARK

Location: Vincennes, Indiana
Acreage: 26
Established: July 23, 1966

As morning dawned on February 25, 1779, a visibly shaken Lieutenant Governor Henry Hamilton emerged from Fort Sackville, a British stronghold near the junction of the Wabash and Ohio rivers, and surrendered his command to American George Rogers Clark and his small, ragged band of men. Stunned, the vanquished officer asked, "Colonel Clark, where is your army?" The young Virginian indicated that what Hamilton saw was all that had come with him, and Hamilton became a prisoner knowing, had he continued to fight, he might well have won.

Clark and his men, called the Big Knives, had trekked across the frozen, drowned lands of what is now southern Illinois from Kaskaskia, on the Illinois River, and in this surprise attack, had compelled the British to give up their fort. It was a marvelous triumph, for not only had Clark successfully brought his men through the frozen winter, but he had also captured a much larger and better-armed British force through trickery and a display of intensity that King George III's men could not match. The seizing of the fort had significant political consequences in the post-Revolutionary period as well, giving the United States a legitimate claim on the Old Northwest Territories during the peace process. Without possession of the fort and the territory it controlled, the Americans were simply in no position to make demands. The psychological impact of its capture was even greater; after Clark's victory, no one ever again believed that the British would limit the American nation to the lands between the eastern seaboard and the Appalachian Mountains.

Beginning in the 1920s, to commemorate the exploits of Clark and his men, the federal government constructed the George Rogers Clark National Memorial in Vincennes, Indiana, on the site of Fort Sackville. In the style of the time, the structure was a massive Greco-Roman cupola designed by Frederick

C. Hirons, an architect from New York. Complete with statues and a mural within the cupola, today, the George Rogers Clark Historical Park is pertinent as a symbol of the way Americans in the 1920s designed public commemorative space. Its primary purpose, to commemorate the actions of Clark and his men, reflected tension between urban and rural America during the 1920s.

Clark epitomized the culture of the first American frontier, an ongoing contest between Anglo-American settlers and Native Americans such as the Shawnee that began when Daniel Boone crossed through the Cumberland Gap into Kain-Tuc-Kee–Kentucky–in 1767. For the remainder of the eighteenth century and until the Battle of Tippecanoe in 1811, the settlers and their Native American neighbors built competing villages in which everyone mattered. As a result, they formed alliances and bonds through trade, marriage, and kinship, creating a joint world. The rise of the American republic and its expansion after 1800 brought this world to an end, but Clark's endeavors harkened back to an earlier, more complicated time.

By the twentieth century, nothing remained of the eighteenth-century wood fort, and the memory of George Rogers Clark's exploits had faded. Only a small marker placed on the site in 1905 by the Daughters of the American Revolution attested to the location of this pivotal event. In a culture grappling with the issues of modernity, and with the sesquicentennial of the capture of Fort Sackville fast approaching, commemoration of a nearly lost moment of heroic dimensions seemed a valuable objective.

By the mid-1920s, local initiative led to the formation of a George Rogers Clark Sesquicentennial Commission to raise funds and oversee the construction of a memorial to Clark's feat. They succeeded in arranging the creation of a federal commission, which received a $1 million appropriation for the

George Rogers Clark's march against Vincennes across the Wabash through wilderness and flood, February 1779. *(National Archives)*

structure. Despite the ongoing Great Depression, it was completed in 1936, when President Franklin D. Roosevelt arrived on June 14 to dedicate the memorial, which was managed by the state of Indiana for the next thirty years. The National Park Service took over administration of the George Rogers Clark National Historical Park in 1966.

The park's visitor center in downtown Vincennes, Indiana, is open daily from 9 A.M. until 5 P.M., and the memorial is open from 9 A.M. until 4:45 P.M. (times are Eastern Standard time; most of Indiana does not observe daylight savings time). Entrance fees are $2 for seven days, and a $4 family permit is also available.

For more information, write George Rogers Clark National Historical Park, 401 S. 2nd Street, Vincennes, IN 47591-1001, or telephone (812) 882-1776. The park's Web site is www.nps.gov/gero.

FURTHER READING

Clark, George Rogers, *The Conquest of the Illinois.* Carbondale: Southern Illinois University Press, 2001.

Harrison, Lowell Hayes. *George Rogers Clark and the War in the West.* Lexington: University Press of Kentucky, 2001.

Rothman, Hal K. *Maintaining a Legacy: An Administrative History of George Rogers Clark National Historical Park.* Omaha, NE: National Park Service, 1994.

GEORGE WASHINGTON BIRTHPLACE NATIONAL MONUMENT

Location: Westmoreland County, Virginia
Acreage: 662
Established: January 23, 1930

On February 22, 1732, the first child of Augustine and Mary Ball Washington was born on his father's tobacco farm at Popes Creek in Westmoreland County on Virginia's "Northern Neck," the peninsula formed by the Potomac and Rappahannock rivers as they flow into Chesapeake Bay. More than a half century later, on April 30, 1789, George Washington took his oath of office as the first president of the United States. In his first inaugural address, the precedent-setting president reminded the country that "the preservation of the sacred fire of liberty, and the destiny of the republican model of government, are justly considered as deeply, perhaps as finally staked, on the experiment entrusted to the hands of the American people."

Washington had distinguished himself as a lieutenant colonel during the French and Indian War, though his service almost cost him his life. During the conflict, in 1755, Wash-

ington narrowly escaped injury, when, while he was serving as an aide to General Edward Braddock, four bullets ripped his coat and two horses were shot from under him. He went on to serve with distinction in the Virginia House of Burgesses, but like many of his fellow planters, Washington felt exploited by British merchants and hampered by British regulations. When the Second Continental Congress convened in Philadelphia in May 1775, Washington was elected commander in chief of the Continental Army, in part to cement Virginia to the cause. On July 3, 1775, he took command of his motley troops and embarked upon a war that was to last six grueling years. Washington's strategy was deceptively simple: harass the British, and avoid devastating losses. He reported to Congress, "we should on all Occasions avoid a general Action, or put anything to the Risque, unless compelled by a necessity, into which we ought never to be drawn." This long-term tactic eventually prevailed, and in 1781, with the aid of French allies, Washington forced the surrender of British General Charles Cornwallis at Yorktown.

Although he longed to retire to the pastoral setting at Mount Vernon, Washington encouraged the convening of the Constitutional Convention at Philadelphia in 1787. When the new Constitution was ratified, the Electoral College unanimously elected George Washington president. After serving his two terms, Washington returned at last to his beloved Mount Vernon, where he enjoyed less than three years of retirement; he succumbed to a throat infection on December 14, 1799. For months, the nation mourned the great man.

In 1930, as part of the bicentennial celebration of Washington's birthday, the federal government authorized the 662-acre monument and constructed a Memorial House on the Popes Creek site. Visitors have described the site as one of America's most serene na-

George Washington Birthplace National Monument. *(Library of Congress)*

tional park properties. The George Washington Birthplace National Monument also preserves the ambience of an eighteenth-century Virginia tobacco plantation as a living colonial farm. Other park facilities include the brick foundation of the historic birthplace home site, the colonial farm area, the Washington family cemetery, hiking trails, a picnic area, and a beach.

Located 38 miles east of Fredericksburg on Virginia Route 3 and Route 204, this day-use site is open year-round, and admission is $2 per person, age seventeen years and older. A comprehensive visitor center contains information, items, and artifacts related to Washington family history, and a fourteen-minute film. In addition to ranger-led talks and walks, the park offers guided living-history tours with costumed interpreters. Each spring, archeologists from the Park Service and other institutions conduct detailed explorations of the areas around Popes Creek plantation, and every February, the site celebrates George Washington's Birthday on President's Day and on his actual birthday with special activities.

There are no food, lodging, or camping facilities at the monument, but the nearby towns of Fredericksburg, Montross, and Colonial Beach have all traveler services. Developed campsites with all amenities can be found at Westmoreland State Park, about 7 miles west of the monument on Virginia Highway 3.

For more information, write George Washington Birthplace National Monument, 1732 Popes Creek Road,

Washington's Birthplace, VA 22443, or telephone (804) 224-1732. The park's Web site is www.nps.gov/gewa.

FURTHER READING

Abbot, W.W. *The Young George Washington and His Papers.* Charlottesville: University of Virginia, 1999.

Freeman, Douglas Southall. *George Washington: A Biography.* Clifton, NJ: A.M. Kelley, 1975.

Lewis, Thomas A. *For King and Country: George Washington: The Early Years.* New York: John Wiley and Sons, 1995.

GEORGE WASHINGTON CARVER NATIONAL MONUMENT

Location: Diamond, Missouri
Acreage: 210
Established: July 14, 1943

> Learn to do common things uncommonly well; we must always keep in mind that anything that helps fill the dinner pail is valuable.
>
> *–G.W. Carver*

Born a slave in the early 1860s, George Washington Carver endured the blatant racism of his time and became an American renaissance man. A long career as an educator, botanist, and agronomist brought him global acclaim for his expertise in painting, music, mathematics, and the natural sciences. Nicknamed the "Plant Doctor," Carver offered holistic interpretations of the relationships between science and art, and science and religion. He successfully melded a child's wonder at nature and the calculating inquiry of a research scientist. In this, he was as much as a full century ahead of his time.

Carver's approach to the world stemmed largely from his home place: the Carver family farm on which he was raised. Confederate guerrilla raiders kidnapped him and his mother shortly after his birth. After they returned him, the Carver family–the white couple who owned him and his family until manumission–raised him as one of their own children. Even as a child, plants flourished

under his care, and although denied entry to at least one college because of his race, he entered Simpson College in Iowa in 1890 and astounded his teachers with his knowledge. He began his career as a research botanist at Iowa Agricultural College, which has since become Iowa State University, and in 1896, he joined Booker T. Washington at the Tuskegee Institute in Alabama, where Carver taught botany and agriculture.

Carver drew national attention for the way he revolutionized the agricultural practices of poor southern farmers, both black and white. He urged the cultivation of protein-rich crops such as peanuts and soybeans over the soil-depleting cotton and tobacco and used his knowledge of chemistry to conceive of new products that people could make from such crops. He sought to be of the greatest good to the greatest number of "my people," and his vision was so broad that it helped many others as well. Although often constrained by the racial codes of the nineteenth- and early-twentieth-century United States, Carver transcended the fixed boundaries of the time. In 1921, he spoke to the U.S. House of Representatives about his work, and the Royal Society of Arts in London, England, later awarded him a fellowship. Despite the many ways that his work improved the life of southern whites as well as blacks, he was bound by the American disease of racism. Although he spoke before Congress, the U.S. government never recognized his achievements and he received few honors in his home region. Yet his work spoke for itself, crossing the firm barriers of American society for the betterment of all.

The park is open throughout the year from 9 A.M. until 5 P.M., and it offers a three-quarter-mile nature trail, a museum, and an interactive exhibit area for students. The cultural setting includes the 1881 historic Moses Carver house as well as the Carver cemetery, and park rangers offer guided tours, interpretive talks, and living-history demonstrations. The monument's rolling hills, woodlands, and prairies are located in southwest Missouri, approximately 2 miles west of Diamond, Missouri. There are no camping or lodging facilities in the park, but all traveler services are available nearby.

For more information, write George Washington Carver National Monument, 646 Carver Road, Diamond, MO 64840-8314, or telephone (417) 325-4151. The park's Web site is www.nps.gov/gwca.

FURTHER READING

Carver, George Washington. *George Washington Carver in His Own Words.* Edited by Gary R. Kremer. Columbia: University of Missouri Press, 1987.

McMurry, Linda O. *George Washington Carver, Scientist and Symbol.* New York: Oxford University Press, 1982.

Perry, John. *Unshakable Faith: Booker T. Washington and George Washington Carver.* Sisters, OR: Multnomah, 1999.

GETTYSBURG NATIONAL MILITARY PARK

Location: Gettysburg, Pennsylvania
Acreage: 5,990
Established: February 11, 1895

On November 19, 1863, President Abraham Lincoln came to Gettysburg, Pennsylvania, to dedicate the national cemetery. A little more than four months before, a fierce and pivotal battle raged across the hills and fields for three long, bloody days. The outcome shattered Robert E. Lee's Army of Northern Virginia and forced the invading Confederate forces back, changing the course of the war and paving the way for the eventual Union victory. The battle of Gettysburg marked the beginning of the end of the Civil War. After Gettysburg, Union victory turned from a question of "if" to one of "when."

In this most famous of his speeches, the Gettysburg Address, Lincoln characterized the struggle that had taken place and its meaning to the nation:

Four score and seven years ago our fathers brought forth on this continent a new nation, conceived in Liberty, and dedicated to the proposition that all men are created equal. Now we are engaged in a great civil war, testing whether that nation, or any nation so conceived and so dedicated, can long endure. We are met on a great battlefield of that war. We have come to dedicate a portion of that field, as a final resting place for those who here gave their lives that that nation might live.

In this portion of his brief address, Lincoln summed up both the meaning of the battle and the war that created it, giving life to a sentiment that ever after shaped how Americans saw their past. Gettysburg signaled the birth of the second American republic, the union that replaced the confederation that preceded it. Born in blood and fire, that second republic became the modern American nation.

The battle at Gettysburg began as Lee's army confidently crossed the Potomac River in mid-June in an attempt to cut Washington, D.C., off from the rest of the North and force the Union to pull its troops out of the South. The Pennsylvania Campaign, as the maneuver was called, forced the Union to respond, and the more than 93,000 men under the command of General George G. Meade crossed the Potomac River and hurried to blunt the Confederate advance. Lee brought his 70,000 men to the vicinity of the strategic crossroads town of Gettysburg in southern Pennsylvania. On July 1, the two huge armies first engaged. The outmanned Union soldiers held their ground until late in the day, when the Confederate advance pushed them southward through the town of Gettysburg. The Confederates passed up the opportunity to seize the elevated ground south of town; Union forces took it and established defensive

The battle of Gettysburg, July 3, 1863. *(Library of Congress)*

positions on Cemetery Ridge. Although the Confederates won the day despite the heavy losses on both sides, Union presence on the high ground shaped the remainder of the battle.

The second day began and remained quiet all morning and most of the afternoon, until Union General Daniel E. Sickles inexplicably moved his men off Cemetery Ridge to what appeared from afar to be an advantageous position. Meade had given no such orders. When Sickles took the position, he found it almost indefensible. He deployed his men in a mile-long line along the Emmittsburg Road, anchored in the south by a peach orchard. In effect his men were strung out along the flat-topped ridge that connected Union and Confederate positions. Rather

than protected, they were closer to the Confederates than before and quite vulnerable to attack. A Confederate general ordered to deploy along the Emmittsburg Road found Union soldiers only a few hundred yards away; General Meade was livid and rode up to confront Sickles. Although Sickles was willing to withdraw, the moment had passed. The Confederate advance had begun.

Under the direction of Lieutenant General James Longstreet, Confederate soldiers in two divisions attacked Cemetery Ridge. Major General John B. Hood led his men toward Little Round Top to the south of Cemetery Ridge, but an astute Union officer, the Army of the Potomac's Chief Engineer Gouverneur K. Warren, recognized the danger and led soldiers to its summit minutes before the Confederates arrived. After a brutal struggle, which one soldier called a "terrible medley of cries, shouts, cheers, groans, prayers, curses, bursting shells, whizzing rifle bullets, and clanging steel," the Confederates retreated. Elsewhere along the line, in a rocky area called Devil's Den, Confederates advanced in fierce hand-to-hand combat. They drove the Union soldiers back and seized the area. In the peach orchard, the Confederates came forward as well, unleashing their rebel yell. In the fierce fighting, Sickles was severely wounded, and he eventually lost a leg. His men took fearsome casualties, but held the line. Confederate Lieutenant General A.P. Hill sent his units up Cemetery Ridge. They reached the top and might have held it, but without reinforcements they were forced to retreat when additional Union troops arrived. Darkness hid their descent as well as a battlefield covered with the bodies of the dead and wounded, many crying for relief. Both sides suffered enormous casualties.

The third and final day of the battle proved decisive. During the night, Union strategists decided to maintain their defensive posture, while Lee and his generals determined to attack. Confederate success would stymie the Union, Lee believed, and force an end to the war. About 1 P.M. on July 3, Lee gave the order and the primary assault of the battle began. Confederate artillery pounded the enemy positions, and Union gunners responded in kind. Noise shattered eardrums, clouds of smoke filled the air, and the rebel assault on the center of the Union position started as wave after wave of Confederate soldiers crossed the open fields in an effort to reach the Union lines. By the thousands, they were gunned down by volley after volley of fire. Despite a few temporary successes during the battle, the impact on the Confederates was devastating. As many as 7,000 of the 12,000 men who attacked the Union lines were left on the field of battle, dead or wounded. After a blood-soaked battle along a bend in a stone wall, an area called the Angle, the Confederate advance subsided, and the beaten, battered troops made their way back to Confederate lines. Major General George Pickett, whose men were at the center of the assault, reported: "General Lee, I have no division now," and he exaggerated only a little. The Army of Northern Virginia was crippled and began its retreat to the south. General Meade did not pursue, but Gettysburg was a clear Union victory. The Confederate army that withdrew was missing one-third of its 75,000 men, killed, wounded, or captured, and the military power of the South was greatly diminished. While the Union could call up thousands of new soldiers, after Gettysburg, the South's remaining pool of men could not replenish the ranks.

Gettysburg National Military Park commemorates this decisive battle and its implications in the shaping of the post–Civil War nation. The adjacent national cemetery memorializes the loss. Statues cover the park and grace the cemetery, and the experience of all is both solemn and invigorating. It is impossible to see Gettysburg without feeling the pain of the birth of the new nation, unified by force in the blood of cousins and brothers, of fathers and sons.

The visitor center offers an Electric Map program and a thirty-minute orientation program, as well as the Gettysburg Museum of the Civil War, featuring one of the largest collections of Civil War relics in the world. Visitors should also plan to see the Gettysburg Cyclorama, a 360-degree painting first exhibited in Boston in 1883, which depicts the climactic event of the battle, *Pickett's Charge*. The military park's visitor center is open year-round, from 8 A.M. until 5 P.M. (and until 6 P.M. in the summer), and admission to the park is free, although there is a charge for the Electric Map and Cyclorama programs. Self-guided auto tour route maps are available at

Gettysburg National Military Park. *(National Park Service)*

the visitor center and Cyclorama center information desks, and commercial bus tours of the park are available through companies near the park. A wide variety of interpretive programs are offered April through October, but the core season for programs is mid-June through mid-August. Subjects include the three days of battle, the national cemetery, the Gettysburg Address, and general Civil War–related topics. There are walking tours, bicycle tours, campfire programs, and living-history demonstrations as well.

For more information, write Gettysburg National Military Park, 97 Taneytown Road, Gettysburg, PA 17325-2804, or telephone (717) 334-1124. The park's Web site is www.nps.gov/gett.

FURTHER READING
Basler, Roy P., ed. *Abraham Lincoln: His Speeches and Writings.* New York: Da Capo, 1990.

Hess, Earl. *Pickett's Charge: The Last Confederate Attack at Gettysburg.* Chapel Hill: University of North Carolina Press, 2001.

Kunhardt, Philip B., Jr. *A New Birth of Freedom, Lincoln at Gettysburg.* Boston: Little, Brown, 1983.

Shaara, Michael. *The Killer Angels.* New York: Ballantine Books, 1993.

Wills, Gary. *Lincoln at Gettysburg, the Words That Remade America.* New York: Simon and Schuster, 1992.

GILA CLIFF DWELLINGS NATIONAL MONUMENT
Location: Silver City, New Mexico
Acreage: 533
Established: November 16, 1907

The ruins at southwestern New Mexico's Gila Cliff Dwellings National Monument date back nearly eight hundred years. They offer a glimpse into the homes and lives of prehistoric people of the Mogollon culture, who constructed these stone and adobe dwellings in caves 180 feet above Cliff Dwelling Creek. Five of the cliff's seven caves contained as many as forty separate rooms, which housed eight to ten families at a time. Skilled farmers and potters, the residents subsisted on squash, beans, and corn grown on the moist bottom land, and supplemented their diet with wild berries, nuts, and game such as turkeys, deer, and elk. The Mogollon people lived in the cliffs and surrounding area for about a hundred and fifty years, then they abandoned the dwellings for reasons unknown.

White settlers discovered the cliff dwellings around 1870, and, over the years, locals removed most artifacts from the dwellings, including turquoise beads, sandals, and stone hammers and axes. In 1907, the federal government set aside the monument as part of the rush to preserve American archeology at the start of the twentieth century. Although many artifacts had been lost by this time, the monument protected both the remains of the cliff dwellings and other important archeological sites.

Gila Cliff Dwellings was among the first national monuments proclaimed under the Antiquities Act, and under its auspices, the agency that administered the land prior to proclamation kept control even after. As a result, Gila Cliff Dwellings was a Forest Service national monument until Franklin D. Roosevelt's reorganization of the federal government in 1933 moved all such areas to National Park Service jurisdiction.

Today, the area surrounding the cliff dwellings looks much like it did centuries ago. The Gila National Forest surrounds the 533-acre monument, and it lies at the edge of the Gila Wilderness, America's first designated wilderness area.

Located 44 miles north of Silver City, New Mexico, Gila Cliff Dwellings National Monument is open year-round, and there is a $3 fee to enter the cliff dwellings. The U.S. Forest Service and the National Park Service jointly operate the small visitor center. It is open daily from 8 A.M. until 5 P.M. Memorial Day through early July, and until 4:30 P.M. for the remainder of the year. The center contains an interpretive museum and sells books, posters, videos, and postcards related to Mogollon culture and the surrounding Gila Wilderness.

A 1-mile, self-guided loop trail begins near the visitor center and leads to the monument's main cliff-dwellings area. Since it is a steep natural footpath, hikers on this trail must wear supportive footwear with substantial soles. During the summer season, park rangers offer daily guided tours to the first 22 people to sign up; on weekends, there are 2 daily tours.

The main access route, New Mexico Highway 15, is a narrow, winding, mountainous road and travel time from Silver City can be as long as two hours. Winter visitors should call ahead for road conditions, since work crews do not plow the roads on weekends or at night.

There are no food, lodging, or camping facilities available at the monument, but nearby Silver City has all traveler facilities. The Forest Service operates 2 small campgrounds between the visitor center and the cliff dwellings. Both are free and open year-round. Two less-developed campgrounds are 5 miles east of the visitor center.

For more information, write Gila Cliff Dwellings National Monument, HC 68, Box 100, Silver City, NM 88061, or telephone (505) 536-9461. The park's Web site is www.nps.gov/gicl.

FURTHER READING

Bradford, James E. *Archeological Survey: Gila Cliff Dwellings National Monument.* Santa Fe, NM: Division of Anthropology, National Park Service, 1992.

Parent, Laurence. *Gila Cliff Dwellings National Monument.* Tucson, AZ: Southwest Parks and Monuments Association, 1992.

Russell, Peter. *Gila Cliff Dwellings National Monument: An Administrative History.* Santa Fe, NM: Southwest Region, Division of History, National Park Service, 1992. Available at www.nps.gov/gicl/adhi/adhi.htm.

GLACIER BAY NATIONAL PARK AND PRESERVE

Location: Gustavus, Alaska
Acreage: 3,283,246
Established: Februrary 25, 1925

One of America's truly spectacular natural preserves, Glacier Bay National Park and Preserve in southeastern Alaska contains some of the most impressive tidewater glaciers in the world. The isolated park also has snow-capped mountains towering over 15,000 feet, coastal beaches with protected coves, deep fjords, coastal and estuarine waters, and freshwater lakes. When Captain George Vancouver first visited and mapped the area in 1794, Glacier Bay was a huge wall of ice extending over 100 miles to the north. By World War I, the same glaciers that Vancouver recorded had receded 65 miles inland. The warming trend continues today, but only on the east side; glaciers on the park's east side continue to recede inland, while glaciers on the cooler west side have either stabilized or have grown larger.

The glaciers within the park are the remnants of what is known as the "little ice age" of about four thousand years ago. Tlingit oral history, along with subsequent investigation, established that this dynamic bay has been completely ice-free at times and was once home to the Huna people, who inhabited the region for thousands of years. Today, nearly one fifth of the park is under water, and no point of land is more than 30 miles from the coast. These diverse land- and seascapes host a mosaic of plant communities, ranging from pioneer species in areas recently exposed by receding glaciers, to climax communities in older coastal and alpine ecosystems. Wildlife is abundant: brown and black bears, seals, mountain goats, humpback whales, and porpoises are frequently seen on or near the shoreline. The park is also home to more than 220 species of birds; more than 25 percent of the total number of avian species in all of North America have been recorded in the park. The sea around the park teems with over 200 species of fish, including all 5 species of Pacific salmon.

Authorized in 1925 as a national monument, Glacier Bay was redesignated as a National Park and Preserve as a result of the Alaska Native Claims Settlement Act and President Jimmy Carter's bold use of the Antiquities Act in 1978. Along with the new Alaska parks, Glacier Bay attained national park status during the lame duck congressional session after Ronald Reagan's 1980 election. Recognizing the sea change the election portended, the departing Congress acted on its pro-preservation leanings and created a national park system for the future—largely in Alaska. After numerous boundary changes, the park now contains nearly 3.3 million acres.

Located about 65 air miles northwest of Juneau, Glacier Bay National Park is only accessible by cruise ship, private or commercial boat, or airplane. While the park is open year-round, the visitor center is only open during the summer. There is no admission charge. Visitor center exhibits illustrate the park's natural and cultural history and include hands-on mammal and rock displays. During the summer, park rangers offer evening programs, guided walks and hikes, and presentations on board tour boats and cruise ships entering the bay. Visitation averages about 500,000 people per year—but nearly 90 percent of these visitors are cruise-ship tourists.

The only road in the park (for taxi, bike, or bus) spans the 10 miles between the Bartlett Cove and Gustavus, where park headquarters and the airport are located. Seven miles of trails wind along the beaches and through the rainforest in the Bartlett Cove area. Concessionaires offer boat and kayak tours from Glacier Bay Lodge that last from eight to nine hours; this is one of the best ways to see the park's inner isles, coves, and 12 tidewater glaciers. Private boaters must have a permit to navigate the park's tricky waters in the summer. The lodge also offers a camper/hiker drop-off service at designated locations in the bay, and various guided kayak, backpacking, and river trips are available.

The Glacier Bay Lodge (800-451-5952) offers overnight accommodations, a restaurant, a gift shop, and fuel sales. Gustavus has several lodges and bed-and-breakfast establishments, as well as groceries, supplies, and a hardware store. Juneau has all traveler services. All campers are required to attend a free camper orientation, which is given on demand at the visitor information station near the dock. Campers may obtain their backcountry permit and check out a bear-resistant food canister at this time; both are required and provided free of charge. Bartlett Cove has a free campground with bear-resistant food caches, firewood, and a warming hut, and permits are issued on a first-come, first-served basis. Anglers with a valid Alaska license are free to fish for various kinds of salmon, trout, and char in the park's freshwater holdings. Halibut fishing is plentiful in the park's saltwater.

For more information, write Glacier Bay National Park and Preserve, P.O. Box 140, Gustavus, AK 99826, or telephone (907) 697-2230. The park's Web site is www.nps.gov/glba.

FURTHER READING

Averkieva, Julia. "The Tlingit Indians." In *North American Indians in Historical Perspective,* 317–42. New York: Random House, 1971.

Boehm, William D. *Glacier Bay: Old Ice, New Land.* Anchorage: Alaska Geographic Society, 1975.

Bohn, Dave. *Glacier Bay: The Land and the Silence.* Anchorage: Alaska Natural History Association, 1997.

Catton, Theodore. *Land Reborn: A History of Administration and Visitor Use in Glacier Bay National Park and Preserve.* Anchorage, AK: National Park Service, 1995. Available at www.nps.gov/glba/adhi/adhi.htm.

Kurtz, Rick S. *Glacier Bay National Park and Preserve: Historic Resources Study.* Anchorage: National Park Service, Alaska System Support Office, 1995.

GLACIER NATIONAL PARK

Location: West Glacier, Montana
Acreage: 1,013,572
Established: May 11, 1910

Aside from its truly spectacular scenery, perhaps the most remarkable aspect of northern Montana's Glacier National Park is that it is a symbol of peaceful international diplomacy. In 1932, the U.S. and Canadian governments voted to rename Glacier and Alberta's Waterton Lakes National Park the Waterton-Glacier International Peace Park, the first park of its kind in the world. More recently, the parks have been designated Biosphere Reserves and World Heritage Sites, as part of an effort to recognize the global importance of this exceptional environment. A combination of magnificent scenery, diverse flora and fauna, and relative isolation from major population centers make Glacier National Park the center of one of the largest and most intact ecosystems in North America.

The park's 1 million–plus acres protect a particularly rich biological diversity of plant and animal species. More than 1,000 plant species, 60 native mammal species, and more than 200 bird species thrive in the park's 2,000 square miles, which naturalist John Muir once called "the best care-killing scenery on the continent." Recent archeological surveys suggest that human use of the area dates back more than ten thousand years. These ancient peoples were likely the ancestors of modern-day Blackfeet, Salish, and Kootenai Indians, and the entire region holds great spiritual significance to them. During the summer months, the Blackfeet tribe hosts the Native America Speaks series.

Established in 1910, Glacier National Park resulted from the unlikely cooperation of the railroads and conservationist George Bird Grinnell, editor of *Forest and Stream,* a prominent conservation newsletter. Grinnell long advocated protection of this area, for he had visited and studied the Blackfeet people who lived there for more than decade. The "Crown of the Continent," as George Bird Grinnell had enthusiastically labeled the area in the 1890s, had become a major national asset. The Great Northern Railroad recognized an economic opportunity in the heavy tourism that rails could bring to the area, and Louis Hill, its president, also pushed for the establishment of a park. The park became reality in May 1910.

Glacier was also important as the scene of some of the most potent fires in the early park system. In 1910, the year of the worst fires to date on the northern plains, the new park was inundated. Complicated by the struggle between Chief of the Forest Service Gifford Pinchot and Secretary of the Interior Richard A.

Fishing at Glacier National Park, 1921. *(Library of Congress)*

Ballinger, the former mayor of Seattle, Washington, Glacier National Park was in the middle of being transferred from the Forest Service to the Department of the Interior when the fires broke out. The response to the fires was muted because of the tension associated with the transfer. Glacier was also the scene of devastating fires in 1919 and 1926.

Glacier National Park is located on the U.S.-Canadian international border about 30 miles north of Kalispell. The park is open year-round, twenty-four hours per day. Some areas of the park, particularly near roads and campgrounds, can get very congested during peak tourist season in the summer. As part of the Recreation Fee Demonstration Program instituted by Congress in 1996, entrance fees are collected year-round. In Glacier these new fees will allow closed campgrounds to re-open, improve accessibility at park facilities, and improve park wayside exhibits, trail

maintenance, and revegetation efforts. Current fees are $5 per person or $10 per vehicle and are valid for seven days; a $20 annual pass is also available.

There are two entrances, east and west, that are connected by the 51-mile Going-to-the-Sun Road (U.S. Highway 2), also known as the Logan Pass Road. Considered one of the most scenic mountain drives in America as it crosses the Rocky Mountains, the road is only open during the summer, and vehicles over 21 feet are prohibited. Another notable, and generally less crowded, scenic drive is Many Glaciers, located on the park's eastern side 9 miles north of St. Mary. The North Fork area—ground zero for fires in both 1988 and 1994—on the park's west side is accessible by one of two dirt roads, both of which are narrow, and the going is slow. The contrast between older forests and recently created meadows are highlights in this remote section of the park. Four of the smaller and more primitive campgrounds—Bowman Lake, Kintla Lake, Logging Creek, and Quartz Creek—are located here. More than 700 miles of trails wind throughout the park, providing excellent opportunities for hiking, wildlife- and bird-viewing, and photography. In the winter, cross-country skiing and showshoeing are popular activities. Snowmobiles are prohibited.

Rangers and volunteers at the Apgar, Logan Pass, and St. Mary visitor centers and the Many Glacier Ranger Station are on duty throughout the summer months to answer questions and provide information. In the winter, information is available weekdays at park headquarters and on weekends at the Apgar Visitor Center. The Logan Pass Visitor Center features exhibits on the alpine ecosystem, which covers almost a third of the park.

Most park services and facilities are available from late May through September. In late fall, winter, and spring very limited services are available in the park; however, surrounding communities provide complete services year-round. Six lodges in the park offer every accommodation style from rustic to elegant. Three lodges are located on the park's west side near Apgar, while the area around Many Glacier on the park's east side contains 2 facilities. Just outside the eastern boundary, in the town of East Glacier, is Glacier Park Lodge. Every lodge has full-service restaurants in or nearby, and all travel services are available in every adjoining park town.

Camping in Glacier is plentiful. Thirteen developed campgrounds provide just under 1,000 sites. Most are operated on a first-come, first-served basis. Campgrounds often fill before noon in July and August; plan to arrive early. In addition, there are 66 primitive backcountry camps accessible only by trail. A backcountry permit is required and can be obtained at all visitor centers. Visitors to these remote campgrounds must exercise extreme caution against bears.

For more information, write Glacier National Park, P.O. Box 128, West Glacier, MT 59936, or telephone (406) 888-7800. For more information on lodging and reservations, call Glacier Park Lodges at (602) 207-6000. The park's informative Web site is www.nps.gov/glac.

FURTHER READING

Fraley, John. *A Woman's Way West: In and Around Glacier National Park, 1925–1990.* Whitefish, MT: Big Mountain, 1998.

Hanna, Warren L. *Montana's Many Splendored Glacierland: All You've Ever Wanted to Know About Glacier Park.* Seattle, WA: Superior, 1976.

———. *Stars over Montana: Men Who Made Glacier National Park History.* West Glacier, MT: Glacier Natural History Association, 1988.

Houk, Rose. *Going-to-the-Sun: The Story of the Highway Across Glacier National Park.* DelMar, MT: Glacier Natural History Association, 1984.

GLEN CANYON NATIONAL RECREATION AREA

Location: Arizona and Utah
Acreage: 1,254,429
Established: April 18, 1958

So, we have a curious ensemble of wonderful features—carved walls, royal arches, glens, alcove gulches, mounds and monuments. From which of these features shall we select a name? We decide to call it Glen Canyon.

—Major John Wesley Powell, 1869

Prior to 1964, Glen Canyon was a long, benign stretch of the Colorado River as it snaked its way through southern Utah. Because of its isolation, few travelers ever visited Glen Canyon to savor its many amphitheaters, lush fern gullies, Native American ruins and artifacts, and narrow side canyons. But in 1964, everything changed. That year, construction was completed on Glen Canyon Dam and water began creeping up the canyon walls. Gone were the amphitheaters, gullies, and Native American ruins, all submerged by the 186-mile-long impoundment. Now Glen Canyon—named by explorer and scientist John Wesley Powell, the first white man to float the entire canyon in 1869 and 1871—was replaced by Lake Powell, a gigantic freshwater reservoir with just under 2,000 miles of shoreline.

The 700-foot-high Glen Canyon Dam was the end result of a compromise by environmental preservationists. When the U.S. Bureau of Reclamation conceived the Colorado River Storage Project (CRSP) after World War II, plans also called for a dam at Echo Park in Dinosaur National Monument. In the mid-1950s, still smarting from the earlier loss of the serene Hetch Hetchy Valley in Yosemite National Park, members of the Sierra Club and their allies forced the bureau to remove Echo Park Dam from the CRSP. Dams, they argued, did not belong in national parks. But the victory had a price. To save Echo Park, the Sierra Club and others agreed to not oppose the construction of a high Glen Canyon Dam, for it and its reservoir would not encroach into any national park property. Construction began in 1956, and before the pool began to fill, David Brower and other Sierra Clubbers toured the doomed canyon. They were stunned. Only then did they realize what they had given away—a geologic marvel, awesome in its silence and solitude. Brower tried a last-minute campaign to stop the dam, but it was too late. He later called the loss of Glen Canyon his greatest regret in life. In 1972, eight years after the dam's completion, Congress authorized the 1.2-million-acre Glen Canyon National Recreation Area (NRA) to provide water-based recreation. Thus, one hundred and three years after Powell first floated the river, Glen Canyon became part of the National Park Service—even though the canyon itself no longer existed.

The debate over Glen Canyon continues to the present day. Some radical preservationists advocate draining Lake Powell and dismantling the dam, in order to begin the process of restoring Glen Canyon to its original state. But this is highly unlikely, since Lake Powell is not only a popular recreation spot, but provides hydroelectric power for the southwest and flood control for the lower Colorado River basin.

Today, recreation at Glen Canyon NRA is almost exclusively water-based. The southern portion of the park is the most accessible. Located 132 miles north of Flagstaff, Arizona, at the lake's southern terminus, is Page. Originally a company town for dam construction workers, Page is now the main center for all activities on the lake's southern reaches. It is here that recreationists have Wahweap Marina, a large developed campground, ranger station, restaurants, motel, and lodge, as well as Dangling Rope Marina. Page has all traveler services, the Carl Hayden Visitor Center, which has information and interpretive exhibits, and the dam itself, for which there are guided tours.

The NRA's northern stretches in Utah are more isolated and have fewer services. This less-crowded end of Lake Powell gets more visitors from points north and east, while the southern portion gets more from the southwest. Here, recreationists can choose from Bullfrog, Hite, and Hall's Crossing marinas, which have all traveler services (except lodging) and ranger stations. Access to these points is easier for travelers coming from Utah or Colorado, while travelers coming from points south have to make a huge circular drive through the Navajo reservation and into Utah, then south to the lake. There is a ferry (fee) at Hall's Crossing that can slightly cut back the driving distance to Bullfrog.

Glen Canyon NRA charges fees for admission and boating; entrance fees are $3 per person or $5 per vehicle and are valid for seven days; boating fees are $10 for the first vessel and $4 for each additional vessel and are valid for seven days. Annual passes are also available. Despite the flooding of the original Glen Canyon, there are still numerous sights to see. More than 100 red-sandstone side canyons still flank the shoreline, offering many opportunities for houseboat camping, swimming, and hiking. Adjacent to the lake's south shore across from Dangling Rope Marina is Rainbow Bridge National Monument. At 290 feet high and 278 feet long, Rainbow is the largest known natural bridge in the world; it is most easily reached by boat and a short hike.

For more information, write Glen Canyon National Recreation Area, P.O. Box 1507, Page AZ 86040-1507, or telephone (928) 608-6404. For information on tours and boat rentals, call (800) 528-6154. The park's informative Web site is www.nps.gov/glca.

FURTHER READING

Gross, Mathew Barrett, ed. *The Glen Canyon Reader.* Tucson: University of Arizona Press, 2003.

Jennings, Jesse David. *Glen Canyon: An Archaeological Summary.* Salt Lake City: University of Utah Press, 1998.

Porter, Eliot. *The Place No One Knew: Glen Canyon on the Colorado.* San Francisco: Sierra Club, 1963.

Reisner, Marc. *Cadillac Desert: The American West and Its Disappearing Water.* New York: Penguin, 1993.

GLEN ECHO PARK

Location: Glen Echo, Maryland
Acreage: 9
Established: April 1, 1970

Located about 2.5 miles northwest of Washington, D.C., Glen Echo has an illustrious history. It began in 1891 as a National Chautauqua Assembly, where people gathered to teach and learn literature, history, sciences, and the arts. In 1899, the Glen Echo Company took over the property and converted it into a premier amusement park. In addition to the roller coaster, bumper cars, and carousel, Glen Echo boasted midway attractions, a pool, and a ballroom, and it served as the Washington area's main amusement park un-til it closed in 1968. Although most of the rides were sold and removed, the historic Dentzel Carousel, built in 1921 and restored through community effort, still remains. In 1971, the Park Service acquired the property as part of the "parks for the people, where the people are" movement. The agency began offering year-round activities in dance, theater, and the arts for the surrounding communities and for visitors from across the country.

Today, the 9-acre park has come full circle. The land and buildings provide a rich historic backdrop for a varied arts education program. Glen Echo Park administers an artist-in-residency program providing the public with an opportunity to see artists at work. The park has also revived its Chautauqua heritage and offers concerts, demonstrations, workshops, and festivals during the summer season. In addition, the antique

Glen Echo Park, 1939. *(Library of Congress)*

hand-carved and hand-painted Dentzel carousel operates four days a week from May through September.

Glen Echo Park is located in Glen Echo, Maryland, on the Potomac Palisades, and is open from 6 A.M. to 1 A.M. year-round. Although there is no admission fee, the park does charge fees to ride the Dentzel carousel and to attend special events. Park rangers conduct guided tours every Sunday at 2 P.M., although tours at other times can be arranged by calling the office in advance. Families with children will want to attend performances of the Adventure Theater and the Puppet Company, and use the playground. Sunday afternoon community dances in the Spanish Ballroom (1931) are for the entire family. The Friday, Saturday, and Sunday dances in the ballroom attract hundreds of people, young and old, couples and singles, to a wide variety of popular music.

Although the park has excellent picnic facilities, there are no food, lodging, or camping facilities. The town of Glen Echo and the surrounding area offer all traveler services. Advance reservations for lodging are advised during the peak late spring–early fall tourist seasons.

For more information, write Glen Echo Park, 7300 MacArthur Boulevard, Glen Echo, MD 20812, or telephone the main office at (301) 492-6229, or the events hotline at (301) 492-6282. The park's Web site is www.nps.gov/glec.

GLORIA DEI (OLD SWEDES') CHURCH NATIONAL HISTORIC SITE

Location: Philadelphia, Pennsylvania
Acreage: 4
Established: November 17, 1942

The present Gloria Dei (Old Swedes') Church in Philadelphia was built between 1698 and 1700. The oldest surviving church in Pennsylvania, it also is the second-oldest Swedish church in America. Although this region of the eastern seaboard would later be claimed by British Quakers, Swedish immigrants arrived here before the English in 1646. The original Gloria Dei was founded in 1677, and for nearly two centuries, the church ministered to the souls of its far-venturing countrymen on behalf of the Church of Sweden. But Sweden was not destined to control North America, and as Swedes were gradually absorbed into the general American population, Gloria Dei became English-speaking. In 1845, it was admitted into the Episcopal Church.

A fine example of seventeenth-century Swiss church architecture, Gloria Dei is owned and maintained by its congregation and contains important historic relics and artifacts. Revolutionary War patriots John Hansen (first president of the Continental Congress under the Articles of Confederation), John Morton (a signer of the Declaration of Independence), and five of General George Washington's officers rest in the churchyard burial grounds. Also buried in the cemetery is the famous naturalist Alexander Wilson, the "Father of American Ornithology."

Gloria Dei is still an active house of worship, and the site is only open to visitors for weekly services and by special arrangement. Admission is free. The church itself contains exhibit items from the early log church, including a baptismal font, the golden sprays on the lectern and pulpit, and the cherubim below the organ. A site bulletin and outdoor signage explain the story of Gloria Dei. Tours of the church and cemetery are available by reservation only.

Located in downtown Philadelphia at the corner of Columbus Boulevard and Christian Street, Gloria Dei was originally set aside as a national historic site in November of 1942. The site is easily accessible by public transportation from the city center, but parking is also available. There are no tourist facilities at the church, but metropolitan Philadelphia has all traveler services, and food and lodging are located nearby. There are also a few private campgrounds in the western suburbs.

For more information, write Gloria Dei Church National Historic Site, Columbus Boulevard and Christian Street, Philadelphia, PA 19147. Since Gloria Dei Church is still an active religious congregation and home to the parish minister, potential visitors must call the rector at (215) 389-1513 for tour information. The park's Web site is www.nps.gov/glde.

FURTHER READING

Cantwell, Robert. *Alexander Wilson: Naturalist and Pioneer, a Biography.* Philadelphia, PA: Lippincott, 1961.

Roak, John Craig. *A Brief Historical Sketch of Gloria Dei Church (Old Swedes'), Philadelphia: Oldest Church in Pennsylvania.* Philadelphia, PA: n.p., 1938.

Wilson, Alexander. *The Life and Letters of Alexander Wilson.* Philadelphia, PA: American Philosophical Society, 1983.

GOLDEN GATE NATIONAL RECREATION AREA

Location: San Francisco, California
Acreage: 74,816
Established: October 27, 1972

As a result of all the ways that it is a composite of all the possible characteristics of American national park areas, Golden Gate National Recreation Area (GGNRA) has become one of the most important national parks in the country. Stretching from the boundaries of Point Reyes National Seashore in the north to San Mateo County in the south, the park contains almost 75,000 acres, about half federally owned and the rest managed by agreement between the federal government and municipal jurisdictions.

The park's location in the San Francisco Bay area, one of the nation's most populous urban areas, has forced the Park Service to address myriad concerns beyond the traditional scope of its mandate. In the U.S. park system, only Golden Gate National Recreation Area contains a former federal prison, Zen Buddhist retreat center, pet cemetery, wilderness areas, clothing-optional beaches, hang-gliding areas, and decommissioned missile sites. Golden Gate is among the very few parks in the system that can reach the America of the future, the multicultural, multiracial urban population that demographers expect to make up 50 percent of the nation by 2050. With its enviable array of resources, its incredible range of constituencies, a location in a major urban area, and—with the addition of the Presidio, the single largest project ever undertaken by the Park Service—Golden Gate has become the laboratory in which the future of American national parks will be determined.

The park itself is a place of beauty and diversity. Its attractions include Fort Point, a Civil War–era installation that guarded the Golden Gate nearly a century before the building of the Golden Gate Bridge, as well as World War II–era gun batteries, a lighthouse, hiking trails, and countless other natural and cultural features. In this remarkable diversity is both promise and peril. GGNRA is both a huge city park and a national park, sharing enough of the traits of both as it seeks to be all things to all people most of the time.

Golden Gate National Recreation Area reflects the changes in public expectations of park management that have defined the National Park Service and the park system during the past twenty-five years. From the day the government established GGNRA in 1972, crucial changes in the Park Service and its policies in one way or another emanated from this multifaceted park or in some way went through it. The demands of management bifurcated the already clumsy formulation of preservation and use embodied in the Park Service's 1916 Organic Act, which have continued to characterized agency management ever since. The urban parks movement, with its idea of parks for the people, had its genesis at Golden Gate National Recreation Area; the shifting management focus of the agency

A 1938 aerial photograph of the San Francisco Bay area with Alcatraz Island in the foreground. Golden Gate National Recreation Area also comprises Marin Headlands, Fort Funston, Fort Mason, Fort Point, Muir Woods National Monument, and the Presidio. *(Library of Congress)*

catapulted the park's thirty-five-year-old general superintendent, William Whalen, to directorship of the agency in 1975. The Presidio may create the kind of public-private and public-public partnerships that will be essential to the survival of national parks in the twenty-first century. Its addition also broadens the intellectual terrain of the park system. GGNRA will be pivotal in charting a course for park management.

The mission of Golden Gate National Recreation Area has both reflected and shaped the way in which the National Park Service has framed the national park system. Since 1963, the Leopold Report, with its vision of parks as vignettes of primitive America, has held the dominant ground in conceptualizing national parks. The experience of GGNRA, with its enormous visita-

tion, impacts on the local, regional, and national scenes, and especially with the economic development possibilities of the Presidio, offers a holistic, comprehensive approach to park management at a time when national parks require innovative management and a broadened constituency. Golden Gate is one of the few parks in the system that can lead the way to new objectives. It is not and has never been a traditional national park; despite its beautiful scenic and natural areas and remarkable natural and cultural resource responsibilities, the park also caters to an enormous day-use, recreational constituency. Blending these diverse missions and responsibilities provides a blueprint for successful survival of national parks in a changing society where a growing number of claimants seek limited federal resources. It is the unit through which the United States will fashion the complicated future of national parks.

The sprawling Golden Gate National Recreation Area boasts several visitor centers: Alcatraz, Cliff House, Marin Headlands, Muir Woods, William Penn Mott, Jr., and the Pacific West Regional Information Center. All are open year-round and offer a wide variety of displays and interpretive programs. The park also offers 4 campgrounds and numerous picnic facilities, and all traveler services can be found in the rich urban environments surrounding San Francisco. Entrance to the park is free, although several sites, such as Alcatraz, charge a visitation fee.

For more information, write Golden Gate National Recreation Area, Fort Mason, Building 201, San Francisco, CA 94123-0022, or telephone (415) 561-4700. The park's Web site is www.nps.gov/goga.

FURTHER READING

Benton, Lisa. *The Presidio: From Army Post to National Park.* Boston: Northeastern University Press, 1998.

Gilliam, Harold, and Ann Gilliam. *Marin Headlands: Portals of Time.* San Francisco: Golden Gate National Park Association, 1993.

Haller, Stephen A. *Post and Park: A Brief Illustrated History of the Presidio.* San Francisco: Golden Gate National Parks Association, 1997.

Rothman, Hal K. *The Park That Makes Its Own Weather: An Administrative History of Golden Gate National Recreation Area.* San Francisco: National Park Service, 2002.

GOLDEN SPIKE NATIONAL HISTORIC SITE

Location: Brigham City, Utah
Acreage: 2,735
Established: April 2, 1957

On May 10, 1869, at a windy promontory summit in the Utah Territory, an event that marked the triumph of human endeavor over a difficult natural world took place: the completion of a transcontinental railroad. Assembled dignitaries posed for pictures. The presidents of the two competing railroad companies, the Union Pacific and the Central Pacific, leaned over to hammer in the ceremonial spikes, two of gold, one of silver, and one of gold, silver, and iron. Leland Stanford of the Central Pacific was first; he swung and missed the spike. To avoid damaging the ceremonial spikes, they were removed and replaced with four ordinary iron spikes. Quickly, workmen completed the process and the telegraph wires sang with the message: "The last spike is driven. The Pacific Railroad is finished." The continent had truly become one nation, joined by the colossus of the railroad. No longer would travelers to California have to sail around Tierra del Fuego or cross the Isthmus of Panama. After the completion of the transcontinental railroad, passengers and freight could travel in relative ease across the continent.

The completion of the transcontinental railroad was the signal event of the last third of the nineteenth century. Before the Civil War, the United States was three nations: North, South, and an unformed West. The war resulted from the differences between the perspectives of the first two. The controversy asked a vexing question: Which word took precedence in the name of the nation, "united" or "states"? The North's triumph was a victory for the idea of a union, not coincidentally an important part of the name of one of the two railroads that sought to build across the West. The completion of the rails offered a telling piece of evidence that this vision of a United States of America would come to dominate national horizons.

Economic, social, and expansionist motives also underpinned the construction of the railroad. As early as the 1840s, efforts to find a possible route to the Pacific Ocean began in earnest, subsidized by the federal government and often tied to the political agenda of the South, eager to capture at least part of the transportation capital used in building and operating a railroad. A route from Texas to

San Diego offered the Southerners what they wanted, while a far northern route across the plains had its advocates. In the end, the impetus for the selection came from the Civil War. When the South seceded and Southern congressmen and senators walked out of Congress, no one remained to defend the Southern agenda. When Abraham Lincoln signed the Pacific Railroad Act in 1862, the only options to cross the continent were in the North. In California, an engineer named Theodore Judah found a route across the forbidding Sierra Nevada mountains.

The federal government supported the railroad's construction, offering huge subsidies and giving the railroads land for each mile of track laid. Building through the mountains, the Central Pacific progressed more slowly than the Union Pacific, which came west from Omaha across the plains, but once into the Great Basin, the Central Pacific built as much as 1 mile of track each day. In 1868, it covered 368 miles, and its construction peaked on April 28, 1869, with the almost unbelievable total of 10 miles in a twenty-four-hour period. The Union Pacific raced westward, covering 425 miles in 1868 alone. The two railroads were in such fierce competition that when they reached Utah, they built separate tracks past each other. After arranging a conference, company officials decided that the rails would meet at the promontory summit. Five days after the "driving of the golden spike," passenger service across the continent began. This inaugurated a new era, in which goods and people could travel with increasing speed across the nation, and remote places could be linked to the core of the nation. In many ways, the twentieth century began at Promontory Summit.

At Golden Spike National Historic Site, a reenactment ceremony occurs each May 10. Fully operating replicas of the engines present at the driving of the spike—the Central Pacific's steam locomotive, the Jupiter, and the Union Pacific's No. 119—are kept in the site engine house. A concrete monument marks the spot of the signing. The government removed the original rails in 1942 and scrapped the original locomotives. A visitor center and other exhibits re-create the history of this momentous event. Entrance fees are $4 per person, or $5 per vehicle in the off-season (roughly mid-September through April), and $7 per vehicle during the summer. And while there are no food or lodging facilities in the park, all traveler services are available nearby.

For more information, write Golden Spike National Historic Site, P.O. Box 897, Brigham City, UT 84302-0897, or telephone (435) 471-2209. The park's Web site is www.nps.gov/gosp.

FURTHER READING

Ambrose, Stephen E. *Nothing Like It in the World: The Men Who Built the Transcontinental Railroad, 1865–1869.* New York: Simon and Schuster, 2000.

Bain, David Howard. *Empire Express: Building the First Transcontinental Railroad.* New York: Viking, 1999.

GRAND CANYON NATIONAL PARK

Location: Grand Canyon, Arizona
Acreage: 1,217,403
Established: January 11, 1908

In 1900, no place spoke to the United States like the Grand Canyon. The Great Chasm of the Colorado, the Grand Cañon, and the other superlatives lavished upon it seemed to embody the identity that Americans sought as they fashioned their place in the world. The canyon's dizzying vistas, rich and moving colors, and mystery, and the nation's ability to master it, confirmed that the continent had substance and depth. Here was the entire package, what the people of the time regarded as God's handiwork, a place that reflected back to Americans what they wanted themselves and their nation to be. It offered assurance as well as wonder, power and humility intertwined; more than any other place, it became the symbol of the moment, the place that Americans looked to explain their complicated relationship with the land they possessed. The Grand Canyon became the personification of American Manifest Destiny.

The more than 1.2 million acres of Grand Canyon National Park contain some of the most beautiful landscapes in the nation. A great upheaval of the earth's crust almost 80 million years ago created the Colorado Plateau. The canyon came into being about 6 million years ago, when the Colorado River sculpted its way through the plateau, creating the deep gorges that astonish the eye today. The combination of clouds, sun, and the many hues of the canyon make it a place that is always changing, a scene that never looks the same twice. The walls of the canyon offer a geological history of the world in its layers.

Before 1860, the Grand Canyon was simply an obstacle to travel, an enormous hole in the ground. The intellectual tools that made its fantastic landscapes, vast loneliness, and remarkable topography meaningful sim-

A man and a woman riding mules on a high trail in the Grand Canyon, c. 1903. *(Library of Congress)*

ply did not have currency in the Western world. European history of the canyon reflected that lack of understanding. Spanish explorer García López de Cárdenas, who in 1540 guided a contingent of the Vázquez de Coronado expedition to its rim, looked over the edge, and perceived not the beauty, mystery, and power of the canyon, but only the obvious: its condition as a barrier to forward movement. López de Cárdenas withdrew disappointed, and he, the men who traveled with him, and ultimately all of Spanish culture, remained indifferent to the canyon's intellectual possibilities. This pose in the face of wonder was hardly callous; it presaged what became a hard-nosed Spanish intellectual and cultural resistance to the Enlightenment, the scientific revolution, and the empiricism that accompanied it. López de Cárdenas's indifference typified a view that can best be described as dogmatically premodern. Only the combination of empirical and sublime, laced with the articulation of science and progress, that defined nineteenth-century thought precipitated an alteration of this outlook, and when it came, it stemmed from the American republic, chock full of expansionist enthusiasm. When John Wesley Powell rafted the Colorado River in 1869, he and his men feared the canyon as well as revered it. By 1880, the context in which Anglo-Americans learned to appreciate and later to understand the Grand Canyon began to take shape.

Geologist Clarence E. Dutton played a key role in creating modern understanding of the canyon. A Yale University graduate, a Civil War veteran, a career army officer, an accomplished raconteur, and a cofounder with Powell of the pivotal Cosmos Club in Washington, D.C., Dutton typified the tradition of military exploration in the intellectual and physical sense. He was both a thinker and a doer. Dutton worked closely with Powell, providing much of the scientific authority that underpinned Powell's famous 1879

Report on the Lands of the Arid Region of the United States, with a More Detailed Account of the Lands of Utah. Dutton's own writing won renown; *The Tertiary History of the Grand Canyon,* a U.S. Geological Survey report, retained lasting significance.

By the mid-1890s, the canyon possessed great cultural significance. Dutton's descriptions rippled like a stone dropped in a pool of water. Thomas Moran, who painted his first picture of the canyon in 1873 at John Wesley Powell's request, returned in the 1880s to color illustrations for *The Tertiary History* drawn by noted artist and ethnographer William Henry Holmes. J.K. Hillers's photographs helped illustrate its meaning. Dutton, Moran, and Powell provided American elites with their interpretation of the Grand Canyon. That information had to be carried to the public. The great popularizer was editor, author, and traveler Charles F. Lummis, who during the 1880s made the Southwest the focus of a concerted effort to present an exotic but uniquely American past in which Europe and its cultural and social history did not share. His writing attracted wide attention, for it melded the era's themes with an appreciation for the exotic. Lummis did not attempt to describe the canyon after his first visit; "there it is; go see it for yourself," he pronounced in the widely read *A Tramp Across the Country,* investing the canyon with a meaning beyond words and simultaneously issuing a challenge to modern America. The visitors who descended upon mining camps in the area were imbued with the spirit of Powell's explorations, Dutton's intellectual mapping, the art of Moran and Hillers, and the combination of nationalism and exhilaration tinged with self-doubt that so affected the privileged of the age.

As the century closed, an awkward situation existed at the Grand Canyon. It had been intellectually delineated, and the canyon held a firm place in the gallery of the extraordinary that Americans relied upon to persuade themselves that they controlled an expansive continent. This idea was part of the cosmology of affirmation, of a piece with the set of signs and symbols that persuaded Americans that all was right in their world—even when evidence to the contrary existed in abundance. The Grand Canyon represented the scope and scale of American civilization and reminded Americans of the spectacular beauty of "their" continent. It announced the nation's importance. Despite this cultural significance, the canyon lacked the amenities associated with meaningful places in the late nineteenth century. No first-class hotel sat on its rim. Its accommodations were crude and rough in an era before the traveling classes found the lack of comfort culturally persuasive. Its various enterprises were poorly run. Even reaching the canyon was an ordeal. The Grand Canyon resonated in fin de siècle American society and culture, and while many would have paid to see it, in 1900, few would endure the rigors of the trip. This enhanced the mythic qualities of the place, but the growth of tourism was hamstrung by the absence of a consistent, comfortable, and efficient form of transportation.

A railroad to the canyon was the most feasible solution. As tourism became an important southwestern economic staple during the 1890s, the Atchison, Topeka, and Santa Fe (AT&SF) railroad recognized both the vast economic potential of tourist rail traffic and the meaning of the Grand Canyon. The AT&SF purchased the old Atlantic and Pacific track through Williams, Arizona, and built a spur to the canyon. On September 17, 1901, a scheduled train made its initial trip from Williams to the Grand Canyon. A ticket for the comfortable three-hour trip cost $3.95, less than the $20 price of the day-long stage ride on rutted roads that departed three times each week from Flagstaff.

The train that reached the rim created the

catalytic moment in the modern history of the Grand Canyon, the moment when the canyon and the cultural, intellectual, social, and economic currents of turn-of-the-century America met in a transformative embrace. The arrival of a national corporation with the power, capital, and impetus to invent a consumable Grand Canyon changed the direction of local and regional history. Instead of remaining an out-of-the-way symbol, the canyon quickly became an American cultural institution, a place that elite Americans felt they must see. Before the AT&SF, the Grand Canyon stayed literally and figuratively distant. Neither the ways to it nor its services met the expectations of any but the most adventurous of the elite. With the AT&SF in charge, upper-class and upper-middle-class Americans could visit it on their own terms, in comfort.

In 1903, President Theodore Roosevelt made his first and only visit to the Grand Canyon. The majesty and power of the canyon overwhelmed this paragon of American values and leader of the conservation movement; nothing seemed to him to more completely reflect the essence of the American nation. From its rim, he proclaimed that no "building of any kind, not a summer cottage, a hotel [should be permitted] to mar the wonderful grandeur, the sublimity, the great loneliness, and beauty of the Canyon. You can not improve it. The ages have been at work on it and man can only mar it. What you can do is keep it for your children, your children's children, and for all those who come after you, as one of the great sites that every American . . . should see." Ever after, the place of the Grand Canyon in the national pageant was secure.

Yet the Grand Canyon's legal standing and its place in national culture did not quite match. Even as it became a symbol, the canyon's legal status reflected only the value of its natural resources. By the 1890s, the public clamored to see it, but weak mechanisms for its protection paralleled the ineffective transportation systems that delivered visitors. Lack of access protected the Grand Canyon, but that same remote character allowed people to file mining claims on the area and convert them to legal title. The canyon's status first as a forest reserve and subsequently as a mining reserve failed to prohibit other uses of reserved land. As long as the canyon had vast economic potential as a tourist destination and a canny politician could easily claim it for extractive purposes, problems ensued.

El Tovar is a resort hotel that sits 20 feet from the edge of the Grand Canyon's South Rim. Opened in 1905, the hotel became the "destination resort" at the Grand Canyon, dramatically increasing tourism. This, in turn, had an indirect bearing on the area's establishment as a national monument in 1908 and a national park eleven years later. *(Library of Congress)*

The railroad also benefited from the minimal legal structure. Even though Theodore Roosevelt demanded a rim devoid of development, the railroad and its ally the Fred Harvey Company soon built the massive 250-room El Tovar Hotel at almost the exact spot where he spoke. Even in 1908, when it passed to the next level of protection after Forest Service chief and leading conservationist Gifford Pinchot told Theodore Roosevelt of David Rust, a Grand Canyon miner, and his plan to construct a tramway to the bottom, the canyon remained wide open. Roosevelt thwarted the project by proclaiming more than 800,000 acres as a national monument under the terms of the Antiquities Act of 1906, but national monument status hardly secured the protection of the canyon from intrusions and economic development.

In 1919, the Grand Canyon became a national park and was transferred by the Forest Service to the jurisdiction of the National Park Service. Only three years old in 1919, the Park Service aimed to become the nation's premier tourist-service agency. An intense construction program followed the February 1919 transfer, with visitor accommodations, staff comforts, and the implementation of visitor control strategies paramount. The Park Service standardized tourism at the Grand Canyon well beyond the efforts of its predecessors and made the park into a tourist destination.

Today, a South Rim shuttle bus provides frequent and convenient access to the park's many visitor centers, viewpoints, and tourist services. Hiking trails (for the bold and the cautious), exhibits, and interpretive programs are plentiful and add significantly to the park experience. Traveler services are available year-round at the South Rim and include groceries, restaurants, gift shops, fuel, banks, and a post office. The park offers lodging at both rims and at Phantom Ranch, at the bottom of the canyon; reservations for all three are available by calling (888) 297-2757. Lodging and all traveler services are also available just outside of the park in Jacob Lake, Arizona, and Kanab, Utah. Camping abounds, both inside and outside of park boundaries; visitors should refer to the park's Web site for contact information and dates. Visitor services and facilities inside the national park on the North Rim are only open from mid-May through mid-October.

For more information, write Grand Canyon National Park, P.O. Box 129, Grand Canyon, AZ 86023, or telephone (928) 638-7888. The park's extensive Web site is www.nps.gov/grca.

FURTHER READING

Beus, Stanley S., and Michael Morales, eds. *Grand Canyon Geology.* New York: Oxford University Press, 2002.

Fletcher, Colin. *The Man Who Walked Through Time.* New York: Vintage Books, 1989.

Pyne, Stephen J. *How the Canyon Became Grand: A Short History.* New York: Penguin, 1999.

Stegner, Wallace Earle. *Beyond the Hundredth Meridian: John Wesley Powell and the Second Opening of the West.* New York: Penguin, 1992.

Worster, Donald. *A River Running West: The Life of John Wesley Powell.* New York: Oxford University Press, 2001.

GRAND PORTAGE NATIONAL MONUMENT

Location: Grand Marais, Minnesota
Acreage: 710
Established: September 15, 1951

In the late eighteenth century, the North West Company, a jointly owned British-Canadian fur-trading venture, controlled a vast area of North America's beaver territory. Headquartered in the northeastern tip of present-day Minnesota at Grand Portage, a vital 8.5-mile link connecting Lake Superior to Fort Charlotte at the upper Pigeon River, the North West Company conducted a lucrative enterprise that shipped furs to eastern and European markets. Between 1785 and 1804, the headquarters was surrounded by a 15-foot-tall palisade built from cedar pickets. It protected a compound comprised of sixteen buildings, including the Great Hall, a business office, kitchen, partners' and manager's house, fur and general stores, blacksmith and woodworker shops, and storage bins for furs and gunpowder. At the height of its operation, the stockade employed as many as 50 traders, 10 guides, and nearly 1,000 canoe men.

The portage itself was originally devised and used by local Ojibway Indians as a means of avoiding the lower Pigeon River's impassable rough rapids and waterfalls; they referred to it as the Kitchi Onigaming, or "great carrying place." The portage allowed traders and trappers unhindered access to Canada's prime fur country and became a major gateway into the interior of the continent for explorers, missionaries, and settlers. Every year, Grand Portage served as the location for a midsummer rendezvous that brought together hundreds of trappers, voyageurs, clerks, agents, and natives. In 1803, the operation came to an end when the United States declared it would levy duties on all furs that passed through Grand Portage, since the area was now south of the new international border (following the Louisiana Purchase). To avoid paying taxes and duties to the United States, the North West Company reluctantly abandoned the locale and moved their operations 40 miles north on Lake Superior's Thunder Bay in Canada.

Today, the 710-acre Grand Portage National Monument preserves the partially reconstructed stockade and the rebuilt Great Hall and kitchen complex, as well as the Grand Portage itself. The monument's grounds, trails, and the Grand Portage are open year-round, and entrance fees are $6 per family or $3 per person. The site has no visitor center. The reconstructed stockade and buildings are open from mid-May to mid-October during daylight hours. The historic buildings have been furnished in the time period of the late 1700s and contain interpretive displays, as well as hands-on exhibits. Nearby, a canoe warehouse houses the vessels, crafted from birch, cedar, and spruce, essential for travel along the east–west fur-trade routes. Video programs are presented throughout the day, and during the summer, costumed interpreters and guides bring living-history programs to the stockade. An annual special event, Rendezvous Days, is a re-creation of the historic fur-trade rendezvous held at Grand Portage. The event includes historic demonstrations and activities and historically costumed reenactors. The event is free, and it is held the second weekend of August. The Grand Portage Band of Minnesota Chippewa also sponsors a traditional American Indian powwow in conjunction with Rendezvous Days. The portage is also a popular destination for hikers, especially in the colorful fall season. A half-mile trail leads to the 300-foot-high summit of Mount Rose, which offers excellent vistas of the Grand Portage and surrounding area.

Grand Portage is located along the magnificent shore and boreal forest of Lake Superior, 150 miles northeast of Duluth on the Grand Portage Indian Reservation—home of the Ojibway nation. Primitive camping is permitted in the monument at Fort Charlotte, at the western end of the Grand Portage. There is no charge for backcountry camping but a permit is required; permits are available at registration boxes located along the Grand Portage, or at the on-site ranger office. No other camping is permitted within the monument. Lodging and food are available at nearby resorts, or at the Ojibway-owned Grand Portage Lodge and Casino just southwest of the monument.

For more information, write Grand Portage National Monument, P.O. Box 668, 315 South Broadway,

Grand Marais, MN 55604-0668, or telephone (218) 387-2788. The park's Web site is www.nps.gov/grpo.

FURTHER READING

Gilman, Carolyn. *The Grand Portage Story.* St. Paul: Minnesota Historical Society, 1992.

Kugel, Rebecca. *To Be the Main Leaders of Our People: A History of Minnesota Ojibwe Politics, 1825–1898.* East Lansing: Michigan State University Press, 1998.

Thompson, Erwin N. *Grand Portage: A History of the Sites, People, and Fur Trade.* Washington, DC: U.S. Office of Archeology and Historic Preservation, Division of History, 1969.

Warren, William W. *History of the Ojibway People.* St. Paul: Minnesota Historical Society, 1984.

GRAND TETON NATIONAL PARK

Location: Moose, Wyoming
Acreage: 309,995
Established: February 26, 1929

The last of the first generation of national parks, Grand Teton at its founding was the quintessential mountaintop park: inside park boundaries lay only the least commercially valuable mountains tops, for the rest of land in the region was part of a marginal ranching regime. Two peaks, the Grand Tetons, dominate the horizon. Towering above northwestern Wyoming, Grand Teton rises 13,770 feet above sea level. It is not alone in its monumental grandeur; twelve other Teton Range peaks reach above 12,000 feet, all high enough to support a dozen mountain glaciers and a varied range of plant and animal communities. The park is also home to the winter feeding grounds of the largest American elk herd. Humans have taken advantage of the area's abundant natural resources for approximately eleven thousand years. Among the region's early white residents were French fur trappers, who arrived around 1820. They named the geologically young Teton Range *Les Trois Tetons* (The Three Breasts). These early residents occupied the Snake River Valley during the short spring, summer, and fall seasons; then they moved to lower elevations and warmer climates in the winter.

In the late 1800s, homesteaders, ranchers, and (later) dude ranch entrepreneurs moved into the valley, bringing irrigation and insulation technologies that allowed them to stay through the long, harsh winters. Soon, the Jackson Hole area (named after trapper David Jackson) became a popular recreation spot; locals encouraged wealthy tourists to come and hunt and fish the area. Struthers Burt, a graduate of Princeton and a well-known American author of the time, became the archetype of dude ranchers. He and others saw a future in preserving the beauty of the region.

During this time, conservationists recognized the area's environmental significance and proposed that the Tetons and surrounding valley be added to Yellowstone National Park. In 1897, President Grover Cleveland established the Teton Forest Reserve, and eleven years later the reserve became Teton National Forest. In 1929, after more than a decade of wrangling and with the support of billionaire industrialist and conservationist John D. Rockefeller, Jr., and the large amount of land he accumulated through a holding company, Congress set aside 96,000 acres of mountains and an adjoining valley as Grand Teton National Park. This initial proclamation was not big enough for Rockefeller. Between 1927 and 1930, he had secretly purchased more than 30,000 acres of private land in the Snake River Valley, both to further his desire for a larger park and to protect certain areas from development. His landgrab angered some local residents, who feared that eastern wealth might swallow up all remaining valley lands and, throughout the 1930s, tension was rife in the valley. Additional rancor between federal agencies made the situation worse. In 1943, President Franklin D. Roosevelt further antagonized local ranchers and residents by establishing the 221,000-acre

The Snake River at Grand Teton National Park. *(National Archives)*

Jackson Hole National Monument, transferring land from the Forest Service to the National Park Service. Despite much anger, including a cattle drive by part-time resident and well-known actor Wallace Beery across the new parklands, the area was moving away from extraction and toward tourism and preservation. Six years later, in 1949, Rockefeller added his acres to the national monument, and in 1950, after boundary adjustments, Congress combined the park and monument into the present-day 309,000-plus-acre national park.

Located between Jackson, Wyoming, and Yellowstone National Park's south entrance, Grand Teton is one of the most heavily vis-

ited national parks in America—more than 4 million visitors annually savor its expansive, alps-like vistas and lush valleys. Most see the park during the warm, sunny summers, for Jackson Hole winters are long, snowy, windy, and very cold. The park and three visitor centers at Moose, Jenny Lake, and Colter Bay are open year-round. Entrance fees are $20 per vehicle or $10 per person, and are good for both Yellowstone and Grand Teton National Parks; a $40 annual pass is also available. Fees are also charged for personal watercraft usage, backcountry camping reservations, and snow planes. The Moose Visitor Center and Park Headquarters features exhibits on the Greater Yellowstone Area, rare and en-

Jimmy Carter fishing in the Grand Tetons, August 1978. *(Courtesy: Jimmy Carter Library)*

dangered species displays, a video room, and an extensive bookstore. The Colter Bay Visitor Center features an Indian Arts Museum, an auditorium, and a large bookstore. Both are open year-round from 8 A.M. until 5 P.M. daily, and for more extended hours during the summer. The Jenny Lake Visitor Center is only open during the summer and features exhibits on Teton Range geology, a relief model, and book sales. Visitors may also wish to stop by the Flagg Ranch Information Station, which has information about John D. Rockefeller and his contributions to the area's preservation. This facility is open only during the summer and winter. During the summer

months, rangers at all of the centers offer tours and talks, guided walks, and evening campfire programs.

Some of the park's more popular activities include fishing, swimming, hiking, photography, boating, mountaineering, and, in the winter, cross-country skiing and snowmobiling. The park has over 200 miles of horseback and hiking trails for all abilities. Activities such as overnight backpacking, boating, floating, canoeing, fishing, and snowmobiling require fee permits, licenses, or registration, obtainable from the visitor centers.

The park and surrounding area contain 6 developed campgrounds: Colter Bay, Jenny

Lake, Gros Ventre, Lizard Creek, Signal Mountain, and Flagg Ranch. Since all are first-come, first-served, they tend to fill fast in the summer, sometimes as early as 8 A.M. at Jenny Lake, and by noon at Signal Mountain. Gros Ventre, in the park's southern end, rarely fills up. There is a $12 per night per site camping fee. The park also has 7 overnight facilities ranging from rustic-rough to rustic-luxurious: Colter Bay Cabins, Dornan's Spur Ranch Cabins, Flagg Ranch Resort (on the Rockefeller Parkway), Jackson Lake Lodge, Jenny Lake Lodge, Signal Mountain Lodge, and Triangle X Ranch. The American Alpine Club Climber's Ranch offers dormitory accommodations, cooking area, and showers for climbers. Further accommodations and traveler services are available in the tourist-oriented town of Jackson. The park is very crowded during the peak summer season, so the park recommends reservations.

For more information, write Grand Teton National Park, P.O. Drawer 170, Moose, WY 83012, or telephone (307) 739-3300. The park's Web site is www.nps.gov/grte.

FURTHER READING

Betts, Robert B. *Along the Ramparts of the Tetons: The Saga of Jackson Hole, Wyoming.* Boulder: University Press of Colorado, 2001.

Craighead, Frank C., Jr. *For Everything There Is a Season: The Sequence of Natural Events in the Grand Teton–Yellowstone Area.* Helena, MT: Falcon, 1994.

Fishbein, Seymour L. *Yellowstone Country: The Enduring Wonder.* Washington, DC: National Geographic Society, 1989.

Fritz, William J. *Roadside Geology of the Yellowstone Country.* Missoula, MT: Mountain, 1985.

Harris, Burton. *John Colter: His Years in the Rockies.* Lincoln: University of Nebraska Press, 1993.

Jackson, John C. *Shadow on the Tetons: David E. Jackson and the Claiming of the American West.* Missoula, MT: Mountain, 1993.

Righter, Robert W. *Crucible for Conservation: The Struggle for Grand Teton National Park.* Boulder: Colorado Association University Press, 1982.

Smith, Robert B., and Lee J. Siegel. *Windows into the Earth: The Geologic Story of Yellowstone and Grand Teton National Parks.* New York: Oxford University Press, 2000.

GRANT-KOHRS RANCH NATIONAL HISTORIC SITE

Location: Deer Lodge, Montana
Acreage: 1,618
Established: August 25, 1972

In the 1850s, Canadian fur trader Johnny Grant bailed out of the rapidly declining fur business in favor of the booming open-range, cattle-ranching trade. Heading south across the border into Montana Territory, Grant settled in the Deer Lodge Valley northwest of Butte to become one of the area's first cattle ranchers. By 1862, Grant and his family-run operation owned more than 2,000 head of cattle and prospered through trade with Oregon Trail emigrants. The same year, he moved the ranch headquarters closer to the young town of Deer Lodge and built the largest home in Montana Territory for his Bannock Indian wife Quarra and seven children.

In 1866, Grant sold his ranch for $19,000 to a German prospector named Conrad Kohrs. Kohrs learned the butcher trade and sold meat to nearby mining camps. Throughout the late nineteenth century, Kohrs and his partner, John Bielenberg, watched as the Montana cattle industry evolved from open ranges to fenced pastures. During this time, the ranch expanded to 25,000 acres and annually shipped about 10,000 cattle east via rail to Chicago. By the early 1920s, however, the rise of fenced farm homesteads had whittled the ranch down to under 1,000 acres. Both Kohrs and Bielenberg died in the 1920s, leaving the ranch to the Kohrs family, who sold it to Conrad Warren in the late 1940s.

In 1972, the Grant-Kohrs Ranch became the first and only unit of the National Park Service designated to commemorate the nation's frontier cattle era. The 1,618-acre ranch includes 90 structures, and it is maintained today as a working ranch, raising Texas longhorns and Herefords, Belgian draft horses, and other livestock and poultry. The day-use-only site is located adjacent to the town of

Deer Lodge off I-90 and is open year-round. Entrance fees are $2 per person or $4 per vehicle during the summer months only. The visitor center houses an impressive collection of artifacts, and exhibits detail the region's ranching history and heritage. A self-guided tour begins here, and major exhibit venues include the furnished main floor of the 1890s Kohrs manor, the 1930s bunkhouse and tack shed, and the thoroughbred barn housing historic wagons, carriages, and sleighs. Rangers also conduct tours of the fully restored and furnished ranch house/headquarters and guided walks to ranch outbuildings. During the peak summer season, the park offers living-history programs on blacksmithing, chuck wagon cooking, and 1890s cowboy life. During the second weekend of July, the historic site and the city of Deer Lodge celebrate Western Heritage Days to commemorate western U.S. history and culture.

There are no food, lodging, or camping facilities at the site, but Deer Lodge has all traveler services, including 2 campgrounds.

For more information, write Grant-Kohrs Ranch National Historic Site, P.O. Box 790, Deer Lodge, MT 59722, or telephone (406) 846-2070. The park's informative Web site is www.nps.gov/grko.

FURTHER READING

Abbott, E.C., and Helen Huntington Smith. *We Pointed Them North: Recollections of a Cowpuncher.* Norman: University of Oklahoma Press, 1978.

Albright, John. *Kohrs and Bielenberg Home Ranch: Grant-Kohrs Ranch National Historic Site, Montana: Historic Resource Study and Historic Structure Report, Historical Data.* Denver, CO: Historic Preservation Division, National Park Service, 1977.

Atherton, Lewis. *The Cattle Kings.* Bloomington: Indiana University Press, 1971.

Ewing, Sherm. *The Ranch: A Modern History of the North American Cattle Industry.* Missoula, MT: Mountain, 1995.

McChristian, Douglas C. *Ranchers to Rangers: An Administrative History of Grant-Kohrs Ranch National Historic Site.* Washington, DC: National Park Service, 1977. Available at www.nps.gov/grko/adhi/adhi.htm.

Meikle, Lyndel, ed. *Very Close to Trouble: The Johnny Grant Memoir.* Pullman: Washington State University Press, 1996.

GREAT BASIN NATIONAL PARK

Location: Baker, Nevada
Acreage: 77,180
Established: January 24, 1922

The West's Great Basin, named by explorer John C. Frémont, is a huge, flat alluvial plain broken only by wide valleys and parallel north–south mountain ranges. It is a vast, arid high-desert landscape encompassing western Utah and most of Nevada, where rivers all flow inland. It is also home to Great Basin National Park. Like the surrounding area, this is a park of stark environmental contrasts. From sagebrush at lower elevations to the treeless 13,063-foot summit of Wheeler Peak, Great Basin National Park includes streams, lakes, alpine plants, abundant wildlife, and a variety of forest types, including groves of ancient bristlecone pines. The park also contains numerous limestone and marble caverns, such as the beautiful Lehman Caves.

The Lehman Caves were formed millions of years ago, when the mountains were higher and the region was more humid. Carbon dioxide–charged water widened and enlarged cracks in the mountain's limestone formation. As the more water-soluble rock dissolved— and the water table dropped—the process of cave formation and decoration accelerated. Large numbers of stalagmites, stalactites, columns, and shields (round discs of calcite) formed inside. The caves were named after local rancher Absalom Lehman, reportedly the first white man to explore these underground geologic treasures. From 1885 until his death in 1891, Lehman guided spelunkers and other explorers throughout the underground rooms. In 1922, President Warren G.

Harding authorized Lehman Caves National Monument to protect the extensive, fragile cave system. In 1986, the monument and surrounding area were incorporated into the 77,180-acre Great Basin National Park.

Great Basin National Park illustrates one of the difficulties of later national parks in the lower forty-eight states. As are peers such as Guadalupe Mountains, it is small for a national park, and, prior to park establishment, its lands were used by local ranchers. As a result, the region remained hostile to the new national park. This local reticence impinged on visitor experience and placed the park in the difficult position of negotiating between its neighbors and the visiting public.

One of the continental United States' more isolated parks, Great Basin National Park is located on U.S. Highway 6/50, 70 miles east of Ely near the Utah border. It is open daylight hours only, year-round, and although there is no park entrance fee, there are fees to tour Lehman Caves (which vary with length) and fees to camp at the 4 developed campgrounds. The park's visitor center is located on Nevada Highway 488, 5 miles from the town of Baker, and a half mile inside the park's boundary. The center is open year-round from 8:30 A.M. until 6 P.M. during the summer, and until 5 P.M. the remainder of the year. Visitors can peruse numerous interpretive exhibits, 2 short audiovisual presentations, the Great Basin Natural History Association bookstore, a concession gift shop, and café. Ranger-led campfire programs, guided bristlecone hikes, and kids programs are offered from Memorial Day through Labor Day. Park officials also offer daily tours of Lehman Cave, ranging from thirty to ninety minutes in length, which are limited to 25 people. During the peak summer season, these tours sell out quickly, and visitors are advised to buy tickets a day in advance or by telephone.

A variety of hiking trails exist throughout the park. Hiking times range from half-hour to several-day trips. Trails lead to the summit of Wheeler Peak, an ancient bristlecone pine grove, the 75-foot-high Lexington Arch, assorted alpine lakes, and various historic features. In the winter, the Wheeler Peak Scenic Drive is only open to the Upper Lehman Creek Campground and Lehman Creek Trailhead. Opening dates of the higher portions of the road depend on the weather. The road usually opens for the summer season starting in May, June, or early July. It usually closes by late October or November.

Very limited motel accommodations and restaurants are available in Baker. The nearest cities that provide full traveler services are Ely, and Delta, Utah, 100 miles east. The park has 4 developed, first-come, first-served campgrounds: Lower and Upper Lehman Creeks, Wheeler Peak, and Baker Creek (fees charged during the summer). The developed campgrounds fill up, especially on summer weekends. Primitive campgrounds along Strawberry Creek and Snake Creek have no potable water. Only Lower Lehman Creek is open year-round. Other campgrounds and primitive sites open as snow levels permit.

For more information, write Great Basin National Park, Highway 488, Baker, NV 89311, or telephone (775) 234-7331. The park's informative Web site is www.nps.gov/grba.

FURTHER READING

Lageson, David R., Stephen G. Peters, and Mary M. Lahren, eds. *Great Basin and Sierra Nevada.* Boulder, CO: Geological Society of America, 2000.

Ryser, Fred A. *Birds of the Great Basin: A Natural History.* Reno: University of Nevada Press, 1985.

Trimble, Stephen. *The Sagebrush Ocean: A Natural History of the Great Basin.* Reno: University of Nevada Press, 1999.

Unrau, Harlan D. *Basin and Range: A History of Great Basin National Park, Nevada.* Denver, CO: National Park Service, 1990.

GREAT SAND DUNES NATIONAL MONUMENT AND PRESERVE

Location: Mosca, Colorado
Acreage: 84,670
Established: March 17, 1932

Great Sand Dunes National Monument and Preserve is a grand, surreal vista of aeolian–wind-shaped–dunes nestled against the lofty peaks of Colorado's southern Rocky Mountains. Here, North America's tallest sand dunes, more than 700 feet in elevation, push hard against the western slope of the rugged Sangre de Cristo mountain range, forming one of the most complex dune systems in the world. Surrounded on three sides by mountain ranges, the San Luis Valley is a natural sand trap. Over the millennia, prevailing southeasterly winds blew sand and dust from the high plains through a gap in the Sangre de Cristos directly east of the monument, creating the towering dunes within the monument. As these tiny particles swirled and accumulated over time, the dunes eventually encompassed 39 square miles and grew to their present height. In March 1932, after considerable effort by local women's groups, President Herbert Hoover declared the dunes a national monument to protect this unique landscape from the threat of gold mining. The monument was greatly enlarged during President Bill Clinton's administration.

Because of the stark textural and visual contrasts between the soft dunes and the craggy mountains, the monument is a photographer's paradise. Professional and amateur photographers from around the world

Great Sand Dunes National Monument and Preserve. These are North America's tallest dunes, rising over 750 feet against the rugged Sangre de Cristo Mountains. *(National Archives)*

flock to the monument, especially in the spring, fall, and winter, when the light is low and mountain snows create surreal images. Beyond its scenic splendor, the park also protects more than 84,000 acres and the diverse flora and fauna that inhabit this terrain, spanning desert to montane life zones. Historically, the Great Sand Dunes were situated along a major route into the San Luis Valley, and archeological evidence, including rare Clovis/Folsom sites, indicates people have inhabited the region since ancient times.

Located in the remote San Luis Valley approximately 38 miles north of Alamosa, Colorado, the monument is open year-round. Entrance fees are $3 per person and are valid for seven days; a $10 annual pass is also available. The visitor center is open from 9 A.M. until 4:30 P.M., year-round, and until 6 P.M. during the summer. Exhibits explain the area's history and geology, and a video presentation and a computer touch screen provide an orientation to the park and its attractions. During the summer months, park rangers lead interpretive programs and conduct evening slide presentations. One of the park's unique attractions is the annual Sand Castle Building/Kite Flying Day on the last Saturday in June. The monument boasts 18 miles of established trails and 39 square miles of unlimited dune hiking. Four-wheeling is another favorite activity, particularly along the Medano Pass Primitive Road, which leaves from the monument and heads east over Medano Pass.

The monument's weather is fairly consistent. In fall, winter, and spring, expect moderate daytime temperatures and freezing to subzero temperatures at night. Summer temperatures during the day average 70 to 80 degrees, and lows may drop to 40 degrees. Out on the dunes in the summer, sand temperatures can reach 140 degrees during the day.

Pinyon Flats Campground is open year-round, on a first-come, first-served basis. There are 88 campsites with fire grates, picnic tables, and access to flush toilets and drinking water, and the fee is $10 per site per night. The campground is in a piñon/juniper forest and has excellent views of the dunes and the Sangre de Cristo mountains. There is also free backcountry camping, available with a permit. Just outside the park is a private campground with full hookups. A general store and dining are available just outside the monument's boundaries during the season, which lasts from May through October. The town of Alamosa, Colorado, has all travel services.

For more information, write Great Sand Dunes National Monument and Preserve, 11500 Highway 150, Mosca, CO 81146, or telephone (719) 378-2312. The park's Web site is www.nps.gov/grsa.

FURTHER READING

Johnson, Ross B. "The Great Sand Dunes of Southern Colorado." *Mountain Geologist* (1968): 23–29.

Trimble, Stephen. *Great Sand Dunes National Monument: The Shape of the Wind.* Tucson, AZ: Southwest Parks and Monuments, 2000.

GREAT SMOKY MOUNTAINS NATIONAL PARK

Location: North Carolina and Tennessee
Acreage: 521,496
Established: June 15, 1934

By the 1920s, the National Park Service was an established agency with a clearly defined domain that competed with other land management agencies for power and position in the federal bureaucracy. As a result of the outstanding promotional efforts of Stephen T. Mather, Horace M. Albright, and Robert Sterling Yard, who Mather persuaded to start an organization called the National Parks Association in 1919, the national parks enjoyed a distinct and lofty place on the itineraries of Americans who traveled. For Mather and Albright, their success was gratifying. It had been for them a rapid and exhilarating rise.

Among the significant problems that re-

Backpacking in the Great Smoky Mountains of Tennessee. *(National Park Service)*

mained were two intertwined issues: the limited geographic range of the national parks, all of which were in the western half of the nation, and their distance from major population centers. Among the biggest parks, only Rocky Mountain, Yosemite, and Mount Rainier could be said to be close to cities. Yosemite was actually quite a distance from the San Francisco Bay Area by the standards of the 1920s, and neither Denver nor Seattle then qualified for the top rank of American cities. The national parks were equally limited by the means through which most were established. In 1920, nearly every national park had been created from public land.

These inherent limitations led to direct conflict with the U.S. Forest Service (USFS) in the Department of Agriculture. The USFS managed the national forests, expanding if not with the vigor of the park system, still

with considerable speed. USFS responsibilities included recreation, although foresters found the triumphant and ebullient style of the 1920s objectionable and favored more down-to-earth options, and the two agencies often found themselves in uncomfortable conflict. Their missions and constituencies overlapped in ways that made an occasional fracas unavoidable.

National park designation had already become a status symbol in American society, a way of saying that the attributes of a place or a region were exceptional, as well as a way for congressional representatives to bring home the bacon of federal projects. For Mather, these situations provided an advantage that allowed the Park Service to outdistance the Forest Service. Mather simply had to find a way to extend national parks east of the Mississippi River, where, not incidentally, the vast majority of the American population lived.

Little public land in the East limited the obvious options for national park creation. Without vast tracts in federal hands, park creation took three primary avenues: gifts of land from willing donors, purchase of private land, and state purchase or donation of land. A gift laid the basis for the first national park in the East, Acadia in Maine. The move to establish an eastern park system, which took shape and came to fruition during the 1920s, required all three of the strategies.

Of the eastern national parks established during the 1920s, Great Smoky Mountains became the showcase. Its genesis combined the factors that usually supported national park establishment and creation, with the new twist that the need for money required a range of fund-raising strategies and attempts. As early as 1919, Mather began to consider national parks in the East, and the Great Smoky Mountains provided an appealing opportunity. The desire of residents of Knoxville, Tennessee, also contributed. One, Mrs. Anne Davis, visited the American West in 1923 and fell in love with the region's spectacular scenic national parks. She believed the Smoky Mountains were the equal of such places, and her desire and position in the community created a base that supported Mather's goals. When the Southern Appalachian National Park Commission assessed potential parks in the southeast in 1924, Great Smoky Mountains came to the fore. The committee ranked it most suited for national park status among the places it reviewed.

Once the Park Service reached a decision to seek a park along the Tennessee–North Carolina border, the question of land acquisition loomed large. The entire region, while including huge areas of unexplored forest, was privately owned, mostly by timber companies. Individuals lived in the region's "hollers," the small valleys and basins that dotted the forests. Much like their ancestors a century before, these people scraped an existence off the land, but retained fierce regional identity and pride in who they were and where they lived. Cherokee people also lived in the area, the last remnants of a nation the federal government expelled and sent west in the 1830s. The Cherokee had an equally powerful claim to the land and as complete an attachment. Finding the money would be difficult, but not as complicated as clearing the land of its prior inhabitants.

Although Congress enacted legislation permitting the secretary of the interior to evaluate and seek donations of land for Great Smoky Mountains National Park in 1925, passing a law and creating a park were two entirely different propositions. The states of Tennessee and North Carolina and two private organizations that supported the park raised more than $3 million for the project, but the federal government did not contribute funds for the purchase of land. Only when John D. Rockefeller, Jr., offered a donation of $5 million in 1927 could the project proceed. In 1929, Horace M. Albright arranged for purchase and options on more than 225,000 acres of the proposed park, and, in 1930, delegations from Tennessee and North Carolina presented Secretary of the Interior Ray Lyman Wilbur with title to more than 300,000 additional acres. In 1933, the federal government supplied another $1.55 million for additional land. With more than 400,000 acres under title, Congress formally established the park in June 1934.

The park and its eastern partners, Shenandoah and Mammoth Cave, broadened the reach of the park system throughout the country and helped extend its constituency. The vast majority of Americans lived much closer to the eastern parks than to their western peers, making the eastern parks the most heavily visited in the park system. Yet these parks were different; scenically beautiful or unique, they had been cleared of people by purchase and no one could claim the areas were pristine, untouched, or primeval. Their political value was great. As the dollars from visitors rolled in, filling state and local coffers, the base of support for national parks in general widened.

Located less than a two-day drive from half of the American population, the over-521,000-acre Great Smoky Mountains National Park is one of the most visited parks in the system. More than 9 million recreational visits occur each year, as visitors view 5,000-foot peaks such as Thunderhead Mountain, Clingaman's Dome, Charlie's Bunion, and Mount Guyot, all along the North Carolina–Tennessee border. A remarkable network of rivers, vast forests, and a range of animals grace the park. Black bears, the recently reintroduced red wolf, white-tailed deer, and wild hogs are among the prime faunal attractions. Although many visitors never turn off their car ignition and even more never venture more than 100 feet from the main road, getting off the beaten track at Great Smoky Mountains National Park offers a rewarding experience. Admission is free.

The park maintains 6 visitor centers that are open year-round. The Cades Cove Visitor Center, located near the midpoint of the 11-mile, one-way Cades Cove Loop Road, is open Monday through Saturday from 9 A.M. until 5 P.M. from March through October, and on weekdays during the remainder of the year. Cades Cove features seasonal ranger-led programs and indoor and outdoor exhibits of southern mountain life and culture, including Cable Mill, a gristmill which operates spring through fall, the Becky Cable house, and other historic structures. The Oconaluftee Visitor Center, located 2 miles north of Cherokee, North Carolina, on U.S. Highway 441, is open daily (hours vary by season) and includes the Mountain Farm Museum, which

contains a fascinating collection of log structures such as a farmhouse, barn, smokehouse, applehouse, corn cribs, and others. Ranger-led programs and demonstrations of farm life are conducted seasonally. The Sugarlands Visitor Center, located 2 miles south of Gatlinburg on U.S. Highway 441, is open daily and offers a twenty-minute film with Dolby Digital Surround Sound and extensive natural history exhibits. The Gatlinburg Welcome Center, located 2 miles outside of Gatlinburg on Highway 441 South; the Smoky Mountain Visitor Center, located at I-40 exit 407 (Highway 66) in the Smokies Stadium complex; and the Townsend Visitor Center, located in Townsend, Tennessee, are open daily, and each has a Great Smoky Mountains Natural History Association bookstore and shop, as well as local tourist information. Recreation opportunities within the park are abundant and include camping, hiking the park's more than 800 miles of trails, picnicking, sightseeing, fishing, auto touring, horseback riding, nature viewing, and photography. Guided horseback rides are available in season at 5 horse stables in the park in Tennessee and North Carolina.

Lodging is available in the park at LeConte Lodge, located atop 6,593-foot Mount LeConte, the park's third highest peak. The lodge is open from mid-March through mid-October and is accessible only by foot; reservations are required (865-429-5704). The park also maintains 10 campgrounds at various sites. Some are open year-round, others for more limited seasons, and fees and facilities vary. In addition, all traveler services, including food and supplies, are available in surrounding communities.

For more information, write Great Smoky Mountains National Park, 107 Park Headquarters Road, Gatlinburg, TN 37738, or telephone (865) 436-1200. The park's Web site is www.nps.gov/grsm.

FURTHER READING

Brown, Margaret L. *The Wild East: A Biography of the Great Smoky Mountains.* Gainesville: University Press of Florida, 2000.

Callahan, North. *Smoky Mountain Country.* Sevierville, TN: Smoky Mountain Historical Society, 1988.

Campbell, Carlos C. *Birth of a National Park in the Great Smoky Mountains.* Knoxville: University of Tennessee Press, 1960.

Frome, Michael. *Strangers in High Places: The Story of the Great Smoky Mountains.* Knoxville: University of Tennessee Press, 1994.

At Home in the Smokies: A History Handbook for Great Smoky Mountains National Park, North Carolina and Tennessee. Washington, DC: National Park Service, 1984.

Houk, Rose. *Great Smoky Mountains National Park: A Natural History Guide.* Boston: Houghton Mifflin, 1993.

Moore, Harry L. *A Roadside Guide to the Geology of the Great Smoky Mountains National Park.* Knoxville: University of Tennessee Press, 1988.

Pierce, Daniel S. *The Great Smokies: From Natural Habitat to National Park.* Knoxville: University of Tennessee Press, 2000.

Williams, Michael Ann. *Great Smoky Mountains Folklife.* Jackson: University Press of Mississippi, 1995.

GREENBELT PARK

Location: Greenbelt, Maryland
Acreage: 1,176
Established: August 3, 1950

Greenbelt Park, located only 12 miles northeast of Washington, D.C., offers urban dwellers and nature lovers access to many forms of outdoor recreation, including year-round hiking, horseback riding, and camping. Established in 1950, the 1,176-acre park is one of America's first federally managed urban recreational areas. During the colonial era, Maryland farmers worked this land intensively. After burning and clearing away trees and vegetation for high-yield crops such as corn and tobacco, they eventually depleted the soils, and the region could no longer sustain an acceptable level of production. In the early 1900s, discouraged farmers abandoned the denuded and eroded landscape. Today, the park's lands are in the long process of recovering from this legacy of exploitation. Only recently has the native coniferous and deciduous woodland begun to flourish. Mammals such as deer, opossum, foxes, beaver, and raccoons now inhabit the area, and many species of birds have also returned, including doves, owls, woodpeckers, warblers, cardinals, tanagers, and wrens.

Located off exits 23 and 24 on I-495/95, Greenbelt Park is open year-round, with no admission fees. The ranger station is at the campground entrance and offers visitor information on the park and other sites in the surrounding metropolitan area. Rangers are on duty during daylight hours year-round. The park's headquarters is open Monday through Friday, and the self-registration campground is open twenty-four hours. The park contains 9 miles of hiking trails, as well as 3 developed picnic areas that can accommodate as many as 200 people. The Sweetgum Picnic Area, the smallest, also has two sets of playground equipment, a baseball field, and a large field.

Greenbelt Park has a 172-site campground that is open all year and offers a convenient retreat from the pressures of city life. The campground fee is $14 per night, per site, with a maximum of 6 campers and 2 tents per site. There are hot showers and bathroom facilities available for registered campers, but no electrical or water hookups. The park accepts campground reservations (800-365-CAMP) from April to November and highly recommends them. Since the park is close to the College Park and Greenbelt Metro rail stations, it is especially popular with campers who visit Washington in the summer. There is no food or lodging in the park, but all travel services are along Greenbelt Road, and off I-95/495 at exit 20.

For more information, write Greenbelt Park, 6565 Greenbelt Road, Greenbelt, MD 20770, or telephone (301) 344-3944. The park's Web site is www.nps.gov/gree.

FURTHER READING
Wirth, Conrad L. *Parks, Politics, and the People.* Norman: University of Oklahoma Press, 1961.

GREEN SPRINGS NATIONAL HISTORIC LANDMARK DISTRICT
Location: Louisa County, Virginia
Acreage: 14,000
Established: December 12, 1977

The 14,000-acre Green Springs National Historic Landmark District preserves the unique cultural landscape of central Virginia's Piedmont region. Originally settled by Quaker families in the early eighteenth century, the region's remarkable fertility continued to attract agriculturalists. The lush, rolling pastures comprised of volcanic soils sustained various levels of grassland farming for nearly three centuries. And along the Green Springs corridor stand the elegant manor-style homes, farms, and buildings that represent a continuum of rural Virginia vernacular architecture, and many generations of agricultural and social history. Altogether, more than 250 eighteenth- and nineteenth-century structures survive in this unmarred landscape. One of the earliest settlers, Richard Morris, built his Green Springs home (visible from Route 617) in 1772. By the 1790s, he had developed the springs into a popular spa, which attracted residents to the area. Respectful of location and scene, and preserved virtually unaltered, the historic landmark district offers a fine example of how the land has been enhanced by human presence.

In 1973, the district was declared a Virginia Historic Site and nominated to the National Register of Historic Places. In 1977, Interior Secretary Cecil Andrus accepted preservation easements for nearly half of the district's total area. As a result, Green Springs

is jointly managed by the Park Service, the Commonwealth of Virginia, private landowners, and their communities. Although many kinds of structures exist in the park, the district contains 35 privately owned, historically significant buildings constructed between the mid-1700s and the early 1900s. These structures are closed to the public.

Green Springs National Historic Landmark District is an early example of the joint management of lands with many uses and users that became an important trend in the national park system during the 1990s. Initially labeled "greenbelt parks," such areas offered a way for the Park Service to expand its holdings in the lower forty-eight states. They also created an opening for Representative Phil Burton to garner support for massive appropriation bills to create new park areas that, for the first time, included privately owned land, which would be managed by agreement. The change encouraged the Park Service to present ongoing human activity, as well as a static historic or natural past, in the park system. By the early 2000s, such parks had become a prominent trend.

There are no entrance fees, visitor, or public facilities at the historic landmark, but a descriptive brochure is available at the district's office in town, or at Maddox Store at the intersection of Virginia Highways 640 and 613. It is a rural cultural landscape of farms and houses best viewed from the many public roads (some gravel) throughout the district. Prospect Hill Inn, on Virginia Highway 613 in the district, is a private bed-and-breakfast lodge, and a variety of hotels and motels are located in either Richmond or Charlottesville. Camping is available nearby. Meals at Prospect Hill Inn require advance reservations. There are other food and traveler facilities at interchanges along I-64, or in Louisa.

For more information, write Green Springs National Historic Landmark District, 22591 Spotswood Trail,

Elkton, VA 22827, or telephone (804) 985-7293, extension 301. The park's Web site is www.nps.gov/grsp.

FURTHER READING

Ayers, Edward L., and John C. Willis, eds. *The Edge of the South: Life in Nineteenth-Century Virginia.* Charlottesville: University Press of Virginia, 1991.

Koons, Kenneth E., and Warren R. Hofstra. *After the Backcountry: Rural Life in the Great Valley of Virginia, 1800–1900.* Knoxville: University of Tennessee Press, 2000.

The Nature Conservancy. *Uncommon Wealth: Essays on Virginia's Wild Places.* Missoula, MT: Falcon, 1999.

GUADALUPE MOUNTAINS NATIONAL PARK

Location: Salt Flat, Texas
Acreage: 86,416
Established: October 15, 1966

Soaring above the west Texas desert, the mountain mass known as Guadalupe contains portions of the world's largest, most exposed Permian-period limestone fossil reef. More than 250 million years ago, this area was a huge inland sea. Over time, the mountains rose and a shoreline formed, and the reef, called Capitan Reef, created a narrow barrier in a horseshoe shape for about 350 miles along the sea's margin. Lime-secreting organisms were the reef's principal agents of creation. By the end of the Permian period, the reef had died and layers of sediment buried it. A few million years later, a general uplift raised the area—including the now-exposed reef—several thousand feet. A long process of wind and water erosion formed and shaped the Guadalupe Mountain range, and only a small portion of the reef remains buried. Today, the almost-87,000-acre Guadalupe Mountains National Park preserves the most outstanding fossil-bed section of this reef, along with other significant natural and cultural features. From the Chihuahuan desert floor to the coniferous forests, the park's diverse ecosystems are home to more than 1,500 species of plants, 60 species of mammals, 303 species of birds, and 55 species of reptiles and amphibians.

Archeologists have discovered evidence of human habitation in the Guadalupe Mountains dating back six thousand years. The bones of prehistoric mammals, now long extinct, including the four-horned antelope, a primitive species of horse, and a prehistoric bison, have also been found in caves. Early inhabitants were hunters and gatherers that lived in the park's caves, which they ornamented with pictographs. Later inhabitants, including Mescalero Apaches and Spanish conquistadors, eked out an agricultural existence in this arid environment. One famous conquistador was New Mexico's colonizer, Don Diego de Vargas, who visited the region in 1692. Eventually, the U.S. military surveyed the region, and emigrants and gold seekers used this route to head west. In the late 1850s, the Butterfield Overland Mail Company also utilized the military route, and the remains of a mail horse-change stop, the "Pinery," exist near the visitor center.

Proclaimed in the 1960s as part of Lyndon B. Johnson's effort to assure Texas received its share of federal perquisites, Guadalupe Mountains became one of the last three traditional national parks in the lower forty-eight states. Along with Redwood and North Cascades, Guadalupe Mountains attempted to preserve a tract of natural land, albeit that had been used many times. In this, such parks mirrored the past of the park system, but were much smaller, tended to be bought back from private ownership, and lack the majesty of Yellowstone and Yosemite. Yet in their own way, they too were important additions to the park system.

Located 55 miles south of Carlsbad, New Mexico, and 110 miles east of El Paso, Texas, on U.S. Highway 62/180, the park is open year-round, and there is no admission fee. The Pine Springs Headquarters Visitor Center is open from 8 A.M. until 4:30 P.M. daily, and contains natural history exhibits and an auditorium slide program. The center has a bilingual park ranger on duty, and the slide program has captions in English and Spanish. The Historic Frijole Ranch Museum features exhibits on local cultural history, and the McKittrick Canyon Contact Station has outdoor exhibits and a slide program on the canyon's history and geology.

Because no roads bisect the park, it is a hiker's paradise. The park contains more than 80 miles of trails, ranging in difficulty from easy to strenuous. Trails are rocky and often steep and rugged. Some lead to Guadalupe Peak, which, at 8,749 feet, is the highest point in Texas. Others wind around the base of El Capitan, up into the high country and across the top of the reef, and into McKittrick Canyon. Self-guided nature trails are at McKittrick Canyon, Pinery Trail at Pine Springs, and Indian Meadow Trail at Dog Canyon.

The park has no commercial food, lodging, or traveler facilities. All visitor centers have water, and rangers advise backcountry travelers to carry plenty of water, especially during the hot summer months. The closest food and lodging facilities are in White's City, New Mexico, 35 miles northeast of the park. The park's 2 developed campgrounds, Pine Springs and Dog Canyon, have tent and RV sites, water, and rest rooms, but no showers or hookups. The fee is $8 per site per night. The park also has 10 primitive backcounty campgrounds that require a free permit, available at the Headquarters Visitor Center or at the Dog Canyon Ranger Station. The park prohibits fires (including charcoal).

For more information, write Guadalupe Mountains National Park, HC 60 Box 400, Salt Flat, TX 79847, or telephone (915) 828-3251. The park's Web site is www.nps.gov/gumo.

FURTHER READING

Fabry, Judith K. *Guadalupe Mountains National Park: An Administrative History.* Santa Fe, NM: Southwest Cultural Resources Center, 1988. Available at www.nps.gov/gumo/adhi/adhi.htm.

Patterson, Patricia. *Queen, New Mexico: A Historical Perspective on the Settlement in the Guadalupe Mountains, 1865–1975.* Roswell, NM: Hall-Poorbaugh, 1985.

Tennant, Alan, and Michael Allender. *The Guadalupe Mountains of Texas.* Austin: University of Texas Press, 1980.

GUILFORD COURTHOUSE NATIONAL MILITARY PARK

Location: Greensboro, North Carolina
Acreage: 229
Established: March 2, 1917

Of all the battles waged in America's Revolutionary War, the two-hour conflict at north-central North Carolina's Guilford Courthouse was the largest, most hotly contested action of the war's climactic southern campaign. Though the fight did not end the war, the serious loss of British manpower suffered at Guilford Courthouse foreshadowed final American victory at Yorktown, less than a year later.

Thwarted in their efforts to capture the northern colonies, the British turned their attention southward in 1778. Generally, the southern campaigns went very well for British and Loyalist forces. In December of that year, the Redcoats crushed the Patriot militia at Savannah and began efforts to reclaim Georgia, the weakest of the colonies. The following year in May, British General Henry Clinton forced the surrender of more than 5,000 troops in Charleston, the most significant American defeat of the war. With Georgia back in the fold, emboldened British General Charles Cornwallis launched a campaign to subdue the Carolina colonies. But his plans unraveled after two major defeats: Kings Mountain in October 1780, and the Cowpens in January 1781. To reassert himself, Cornwallis became more aggressive, relentlessly pursuing the southern Continental Army

Guilford Courthouse National Military Park. The battle fought here on March 15, 1781, was the largest, most hotly contested action of the Revolutionary War's climactic southern campaign. The battle's outcome foreshadowed Lord Cornwallis's final defeat at Yorktown seven months later. *(National Park Service)*

forces commanded by the crafty, resourceful General Nathanael Greene. Greene, however, had already succeeded in frustrating and dividing British and Loyalist forces by keeping on the run throughout Virginia and North Carolina. In early March 1781, Greene's forces took position at Guilford Courthouse and invited Cornwallis to attack. On March 15, 1781, 4,400 American soldiers and militia dealt a huge setback to England's hopes of retaining even her southern colonies. Although Cornwallis won this battle, he began to realize that he could not win the war. Seven months later, Cornwallis surrendered his troops at Yorktown. When Lord North received the news, he cried, "Oh God, it is all over!"

Established in 1917, the 229-acre Guilford

Courthouse National Military Park (NMP) protects the site of this pivotal battle that opened the campaign to end the Revolutionary War. It was initially managed by the War Department, but was transferred to the National Park Service as part of Franklin D. Roosevelt's reorganization of the federal government in 1933. Guilford Courthouse NMP and its peers provided the fledgling Park Service with a national history the agency could interpret to the public. Even more, the acquisition of such land helped expand the range of areas included in the park system.

Located 6 miles northwest of Greensboro, North Carolina, the park is open year-round during daylight hours, and there is no admission fee. The park's visitor center and headquarters are located at the entrance on New

Garden Road and feature 28 monuments honoring Revolutionary heroes and heroines. Visitors should also see the twenty-minute film *Guilford Letters* and peruse the museum exhibits. There is a 2.25-mile, self-guided, automobile/bicycle tour that begins at the visitor center. Seven informational stops along the route provide on-site interpretive and descriptive information. The historic New Garden Road and more than 2 miles of paved foot trails provide access to important points on the battlefield. Every March 15, the park observes the annual anniversary of the battle, and additional living-history programs are scheduled on Memorial Day, Independence Day, and in the fall.

The park has no food, lodging, or camping facilities, but Greensboro has all traveler services, including a developed city campground located south of town.

For more information, write Guilford Courthouse National Military Park, 2332 New Garden Road, Greensboro, NC 27410-2355 or call (336) 288-1776. The park's Web site is www.nps.gov/guco.

FURTHER READING

Baker, Thomas E. *Another Such Victory: The Story of the American Defeat at Guilford Courthouse That Helped Win the War for Independence.* New York: Eastern Acorn, 1981.

Davis, Burke. *The Cowpens–Guilford Courthouse Campaign.* Philadelphia: University of Pennsylvania Press, 2002.

Rankin, Hugh F. *Greene and Cornwallis: The Campaign in the Carolinas.* Raleigh, NC: Department of Cultural Resources, Division of Archives and History, 1976.

GULF ISLANDS NATIONAL SEASHORE

Location: Florida and Mississippi
Acreage: 137,991
Established: January 8, 1971

Gulf Islands National Seashore protects a stunningly beautiful barrier island system, which stretches from Cat Island in Mississippi to the eastern tip of Santa Rosa Island in Florida. Comprising 137,000-plus acres in multiple units spread over two states, this sprawling park boasts sparkling blue waters, magnificent snowy white beaches, fertile coastal marshes, and dense maritime forests. The islands that comprise the national seashore are made of quartz sand eroded from the Appalachian Mountains and washed downstream into the Gulf of Mexico. More than 250 species of birds inhabit the park's dunes, lagoons, salt marshes, and pine forests, and huge, rare sea turtles crawl ashore to lay their eggs in the warm sandy beaches. The park is also home to the Naval Live Oaks Reservation south of Pensacola, one of America's first attempts at sustained-yield forest conservation; in 1828, the Naval Live Oaks Reservation was placed under protective management by the War Department to provide timbers for constructing naval ships.

The islands also have a rich cultural heritage. Although many native tribes had called the area home—as evidenced by the prehistoric shell mounds—Spanish explorers claimed the area as their own in the early 1500s and encouraged settlement. In 1699, the French-Canadian explorer Pierre Le Moyne d'Iberville landed at Ship Island to lay claim to what would eventually become the colony of French Louisiana. More than a century later, in 1821, the United States purchased the last section of West Florida to permanently exclude further French and Spanish involvement or control in the region. And within a year, the new owners began constructing a series of coastal fortifications along the Gulf, including Fort Massachusetts and Fort Pickens, which remain to the present day.

One of America's most heavily used park properties, Gulf Island is open year-round. Entrance fees are $3 per person or $6 per vehicle and are valid for seven days; a $20 annual pass is also available. Roadways connect the 6 separate geographic locations in

Florida. In Mississippi, a passenger ferry service from Gulfport to West Ship Island operates from March through October. The mainland portion of Davis Bayou in Mississippi can be reached by different roads. Since Hurricane Opal in 1995, new roads have been constructed at Santa Rosa and the Fort Pickens areas.

Gulf Islands National Seashore maintains 4 visitor centers. Mississippi's Davis Bayou area, east of Biloxi, has a visitor center that contains information, interpretive exhibits on the area's history, and publications. A heavy day-use area during the peak summer season, Davis Bayou also has picnic facilities, a ball field, a self-guided nature trail, and boat ramps. It is also one of the few areas in the seashore without sandy beach swimming. The most heavily used section in the park is around historic Fort Pickens in the Florida section. Tours of the old coastal fortification are conducted daily from March through October. The Fort Pickens unit also has a visitor center, a developed campground, stores, and other traveler services. Access is via U.S. Highway 98 south of Pensacola. The Naval Live Oaks Visitor Center is located in Gulf Breeze, and the Fort Barrancas Visitor Center is at the Pensacola Naval Air Station. Self-guiding nature trails are located in Davis Bayou, Mississippi, and Florida's Fort Pickens, Perdido Key, Fort Barrancas, and Naval Live Oaks. Live Oak Bicycle Trail at Davis Bayou and the bike trail at Fort Pickens area offer scenic byways for bicyclists.

The park's 2 campgrounds are located at Davis Bayou in Mississippi and at Fort Pickens in Florida. Davis Bay has 51 sites with hot showers, hookups for water and electricity, and a dump station. Campsites are on a first-come, first-served basis and cost $16 for electric sites and $14 for nonelectric sites. Fort Pickens is a reservation campground (call 800-365-CAMP) featuring paved parking pads, picnic tables, grills, and water and electric hookups. Fees are $20 for electric sites and $15 for nonelectric sites. Picnic areas are located throughout the park. In 1978, the federal government designated Horn Island and Petit Bois Island in Mississippi as wilderness areas. Primitive camping is permitted on these islands, as well as Mississippi's East Ship Island. Primitive camping is also allowed on the beach at the east end of the Perdido Key area in Florida. Food, lodging, and all other traveler services are available in all nearby Florida and Mississippi towns and cities.

For more information, write Gulf Islands National Seashore, 1801 Gulf Breeze Parkway, Gulf Breeze, FL 32561, or telephone (850) 934-2600. The park's informative Web site is www.nps.gov/guis.

FURTHER READING

Bearss, Edwin C. *Fort Barrancas, Gulf Islands National Seashore, Florida.* Denver, CO: Denver Service Center, National Park Service, 1983.
——. *Fort on Ship Island (Fort Massachusetts), 1857–1935: Gulf Islands National Seashore, Harrison County, Mississippi.* Denver, CO: Denver Service Center, National Park Service, 1984.

H

HAGERMAN FOSSIL BEDS NATIONAL MONUMENT

Location: Hagerman, Idaho
Acreage: 4,351
Established: November 18, 1988

Among the mammalian curiosities that existed during Earth's late Pliocene era was a strange combination of zebra and small horse, now known as the Hagerman Horse. This unusual creature was about the size of the present-day Arabian horse and had a single toe instead of a hoof. Given the scientific name of *Equus simplicidens*, the Hagerman Horse has the distinction of being the earliest record of Equus, the genus that includes all modern horses, zebras, and donkeys. South-central Idaho's Hagerman Fossil Beds National Monument contains the largest known concentration of Hagerman Horse fossils in North America and is internationally renowned for protecting the world's richest fossil deposits from the late Pliocene, almost 3.5 million years ago. The fossilized plants and animals found here represent not only the last glimpse of this pre–Ice Age era, but also the earliest appearances of modern flora and fauna.

At the Pliocene's end, the entire region was part of a huge flood plain near a large lake. Heavy precipitation helped produce thick grasslands and streams, which supported a variety of wildlife: small camels, antelopes, ducks, egrets, the Hagerman Horse, mastodons, storks, and swans. Regular seasonal floods buried their skeletons and loose bones under layers of sediment. Because the fossil-laden bluffs were on the west bank of the Snake River, they went largely unnoticed until 1928. At that time, a local rancher showed some fossils he had stumbled across to a U.S. Geologic Survey employee. Subsequent excavations revealed a plethora of almost perfectly preserved fossils, including the largest single deposit of the extinct Hagerman Horse; Smithsonian researchers recovered more than 200 individuals of both sexes and all ages.

Established in 1988, the 4,351-acre Hagerman Fossil Beds National Monument was part of an ongoing effort to represent the natural past as broadly as possible within the park system. Entry does not require an admission fee. The visitor center is open from 9 A.M. to 5 P.M. daily from Memorial Day through Labor Day, and from 10 A.M. to 4 P.M. Thursday through Sunday for the remainder of the year. The center has fossil exhibits and video programs, and park rangers lead regularly scheduled park tours during the summer. Fossils are not on exhibit in the field area. During Memorial Day weekend, the park is home to the Hagerman Fossil Days Celebration. A trail system is available on the north end of the monument that provides access along the bluffs and Snake River. Trail lengths vary from 2 miles up to 20, depending on visitor interests. These trails are open to mountain bikes, hikers, and equestrians. Travelers can obtain directions and maps at the visitor center or at brochure boxes at the trailheads.

The monument has no food, lodging, or camping facilities, but the town of Hagerman has all traveler services. Three Island State Park, 25 miles northwest of the monument in Glenns Ferry, has a large developed campground. There are several commercial RV parks along U.S. Highway 30 between Hagerman and Twin Falls.

For more information, write Hagerman Fossil Beds National Monument, 221 North State Street, Hagerman, ID 83332, or telephone (208) 837-4793. The park's Web site is www.nps.gov/hafo.

FURTHER READING

McDonald, H.G. "More Than Just Horses: Hagerman Fossils Beds." *Rocks and Minerals* 68 (1993): 322–26.

Shallat, Todd A., and Kathryn Ann Baxter. *Secrets of the Magic Valley and Hagerman's Remarkable Horse.* Boise, ID: Black Canyon Communications, 2002.

White, J.A. "The Hagerman Zebra and Other Wildlife." *Idaho Yesterdays* 11:1 (1967): 20–21.

HALEAKALA NATIONAL PARK

Location: Kula, Maui, Hawaii
Acreage: 29,094
Established: August 1, 1916

Few volcanic landscapes in the world are as breathtaking as Haleakala National Park on the Hawaiian island of Maui. According to legend, it was here that the demigod Maui captured the sun, releasing it only after it promised to move more slowly across the sky–Haleakala (emphasis on the last syllable) means "house of the sun." Established in 1916, the national park preserves the outstanding volcanic landscape of the upper slopes of Haleakala and protects the unique and fragile ecosystems of Kipahulu Valley, the scenic pools along O'heo Gulch, and many rare and endangered species.

Rising 10,023 feet above sea level, Haleakala is the larger of the two volcanoes that make up Maui. One of Earth's largest mountain landmasses, Haleakala once stood more than 13,000 feet above sea level, with another 20,000 feet of its height hidden by the Pacific Ocean. As both volcanoes spewed lava and magma, the molten rock coalesced to form a connecting landmass between the

mountains. During an extended dormancy, heavy rains cut streams and valleys down Haleakala's slopes and created a large valley, or crater, near the summit. Although subsequent eruptions formed a series of cinder cones in the crater, geologists estimate that Haleakala's last volcanic activity occurred five hundred to one thousand years ago. Considering the relative instability and potential activity of all Hawaiian volcanoes, it is not considered dormant.

Haleakala was added to the park system in the great burst of energy that accompanied the creation of the National Park Service (NPS). Following the Hetch Hetchy debacle in 1913, when a part of Yosemite National Park was dammed for a water supply for San Francisco, a combination of progressive interests and conservation advocates united to create a bureau to manage the growing number of national parks and monuments. They also sought spectacular scenic places to add to the system, with the important caveat that such areas belong to the federal government. Haleakala nicely fit within this category and was added to the park system just a few short weeks before the establishment of the NPS.

The 29,094-acre park is open year-round, with peak visitation usually occurring in the dryer summer season. Entrance fees are $5 per person or $10 per vehicle for the park's Summit area, and a $20 annual pass is available. Park headquarters, the Haleakala Visitor Center, and the Kipahulu Ranger Station Visitor Center have numerous cultural and natural history exhibits, and rangers are on duty during business hours to answer questions. Both park areas offer guided walks and programs on geology, and natural and cultural history. The park has a significant system of hiking trails and guided walks, and most depart from the visitor centers or park headquarters. Many lead in and around the crater, as well as through the lush valleys on the park's east side, where more than 250 inches of rain fall annually. The park recommends hikers bring rain gear, especially during the monsoon season. Haleakala's summit is also a stargazer's paradise. The visual horizon often extends 115 miles out to sea, and it is so high and clear here—and completely free of urban and other light pollution—that anyone with a set of powerful binoculars, for rent at one of the island's dive shops, can see Jupiter's larger moons.

Haleakala National Park extends from the summit of Haleakala down the mountain's southeast flank to the Kipahulu coast near Hana. There are no direct connecting roads between these 2 sections of the park, but travelers can reach both from Kahului. The summit of Haleakala is a three-hour, round-trip drive from Kahului, via roads 37, 377, and 378. The Kipahulu area is at the east end of Maui between Hana and Kaupo. Visitors can reach it via Highway 36, a curvy, often wet road. Kipahulu is about 90 miles from the resort areas of Wailea or Kaanapali and 60 miles from central Maui. Driving time is about three to four hours each way.

Haleakala has 2 semideveloped campgrounds: Hosmer Grove on the west end and Kipahula (no water) on the east. In addition, the park maintains 3 wilderness cabins for visitor use by advanced reservation lottery. Reaching the cabins requires a hike of 4, 6, or 10 miles for Holua, Kapalaoa, and Paliku, respectively. The park allots each cabin to a party as a unit and can accommodate 12 people a night. Fees are based on the number of people in the party, and travelers must make reservations at least ninety days prior to the trip. There are no food, lodging, gas, or other traveler services in the park, but Hana, Kahului, and Pukalani have all traveler services.

For more information, write Haleakala National Park, P.O. Box 369, Makawao, HI 96768, or telephone (808) 572-4400. The park's Web site is www.nps.gov/hale.

FURTHER READING

Jackson, Frances O. *An Administrative History of Hawaii Volcanoes National Park, Haleakala National Park.* Honolulu, HI: National Park Service, 1972.

Macdonald, Gordon A., and Douglas H. Hubbard. *Volcanoes of the National Parks in Hawaii.* Hawaii Volcanoes National Park: Hawaii Natural History Association in cooperation with the National Park Service, 1982.

Mack, Jim. *Haleakala: The Story Behind the Scenery.* Las Vegas, NV: KC Publications, 1993.

HAMILTON GRANGE NATIONAL MEMORIAL

Location: New York, New York
Acreage: 1
Established: April 27, 1962

Of the early American leaders, no one more clearly anticipated the economic future of the nation than Alexander Hamilton. Born in the West Indies in 1757, Alexander Hamilton began working at the age of thirteen as a clerk in a St. Croix shipping firm, and he quickly rose to become company manager. Recognizing Hamilton's business acumen, his associates decided to finance his education. At seventeen, he enrolled in King's College, now Columbia University, in New York City. Hamilton soon became an ardent defender of American patriotic causes, writing pamphlets and newspaper articles. When the American Revolution began, Congress commissioned him a captain of artillery, and he soon became an aide-de-camp to General George Washington. After the war, Hamilton served as a congressional delegate and was instrumental in creating the new Constitution. He went on to serve as the first secretary of the treasury (1789–1795), where he devised plans for funding the national debt, securing increased federal credit, encouraging expansion of American manufacturing, and organizing a national banking system. He was the primary author of the *Report on Manufactures,* a 1790 document that envisioned the United States as a commercial republic. This report solidified Hamilton's reputation as the intellectual opponent of Thomas Jefferson, who advocated an agrarian economic model for the new nation.

At the end of the eighteenth century, Hamilton commissioned New York City Hall architect John McComb to design a federal-style house in upper Manhattan. Named after the Hamilton family's ancestral home in Scotland, the Grange was completed in 1802 and served as Hamilton's "refuge from politics" for only two years. On July 11, 1804, he was fatally wounded in the "Incident at Weehawken," a duel with his political rival Aaron Burr. He died the next day.

The 1-acre memorial, authorized by Congress in April 1962, is on Convent Avenue between West 141st and West 142nd streets in Manhattan. The Grange is open from 9 A.M. to 5 P.M. Friday through Sunday, and admission is free. The memorial recently underwent a three-year renovation project,

which restored the home with period furnishings, some of which belonged to Hamilton. The facility includes exhibits on the history of Hamilton's life and the Grange.

The memorial has no traveler facilities, but food and lodging are available throughout New York City, and camping is available in the suburbs. Since street parking is scarce, the Park Service strong encourages visitors to use public transportation.

For more information, write the superintendent, Hamilton Grange National Memorial, 287 Convent Avenue, New York, NY 10005, or telephone (212) 666-1640. The park's Web site is www.nps.gov/hagr.

FURTHER READING

Fleming, Thomas J. *Duel: Alexander Hamilton, Aaron Burr, and the Future of America.* New York: Basic Books, 1999.

Flexner, James Thomas. *The Young Hamilton: A Biography.* New York: Fordham University Press, 1997.

Hamilton, Alexander, James Madison, and John Jay. *The Federalist Papers.* Edited by Clinton Rossiter. New York: Mentor Books, 1999.

Knott, Stephen F. *Alexander Hamilton and the Persis-*

Hamilton Grange, built in 1802, features period furnishings and historical exhibits. *(National Park Service)*

tence of Myth. Lawrence: University Press of Kansas, 2002.

HAMPTON NATIONAL HISTORIC SITE

Location: Towson, Maryland
Acreage: 62
Established: June 22, 1948

Upon its completion in 1790, the ornate mansion known as Hampton became the largest private home in the United States. Built over a seven-year period by agriculturalist and merchant Charles Ridgley—who also owned an ironworks facility that supplied cannon and ammunition to American forces in the Revolutionary War—the home and estate remained in the Ridgley family for seven generations. Ridgely's empire rested on the twin pillars of eighteenth-century and antebellum wealth: rich land and the slave labor that worked it. At 24,000 acres, Ridgley's plantation was once the largest in central Maryland, the kind of property that illustrates why Maryland was long considered a southern state. In addition to the house, the vast estate contained numerous outbuildings, large shade trees, extensive English-styled ornamental gardens and topiary, vineyards, orchards, and pastures on which the family raised prize-winning thoroughbred racehorses. A combination of slave labor and indentured workers—people who contracted for a set time to repay the cost of Atlantic passage—accomplished all of this.

Ridgley's support of the American Revolution and his ownership of slaves seem difficult to reconcile, but in his time, this odd combination was typical. When the founding fathers of the United States conceived of democracy, their view was far narrower than today's definition of the concept. As a result, a man like Ridgley, with the best intentions, could support "liberty" without feeling any obligation to extend it to all the people working for him. This contradiction between the language and the meaning of the Declaration of Independence and the U.S. Constitution ultimately divided the nation and led to the Civil War. Long after the Civil War brought about the end of slavery, however, the house remained a symbol of the antebellum lifestyle. The Ridgley family occupied the house until 1948, four years after the Park Service assumed official responsibility for its maintenance and interpretation. In the decades since, it has become an important destination for visitors to the Baltimore area.

Today, the 62-acre site's centerpiece is the cupola-capped, three-story Hampton mansion, an unusually ornate version of the period's typically conservative Georgian architectural style. The nearby slave quarters remind visitors of the way that owners accumulated their wealth, not only from the land, but from the hard work of people who had no choice and received no pay for their labor. Admiring the enormous house is easy; it is harder to recall the pain and suffering that underpinned the idyllic lifestyle within.

Located in Towson, Maryland, north of Baltimore, Hampton National Historic Site preserves this remnant of a once-vast, eighteenth-century plantation estate, an extraordinary example of the power and wealth that landowners could amass in the era of slavery. The site is open daily, year-round, during daylight hours, and is closed on major federal holidays in winter. The Park Service charges a $5 fee to tour the mansion. Period furnishings fill the mansion's many rooms, along with assorted pieces of elegant furniture, carpets, china, chandeliers, and pictures that belonged to the Ridgley family. The house also has a small gift shop and a tea room that serves light lunches.

In addition to touring the mansion, visitors can stroll the remaining estate grounds and elaborate gardens and view the 24 outbuildings. Among these buildings, the slave quarters and stables are the most interesting and well preserved.

All traveler services are available in nearby Towson and Baltimore, and Patapsco State Park, near I-695 in west Baltimore, offers developed camping facilities.

For more information, write Hampton National Historic Site, 535 Hampton Lane, Towson, MD 21286-1397, or telephone (410) 823-1309. The park's Web site is www.nps.gov/hamp.

FURTHER READING
Peterson, Charles E. *Notes on Hampton Mansion.* College Park: National Trust for Historic Preservation Library Collection of the University of Maryland Libraries, 2000.

HARPERS FERRY NATIONAL HISTORICAL PARK

Location: Maryland, Virginia, and
  West Virginia
Acreage: 2,504
Established: June 30, 1944

With its beautiful forests, rivers, valleys, and sheer cliffs, Harpers Ferry was once described by President Thomas Jefferson as "perhaps one of the most stupendous scenes in Nature." Throughout its history, the area has been the backdrop for several significant events in America's history. The Harpers Ferry National Historical Park captures, in

Soldier of the 22nd New York State Militia near Harpers Ferry, West Virginia, 1861. *(Library of Congress)*

this single setting, the convergence of several historical themes: Native Americans, industry and transportation, African Americans, John Brown and slavery, the Civil War, and the natural environment.

Located at the confluence of the Potomac and Shenandoah rivers in West Virginia, Harpers Ferry was founded in 1747 by Philadelphian Robert Harper, who quickly expanded an existing ferry service at the site. In 1796, President George Washington convinced Congress to establish a national armory and arsenal at Harpers Ferry, which soon was producing thousands of small arms annually. By the 1830s, the ferry crossing was caught in the middle of a feverish westward transportation expansion. Not only did the Chesapeake and Ohio Canal towpath pass on

the opposite shore of the Potomac, but the Baltimore and Ohio Railroad (B&O) crossed a bridge from Maryland through Harpers Ferry on its way to the Ohio River Valley. Yet another rail line, the Winchester and Potomac, connected with the B&O at Harpers Ferry. This expansion greatly enhanced the area's economic growth.

It was the events leading up to and including the Civil War that secured Harpers Ferry a distinctive spot in the annals of American history. On October 16, 1859, abolitionist John Brown, a wild-eyed antislavery zealot who had been at the center of the violence in "Bleeding Kansas," and his twenty-man "army of liberation" launched a raid on the federal armory, determined to seize the 100,000 weapons cached there to arm slaves

John Brown's Fort, Harpers Ferry, West Virginia. *(Library of Congress)*

and incite a revolt throughout the South that would free blacks from bondage. Eventually defeated and captured, Brown was tried, found guilty of treason, and hung. While the raid failed, Brown became a martyr for the abolitionist cause, and the event further polarized American public opinion on the moral issue of slavery, pushing the nation inevitably toward civil war.

Harpers Ferry's strategic location between the North and the South played a significant role in the Civil War. On April 18, 1861, less than twenty-four hours after Virginia seceded from the Union, federal troops torched the armory to keep the facility and its 15,000 weapons out of Confederate hands. The Confederacy managed to salvage most of the arsenal's weapons manufacturing equipment, which it moved to a safer location near Richmond. During the course of the Civil War, Harpers Ferry changed hands eight times. Because of its prime location near the Confederate-held Shenandoah Valley, the Union fought with determination to retain the ferry as a staging point for Southern campaigns. After the 1862 battle of Antietam, Union forces built fortifications and retained control over Harpers Ferry; the 1863 creation of West Virginia as a northern state helped keep the ferry in Union hands for the remainder of the war. When held by the Union, Harpers Ferry also became a refuge for runaway slaves. In 1864, Storer Normal School (later Storer College) was founded there to help educate these slaves. Although it closed in 1955, part of the campus is now used as a Park Service training facility.

Established as a national monument in 1944 and redesignated as a national historic park in 1963, the 2,504-acre Harpers Ferry National Historical Park explores the above-mentioned themes through a wide variety of interpretive programs, exhibits, and self-guided hiking tours. Located twenty miles southwest of Frederick, Maryland, on U.S.

Highway 340, the park is open year-round, and entrance fees are $5 per vehicle or $3 per person. The Cavalier Heights Visitor Center is open from 8 A.M. until 5 P.M. daily and houses museum displays on John Brown, black voices, industry, restoration, and the Civil War, as well as a wetlands exhibit. Shuttle buses transport visitors to other sites, including Lower Town, Harper house, the old federal armory buildings, and the ruins of the old industrial center. In addition, many hiking and biking trails are available, and technical rock climbers can scale the sheer rock cliffs on Maryland Heights (permit required). The park also schedules many living-history and special programs throughout the year including Earth Day, July 4, Election Day 1860, and Christmas Day.

There are no food, lodging, or camping facilities in the park, but the town of Harpers Ferry and other nearby communities offer all traveler services. Camping is available nearby in private campgrounds.

For more information, write Harpers Ferry National Historical Park, P.O. Box 65, Harpers Ferry, WV 25425, or telephone (304) 535-6298. The park's informative Web site is www.nps.gov/hafe.

FURTHER READING

Gilbert, Dave. *Waterpower: Mills, Factories, Machines and Floods at Harpers Ferry, West Virginia, 1762–1991.* Harpers Ferry, WV: Harpers Ferry Historical Association, 1999.

Oates, Stephen B. *To Purge This Land with Blood: A Biography of John Brown.* Amherst: University of Massachusetts Press, 1984.

Renehan, Edward J. *The Secret Six: The True Tale of the Men Who Conspired with John Brown.* Columbia: University of South Carolina, 1996.

HARRY S TRUMAN NATIONAL HISTORIC SITE

Location: Independence, Missouri
Acreage: 7
Established: May 23, 1983

America's thirty-third president, fondly known as "Give 'em Hell Harry" for his vo-

Harry S Truman National Historic Site. *(Library of Congress)*

ciferously direct "The Buck Stops Here" leadership style, came from modest, midwestern, agrarian stock. Truman was born in 1884 in Lamar, Missouri, and six years later the family moved to Grandview, Missouri. There he helped work the family farm, met his future wife, Elizabeth "Bess" Wallace, and graduated from high school. During World War I, he served in France as a captain in the field artillery, and then returned home, married Bess, and opened a haberdashery in Kansas City. After attending law school and serving a few terms as a Jackson County judge, Truman was elected to the U.S. Senate in 1935. During World War II, he headed a Senate war investigating committee, checking into waste and corruption, that saved the country as much as $15 billion. In 1944, when voters reelected President Franklin D. Roosevelt for

an unprecedented fourth term, his running mate Harry S Truman became vice president. During Truman's first few weeks in office, he scarcely saw Roosevelt and received no briefing on the development of the atomic bomb or the mounting difficulties with Soviet Russia. Suddenly, these issues became Truman's concerns when, on April 12, 1945, Roosevelt died and Truman became president of the United States. "I felt like the moon, the stars, and all the planets had fallen on me," he remembered.

As president, Truman made some of the most critical decisions in modern history. Soon after V-E Day, he ordered atomic bombs dropped on two Japanese cities, Hiroshima and Nagasaki. The horror of the attacks stunned the empire of Japan, which surrendered soon after, ending the terrible war. His practical, at times confrontational, leadership style in the early Cold War era appealed to voters. In an election famous for the picture of Truman holding a newspaper trumpeting his defeat, he was elected president in 1948 and served until 1953. He helped promote the creation of NATO (North Atlantic Treaty Organization), successfully implemented the Marshall Plan that helped rebuild postwar Europe, devised the Truman Doctrine that helped Greece, Turkey, and other Mediterranean countries check Communist aggression, and gained UN approval for a peacekeeping force in South Korea after North Korea's 1950 invasion. At home, Truman championed the Fair Deal, a twenty-one-point domestic program to promote full employment, expand Social Security, and provide public housing. Although a third term beckoned the popular president, Truman chose to return to his home in Independence with his wife, Bess, where he lived until his 1972 death. Bess Truman died in 1982.

Established in 1982, the Harry S Truman National Historic Site includes the Truman Home in Independence, Missouri, and the Truman farm home located 20 miles south in Grandview. Both units are located within the Kansas City metropolitan area. Truman lived in the 219 North Delaware Street house from 1919 until his death. The white Victorian house was built by the maternal grandfather of Bess Wallace Truman, and it was known as the "Summer White House" during the Truman administration. The site also includes the 2 adjacent homes of Bess Truman's brothers and, across Delaware Street, the home of the president's favorite aunt and cousins. The Truman farm home was built in 1894 by Harry Truman's maternal grandmother. The farm home is the centerpiece of a 5-acre remnant of the family's once 600-acre farm. His mother claimed that it was here that Harry got his "common sense." Several outbuildings

also remain on the site. Admission to the historic site is $2 per person, which includes the guided tours offered at both sites. Self-guided tours of the grounds are available daily, and between Memorial Day and Labor Day, the park offers guided walking tours of historic Independence and the Truman neighborhood. The Independence Visitor Center has an introductory audiovisual program, interpretive exhibits, and a bookstore. There is no visitor center in Grandview.

The park has no food, lodging, or camping facilities, but Independence, Grandview, and the metropolitan Kansas City area have all traveler services, and there also are numerous private, developed campgrounds in the region.

For more information, write Harry S Truman National Historic Site, 223 North Main Street, Independence, MO 64050, or telephone (816) 254-9929. The park's Web site is www.nps.gov/hstr.

FURTHER READING

Beschloss, Michael R. *The Conquerors: Roosevelt, Truman and the Destruction of Hitler's Germany, 1941–1945.* New York: Simon and Schuster, 2002.

Hamby, Alonzo L. *Man of the People: A Life of Harry S Truman.* New York: Oxford University Press, 1995.

McCullough, David. *Truman.* New York: Simon and Schuster, 1992.

Truman, Harry, and Margaret Truman, ed. *Where the Buck Stops: The Personal and Private Writings of Harry S Truman.* New York: Warner Books, 1989.

HAWAII VOLCANOES NATIONAL PARK

Location: Hilo, Hawaii
Acreage: 323,431
Established: August 1, 1916

Established in 1916, Hawaii Volcanoes National Park displays the awesome results of 70 million years of volcanism, migration, and evolution—the fundamental processes that thrust bare land from the sea and colonized it with unique ecosystems and distinctive human cultures. Located on the southeastern corner of the island of Hawaii, the park contains not only the world's most massive volcano, the 13,677-foot Mauna Loa, but also the world's most continuously active volcano, the 4,900-foot Kilauea, which has been in various stages of eruptive activity since January 1983. More than half of the park is designated wilderness, and it is home to plant and animal species found nowhere else on earth.

The park is part of the first generation of national park areas, a scenically spectacular place for which there was no apparent commercial economic use at the time of its establishment. Established just two short weeks before the founding of the Park Service, Hawaii Volcanoes reflected the Progressive-era enthusiasm for spectacular nature and the powerful conservation sentiment of the legislatures of that era. Hawaii was a territory at the park's establishment, but this was hardly an obstacle and in fact may have made founding the park politically easier. Here was a place of beauty and power; creating a national park added both it and the Hawaiian islands to the pantheon of the American spectacular.

Not surprisingly, most activities at Hawaii Volcanoes focus on the park's namesake. Kilauea, whose name means "spreading, much spewing," offers scientists valuable insight into the birth and creation of the Hawaiian island chain, while visitors can enjoy dramatic—sometimes terrifying—views of an active volcanic process. Along Kilauea's slopes, patches of vegetation border recent flows,

"Devastation Trail" is the name given to this boardwalk through skeletons of trees destroyed by the 1969 volcanic eruption in Hawaii Volcanoes National Park. *(National Archives)*

providing a natural laboratory in which to study plant succession. Although less dramatic in recent years than its smaller neighbor, Mauna Loa is still considered an active volcano; it last erupted in 1984. Its name means "long mountain" and it has a long history, one key to the island's formation. Millions of years ago, a hot spot in the earth's mantle caused lava and gases to spurt from cracks located 18,000 feet below the ocean's surface. As more layers of lava piled on top of one another, the island of Hawaii emerged. Mauna Loa's size is staggering; this massive mountain rises 32,000 feet from the ocean floor to the summit. In this sense, it is more massive than the world's highest mountain, Mount Everest. (Mauna Kea, north of the park, is even higher at 13,800 feet above sea level, but it is not an active volcano.)

A popular locale with natives and mainland tourists alike, the 323,431-acre Hawaii Volcanoes National Park is open all day, year-round. Entrance fees are $10 per vehicle or $5 per individual and are valid for seven days. A $20 annual pass is also available. The Kilauea Visitor Center, located just inside the park entrance, offers visitor information and interpretive exhibits, and films and videos are shown in the auditorium throughout the day. Park rangers offer daily talks and guided walks, as well as occasional evening programs as part of the "After Dark in the Park" series. Free educational programs on biological and geological subjects and Hawaiian cultural and historical topics are held in the Kilauea Visitor Center auditorium. The annual Hawaii Native Cultural Heritage festival celebrates Hawaii's native population. The Thomas A. Jaggar Museum, located about 3 miles from the park's entrance, offers earth science displays and features murals depicting Hawaiian culture. An adjacent overlook offers a panoramic view of Kilauea Caldera and Mauna Loa.

Near Kilauea, the 11-mile Crater Rim Drive winds through lush forests, craters, and areas of total volcanic devastation. Many interesting hiking trails and overlooks take off from this road, including 1 that leads through the Thurston lava tube. Visitors can also drive part-way up Mauna Loa, which leads to many scenic hiking trails and overlooks. Experienced mountaineers can hike Mauna Loa to the summit, but they should be prepared for extreme weather shifts, including high winds and year-round snowstorms. Since the park is situated on 2 active volcanoes, there are many hidden hazards for those unfamiliar with volcanic environments. The Park Service advises visitors to wear adequate clothing and sturdy shoes, to stay on designated trails, and not to enter closed areas or lava tubes (except Thurston). Some sections of the park near the Kilauea caldera and lava flow can be evacuated on a moment's notice if increased volcanic activity poses a direct threat. Because volcanic fumes are very hazardous to human health, visitors with heart or breathing problems, infants, young children, and pregnant women should avoid stopping at Sulphur Banks, Halema'uma'u Crater, and other areas where gaseous fumes can overwhelm.

Lodging is available in the park at the historic Volcano House (808-967-7321), located on the rim of the Kilauea caldera. Facilities include 42 rooms and 10 cabins, some with spectacular views of the crater, gift shops, and a restaurant/bar. Prices range from $40 to $185 per day and reservations are required. All other traveler services are located in the town of Volcano, 1 mile outside the park on road 11, and in Hilo, 30 miles northeast.

The park maintains 2 developed campgrounds, and both operate on a first-come, first-served basis. Namakani Paio is open all year and has rest rooms, water, picnic tables, and barbecue pits. Kulanaokuaiki is also open all year, and it has 3 sites with barbecue grills, picnic tables, and a vault toilet. There is no water at this location. Backcountry wilderness camping is available with a free permit.

For more information, write Hawaii Volcanoes National Park, P.O. Box 52, Hawaii National Park, HI 96718-0052, or telephone (808) 985-6000. The park's Web site is www.nps.gov/havo.

FURTHER READING

Jackson, Frances. *National Parks in Hawaii: 50 Years, 1916–1966: A Short History of Hawaii Volcanoes National Park.* Honolulu: Hawaii Natural History Association, 1966.

MacDonald, Gordon. *Volcanoes in the Sea: The Geology of Hawaii.* Honolulu: University of Hawaii Press, 1983.

Stone, Charles P. *Hawaii's Plants and Animals: Biological Sketches of Hawaii Volcanoes National Park.* Honolulu: Hawaii Natural History Association, 1994.

HERBERT HOOVER NATIONAL HISTORIC SITE

Location: West Branch, Iowa
Acreage: 187
Established: August 12, 1965

Born August 10, 1874, in West Branch, Iowa, Herbert Clark Hoover was the first American president to hail from west of the Mississippi River. He experienced a traumatic childhood. Orphaned by the age of ten, the young Hoover and his two siblings bounced around from one family member to another, eventually ending up in Oregon to live with an aunt and uncle. When he was seventeen, Hoover enrolled in the first class of Stanford University's School of Engineering as a geology major. There he met his wife, Lou Henry, and after his 1895 graduation, they went to China, where he worked for a private corporation as China's leading engineer. During the 1900 Boxer Rebellion, Hoover directed the building of barricades and once risked his life to rescue Chinese children caught in the cross-fire. By the age of twenty-seven, he had become a junior partner in an international mining consulting firm. When World War I broke out, Hoover was called upon to help

stranded American tourists escape from Europe. In just six weeks, he coordinated the safe return of nearly 120,000 Americans. Hoover then turned his attention toward the people of Europe, supervising various international relief agencies that helped feed people around the world. In 1921, Hoover was selected by President Warren Harding as secretary of commerce, a post he held until his election to the presidency in 1928. When he ascended to office, he was the most qualified person to ever attain the White House.

During the 1928 campaign, Hoover had confidently predicted that "we in America today are nearer to the final triumph over poverty than ever before in the history of any land." To Americans, their choice for president seemed obvious—"Who, but Hoover!" the slogan went. A national economic collapse and the subsequent Great Depression challenged Hoover. His limited responses, based in his Quaker principles that people should help themselves, doomed his presidency. Voters considered his well-intentioned —if belated—efforts to reduce the disastrous impact of the stock market crash, to be inadequate. He quickly became the scapegoat for the Depression; indeed, the man who had fed Europe was roundly vilified at home. A sculptor gave the fitting epitaph for his presidency: "if you put a rose a in Hoover's hand," he observed, "it would wilt." In November 1932, he was soundly defeated by Democrat Franklin D. Roosevelt, who promised a "New Deal" for the American people. After his defeat, Hoover retired to California, where he devoted his time to organizing the Hoover Institute on War, Revolution, and Peace. After World War II, President Harry S Truman called upon Hoover to help oversee administration strategies to check postwar famine. Hoover also chaired various commissions to help improve the efficiency of the federal government's executive branch. Herbert Hoover died in October 1964, at the age of ninety, and is buried with his wife on a hillside overlooking his West Branch birthplace.

Established in August 1965, the 187-acre national historic site preserves Hoover's birthplace, the Friends Meetinghouse, Hoover's boyhood neighborhood, and the grave sites of President and Mrs. Hoover. In addition, the site also houses the Hoover Presidential Library and Museum, which is administrated by the National Archives and Records Administration. Located 10 miles east of Iowa City along I-80, the Herbert Hoover National Historic Site is open year-round, and the $2-per-person entrance fee admits visitors to both the historic site and the presidential library-museum. A replica of a typical blacksmith shop, similar to the one operated by Herbert Hoover's father, is located near the Birthplace Cottage. Next to it is the oldest schoolhouse in West Branch. Four of the historic buildings, including the Birthplace Cottage, are open to the public. The site also has natural features for hiking (and cross-country skiing in the winter), including 1.7 miles of hiking trails amid the park's restored 76-acre tall-grass prairie. The visitor center is open daily from 9 A.M. until 5 P.M., and it provides an orientation video, interpretive exhibits, programs, and information. Park rangers offer daily guided tours of the site and prairie walks. The library and museum also have a variety of exhibits. Hooverfest is held the first weekend in August and celebrates the president's birthday with craft demonstrations. Other special activities include a fall apple cider pressing on the first weekend in October, and Christmas Past, on the first weekend in December.

There are no food, lodging, or camping facilities in the park, but West Branch and Iowa City have all traveler services. Several private campgrounds are located nearby, and Lake McBride State Park, 25 miles northwest of West Branch, has a developed campground.

For more information, write Herbert Hoover National Historic Site, 110 Parkside Drive, P.O. Box 607, West Branch, IA 52358, or telephone (319) 643-2541. The park's Web site is www.nps.gov/heho.

FURTHER READING

Fausold, Martin L. *The Presidency of Herbert C. Hoover.* Lawrence: University Press of Kansas, 1985.
Nash, George H. *Life of Herbert Hoover: The Humanitarian, 1914–1917.* New York: W.W. Norton, 1996.
Wilson, Joan Hoff. *Herbert Hoover: Forgotten Progressive.* Boston: Little, Brown, 1975.

HISTORIC CAMDEN

Location: Camden, South Carolina
Acreage: 107
Established: May 24, 1982

Originally known as Fredericksburg Township, the area around Camden, South Carolina, was laid out during the winter of 1731–1732 under instructions from King George II. By 1768, the Wateree River town had become a vibrant center of inland trade and commerce. That same year, the town's current name was adopted in honor of a member of the British parliament who championed American colonial rights: Charles Pratt, Lord Camden.

Following the 1780 fall of Charleston in the Revolutionary War, Camden was occupied by British troops. In his quest to save the southern colonies from American takeover, British General Charles Lord Cornwallis established several fortified military posts inland, one of which was Camden. Although the British and their Loyalist allies successfully defended Camden against the intrusion of determined American forces, heavy casualties throughout the South (see Kings Mountain and Guilford Courthouse National Military Parks and Cowpens National Battlefield) forced the British to burn their fortifications and evacuate, leaving Camden to the Americans in May 1781.

Authorized in 1982, the 107-acre Historic

Camden site protects and interprets this eighteenth-century colonial village. The park is open daily, and although there is no admission fee, the Park Service does charge a guided-tour fee. Historic Camden includes several period buildings and structures that have been reconstructed or moved to their present location. The Cunningham House (1840) serves as both the park and tour headquarters. The original town site, next to the museum center, offers archeological findings, including partial reconstructions of the town wall and powder magazine, as well as the reconstructed home of the town's founder.

The park has no food, lodging, or camping facilities, but the town of Camden has all traveler services. Three state parks located near Camden—Lee, Lake Wateree, and Sesquicentennial—have developed campgrounds with water and electrical hookups.

For more information, write Historic Camden, P.O. Box 710, Camden, SC 29020, or telephone (803) 432-9841. The park's Web site is www.historic-camden. org.

FURTHER READING

Kirkland, Thomas J. *Historic Camden.* Camden, SC: Kershaw County Historical Society, 1994.
McKain, James D. *Index to Historic Camden, Colonial and Revolutionary and Nineteenth Century.* Columbia: The South Carolina Magazine of Ancestral Research, 1995.

HOME OF FRANKLIN D. ROOSEVELT NATIONAL HISTORIC SITE

Location: Hyde Park, New York
Acreage: 800
Established: January 15, 1944

The thirty-second president of the United States, Franklin Delano Roosevelt, was born in 1882 at Springwood mansion in Hyde Park, New York. This sumptuous estate was originally built around 1800 as a large farmhouse, and Franklin's father, James Roosevelt, purchased it in 1867. Eventually, the Roosevelt family expanded and altered the farmhouse into the spacious mansion preserved today. Following his father's death in 1900, Franklin and his mother continued to live in the house. In 1905, after graduating from Harvard Law School, he married his distant cousin Eleanor Roosevelt, and began practicing law. Franklin soon followed the example of another distant cousin—Theodore Roosevelt—and entered public service; in 1910, he was elected to the New York state senate. President Woodrow Wilson later appointed him assistant secretary of the navy (a position also held by Theodore Roosevelt), and in 1920, Franklin Roosevelt was the Democratic nominee for vice president.

The following year, disaster hit when Franklin was stricken with polio as he sailed a boat. With the sheer force of will, he was able to guide the boat to shore as he lost control over his legs. The illness made him a different person. Instead of the privileged dilettante he had been, he emerged as a fighter in the truest sense of the word. Determined to continue with his political career, he fought to regain the use of his legs and was elected governor of New York in 1928 and 1930. The timing of national events proved fortuitous for Franklin Roosevelt. As America's economy collapsed—and President Herbert Hoover's belated economic recovery policies were deemed inadequate by voters—Roosevelt ascended to the White House by promising Americans a "New Deal" in the 1932 election. Roosevelt's New Deal ushered in a new era of government—the welfare state—and his foreign policy transformed the aggressive Monroe Doctrine into a "good neighbor" policy in the Western Hemisphere. When the Japanese attacked Pearl Harbor on December 7, 1941, Roosevelt directed the nation's war effort, declaring that this day would "live in infamy." As the war drew to a close, however, Roosevelt's health deteriorated, and on April 12, 1945, he died of a cerebral hem-

Lifelong residence of President Franklin D. Roosevelt in Hyde Park, New York. *(Library of Congress)*

orrhage. Throughout his four terms as president, Roosevelt and his family were never very comfortable with living in the White House, and they frequently retreated to his Hyde Park home. Three days after his death, Roosevelt was buried at Springwood in the Rose Garden, and seventeen years later Eleanor was buried beside him.

In 1944, Congress designated this 800-acre estate as a national historic site to preserve the birthplace and lifetime residence of President Franklin D. Roosevelt. Located in southeastern New York, about 6 miles north of Poughkeepsie on U.S. Highway 9 in Hyde Park, the site is open year-round. The $10 entrance fee is valid for seven days and includes a guided tour of the FDR home and admission to the presidential museum. Exhibits include the furnished home, the Rose Garden and Gravesite, the Ice House, and

stables maintained and operated by the National Park Service. The FDR Presidential Museum and Library is maintained and operated by the National Archives and Records Administration. In addition to the regularly scheduled guided tours of the home, the park occasionally offers programs on themes dealing with Roosevelt's presidency, policies, conservation, home life, and personal and political challenges. The Dutchess County Tourist Information Center, located on the grounds, is open from 9 A.M. until 5 P.M. from April through October and has exhibits, maps, and information about tourist sites in New York's historic Hudson River Valley.

There are no food, lodging, or camping facilities at the site, but lodging and meals are available in the surrounding Hyde Park and Poughkeepsie area, and Mills-Norrie State

Park, 5 miles north on U.S. Highway 9, offers developed campsites.

For more information, write Home of Franklin D. Roosevelt National Historic Site, 4097 Albany Post Road, Hyde Park, NY 12538, or telephone (845) 229-9115. The park's Web site is www.nps.gov/hofr.

FURTHER READING

Beschloss, Michael R. *The Conquerors: Roosevelt, Truman and the Destruction of Hitler's Germany, 1941–1945*. New York: Simon and Schuster, 2002.

Freidel, Frank. *Franklin D. Roosevelt: A Rendezvous with Destiny*. Boston: Little, Brown, 1990.

Leuchtenburg, William E. *Franklin D. Roosevelt and the New Deal, 1932–1940*. New York: Harper and Row, 1963.

Schlesinger, Arthur M., Jr. *The Crisis of the Old Order, 1919–1933*. Boston: Houghton Mifflin, 1988.

——. *The Coming of the New Deal*. Boston: Houghton Mifflin, 1988.

——. *The Politics of Upheaval*. Boston: Houghton Mifflin, 1988.

HOMESTEAD NATIONAL MONUMENT OF AMERICA

Location: Beatrice, Nebraska
Acreage: 195
Established: March 19, 1936

On May 20, 1862, President Abraham Lincoln signed into law the Homestead Act. Designed to alleviate decades of public pressure on the government to donate public lands to ever-increasing numbers of westward moving settlers, the act allowed a U.S. citizen—or immigrant who declared intentions to become a citizen—to settle, improve, and attempt an agrarian life on 160 acres of unappropriated government land.

The act, however, was not without certain conditions. To gain full title to the parcel, a claimant was required to pay a minimal filing fee, maintain a physical presence on the land, build and live in a house, cultivate a minimum of 10 acres of crops, and make substantial improvements over a five-year period. There were also some conceptual shortcom-

ings to the Homestead Act. While 160 acres was usually sufficient to develop and work a farm in the humid regions (roughly) east of the Missouri and Mississippi rivers, 160 acres was inadequate for crop production or livestock maintenance in the arid Great Plains and many sections of the West without supplemental irrigation. As a result, many homesteaders in the dryer sections of the country, who could not afford irrigation technology, found it impossible to eke out a living on a mere quarter section. Nevertheless, though racked with land-speculation fraud and squatting problems, the Homestead Act was generally successful. Between 1863 and 1935, the government deeded more than 275 million acres of public domain—10 percent of the area of the United States—to homesteaders under the Homestead Act and other subsequent land disposal legislation. The act remained in effect until 1976, with provisions for homesteading in Alaska until 1986.

Authorized in 1936, the 195-acre Homestead National Monument commemorates the impact of the Homestead Act of 1862 upon the nation. Located 4 miles west of Beatrice, Nebraska, on Nebraska 4, the monument is open year-round, and admission is free. The site itself preserves one of the first homesteads claimed—Daniel and Agnes Freeman's claim from January 1, 1863. Although the Freemans raised six children and worked the farm—and are buried on the site's eastern boundary—nothing remains of the original buildings. The monument includes the original homestead foundations and grounds, the Freeman School, a 1-room schoolhouse, and the Palmer-Epard cabin, an 1800s structure moved from another site. The park also contains nearly 100 acres of restored tall-grass prairie. Begun in 1939, this is the oldest prairie restoration in the National Park System and the second oldest of any in the nation. The Homestead Visitor Center, near the en-

The Palmer-Epard cabin at Homestead National Monument of America. *(National Park Service)*

trance, contains information, exhibits, and a short video that explains the Homestead Act and the site. An easy, two-and-a-half-mile trail leads to the Freeman building foundations, through the tall-grass prairie, and up to the Freemans' graves. The gravesite also offers outstanding vistas of the site. The park periodically offers guided walks and living-history programs. Other special events include Homestead Days on the last full weekend in June, and the Winter Festival of Prairie Cultures in early December.

There is no lodging, camping, or food onsite, but the town of Beatrice has all traveler services, including 2 city parks with camping facilities.

For more information, write Homestead National Monument of America, 8523 West State Highway 4, Beatrice, NE 68310, or telephone (402) 223-3514. The park's Web site is www.nps.gov/home.

FURTHER READING

Homestead National Monument of America, Beatrice, Nebraska: Cultural Landscape Report. Omaha, NE: National Park Service, Midwest Systems Support Office, 2000.

Layton, Stanford J. *To No Privileged Class: The Rationalization of Homesteading and Rural Life in the Early Twentieth-Century American West.* Salt Lake City, UT: Signature Books, 1988.

Lee, Lawrence Bacon. *Kansas and the Homestead Act, 1862–1905.* New York: Arno, 1979.

HOPEWELL CULTURE NATIONAL HISTORICAL PARK

Location: Chillicothe, Ohio
Acreage: 1,170
Established: March 2, 1923

Hopewell Culture National Historical Park preserves an important piece of the human history of the continent. When Europeans arrived in the Midwest, they found mounds that pointed to the existence of a sophisticated society before them. Places such as Hopewell Culture—named for the prehistoric mound-building society—reveal a history that is hard for Americans to fathom. Between about 200 B.C.E. and 500 C.E., the Ohio River Valley was the focal point of the Hopewell Culture a term used by archeologists and anthropologists to describe the distinctive North American Indian communities across the eastern stretches of the continent that shared a common set of beliefs and practices expressed in this unique mound-building construction. Many of these structures, which served as ceremonial grounds for interring the dead, were built on a monumental scale, with earthen walls as high as 12 feet outlining geometric figures more than 1,000 feet across.

Items found within these burial mounds suggest that the Hopewell people surpassed most native peoples of the time in their level of artistic development. In addition to their high-grade pottery and stone tobacco pipes, the Hopewellians fashioned many of their elaborate and finely crafted objects from exotic raw materials, including headdresses and breastplates of copper from the Great Lakes area, carved obsidian from the Rocky Mountains, mirrors of mica from the Appalachians, marine shells from the Gulf of Mexico, and grizzly bear teeth from the West. Thousands of these treasures are now held in the park's museum and archives, along with numerous artifacts from more recent historic time periods.

One of the greatest concentrations of earthen mounds, hilltop enclosures, and geometric earthworks in the form of circles, squares, and octagons is found in the Scioto River Valley near present-day Chillicothe, Ohio. Five of these major centers are now preserved and protected as the 1,170-acre Hopewell Culture National Historical Park.

First established in 1923 as the 57-acre Mound City Group National Monument, the park was renamed in 1992 as the site expanded to include 3 other units.

The park's visitor center is located 3 miles north of Chillicothe and features permanent museum exhibits displaying Hopewellian artifacts excavated at the Mound City Group and the award-winning seventeen-minute orientation video *Legacy of the Mound Builders*. A 1.5-mile self-guided trail through the Mound City starts at the visitor center, and during the peak summer season, park rangers lead guided tours. The park also offers special programs throughout the year, mostly featuring American Indian and archeological themes.

The visitor center is open daily from 8:30 A.M. until 6 P.M. from Memorial Day through Labor Day, and until 5 P.M. the rest of the year; from December through February, the park is closed on Mondays and Tuesdays. Entrance fees are $2 per person or $4 per vehicle, and a $20 annual pass also is available.

There are no food, lodging, or camping facilities at the park, but Chillicothe has all traveler services, including private campgrounds.

For more information, write Hopewell Culture National Historical Park, 16062 State Route 104, Chillicothe, OH 45601-8694, or telephone (740) 774-1126. The park's Web site is www.nps.gov/hocu.

FURTHER READING

Cockrell, Ron. *Amidst Ancient Monuments: The Administrative History of Mound City Group National Monument/Hopewell Culture National Historical Park, Ohio.* Omaha, NE: National Park Service, Midwest Support Office, 1999. Available at www.nps.gov/hocu/adhi/adhi.htm.

Greber, N'omi. *The Hopewell Site: A Contemporary Analysis Based on the Work of Charles C. Willoughby.* Boulder, CO: Westview, 1989.

Korp, Maureen. *The Sacred Geography of the American Mound Builders.* Lewiston, NY: E. Mellen, 1990.

Romain, William F. *Mysteries of the Hopewell: Astronomers, Geometers, and Magicians of the Eastern Woodlands.* Akron, OH: University of Akron Press, 2000.

HOPEWELL FURNACE NATIONAL HISTORIC SITE

Location: Elverson, Pennsylvania
Acreage: 848
Established: August 3, 1938

One of the finest remaining examples of a nineteenth-century, rural, iron plantation, Hopewell Furnace National Historic Site preserves the facility built by ironmaster Mark Bird in late 1771, at the headwaters of southeastern Pennsylvania's French Creek. Bird's construction of Hopewell Furnace defied an English law that prohibited the manufacture of finished iron products by colonists. Yet the law was rarely—and poorly—enforced, and soon after its completion, Hopewell was in production, making cast-iron stove plates. To make his style of cast-iron products and molds, Bird used iron ore, limestone (to eliminate impurities), and charcoal. Much like other early American industrial enterprises, the facility was powered by a water wheel on French Creek.

During the Revolutionary War, Hopewell Furnace provided George Washington's Continental Army with cannons, shells, and other armament. And though the postwar depression (and a flood) forced Bird out of business in 1786, Hopewell Furnace restarted operations in 1816 under new owner Clement Brooke. Until 1844, the facility roared twenty-four hours a day, using tenant workers to produce tens of thousands of cast-iron wood-burning stoves, kettles, pots, and pans. During this time, the facility consumed the equivalent of 1 acre of hardwood forest—converted into charcoal—to process 6 tons of ore. Hopewell's prosperity, however, could not continue. In the two decades before the Civil War, Hopewell Furnace's production declined, due to frequent economic recessions, reduced demand for finished iron goods, and increased competition from larger ironworks located near major transportation centers like Pittsburgh. Although the small plant tried to compete, it could not. After producing 65,000 stoves, Hopewell Furnace closed for good in the summer of 1883, as technological improvements in iron production rendered the charcoal process obsolete.

Originally established in 1938 as Hopewell Village National Historic Site, this wooded 848-acre park preserves one of the finest examples of nineteenth-century rural American industrial history. Located about 45 miles northwest of Philadelphia, the historic site is open year-round, and entrance fees are $4 per person (additional fees are charged for special programs); a $20 annual pass is also available. The park's visitor center features an introductory slide program and interpretive exhibits that explain the iron-making process at Hopewell. The center is also the starting point for a self-guided tour of the restored community, including the charcoal cooling house, blast furnace, water wheel, tenant houses, company store, and ironmaster's house. Additional trails provide opportunities for woodland recreation and visiting other historic features like the charcoal hearths and collier pits. More than 10 buildings are open daily as museums, and audio programs in the buildings tell the story of the structure or its relationship to the operation of the furnace. Other buildings are used by staff in period attire to conduct living-history demonstrations, and the working farm introduces visitors to the livestock so important to the plantation. The park also boasts a historic orchard that produces more than twenty-five varieties of apples, which are available to visitors during the late summer and fall.

There are no food, lodging, or camping facilities at the park. Rooms and meals are available in nearby Pottstown, Reading, and Morgantown, as well as in metropolitan Philadelphia. Camping is available in the adjacent French Creek State Park.

For more information, write Hopewell Furnace National Historic Site, 2 Mark Bird Lane, Elverson, PA 19520, or telephone (610) 582-8773. The park's Web site is www.nps.gov/hofu.

FURTHER READING
Gordon, Robert B. *American Iron, 1607–1900.* Baltimore, MD: Johns Hopkins University Press, 1996.
National Park Service. *Hopewell Furnace: A Guide to Hopewell Village National Historic Site, Pennsylvania.* Washington, DC: National Park Service, 1983.
Walker, Joseph E. *Hopewell Village: A Social and Economic History of an Iron-making Community.* Philadelphia: University of Pennsylvania Press, 1966.

HORSESHOE BEND NATIONAL MILITARY PARK

Location: Daviston, Alabama
Acreage: 2,040
Established: July 25, 1956

The War of 1812 inflamed the American frontier, distracting the nation from its nascent westward expansion and revealing the limits of the power of settlers in ways Native American people had not seen since the American Revolution. The British capitalized on this tension, recruiting Native American allies all across the nation, but especially in places where frontier society was at its weakest. Groups such as the Red Sticks, a traditional branch of the Creek people denoted by the red war clubs they carried into battle, saw the war as an opportunity to reverse their fortunes. They sought to recapture land they had lost to settlers and to reinstate their cultural traditions.

In the Creek homeland in the Alabama–southern Tennessee area, where white settlers felt especially threatened by British recruitment of the Creek, the tension spilled over into violence. In a preemptive strike, a group of whites attacked a party of Creek near Burnt Corn Creek in southern Alabama, sparking the First Creek War. Already unhappy with American expansion, the Creek retaliated. On August 30, 1813, they attacked Fort Mims, a stockade about 30 miles upriver from Mobile, Alabama, occupied by settlers and several companies of Mississippi volunteers. The defenders never even got the gates to the fort closed, and after a few hours of brutal fighting, almost 500 people lay dead in the stockade. About fifty escaped to tell the tale of the "massacre at Fort Mims."

The American response was immediate, for the "Creek uprising," as Americans called it, challenged them in two ways: it reintroduced Native Americans as a threat to westward expansion and it gave comfort to the British during a part of the War of 1812 when American forces were in disarray and the nation's ability to survive was in question. In October 1813, Major General Andrew Jackson, by then a well-known military figure, led a group of 3,500 Tennessee militiamen, including the soon-to-be-widely-known Davy Crockett, from Tennessee towards Alabama to quell the Red Sticks. Under Jackson, the pursuit was both effective and relentless. After a series of successful attacks, Jackson's men, aided by U.S. regulars, and some native allies—typically enemies of the Creek—cornered more than 1,000 Red Sticks in a village called Tohopeka, at Horseshoe Bend, a 100-acre tract surrounded on three sides by the Tallapoosa River.

The Americans enjoyed superior numbers, and on March 27, 1814, 2,000 soldiers under Jackson began a siege. They pounded the village with their two small cannons, but the sturdy structures withstood the assault. A 5- to 8-foot-high barricade through which defenders could fire their rifles protected the open area in front of the village and this too held in the face of the cannon fire. After sending 700 cavalrymen and nearly as many Cherokee allies to fan out to prevent an escape, the Americans did the only thing they could: they stormed the barricade and went over the top. The vicious hand-to-hand fighting that lasted hours left more than 800 Red Sticks dead against 49 of Jackson's men.

The victory at Horseshoe Bend ended the First Creek War and introduced Andrew Jackson to a national audience; his subsequent triumph at the Battle of New Orleans made him nationally prominent and began the long process that led him to the White House in 1828. There Jackson remained an implacable foe of Native Americans, engineering their removal from the East to the Indian Territory, now Oklahoma. Like everyone else, he was a product of his time and experiences, and he generally regarded Native Americans as his enemies and treated them as such.

Horseshoe Bend National Military Park offers a small museum that features exhibits related to the history of the Creek Indians, the events that led up to the battle, the battle itself, and its aftermath. The park also offers a major living-history event during the last weekend of March, which includes musket and cannon firings, Native American and early frontier cultural demonstrations, and interpretive programs to observe the anniversary of the battle. The park is open year-round, from 9 A.M. until 4:30 P.M., and admission is free.

For more information, write Horseshoe Bend National Military Park, 11288 Horseshoe Bend Road, Daviston, AL 36256-9751, or telephone (256) 234-7111. The park's Web site is www.nps.gov/hobe.

FURTHER READING

Adams, Henry. *The War of 1812.* Edited by H.A. DeWeerd. New York: Cooper Square, 1999.

Brantley, W.H. *Battle of Horseshoe Bend.* Birmingham, AL: Southern University Press, 1955.

Elting, John R. *Amateurs to Arms! A Military History of the War of 1812.* Chapel Hill, NC: Algonquin Books of Chapel Hill, 1991.

Saunt, Claudio. *A New Order of Things: Property, Power, and the Transformation of the Creek Indians, 1733–1816.* Cambridge, UK, and New York: Cambridge University Press, 1999.

HOT SPRINGS NATIONAL PARK
Location: Hot Springs, Arkansas
Acreage: 5,550
Established: April 20, 1832

Hot Springs National Park holds an unusual distinction in American park history. Although Yellowstone was the first area to be established as a national park, forty years prior to its creation, Congress saw fit to set aside Hot Springs as one. In April 1832, Congress established Hot Springs Reservation to protect the medicinal waters that flowed from the southwestern slope of Hot Springs Mountain in central Arkansas. The springs' curative powers had been utilized for centuries by native peoples and had taken on legendary status. Local lore maintains that Spanish explorer Hernando de Soto visited the springs on his many expeditions, and later, when the region was under France's flag, French trappers and traders used the thermal baths to rest and relax.

In 1803, President Thomas Jefferson purchased the expansive Louisiana Territory from France, which included this collection of forty-seven natural springs. Word about the therapeutic thermal waters spread like wildfire. Soon after the reservation's 1832 creation, the hot springs' reputation as a place where the waters healed the sick and lame soared. Cure seekers from across America came to the springs by stagecoach and railroad to soak in the odorless, bubbling, 143-degree waters.

In the early years, on-site bathhouses were no more than crude huts with little privacy. After the Civil War, however, some private stone bathhouses were constructed and operated as concessions by the federal government. By the early 1900s, the hot springs reached its apex of popularity as the place where any physical malady could possibly be cured, from arthritis to syphilis. The adjacent town of Hot Springs also boomed into a tourist-oriented mecca of recreation and gambling. The reservation eventually developed into a well-known resort nicknamed "The American Spa," because it attracted not only the wealthy but also indigent health seekers from around the world.

Because of this popularity, in 1921 the federal government officially redesignated the 5,550-acre reserve as Hot Springs National Park, America's smallest national park. Hot Springs National Park is also unique in that it is the only national park in America to include part of an urban area–the downtown area of Hot Springs, which contains the famed Bathhouse Row. The former Fordyce Bathhouse has been fully restored as the park's museum/visitor center; it is open daily from 9 A.M. until 5 P.M., and until 6 P.M. during the peak summer season. Considered the row's most elegant bathhouse when completed in 1915, Fordyce contains mosaic tile floors, marble, stained glass, and restored bathhouse rooms. There are interpretive exhibits and displays on the hot springs' history, a fifteen-minute orientation movie called *Valley of the Vapors*, and a nine-minute video demonstrating the traditional bath routine. Bathhouse Row also contains many wayside exhibits. There are no admission fees.

Not surprisingly, the park's main attractions have always been the hot spring baths, given at eight magnificent houses on Bathhouse Row. Since the bathhouse business declined after the advent of modern medicines, only the Buckstaff Bathhouse remains open for traditional baths. Visitors can also take in a hot spring bath, sit in whirlpools, or partake of a massage at a number of bathhouses operated by concessionaires and permittees. The visitor center maintains a list of these private bathhouses, and all are operated in strict accordance to Park Service regulations.

In addition to the baths, the park has many hiking trails and scenic roads. The Grand Promenade is a landscaped walkway located behind Bathhouse Row that offers a glimpse of the protected springs and historic landscape features. Visitors can also wander along approximately 26 miles of day-use hiking trails that wind through dense oak-hickory forests. Scenic mountain drives on West Mountain, Hot Springs, and North Mountain offer spectacular views, and one notable attraction is the observation tower atop Hot Springs Mountain (fee charged.)

There are no food or lodging facilities located in the national park, but the town of Hot Springs has all traveler services. The park's only developed campground is Gulpha Gorge, which is open year-round on a first-come, first-served basis. Campsites have picnic tables, grills, water, modern rest rooms, and access to a dump station; the fee is $10 per night. Campgrounds are also available in the surrounding area, including the Lake Ouachita, Corps of Engineers, and Arkansas state parks.

For more information, write Hot Springs National Park, P.O. Box 1860, Hot Springs, AR 71902-1860, or telephone (501) 624-3383, extension 640. The park's Web site is www.nps.gov/hosp.

FURTHER READING
Bedinger, M.S., et al. *The Waters of Hot Springs National Park, Arkansas–Their Nature and Origin.* Washington, DC: U.S. Government Printing Office, 1979.
Brown, Dee Alexander. *The American Spa: Hot Springs, Arkansas.* Little Rock, AR: Rose, 1982.
Hanor, Jeffrey S. *Fire in Folded Rocks.* Hot Springs, AR: Hot Springs National Park, 1980.
Phillips, Marcus. *Indian Folklore Atlas of Hot Springs National Park.* Hot Springs, AR: Garland County Historical Society, 1994.
Scully, Francis J. *Hot Springs, Arkansas and Hot Springs National Park: The Story of a City and the Nation's Health Resort.* Little Rock, AR: Hanson, 1966.

HOVENWEEP NATIONAL MONUMENT

Location: Colorado and Utah
Acreage: 785
Established: March 2, 1923

Noted for its solitude and unspoiled, natural environment, Hovenweep National Monument protects and preserves six clusters of towers, pueblos, and cliff dwellings that represent some of the Southwest's finest remnants of pre-Columbian stone architecture. The monument's prehistoric inhabitants—and those of nearby Mesa Verde National Park—were part of the Puebloan group, an extensive farming culture that occupied the Four Corners region of Utah, Colorado, New Mexico, and Arizona from around 500 B.C.E. until 1300 C.E. Human habitation in the Hovenweep area dates back even further—more than ten thousand years. Nomadic Paleo-Indians visited the mesa now known as Cajon to gather food and hunt game. Following the seasonal weather patterns, these Paleo-Indians hunted and gathered on Cajon Mesa for centuries. By about 900 C.E., these pre-Columbian foragers started settling on Cajon Mesa year-round, planting and harvesting crops in the mesa's rich soil. At its cultural peak in the mid-thirteenth century, more than 2,500 Puebloans called the mesa home.

The inhabitants of the region at that time, now referred to as the ancestral Puebloans (formerly Anasazi), also excelled in architectural skills. The buildings that survive today are the remnants of settlements built during the apex of Puebloan regional occupation. Structures are numerous and varied; some are square, D-shaped, oval, and round, while some measure four stories tall. Portions of towers, kivas, room blocks, granaries, check dams, and farming terraces also remain. Scholars have proffered multiple theories as to how the Puebloan culture used Hovenweep's buildings. The towers might have been used as celestial observatories, defensive structures, storage facilities, civil buildings, homes, or any combination thereof. Archeologists have found that most of the towers were associated with kivas (religious and social structures), pointing to possible ceremo-

Ancient dwelling of native peoples at Hovenweep National Monument. *(National Archives)*

nial use. Surrounding the towers are piles of rubble indicating that many more structures existed than survive today.

While building use is speculative, land use is not, for the Puebloans were successful farmers. They terraced their land into farmable plots, formed catch basins to hold water runoff, and erected check dams to retain soils that would normally wash off the cliff edges. Some storage caches along the canyon rims still exist; these caches held dried corn, beans, and squash crops for later use. By 1300, the people of Hovenweep and the surrounding region left, presumably moving south and joining with the Hopi and Zuni cultures. Several theories exist as to why they departed. Some believe that they were forced out by hostile, nomadic neighbors, while others think a combination of overpopulation, land overuse, and a twenty-year drought beginning around 1276 made the area uninhabitable. "Hovenweep" is a Ute word meaning "deserted valley."

Located in 6 separate units on the Utah-Colorado border west of Cortez, Colorado, Hovenweep National Monument is open year-round, and admission fees are $3 per person or $6 per vehicle. While the park does not have a formal visitor center, the ranger station at Square Tower has educational information for visitors, a video presentation, limited exhibits, and a small book sales area. Improved roads lead from both Cortez and Blanding, Utah; however, some dirt and gravel roads in the area remain very rough and may be impassable in stormy weather. Hiking trails lead throughout the monument's 6 units: Square Tower and Cajon in Utah, and the Holly, Hackberry, Cutthroat Castle, and Goodman Point ruins in Colorado. All of the units except Square Tower are isolated and hard to reach. Square Tower is the best-preserved ruin, and has a self-guided trail and rangers on duty to answer questions. A 4-mile trail leads from Square Tower to Holly Ruin.

Hovenweep has no food or lodging facilities in the park, but gasoline and some grocery items are available in most of the small towns near the monument. Blanding, Utah, and Cortez offer a wide variety of traveler services. There is a small campground located near the ranger station, which is open seasonally on a first-come, first-served basis. The sites are designed for tent camping, although a few sites will accommodate some smaller RVs, and the fee is $10 per night. Flush toilets and running water are available.

For more information, write Hovenweep National Monument, McElmo Route, Cortez, CO 81321, or telephone (970) 562-4282. The park's Web site is www.nps.gov/hove.

FURTHER READING

Noble, David Grant. *Understanding the Anasazi of Mesa Verde and Hovenweep.* Santa Fe, NM: Ancient City, 1985.

Olsen, Nancy H. *Hovenweep Rock Art: An Anasazi Visual Communication System.* Los Angeles: Institute of Archaeology, University of California, Los Angeles, 1985.

Thompson, Ian. *The Towers of Hovenweep.* Mesa Verde National Park, CO: Mesa Verde Museum Association, 1993.

HUBBELL TRADING POST NATIONAL HISTORIC SITE

Location: Ganado, Arizona
Acreage: 160
Established: August 28, 1965

In addition to being a national historic site, the Hubbell Trading Post is the oldest continuously operating trading post on the Navajo reservation. The post itself was established in 1871, shortly after the federal government returned the Navajos to their homeland from military confinement at central New Mexico's Fort Sumner. In 1878, trader John Lorenzo Hubbell purchased the post from its original owner as a 160-acre homestead. Hubbell then established a series of trading posts, a wholesale house in Winslow, and stage and freight lines. Fondly known as "Don Lorenzo" by the Navajos, he provided food and other basic supplies in exchange for blankets and jewelry. The post was also an important cultural meeting place, where Hubbell helped nurture a deeper sense of understanding and trust between Anglos and Navajos after decades of animosity. Through his business, Hubbell encouraged the revival of artistic excellence in traditional Navajo arts and crafts; this is most evident in the weaving of rugs and blankets in the Two Grey Hills, Crystal, Ganado, Wide Ruin, and Chinle styles and the crafting of high-quality silver and turquoise jewelry.

After Hubbell's 1930 death, his family

continued to run the post until it was sold to the National Park Service in 1967 and set aside as a historic site. Today, the park protects the stone trading post building, the Hubbell family's adobe home built in 1901, a small hogan constructed in 1934 to honor Hubbell, and various corrals and barns. The active trading post is operated for the Park Service by the Southwest Parks and Monuments Association, a nonprofit organization that helps maintain the Hubbell family's trading traditions.

Located on the Navajo Indian reservation on Highway 264, 1 mile west of Ganado, Arizona, the Hubbell Trading Post National Historic Site is open year-round during daylight hours, and admission is free (the Navajo Nation, unlike the rest of Arizona, observes daylight saving time). The visitor center has interpretive exhibits, a small bookstore, and silversmithing and rug-weaving demonstrations. The post also offers the visitor an opportunity to experience traditional trading activities that have gone on for over a century, and a variety of American Indian arts and crafts, such as rugs, baskets, kachinas, jewelry, drums, and pots, are available for purchase. Rangers offer tours of the Hubbell family home and guided walks during the summer months, and in the winter as staffing permits.

The historic site has a small grocery store, and food and supplies are also available in Ganado. There are no camping or lodging facilities on-site or in Ganado. The closest camping is at Canyon de Chelly National Monument near Chinle, and the nearest lodging is 30 miles north in Chinle or 30 miles east in Window Rock. Gallup, New Mexico, 55 miles to the southeast, has all traveler services.

For more information, write Hubbell Trading Post National Historic Site, P.O. Box 150, Ganado, AZ 86505, or telephone (520) 755-3475. The park's Web site is www.nps.gov/hutr.

FURTHER READING

Brugge, David M. *Hubbell Trading Post: National Historic Site.* Tucson, AZ: Southwest Parks and Monuments Association, 1993.

Cloyd, Paul C. *The Two-Story Barn: Hubbell Trading Post National Historic Site, Arizona.* Denver, CO: National Park Service, 1997.

Manchester, Albert, and Ann Manchester. *Hubbell Trading Post National Historic Site: An Administrative History.* Santa Fe, NM: Southwest Cultural Resources Center, National Park Service, 1993. Available at www.nps.gov/hutr/adhi/adhi.htm.

Peterson, Charles S. *Hubbell Trading Post National Historic Site, Arizona.* Tucson, AZ: Southwest Parks and Monuments Association, 1983.

INDEX

A

Abbey, Edward, **1**:60–61, 116
Abraham Lincoln. *See* Lincoln,
  Abraham
Abraham Lincoln Birthplace
  National Historic Site,
  1:33–35
Abraham Lincoln National
  Historical Park, **1**:34
Abraham Lincoln National
  Park, **1**:34
Abraham Lincoln: The War Years
  (Sandburg), **1**:126
Acadia National Park, **1**:4,
  35–38, 250, 295; **2**:504
Acadian Cultural Centers,
  1:342–43
Adams, Abigail Smith, **1**:39–40
Adams, Charles Francis, **1**:40
Adams, Henry, **1**:40
Adams, James Brooks, **1**:40
Adams, John, **1**:38–40
Adams, John Quincy, **1**:38–40
Adams, Louisa Catherine, **1**:40
Adams, Samuel, **1**:100
Adams Mansion National
  Historic Site, **1**:38
Adams National Historical
  Park, **1**:38–41
African American historical
  people and sites
    African Meeting House,
    1:97–98

African American historical
  people and sites *(continued)*
    Black Heritage Trail,
    1:97–98
    Booker T. Washington
    National Monument,
    1:95 96
    Boston African American
    National Historic Site,
    1:96–98
    Brown Foundation for
    Educational Equity,
    Excellence, and
    Research, **1**:104
    Brown v. Board of Education
    National Historic Site,
    1:103–4, 137; **2**:525
    Central High School
    National Historic Site,
    1:137–38
    Frederick Douglass
    National Historic Site,
    1:7, 247–49; **2**:431, 439
    George Washington Carver
    National Monument,
    1:264–65
    Maggie L. Walker National
    Historic Site, **2**:393–94
    Martin Luther King, Jr.
    National Historic Site,
    2:403–4
    Mary McLeod Bethune
    Council House National
    Historic Site, **2**:406–8,
    431

African American historical
  people and sites *(continued)*
    Monroe Elementary
    School, **1**:103–4
    National Archives for
    Black Women's History,
    2:406
    Nicodemus National
    Historic Site, **2**:443–45
    Selma To Montgomery
    National Historic Trail
    and All-American
    Road, **2**:523–27
    Tuskegee Airmen National
    Historic Site, **2**:561–62
    Tuskegee Institute National
    Historic Site, **1**:95, 264;
    2:562–64
African Meeting House, **1**:97–98
Agate Fossil Beds National
  Monument, **1**:41–42
Alaska brown bear, **2**:360
Alaska National Interest Lands
  Conservation Act (1980), **1**:21,
  29; **2**:362, 371, 585, 587, 613
Alaskan Native Claims
  Settlement Act of 1978, **1**:255,
  270; **2**:601
Albright, Horace M., **1**:2–3, 9,
  15–16, 18–19, 27, 29, 60, 74,
  136, 154, 293, 295; **2**:348, 502,
  610
Alcott, Louisa May, **2**:412–13
Aleutian World War II National
  Historic Area, **1**:42

Alibates Flint Quarries National Monument, **1**:42–43

Allegheny Portage Railroad National Historic Site, **1**:43–45

Alliance for Progress, **2**:350

American Academy of Science, **1**:6

American alligator, **1**:86

American Ark, **1**:86

American Civic Association, **1**:2

American Ethnological Society, **1**:254

American Fur Company, **1**:245

American Memorial Park, **1**:45–47

American Recreation Coalition, **1**:23

American Red Cross, **1**:153; **2**:353

American Renaissance, **2**:388

American Revolution. *See* Revolutionary War sites

American Revolution Bicentennial tribute, **1**:158

American war with Mexico. *See* Mexican-American War

American war with Spain. *See* Spanish-American War

Amistad Dam, **1**:47–48

Amistad National Recreation Area, **1**:47–48

Anacostia Park, **2**:431

Anasazi Indian culture, **1**:113, 123, 138, 203; **2**:408–9, 509

Anastasia Island, **1**:228

Anderson, Robert, **1**:242–43

Andersonville National Cemetery, **1**:49, 153

Andersonville National Historic Site, **1**:48–49

Andrew Johnson. *See* Johnson, Andrew

Andrew Johnson National Historic Site, **1**:49–52

Andrus, Cecil, **1**:29, 298

Aniakchak Caldera, **1**:52

Aniakchak National Monument & Preserve, **1**:52–53

Aniakchak National Wild River, **1**:52–53

Antebellum South, **2**:429

Antietam National Battlefield, **1**:53–56

Antietam National Cemetery, **1**:54–55

Antiquities Act of 1906, **1**:2, 21, 107, 125, 129, 203, 269–70, 284; **2**:550, 559, 585, 613

Apache Indians, **1**:216–17, 220–21

   See also Chiricahua Apache Indians

Apostle Islands National Lakeshore, **1**:56–58

Appalachian Mountains, **1**:93, 166

Appomattox Court House National Historical Park, **1**:58–60

Arbuckle National Recreation Area, **1**:146

Archaeological Institute of America, **1**:21

Archaeological Resources Protection Act of 1979, **2**:409

Archeo-astronomical site, **1**:73

Archeological sites and deposits, **1**:88, 144, 293, 323; **2**:555, 613

   Amistad National Recreation Area, **1**:47–48

   Aztec Ruins National Monument, **1**:67–69

   Bandelier National Monument, **1**:4, 27, 73–75

   Big Bend National Park, **1**:76–79

   Canyon de Chelly National Monument, **1**:113–14

   Canyonlands National Park, **1**:114–17

   Casa Grande Ruins National Monument, **1**:26, 129–30

   Effigy Mounds National Monument, **1**:195–96

   Fossil Butte National Monument, **1**:247

   Gila Cliff Dwellings National Monument, **1**:268–69

Archeological sites and deposits *(continued)*

   Guadalupe Mountains National Park, **1**:299–300

   Mesa Verde National Park, **1**:328; **2**:408–10

   Montezuma Castle National Monument, **2**:419–20

   Ocmulgee National Monument, **2**:451–52

   Pecos National Historical Park, **2**:466–67

   Poverty Point National Monument/State Commemorative Area, **2**:481–82

   Russell Cave National Monument, **2**:499

   See also Fossil sites

Arches National Park, **1**:60–62

Arista, Mariano, **2**:462

Arkansas Post National Memorial, **1**:62–63

Arlington House, The Robert E. Lee Memorial, **1**:63–65

Arlington National Cemetery, **1**:64–65

Armistead, George, **1**:229

Armstrong, Louis, **2**:440

Arnold, Benedict, **1**:240

Articles of Confederation, **2**:333–34, 538, 552

Aspinall, Wayne, **1**:87, 168–69

Assateague Island National Seashore, **1**:65–67

Assateague Lighthouse, **1**:66

Astor, John Jacob, **1**:245

Atchison, Topeka, and Santa Fe (AT&SF) railroad, **1**:282–83

Atlanta Compromise, **1**:95

Atrisco Land Grant of 1680, **2**:471

Avalon Foundation, **1**:120

Aviation sites

   Dayton Aviation Heritage National Historical Park, **1**:173–74

   White Sands National Monument, **2**:591–92

Aviation sites (continued)
Wright Brothers National Memorial, **2:**603–5
Ayres, Thomas A., **2:**610
Aztec Ruins National Monument, **1:**67–69

B

Badlands National Park, **1:**71–73
Bailly, Joseph, **2:**336
Ballinger, Richard A., **1:**2, 272
Baltimore and Ohio Railroad (B&O), **1:**311
Bandelier, Adolphe F. A., **1:**73–74
Bandelier National Monument, **1:**4, 27, 73–75
Banks, Nathaniel, **1:**112
Bar Harbor, **1:**37
Barataria Preserve, **2:**342–43
Barrier Canyon style rock art, **1:**114, 116
Barrier islands, **1:**121, 167, 228, 302; **2:**461
Bartholdi, Auguste, **2:**539
Barton, Clara, **1:**153–54; **2:**353
Barton National Historic Site. See Clara Barton National Historic Site
Bascomb, George, **1:**217
Bascomb Affair, **1:**217
Bat Cave, **1:**127
Battle of Big Hole, **1:**80–82; **2:**441–43
Battle of Bull Run, **1:**53, 58, 153; **2:**397–98
Battle of Bunker Hill, **1:**100
Battle of Chattanooga, **1:**144
Battle of Chickamauga, **1:**144–45
Battle of Fort Donelson, **1:**222
Battle of Guam, **2:**580
Battle of Lookout Mountain, The (Walker), **1:**145
Battle of New Orleans, **1:**326; **2:**343
Battle of the Little Bighorn, **1:**226; **2:**384–86, 441
Battle of Tippecanoe, **1:**261
Battle of Tupelo, **2:**560

Battle of Washita, **1:**227
Battle of Yorktown, **1:**154–55
Bear Lodge, **1:**184–85
Beauregard, Pierre G. T., **1:**241–42; **2:**532
Bee, Bernard, **2:**397
Beery, Wallace, **1:**287
Bell Vue Point, **1:**246
Bent, Charles, **1:**75
Bent, William, **1:**75
Bent's Old Fort National Historic Site, **1:**75–76
Bentsen, Lloyd, **1:**87
Bering Land Bridge National Preserve, **2:**585–86
Berkeley, William, **1:**155
Bermuda Plantation, **1:**112
Bethany Church cemetery, **1:**103
Bethune, Mary McLeod, **2:**406–8
Bethune Council House National Historic Site. See Mary McLeod Bethune Council House National Historic Site
Bielenberg, John, **1:**289
Bierstadt, Albert, **2:**388
Big Bend National Park, **1:**76–79
Big Cinder Butte, **1:**165
Big Cypress National Preserve, **1:**79–80, 207
Big Cypress Watershed, **1:**79
Big Hole National Battlefield, **1:**80–82; **2:**441–43
Big South Fork National River and Recreation Area, **1:**85–86
Big Thicket National Preserve, **1:**86–88
Bighorn Canyon National Recreation Area, **1:**83–85
Bighorn Lake, **1:**83
Billings, Frederick, **2:**401
Billings National Historical Park. See Marsh-Billings-Rockefeller National Historical Park
Biltmore estate, **1:**250
Bird, Mark, **1:**324
Bird Island Basin, **2:**462
Biscayne National Park, **1:**88–89

Black Canyon of the Gunnison National Park, **1:**89–91
Black Codes, **1:**51
Black Heritage Trail, **1:**97–98
Black-footed ferret, **1:**71
Blackstone River Valley National Heritage Corridor, **1:**91–93
Bleeding Kansas, **1:**236–37, 311
Bloody Lane, **1:**54–55
Bloody Sunday, **2:**525
Blue Mesa Lake, **1:**168–69
Blue Ridge Parkway, **1:**19, 93–95
Booker T. Washington National Monument, **1:**95–96
Boone, Daniel, **1:**166, 261
Booth, John Wilkes, **1:**188, 215–16
BOR. See Bureau of Outdoor Recreation
Borax deposits, **1:**173
Borglum, Gutzon, **2:**427–28
Boston African American National Historic Site, **1:**96–98
Boston Harbor Islands National Recreation Area, **1:**98–100
Boston National Historical Park, **1:**100–102
Boulder Dam National Recreation Area, **2:**374
Bowles, Samuel, **2:**610
Braddock, Edward, **1:**262
Bradford, William, **1:**117
Brady, John G., **2:**534
Bragg, Braxton, **1:**145; **2:**541–42
Brewer, James L., **1:**4
Brices Cross Roads National Battlefield, **1:**102–3
Bridger, Jim, **2:**607
Brooke, Clement, **1:**324
Brooks Range, **1:**255
Brooks River National Historic Landmark, **2:**360
Brower, David, **1:**5, 274
Brown, Cheryl, **1:**103
Brown, John, **1:**248, 311–12; **2:**443
Brown, Linda, **1:**103
Brown, Oliver, **1:**103

Brown Foundation for Educational Equity, Excellence, and Research, 1:104

Brown pelicans, 1:107

Brown v. Board of Education National Historic Site, 1:103–4, 137; 2:525

Bryan, William Jennings, 1:34

Bryce, Ebenezer, 1:105

Bryce Canyon National Park, 1:3, 104–7

Buard, Julia, 1:112

Buck Island Reef National Monument, 1:107–8

Buckner, Simon, 1:223

Buell, Don, 2:532

Buell, Dorothy, 2:336

Buffalo soldier cavalry (Troop H), 1:221

Bull Moose Republicanism, 1:24

Bull Run, 1:53, 58, 153; 2:397–99

Bulow, William J., 2:427

Bunker Hill Monument, 1:100

Bureau of Land Management, 1:201; 2:355, 417

Bureau of Outdoor Recreation (BOR), 1:30; 2:590

Bureau of Reclamation, 1:1, 5, 83–84, 187, 273

Burgoyne, John, 1:240; 2:519, 547

Burnside, Ambrose E., 1:251

Burr, Aaron, 1:308

Burt, Struthers, 1:286

Burton, Philip, 1:9, 97, 143, 205, 254, 298; 2:552–53, 600

Bush, George H. W., 1:87

Bush, George W., 1:22–23

Butterfield Overland Mail, 1:217

Byrd, Harry Flood, 2:530

C

Cabrillo, Juan Rodriguez, 1:109

Cabrillo National Monument, 1:109–10

Cadillac Mountain, 1:35–36

California Department of Parks and Recreation, 1:25

California Desert Plan (1980), 2:417

California Desert Protection Act (1994), 1:174; 2:355, 417

California Gold Rush, 2:367, 490–91, 589–90

California Trail, 1:151–52

Calumet, 2:365

Calusa Culture Mounds, 1:207

Cammerer, Arno B., 1:16–17

Camp David, 1:28

Camp Sumpter, 1:49

Campbell, John, 2:421

Canaveral National Seashore, 1:110–11

Cane River Creole National Historical Park and Heritage Area, 1:111–13

Cañon de Santa Elena, 1:76

Canyon de Chelly National Monument, 1:113–14

Canyonlands National Park, 1:114–17

Cape Cod National Seashore, 1:117–19

Cape Hatteras Lighthouse, 1:119

Cape Hatteras National Seashore, 1:30, 119–21, 236

Cape Krusenstern National Monument, 2:586–87

Cape Lookout Lighthouse, 1:222

Cape Lookout National Seashore, 1:121–23

Capitan Reef, 1:299

Capitol Hill Parks, 2:431

Capitol Reef National Park, 1:123–25

Capulin Volcano National Monument, 1:125–26

Carl Sandburg. *See* Sandburg, Carl

Carl Sandburg Home National Historic Site, 1:126–27

Carlsbad Caverns National Park, 1:3, 8, 127–29

Carlsen, Emil, 2:584

Carnegie, Andrew, 1:167

Carnegie, Thomas, 1:167

Carnegie family, 1:167

Carnegie Museum, 1:186

Carnifex Ferry Battlefield State Park, 1:258

Carter, Earl, 2:347

Carter, Jimmy, 1:19, 21, 52, 107, 198, 255, 270; 2:346–47, 360, 371, 585

Carter, Rosalynn, 2:346–47

Carter National Historic Site. *See* Jimmy Carter National Historic Site

Carver, George Washington, 1:264–65; 2:563

Carver National Monument. *See* George Washington Carver National Monument

Casa Grande Ruins National Monument, 1:26, 129–30

Cascade Range, 2:379–80

Cassidy, Butch, 1:116

Castillo de San Marcos National Monument, 1:130–32

Castle Clinton National Monument, 1:132–34

Castolon District, 1:78

Caswell, Richard, 2:421

Catoctin Mountain Park, 1:28, 134–35

Cattle ranching, 1:289; 2:466

Caves and caverns
    Bat Cave, 1:127
    Carlsbad Caverns, 1:3, 8, 127–29
    Crystal Cave, 2:529
    Cueva Pintada (painted cave), 1:73
    Flatt's Cave, 2:396
    Jewel Cave, 2:345–46
    Lehman Caves, 1:290–91
    Mammoth Cave, 1:4, 37, 295; 2:395–97
    Oregon Caves, 2:457–59
    Russell Cave, 2:499
    Timpanogos Cave, 2:553–54
    Wind Cave, 2:597–99

Cayuse Indians, 2:593

CCC. *See* Civilian Conservation Corps

Cedar Breaks National Monument, 1:104, 136–37

Central High School National Historic Site, 1:137–38

Central Pacific Railroad, 1:279–80

Central Park, New York City, **1:**249–50

Cerro Grande fire (2000), **1:**27

Chaco Canyon culture, **1:**67

Chaco Culture National Historical Park, **1:**138–39

Chalmette Battlefield and National Cemetery, **1:**342–43

Chamizal controversy, **1:**140

Chamizal National Memorial, **1:**139–41

Champlain, Samuel de, **1:**35; **2:**504

Channel Islands National Park, **1:**141–42

Channing, Edward, **2:**422

Chapman, Oscar, **1:**19

Charles Pinckney National Historic Site, **1:**142–43

Charlestown Navy Yard, **1:**100–101

Charley River National Preserve. *See* Yukon-Charley Rivers National Preserve

Chatham Manor, **1:**253

Chattahoochee River National Recreation Area, **1:**143–44

Chattanooga National Military Park. *See* Chickamauga and Chattanooga National Military Park

Chellberg, Anders and Joanna, **2:**336

Cherokee Indians, **1:**238, 285; **2:**364, 464

Chesnut, Mary Boykin, **2:**363

Chester, Daniel, **2:**412

Cheyenne Indians, **2:**513–14

Chicago Exposition (1893), **1:**250

Chicago Portage National Historic Site, **2:**331

Chickamauga and Chattanooga National Military Park, **1:**144–46

Chickasaw Indians. *See* Choctaw-Chickasaw Indians

Chickasaw National Recreation Area, **1:**146–47

Chief Black Kettle, **2:**513, 581–83

Chief Joseph, **1:**80–81; **2:**441–42

Chigmit Mountains, **2:**371

Chihuahuan Desert, **1:**76–77

Chimney Rock National Historic Site, **1:**147–48

Chiricahua Apache Indians, **1:**216–17, 221

Chiricahua National Monument, **1:**148–50

Chisos Mountains, **1:**77–79

Chivington, John M., **2:**513, 581

Choctaw-Chickasaw Indians, **2:**464

Chopawamsic Recreational Demonstration Area, **2:**482

Chopin, Kate, **1:**112

Christ Church, **2:**334

Christiansted National Historic Site, **1:**150–51

Church of Jesus Christ of Latter-Day Saints, **1:**105; **2:**476

Churches, synagogues, and temples

Bethany Church cemetery, **1:**103

Christ Church, **2:**334

Congregation Mikveh Israel, **2:**334

Gloria Dei (Old Swedes') Church, **1:**276–77

Heiau (Hawaiian temples), **2:**359

Old North Church, **1:**100; **2:**411

Saint Paul's Church, **2:**506–7

Touro Synagogue, **2:**557–58

United First Parish Church, **1:**38, 40

City of Rocks National Reserve, **1:**151–52

Civil War historical sites and battlefields

Andersonville National Historic Site, **1:**48–49

Antietam National Battlefield, **1:**53–56

Appomattox Court House National Historical Park, **1:**58–60

Arlington House, The Robert E. Lee Memorial, **1:**63–65

Civil War historical sites and battlefields *(continued)*

Brices Cross Roads National Battlefield, **1:**102–3

Carnifex Ferry Battlefield State Park, **1:**258

Chickamauga and Chattanooga National Military Park, **1:**144–46

Fort Donelson National Battlefield, **1:**222–23

Fort Pulaski National Monument, **1:**233–35

Fort Sumter National Monument, **1:**241–43

Fredericksburg and Spotsylvania National Military Park, **1:**251–53

Gettysburg National Military Park, **1:**265–68

Harpers Ferry National Historical Park, **1:**248, 310–12; **2:**443, 538

Kennesaw Mountain National Battlefield Park, **2:**362–64

Manassas National Battlefield Park, **2:**397–99

Monocacy National Battlefield, **2:**418–19

Pea Ridge National Military Park, **2:**464–66

Petersburg National Battlefield, **2:**467–69

Richmond National Battlefield Park, **2:**492–93

Robert Gould Shaw Memorial, **1:**97

Shiloh National Military Park, **2:**532–33

Stones River National Battlefield, **2:**541–42

Tupelo National Battlefield, **2:**560–61

Vicksburg National Military Park, **2:**572–74

Wilson's Creek National Battlefield, **2:**595–97

Civilian Conservation Corps (CCC), **1:**4, 16, 29, 135, 146, 187; **2:**364, 385–86, 470, 482, 599

Claims Settlement Act of 1971, **2:**371

Clara Barton. *See* Barton, Clara

Clara Barton National Historic Site, **1:**153–54

Clark, George Rogers, **1:**260–61

Clark, William, **1:**219; **2:**343

Clark National Historical Park. *See* George Rogers Clark National Historical Park

Clay, Henry, **1:**40

Clemm, Virginia, **1:**193

Cleveland, Grover, **1:**162, 286; **2:**454

Clinton, Bill, **1:**22, 26, 107, 170, 292

Clinton, DeWitt, **1:**132

Clinton, Henry, **1:**300

Coahuiltecans, **2:**511

Cochise, **1:**217

Cochrane, Alexander, **1:**229

Collier, Robert, **1:**34

Colonial American historic sites
  Adams National Historical Park, **1:**38–41
  Boston National Historical Park, **1:**100–102
  Cape Cod National Seashore, **1:**117–19
  Charles Pinckney National Historic Site, **1:**142–43
  Christiansted National Historic Site, **1:**150–51
  Colonial National Historical Park, **1:**154–56
  Federal Hall National Memorial, **1:**211–12
  Fort Frederica National Monument, **1:**223–24
  Fort Necessity National Battlefield, **1:**230–31
  Fort Raleigh National Historic Site, **1:**235–36
  Fort Stanwix National Monument, **1:**240–41
  Friendship Hill National Historic Site, **1:**253–54

Colonial American historic sites (*continued*)
  George Rogers Clark National Historical Park, **1:**260–62
  Gloria Dei (Old Swedes') Church National Historic Site, **1:**276–77
  Green Springs National Historic Landmark District, **1:**298–99
  Guilford Courthouse National Military Park, **1:**300–302, 318
  Hamilton Grange National Memorial, **1:**307–9
  Hampton National Historic Site, **1:**309–10
  Historic Camden, **1:**318–19
  Hopewell Furnace National Historic Site, **1:**324–25
  Independence National Historical Park, **2:**332–35
  Kings Mountain National Military Park, **2:**365–67
  Minute Man National Historical Park, **2:**411–13
  Morristown National Historical Park, **2:**422–24
  New Bedford Whaling National Historical Park, **2:**439–40
  Ninety Six National Historic Site, **2:**445–46
  Roger Williams National Memorial, **2:**496–97
  Saint Paul's Church National Historic Site, **2:**506–7
  Salem Maritime National Historic Site, **2:**507–9
  Thomas Stone National Historic Site, **2:**552–53
  Touro Synagogue National Historic Site, **2:**557–58
  See also Revolutionary War sites

Colonial National Historical Park, **1:**154–56

Colonial Williamsburg, **2:**347

Colorado National Monument, **1:**156–57

Colorado River, **1:**114–16, 169, 187, 273, 281

Colorado River Storage Project (CRSP), **1:**5, 169, 187, 273

Colter, John, **2:**607

Columbia River, **2:**376

Columbus, Christopher, **2:**510

Columnar basalt, **1:**183

Condon, Thomas, **2:**348–49

Congaree National Park, **1:**157–58

Congregation Mikveh Israel, **2:**334

Congress Hall, **2:**334

Connemara farm (Carl Sandburg Home), **1:**126

Conservation movement, **1:**1, 5; **2:**402

Consolidated Bank and Trust Company, **2:**394

Constitution Gardens, **1:**158–59

Continental Congress, **1:**211; **2:**333, 547, 552

Continental Divide, **2:**496

Cook, Charles W., **2:**607

Cook, James H., **1:**41

Cook Collection of American Indian artifacts, **1:**41; **2:**607

Coolidge, Calvin, **2:**527

Copper mining, **2:**364

Coquina Beach, **1:**119

Coral grottoes and reefs, **1:**107, 188; **2:**574

Cornwallis, Charles, **1:**155, 262, 300–301, 318; **2:**365

Coronado, Francisco Vásquez de, **1:**159–60, 281; **2:**471

Coronado National Memorial, **1:**159–60

Cosmos Club, **1:**281

Cotton textile industry, **2:**388–89

Cowles, Henry, **2:**336

Cowpens National Battlefield, **1:**160–62, 318

Cramton, Louis, **2:**476

Cranberry Isles, **1:**37

Crater Lake National Park, **1:**162–64

Craters of the Moon National Monument and Preserve, 1:164–66

Crawford, Medorem, 2:523

Crazy Horse, 2:384

Creek Indians, 1:325–26; 2:451–52, 481

Creole culture, 1:111–13

Crockett, Davy, 1:325

CRSP. See Colorado River Storage Project

Crystal Cave, 2:529

Crystal Lake, 1:168–69

Cuban missile crisis, 2:350

Cueva Pintada (painted cave), 1:73

Cumberland Gap National Historical Park, 1:166–67

Cumberland Island National Seashore, 1:167–68

Cumberland River, 1:85, 222

Cunningham House, 1:319

Curecanti National Recreation Area, 1:90, 168–70

Curtis, Samuel R., 2:464

Custer, George Armstrong, 1:59, 227; 2:384–85, 581, 583

Custer, Libby, 1:59

Custis, George Washington Parke, 1:63–64

Custis, John Parke, 1:63

Custis, Mary Anna Randolph, 1:64–65

Cuyahoga Valley National Park, 1:170–72

D

Dakota Internment Camp, 2:415

Dakota Sioux, 2:478

Dana, Charles A., 1:23

Dare, Virginia, 1:236

Darwin, Charles, 2:348

Daughters of the American Revolution, 1:261

Davis, Anne, 1:295

Davis, Jefferson, 1:220, 242

Davis, Miles, 2:440

Dawes, William, 2:411

Day Fossil Beds National Monument. See John Day Fossil Beds National Monument

Dayton Aviation Heritage National Historical Park, 1:173–74

De Fuca, Juan, 2:454

De Iturbide, Agustín, 2:471

De Leon, Ponce, 1:188

De Oñate, Don Juan, 1:203; 2:471

De Soto, Hernando, 1:157, 182–83, 326

De Soto National Memorial, 1:182–83

De Vargas, Don Diego, 1:299

De Veuster, Joseph (Father Damien), 2:357

De Villiers, Joseph Coulon, 1:231

Deadwood Stage route, 1:225

Death Valley National Monument, 1:174, 2:355

Death Valley National Park, 1:174–76

Death Valley Wilderness Area, 1:174

Declaration of Independence, 1:158; 2:332–34

Declaration of Independence Memorial, 1:158

"Defense of Fort McKenry, The" (Key), 1:229

Del Norte Coast Redwoods State Park, 2:489, 491

Delaware and Lehigh Navigation Canal National Heritage Corridor, 1:177–78

Delaware National Scenic River, 1:178–79

Delaware Water Gap National Recreation Area, 1:178–79

Demaray, Arthur E., 1:17

Denali National Park and Preserve, 1:179–82

Dentzel Carousel, 1:275–76

Derby, Elias Hasket, 2:507

Desert Solitaire (Abbey), 1:60

Devils Postpile National Monument, 1:183–84

Devils Tower, climbing, 1:186

Devils Tower National Monument, 1:184–86

DeVoto, Bernard, 1:6, 187

D'Iberville, Pierre Le Moyne, 1:302

Dickens, Charles, 2:388

Dickenson, Russell E., 1:10, 17–18, 22, 25, 27

Dingmans Falls area, 1:179

Dinosaur National Monument, 1:5, 19, 186–88, 273

Division of Urban and Environmental Activities, 1:28

Doane, Gustavus, 2:608

Dodge, Richard, 1:185

Dominguez-Escalante expedition, 1:115

Dorr, George B., 1:36

Douglas, Paul H., 2:336

Douglass, Earl, 1:186

Douglass, Frederick, 1:7, 247–49; 2:431, 439

Douglass National Historic Site. See Frederick Douglass National Historic Site

Drake, Sir Francis, 1:235; 2:478

Dred Scott case, 2:344

Drury, Newton B., 1:5, 7, 9, 18–19; 2:491

Dry Tortugas National Park, 1:188–89

Dude ranch, 1:286

Dunbar, Paul Laurence, 1:173

Duncan, John, 1:260

Dutton, Clarence E., 1:281–82

E

Earl Douglass Quarry, 1:186

Early, Jubal A., 2:418

Earth First!, 1:61; 2:503

East Bay Regional Park District, 1:25

Eastern Wilderness Act (1975), 2:531

Ebey, Isaac, 1:191

Ebey's Landing National Historical Reserve, 1:191–92

Echo Canyon, 1:186–87

Echo Park Dam, **1:**5, 7, 19, 187, 273

Ecological preserves. *See* National preserves and reserves

Edgar Allan Poe. *See* Poe, Edgar Allan

Edgar Allan Poe National Historic Site, **1:**192–93

Edison, Thomas Alva, **1:**193–95

Edison National Historic Site, **1:**193–95

Effigy Mounds National Monument, **1:**195–96

Eiffel, Alexandre Gustave, **2:**539

Eisenhower, Dwight D., **1:**137, 196–98

Eisenhower, Mamie, **1:**197

Eisenhower National Historic Site, **1:**196–98

El Malpais National Monument, **1:**201–2

El Morro National Monument, **1:**202–4

Eleanor Roosevelt. *See* Roosevelt, Eleanor

Eleanor Roosevelt National Historic Site, **1:**198–99

Ellington, Duke, **2:**440

Elliot, Joel, **2:**583

Ellis Island, **1:**133, 200–201; **2:**539–40

Ellis Island Immigration Museum, **1:**200–201

Ellis Island National Monument, **1:**200–201

Emancipation Proclamation, **1:**55

Emerald Mound, **2:**560

Emerson, Ralph Waldo, **2:**387–88

Endangered species, **1:**71, 86, 107, 121, 207; **2:**359, 461, 478–79

Endangered Species Act of 1973, **2:**536

Environmental groups and movement, **1:**60–61, 79; **2:**503

Equal Rights Party, **1:**248

Erie Canal, **1:**132, 171; **2:**540

Erie Canal Towpath Trail, **1:**171

Escalante expedition. *See* Dominguez-Escalante expedition

Eugene O'Neill National Historic Site, **1:**204–5

Evans, Rudolph, **2:**433

Everglades National Park, **1:**79, 205–9

Everhardt, Gary, **1:**19–20

Exploration and Empire: The Explorer and the Scientists in the Winning of the American West (Goetzmann), **1:**227

Expositions
    Chicago Exposition (1893), **1:**250
    Panama-California Exposition (1915), **1:**109

F

Faneuil Hall, **1:**100

Faribault, Jean Baptiste, **2:**415

Father Damien (Joseph De Veuster), **2:**357

Faubus, Orval, **1:**137

Federal Customs House, **1:**212

Federal Hall National Memorial, **1:**211–12

Federal land management, **1:**111

Federal Reserve Bank, **1:**212

Fenway Park, Boston, MA, **1:**250

Ferguson, Patrick, **2:**365–66

Fernald Point, **1:**35

Fessenden, Reginald, **1:**236

Fire Island Light Station, **1:**213–14

Fire Island National Seashore, **1:**212–14

First Bank of the United States, **2:**334

Fitzhugh, Mary Lee, **1:**63

Five Civilized Tribes, **1:**238

F.L. Caeppart et al. v. U.S., **1:**175

Flagler, Henry, **1:**131

Flatt's Cave, **2:**396

Flint quarries, **1:**42–43

Flood, Harry, **2:**530

Florida Jetport, **1:**79

Florida Keys, **1:**88

Florida State Parks, **1:**22

Florissant Fossil Beds National Monument, **1:**214–15

Floyd, William, **1:**213–14

Floyd Bennett Field, **1:**257

Folsom, David E., **2:**607

Ford, Gerald R., **1:**110; **2:**346

Ford, Henry, **2:**535

Ford Foundation, **1:**22

Ford's Theatre National Historic Site, **1:**215–16

Forest Park, Prince William, **2:**482–83

Forked Lightning Ranch, **2:**466

Forrest, Nathan Bedford, **1:**102; **2:**560

Fort Bowie National Historic Site, **1:**216–17

Fort Caroline National Memorial, **1:**217–19, 228

Fort Clatsop National Memorial, **1:**219–20

Fort Davis National Historic Site, **1:**220–22

Fort Donelson National Battlefield, **1:**222–23

Fort Duquesne, **1:**230

Fort Frederica National Monument, **1:**223–24

Fort Hancock, **1:**257

Fort Hindman, **1:**62

Fort Jefferson, **1:**188–89

Fort Laramie National Historic Site, **1:**224–26

Fort Larned National Historic Site, **1:**226–27

Fort Marion National Monument, **1:**131–32

Fort Matanzas National Monument, **1:**228–29

Fort McHenry National Monument and Historic Shrine, **1:**229–30

Fort Mims, **1:**325

Fort Necessity National Battlefield, **1:**230–31

Fort Nonsense, **2:**422–23

Fort Piute, **2:**417

Fort Point Museum Association, **1:**233

Fort Point National Historic Site, 1:231–33

Fort Pulaski National Monument, 1:233–35

Fort Raleigh National Historic Site, 1:235–36

Fort Rosalie, 2:429

Fort Sackville, 1:260–61

Fort Schwatka, 1:42

Fort Scott National Historic Site, 1:236–37

Fort Smith National Historic Site, 1:237–40

Fort Snelling State Park, 2:415

Fort Stanwix National Monument, 1:240–41

Fort Sumter National Monument, 1:241–43

Fort Tilden, 1:257

Fort Union National Monument, 1:243–45

Fort Union Trading Post National Historic Site, 1:245–46

Fort Vancouver National Historic Site, 1:246–47

Fort Wadsworth, 1:257

Fort William, 1:224

Fossil Butte National Monument, 1:247

Fossil sites
Agate Fossil Beds National Monument, 1:41–42

Badlands National Park, 1:71–73

Dinosaur National Monument, 1:5, 19, 186–88, 273

Fossil Butte National Monument, 1:247

Florissant Fossil Beds National Monument, 1:214–15

Hagerman Fossil Beds National Monument, 1:305–6

John Day Fossil Beds National Monument, 2:348–49

Olgocene-epoch beds, 1:71

Permian-period reef, 1:299

Fossil sites (continued)
Petrified Forest National Park, 1:215; 2:351, 469–70

See also Archeological sites and deposits

Four Corners region, 1:328; 2:487

Franklin, Benjamin, 2:332, 334

Franklin Delano Roosevelt. See Roosevelt, Franklin Delano

Franklin Delano Roosevelt Memorial, 2:432, 434

Fred Harvey Company, 1:284

Frederick Douglass. See Douglass, Frederick

Frederick Douglass National Historic Site, 1:7, 247–49; 2:431, 439

Frederick Law Olmsted. See Olmsted, Frederick Law

Frederick Law Olmsted National Historic Site, 1:249–51

Fredericksburg and Spotsylvania National Military Park, 1:251–53

Freedman's colony, 1:236

Freedom Trail, 1:100

Freemans' claim, 1:321

Frémont, John C., 1:75, 290; 2:523

Fremont Culture, 1:123

French, Daniel Chester, 2:433

French and Indian War (Seven Years' War), 1:36, 230, 262; 2:504

French Huguenots, 1:218, 228

Friendship Hill National Historic Site, 1:253–54

Frigate birds, 1:107

Frijoles Canyon, 1:73–74

Fruita orchards, 1:124

Fry, Walter, 2:527

G

Gage, Thomas, 2:411

Gallatin, Albert, 1:253–54

Gamble, Robert J., 2:597

Gansevoort, Peter, 1:240

Garfield, James A., 1:248; 2:341–42

Garfield National Historic Site. See James A. Garfield National Historic Site

Garrison, William Lloyd, 1:248

Garrucho, Joseph, 2:559

Gates, Horatio, 2:365, 519–20

Gates, The, 1:53

Gates of the Arctic National Park and Preserve, 1:255–56

Gateway Arch, 1:20; 2:344

Gateway National Recreation Area, 1:9, 20, 256–57; 2:374

Gauley River National Recreation Area, 1:257–58

General Education Board, 2:347

General Grant National Memorial, 1:258–60

General Grant National Park, 2:527

General Land Office, 1:1

George Mason Memorial, 2:431

George Rogers Clark. See Clark, George Rogers

George Rogers Clark National Historical Park, 1:260–62

George Washington. See Washington, George

George Washington Birthplace National Monument, 1:262–64

George Washington Carver. See Carver, George Washington

George Washington Carver National Monument, 1:264–65

George Washington Memorial Parkway, 1:65

Geronimo, 1:217, 221

Gettysburg Address, 1:265; 2:433

Gettysburg National Military Park, 1:265–68

Ghost Dance sites, 1:71

Gibbon, John, 1:80

Gibbons Battlefield Administrative Site, 1:82

Gila Cliff Dwellings National Monument, 1:268–69

Gila Wilderness, 1:269

Gillmore, Quincy Adams, **1:**234

Glacier Bay National Park and Preserve, **1:**269–71

Glacier International Peace Park. *See* Waterton-Glacier International Peace Park

Glacier National Park, **1:**271–73

Glen Canyon Dam, **1:**5–7, 273; **2:**488

Glen Canyon National Recreation Area, **1:**273–75; **2:**374, 488

Glen Echo Park, **1:**275–76

Glickman, Dan, **2:**545

Gloria Dei (Old Swedes') Church National Historic Site, **1:**276–77

Glorieta Pass, **2:**517

Glorieta Unit, **2:**466

Goetzmann, William H., **1:**227

Gold rushes
    California Gold Rush, **2:**367, 490–91, 589–90
    Klondike Gold Rush, **2:**367–69, 613–14

Golden Gate Bridge, **1:**232–33

Golden Gate National Recreation Area, **1:**9, 20, 29, 232–33, 256, 277–79; **2:**374, 479, 514

Golden Spike National Historic Site, **1:**279–80

Gompers, Samuel, **1:**34

Goodman, Benny, **2:**440

Gordon, John, **2:**418

Gore, Al, **1:**10, 22

Gran Quivira National Monument, **2:**510

Grand Canyon National Park, **1:**3–4, 17, 104, 280–84; **2:**351

Grand Coulee Dam, **2:**376

Grand Marais Coast Guard Station, **2:**473

Grand Marais Maritime Museum, **2:**473

Grand Portage National Monument, **1:**284–86

Grand Teton National Park, **1:**4, 19, 27, 286–89; **2:**348

Grant, Johnny, **1:**289

Grant, Julia Dent, **1:**258; **2:**566

Grant, Ulysses S., **1:**58, 102, 145, 222–23, 248, 251–52, 258–60; **2:**362–63, 464, 467–68, 492, 532, 565–66, 572, 608

Grant-Kohrs Ranch National Historic Site, **1:**82, 289–90

Grant National Historic Site. *See* Ulysses S. Grant National Historic Site

Grant National Memorial. *See* General Grant National Memorial

Grant's Tomb, **1:**258–60

Graveyard of the Atlantic, **1:**119–20

Great American Desert, **1:**75

Great Basin National Park, **1:**290–91

Great Depression, **1:**36, 186, 261, 317; **2:**344, 376, 433

Great houses (dwellings), **1:**138–39

Great Migration (1629), **2:**496

Great Northern Railroad, **1:**271

Great Outdoors Award, **1:**23

Great Plains, homesteading, **1:**321

Great Plains Indians, **2:**581

Great Sand Dunes National Monument and Preserve, **1:**292–93

Great Smoky Mountains National Park, **1:**4, 28, 37, 93–94, 250, 293–97

Great Society programs, **1:**213; **2:**346, 391

Green River, **1:**114–16, 186–87, 247; **2:**396–97

Green River Formation, **1:**247

Green Springs National Historic Landmark District, **1:**298–99

Green turtles, **1:**107

Greenbelt Park, **1:**297–98; **2:**431

Greene, Nathanael, **1:**301; **2:**445

Greenline parks, **1:**92, 191

Grinnell, George Bird, **1:**271

Guadalupe Mountains National Park, **1:**299–300

Guam, **1:**46; **2:**580

Guano fertilizer, **1:**127–28

Guilford Courthouse National Military Park, **1:**300–302, 318

Guiteau, Charles, **2:**341

Gulf Islands National Seashore, **1:**302–3

Gunnison, John, **1:**90

Gunnison Diversion Tunnel National Historic Civil Engineering Landmark, **1:**169

Gunnison River, **1:**168–69

H

Hagerman Fossil Beds National Monument, **1:**305–6

Hagerman Horse, **1:**305

Haleakala National Park, **1:**306–7

Halleck, Henry W., **2:**532

Hamilton, Alexander, **1:**253, 307–9

Hamilton, Henry, **1:**260

Hamilton Grange National Memorial, **1:**307–9

Hampton Institute, **1:**95

Hampton National Historic Site, **1:**309–10

Hancock, John, **1:**100

Hancock County Trustees of Public Preservations, **1:**36

"Hanging Judge," (Isaac C. Parker), **1:**239

Hanna, Mark, **2:**549

Hansen, John, **1:**276

Hansen, Martin, **2:**554

Hansen's disease (leprosy), **2:**357

Harding, Warren G., **1:**291, 317; **2:**594

Harding Icefield, **2:**361

Harper, Robert, **1:**311

Harpers Ferry National Historical Park, **1:**248, 310–12; **2:**443, 538

Harrison, Benjamin, **1:**248

Harrison, Peter, **2:**557

Harry S Truman. *See* Truman, Harry S

Harry S Truman National Historic Site, **1:**312–14

Hart, Fredrick, **2:**435

Hart, Philip A., **2:**536

Hartwell Tavern, **2:**412

Hartzog, George B., Jr., **1:**7–9, 20–21, 28

Hassam, Childe, **2:**584

Hawaii Volcanoes National Park, **1:**314–17

Hawaiian Islands, about **2:**357
   See also sites in the Hawaiian Islands.

Hawaiian temples (Heiau), **2:**359

Hawksbill, **1:**107

Hawthorne, Nathaniel, **2:**387, 412–13, 507

Hayden, Ferdinand V., **2:**608

Hayes, Rutherford B., **1:**248

Hazen, William B., **2:**582–283

HBC. *See* Hudson Bay Company

Heiau (Hawaiian temples), **2:**359

Hell on the Border, **1:**239

Herbert Hoover. *See* Hoover, Herbert Clark

Herbert Hoover National Historic Site, **1:**317–18

Heritage areas
   Blackstone River Valley National Heritage Corridor, **1:**91–93
   Cane River Creole National Historical Park and Heritage Area, **1:**111–13
   Chaco Culture National Historical Park, **1:**138–39
   Dayton Aviation Heritage National Historical Park, **1:**173–74
   Delaware and Lehigh Navigation Canal National Heritage Corridor, **1:**177–78
   Historic Camden, **1:**318–19
   Illinois and Michigan Canal National Heritage Corridor, **2:**331–32
   Lowell National Historical Park, **2:**388–90
   Natchez National Historical Park, **2:**429–30

Heritage areas *(continued)*
   New Bedford Whaling National Historical Park, **2:**439–40
   New Orleans Jazz National Historical Park, **2:**440–41

Hetch Hetchy Valley, **1:**2, 5, 183–84, 187, 273, 306; **2:**352, 610–11

Hewett, Edgar L., **1:**21, 74

Hickel, Walter J., **1:**8, 27

Hidatsa Indians, **2:**369

Highland Lighthouse, **1:**118

Hiler, Hilaire, **2:**514

Hill, Alfred J., **1:**195

Hill, A.P., **1:**267

Hill, Louis, **1:**271

Hillers, J. K., **1:**282

Hirons, Frederick C., **1:**261

Historic Camden, **1:**318–19

Historic trails
   Black Heritage Trail, **1:**97–98
   California Trail, **1:**151–52
   Freedom Trail, **1:**100
   National Trails System Act of 1968, **2:**526
   Ohio and Erie Canal Towpath Trail, **1:**171
   Oregon Trail, **1:** 147–48, 289; **2:**522–23, 593
   Santa Fe National Historic Trail, **1:**75, 226–27, 243–44; **2:**466, 516–18
   Selma To Montgomery Trail and All-American Road, **2:**523–27
   Tamiami Trail, **1:**79
   Trail of Tears National Historic Trail, **1:**238–39; **2:**364, 464
   Wilderness Trail, **1:**166

Hite, Cass, **2:**437

Hohokam Indians, **1:**129–30

Holmes, William Henry, **1:**282; **2:**612

Home of Franklin D. Roosevelt National Historic Site, **1:**319–21

Home of Theodore Roosevelt. *See* Sagamore Hill National Historic Site

Homestead Act, **1:**50, 321

Homestead National Monument of America, **1:**321–22

Honokohau settlement, **2:**359

Hood, John B., **1:**266

Hoodoos, **1:**104

Hooker, Joseph, **1:**55

Hoover, Herbert Clark, **1:**90, 113, 292, 317–318, 319; **2:**502, 592

Hoover Dam, **2:**374

Hoover National Historic Site. *See* Herbert Hoover National Historic Site

Hopewell Culture National Historical Park, **1:**322–23

Hopewell Furnace National Historic Site, **1:**324–25

Hopi Indians, **2:**487

Hornbek Homestead, **1:**215

Horses of Assateague, **1:**66

Horseshoe Bend National Military Park, **1:**325–26

Horseshoe Canyon, **1:**116

Hot Springs National Park, **1:**326–27

Houston, Jeanne Wakatsuki, **2:**400

Hovenweep National Monument, **1:**327–29

Howard, J. D., **2:**381

Howe, Julia Ward, **2:**387

Howe, William, **1:**240

Hubbell, John Lorenzo, **1:**329–30

Hubbell Trading Post National Historic Site, **1:**329–30

Hudson Bay Company (HBC), **1:**246

Hudson River School, **1:**36

Hughes, Sarah, **2:**391

Hulls Cove Visitor Center, **1:**37

Hurricane Hugo, **1:**157

Hutchinson, Ira, **1:**29

Huxman, Walter, **1:**103

I

Ice Age Clovis culture, **1:**43

Ice caps, **2:**361

Ickes, Harold L., **1:**16, 18–19

Illinois and Michigan Canal National Heritage Corridor, **2:**331–32

Illinois River, **2:**331

Independence Hall, **2:**334

Independence National Historical Park, **2:**332–35

Independent Order of St. Luke, **2:**393–94

Indian removal, **2:**512–13

Indian Wars, **1:**217, 227; **2:**441, 513
    See also French and Indian War

Indiana Dunes National Lakeshore, **2:**335–38

Industrial America
    Allegheny Portage Railroad National Historic Site, **1:**43–45
    Blackstone River Valley National Heritage Corridor, **1:**91–93
    Dayton Aviation Heritage National Historical Park, **1:**173–74
    Edison National Historic Site, **1:**193–95
    Golden Spike National Historic Site, **1:**279–80
    Lowell National Historical Park, **2:**388–90
    Saugus Iron Works National Historic Site, **2:**520–22
    Steamtown National Historic Site, **2:**540–41
    Wright Brothers National Memorial, **2:**603–5
    See also Railroad sites

Inscription Rock, **1:**203–4

Institute for the Prevention of Terrorism, **2:**453

International Biosphere Reserves
    Big Thicket National Preserve, **1:**86
    Congaree National Park, **1:**157
    Glacier National Park, **1:**271
    Redwood National Park, **2:**491

International Boundary and Water Commission, **1:**47

Internment camps
    Dakota Internment Camp, **2:**415
    Manzanar National Historic Site, **2:**399–401
    Minidoka Internment National Monument, **2:**410–11

Iowa Conservation Commission, **1:**196

Iron plantation, **1:**324

Iron works, **2:**522

Iroquois Indians, **1:**240

Isle au Haut, **1:**37–38

Isle of Bare Mountains (*L'Isle des Monts-desert*), **1:**35

Isle Royale National Park, **2:**338–39

Islesford Historical Museum, **1:**37

J

Jackson, Andrew "Old Hickory," **1:**40, 325–26; **2:**343, 391, 405, 561

Jackson, Claiborne F., **2:**595

Jackson, David, **1:**286

Jackson, Jimmie Lee, **2:**526

Jackson, Thomas J. "Stonewall," **1:**55, 251, 253; **2:**397–98, 418

Jackson, William Henry, **2:**523, 608

Jackson Hole National Monument, **1:**286–87

Jacob Ford Mansion, **2:**423

Jacob Riis Park bathhouse, **1:**257

Jagt, Guy Vanger, **2:**536

James A. Garfield. *See* Garfield, James A.

James A. Garfield National Historic Site, **2:**341–42

Jamestown, **1:**154–55

Jazz Age, **2:**440

Jean Lafitte. *See* Lafitte, Jean

Jean Lafitte National Historical Park and Preserve, **2:**342–43

Jedediah Smith Redwoods State Park, **2:**489, 491

Jefferson, Thomas, **1:**39, 142, 219, 253, 308, 310, 326; **2:**333–34, 343, 388, 427, 433, 547

Jefferson Memorial, **1:**159, 250; **2:**432–33

Jefferson National Expansion Memorial, **1:**20, 166; **2:**343–45

Jewel Cave National Monument, **2:**345–46

Jim Crow laws, **1:**95, 103, 173; **2:**404, 440, 561

Jimmy Carter. *See* Carter, Jimmy

Jimmy Carter National Historic Site, **2:**346–47

Job Corps Conservation Center, **1:**28

John D. Rockefeller, Jr. *See* Rockefeller, John D., Jr.

John D. Rockefeller, Jr. Memorial Parkway, **2:**347–48

John Day Fossil Beds National Monument, **2:**348–49

John Fitzgerald Kennedy. *See* Kennedy, John Fitzgerald

John Fitzgerald Kennedy National Historic Site, **2:**349–51

John Muir. *See* Muir, John

John Muir National Historic Site, **2:**351–53

John Wesley Memorial, **1:**234

Johnson, Andrew, **1:**49–52

Johnson, Frank M., Jr., **2:**526

Johnson, Lyndon B., **1:**21, 47–48, 116, 212, 256, 299; **2:**375, 390–92, 434, 525–26

Johnson, William, **2:**429

Johnson Farm, **1:**93

Johnson National Historic Site. *See* Andrew Johnson National Historic Site

Johnson National Historical Park. *See* Lyndon B. Johnson National Historical Park

Johnston, Albert Sidney, **2:**532

Johnston, Joe, **2:**363

Johnstown Flood National Memorial, **2:**353–54

Jolie Prairie, **1:**246

Jolliet, Louis, **2:**331

José, Juan, **1:**73

Joshua Tree National Park, **2**:354–56

Judah, Theodore, **1**:280

Julien, Denis, **1**:115

K

Kabotie, Fred, **2**:470

Kaibab Paiute Indians, **2**:476, 487

Kaiser, Henry J., **2**:498

Kalaupapa National Historical Park, **2**:357–58

Kaloko-Honokohau National Historical Park, **2**:358–59

Kamehameha I, **2**:484

Kamehameha II, **2**:484

Kamehameha V, **2**:357

Kate Chopin House, **1**:113

Katmai National Park and Preserve, **2**:359–61

Kearney, Stephen W., **1**:75

Kemp's ridley sea turtles, **2**:461

Kenai Fjords National Park, **2**:361–62

Kennedy, Jacqueline Bouvier, **2**:349

Kennedy, John Fitzgerald, **1**:30, 140, 199; **2**:349–51, 391, 433–34, 479, 589

Kennedy, Joseph P., **2**:350

Kennedy, Roger, **1**:10, 22

Kennedy, Rose Fitzgerald, **2**:350

Kennedy National Historic Site. *See* John Fitzgerald Kennedy National Historic Site

Kennedy Space Center, **1**:110

Kennesaw Mountain National Battlefield Park, **2**:362–64

Kettle Falls Hotel, **2**:578

Keweenaw National Historical Park, **2**:364–65

Key, Francis Scott, **1**:229

Kilauea, **1**:315

King, Martin Luther, Jr., **1**:28, 34, 137; **2**:403–4, 524–25

King National Historic Site. *See* Martin Luther King, Jr. National Historic Site

Kings Canyon National Park. *See* Sequoia and Kings Canyon National Parks

Kings Mountain National Military Park, **2**:365–67

Kingsley Plantation, **1**:218; **2**:555

Kino, Eusebio Francisco, **1**:129; **2**:558–59

Klondike Gold Rush, **2**:367–69, 613–14

Klondike Gold Rush National Historical Park, **2**:367–69

Knife River Indian Villages National Historic Site, **2**:369–70

Kobuk Valley National Park, **2**:587–88

Kohrs, Conrad, **1**:289

Kohrs Ranch National Historic Site. *See* Grant-Kohrs Ranch National Historic Site

Kolob Arch, **2**:616

Korean War Veterans Memorial, **2**:432, 434

Kosciuszko, Thaddeus, **2**:546–48

Kosciuszko National Monument. *See* Thaddeus Kosciuszko National Monument

L

Lacey, John F., **2**:597

Lafayette National Park, **1**:4, 35, 37

Lafitte, Jean, **2**:342–43

Lafitte, Pierre, **2**:342

Lafitte National Historical Park and Preserve. *See* Jean Lafitte National Historical Park and Preserve

Lake Champlain, **1**:240

Lake Clark National Park and Preserve, **2**:371–72

Lake Conemaugh, **2**:353

Lake Florissant, **1**:214

Lake Mead National Recreation Area, **2**:372–75

Lake Meredith National Recreation Area, **2**:375–76

Lake Michigan, **2**:331, 335, 535

Lake Powell, **1**:7, 123, 273–74; **2**:487–88

Lake Roosevelt National Recreation Area, **2**:376–78

Lake Superior, **1**:56; **2**:338, 473

Lakeshore areas

Apostle Islands National Lakeshore, **1**:56–58

Indiana Dunes National Lakeshore, **2**:335–38

Pictured Rocks National Lakeshore, **2**:473–74

Sleeping Bear Dunes National Lakeshore, **2**:535–37

Lakota (Sioux) Indians, **1**:225–26; **2**:384, 415, 550

Land and Water Conservation Fund, **1**:21, 124

Landmark sites

Brooks River National Historic Landmark, **2**:360

Green Springs National Historic Landmark District, **1**:298–99

Gunnison Diversion Tunnel National Historic Civil Engineering Landmark, **1**:169

Landscape architecture, **1**:4, 249–51

Lane, Franklin K., **1**:2, 15, 24

Langford, Nathaniel Pitt, **2**:607

Larned, Benjamin, **1**:226

Lassen, Peter, **2**:379

Lassen Volcanic National Park, **2**:378–80

Laumet, Antoine (Sieur de la Mothe Cadillac), **1**:36

Lava Beds National Monument, **2**:380–81

Lazo, Ralph, **2**:400

Least-Heat Moon, William, **2**:545

Leatherback sea turtles, **1**:107

Lecomte, Ambroise, **1**:112

Lee, George Washington Custis, **1**:64

Lee, Henry "Light Horse Harry," **2**:445

Lee, Richard Henry, **2**:333

Lee, Robert E., **1**:53–54, 58, 60, 63–65, 215, 234, 251–52, 259, 265, 267; **2**:398, 418, 467, 492, 565

Lee Memorial. *See* Arlington House, The Robert E. Lee Memorial

Lehigh Navigation Canal National Heritage Corridor. *See* Delaware and Lehigh Navigation Canal National Heritage Corridor

Lehigh Navigation System, **1:**177

Lehman, Absalom, **1:**290

Lehman Caves National Monument, **1:**290–91

L'Enfant, Pierre, **2:**430–31

Leopold, A. Starker, **1:**6

Leopold Report (1963), **1:**6, 278; **2:**503

Leper (sufferer of Hansen's Disease) colony, **2:**357

Let burn strategy, **1:**25

Levander, Harold, **2:**577

Lewis, John, **2:**525

Lewis, Meriwether, **1:**219; **2:**343, 561

Lewis, Theodore, **1:**195

Lewis and Clark Expedition, **1:**219–20, 253; **2:**344, 369, 433, 607

Liberty Bell, **2:**332–33

Liberty Bell Center, **2:**334–35

Liberty Hall, **2:**334

Lighthouses, largest collection, **1:**56

Lillington, Alexander, **2:**420–21

Limited Nuclear Test-Ban Treaty (1963), **2:**350

Lin, Maya Ying, **2:**435

Lincoln, Abraham, **1:**33–35, 50–51, 54–55, 188, 215, 222, 241–42, 248–49, 259, 265, 280, 321; **2:**362, 381–83, 388, 391, 397, 427, 433, 492, 542, 565, 572, 595

Lincoln, Mary Todd, **2:**381, 383

Lincoln, Nancy Hanks, **1:**33; **2:**381–82

Lincoln, Sarah Bush Johnston, **2:**381

Lincoln, Thomas, **1:**33; **2:**381

Lincoln Birthplace. *See* Abraham Lincoln Birthplace National Historic Site

Lincoln Boyhood National Memorial, **2:**381–83

Lincoln Farm Association, **1:**34

Lincoln Highway, **1:**5

Lincoln Home National Historic Site, **2:**383–84

Lincoln Memorial, **2:**432–33

Linenthal, Edward, **2:**441

L'Isle des Monts-desert (Isle of Bare Mountains), **1:**35

Little Arkansas Treaty, **2:**582

Little Bighorn Battlefield National Monument, **1:**226; **2:**384–86, 441

Little River Canyon National Preserve, **2:**386–87

Llano Estacado (Staked Plains), **2:**375

Loggerhead turtle, **1:**121

Longfellow, Henry Wadsworth, **2:**387–88, 411

Longfellow National Historic Site, **2:**387–88

Longmire Museum, **2:**425

Longstreet, James, **1:**266

López de Cárdenas, García, **1:**281

Lopez Mateos, President, **1:**140

Los Alamos, **1:**74

Lost Colony, **1:**119, 235–36

Lothrop, Harriet, **2:**413

Louisiana Purchase, **1:**142, 219; **2:**343–44, 433

Louisiana Territory, **1:**62, 238, 253, 326

Lowell, Francis Cabot, **2:**388–89

Lowell National Historical Park, **2:**388–90

Lummis, Charles F., **1:**282

Lyndon B. Johnson. *See* Johnson, Lyndon B.

Lyndon B. Johnson National Historical Park, **2:**390–92

Lyon, Nathaniel, **2:**595, 597

M

MacArthur, Douglas, **1:**45, 197

Maderas del Carmen, **1:**76

Madison, James, **1:**40, 132, 253

Maggie L. Walker. *See* Walker, Maggie L.

Maggie L. Walker National Historic Site, **2:**393–94

Magnolia Plantation, **1:**112

Mainella, Fran P., **1:**22–23

Mammoth Cave National Park, **1:**4, 37, 295; **2:**395–97

Man and Nature (Marsh), **2:**402

Manassas National Battlefield Park, **2:**397–99

Mandan Indians, **2:**369

Mangas Coloradas, **1:**217

Manhattan Project, **2:**591

Manifest Destiny, **1:**234, 236, 281; **2:**516, 581

Mansfield, Joseph, **1:**55

Manzanar National Historic Site, **2:**399–401

Marble Halls of Oregon, **2:**457

Mariana Islands, **1:**45–47; **2:**580

Marion, Francis, **2:**366

Marquette, Father Jacques, **2:**331

Marsh, George Perkins, **2:**401–3

Marsh, Othniel, **2:**348

Marsh-Billings-Rockefeller National Historical Park, **2:**401–3

Marshall, Robert, **1:**255

Martin, Josiah, **2:**420

Martin Luther King, Jr. *See* King, Martin Luther, Jr.

Martin Luther King, Jr. National Historic Site, **2:**403–4

Martin Van Buren. *See* Van Buren, Martin

Martin Van Buren National Historic Site, **2:**404–6

Mary McLeod Bethune. *See* Bethune, Mary McLeod

Mary McLeod Bethune Council House National Historic Site, **2:**406–8, 431

Mason, Samuel, **2:**561

Massachusetts Bay Colony, **2:**521

Massachusetts 54th Regiment, **1:**98

Massasoit, **1:**118

Matanzas massacre, **1:**228

Mather, Stephen T., **1:**2–3, 8–9, 15–16, 18, 21, 23–24, 105, 136, 293–95; **2:**336, 476, 610, 613–16

Mauna Loa, **1:**315–16

Mayflower Compact, **1:**117

McArdle, Eliza, **1:**50

McClellan, George B., **1:**53–54, 251; **2:**492

McComb, John, **1:**308

McCulloch, Benjamin, **2:**595

McFarland, Horace, **1:**2

McKinley, William, **2:**425, 548–49

McLean, Wilmer, **1:**58–59

M'Clintock House, **2:**600

McLoughlin, John, **1:**246

McMurran, John T., **2:**429

McPhee, John, **2:**587

Meade, George G., **1:**265–67

Medicine Lodge Treaty (1867), **2:**581–82

Meek, Joe, **2:**607

Mellon family, **1:**118, 122

Melrose estate, **2:**429

Melville, Herman, **2:**439

Merriam, John C., **2:**349

Merritt, Wesley, **1:**221

Merritt Island National Wildlife Refuge, **1:**110–11

Mesa Verde National Park, **1:**328; **2:**408–10

Mesa Verde Pueblo people, **1:**67–68, 328; **2:**408–10

Mexican-American War, **1:**75, 239, 243, 259; **2:**462–63, 466, 517, 565

Mexican Revolution, **1:**78

Mezes, Sidney, **1:**24

Michaud, Frank and Albert, **2:**345

Michigan Canal National Heritage Corridor. *See* Illinois and Michigan Canal National Heritage Corridor

Micro Beach, **1:**46

Miles, Nelson A., **1:**81

Military sites and memorials
   Chickamauga and Chattanooga National Military Park, **1:**144–46
   Fredericksburg and Spotsylvania National Military Park, **1:**251–53
   Gettysburg National Military Park, **1:**265–68

Military sites and memorials *(continued)*
   Guilford Courthouse National Military Park, **1:**300–302, 318
   Horseshoe Bend National Military Park, **1:**325–26
   Kings Mountain National Military Park, **2:**365–67
   Little Bighorn Battlefield National Monument, **2:**384–86
   Manassas National Battlefield Park, **2:**397–99
   Minute Man National Historical Park, **2:**411–13
   Moores Creek National Battlefield, **2:**420–22
   Morristown National Historical Park, **2:**422–24
   Palo Alto Battlefield National Historic Site, **2:**462–64
   Pea Ridge National Military Park, **2:**464–66
   Port Chicago Naval Magazine National Memorial, **2:**480–81
   Richmond National Battlefield Park, **2:**492–93
   Saratoga National Historical Park, **2:**518–20
   Shiloh National Military Park, **2:**532–33
   Springfield Armory National Historic Site, **2:**537–38
   Stones River National Battlefield, **2:**541–42
   Tupelo National Battlefield, **2:**560–61
   Tuskegee Airmen National Historic Site, **2:**561–62
   USS *Arizona* Memorial, **2:**566–68
   Valley Forge National Historical Park, **2:**569–70

Military sites and memorials *(continued)*
   Vicksburg National Military Park, **2:**572–74
   War in the Pacific National Historical Park, **2:**580–81
   Washita Battlefield National Historic Site, **2:**581–84
   See also Civil War historical sites and battlefields; National battlefields; Revolutionary War sites; World War II sites

Millbrook Village, **1:**178

Miller Field, **1:**257

Mills, Enos A., **2:**495

Mineral springs, **1:**146; **2:** 607

Minidoka Bird Refuge, **1:**152

Minidoka Internment National Monument, **2:**410–11

Mining in the Parks Act (1976), **1:**173

Minnesota Federation of Women's Clubs, **2:**576

Minute Man National Historical Park, **2:**411–13

Mission 66 program, **1:**6, 20, 29–30; **2:**438, 495, 535–36

Mississippi National River and Recreation Area, **2:**413–15

Miwok Indians, **2:**478

Mixed grass prairie, **1:**71–72

Miyatake, Toyo, **2:**400

Modoc Indian War (1872–1873), **2:**380–81

Mogollon culture, **1:**268

Mojave Desert, **2:**355, 415

Mojave National Preserve, **2:**415–18

Molokai, **2:**357

Molokai Light, **2:**357

Mondale, Walter, **2:**577

Monk, Thelonius, **2:**440

Monocacy National Battlefield, **2:**418–19

Monocacy River Valley, **1:**134

Monocline, **1:**123

Monroe, James, **1:**40

Monroe Doctrine, **1:**40, 319

Monroe Elementary School, **1:**103–4

Montezuma Castle National Monument, **2:**419–20

Montgomery bus boycott, **2:**403

Monument Valley, **1:**156

Moody, Paul, **2:**388

Moores Creek National Battlefield, **2:**420–22

Moran, Thomas, **1:**282; **2:**608

Morgan, Daniel, **1:**160–61; **2:**520

Morris, Earl, **1:**68

Morris, Richard, **1:**298

Morristown National Historical Park, **2:**422–24

Morrow Point Lake, **1:**168–69

Morton, C. B. Rogers, **1:**8, 19

Morton, John, **1:**276

Mott, Lucretia, **2:**599

Mott, William Penn, Jr., **1:**25

Mound Builders, **1:**195, 323; **2:**452, 612

Mount Desert Island, **1:**36–37

Mount Mazama, **1:**162

Mount McKinley, **1:**179–80

Mount Olympus National Monument, **2:**454–55

Mount Rainier National Park, **1:**294; **2:**351, 424–26

Mount Rushmore National Memorial, **2:**426–28

Mount St. Elias, **2:**601

Mount Saint Helens, **1:**148, 162; **2:**379

Mount Vernon, **2:**430

Mudd, Roger, **1:**188

Mudd, Samuel, **1:**188

Muir, John, **1:**1, 183, 271; **2:**351–53, 491, 610–11

Muir National Historic Site. *See* John Muir National Historic Site

Mukuntuweap National Monument, **2:**615

Munemori, Sadao, **2:**400

Murrah Federal Building, Oklahoma City, **2:**453

Murrell, John, **2:**561

Museum of Fine Arts, Santa Fe, **1:**21

Museum of New Mexico, **1:**21

Museum of Westward Expansion, **2:**344

N

NAACP. *See* National Association for the Advancement of Colored People

NACW. *See* National Association of Colored Women

NANA Regional Corporation, **2:**587

Napoleon Bonaparte, **1:**62

NASA. *See* National Aeronautics and Space Administration

Natchez Indians, **2:**481

Natchez National Historical Park, **2:**429–30

Natchez Trace Parkway, **2:**560–61

National Aeronautics and Space Administration (NASA), **1:**110; **2:**592

National anthem, **1:**229

National Archives for Black Women's History, **2:**406

National Association for the Advancement of Colored People (NAACP), **1:**103; **2:**394, 561

National Association of Colored Women (NACW), **2:**394, 407

National battlefields

    Antietam National Battlefield, **1:**53–56

    Big Hole National Battlefield, **1:**80–82; **2:**441–43

    Brices Cross Roads National Battlefield, **1:**102–3

    Cowpens National Battlefield, **1:**160–62

    Fort Donelson National Battlefield, **1:**222–23

    Fort Necessity National Battlefield, **1:**230–31

National battlefields *(continued)*

    Kennesaw Mountain National Battlefield Park, **2:**362–64

    Monocacy National Battlefield, **2:**418–19

    Moores Creek National Battlefield, **2:**420–22

    Petersburg National Battlefield, **2:**467–69

    Richmond National Battlefield Park, **2:**492–93

    Stones River National Battlefield, **2:**541–42

    Tupelo National Battlefield, **2:**560–61

    Wilson's Creek National Battlefield, **2:**595–97

National Capital Park and Planning Commission (1928), **1:**29

National Capital Parks, **1:**28; **2:**430–31

National Capital Region, **1:**27

National Council of Negro Women, **2:**406

National Environmental Policy Act (NEPA), **1:**27; **2:**455–56

National Forest Service (NFS), **1:**74

National Geographic Society, **2:**491

National Historic Civil Engineering Landmark, **1:**169

National historic sites and areas

    Abraham Lincoln Birthplace National Historic Site, **1:**33–35

    Aleutian World War II National Historic Area, **1:**42

    Allegheny Portage Railroad National Historic Site, **1:**43–45

    Andersonville National Historic Site, **1:**48–49

    Andrew Johnson National Historic Site, **1:**49–52

    Bent's Old Fort National Historic Site, **1:**75–76

National historic sites and areas
(continued)

Boston African American
National Historic Site,
1:96–98

Brown v. Board of Education
National Historic Site,
1:103–4, 137; **2**:525

Carl Sandburg Home
National Historic Site,
1:126–27

Central High School
National Historic Site,
1:137–38

Charles Pinckney National
Historic Site, **1**:142–43

Chimney Rock National
Historic Site, **1**:147–48

Christiansted National
Historic Site, **1**:150–51

Clara Barton National
Historic Site, **1**:153–54

Edgar Allan Poe National
Historic Site, **1**:192–93

Edison National Historic
Site, **1**:193–95

Eleanor Roosevelt
National Historic Site,
1:198–99

Eugene O'Neill National
Historic Site, **1**:204–5

Ford's Theatre National
Historic Site, **1**:215–16

Fort Bowie National
Historic Site, **1**:216–17

Fort Davis National
Historic Site, **1**:220–22

Fort Laramie National
Historic Site, **1**:224–26

Fort Larned National
Historic Site, **1**:226–27

Fort Point National
Historic Site, **1**:231–33

Fort Raleigh National
Historic Site, **1**:235–36

Fort Scott National
Historic Site, **1**:236–37

Fort Smith National
Historic Site, **1**:237–40

Fort Union Trading Post
National Historic Site,
1:245–46

National historic sites and areas
(continued)

Fort Vancouver National
Historic Site, **1**:246–47

Franklin D. Roosevelt
National Historic Site,
1:319–21

Frederick Douglass
National Historic Site,
1:7, 247–49; **2**:431, 439

Frederick Law Olmsted
National Historic Site,
1:249–51

Friendship Hill National
Historic Site, **1**:253–54

Gloria Dei (Old Swedes')
Church National
Historic Site,
1:276–77

Golden Spike National
Historic Site, **1**:279–80

Grant-Kohrs Ranch
National Historic Site,
1:82, 289–90

Hampton National
Historic Site, **1**:309–10

Harry S Truman National
Historic Site, **1**:312–14

Herbert Hoover National
Historic Site, **1**:317–18

Hopewell Furnace
National Historic Site,
1:324–25

Hubbell Trading Post
National Historic Site,
1:329–30

James A. Garfield National
Historic Site, **2**:341–42

Jimmy Carter National
Historic Site, **2**:346–47

John Fitzgerald Kennedy
National Historic Site,
2:349–51

John Muir National
Historic Site, **2**:351–53

Knife River Indian Villages
National Historic Site,
2:369–70

Lincoln Home National
Historic Site, **2**:383–84

Longfellow National
Historic Site, **2**:387–88

National historic sites and areas
(continued)

Maggie L. Walker National
Historic Site, **2**:393–94

Manzanar National
Historic Site, **2**:399–401

Martin Luther King, Jr.,
National Historic Site,
2:403–4

Martin Van Buren National
Historic Site, **2**:404–6

Mary McLeod Bethune
Council House
National Historic Site,
2:406–8, 431

Nicodemus National
Historic Site, **2**:443–45

Ninety Six National
Historic Site, **2**:445–46

Palo Alto Battlefield
National Historic Site,
2:462–64

Puukohola Heiau National
Historical Site, **2**:484–85

Sagamore Hill National
Historic Site, **2**:501–2

Saint Croix Island
International Historic
Site, **2**:503–4

Saint Paul's Church
National Historic Site,
2:506–7

Saint-Gaudens National
Historic Site, **2**:504–6

Salem Maritime National
Historic Site, **2**:507–9

San Juan National Historic
Site, **2**:515–16

Sand Creek Massacre
National Historic Site,
2:512–14, 581

Saugus Iron Works
National Historic Site,
2:520–22

Springfield Armory
National Historic Site,
2:537–38

Steamtown National
Historic Site, **2**:540–41

Theodore Roosevelt
Birthplace National
Historic Site, **2**:548–49

National historic sites and areas
   (*continued*)
   Theodore Roosevelt
      Inaugural National
      Historic Site, **2:**549–50
   Thomas Stone National
      Historic Site, **2:**552–53
   Touro Synagogue National
      Historic Site, **2:**557–58
   Tuskegee Institute National
      Historic Site, **1:**95, 264;
      2:562–64
   Ulysses S. Grant National
      Historic Site, **2:**565–66
   Vanderbilt Mansion
      National Historic Site,
      2:570–72
   Weir Farm National
      Historic Site, **2:**584–85
   Whitman Mission National
      Historic Site, **2:**592–94
National historical parks, **1:**7
   Adams National Historical
      Park, **1:**38–42
   Appomattox Court House
      National Historical
      Park, **1:**58–60
   Boston National Historical
      Park, **1:**100–102
   Cane River Creole
      National Historical
      Park and Heritage Area,
      1:111–13
   Chaco Culture National
      Historical Park, **1:**138–39
   Colonial National
      Historical Park,
      1:154–56
   Cumberland Gap National
      Historical Park,
      1:166–67
   Dayton Aviation Heritage
      National Historical
      Park, **1:**173–74
   George Rogers Clark
      National Historical
      Park, **1:**260–62
   Harpers Ferry National
      Historical Park, **1:**248,
      310–12; **2:**443, 538
   Hopewell Culture National
      Historical Park,
      1:322–23

National historical parks
   (*continued*)
   Independence National
      Historical Park,
      2:332–35
   Jean Lafitte National
      Historical Park and
      Preserve, **2:**342–43
   Kalaupapa National
      Historical Park,
      2:357–58
   Kaloko-Honokohau
      National Historical
      Park, **2:**358–59
   Keweenaw National
      Historical Park,
      2:364–65
   Klondike Gold Rush
      National Historical
      Park, **2:**367–69
   Lowell National
      Historical Park,
      2:388–90
   Lyndon B. Johnson
      National Historical
      Park, **2:**390–92
   Marsh-Billings-
      Rockefeller National
      Historical Park,
      2:401–3
   Minute Man National
      Historical Park,
      2:411–13
   Morristown National
      Historical Park,
      2:422–24
   Natchez National
      Historical Park,
      2:429–30
   New Bedford Whaling
      National Historical
      Park, **2:**439–40
   New Orleans Jazz National
      Historical Park,
      2:440–41
   Nez Perce National
      Historical Park, **1:**82;
      2:441–43
   Pecos National Historical
      Park, **2:**466–67
   Pu'uhonua O Honaunau
      National Historical
      Park, **2:**483–84

National historical parks
   (*continued*)
   Rosie the Riveter World
      War II Home Front
      National Historical
      Park, **2:**497–99
   Salt River Bay Park
      National Historical
      Park and Ecological
      Preserve, **2:**510–11
   San Antonio Missions
      National Historical
      Park, **2:**511–12
   San Francisco Maritime
      National Historical
      Park, **2:**514
   Saratoga National
      Historical Park,
      2:518–20
   Sitka National Historical
      Park, **2:**533–35
   Tumacácori National
      Historical Park,
      2:558–60
   Valley Forge National
      Historical Park,
      2:569–70
   Women's Rights National
      Historical Park, **1:**7;
      2:599–601
National Law Enforcement
   Officers Memorial, **2:**431
National Mall, **2:**431–35
National memorials
   Arkansas Post National
      Memorial, **1:**62–63
   Chamizal National
      Memorial, **1:**139–41
   Coronado National
      Memorial, **1:**159–60
   De Soto National
      Memorial, **1:**182–83
   Federal Hall National
      Memorial, **1:**211–12
   Fort Caroline National
      Memorial, **1:**217–19, 228
   Fort Clatsop National
      Memorial, **1:**219–20
   General Grant National
      Memorial, **1:**258–60
   Hamilton Grange National
      Memorial, **1:**307–9

National memorials *(continued)*

Johnstown Flood National Memorial, **2:**353–54

Lincoln Boyhood National Memorial, **2:**381–83

Mount Rushmore National Memorial, **2:**426–28

National Law Enforcement Officers Memorial, **2:**431

National World War II Memorial, **2:**431

Oklahoma City National Memorial, **1:**145; **2:**452–54

Roger Williams National Memorial, **2:**496–97

Wright Brothers National Memorial, **2:**603–5

See also National tragedies

National monuments, **1:**2–4

Agate Fossil Beds National Monument, **1:**41–42

Alibates Flint Quarries National Monument, **1:**42–43

Aniakchak National Monument & Preserve, **1:**52–53

Aztec Ruins National Monument, **1:**67–69

Bandelier National Monument, **1:**4, 27, 73–75

Buck Island Reef National Monument, **1:**107–8

Cabrillo National Monument, **1:**109–10

Canyon de Chelly National Monument, **1:**113–14

Capulin Volcano National Monument, **1:**125–26

Casa Grande Ruins National Monument, **1:**26, 129–30

Castillo de San Marcos National Monument, **1:**130–32

Cedar Breaks National Monument, **1:**104, 136–37

Chiricahua National Monument, **1:**148–50

National monuments *(continued)*

Colorado National Monument, **1:**156–57

Craters of the Moon National Monument and Preserve, **1:**164–66

John Day Fossil Beds National Monument, **2:**348–49

Devils Postpile National Monument, **1:**183–84

Devils Tower National Monument, **1:**184–86

Dinosaur National Monument, **1:**5, 19, 186–88, 273

Effigy Mounds National Monument, **1:**195–96

El Malpais National Monument, **1:**201–2

El Morro National Monument, **1:**202–4

Ellis Island National Monument, **1:**200–201

Florissant Fossil Beds National Monument, **1:**214–15

Fort Frederica National Monument, **1:**223–24

Fort Matanzas National Monument, **1:**228–29

Fort McHenry National Monument and Historic Shrine, **1:**229–30

Fort Pulaski National Monument, **1:**233–35

Fort Stanwix National Monument, **1:**240–41

Fort Union National Monument, **1:**243–45

Fossil Butte National Monument, **1:**247

George Washington Birthplace National Monument, **1:**262–64

Gila Cliff Dwellings National Monument, **1:**268–69

Grand Portage National Monument, **1:**284–86

Great Sand Dunes National Monument and Preserve, **1:**292–93

National monuments *(continued)*

Hagerman Fossil Beds National Monument, **1:**305–6

Homestead National Monument of America, **1:**321–22

Hovenweep National Monument, **1:**327–29

Jewel Cave National Monument, **2:**345–46

John Day Fossil Beds National Monument, **2:**348–49

Lava Beds National Monument, **2:**380–81

Little Bighorn Battlefield National Monument, **1:**226; **2:**384–86, 441

Minidoka Internment National Monument, **2:**410–11

Montezuma Castle National Monument, **2:**419–20

Natural Bridges National Monument, **2:**436–37

Navajo National Monument, **2:**437–39

Ocmulgee National Monument, **2:**451–52

Oregon Caves National Monument, **2:**457–59

Organ Pipe Cactus National Monument, **2:**459–60

Petroglyph National Monument, **2:**471–73

Pinnacles National Monument, **2:**474–76

Pipe Spring National Monument, **2:**476–77

Pipestone National Monument, **2:**477–78

Poverty Point National Monument/State Commemorative Area, **2:**481–82

Rainbow Bridge National Monument, **2:**487–89

Russell Cave National Monument, **2:**499

National monuments (continued)
    Salinas Pueblo Missions
        National Monument,
        2:509–10
    Scotts Bluff National
        Monument, 2:522–23
    Statue of Liberty National
        Monument, 1:200;
        2:539–40
    Sunset Crater Volcano
        National Monument,
        2:542–43, 579, 605
    Thaddeus Kosciuszko
        National Monument,
        2:546–48
    Timpanogos Cave National
        Monument, 2:553–54
    Tonto National Monument,
        2:555–57
    Tuzigoot National
        Monument, 2:564
    Walnut Canyon National
        Monument, 2:579–80
    White Sands National
        Monument, 2:591–92
    Wupatki National
        Monument, 2:605–6
    Yucca House National
        Monument, 2:612–13
National Monuments Act, 2:550
National Park Service (NPS)
    challenges of, 1:10–11
    conservation efforts of, 1:5
    contributions of Albright
        and Mather, 1:2–3, 15,
        23–24
    founding of, 1:1–3
    inclusion of ignored
        minorities, 1:7
    inviolability principle, 1:5
    landscape architecture of,
        1:4, 249–51
    Leopold Report (1963), 1:6,
        278; 2:503
    mission of, 1:1, 8
    Mission 66 capital
        development program,
        1:6
    New Deal era parkitecture,
        1:4
    1920s, 1:3
    1930s New Deal era, 1:4

National Park Service
    (continued)
    1950s, 1:5, 8
    1960s growth, 1:7–8
    1970s politics, 1:9–10
    1980s, 1:9–10
    1990s reorganization, 1:10
    overview and history, 1:1–11
    people-management focus,
        1:6
    post-September 11th, 1:23
    post-World War II era,
        1:4–5
    recreational playgrounds,
        1:5–7
    Robbins Report, 1:6
    urban areas and, 1:8–9
    Vail Agenda, 1:10
    Web site development, 1:22
National Park Service Act, 1:2
National Park Service Organic
    Act, 2:379
National Park Trust, 2:546
National parks
    Acadia National Park, 1:4,
        35–38
    Arches National Park,
        1:60–62
    Badlands National Park,
        1:71–73
    Big Bend National Park,
        1:76–79
    Biscayne National Park,
        1:88–89
    Black Canyon of the
        Gunnison National
        Park, 1:89–91
    Bryce Canyon National
        Park, 1:3, 104–7
    Canyonlands National
        Park, 1:114–17
    Capitol Reef National
        Park, 1:123–25
    Carlsbad Caverns National
        Park, 1:3, 8, 127–29
    Channel Islands National
        Park, 1:141–42
    Congaree National Park,
        1:157–58
    Crater Lake National Park,
        1:162–64

National parks (continued)
    Cuyahoga Valley National
        Park, 1:170–72
    Death Valley National
        Park, 1:174–76
    Denali National Park and
        Preserve, 1:179–82
    Everglades National Park,
        1:79, 205–9
    Gates of the Arctic
        National Park and
        Preserve, 1:255–56
    Glacier Bay National Park
        and Preserve, 1:269–71
    Glacier National Park,
        1:271–73
    Grand Canyon National
        Park, 1:3–4, 17, 104,
        280–84; 2:351
    Grand Teton National
        Park, 1:4, 19, 27, 286–89;
        2:348
    Great Basin National Park,
        1:290–91
    Great Smoky Mountains
        National Park, 1:4, 28,
        37, 93–94, 250, 293–97
    Guadalupe Mountains
        National Park,
        1:299–300
    Haleakala National Park,
        1:306–7
    Hawaii Volcanoes National
        Park, 1:314–17
    Hot Springs National Park,
        1:326–27
    Isle Royale National Park,
        2:338–39
    Joshua Tree National Park,
        2:354–56
    Katmai National Park and
        Preserve, 2:359–61
    Kenai Fjords National
        Park, 2:361–62
    Lake Clark National Park
        and Preserve, 2:371–72
    Lassen Volcanic National
        Park, 2:378–80
    Mammoth Cave National
        Park, 1:4, 37, 295;
        2:395–97
    Mesa Verde National Park,
        1:328; 2:408–10

National parks (*continued*)

Mount Rainier National Park, **1:**294; **2:**351, 424–26

North Cascades National Park, **2:**446–49

Olympic National Park, **2:**454–57

Petrified Forest National Park, **1:**215; **2:**351, 469–70

Redwood National and State Parks, **1:**25; **2:**489–91

Rocky Mountain National Park, **1:**294; **2:**494–96

Saguaro National Park, **2:**502–3

Sequoia and Kings Canyon National Parks, **1:**1 2; **2:**527–29

Shenandoah National Park, **1:**4, 37, 93, 295; **2:**529–32

Theodore Roosevelt National Park, **2:**550–52

Virgin Islands National Park, **2:**574–76

Voyageurs National Park, **2:**576–78

Western Arctic National Parklands, **2:**585–89

Wind Cave National Park, **2:**597–99

Wrangell-St. Elias National Park and Preserve, **2:**601–3

Yellowstone National Park, **1:**1, 4, 9–10, 15, 18, 21, 25, 82, 121, 171, 286–87; **2:**348, 607–9

Yosemite National Park, **1:**8, 18, 294; **2:**351–52, 609–12

Zion National Park, **1:**3, 104; **2:**615–17

National Parks Association, **1:**293

National preserves and reserves

Aniakchak National Monument & Preserve, **1:**52–53

Barataria Preserve, **2:**342–43

National preserves and reserves (*continued*)

Bering Land Bridge National Preserve, **2:**585–86

Big Cypress National Preserve, **1:**79–80, 207

Big Thicket National Preserve, **1:**86–88

City of Rocks National Reserve, **1:**151–52

Craters of the Moon Monument and Preserve, **1:**164–66

Denali National Park and Preserve, **1:**179–82

Ebey's Landing National Historical Reserve, **1:**191–92

Gates of the Arctic National Park and Preserve, **1:**255–56

Glacier Bay National Park and Preserve, **1:**269–71

Great Sand Dunes National Monument and Preserve, **1:**292–93

Jean Lafitte National Historical Park and Preserve, **2:**342–43

Katmai National Park and Preserve, **2:**359–61

Lake Clark National Park and Preserve, **2:**371–72

Little River Canyon National Preserve, **2:**386–87

Mojave National Preserve, **2:**415–18

Noatak National Preserve, **2:**588–98

Pacific Forest Reserve, **2:**424

Salt River Bay National Historical Park and Ecological Preserve, **2:**510–11

Tallgrass Prairie National Preserve, **2:**545–46

Timucuan Ecological and Historic Preserve, **1:**218; **2:**554–55

Wrangell-St. Elias National Park and Preserve, **2:**601–3

National preserves and reserves (*continued*)

Yukon-Charley Rivers National Preserve, **2:**613–14

National Prisoner of War Museum, **1:**49

National recreation areas

Amistad National Recreation Area, **1:**47–48

Big South Fork National River and Recreation Area, **1:**85–86

Bighorn Canyon National Recreation Area, **1:**83–85

Boston Harbor Islands National Recreation Area, **1:**98–100

Chattahoochee River National Recreation Area, **1:**143–44

Chickasaw National Recreation Area, **1:**146–47

Curecanti National Recreation Area, **1:**90, 168–70

Delaware Water Gap National Recreation Area, **1:**178–79

Gateway National Recreation Area, **1:**9, 20, 256–57; **2:**374

Gauley River National Recreation Area, **1:**257–58

Glen Canyon National Recreation Area, **1:**273–75; **2:**374, 488

Golden Gate National Recreation Area, **1:**9, 20, 29, 232–33, 256, 277–79; **2:**374, 479, 514

Lake Mead National Recreation Area, **2:**372–75

Lake Meredith National Recreation Area, **2:**375–76

Lake Roosevelt National Recreation Area, **2:**376–78

Mississippi National River and Recreation Area, **2:**413–15

National recreation areas
(continued)
   Santa Monica Mountains
      National Recreation
      Area, 2:518
   Whiskeytown National
      Recreation Area,
      2:589–91
   See also Lakeshore areas;
      National seashores
National Register of Historic
   Places, 1:78, 215, 257, 298;
   2:359
National Resource Challenge,
   1:27
National Road, 1:231
National seashores
   Assateague Island
      National Seashore,
      1:65–67
   Canaveral National
      Seashore, 1:110–11
   Cape Cod National
      Seashore, 1:117–19
   Cape Hatteras National
      Seashore, 1:30, 119–21,
      236
   Cape Lookout National
      Seashore, 1:121–23
   Cumberland Island
      National Seashore,
      1:167–68
   Fire Island National
      Seashore, 1:212–14
   Gulf Islands National
      Seashore, 1:302–3
   Padre Island National
      Seashore, 2:461–62
   Point Reyes National
      Seashore, 2:478–80
National Sporting Goods
   Association, Gold Medal for
   State Parks, 1:22
National tragedies
   American Memorial Park,
      1:45–47
   Andersonville National
      Historic Site, 1:48–49
   Ford's Theatre National
      Historic Site,
      1:215–16
   Johnstown Flood National
      Memorial, 2:353–54

National tragedies (continued)
   Kalaupapa National
      Historical Park,
      2:357–58
   Little Bighorn Battlefield
      National Monument,
      1:226; 2:384–86, 441
   Manzanar National
      Historic Site, 2:399–401
   Minidoka Internment
      National Monument,
      2:410–11
   Nez Perce National
      Historical Park, 1:82;
      2:441–43
   Oklahoma City National
      Memorial, 1:145;
      2:452–54
   Sand Creek Massacre
      National Historic Site,
      2:512–14, 581
   USS Arizona Memorial,
      2:566–68
   Washita Battlefield
      National Historic Site,
      2:581–84
   Whitman Mission National
      Historic Site, 2:592–94
National Trails System Act of
   1968, 2:526
National Wild and Scenic Rivers
   Aniachak National Wild
      River, 1:52–53
   Charley River, 2:613–14
   Delaware River, 1:178
   Noatak River, 1:588
National Wilderness
   Preservation System, 2:531
National World War II
   Memorial, 2:431
Native American sites
   Aztec Ruins National
      Monument, 1:67–69
   Badlands National Park,
      1:71–73
   Bandelier National
      Monument, 1:4, 27,
      73–75
   Big Hole National
      Battlefield, 1:80–82;
      2:441–43
   Canyon de Chelly National
      Monument, 1:113–14

Native American sites
(continued)
   Casa Grande Ruins
      National Monument,
      1:26, 129–30
   Chaco Culture National
      Historical Park, 1:138–39
   Cook Collection of
      American Indian
      artifacts, 1:41; 2:607
   Hopewell Culture National
      Historical Park, 1:322–23
   Hovenweep National
      Monument, 1:327–29
   Hubbell Trading Post
      National Historic Site,
      1:329–30
   Knife River Indian Villages
      National Historic Site,
      2:369–70
   Little Bighorn Battlefield
      National Monument,
      1:226; 2:384–86, 441
   Mesa Verde National Park,
      1:328; 2:408–10
   Navajo National
      Monument, 1:4; 2:437–39
   Nez Perce National
      Historical Park, 1:82;
      2:441–43
   Ocmulgee National
      Monument, 2:451–52
   Pecos National Historical
      Park, 2:466–67
   Petroglyph National
      Monument, 2:471–73
   Pipestone National
      Monument, 2:477–78
   Salinas Pueblo Missions
      National Monument,
      2:509–10
   San Antonio Missions
      National Historical
      Park, 2:511–12
   Sand Creek Massacre
      National Historic Site,
      2:512–14, 581
   Tonto National Monument,
      2:555–57
   Tuzigoot National
      Monument, 2:564
   Walnut Canyon National
      Monument, 2:579–80

Native American sites
(continued)
    Washita Battlefield
        National Historic Site,
        2:581–84
    Wupatki National
        Monument, 2:605–6
    Yucca House National
        Monument, 2:612–13
Natural Bridges National
    Monument, 2:436–37
Natural Resource Challenge,
    1:27
Naturalization ceremony, 1:158
Nauset Lighthouse, 1:118
Navajo Indians, 1:113, 329;
    2:487–88
Navajo National Monument,
    1:4; 2:437–39
Naval Life Oaks Reservation,
    1:302
NEPA. See National
    Environmental Policy Act
Neuberger, Richard, 1:122;
    2:536
New Bedford Whaling National
    Historical Park, 2:439–40
New Deal era, 1:1, 4, 15–16, 18,
    29, 74, 93, 146, 154, 162, 186,
    195, 317, 319; 2:344, 395, 419,
    433, 561, 576
New Frontier program, 2:350
New Orleans Jazz National
    Historical Park, 2:440–41
New York City Five-Borough
    Bike Tour, 1:257
New York City Marathon, 1:257
Nez Perce National Historical
    Park, 1:82; 2:441–43
Nez Perce War of 1877, 1:80–81
NFS. See National Forest Service
Nicodemus National Historic
    Site, 2:443–45
Nightingale reed-warbler, 1:46
Nimitz, Chester W., 1:45
Ninety Six National Historic
    Site, 2:445–46
Nixon, Richard M., 1:8–9, 21, 25,
    27–28, 124, 158, 165, 256;
    2:350
Noatak National Preserve,
    2:588–98

Nobel Peace Prize, 2:346, 501
Nobles, William, 2:379
Nordenskiöld, Gustav, 2:408
North, Lord, 1:301
North Cascades National Park,
    2:446–49
North Plains Indians, 2:369
Northern Mariana Islands,
    1:46–47
Northwest Ordinance, 1:211
Novarupta Volcano, 2:360
NPS. See National Park Service

O

Oakland Plantation, 1:112
Ocmulgee National Monument,
    2:451–52
Oglala Sioux Nation, 1:71–72
Oglethorpe, James Edward,
    1:223–24
Ohio and Erie Canal Towpath
    Trail, 1:171
Ojibway Indians, 1:285
Oklahoma City National
    Memorial, 1:145; 2:452–54
Old Dominion Foundation, 1:120
Old Faithful geyser, 2:608
Old Ironsides (USS
    Constitution), 1:100–101
Old North Church, 1:100; 2:411
Old Point Loma Lighthouse,
    1:109–10
Old Post Office Tower, 2:431
Old State House, 1:100
Old Stone House, 2:493
Old Swedes' Church. See Gloria
    Dei Church National Historic
    Site
Oligocene-epoch fossil beds,
    1:71
Olmsted, Charles, 1:234
Olmsted, Frederick, Jr., 1:250
Olmsted, Frederick Law,
    1:249–51
Olmsted, John Charles, 1:250
Olmsted National Historic Site.
    See Frederick Law Olmsted
    National Historic Site
Olympic National Park, 2:454–57
Omnibus Act of 1978, 2:552

Oñate, Juan de, 2:509
O'Neill, Carlotta, 1:205
O'Neill, Eugene, 1:204–5
O'Neill National Historic Site.
    See Eugene O'Neill National
    Historic Site
O'odham Indians, 2:558–59
Order of Panama civic
    organization, 1:109
Oregon Caves National
    Monument, 2:457–59
Oregon Trail, 1:147–48. 289;
    2:522–23, 593
Organ Pipe Cactus National
    Monument, 2:459–60
Organic Act (1916), 1:277
Orr, Elison, 1:195
ORRRC. See Outdoor Recreation
    Resources Review
    Commission
Ory, Kid, 2:440
Otis Pike Wilderness Area, 1:213
Our Fourth Shore: Great Lakes
    Shoreline Recreation Area
    Survey, 1:122
Our Vanishing Shoreline, 1:30,
    118, 122; 2:535–36
Outdoor Recreation Resources
    Review Commission
    (ORRRC), 1:30, 122
Outer Banks, 1:119, 121
Ouzel fire (1978), 2:496

P

Pacific Coast Recreation Area
    Survey, 1:122
Pacific Forest Reserve, 2:424
Pacific Railroad Act (1862),
    1:280
Paddlefish, 1:86
Padre Island National Seashore,
    2:461–62
Painted cave (Cueva Pintada),
    1:73
Painted Desert, 2:469
Paiute people, 2:476
    Also see Kaibab Paiute
        Indians
Paleontological research site,
    1:247

Palo Alto Battlefield National
    Historic Site, **2:**462–64
Panama Canal Treaty, **2:**346
Panama-California Exposition
    (1915), **1:**109
Park barreling, **1:**9, 18; **2:**374–75
Park Restoration and
    Improvement Program
    (PRIP), **1:**9, 18
Parker, Charlie, **2:**440
Parker, Ely, **1:**58
Parker, Isaac C. "Hanging
    Judge," **1:**239
Parkitecture, **1:**4, 74
Parks, Rosa, **2:**403
Parkways
    Blue Ridge Parkway, **1:**19,
        93–95
    George Washington
        Memorial Parkway, **1:**65
    John D. Rockefeller, Jr.
        Memorial Parkway,
        2:347–48
    Natchez Trace Parkway,
        2:560–61
Partnership parks, **2:**331
Paul Revere House, **1:**100–101
Pea Island National Wildlife
    Refuge, **1:**120
Pea Ridge National Military
    Park, **2:**464–66
Peace Corps, **2:**350
Peale, Arthur C., **1:**214
Pearl Harbor, **1:**45, 197, 319;
    2:400, 410, 433, 480, 566–68
Pecos National Historical Park,
    2:466–67
Pectol, Ephraim Porter, **1:**123
Penitente Brotherhood, **2:**471
Penn, William, **1:**177
Pennsylvania Main Line Canal,
    1:44
People in American history,
    sites honoring
    Carl Sandburg Home
        National Historic Site,
        1:126–27
    Charles Pinckney National
        Historic Site, **1:**142–43
    De Soto National
        Memorial, **1:**182–83

People in American history,
    sites honoring (*continued*)
    Edgar Allan Poe National
        Historic Site, **1:**192–93
    Edison National Historic
        Site, **1:**193–95
    Eugene O'Neill National
        Historic Site, **1:**204–5
    Frederick Law Olmsted
        National Historic Site,
        1:249–51
    George Rogers Clark
        National Historical
        Park, **1:**260–62
    Hamilton Grange
        National Memorial,
        1:307–9
    Jean Lafitte National
        Historical Park and
        Preserve, **2:**342–43
    John D. Rockefeller, Jr.,
        Memorial Parkway,
        2:347–48
    John Day Fossil Bed
        National Monument,
        2:348-9
    John Muir National
        Historic Site, **2:**351–53
    Longfellow National
        Historic Site, **2:**387–88
    Lowell National Historical
        Park, **2:**388–90
    Marsh-Billings-Rockefeller
        National Historical
        Park, **2:**401–3
    Roger Williams National
        Memorial, **2:**496–97
    Saint-Gaudens National
        Historic Site, **2:**504–6
    Thaddeus Kosciuszko
        National Monument,
        2:546–48
    Thomas Stone National
        Historic Site, **2:**552–53
    Vanderbilt Mansion
        National Historic Site,
        2:570–72
    Wright Brothers National
        Memorial, **2:**603–5
    See also African American
        historical people and
        sites; Presidential sites;
        Women in American
        history, sites honoring

Perez, Juan, **2:**454
Permanent Indian Frontier,
    1:238
Permian-period fossil reef, **1:**299
Petersburg National Battlefield,
    2:467–69
Petersen Boarding House,
    1:215–16
Peterson, William, **2:**607
Petrified Forest National Park,
    1:215; **2:**351, 469–70
Petroglyph National
    Monument, **2:**471–73
Philip Schuyler Country House,
    2:519–20
Pickett, George, **1:**267
Pickney, Charles, **1:**142
Pictured Rocks National
    Lakeshore, **2:**473–74
Piedras Marcadas people, **2:**471
Pierce, Franklin, **1:**220
Pilgrims, **1:**117–18
Pinchot, Gifford, **1:**250, 271,
    284; **2:**501, 594, 611
Pinckney National Historic Site.
    See Charles Pinckney
    National Historic Site
Pinkley, Frank "Boss," **1:**26, 130
Pinnacles National Monument,
    2:474–76
Pinto Culture, **2:**355
Pioneer artifacts, **1:**93
Pipe Spring National
    Monument, **2:**476–77
Pipestone National Monument,
    2:477–78
Piping plover, **1:**121
Piscataway Park, **2:**430–31
Pit houses, **1:**113
Plains Indians, **1:**224–27, 243;
    2:385, 477, 517
Platt, Orville, **1:**146
Platt, Thomas, **2:**548
Platt National Park, **1:**146
Plessy v. Ferguson decision,
    1:103–4; **2:**561
Plymouth colony, **1:**117
Poe, Edgar Allan, **1:**192–93
Poe National Historic Site. *See*
    Edgar Allan Poe National
    Historic Site

Point Reyes National Seashore, **2:**478–80

Pony Express, **1:**225

Pony Penning, **1:**66

Pope, John, **2:**399

Poplar Grove National Cemetery, **2:**467–68

Port Chicago Naval Magazine National Memorial, **2:**480–81

Poverty Point National Monument/State Commemorative Area, **2:**481–82

Powell, John Wesley, **1:**114–15, 186, 273, 281–82

Prairie Creek Redwoods State Park, **2:**489, 491

PrairyErth (Least-Heat Moon), **2:**545

Pratt, Charles, **1:**318

Prehistoric dwellings, **2:**360

Prehistoric mammal fossils, **1:**41

Preis, Alfred, **2:**567

Presidential sites
 Abraham Lincoln Birthplace National Historic Site, **1:**33–35
 Adams National Historical Park, **1:**38–41
 Andrew Johnson National Historic Site, **1:**49–52
 Eisenhower National Historic Site, **1:**196–98
 Franklin Delano Roosevelt Memorial, **2:**432, 434
 General Grant National Memorial, **1:**258–60
 George Washington Birthplace National Monument, **1:**262–64
 Harry S Truman National Historic Site, **1:**312–14
 Herbert Hoover National Historic Site, **1:**317–18
 Home of Franklin D. Roosevelt National Historic Site, **1:**319–21
 James A. Garfield National Historic Site, **2:**341–42
 Jefferson Memorial, **1:**159, 250; **2:**432–33

Presidential sites *(continued)*
 Jefferson National Expansion Memorial, **1:**20, 166; **2:**343–45
 Jimmy Carter National Historic Site, **2:**346–47
 John Fitzgerald Kennedy National Historic Site, **2:**349–51
 Lincoln Boyhood National Memorial, **2:**381–83
 Lincoln Home National Historic Site, **2:**383–84
 Lincoln Memorial, **2:**432–33
 Lyndon B. Johnson National Historical Park, **2:**390–92
 Martin Van Buren National Historic Site, **2:**404–6
 Mount Rushmore National Memorial, **2:**426–28
 Sagamore Hill National Historic Site, **2:**501–2
 Theodore Roosevelt Birthplace National Historic Site, **2:**548–49
 Theodore Roosevelt Inaugural National Historic Site, **2:**549–50
 Theodore Roosevelt National Park, **2:**550–52
 Ulysses S. Grant National Historic Site, **2:**565–66
 William Howard Taft National Historic Site, **2:**594–95

Presidio, **1:**232–33, 277–78

Primitive areas, **2:**576

Prince William Forest Park, **2:**482–83

PRIP. *See* Park Restoration and Improvement Program

Prisoners of war memorial, **1:**48–49

Progressive Era, **1:**1, 3, 24, 315; **2:**379, 424, 495, 594

Promontory Summit, **1:**280

Protoecological parks, **2:**460

Prudhomme, Pierre Emmanuel, **1:**112

Public-private management partnership, **2:**546

Pueblo culture, **1:**113, 138, 201, 328; **2:**419, 466, 509–10, 579

Pueblo of Pecos, **2:**466

Pueblo Revolution of 1680, **2:**471

Pulaski, Casimir, **1:**233

Puritans, **2:**496–97, 507

Putnam, Sallie, **2:**492

Pu'uhonua O Honaunau National Historical Park, **2:**483–84

Puukohola Heiau National Historical Site, **2:**484–85

Q

Quaker settlers, **1:**298

Queen Elizabeth I, **1:**235

Quincy, **2:**364–65

Quiet Crisis, The (Udall), **1:**116

R

Railroad sites, **2:**571
 Allegheny Portage Railroad National Historic Site, **1:**43–45
 Golden Spike National Historic Site, **1:**279–80
 Staple Bend Tunnel, **1:**45
 Steamtown National Historic Site, **2:**540–41

Rainbow Bridge National Monument, **2:**487–89

Raker, John F., **2:**378

Raleigh, Walter, **1:**119, 235

Rattlesnake Island, **1:**228

Reagan, Ronald, **1:**18, 25, 28, 158, 255, 270

Reclamation Service, **1:**1

Reconstruction era, **1:**51

Red-cockaded woodpecker, **1:**86

Red Sticks, **1:**325–26

Redwood National and State Parks, **1:**25; **2:**489–91

Reeb, James, **2:**526

Report on the Lands of the Arid Region of the United States (Powell), **1:**282

Report on the Seashore Recreation Survey of the Atlantic and Gulf Coasts, **1:**122

Revere, Paul, **1**:100; **2**:411

Revolutionary War sites, **1**:142, 228, 240, 307, 309

Boston National Historical Park, **1**:100–102

Colonial National Historical Park, **1**:154–56

Cowpens National Battlefield, **1**:160–62, 318

Federal Hall National Memorial, **1**:211–12

Guilford Courthouse National Military Park, **1**:300–302, 318

Historic Camden, **1**:318–19

Independence National Historical Park, **2**:332–35

Kings Mountain National Military Park, **2**:365–67

Minute Man National Historical Park, **2**:411–13

Moores Creek National Battlefield, **2**:420–22

Morristown National Historical Park, **2**:422–24

Ninety Six National Historic Site, **2**:445–46

Saratoga National Historical Park, **2**:518–20

Springfield Armory National Historic Site, **2**:537–38

Thaddeus Kosciuszko National Monument, **2**:546–48

Thomas Stone National Historic Site, **2**:552–53

Valley Forge National Historical Park, **2**:569–70

See also Colonial American historic sites

Ribault, Jean, **1**:218

Richmond National Battlefield Park, **2**:492–93

Ridenour, James, **1**:22

Ridgley, Charles, **1**:309

Rio Grande River, **1**:76–77, 139–40

Rivers

Aniakchak National Wild River, **1**:52–53

Big South Fork River, **1**:85–86

Blackstone River, **1**:91–93

Brooks River, **2**:360

Cane River, **1**:111–13

Charley River, **2**:613–14

Chattahoochee River, **1**:143–44

Colorado River, **1**:5, 114–16, 169, 187, 273, 281

Columbia River, **2**:376

Cumberland River, **1**:85, 22

Delaware River, **1**:178–79

Lehigh River, **1**:178–79

Gauley River, **1**:257–58

Green River, **1**:114–16, 186–87, 247; **2**:396–97

Gunnison River, **1**:168–69

Illinois River, **2**:331

Knife River, **2**:369–70

Little River, **2**:386–87

Mississippi River, **2**:413–15

Salt River Bay, **2**:510–11

Stones River, **2**:541–42

Yukon River, **2**:613–14

Roanoke Island, **1**:235–36

Roanoke settlement, **1**:119

Robber Barons, **2**:571

Robbins Report (American Academy of Sciences), **1**:6; **2**:503

Robert E. Lee. *See* Arlington House, The Robert E. Lee Memorial; Lee, Robert E.

Robert Gould Shaw Memorial, **1**:97

Rock Creek Nature Center, **2**:493

Rock Creek Park, **2**:493–94

Rock of Ages, **1**:8

Rockefeller, John D., **2**:347–48

Rockefeller, John D., Jr., **1**:285–88; **2**:347–48

Rockefeller, Jr. Memorial Parkway. *See* John D. Rockefeller, Jr. Memorial Parkway

Rockefeller, Laura Spellman, **2**:347

Rockefeller, Laurence S., **2**:348, 402

Rockefeller, Mary French, **2**:402

Rockefeller Center, **2**:347

Rockefeller Foundation, **2**:347

Rockefeller Institute for Medical Research, **2**:347

Rockefeller National Historical Park. *See* Marsh-Billings-Rockefeller National Historical Park

Rocky Mountain National Park, **1**:294; **2**:494–96

Roger Williams. *See* Williams, Roger

Roger Williams National Memorial, **2**:496–97

Roosevelt, Eleanor, **1**:198–99, 319; **2**:407

Roosevelt, Franklin Delano, **1**:4, 15, 45, 71, 81, 123–24, 145, 162, 188, 198–99, 223, 252, 261, 269, 286, 301, 313, 317, 319–21; **2**:376, 395, 399–400, 407, 410, 433, 454–55, 502, 561, 566

Roosevelt, James, **1**:319

Roosevelt, Ted, Jr., **2**:501

Roosevelt, Theodore, **1**:1–2, 34, 162, 184, 283–84, 319; **2**:345, 427, 436, 454, 501–2, 505, 548–52, 563, 594, 597

Roosevelt Birthplace. *See* Theodore Roosevelt Birthplace National Historic Site

Roosevelt (Franklin D.) Home. *See* Home of Franklin D. Roosevelt National Historic Site

Roosevelt (Theodore) Home. *See* Sagamore Hill National Historic Site

Roosevelt Inaugural National Historic Site. *See* Theodore Roosevelt Inaugural National Historic Site

Roosevelt Memorial. *See* Franklin Delano Roosevelt Memorial

Roosevelt National Historic Site. *See* Eleanor Roosevelt National Historic Site

Roosevelt National Park. *See* Theodore Roosevelt National Park

Rosencrans, William, **1:**145; **2:**541–42

Rosie the Riveter World War II Home Front National Historical Park, **2:**497–99

Rosier, Lance, **1:**87

Ross, Robert, **1:**229

Ross Lake National Recreation Area, **2:**447–48

Russell, William Howard, **2:**398

Russell Cave National Monument, **2:**499

Rust, David, **1:**284

Ryder, Albert Pinkham, **2:**584

S

Saarinen, Eero, **2:**344

Sacred Ground (Linenthal), **2:**441

Sagamore Hill National Historic Site, **2:**501–2

Sagebrush Rebellion, **1:**255

Saguaro National Park, **2:**502–3

St. Augustine, **1:**130–31, 218, 228

St. Elias National Park and Preserve. *See* Wrangell-St. Elias National Park and Preserve

St. Clair, Arthur, **2:**423

Saint Croix Island International Historic Site, **2:**503–4

St. Leger, Barry, **1:**240

St. Luke Penny Savings Bank, **2:**393

Saint Paul's Church National Historic Site, **2:**506–7

St. Vrain, Ceran, **1:**75

Saint-Gaudens, Augustus, **1:**98; **2:**504–5

Saint-Gaudens National Historic Site, **2:**504–6

Saipan Island, **1:**45–47

Salado people, **2:**556

Salem Maritime National Historic Site, **2:**507–9

Salinas Pueblo Missions National Monument, **2:**509–10

Salt River Bay National Historical Park and Ecological Preserve, **2:**510–11

San Antonio Missions National Historical Park, **2:**511–12

San Francisco Maritime National Historical Park, **2:**514

San Francisco Peaks Volcanic Field, **2:**543

San Juan National Historic Site, **2:**515–16

San Juan Southern Paiute, **2:**487

Sand Creek Massacre National Historic Site, **2:**512–14, 581

Sandburg, Carl, **1:**126–27

Sandburg Home. *See* Carl Sandburg Home National Historic Site

Sanford Dam, **2:**375

Sangre de Cristo mountain range, **1:**292

Santa Fe National Historic Trail, **1:**75, 226–27, 243–44; **2:**466, 516–18

Santa Monica Mountains National Recreation Area, **2:**518

Saratoga National Historical Park, **2:**518–20

Saugus Iron Works National Historic Site, **2:**520–22

Save-the-Redwoods League, **1:**18; **2:**491

Schoodic Peninsula, **1:**37

School of American Research, **1:**21

Schuyler, Philip, **2:**519–20

Scott, Hiram, **2:**522

Scotts Bluff National Monument, **2:**522–23

Sea turtles, **1:**107, 121; **2:**461

Second Bank of the United States, **2:**405

Second Great Awakening, **2:**593

Second World Conference on National Parks, **1:**21

See America First movement, **1:**105

Selma To Montgomery National Historic Trail and All-American Road, **2:**523–27

Seminole Wars, **1:**207

Seneca Falls Convention, **2:**599–600

Sequoia and Kings Canyon National Parks, **1:**1–2; **2:**527–29

Sequoia gigantea, **2:**489

Sequoia sempervirens, **2:**489

Seven Years' War. *See* French and Indian War

Shaw, Robert Gould, **1:**97

Shawnee Indians, **2:**481

Shays, Daniel, **2:**538

Shays' Rebellion, **2:**538

Shenandoah National Park, **1:**4, 37, 93, 295; **2:**529–32

Sheridan, Philip H., **1:**59; **2:**582–83

Sherman, William Tecumseh, **1:**102, 145, 243; **2:**363–64, 560, 565

Shiloh National Military Park, **2:**532–33

Shrine of the Stone Lions, **1:**73

Shriver, Sargent, **1:**28

Sibley, Henry Hastings, **2:**415

Sickles, Daniel E., **1:**266–67

Sidney, Margaret, **2:**412–13

Sierra Club, **1:**1, 5, 7, 157, 273–74; **2:**351–52, 491, 610

Sieur de la Mothe Cadillac (Antoine Laumet), **1:**36

Sieur de Mons, Pierre Dugua, **2:**504

Sieur de Monts National Monument, **1:**35

Sieur de Monts Nature Center, **1:**37

Sinagua people, **2:**419–20, 564, 579, 605

Sioux Indians. *See* Dakota Sioux; Lakota Indians; Oglala Sioux Nation; Sioux Uprising

Sioux Uprising (1862), **2:**415

Sitka National Historical Park, **2:**533–35

Sitting Bull, **2:**384–285

Skidmore, Owings, and Merrill, **1:**158

Skinner, John, **1:**229
Slater Mill, **1:**91–92
Sleeping Bear Dunes National Lakeshore, **2:**535–37
Smith, Andrew Jackson, **2:**560
Smith, Bessie, **2:**440
Smith, Francis Marion, **1:**23–24
Smithsonian Institution, **2:**499
Smithsonian National Museum, **1:**22
Snake River, **1:**286, 305
Sonoran Desert, **2:**459–60
South Fork Dam, **2:**353
South Fort Fishing and Hunting Club, **2:**353
Southern Appalachian National Park Commission, **1:**295
Southern Christian Leadership Conference, **2:**403
Southwestern National Monuments, **1:**26
Spanish Ballroom, **1:**276
Spanish-American War, **1:**153; **2:**548–49
Spotsylvania National Military Park. *See* Fredericksburg and Spotsylvania National Military Park
Springfield Armory National Historic Site, **2:**537–38
Squanto, **1:**118
St. *See* Saint
Staked Plains (Llano Estacado), **2:**375
Stamp Act Congress, **1:**211
Stanford, Leland, **1:**279
Stanford University, **1:**250
Stanley, F. O., **2:**495
Stanley Steamer automobile, **2:**495
Stansbury expedition, **1:**90
Stanton, Edwin, **1:**51–52
Stanton, Elizabeth Cady, **2:**599–600
Stanton, Robert M., **1:**26–27
Staple Bend Tunnel, **1:**45
"Star-Spangled Banner, The" (Key), **1:**229
Statue of Liberty National Monument, **1:**200; **2:**539–40

Steam locomotive era, **2:**540
Steamtown National Historic Site, **2:**540–41
Steel, William Gladstone, **1:**162–63
Stone, Thomas, **2:**552–53
Stone National Historic Site. *See* Thomas Stone National Historic Site
Stoneman Meadows riot, **1:**6, 28
Stones River National Battlefield, **2:**541–42
Stowe, Harriet Beecher, **1:**249
Strauss, Joseph, **1:**232
Stuart, Gilbert, **2:**388
Sturgis, Samuel, **1:**102
Sturgis Motorcycle Rally, **1:**186
Sulphur Springs Reservation, **1:**146
Summer in the Parks program, **1:**28
Sumner, Charles, **2:**387
Sumner, Edwin V., **1:**243
Sunken Forest, **1:**213
Sunset Crater Volcano National Monument, **2:**542–43, 579, 605
Superior National Forest, **2:**576
Synagogues. *See* Churches, synagogues, and temples

T

Taft, Charlie, **2:**595
Taft, Helen Herron, **2:**594
Taft, William Howard, **1:**2, 34; **2:**487, 594–95
Taft National Historic Site. *See* William Howard Taft National Historic Site
Tallgrass Prairie National Preserve, **2:**545–46
Tamiami Trail, **1:**79
Tao House, **1:**204–5
Taos uprising (1847), **1:**75
Tarleton, Danastre, **1:**160
Taylor, Richard C., **1:**195
Taylor, Zachary, **2:**462–63, 565
Temples. *See* Churches, synagogues, and temples

Tennessee Archeological Society, **2:**499
Tenure of Office Act, **1:**51
Terrorism, **2:**453
Tertiary History of the Grand Canyon, The (Dutton), **1:**282
Teton National Forest, **1:**286
Texas Panhandle Pueblo Culture National Monument, **1:**43; **2:**375
Textile manufacturing, **2:**389
Thaddeus Kosciuszko. *See* Kosciusko, Thaddeus
Thaddeus Kosciuszko National Monument, **2:**546–48
Theodore Roosevelt. *See* Roosevelt, Theodore
Theodore Roosevelt Birthplace National Historic Site, **2:**548–49
Theodore Roosevelt home. *See* Sagamore Hill National Historic Site
Theodore Roosevelt Inaugural National Historic Site, **2:**549–50
Theodore Roosevelt National Park, **2:**550–52
Third System network, **1:**234
Thomas, George H., **1:**145
Thomas Bond House, **2:**335
Thomas Stone. *See* Stone, Thomas
Thomas Stone National Historic Site, **2:**552–53
Thompson Island Information Center, **1:**37
Thoreau, Henry David, **1:**118
Three Servicemen Statue, **2:**435
Tidewater glaciers, **1:**269
Timbisha Shoshone Indians, **1:**174–75
Timpanogos Cave National Monument, **2:**553–54
Timucuan Ecological and Historic Preserve, **1:**218; **2:**554–55
Timucuan Indians, **1:**218
Tinian, **1:**46
Tlingit clan, **2:**533–34
Tocks Island Dam, **1:**178

Tojo, Hideki, **2:**566
Toll, Roger W., **2:**495
Tonto National Monument, **2:**555–57
Touro Synagogue National Historic Site, **2:**557–58
Town of Alameda land grant of 1710, **2:**471
Trading post, **1:**75, 329
Trail of Tears National Historic Trail, **1:**238–39; **2:**364, 464
Tramp Across the Country, A (Lummis), **1:**282
Transcontinental railroad, **1:**279
Transcontinental telegraph, **1:**225
Treaty of Fort Stanwix, **1:**240
Treaty of Guadalupe-Hidalgo, **1:**139; **2:**462, 472
Treaty of Paris, **1:**155
Troop H (Buffalo soldier cavalry), **1:**221
Truman, Elizabeth "Bess" Wallace, **1:**313–14
Truman, Harry S, **1:**133, 151, 195, 198, 206, 313–14, 317; **2:**434
Truman National Historic Site. *See* Harry S Truman National Historic Site
Tumacácori National Historical Park, **2:**558–60
Tupelo National Battlefield, **2:**560–61
Turkey Creek Caldera, **1:**148
Tuskegee Airmen National Historical Site, **2:**561–62
Tuskegee Institute National Historic Site, **1:**95, 264; **2:**562–64
Tuzigoot National Monument, **2:**564
Twachtman, John, **2:**584
Twain, Mark, **1:**34

U

Udall, Morris "Mo," **1:**29
Udall, Stewart, **1:**30, 116; **2:**546
Ulysses S. Grant. *See* Grant, Ulysses S.

Ulysses S. Grant National Historic Site, **2:**565–66
Underground Railroad, **1:**248; **2:**439
Union Pacific Railroad, **1:**106, 279–80; **2:**616
United First Parish Church, **1:**38, 40
United Nations, **2:**348, 491
Upjohn, Richard, **2:**405
Urban parks, **1:**8–9, 20, 28, 249
   Central Park, New York City, **1:**249–50
   Constitution Gardens, **1:**158–59
   Cuyahoga Valley National Park, **1:**170–72
   Gateway National Recreation Area, **1:**9, 20, 256–57; **2:**374
   Glen Echo Park, **1:**275–76
   Golden Gate National Recreation Area, **1:**9, 20, 29, 232–33, 256, 277–79
   Greenbelt Park, **1:**297–98; **2:**431
   Lake Mead National Recreation Area, **2:**373–75
   National Capital Parks, **1:**28; **2:**430–31
   National Mall, **2:**431–35
   Rock Creek Park, **2:**493–94
   Santa Monica Mountains National Recreation Area, **2:**518
U.S. Army Corps of Engineers, **1:**63, 85, 115, 158, 231, 258
U.S. Army Corps of Topographical Engineers, **1:**90, 115
U.S. Capitol, **1:**250
U.S. Coast Guard, **1:**118
U.S. Congress, **1:**2–3, 6–7, 9, 15, 24, 27, 51–52, 107, 122, 129, 157, 162, 187, 205, 221, 255, 285; **2:**338, 351, 371, 444, 491, 535
U.S. Constitution, **1:**142, 158, 212; **2:**334

U.S. Customs House, **2:**507–8
U.S. Department of Agriculture, **1:**2, 294
U.S. Department of the Interior, **1:**1–2, 5, 10, 24, 27, 65, 167, 272; **2:**482, 546, 597
U.S. Fish and Wildlife Service, **1:**111
U.S. Forest Service, **1:**1–3, 15, 82, 136, 269, 272, 284, 287, 294; **2:**454, 576
U.S. Geological Service, **1:**17
U.S. Geological Survey, **2:**608
U.S. House of Representatives, **1:**6, 40, 50, 52, 87, 233, 254; **2:**476
U.S. Indian Bureau, **1:**227
U.S. Lifesaving Service, **1:**118–19
U.S. Military Academy at West Point, **2:**547
U.S. Navy, **2:**481
U.S. Senate, **1:**6, 50, 87, 233
U.S. Supreme Court, **1:**103–4, 137, 175; **2:**334, 344, 403, 525
U.S. Virgin Islands, **1:**107
USS *Arizona* Memorial, **2:**566–68
USS *Cairo*, **2:**573
USS *Cassin Young*, **1:**100
USS *Constitution* (Old Ironsides), **1:**100–101
USS *E.A. Bryan*, **2:**481
USS *Maine*, **1:**153
USS *Oklahoma*, **2:**566
USS *Quinault Victory*, **2:**481
USS *Red Oak Victory*, **2:**498

V

Vail Agenda, **1:**10
Val-Kill Cottage, **1:**198–99
Valley Forge National Historical Park, **2:**569–70
Valley of Ten Thousand Smokes, **2:**360
Van Buren, Martin, **2:**404–6
Van Buren National Historic Site. *See* Martin Van Buren National Historic Site
Van Dorn, Earl, **2:**464

Vancouver, George, **1:**191, 246, 269

Vanderbilt, Cornelius, **2:**571

Vanderbilt, Frederick W., **2:**571

Vanderbilt, George, **1:**250

Vanderbilt, William Henry, **2:**571

Vanderbilt Mansion National Historic Site, **2:**570–72

Vaux, Calvert, **1:**249

Verrazano, Giovanni da, **1:**35

Vicksburg National Military Park, **2:**572–74

Vietnam Veterans Memorial, **1:**145; **2:**432, 435

Vietnam Women's Memorial, **2:**435

Virgin Islands National Park, **2:**574–76

Virginia Historic Site, **1:**298

Vital Signs program, **1:**27

Volcanoes and volcanic sites, **1:**148, **2:**380

   Aniakchak National Monument & Preserve, **1:**52–53

   Capulin Volcano National Monument, **1:**125–26

   Craters of the Moon National Monument and Preserve, **1:**164–66

   Devils Postpile National Monument, **1:**183–84

   El Malpais National Monument, **1:**201–2

   Haleakala National Park, **1:**306–7

   Hawaii Volcanoes National Park, **1:**314–17

   Lassen Volcanic National Park, **2:**378–80

   Lava Beds National Monument, **2:**380–81

   Mount Saint Helens, **1:**148, 162; **2:**379

   Novarupta Volcano, **2:**360

   Pinnacles National Monument, **2:**474–76

   Sunset Crater Volcano National Monument, **2:**542–43, 579, 605

Voting Rights Act (1965), **2:**526

Voyageurs National Park, **2:**576–78

W

Walker, James, **1:**145

Walker, Maggie L., **2:**393–94

Walker, Ronald H., **1:**9, 18, 27–28

Walker National Historic Site. *See* Maggie L. Walker National Historic Site

Wall Street, **1:**211

Wallace, George, **2:**525

Wallace, Lew, **2:**418

Walnut Canyon National Monument, **2:**579–80

Wampanoag Indians, **1:**118

War Department, **1:**2, 4, 15, 55, 65, 81–82, 102, 145, 162, 197, 227, 252, 301–2; **2:**366, 560

War in the Pacific National Historical Park, **2:**580–81

War of 1812, **1:**132, 230, 234, 242, 253, 325; **2:**342–43, 507

War on Poverty, **1:**28

War Relocation Authority, **2:**400

Ward, John Quincy Adams, **1:**212

Warren, Conrad, **1:**289

Warren, Earl, **1:**103–4

Warren, Gouverneur K., **1:**266

Washburn, Henry D., **2:**607–8

Washington, Booker T., **1:**95–96, 264; **2:**562–63

Washington, George, **1:**38, 63, 155, 212, 230–31, 262–63, 276, 307, 311, 324; **2:**333–34, 388, 422–23, 427, 430, 432, 519, 547, 557, 569–70

Washington Birthplace. *See* George Washington Birthplace National Monument

Washington Monument, **1:**23, 159; **2:**344, 432–33

Washington (Booker T.) National Monument. *See* Booker T. Washington National Monument

Washita Battlefield National Historic Site, **2:**581–84

Water rights, **1:**175

Waterpocket Fold, **1:**123

Waterton-Glacier International Peace Park, **1:**271

Watt, James, **1:**9–10, 18

Wayne Aspinall Storage Unit, **1:**168

Wayside, **2:**412–13

Weir, Dorothy, **2:**584

Weir, Julian Alden, **2:**584

Weir Farm National Historic Site, **2:**584–85

West Point Military Academy, **2:**547

Western Arctic National Parklands, **2:**585–89

   Bering Land Bridge National Preserve, **2:**585–86

   Cape Krusenstern National Monument, **2:**586–87

   Kobuk Valley National Park, **2:**587–88

   Noatak National Preserve, **2:**588–89

Wetherill, Richard, **1:**138; **2:**408

Whalen, William J., **1:**28–29, 278

Wheeler Peak, **1:**290–91

Whidbey Island, **1:**191–92

Whiskeytown National Recreation Area, **2:**589–91

White, James Larkin, **1:**127–28

White, John, **1:**235

White Mesa Ute, **2:**487

White Sands National Monument, **2:**591–92

White Sands Proving Ground, **2:**591

Whitman, Marcus, **2:**592–93

Whitman Massacre, **2:**593

Whitman Mission National Historic Site, **2:**592–94

Whitney, Samuel, **2:**413

Wilbur, Ray Lyman, **1:**295

Wilderness Act (1964), **1:**7–8; **2:**425, 530, 536

Wilderness area, **1:**174, 269; **2:**360, 372

Wilderness Society, **1:**7, 255

Wilderness Trail, **1:**166

Wildlife refuge, **1:**66, 79, 141, 207

Wilkins, James, **1:**151

William Howard Taft. *See* Taft, William Howard

William Howard Taft National Historic Site, **2:**594–95

William Johnson House, **2:**429

Williams, Hosea, **2:**525

Williams, Roger, **2:**496–97, 557

Williams National Memorial. *See* Roger Williams National Memorial

Wilson, Alexander, **1:**276

Wilson, Woodrow, **1:**2, 24, 186, 319; **2:**594

Wilson's Creek National Battlefield, **2:**595–97

Wind Cave National Park, **2:**597–99

Windsor Castle, **2:**476

Winthrop, John, **2:**496

Winthrop, John, Jr., **2:**521

Wirt, Frederick, **1:**49

Wirth, Conrad L., **1:**7–9, 20, 29 30, 134; **2:**576

Wirth, Theodore, **1:**29; **2:**576

Women in American history, sites honoring

    Clara Barton National Historic Site, **1:**153–54

    Eleanor Roosevelt National Historic Site, **1:**198–99

    Maggie L. Walker National Historic Site, **2:**393–94

    Mary McLeod Bethune Council House National Historic Site, **2:**406–8, 431

    Rosie the Riveter World War II Home Front National Historical Park, **2:**497–99

    Women's Rights National Historical Park, **1:**7; **2:**599–601

Women's Rights National Historical Park, **1:**7; **2:**599–601

Women's suffrage movement, **1:**153

Woodhull, Victoria, **1:**248

Woodland culture, **1:**195

Works Progress Administration (WPA), **1:**4, 135

World Heritage sites

    Aztec Ruins National Monument, **1:**68

    Glacier National Park, **1:**271

    Redwood National Park, **2:**491

World War II sites

    Aleutian World War II National Historic Area, **1:**42

    American Memorial Park, **1:**45–47

    Manzanar National Historic Site, **2:**399–401

    Minidoka Internment National Monument, **2:**410–11

    Port Chicago Naval Magazine National Memorial, **2:**480–81

    Rosie the Riveter World War II Home Front National Historical Park, **2:**497–99

    Tuskegee Airmen National Historic Site, **2:**561–62

    USS *Arizona* Memorial, **2:**566–68

    War in the Pacific National Historical Park, **2:**580–81

WPA. *See* Works Progress Administration

Wrangell-St. Elias National Park and Preserve, **2:**601–3

Wright, Orville, **1:**173; **2:**603–4

Wright, Wilbur, **1:**173; **2:**603–4

Wright Brothers National Memorial, **2:**603–5

Wupatki National Monument, **2:**605–6

Y

Yahi Indians, **2:**379

Yamassee War (1715), **2:**451

Yampa River, **1:**186–87

Yankton Lakota Indians, **2:**477

Yarborough, Ralph, **1:**87

Yard, Robert Sterling, **1:**293

Yellowstone National Park, **1:**1, 4, 9–10, 15, 18, 21, 25, 82, 121, 171, 286–87; **2:**348, 607–9

Yellowtail, Robert, **1:**83

Yellowtail Dam, **1:**83–84

Yosemite National Park, **1:**8, 18, 294; **2:**351–52, 609–12

    early management of, **1:**1–2

    Hetch Hetchy Valley, **1:**2, 5, 183–84, 187, 273, 306; **2:**352, 610–11

    Stoneman Meadows riot, **1:**6, 28

Yosemite River Valley, **1:**250

Young, John, **2:**484

Young, Mahonri, **2:**584–85

Yucca House National Monument, **2:**612–13

Yukon-Charley Rivers National Preserve, **2:**613–14

Z

Z-Bar ranch, **2:**546

Zenger, John Peter, **2:**506

Zion National Park, **1:**3, 104; **2:**615–17

9/13→H